THE FOUNDATIONS OF CHRISTIAN BIOETHICS

To my mother,
Beulah Lillie Karbach Engelhardt,
who reposed March 8, 1992,
and to my father,
Hugo Tristram Engelhardt,
who reposed May 27, 2000.
May the readers of this book remember them in their prayers.

THE FOUNDATIONS OF CHRISTIAN BIOETHICS

H. Tristram Engelhardt, Jr.

SWETS & ZEITLINGER
PUBLISHERS

LISSE   ABINGDON   EXTON (PA)   TOKYO

Library of Congress Cataloging-in-Publication Data

Engelhardt, H. Tristram (Hugo Tristram), 1941-
 The foundations of Christian bioethics / H. Tristram Engelhardt, Jr.
  p. cm.
 Includes index.
 ISBN 902651557Xp
  1 Medical ethics. 2. Christian ethics. 3. Medicine--Religious aspects--Christianity. I.
Title.

R725.56. E54 2000
174'.2--dc21

00-033848

Cover design: Concept & Grafische Vormgeving, Amsterdam, The Netherlands.
Typesetting: Grafische Vormgeving Kanters, Sliedrecht, The Netherlands.
Printed in the Netherlands by Krips, Meppel.

© 2000 Swets & Zeitlinger Publishers b.v. Lisse

ISBN 90 265 1557 X

Contents

The Holy Spirit provideth all; overfloweth with prophecy; fulfilleth the Priesthood; and hath taught wisdom to the illiterate. He hath revealed the fishermen as theologians.

Vespers for Pentecost

Biblical Quotations

Passages from the New Testament are taken from the edition with footnotes, *The Orthodox New Testament*, vol. 1, *The Holy Gospels*, and vol. 2, *Acts, Epistles, and Revelation*, trans. Holy Apostles Convent (Buena Vista, Colorado: Holy Apostles Convent, 1999). I appreciate the kind permission of the Holy Apostles Convent to use this text. Quotations from the Old Testament are taken from the edition of the Septuagint translated by Sir Lancelot Charles Lee Brenton (London: Samuel Bagster, 1851). This is currently available as *The Septuagint with Apocrypha*, trans. Brenton (Peabody, MA: Hendrickson Publishers, 1997). The passages from the Psalms are those of *The Psalter According to the Seventy*, trans. Holy Transfiguration Monastery (Boston, MA: Holy Transfiguration Monastery, 1987).

Abbreviations

AK   Immanuel Kant, *Kants Werke* (Berlin: Preussische Akademie der Wissen-schaften, 1902).

ANF   *Ante-Nicene Fathers*, eds. Alexander Roberts and James Donaldson (Pea-body, MA: Hendrickson Publishers, 1994).

LXX   Septuagint

NPNF1   *Nicene and Post-Nicene Fathers*, First Series, ed. Philip Schaff (Peabody, MA: Hendrickson Publishers, 1994).

NPNF2   *Nicene and Post-Nicene Fathers*, Second Series, eds. Philip Schaff and Henry Wace (Peabody, MA: Hendrickson Publishers, 1994).

Preface

This book is as much about a philosophical puzzle as it is about bioethics. This book is more about a religious quest than it is about a philosophical puzzle. Yet, it is directed to a philosophical puzzle which it approaches through philosophical reflection and analysis. The philosophical puzzle is this: if we are trapped in immanence, can moral truth be anything but ambiguous? If one ranks cardinal values somewhat differently, one affirms a different moral vision, a different understanding of what it is to act appropriately. Public policy controversies and moral debates show that, given the diversity of moral considerations, there are always different accounts of the moral life. Political struggles often concern which moral understanding will be established (e.g., pro-life or pro-choice). Alternative moralities compete without an apparent principled basis for definitively choosing one as canonical. If truth cannot break through to us and personally direct us, will we not always be lost in a plurality of diverse moral and religious views in the sense of not knowing which norms should govern? Will morality then be more a matter of taste, cultural inclination, and communal preference? Will not acquiescence in true moral diversity be acquiescence in a moral relativity beyond the redemption of a final truth? Who but a true post-modern could without regret live in such a context?

Yet, is our moral condition not exactly this: an irresolvable plurality of moral understandings? Is our moral context framed not merely by controversies regarding theoretical justifications, but by substantive and foundational moral disagreements on matters ranging from abortion and cloning to health care reform, from different views about human reproduction to divergent understandings of the moral significance of equality? Protestations to the contrary, and in the face of moral fashions and established canons of political correctness, there is a diversity of moral visions, a plurality of understandings of moral flourishing. In attempts to settle differences by sound rational argument, each side presupposes different fundamental moral premises as well as rules of evidence and inference. Each speaks past the other without a final, rationally principled resolution. The result is that bioethical controversies fuel engaging but insoluble debates. As Alasdair MacIntyre observes:

> The most striking feature of contemporary moral utterance is that so much of it is used to express disagreements; and the most striking feature of the debates in which these disagreements are expressed is their intermin-

able character. I do not mean by this just that such debates go on and on
and on – although they do – but also that they apparently can find no
terminus. There seems to be no rational way of securing moral agreement
in our culture.[1]

Despite desperate claims of consensus and impassioned attempts to impose uniform
moral views, moral diversity persists. Disagreement defines our moral context, even in
the face of an emerging liberal cosmopolitan ethos celebrating liberty, equality, and
self-fulfillment.

Disagreement also defines the field of bioethics, which focuses on what is morally at
stake in sexuality, the procreation of children, suffering, treating patients appropriately, establishing health care institutions, acting justly in the allocation of health care
resources, and facing death. Because of substantive disagreements, the focus of secular
bioethics in the clinic is primarily on matters of procedure, such as free and informed
consent and the use of advance directives. With issues such as cloning and germline
genetic engineering, there is often a tortured sense that clear, definitive, and substantive
answers should be forthcoming from bioethics, though they prove elusive. Substantive
moral guidance requires particular moral assumptions. In the absence of a moral view
materially equivalent to an intact religious moral and metaphysical vision with a thick
appreciation of the good life and the good death, one finds questions asked that cannot
be answered with content in the context they are now posed. The questions only make
sense and could only secure substantive answers within an intact and functioning
religious worldview. After all, ours is a post-Christian culture. We often inherit questions from our Christian past that traditional Christianity could have taken seriously
and to which Christianity could have responded. However, one does not find the
Christianity to provide the answers for which one hoped.[2] For example, can voluntary
active euthanasia be part of a good death? Is germline genetic engineering morally
praiseworthy? Is artificial insemination from a donor adultery? Though these questions engage considerable interest, definitive, principled, and content-full secular moral answers remain elusive. Secular morality has lost a sense of the final importance of a
good death for salvation. There is no guiding vision of the normatively human. Nor is
there a common sense of the sacredness of sexual reproduction. The disjunction of
urgent puzzles from available non-procedural moral guidance generally characterizes
post-traditional societies. In our society, it takes on a particular character. After all, we
live in the ruins of Christendom. We are left with fragments of moral intuitions from a
once intact way of life. These fragments remain as hesitations that cannot ultimately be
defended but nevertheless persist as powerful but unsecured taboos (e.g., the condemnation of neonatal infanticide in the face of a liberal abortion policy, including partial-
birth abortions).[3]

Christian insights into morally appropriate conduct cannot function coherently in a
framework of post-Christian moral commitments: one no longer possesses the moral
framework that once gave sense to these insights. For that matter, in a post-Christian,
amorphously neo-pagan[4] world it is far from clear which Christianity one should
accept or what religious understanding one should embrace. In the absence of a veridical experience of the truth, moral arguments beg the question, proceed in a circle, or
involve an infinite regress. The justification of any particular moral obligations be-

comes contingent on the premises one happens to affirm. This state of affairs gives grounds for moral epistemic skepticism, yet not for metaphysical moral skepticism.[5] Though philosophy and speculative theology are unable to reason their way through this impasse without a *petitio principii*, and though many philosophers and theologians settle for the expedient of appealing to intuitions or to their own favorite balance of moral appeals, there remains a sense that a final and enduring truth must exist in these matters. Yet, this truth is hidden by immanence. Even our sense that morality should have an integrity or coherence, not to mention a deep command on our consciences, is a remnant of the Christian understanding that once framed the West.

The cardinal philosophical and theological puzzle is: can one break through immanence to truth? And if so, how? By addressing this puzzle, this volume invites the reader to the Christianity of the first millennium, a Christianity rooted in mysticism, or better stated, in a noetic theology.[6] It is here that the puzzle is solved and the door found in the horizon of immanence: Christianity's disclosure of an immediate experience of the uncreated energies of a radically transcendent, personal God. Here philosophical solutions and theological truth coincide: the truth is a Who. Such a theology is pursued ascetically through prayer bound to repentance expressed in worship. Within such a theology, bioethics is a way of life. It can only be introduced via an invitation to enter. To the question of "How can I know the truth?" one receives first and foremost instruction in ascetic transformation. It is the "pure of heart who shall see God" (Matt 5:8).

Bioethics depends on having made sense of ethics. One cannot give reliable bioethical advice unless one knows which ethics or whose morality should guide. Bioethics is so controverted, it is fundamentally unclear how reliably to determine what is reliable. Depending on whom one asks, one will be informed either that having an abortion is a way of murdering one's unborn child, or that forbidding abortion by law is a form of enforced pregnancy violative of the basic rights of women. So, too, with issues of social justice. The advice may range from warning that anything but a single-payer system providing equal care to all violates basic human rights to advising that such a system is itself violative. Matters are no better with regard to issues of physician-assisted suicide and euthanasia. Some will advise that these are forms of murder or assisted murder, and others will advise that they can be forms of compassionately treating a suffering patient. Concerning issues of life and death, justice and injustice, there are foundational and persistent disagreements. Christian bioethics depends on knowing what Christianity is and which Christianity should guide. This volume begins by examining this cluster of issues through exploring the recent emergence of Christian bioethics and its eclipse by the worldwide dominance of a philosophical, secular bioethics. This volume argues that this emergence and subsequent marginalization of Christian bioethics must be explored against a more fundamental phenomenon: the social marginalization of Christian moral theology and the development of a global, secular, cosmopolitan culture. This cosmopolitan culture not only relocates Christian sentiments within the assumptions of a dominant, global, secular ethos, it aspires to transform Christianity itself.

The mainline Protestant religions, along with many Roman Catholics, have drunk deeply of the passion of *aggiornamento*. Rather than finding themselves at home in the emerging global liberal cosmopolitan culture as they expected, they are marked by a double alienation. On the one hand, they are estranged from the moral framework within which the authors of the New Testament and the Fathers of the Church lived and breathed. That world is for them too sexist and unconcerned with political liberation to be anything but deeply politically incorrect, if not profoundly embarrassing. Imagine a culture in which wives submit respectfully to their husbands and slaves recognize that the tyrant from which they should free themselves is first and foremost their own passions. On the other hand, when religions accommodate to the pretensions of the secular culture, they become irrelevant. They have nothing of their own to offer. The choice is an unappealing one: Christianity and its bioethics are either in their traditional form a secular scandal or in their secularly reformed versions largely beside the point. After all, if one wanted accounts of social justice, secular philosophy should do at least as well as, if not better than, Christian moral theology – a point made by many Christian moralists, as we shall see.

To write a book that takes traditional Christianity and its bioethics seriously is counter-cultural. We live in a largely post-traditional world in which transcendent claims are eclipsed by the immanent. We find ourselves at the end of an age and at the cusp of a new era. Age-old social expectations have been brought into question.[7] We are after Christendom and at the beginning of a frankly post-traditional secularity. For example, many now experience once-taken-for-granted understandings of sexual morality as both homophobic and patriarchal. Others can no longer appreciate what could be morally inappropriate in physician-assisted suicide or euthanasia.[8] Few would regard an ascetic retreat to a high pillar, emulating St. Symeon the Stylite (+Sept. 1, 459),[9] whose feast begins the ecclesiastical year (September 1), as anything but deeply misguided.[10] The Christian metaphysical assumptions that once legitimated ways of life, institutions, and law no longer command general assent. Much of what once gave deep meaning to the ordinary routines of life (e.g., saying grace before meals, praying before a journey, or drinking holy water when ill) has fallen into desuetude.[11] There has been a profound desanctification of everyday life. All of this conspires to make traditional Christianity appear in need of reformation. The Roman Catholic moral theologian Edward Schillebeeckx sees traditional Christianity as irrelevant.[12] He appreciates the profound gulf separating the moral and spiritual yearning of the dominant culture from that of traditional Christianity. For the post-traditional, the Tradition is misguiding.

This cultural loss of traditional spirituality, the societal dislocation from the transcendent, and the dissociation of traditional belief from the contemporary global secular culture are not experienced as a delegitimation by traditional Christians. To the contrary. This change in moral and spiritual expectations discloses the impossibility of a viable Christianity outside of traditional worship and belief. It sets traditional Christianity over against Christianity in its post-traditional forms. Traditional Christianity presumes that its bioethics will be at odds with the dominant secular morality as well as with post-traditional Christianity. For their part, post-traditional Christians are puzzled by the persistence of traditional Christianity and its bioethics.

A bioethics rooted in the Christianity of the first millennium will understand itself within an all-encompassing way of life aimed at union with God. No decision, no matter how trivial, should lack connection with this goal. The result is a Christian bioethics poorly accessible to those who do not live the Christian life within which this

bioethics is located. Where other religious approaches to morality may offer academically domesticated intellectual undertakings under the rubric of moral theology and
bioethics as if these were primarily areas of conceptual interest, traditional moral
theology and bioethics are first and foremost integral to the pursuit of salvation.
Because the morality of contemporary life is thisworldly, a traditional Christian bioethics discloses concerns out of harmony with the secular world. Moral theology and
bioethics set within the Christianity of the first millennium will be one with an all-
encompassing, transcendently-oriented lifeworld, regarding which only limited instruction can be given from the outside.

Secular bioethics is, in contrast, framed by the immanent. From the search for self-
satisfaction to the advancement of autonomous lifestyles, to the pursuit of social
justice, such value-concerns need not rely on an acknowledgement of a transcendent
God, much less on the bodily resurrection of Jesus Christ. These value-concerns are
considered to have a legitimacy of their own: a matter of consolation for post-traditional Christians no longer anchored in the metaphysical commitments of traditional
Christianity. Indeed, ours is a post-metaphysical age beyond the passions of either
Christianity or communism. Both have fallen. Our post-Christian, post-communist age
and its bioethics are largely bereft of a sense of metaphysical urgency: our concerns are
located within the horizon of the tangible. In this context, the 20th-century secular
reformation of Christianity, the relocation of mainline Christianity within an emerging
secular cosmopolitan culture, gives energy to an ecumenist search for Christian unity
that discounts the plausibility of a sectarian bioethics.[13] As the influence of Christianity has diminished, the various Christianities have found their members believing in
ever less, and therefore less disposed to regard themselves as different and separate. At
the same time, there are contrary attempts within the various Christian religions to
assert fundamental commitments over against the secular forces of our age. These
phenomena have especially marked the Protestant religions, which have ruptured into
conservative and liberal denominations, producing in the process conservative and
liberal Christian bioethics. The various liberal Christian groups have sought to go into
communion, as their former conservative brethren have departed as entire congregations to more traditional Christian religions. Christians at the traditional or liberal
poles of the spectrum, respectively, frequently find that they share more with others at
the same pole than they do with their co-religionists. These disagreements involve not
only the Protestant religions, but Roman Catholics as well, as illustrated by the followers of Archbishop Marcel Lefebvre and the Society of St. Pius X.[14] In reaction, secularists have recast "fundamentalist" into both a religious and a political opprobrium: to
be a fundamentalist in the terms of secular society is to have religious commitments
fundamentally out of harmony with the dominant, global, secular ethics.

Against the spirit of this opprobrium, this volume and its bioethics are fundamentalist. It looks to the foundations of Christianity in the roots of the first millennium, the
origin of Christianity. This point of departure contrasts with the Christianity of the
West that set reason along with Scripture at the center of its faith (*sola scriptura*, if not
nuda scriptura). If reason is at the center of theology, one will rationally reconstruct
the content of any Christian bioethics in the image and likeness of secular moral
rationality. In purifying moral theology of seemingly irrational elements, a more secularly congenial Christian bioethics will be produced, as the content of traditional

bioethics is evacuated. Claims based in post-religious experience, but without a discursive rational justification, will be rejected. If Scripture is at the core of theology, its authoritative claims will be deconstructed through text-critical and sociohistorical reassessments of the Scriptures, thus rendering it congenial to the assumptions of our age. Instead, traditional Christian bioethics is grounded in unbroken veridical experience of God. This Christianity is radically historical in affirming the unity of Christianity over two millennia. It is radically anti-historicist in affirming that the truth it reveals is independent of the pretensions, aspirations, and forces of particular times and places. It asserts possession of the "faith which was once delivered to the saints" (Jude 1:3).

The Christianity at the foundation of this volume's bioethics is one that few in the West have ever encountered, much less experienced. Its theology is not primarily one of academicians advancing their considered intuitions. It is a theology won by asceticism and through experience of the God Who unites His theologians over space and across the millennia. It understands that to know truly is not a matter of discursive or scholastic reasoning, but of changing the knower and of being granted illumination by God. Not only must this theology be presented as *the* foundation of a Christian bioethics despite the plurality of Christianities and their bioethics, it must also recognize itself as unique, original, and unaltered. The message is given through this manner of expression as truly as it is in its content. Unlike the guarded claims of academics, this Christianity lives in the certainty of its Truth, without repentance for this political incorrectness. It teaches with an authority not of this world.

As to repentance, the readers of my previous book, the second edition of *The Foundations of Bioethics*, may recall that I wrote "I am, after all, a born-again Texian Orthodox Catholic, a convert by choice and conviction, through grace and in repentance for sins innumerable."[15] Though there is surely also much in the second edition for which to repent, I hoped at least to have made matters clearer: *The Foundations of Bioethics* does not celebrate the sparse fabric of the secular morality available to bind moral strangers,[16] people who do not share a common moral vision.[17] For this reason I noted that "If one wants more than secular reason can disclose – and one should want more – then one should join a religion and be careful to choose the right one."[18] Even in the first edition, I stressed that "Some may wish to see this volume as a defense of a secular pluralist ethic. That would be a mistake."[19] While addressing the sparse secular morality that can bind moral strangers when they are deaf to God, both editions stressed that there should be, and indeed that there truly is, the thick morality of moral friends. This volume speaks to what that morality should be.

To dispel at least one confusion from the outset, the Orthodox Catholicism of this volume is that which unites in true worship and belief the Patriarch of Antioch, the Archbishop of Athens and of all Greece, the Patriarch of Moscow, the Catholicos of Georgia, the Pope of Alexandria and all Africa, and the Metropolitan of Washington, not to mention the bishop of Dallas and the South, among others.[20] Many may think of this belief as isolated within various ethnic enclaves such as Czech Orthodox, Japanese Orthodox, Polish Orthodox, and Serbian Orthodox churches. In the West, the immigrant character of some congregations frequently obscures the truth. Yet, there is even an Orthodox Church in America. In the United States the Antiochian Orthodox Church successfully compasses members from all races with a clergy who have come to the altar primarily as converts.[21] It is to this Church, sinner that I am, that I owe my nurturing in the faith: this truly miraculous faith, which discloses a world alive with the wonder of grace, and of cosmic conflict with diabolic evil. This faith of the Apostles has no one as its head save Christ, and no pope in the contemporary Western sense of the term, only a patriarch in an impoverished remnant of Constantinople to chair meetings of patriarchs and bishops, united in a single experience of faith. This faith, at one with its roots in the first centuries, supplies the vision of this volume.

This volume grounds bioethics within an ascetic and liturgical theology confident that its inspiration is from the same Spirit Who inspired the Scriptures and directed the Apostles. It celebrates the great gift of the Scriptures but recognizes that they are not essential to Christianity. Its theology is fundamentally out of step with the Christian religions of the West, though this Christianity lies at their roots. After all, Christianity is in its place of origin an oriental, not a Western European, faith. This means that the reader of this volume will encounter such figures as Sts. Ephraim the Syrian (A.D. 306-373) and Isaac the Syrian (A.D. 613-?) as cardinal epistemologists in the service of explicating Christianity's normative morality along with its bioethics. If nothing else, the non-Christian reader as well as the post-Christian bioethicist will find an introduction to a world of bioethical reflections well articulated in the first thousand years of the Faith, which shaped moral practices that came to define the Christianity of the West.

It will not take the reader long to conclude that in this volume "traditional Christianity" is generally used as a code word for Orthodox Christianity.[22] Fair enough. Now for a defense of my usage. The term is chosen to identify the Christianity that sustained the expectations of the Church of the first seven Councils, indeed, of the Christianity of the Levant and Greece, out of which Western Christianity and even Western philosophy drew much of their substance. In this sense, traditional Christianity is not just Orthodox Christianity, at least if this is understood as only one among a plurality of Christian religions. Traditional Christianity is the historical and indeed philosophical key to the metaphysics and epistemology that allowed religion to start anew two millennia ago. The term "traditional Christianity" invites the reader from whatever religion to enter into the religious experience alive in the texts, prayers, moral understandings, and spiritual concerns of Christianity's first millennium. Some might regard these texts and usages as only historical relics. Others might consider a call to return to the sources primarily as an invitation to study and reorient an academically framed theology. Here the invitation is to enter into a lifeworld that knows without doubt that St. Basil the Great (329-379), St. John Chrysostom (334-407), St. Gregory the Theologian (329-390), and St. Symeon the New Theologian (949-1022) are constant, living companions.

Post-traditional Christianity has stepped away from these understandings of first millennium Christianity. This rupture of separation from the Christianity of the seven Ecumenical Councils had already opened wide with the discursive rationality of the Western High Middle Ages. This break from the first millennium eventually gave birth to the individualism of the Reformation and the pagan sense of culture recaptured by the Renaissance. When the Enlightenment's confidence in a rational unity is broken[23] by the fragmentation of post-modernity, a polytheism of moral vision is reborn. Because post-traditional culture no longer possesses a unified, morally normative understanding of family structure, sexuality, asceticism, and death, the plurality of moral visions must be located within free choice and the value of liberty. The post-traditional bioethics of our contemporary world is defined by moral pluralism's being lodged within a liberal cosmopolitan ethos that seeks to embrace and redefine this pluralism. It is an ethos at peace with a diversity of moral visions and a multiplicity of moral understandings, as long as none makes an absolute claim to the truth. The liberal cosmopolitan, by privileging autonomy, equality, and self-fulfillment, domesticates moral diversity. The emerging dominance of the liberal cosmopolitan ethos provided the energy for the phenomenal flowering of bioethics in the 1970s.

Bioethics as a term was likely coined in 1970 by Van Rensselaer Potter,[24] though it found its contemporary meaning in the same year through André Hellegers, who brilliantly appreciated the needs of the time.[25] Potter hoped to introduce bioethics as a global way of life. Hellegers turned bioethics into an academic discipline designed to function as a secular theology for an emerging high-technology culture. Through intensive courses, he provided one of the first "seminaries" to train the ethicists or bioethicists needed as secular chaplains for a morally transformed health care. Edmund Pellegrino saw what others did not see: the importance of embedding bioethics in the general concerns of the humanities.[26] He more than anyone appreciated the connection with the *humanitas* of ancient Rome and the sentiments of the Renaissance. A new secular moral framework was emerging with deep connections with Europe's pagan past and the recapture of its cultural richness. Against this birth of a vigorous secular bioethics, Christian bioethics showed failure to thrive. After a brief flowering, Christian bioethics became largely indistinguishable from its secular versions. As should now be clear to the reader, this sojourn into Christian bioethics relocates the field yet once more. Like Potter's work, this volume indicates the possibility of bioethics as a way of life, sustained by a particular moral experience, albeit one of a transcendent God. The goal is to lead Christian bioethics back to where Christian reflections found themselves in the first millennium.

Houston, Texas   H. Tristram Engelhardt, Jr.
March 12, 2000, Feast of St. Symeon the New Theologian

Notes

1. Alasdair MacIntyre, *After Virtue* (Notre Dame, IN: University of Notre Dame Press, 1981), p. 6.
2. Alasdair MacIntyre contends that the practices within which traditional moral concerns were lived and understood are now broken and dysfunctional.

   A key part of my thesis has been that modern moral utterance and practice can only be understood as a series of fragmented survivals from an older past and that the insoluble problems which they have generated for modern moral theorists will remain insoluble until this is well understood. If the deontological character of moral judgments is the ghost of conceptions of divine law which are quite alien to the metaphysics of modernity and if the teleological character is similarly the ghost of conceptions of human nature and activity which are equally not at home in the modern world, we should expect the problems of understanding and of assigning an intelligible status to moral judgments both continually to arise and as continually to prove inhospitable to philosophical solutions. *Ibid.*, pp. 104-105.

Given the disarray of many moral practices (e.g., does the practice of responsible parenting include the use of prenatal screening and selective abortion?) and the broken character of the cultural framework in which they are found (e.g., in a post-Christian culture, mixed signals are sent: some hearken back to traditional Christian roots, others look forward to a fully secular society), there often remains a passionate hunger for concrete moral guidance, and only deep puzzlement when it cannot be found. The searching becomes intense and repetitive. A post-traditional Christian culture may thus retain a sense that surrogate motherhood and cloning are improper ways of reproducing, but no longer possess an intact understanding why they are wrong.

3. As Alasdair MacIntyre observes, contemporary Western hesitations regarding many immoral activities remain as deep but unjustifiable intuitions on an analogy with the taboos of the Hawaiians of the late 18th and early 19th centuries (*After Virtue*, p. 105). As Captain Cook recorded in his diaries:

The women never upon any account eat with the men, but always by themselves. What can be the reason of so unusual a custom, it is hard to say; especially as they are a people in every other instance, fond of Society and much so of their Women. They were often asked the reason, but they never gave no other Answer, but that they did it because it was right, and expressed much dislike at the custom of Men and Women eating together of the same Victuals ... more than one-half of the better sort of the inhabitants have entered into a resolution of enjoying free liberty in Love, without being troubled or disturbed by its consequences ... both sexes express the most indecent ideas in conversation without the least emotion, and they delight in such conversation beyond any other. Chastity, indeed, is but little valued.
J. Cook, *Captain Cook's Journal 1758-71*, ed. Capt. W. S. L. Wharton (London: Elliot Stock, 1893), pp. 91-95.

Similarly, many secularized persons in the West retain some hesitations regarding abortion, especially particular forms such as partial-birth abortions (i.e., which are performed late in pregnancy and require the delivery of enough of the baby's head to allow its brains to be sucked out prior to removing the dead fetus). Under such circumstances, some condemn such procedures on the basis of a moral intuition or a sense of revulsion for which they cannot give a justification.

4. The term neo-pagan is used to identify a syncretical approach to issues religious and spiritual. Pagan religions, whether those of the Mediterranean littoral, India, or Japan, have been disposed to see all gods and religions as manifestations of a deeper truth in terms of which the diversity of religious and spiritual sentiments can be respected and maintained, though transported and placed within a polytheism affirming a diversity of perspectives. Hospital chaplain programs that attempt to address the "spiritual needs" of patients without attending to the truth of the religious issues involved are neo-pagan in this fashion. Often, the neo-paganism takes on a quite specific, self-conscious character. Consider, for example, a recent volume: Patricia Telesco, *The Urban Pagan* (St. Paul, MN: Llewellyn Publications, 1995). Among other things, the author, a trustee for the Universal Federation of Pagans, suggests, "From working magic into our daily routine, the next logical step is to look at various celebrations throughout the year as opportunities to honor the Earth and the God/dess in all their aspects" (p. 285).

5. Moral epistemic skepticism acknowledges the difficulty, if not impossibility, of resolving moral controversies by sound rational argument. Metaphysical moral skepticism doubts whether there is a moral truth. One can be skeptical about discursive moral rationality's ability to establish a canonical moral understanding without being a metaphysical moral skeptic.

6. The recognition of the mystical is crucial for this book; it points to an experience of the divine, in particular, of the very energies of God, which transform both body and soul. The mystical in this sense does not identify an experience of a quasi-platonic sphere transcendent

to the material world, nor a world of ideas in the mind of God that can be dispassionately contemplated. To capture what is at stake, a special sense of noesis is employed to identify a direct experience of God. Much more will be said about these matters in chapter 4.

7. A. J. Conyers, *Eclipse of Heaven* (South Bend, IN: St. Augustine's Press, 1999).

8. By the mid 1990's, there was in many parts of America acceptance by any persons, in at least some circumstances, of physician-assisted suicide. See, for example, Jerald Bachman, Kirsten Alcser, David Doukas, *et al.*, "Attitudes of Michigan Physicians and the Public Toward Legalizing Physician-Assisted Suicide and Voluntary Euthanasia," *New England Journal of Medicine* 334 (February 1, 1996), 303-309, and Melinda Lee, Heidi Nelson, Virginia Tilden, *et al.*, "Legalizing Assisted Suicide – Views of Physicians in Oregon," *New England Journal of Medicine* 334 (February 1, 1996), 310-315.

9. For the life of St. Symeon the Stylite, see *The Great Collection of the Lives of the Saints*, trans. Fr. Thomas Marretta (House Springs, MO: Chrysostom Press, 1994), vol. 1, *September*, pp. 20-42.

10. Walter Percy provides a contemporary exploration of the flight from temptation undertaken by the stylites, albeit within a somewhat corrupt understanding of the pursuit of sanctity, in *The Thanatos Syndrome* (New York: Farrar, Straus, Giroux, 1987).

11. Peter L. Berger, *The Social Reality of Religion* (London: Penguin, 1969).

12. Edward Schillebeeckx, "Silence and Speaking about God in a Secularized World," in *Christian Secularity*, ed. Albert Schlitzer (Notre Dame, IN: University of Notre Dame Press, 1969), especially p. 156.

13. The ecumenist passions of the 20th and early 21st century are surely complex in their roots and diverse in their goals (i.e., all are not in agreement about the kind of unity that should achieved). In part, there has been a sense of ennui regarding denominational differences. It is not only that many Episcopalians, Methodists, and Presbyterians have forgotten what once divided their denominations, but even Roman Catholics can often not recall why they should find themselves so distant from Protestants, other than that the others lack a pope. When doctrinal differences no longer arouse passion, ecumenical movements take on greater plausibility. In addition, there is an argument that the multiplicity of Christianities is a scandal that should be cured by ecumenical unity. Surely, every serious Christian would hold that differences should be cured by all coming back to true belief. The difficulty is gaining agreement as to what beliefs should be abandoned and what unity embraced. A special impetus is added when one is no longer committed to the differences that once separated, and is therefore embarrassed that they should still divide.

14. For an account of the reaction of conservative Roman Catholics to the liturgical innovations of the 1960's and 1970's, see the three volume study, *Liturgical Revolution* by Michael Davies, *Cranmer's Godly Order* (Ft. Collins, CO: Roman Catholic Books, 1995), *Pope John's Council* (Kansas City, MO: Angelus Press, 1992), and *Pope Paul's New Mass* (Dickenson, TX: Angelus Press, 1980). For example, a traditionalist Roman Catholic guide suggests that the faithful attend Orthodox Liturgies rather than Novus Ordo, post-1970 masses. Radko Jánsky (ed.), *Catholic Traditionalist Directory* (St. Louis, MO: SFIU-MvC, 1989). To appreciate the strength of the polarization between traditional and post-traditional Roman Catholics, consider the condemnation of the contemporary Roman Catholic liturgy, the Novus Ordo mass (established in 1970 [*Missale Romanum: ex decreto sacrosancti oecumenici concilii Vaticani II instauratum auctoritate Pauli PP. VI promulgatum*, editio typica (Vatican City: Typis Polyglottis Vaticanis, 1970)] and indicated in the quotation as N.O.M.) by the author of the Directory. "Most of the vernacular versions of the N.O.M. and their accompanying practices are imbecilic, blasphemous, sacrilegious, and at least implicitly heretical, distorting knowingly the words of Christ, and thus are properly avoided by those who refuse to participate in a disgraceful mockery of the sacred and in insulting God" (p. 2).

15. H. T. Engelhardt, Jr., *The Foundations of Bioethics*, 2nd ed. (New York: Oxford University Press, 1996), p. xi.
16. The phenomenon of secular morality and its culture is addressed in H. T. Engelhardt, Jr., *Bioethics and Secular Humanism: The Search for a Common Morality* (Philadelphia: Trinity Press International, 1991).
17. The term moral strangers recognizes that, in the absence of common moral premises or a common understanding of the moral life, individuals meet without the possibility of resolving important moral controversies either through sound rational argument or through an appeal to jointly recognized moral authorities. When individuals share neither moral premises nor moral authorities, they can still in limited areas agree how to act together, even if they cannot discover how they should collaborate. Moral friends are those who do share a moral vision so as to be able to resolve their moral controversies either by sound rational argument or through appeal to a commonly acknowledged moral authority. In our broken world, moral strangers are often affective friends, if not even spouses. See Engelhardt, *The Foundations*, 2nd ed., especially pp. 6-7.
18. *Ibid.*, p. xi.
19. Engelhardt, *The Foundations of Bioethics* (New York: Oxford, 1986), p. viii.
20. The Orthodox Catholicism of this volume is that of the Orthodox Church, the ancient Roman Church whose bishops assemble presided over by the Bishop of New Rome, the Ecumenical Patriarch of Constantinople.
21. In great measure, the Antiochian Orthodox Church in America under Metropolitan Philip reclaimed Orthodox Christianity's Christ-given mission to bring all to true worship and belief, an obligation on which She acted with difficulty (i.e., with the prize of winning martyrdom) after the fall of New Rome to the Mohammedans and of Moscow to the Bolsheviks. In America, before Moscow's fall, one can think of the missionary work to the Roman Catholics of St. Alexis of Wilkes-Barre, Pennsylvania (1854-1909). In the latter part of the 20th century, the turning point was taken by Metropolitan Philip, the primate of the Antiochian Orthodox Christian Archdiocese in America, who understood the obligation to reach out and bring all to Orthodoxy. The result of this rebirth of Orthodox evangelism has been a church receiving thousands of converts, including whole communities of worshipers. See Peter E. Gillquist, *Becoming Orthodox* (Ben Lomond, CA: Conciliar Press, 1992), rev. ed., as well as Gillquist, *Metropolitan Philip* (Nashville: Thomas Nelson Publishers, 1991). This rebirth of Orthodox evangelization has changed Orthodoxy throughout the world.
22. Orthodox Christianity is often defined as the religion directed in right belief to give right worship to God. More fundamentally, it is the religion that leads to right glory, glory with God the Father. "And now, O Father, glorify thou me with thine own self with the glory which I had with thee before the world was" (John 17:5).
23. The Enlightenment was many things in many countries. Yet there were commonalities. In different ways, the authors of the *Encyclopédie*, Scottish philosophers, and Immanuel Kant sought to guide morality and political life on bases that would "be found undeniable by all rational persons." Alasdair MacIntyre, *Whose Justice? Which Rationality?* (Notre Dame, IN: University of Notre Dame Press, 1988), p. 6. As MacIntyre argues, the central aspiration of the Enlightenment was

> to provide for debate in the public realm standards and methods of rational justification by which alternative courses of action in every sphere of life could be adjudged just or unjust, rational or irrational, enlightened or unenlightened. So, it was hoped, reason would displace authority and tradition. Rational justification was to appeal to principles undeniable by any rational person and therefore independent of all those social and cultural particularities which the Enlightenment thinkers took to be the mere accidental clothing of reason in particular times and places. *Ibid.*, p. 6.

The Enlightenment involved a rejection of "morality as interpreted by churches" (J.B. Schnee-wind, *The Invention of Autonomy* [New York: Cambridge University Press, 1998], p. 7) in favor of a "morality of self-governance", which in the end would be justified by "philosophy, appealing to reason and not to any authority" (*ibid.*). The unity of the Enlightenment was the unity of this rational project, a faith in a community of individuals bent on rational self-governance, though the participants had quite different understandings of both rationality and appropriate self-government.

24. Van Rensselaer Potter, "Bioethics, the Science of Survival," *Perspectives in Biology and Medicine* 14 (1970), 127-53; "Biocybernetics and Survival," *Zygon* 5 (1970), 229-46; and *Bioethics, Bridge to the Future* (Englewood Cliffs, NJ: Prentice-Hall, 1971). Potter developed his ideas further in *Global Bioethics* (East Lansing: Michigan State University Press, 1988). For an overview of the development of bioethics, see Albert Jonsen, *The Birth of Bioethics* (New York: Oxford, 1998).

25. Warren Reich, "The Word 'Bioethics': Its Birth and the Legacies of Those who Shaped its Meaning," *Kennedy Institute of Ethics Journal* 4 (1994), 319-336.

26. For Pellegrino's early, important, and influential appreciation of the role of the humanities in framing the context for bioethics, see the collection of his essays in Pellegrino, *Humanism and the Physician* (Knoxville: University of Tennessee Press, 1979).

Acknowledgements

There are many to whom I owe profound gratitude. Without their love, friendship, support, and guidance, this volume would never have taken shape. Needless to say, it would have been a better volume if I had consistently followed their advice. Anything worthwhile in this book should be attributed to them. The shortcomings are mine, due to my hardheaded failure to follow their suggestions. First and foremost, my enduring gratitude is to my wife Susan, who for more than a third of a century has sustained me with her unfailing love. She typed, edited, and reshaped this manuscript more times than either of us can remember. I am deeply grateful as well for the advice and editorial suggestions of my daughters, Christina Tristram Engelhardt Partridge, and Dorothea Tristram Engelhardt Anitei. I bear a special debt to my son-in-law, I. Julian Anitei. Then there is the deep gratitude I owe to my spiritual father, the Rev. Thomas Joseph. I ask for his prayers and for his forgiveness for my having fallen short of his guidance regarding this book and my life. May God forgive me for the errors I have unwittingly placed in this volume, for which I sincerely repent.

Many spent considerable time reading the ancestral manuscripts of this book. These include Archpriest John Breck, Archimandrite Constantin Chirila, Fr. Joseph Copeland, Corinna Delkeskamp-Hayes, Christopher Earler, Archpriest George Eber, Archpriest Edward Hughes, Fr. Paul Jaroslaw, Vigen Guroian, Archpriest Stanley Harakas, B. Andrew Lustig, Laurence B. McCullough, Timothy F. Mulligan, John F. Peppin, Josef Seifert, Rev. Allyne L. Smith, Jr., and Stuart F. Spicker, as well as Sebastian Moldovan, who by e-mail patiently provided a wealth of advice, which I have only inadequately followed. A constant companion in the framing of these arguments has been my friend for over a third of a century, Thomas J. Bole, III. I have special debts to my students and former students. Here I mention in particular Mark J. Cherry, Ruiping Fan, Ana Smith Iltis, George Khushf, Lisa Rasmussen, Stephen E. Wear, and Kevin Wm. Wildes, S.J. Their reflections, suggestions, and our debates about issues have enriched this work. I have learned from them; they have been my generous teachers. My gratitude to Iltis and Rasmussen for their heroic work in copy-editing the manuscript requires underscoring. I must make special acknowledgement to Baruch A. Brody for his friendship, collegiality, learning, and prayers. There are others who patiently read and re-read various versions of this work, including my generous and long-suffering friend Stephen Erickson. Others were conversation partners who helped me to see my ideas more clearly, including first and foremost Joseph Boyle, Nicholas Capaldi, and Emilio Pacheco.

In some sense, this book began to take shape on Great Saturday, April 6, 1991, when I entered into the Orthodox Church. To those who guided me to that morning, I bear an eternal debt, as I do to those who over the years have been my guides even when I have not adequately followed their guidance. Here I must especially mention Geronda Dositheos of Holy Archangels Monastery, Monk Issidore of the Great and Holy Monastery of Vatopaidi, Reader C. L. Kennedy, and Archpriest Joseph Shahda. Again, my sins and my errors in this book are not theirs. In the nine years since that Saturday, I made numerous presentations that were transformed into the material of this volume. Distantly ancestral drafts of what became some of the chapters appeared in various forms in *Christian Bioethics,* which journal would never have come into existence without the encouragement of Martin Scrivener of Swets and Zeitlinger Publishers. I owe a very special debt of gratitude to the Internationale Akademie für Philosophie im Fürstentum Liechtenstein, where through the generosity of His Magnificence, Josef Seifert, I enjoyed six months of animated discussions concerning the developing manuscript of this volume in the fall of 1997. I am similarly in debt to Liberty Fund, Inc., where in the spring of 1998 I sojourned as a Visiting Scholar. The invitation extended by T. Alan Russell and George B. Martin allowed me the opportunity with a splendid coterie of scholars to explore ideas raised by this volume. Kurt Schmidt was especially gracious; he brought together a group of German theologians for a colloquium on a draft of the manuscript on October 23, 1999, at the Zentrum für Ethik in der Medizin, Frankfurt/Main. In various fashions, my discussions with colleagues at Baylor College of Medicine, the Department of Philosophy at Rice University, and Gerald McKenny from the Department of Religious Studies aided me crucially as I both formulated this project and brought it to conclusion. The final proofreading is due to the careful eye of Jenny Bambakidis.

Those who come later have a special debt to those who blaze the way. Here I single out the work of V. Rev. Stanley Harakas, in particular *Health and Medicine in the Eastern Orthodox Tradition* (1990) and *Living the Faith* (1992), the work of Vigen Guroian, especially *Incarnate Love* (1989) and *Life's Living Toward Dying* (1996), and V. Rev. John Breck's *The Sacred Gift of Life: Orthodox Christianity and Bioethics* (1998).

Last but not least, I want to thank all who prayed for me as I engaged in this undertaking. Chief among these is my patron, St. Herman of Alaska, whose name I bear.

1 From Christian Bioethics to Secular Bioethics: The Establishment of a Liberal Cosmopolitan Morality

Can Morality be Sectarian?

Christian bioethics is a puzzle. The very name suggests an ethics other than one for humans generally. Can there be an ethics just for certain humans? Has a special ethics been given to Christians as the Torah was given to Israel?[1] Can there be an ethics for all people, but which only some people can know or know fully? Could or should a Christian bioethics differ from a secular bioethics?[2] If so, how? Should Christian bioethics differ from other religiously grounded bioethics? What implications would any differences have for secular morality or ecumenical reflections? More fundamentally, what implications would any differences between secular and Christian bioethics have for our understanding of ethics? For example, a Christian bioethics not materially equivalent to a secular bioethics appears particular and sectarian rather than universal. What would it mean to claim that one can come to know morality fully only if one is a Christian? At the very least, such an ethic would be divisive rather than all-embracing. If it placed moral matters in a traditional, Christian context, Christian bioethics would locate human reproduction, suffering, health care allocation, and death in a very particular narrative of sin and salvation, of redemption by Christ and of our reconciliation with God.

All of this has a particularity troublesome in many ways for the secular mind. It has a sectarian character offensive to an ecumenical spirit. The personal character of the Christian narrative, which is attractive to many, is for this very reason also disturbing. Traditional Christianity promises to locate all moral concerns, all encounters with moral and natural evil, within a very particular history of creation, the fall, and redemption. Though this account does not avoid any of the particulars of the human drama, it excludes competing non-Christian understandings, which may be similar but not the same. The very thickness of Christianity's moral power is tied to its exclusiveness. The bioethics offered by the Christian narrative leaves no question unaddressed, not even the existential cry, "Why is this happening to me?" Even so, the philosopher's concern is heightened. How can a Christian bioethics properly be an ethics, if it is sectarian? Yet, how can a bioethics be Christian unless it differs at least in some respect from a secular bioethics, unless it is in some sense sectarian? If Christian ethical claims were the same as those of a general secular ethics, one could find what one needed in a secular account.

An exploration of Christian bioethics at the beginning of the 21st century might with relief be regarded as anachronistic, as a matter of the past. This side of the Renaissance and the French Revolution, the once-Christian West is increasingly post-Christian. Though in some countries a particular Christianity is still established – in Germany, two – their role and force for public policy are progressively marginalized in the framing of law and public policy. Western Christendom has become secular. Strictly speaking, Christianity is no more. There is no society that is unabashedly Christian, as Spain under Franco or Portugal under Salazar had been Christian.[3] Christendom's public institutions are guided in largely secular terms. As health policy is no longer religious in orientation, a Christian bioethics in such circumstances may appear to have a merely historical significance. It invites being perceived as only an elaboration of the moral assumptions that once governed Western law and that still lie hidden at its roots. A Christian bioethics may also be seen as a vexatious thorn in the side of secular health care policy. An account of Christian bioethics in either guise is still worthwhile. On the one hand, it provides insight into the roots of contemporary health care debates regarding abortion, third-party-assisted reproduction, physician-assisted suicide, and euthanasia. As a matter of historical circumstance, the framing assumptions of the West remain Christian. These assumptions have been exported throughout the world via European and American political, cultural, and economic dominance. On the other hand, Christianity in its zealous forms is still a challenge to secular health care policy. A better understanding of this challenge is no mean contribution. This volume, in exploring the foundations of Christian bioethics, offers a bit of both: it explores the Christian roots of contemporary health care policy and investigates the ways in which Christian bioethics is likely to conflict with secular bioethics and health care policy. This volume addresses these two goals through pursuing a more foundational project: an exploration of the possibility of a Christian bioethics.

Because philosophy and ethics in the West have come to be understood as secular, intellectual endeavors, the possibility of a Christian bioethics must be gauged through exploring the possibility of a secular bioethics: One must see how and where the two may differ. By recognizing where a secular bioethics can succeed, one can then determine if and when a Christian bioethics in some sense supplements a secular bioethics, as well as the reverse. This exploration will show that secular bioethics emerged to remedy difficulties posed by Christian bioethics. A Christian bioethics has the difficulty of being (1) plural, since there is not one Christianity, but many, and therefore many Christian bioethics, and (2) particular, since Christian bioethics as Christian is not open to all but only to those who accept its premises, embrace its faith, and are transformed by its Grace. Secular bioethics promised to overcome the difficulties of a Christian bioethics by providing a single universal moral account accessible to all and therefore appropriate for a secular society.

A reassessment of the possibility of Christian bioethics must be undertaken against this failure of secular bioethics, which in many ways mirrors the difficulties facing a Christian bioethics: secular bioethics is plural.[4] The reason is simple: when secular bioethics possesses content, this content is also always particular, and it is not possible to establish one particular content as canonical without begging the question as to which ranking of values or right-making conditions should be normative (the details of this difficulty will be explored presently). Here it is enough to note that the problem is not merely a lack of certainty in matters moral, but of fundamental disagreements about the character of moral obligations, particularly as these express themselves in bioethical understandings. One is therefore confronted with a diversity of secular bioethics without the possibility of reliable guidance as to which bioethics to affirm and which guidance to follow (e.g., consider the problem of someone wanting to have reliable guidance regarding whether to have an abortion or to use physician-assisted suicide: everything will turn on whom one asks). The reason is this: given a plurality of possible foundational premises, as well as diverse rules of evidence and inference, for establishing a canonical secular ethics, there is no rationally principled fashion in which one can definitively choose among competing alternatives. Any attempt to justi-fy a choice argues in a circle or engages an infinite regress. If, for example, one ranks differently the moral importance of liberty, equality, prosperity, and security, one will affirm substantively different concrete moral understandings. Affirming one value-order over the other requires a particular understanding of proper ordering. But which value-order should one affirm? To determine that, one needs a higher-level value sense, ad infinitum. There is no way to choose among such rankings without begging the question. A secular bioethics with content becomes only one among many, thus recap-turing the diversity and plurality that characterizes religious bioethics. Recasting Alas-dair MacIntyre, one must ask: which morality, whose bioethics?[5] Depending on the choice one makes, one can receive radically different moral guidance and advice.

In such circumstances a secular bioethics can still be maintained, but only if ground-ed in content-less procedures for deriving authority from the permission of individuals, the only moral authority possible for collaboration among moral strangers.[6] We face a dilemma; if one gains universality in secular ethics by affirming a morality within which all can collaborate despite the diversity of their moral visions, one loses moral content. If one gains content, one does so at the price of universality: not all will agree to collaborate. On the one hand, a secular bioethics can succeed in achieving universal-ity by being grounded in a procedure for collaboration that eschews particular moral content. However, if secular bioethics eschews content, it forgoes the substance neces-sary to structure a full-bodied understanding of the good, the right, duty, virtue, character, and the good life. On the other hand, particular, content-full, secular ac-counts of the good, the right, duty, virtue, character, and the good life cannot find a warrant in general secular rationality. [7] Or more precisely, one must choose one among many alternative moral rationalities, allowing one to select the morality one wants in order to justify the action one wants to undertake. At best, a secular bioethics can draw its roots, as Rorty claims, from the contingency of history and place.[8] Such contingen-cy has no principled canonical normative force. Moreover, in our increasingly global culture, the contingencies of ethnicity, history, and place that give content to particular views of the good carry ever less motivational force. The language of the cosmopolitan liberal occupies center stage.[9] His discourse invites the progressive evacuation of any moral content not justifiable in general rational terms. The morality of the particular has become merely a matter of happenstance. Content has no deep anchor and tradi-tion little persuasive force.

A religious bioethics in the sense of a bioethics grounded in the recognition or experience of a transcendent God and in one's obligations to that God offers the possibility of a deep anchor for a content-full morality. This volume explores the possibility of a Christian bioethics providing such an anchor. It opens with the Christian bioethics that began to take shape in the second half of the 20th century. This chapter gives special attention to Roman Catholic reflections not only because of their salience in the 20th century, but also because of their rich literature reaching back to their flowering in the 16th century.[10] All of this is placed under the rubric bioethics, even though the term is of recent origin (i.e., the early 1970s). In many ways, it is anachronistic to use this term prior to the 1970s, for the phenomenon of bioethics was in many ways associated with the deprofessionalization of medical ethics and its reconceptualization as a secular, philosophically oriented discipline independent of the health care professions.[11] Bioethics is employed to identify a range of moral concerns regarding health care and the biomedical resources that transcend those internal to the health care professions.

The brief flowering of Christian bioethics in the 1960s and 1970s is explored against the background of the secularization of Western European and North American society, the chaos engendered by Vatican II, and the emerging moral philosophical conviction that the substance of Christian bioethics should be knowable within the assumptions of secular morality. As this chapter shows, secular bioethics emerged out of the Enlightenment hope to disclose a secular ethic that could transcend the multiplicity of Christianities and their moralities.[12] This Enlightenment hope has persisted despite the bloodshed of the French and October Revolutions, leading among other things to the emergence of the medical humanities and the contemporary high expectations from a secular bioethics. Though a canonical moral content for secular bioethics cannot be justified, a liberal cosmopolitan ethic has emerged with aspirations to global governance. It frames the moral context and supplies the moral content for the dominant, standard account of bioethics. This liberal cosmopolitan ethic, which displaced the hegemony of the ethos of established Christendom, is examined in greater detail in chapter 3. This chapter concludes by gauging the challenges facing a secular bioethics to secure a canonical content and to avoid breaking into a plurality of bioethics. This assessment of the character and limits of a secular bioethics serves as an invitation to explore what a Christian bioethics would need to be, as well as what commitments it must embrace, to be a plausible source of content-full morality.

The second chapter explores the roots of secular ethics in order to understand why secular morality fails to provide what Christian moral thought had once secured: the harmony of the right and the good, the justification of morality and the motivation to be moral, and a canonical content for the moral life. In the absence of these desiderata, the right conflicts with the good, the motivation to act morally is defeated by non-moral reasons, and the content of morality is ambiguously plural. Moral guidance is contradictory, inadequate, arbitrary, and indeed useless unless one wholeheartedly embraces the particular morality of a particular moral community. Again, the question is which moral community and why one should embrace it. Kant's secular belief in an as-if God and immortality and Hegel's defense of the rational necessity of the contingent character of moral content, as well as Kierkegaard's grounding of faith in an act of the will, are employed as case examples of attempts to restore the moral wholeness and canonical moral authority lost to the post-medieval West. Neither Kant nor Hegel succeeds in providing a deep unity for the dimensions of the moral life. Nor does Kierkegaard give an adequate account of Christian knowledge born of faith that can successfully bring the individual beyond the horizon of the immanent to an ultimate grounding of morality in a fully transcendent personal God. While Kant collapses society and community, and though Hegel attempts to sustain a moral distinction between the two, Kierkegaard loses an anchor in either. As a protestor against the established church of Denmark and without a substantive sense of the community of saints, Kierkegaard becomes, despite his best intentions, a harbinger of the rootless, post-modern individual who has no overriding identification with any actual, particular society or community. From the outside, Kierkegaard's story becomes one individual narrative alongside numerous other individual narratives in the growing cacophony of a post-Enlightenment world.

These attempts to secure a perspective that can guide life are plagued by the cardinal problem of post-Enlightenment culture: the inability to reach beyond immanence so as to establish a canonical, content-full morality and a harmony of the right and the good, which can form the basis of moral community. Philosophical attempts to reach to the transcendent go aground within a horizon of conditioned, immanent reality. God becomes invisible, and any image of God at best a human projection. These fundamental difficulties disclose the unity and explanatory power once sought from an account of morality rooted in a personal God. The failure to secure an integrated, canonical, content-full morality invites reconsidering both secular and Christian bioethics.

As the third chapter shows, a generally justifiable secular morality is by default libertarian: moral diversity is nested in a libertarian cosmopolitan ethic grounded in permission. Within this moral vision, there are only the sparse webs of moral authority established by agreement. The hunger for more direction than this sparse ethic of consent and contrast can sustain leads to a liberal cosmopolitan ethic which affirms individual autonomous choice as a cardinal value, thus endorsing freedom from constraints imposed on the pursuit of self-satisfaction and fulfillment. Though the libertarian cosmopolitan ethic can justify a sparse commitment to respect permission as a source of authority, the liberal cosmopolitan ethic engenders a full-fleshed ethos, an all-encompassing way of life. Within this moral vision, Christianity is transformed, producing an immanentized Christian bioethics. This offers the possibility of radically reconceiving, reimaging, and democratizing the project of Christian morality and thereby of Christian bioethics. On the one hand, Christian bioethics can be grounded in liberty as the cardinal human good. On the other hand, the received content of Christian images, narratives, and concerns with the sacred can be recast free of the constraints of the past through an affirmation of autonomy and equality. Such a Christian bioethics is directed to liberating, sustaining, and empowering persons in terms rooted in a revised Christian humanism. This reconceptualization of Christian bioethics as an ethics of immanence constitutes a radical departure from traditional Christian aspirations. Such a post-traditional Christianity and its bioethics are radically at odds with the Christianity of the first millennium and are unable to cure the tensions at the root of secular morality or to respond to the human hunger that in many remains unextinguished.

The fourth chapter addresses the possibility of a Christianity and its bioethics grounded in the noetic experience[13] of a transcendent, personal God. This chapter draws on the Christianity of the first millennium to show that it can reach beyond the horizon of immanence. The reality of this vantage point is examined in terms of: (1) the epistemological commitments, (2) the underlying metaphysics, (3) the social context of knowing and valuing, (4) the axiological understandings, (5) the account of narrative and history, and finally, (6) the exemplars of knowing and valuing that should guide a Christian bioethics. This account discloses the grounding required for a Christian bioethics to be an ethics with canonical moral content: an actual and ongoing experience of God. The content secured is the one that framed the Christianity of the first seven ecumenical councils.[14] Given Orthodox Christianity's continued bond to the epistemology and metaphysics of this Christianity, the account draws on Orthodox Christian theologians, even when they write after the schism that emerged in the 9th century and permanently divided Christianity after the 13th century. This partiality to Orthodoxy in exploring the grounding of a Christian bioethics may be seen as more compelling, given that the epistemic and metaphysical assumptions of Western Christianity provided the basis for a morality that could only succeed by becoming secular. Western secular morality developed out of a fragmented Western Christianity. Against a background of disunity and deep differences, it aspired to a rationally grounded universality.[15] The fragmentation and diversity of Western Christianity invited a secular morality that could transcend the divisions within Western Christianity and compass all in a single, secular morality. Orthodox Christianity never experienced this fragmentation. Nor did it assume that secular moral reflection, which it experienced as primarily polytheistic, and therefore plural, could provide a unity superior to that available only through the Christian life itself. Instead, this Christianity lives in a theology that is ascetic, experiential, liturgical, and noetic.

Issues of sexuality and the procreation of new human life, including contraception, sterilization, abortion, artificial insemination, *in vitro* fertilization, and embryo transfer, as well as cloning and genetic engineering, are the focus of the fifth chapter. Matters connected with abortion are also addressed, such as experimentation with embryos. This, as well as the subsequent chapters, examines these bioethical topics not as isolated moral challenges, but in terms of the central Christian task of transfiguring union with God. "That all may be one, as even as Thou, Father, art in me, and I in Thee, that they also may be one in Us" (John 17:21). This focus on holiness transforms the question of how correctly to make reproductive choices from a merely legalistic engagement to the ascetic task of finding spiritual wholeness in a morally broken world. Over against the liberal cosmopolitan consensus regarding reproductive morality, which emphasizes individual choice free of the constraints of tradition and nature, the Church of the first millennium gives an account of the relation of man and woman that reaches from Eden and the Fall through redemption to the kingdom of heaven. Traditional Christianity introduces a narrative into which all humans have been told and in which alone they can find ultimate meaning.

So, too, suffering, illness, disability, and death are placed within the cosmic Christian narrative of sin, redemption, and grace. In chapter six, the moral and religious significance of finitude and suffering are examined within the consequences of both the sin of Adam and Eve and the sins of all humans. The traditional Christian concern that the pursuit of health and the postponement of death not be all-consuming undertakings sets important limits to secular technological imperatives. By locating suffering and death within a life aimed at transcendence, immanent concerns, including those of health care, are radically relativized. As a consequence, traditional Christian approaches to such issues as withholding treatment, withdrawing treatment, using advance directives, providing physician-assisted suicide, and offering euthanasia have a significance that contrasts with their taken-for-granted meaning within an immanent secular morality. The chapter also addresses issues in transplantation and the definition of death.

In chapter seven, informed consent is relocated within views rooted in the first millennium. Consent by children and proxies is examined in terms of Christian concerns regarding family, community, and salvation, so that family values, autonomy, and truth-telling are considered within the context of the pursuit of holiness. The chapter then turns to the challenges to being a Christian physician, health care professional, or patient in a post-Christian age. Because traditional Christians will not only refuse to provide immoral services but also even to refer for them, they will be stumbling blocks to the ordinary realization of secularly appropriate health care. If they do not reach into public discourse and public space, traditional Christians may grudgingly be granted limited space for their own private beliefs. However, if traditional Christians proceed to impose transaction costs on what secular bioethics takes to be choices appropriately left to patients, traditional Christians will be fundamentalists in the invidious sense of persons whose basic commitments are disruptively at odds with the secular society within which they live. If traditional Christians in addition take advantage of their relations with patients to introduce them to Christianity and the possibility of salvation, they will violate secular professional commitments to moral neutrality. The secular, post-traditional, post-Christian world not only offers innumerable opportunities for cooperation with evil, it is committed to domesticating religious belief and resisting claims to spheres of privacy within which traditional Christians can maintain enclaves for the peaceable pursuit of their spiritual commitments.

The final chapter reassesses the cleft between the Christian and the secular, as well as between traditional and post-traditional Christian bioethics. It looks to the bioethical battles in the culture wars[16] of the future and the place of Christian bioethics in a post-Christian, post-traditional world. The chapter closes with the recognition that a traditional Christian bioethics is one taught through asceticism and prayer.

Christian Bioethics: Confused and Eclipsed

Christian reflections about abortion, infanticide, and preparation for death extend back to the writings of the Apostolic Fathers.[17] There is a substantial body of Roman Catholic theological reflections bearing on health care, reaching back centuries. In presenting this, as well as the other historical accounts in this book, the events are displayed from a particular perspective. As with all histories, the one offered here is nested within its own commitments. Assumptions or commitments regarding the basic character of reality are always necessary in order to guide in sorting information from noise. To see, one must know in general what one is looking for. To recognize anything, one must see it from a particular perspective. As already confessed, the perspective of this volume is that of a traditional Christian. Again, perspective is everything. What for one historian will be a history of decadence will for another be a history of moral progress. When different histories are sustained by divergent metaphysical commitments, these histories will be as different as divergent accounts of physics (consider, for example, how different the universe appears through the lens of the physics of Aristotle, Newton, or Einstein).

The Roman Catholic medical-ethical handbooks and compendia of moral theology that emerged at the end of the 19th century and enjoyed a flourishing in the 1950s have a continuity with Roman Catholic moral theological reflections, reaching to the beginning of the 16th century and to the flowering of Western scientific interest in medicine and its foundational sciences.[18] From the 16th century onward, moral theological interest in medicine was driven by the remarkable medical progress after the Renaissance. Even Descartes (1596-1650) thought he could extend life, given the promise of medical knowledge.[19] Medicine claimed importance before it could convey much benefit. Though therapeutic benefits came later, there were striking advances in knowledge. From Vesalius[20] to Harvey[21] to Morgagni[22] through Bichat[23] and Virchow[24] and the explosion of medical science in the 19th century, new construals of medical research and science altered the very meaning of medical knowledge.

In contrast, in the wake of the Council of Trent (1545-1563) there developed a continuity in Roman Catholic moral theological reflections that extended unbroken into the early 1960s.[25] Roman Catholic moral thought had a previous substantial change in its character when it passed from the pre-Scholastic to the Scholastic period. The pre-Scholastic era, which was pastoral in its character, was much closer in its theological spirit to that of the Church of the first millennium.[26] The Scholastic period, which began in the 12th century and extended to the Council of Trent, was marked by a concern with discursive rational reflection and systematization. The modern period, which began with Trent, in great measure carried forward the Scholastic tradition, but now more fully developed. It was in this period that reflections on medicine became the focus of whole works and began to constitute a sub-discipline of moral theology.[27] This post-Tridentine, medical-ethical, moral theological literature was insightful. It constituted much more than merely wooden applications of past reflections. This significant body of Roman Catholic medical ethical reflection and scholarship was characterized by its constituting a single coherent community of research. Those who participated shared a common set of assumptions and procedures.[28] Moreover, they possessed a common understanding of who was in moral authority to settle moral controversies (i.e., the magisterium, in particular, the Pope). Controversies could and did arise, but by and large the constraints were accepted. To employ metaphors taken from Thomas Kuhn's account of scientific revolutions, Roman Catholic medical moral theologians possessed a common paradigm. They were engaged not in crisis moral reflection, but in normal moral and theological reflection, rather than one marked by disputes regarding foundations.[29] Fundamental assumptions were not at stake; fundamental principles could be applied with confidence. The general framework and assumptions for moral reasoning were not called into question. Instead, particular problems were articulated, explored, and solutions produced within a taken-for-granted background understanding of the nature of moral science. There were problems to face, but not a sense of crisis in the mode of approach. A common sense of doing Christian medical ethics or bioethics was available for Roman Catholics until the mid-1960s.[30] As John Berkman observes, "The conceptual continuity in moral theology is clearly visible from the manuals themselves, which in 1950 maintained the same basic structure and categories of the manuals which begin in 1605."[31] There was a confidence in the ability of moral theological reflection to answer the questions posed by new technological and scientific developments.

At the end of the 19th century, there was a significant increase in Roman Catholic moral theological investigations concerning matters medical. The moral theological handbook tradition turned to the needs of physicians, priests, and nurses.[32] During this same period, new medical techniques were being developed and new understandings of etiology, pathogenesis, and therapy were gaining salience. A good proportion of contemporary surgical procedures trace their roots to this period, which enjoyed the combination of anesthesia with Lister's asepsis. During this period the germ theory became well established and the first steps were taken in the development of antisera as medical treatments. The emergence of contemporary medicine motivated theological reflections. This was a period within which various aspirations to progress, secularization, and modernization brought into question traditional Christian commitments.[33] After the Second World War, there was continued acceleration in the tempo of scientific and technological progress. The response was a further development of the religious medical-ethical literature, to which not only Roman Catholics, but also Protestants and Jews[34] began to make numerous contributions.[35] Initially, the Roman Catholic response was both vigorous and in continuity with its manualist tradition.

The Christian bioethics that took shape in the 1970s developed a character quite different from the Roman Catholic medical-ethical tradition of the past. It did not so much produce manuals or guides for the perplexed physician, nurse, or believer, as it did reports of theological perplexity. The guides were themselves often disoriented: the moral theologians on whom bioethicists might draw were frequently unsure as to the character of appropriate moral guidance. Roman Catholic bioethical scholarship took on the character of a moral science in confusion: moral theology was in search of its foundations. As Roman Catholicism passed through the aftermath of Vatican II, it became impossible to carry forward the tradition of medical-ethical reflection that had taken shape at the beginning of the 17th century. This rupture in the tradition of Roman Catholic bioethical reflections was associated with the religious changes that occurred in Roman Catholicism following Vatican II.[36] Pope John XXIII (1958-1963) began a revolution as he sought to bring "ecclesiastical discipline into closer accord with the needs and conditions of our times."[37]

The Second Vatican Council was welcomed as a source of renewal and as the beginning of a second Pentecost. It was followed by significant social and institutional changes, including a large-scale departure of priests and nuns.[38] There was a fundamental reexamination of church traditions and ways of doing theology, including bioethics. There were changes in piety, belief, and church structure. The result was that Roman Catholic moral theological and bioethical reflections entered a period of crisis. This crisis was part and parcel of a deeper crisis of self-identity, which expressed itself in and drew force from changes in the Roman Catholic life of worship. As the Orthodox theologian Alexander Schmemann observes, the character of Roman Catholic liturgics became marked by experimentation and anarchy that drew from an "... indeed deeply anti-traditional set of aspirations".[39] An institution and a body of scholarship that had resisted modernism[40] now embraced it. In calling for *aggiornamento*,[41] the emphasis of much Roman Catholic moral reflection moved from either sanctifying the world, retreating from the world, or engaging the world, to acculturating to the world. Despite the best efforts of many in the Roman Catholic hierarchy, the result was an institutional environment that invited a critical reexamination of the fundamental moral and theological commitments that defined Roman Catholicism. New forms of worship and theological reflection promised novel ways of coming to terms with contemporary secular culture and its technologies.

These changes profoundly influenced subsequent Roman Catholic moral thought and restructured Christian thought generally. The reexaminations of theology that became prominent were both a contribution to as well as the result of the cultural upheavals that marked the 1960s, and within which contemporary bioethics emerged. What followed was a cultural revolution in Western Christianity comparable to the Reformation. Vatican II shook not only Roman Catholicism to its core, it sent shock waves into other Christian religions. Because of its very size and influence, Roman Catholicism's commitment to the changes that occurred in the wake of Vatican II, changes that internalized the cultural crisis of the period, unbalanced other Western Christian religions, which at that same time were feeling the pressure of powerful cultural forces.[42] As the Red Guards during the same period sought a new social order free from the mistakes of the past, so, too, many Christians attempted to reach back to what they considered the origins of Christianity so as to start afresh. Vatican II was completed with a confidence in the task of re-imaging Christianity. These changes further secularized the cultural character of the West, so that Pope John Paul II could lament, "Dechristianization, which weighs heavily upon entire peoples and communities once rich in faith and Christian life, involves not only the loss of faith or in any event its becoming irrelevant for everyday life, but also, and of necessity, a decline or obscuring of the moral sense."[43] A new moral sense took center stage: a sense of crisis and fundamental revision. It is within these changes that moral theorists turned to medical morality. The Christian bioethics that took shape in the 1970s and beyond was fashioned within a new moral context.

Many would dispute whether the Second Vatican Council played so cardinal a role in the widespread changes in religious and moral consciousness during the late 1960s with such fateful implications for the subsequent character of Christian bioethics. They would regard Vatican II and/or its consequences as a symptom of a cultural change, not as one of its principal causes. They would instead attribute the changes to the emergence of a post-traditional global culture, the development of a robustly materialistic market economy, or the collapse of an outworn metaphysics. As the Roman Catholic theologian Edward Schillebeeckx observes,

> The Christian revelation, in the form in which it has been handed down to us, clearly no longer provides any valid answer to the questions about God asked by the majority of people today. Neither would it appear to make any contribution to modern man's meaningful understanding of himself in this world and in human history. It is at once evident that more and more of these people are becoming increasingly displeased and dissatisfied with the traditional Christian answers to their questions.[44]

This perception with regard to Christianity led in many of its denominations to the evacuation of traditional doctrinal commitment, as Steve Bruce observes. "Major elements of the Christian faith – the miracles, the Virgin Birth, the bodily resurrection of Christ, the expectation of Christ's return, the reality of eternal damnation – have quietly been dropped from the teachings of the major Christian churches."[45] There is no question that a profound change in moral, religious, and metaphysical consciousness characterized the self-perception of the 1960s. This perception possessed an energy that transformed religious understanding in the West. It framed the culture within which Vatican II was held and applied. Peter Berger saw this change in stark terms:

> Probably for the first time in history, the religious legitimations of the world have lost their plausibility not only for a few intellectuals and other marginal individuals, but for broad masses of entire societies. This opened up an acute crisis not only for the nomization of the large social institutions but for that of individual biographies. In other words, there has arisen a problem of "meaningfulness" not only for such institutions as the state or the economy but for the ordinary routines of everyday life.[46]

All of these considerations give grounds for holding that Vatican II was itself shaped by these larger cultural changes rather than contributing to them and to the context for contemporary bioethics, including Christian bioethics.

Some thirty years later, Berger observes the shipwreck of *aggiornamento* and the power of traditional religious movements, especially outside of Western Europe.

> On the international religious scene, it is conservative or orthodox or traditionalist movements that are on the rise almost everywhere. These movements are precisely the ones that rejected an *aggiornamento* with modernity as defined by progressive intellectuals. Conversely, religious movements and institutions that have made great efforts to conform to a perceived modernity are almost everywhere on the decline.[47]

The ability of traditional religion not only to survive but thrive is evidence that Vatican II was not just moved by history, but indeed moved history, and in so doing damaged traditional Christianity. A religion, if it is determined to defend its character, can do so. Orthodox Judaism has preserved itself in the midst of Christian and secular cultures indifferent to, when not deeply hostile to, its presence. Its members have been able to participate in the scientific, technological, and economic world around them while maintaining, often at great personal cost, their own religious moral identity. Islam, whose secularization had been anticipated by many accounts of the passing of traditional society, has sustained its traditional commitments.[48] It has not been secularized by the forces of the age. However one might judge their methods and goals, individuals such as Ayatollah Khomeini (1900-1989) caused the religious history of their countries to go in a different direction. The choices of people individually and corporately shape history. The dramatic changes in Roman Catholicism on the heels of Vatican II at least support the Council's role as a significant contributory factor in the shift of Christian moral theological vision, and consequently in religious bioethical understandings that occurred in the late 1960s and 1970s. Mainline Christians came to reconsider the nature of morality and moral reflection.

Joseph Fletcher, a one-time Episcopal priest, played prophet for many of the changes that would define the moral context and mark the biomedical ethics of the 1960s. In the 1950s Fletcher anticipated the moral tumult that would occur in the subsequent decades.[49] He heralded the crisis that was beginning, and contributed to it a form of Christian moral theology that in the end became unabashedly secular humanist. The Christian moral theological literature that emerged was marked by a questioning of authority and of once-taken-for-granted moral traditions.[50] The neo-Christian criticisms of traditional Christianity were often so substantive as to impeach the very reasonableness of remaining Christian. For example, assessing James Gustafson's view that God lacks intention in action but possesses purpose, Jeffrey Stout concludes that "Gustafson's desire to avoid anthropomorphic conceptions of the Deity leads him, in the end, to the view that in one important respect the Deity is more like a dog than like a human being."[51] Indeed, Stout suggests that Gustafson's Christian theology functions as a prolegomenon to disbelief.[52] "Gustafson's criticisms of traditional religious doctrines create a momentum that seems bound to carry us beyond his own position to atheism."[53] Against the background of such challenges to its moral theology, Christian bioethics could not provide unambiguous guidance. Christian bioethics as a coherent and constructive enterprise was doomed from the start.

Despite these considerable difficulties, Christian bioethics as a family of bioethics had a brief and significant flowering. For some two decades, it commanded a centrality in the public debates regarding the new medicine. It then receded from public policy discussions. This is not to deny that a rich and often thoughtful literature continued to grow, nurtured by authors from evangelical as well as other perspectives.[54] Christian bioethics simply no longer commands the public policy notice it once enjoyed. During its flourishing, Protestant bioethicists such as Paul Ramsey and Stanley Hauerwas claimed a prominent place for a Christian bioethics.[55] Their reflections garnered broad attention. Initially, the novelty of the debates was itself engaging, even as an old paradigm of Christian bioethics collapsed, and many scholars energetically struggled to erect diverse new ones. During the 1960s and early 1970s the various Christian bioethics flourished at the vanguard of bioethical scholarship, so that in this period one could not have given an adequate account of medical ethics or bioethics without taking account of the work of Christian thinkers such as Ramsey and Hauerwas. Yet, just as secular bioethics assumed an important role for public policy, Christian bioethics receded in cultural significance and force. Christian bioethics served as an intermediate step in the emergence of secular bioethics. In part, this was due to Christian bioethics attempting to speak to the world in secular rather than in Christian terms. By discounting its particularity, Christian bioethics marginalized the importance of what it could offer. As Stanley Hauerwas has argued, this has been one of the major forces in the recent decline of Christian bioethics.[56]

Other factors were also influential in making a secular bioethics appear more attractive than a Christian bioethics. The secularization of the culture made the consideration of a Christian bioethics as a source for moral guidance unappealing. Reliance on traditional authority figures came to be regarded as pejoratively paternalistic, if not as an expression of a false consciousness. Traditional Christian morality interpreted by an authoritative hierarchy was at loggerheads with the view that society should be open, liberal, and pluralist. The very notion of a religious tradition as a source of moral judgment collided with an emerging sense of autonomy and individual rights. Indeed, traditional Christianity is not only hierarchical but robustly patriarchal. It takes seriously the declaration of St. Paul that "the head of the woman is the man" (I Cor 11:3) and that "man was not created on account of the woman, but woman on account of the man" (I Cor 11:9). Although accepting men and women as equally called to salvation, traditional Christianity recognizes them in a hierarchy of honor and authority. Against the backdrop of the rights movements of the 1960s and their rejection of traditional claims of social authority, traditional Christian understandings were not only unacceptable and embarrassing, but to be positively rejected. Traditional Christian commitments came to be regarded as exploitative, thus driving a deep cultural wedge between traditional and post-traditional Christianities.

With this rupture separating traditional and post-traditional Christianity, Christian morality became ever more pluralist. The moral diversity unleashed by the fragmentation of Western Christianity in the Reformation had long expressed itself in various Christian bioethics. The cleft between traditional and post-traditional Christian moral views further complicated the situation. By making the divisions within particular Christian religions often more stark than those separating these religions, traditional Roman Catholics, Episcopalians, and Presbyterians found themselves in many respects sharing more of an understanding of morality and bioethics than they had in common with the more liberal theologians and members of their own religion. Ecumenical aspirations to the contrary notwithstanding, a puzzled physician seeking moral guidance was confronted with a plurality of Western Christian moral understandings. It was unclear which among the Christian religions should give guidance. Roman Catholics and Protestants, for example, were divided regarding what is morally at stake in contraception, sterilization, and third-party-assisted reproduction. It was also unclear how such guidance should be understood in an increasingly secular Western culture.

In an age that endorses diversity, while considering real disparities of belief as threatening, Christian bioethics, or at least traditional Christian bioethics, presented differences that matter, and that are therefore threatening. The Western history of religious wars and inquisitorial coercion encumbered Christian bioethics with a past that made its contemporary undertaking suspect. In a world bloodied by its response to difference, Christian bioethics offered to divide Christian from non-Christian, and Christian from Christian, seeming to endanger the fabric of a peaceable society. The particular content of Christian bioethics was a possible enemy of tolerance and a friend of conflict. Having engendered the religious wars of the past, Christianity of the mid-20th century was engendering the culture wars of the future. From the perspective of post-traditional Christians, and indeed in terms of many of the rights movements of the 1960s and 70s, traditional Christianity was reactionary at best. It resisted progressive liberalism's commitment to freeing persons and social structures from the constraining hands of the past. It saw in abortion and the emerging contraceptive ethos not avenues of liberation but roads to damnation. Rather than celebrating this ethos of choice as a liberation from the tyranny of biological forces, which had subjected women to men, traditional Christianity recognized in the sexual revolution's affirmation of extramarital sex, the contraceptive ethos, and abortion, as only a further enslavement to the passions and the chaos they bring. Disagreements about these matters within Christianity itself heightened the moral confusion of the time. Christian bioethics, rather than providing a means to resolve bioethical controversies and to achieve a general consensus concerning health care policy, fueled further controversy.

To summarize, when Christian bioethics turned to the challenges of providing moral guidance for the new high-technology medicine, it found itself unequal to the task. The difficulties were multiple and deeply rooted in contemporary Christianity. Christianity was divided into a diversity of Christianities; it could not give unambiguous guidance. Given the plurality of visions, one could disingenuously select within rather broad constraints the religious perspective to approve behavior one wanted to embrace (e.g., if one wanted to find religious approval of artificial insemination by a donor, one needed only to select the appropriate Christian theologian). The mainline Christian religions were themselves in disarray about what it meant to be Christian: from within many Christian religions unambiguous guidance was often unavailable because centuries-old approaches to resolving moral controversies had been abandoned or rejected. Just as Christian bioethics had the opportunity to provide guidance for contemporary health care policy, Christianity seemed unclear as to what ethics it should offer. In consequence, the relevance of Christianity to the modern world could only be doubted. As if this were not bad enough, the surrounding culture had grounds to regard Christianity as a threat to a democratic and open polity for several reasons. First, traditional Christianity sought answers to moral problems within a hierarchical structure, rather than from individual reasoning and choice unfettered by the constraints of the past. Second, Christianity's hierarchical structure was patriarchal. Third, Christianity, by the particularity of its moral commitments, accented differences rather than encouraging the emergence of a moral consensus to which all could subscribe. Fourth, Christianity, insofar as it offered an ethics that contrasted with a secular ethics, could not provide guidance for public institutions or policy in the secular pluralist societies that had emerged in the West after the Second World War. The Christianness of Christian bioethics was itself problematic.

Christian vs. Secular Bioethics: The Disappearance of a Difference

As if to remedy the difficulties of a Christian bioethics that seemed too Christian, many Christian moral theologians directed their energies to showing that there is nothing morally to distinguish a Christian ethics from a secular ethics. The Jesuit moral theologian Joseph Fuchs reasoned,

> ... Christians and non-Christians face the same moral questions, and ... both must seek their solution in genuinely human reflection and according to the same norms; e.g., whether adultery and premarital intercourse are morally right or can be so, whether the wealthy nations of the world must help the poor nations and to what extent, whether birth control is justified and should be provided, and what types of birth control are worthy of the dignity of the human person. Such questions are questions for all of humanity. If, therefore, our church and other human communities do not

always reach the same conclusions, this is not due to the fact that there exists a different morality for Christians from that for non-Christians.[57]

A similar conclusion regarding the material equivalence of a secular and Christian ethics was reached as well by the theologian James Walter: "It has been my contention that there is neither anything distinctive nor specific to Christian ethics at the level of ground of ethics."[58] These claims by Fuchs and Walters are in accord with much of Western Christian natural-law-oriented, moral theological reflections, which identified the content of Christian morality with what natural reason can disclose.[59]

Within this framework of analysis, the moral distance between Christian moral theology and secular moral philosophy disappears. Christian ethics, which might have seemed (1) plural, (2) different from secular ethics, and (3) threatening to divide Christian from non-Christian by accenting moral differences, can be unified through reason, acknowledged as materially equivalent to a secular ethics, and regarded as affirming the moral community of all humans. As Charles Curran puts it:

> Obviously a personal acknowledgement of Jesus as Lord affects at least the consciousness of the individual and his thematic reflection on his consciousness, but the Christian and the explicitly non-Christian can and do arrive at the same ethical conclusions and can and do share the same general ethical attitudes, dispositions and goals. Thus, explicit Christians do not have a monopoly on such proximate ethical attitudes, goals and dispositions as self-sacrificing love, freedom, hope, concern for the neighbor in need or even the realization that one finds his life only in losing it. The explicitly Christian consciousness does affect the judgment of the Christian and the way in which he makes his ethical judgments, but non-Christians can and do arrive at the same ethical conclusions and also embrace and treasure even the loftiest of proximate motives, virtues, and goals which Christians in the past have wrongly claimed only for themselves. This is the precise sense in which I deny the existence of a distinctively Christian ethic; namely, non-Christians can and do arrive at the same ethical conclusions and prize the same proximate dispositions, goals and attitudes as Christians.[60]

This view of the material equivalence of Christian and secular morality was elaborated by many other Christian moralists.[61] Given such an understanding, Christian bioethics should cease to be a puzzle to secular thought or a source of division in secular society. Both in principle would share the same basic premises, as well as rules of moral evidence and inference. Rightly understood, Christian bioethics would not be plural, if secular bioethics were singular. A successful natural law account of morality should exorcise moral pluralism.

The concern is then whether being a Christian might at least communicate a particular style of moral life that would otherwise not be available to everyone and thus to every bioethicist.[62] To build on a set of points made by Aubert,[63] even if Christian and non-Christian morality are in general materially the same, they can still possess certain differences. The existential character of Christian belief in this account ties Christians to an experience of the God-directed nature of ethical demands, such that the manner and intentionality of Christian moral conduct differ from that of non-believers. Non-Christians would not be obeying moral rules for the sake of Christ. In addition, Christian theological understandings would transform the significance of actions. For example, Christians would regard the breaking of moral norms (e.g., intentionally harming a patient) as involving an estrangement from Christ. There would still be certain moral norms that would by definition be connected to being Christian, such as the obligation to join with other Christians in prayer. Being a Christian would also guide individual choices, such as the decision to join a Christian religious order so as to provide health care to the poor. Such individual decisions could only be fully under-stood within the context of Christian belief. All of this can be conceded while still holding that the general substance of Christian norms and therefore the general sub-stance of a Christian bioethics are the same as that of a non-Christian bioethics.[64]

In such circumstances, a Christian bioethics should not challenge a secular moral consensus. A Christian bioethics materially equivalent to a secular bioethics would not offer different moral rules concerning third-party-assisted reproduction, abortion, the allocation of medical resources, physician-assisted suicide, or euthanasia. Properly understood, there should not be particular confessional bioethical norms. The plurality of Christian bioethical rules could be brought in line with secular morality, given sufficient conceptual analysis and philosophical investigation. As a consequence, ener-gies could be directed in the universal service of social justice rather than that of a false moral particularity. The seeming divisiveness of Christian bioethics could be overcome through focusing on a morality endorsable by all and available to open philosophical examination and democratic appraisal.

Rather than working to the advantage of Christian bioethics, this approach further strengthened the case for a secular bioethics. Again, a secular bioethics was attractive either (1) because a Christian bioethics is particular and therefore plural and less congenial to policymakers than a secular ethic, which would unite persons as such and avoid religious divisiveness, or (2) because Christian morality is in substance equiva-lent to a secular morality and can therefore be adequately addressed by secular philo-sophical reflection. Christian bioethics would then be either divisive and dangerous or harmless and irrelevant. In either case, a secular rather than a distinctively Christian morality recommended itself. For many, secular bioethics is an appropriate religious choice because of its universal claims and ecumenical promises. This construal of Christian bioethics appears to have the advantage of freeing Christian bioethics from its divisions by anchoring it in a hoped-for unity achievable through secular moral philosophical analysis and argument.

Moral Crises and the Medieval Faith in Reason

The emergence of secular bioethics as a field of scholarship and as a foundation for health care policy has been among the dramatic cultural developments in post-World-War-II America, and indeed across the world. Though the term bioethics appeared only in the early 1970s, there was already in the 1940s, 50s, and 60s a dramatic resurgence of interest in both medical ethics and the medical humanities. As with all historical phenomena, this engagement in the medical humanities, medical ethics, and bioethics was associated with numerous cultural changes. Had it not been tied to a profound need to gain moral clarification and guidance, interest in bioethics would not have spread as quickly as it did across the world, gaining a place for bioethics both in the academy and in the framing of health care policy. It is easy to regard this constellation of concerns as primarily a response to the dramatic developments in medical science and technology following the Second World War or as a reaction to the atrocities of the National Socialists.[65] These explanations are too simple. It was not just that new technologies produced new moral challenges or that physicians had abetted the horrors of National Socialism, thus stimulating moral reflections and reactions in response to these atrocities. More significantly, taken-for-granted traditions were collapsing, creating a moral vacuum.

The profession of medicine itself was changing in terms of its social status and its self-understanding. Physicians were no longer accepted as in authority to make a wide range of decisions regarding the treatment of their patients. Traditional medical decision-making became characterized as paternalistic, and the test for informed consent moved from the professional standard to that of the reasonable and prudent person.[66] The 20th century was witnessing the substantive deprofessionalization of the health care professions. Medicine had entered the 20th century with many of its prerogatives as a quasi-self-governing guild still intact. American medicine conceived of itself as uniting independent (in the sense of unsalaried single practitioners) professionals who shared the self-regulation of their scientific art on behalf of the good of their patients and their society. The expectation was that all features of medical services should be directly under the control and supervision of the medical profession. In the United States with the emergence of health care insurance and the application of anti-trust law to the medical profession, medicine's character as an independent, self-governing profession was radically altered. Under American law, medicine came to be regarded no longer as a guild or as a self-regulating profession, but as a regulated trade.[67] Attempts by the medical profession to constrain its practitioners around a particular ethos, such as avoiding commercially oriented advertising, were forbidden at law.[68] By law, the medical profession was forbidden to impose its medical ethics on its members. It became increasingly difficult to induce membership in county and state medical associations, much less in the American Medical Association.

The ethics of the medical profession was both marginalized and brought into question. It was marginalized in that ever fewer physicians (at the close of the millennium barely a half) belonged to the American Medical Association, the author of the code of professional ethics supposedly governing the profession in the United States.[69] More fundamentally, ethics grounded in the insights and concerns of a particular professional organization was brought into question to the extent that one aspired to an ethics to guide a society as a whole in meeting its public policy challenges. It was only natural that in such circumstances concerns with medical ethics as a professional undertaking would be eclipsed by bioethics both in substance and in name. The term "medical ethics" took on a limited significance in reflecting the internal and generally unenforceable moral norms of one profession over against the universal aspirations of bioethics. These changes were part of a complex fabric of developments, which included the transformation of the once binary relationship of physician and patient into a complex association of physician, patient, insurer, payer (now usually the employer of the patient or increasingly a governmental agency), institutional provider (e.g., hospital), and governmental regulator. During this period of time, the physician solo practitioner was progressively relocated into group practice settings, managed health care plans, and institutional employers of physician services. Numerous third parties assumed authority over the physician-patient relationship, if not over the physicians themselves. An increasing number of non-physician experts came to play central roles in the conduct of medicine.[70] As Western Christian bioethics faced the social, technological, and economic challenges of the 1960s and 70s, it found physicians, dentists, nurses, and others whose professional identity was under revision, if not in question. The medicine of the 1960s and 1970s was becoming not only post-traditional, but post-professional. In this environment of moral, professional, and technological change, moral uncertainty became salient. There was a sense of an obligation to use responsibly the new powers provided by technological development but with fundamental unclarity, indeed disagreement, about the nature of those obligations. Just as it was called to give guidance, Western Christianity also found itself uncertain about what moral guidance it could or should provide. In this moral vacuum, secular morality offered itself as a plausible alternative source of guidance.

Western European expectations regarding bioethics and the moral life developed out of what had been a bold medieval attempt to bring faith and reason into synergy: each supported the other while allowing reason independently of a religious confession to disclose a morality common to all. Though the West had faith in faith, it came to possess an equal faith in reason's capacity to disclose a content-full morality binding all.[71] Despite the skepticism of figures such as Hume, the West would preserve from this tradition a continuing faith in universal human rights and even the possibility of a global bioethics. The Christian West had read St. Paul's reference in Romans 2:15 to "the law written in their hearts" as identifying an intellectual capacity to discover discursively a moral truth independent of humans. Western Christianity could then attempt to fulfill a promise made by the Stoics in their philosophical reflections, as well as in Roman law.[72] It was not just that a *jus naturale* was assumed as the backdrop for a proper *jus gentium*. It was also assumed that the substance of a Christian bioethics should be available through natural reason. This is not to say that Thomas Aquinas and others did not recognize that corrupted cultures and minds could not fully appreciate the natural law. They recognized that the passions could cloud the mind.[73] They also initially recognized a role for grace in all cognition.[74] But emphasis came to be placed on moral truths that discursive reason could disclose by examining human nature. The result was a shift in the understanding of morality so that moral knowledge was construed on the model of the impersonal rationality of logical or empirical scientific investigation. What came to be important was not the character of the reasoner, but the character of the argument and analysis.

Just as a logician or mathematician may succeed theoretically, though possessed of a personal dislike for logic and mathematics, so, too, the success of the moralist came to be seen to depend not on the life of the moralist, but on the character of the moralist's arguments. Moral truths could then be better explored and understood through developing better intellectual skills, rather than through developing a better moral life. One could not only be a good moral philosopher and bioethicist, but even a good moral theologian, although a moral reprobate and an unrepentant sinner. The conduct of one's moral and spiritual life was becoming disconnected from the conduct of moral philosophy and of theology. The further implication was that, through morally disinterested, discursive secular reasoning, one could establish the lineaments of a secular morality that should in general be coincident with the requirements of Christian moral theology. This disconnection of morality as a science from the moral life was abetted by the ways in which Roman Catholic moral theological reflection developed from its medieval confidence in reason to a strong affirmation of reason's role in morality as a special science.

Consider, for example, the following pre-Vatican II, mid-20th century reflection on the capacities of Roman Catholic moral theologians. The enterprise of morality and of bioethics is appreciated as a scientific one, suggesting that it can be undertaken in great measure by relying on rational principles accessible to all. Success in seeing moral truths is not directly dependent on the investigator's success in living a good moral life, but on reasoning well.

> But the [Roman] Catholic moralists do have a just claim to special competence in the science of ethics, the science of moral right and wrong, the science of applying the moral law to the problems of human living. They are highly trained and experienced men in this particular field. Their preparation for this professional capacity is intense and comprehensive; they usually teach the science of morality over a number of years; and they are constantly dealing with practical applications of this science. Aside from any question of religion, the [Roman] Catholic moralists represent by far the world's largest group of specialists in the science of ethics. And they have a tradition of scientific study that extends over centuries.[75]

Again, the claim is not just of a near coincidence of the morality known by discursive reason and that known by faith, but also the view that morality can be known without attempting to live morally. This approach also suggested that one could live a moral life, even in the absence of living a good religious life. In addition, there is the implication that one can be a successful scholar of Christian bioethics by reasoning well, whether or not one is Christian, whether or not one lives a moral life, or for that matter whether or not one lives a life of religious dedication. The religious life, the moral life, and the enterprise of moral theology were separated. Moral theological knowing depended on discursive reasoning, not on a noetic knowing influenced by the character of one's life.

This confidence in discursive moral rationality supported a moral universalism that could claim, on the basis of right reason, to be the foundation of a universal society. The Middle Ages assumed a unity of faith, discursive reason, and society. As the history of the high Middle Ages showed, this unity required coercive force and inquisitional supervision.[76] Western Christianity was united under a Western Christian emperor and Christian kings.[77] In addition, discursive reason could disclose a moral fabric that all could share, even heretics. A morality grounded in discursive rationality offered the promise of a four-fold successful unity. First, morality and rationality would be materially equivalent: those who disagreed with the fabric of morality (and thus of bioethics) would be making irrational claims in the sense of claims that could not be rationally justified. Second, since rational argument buttressed the fabric of morality, morality (including bioethics) could carry with it the authority of reason in addition to the authority of God. Third, coercive force (e.g., imposing a rationally justified health care policy) against behavior contrary to right reason would not be alien to those subject to it. Rather, such coercive force would restore true autonomy. The behavior imposed would not be heteronomous, but in principle congenial to the true nature of those who were thus reformed. Finally, all would be shown to be bound in a single moral community defined not just by Western Christian morality, but also disclosable through rational reflection. All of these assumptions with regard to rationality and morality would later be embraced by Kant. They came to provide a basis for expecting that one could establish a canonical content-full morality as the basis for a universally authoritative bioethics and health care policy, even without faith. Its keystone was discursive rationality. This keystone decisively marginalized the noetic form of knowing that had previously been at the core of Christian claims to knowledge.[78]

From the Reformation and the Enlightenment to Secular Bioethics

When the Reformation forced the West to undergo a foundational experience of diversity, there was a fundamental recasting of Western moral experience with profound implications for bioethics, both secular and Christian. After a half millennium of unity, Western moral experience became defined in terms of rupture, fragmentation, and novelty. The Western Christian unity of prayer, liturgy, and life was shattered into numerous and competing accounts concerning the significance of human suffering (e.g., disputes regarding purgatory and indulgences), the character of human salvation (e.g., the roles played by faith and works), and the character of appropriate Christian behavior (e.g., the celibacy of priests and the place of fasting in the Christian life). In addition, the multitude of Christianities and their traditions of Christian moral reflection began each on its own to address issues in medical ethics. The significant body of biomedical moral analyses generated within Roman Catholic moral theology in the 16th and 17th centuries became significant for that religion, but not for the other Christian religions. The experience of the moral life and its systematic understanding became plural.

Against this fragmentation,[79] the West reached back to a cardinal element of its defining self-understanding: the role of discursive reasoning. Even if Western Christianity were fragmented into numerous competing religious moral communities, secular moral thought should still disclose a unity through rational moral reflection. Faith in secular moral rationality was underscored just as religious reason fragmented into a plurality of competing understandings. As the Reformation broke the unity of European religious consciousness, the Renaissance gave strength to secular rational aspirations. These aspirations were then fortified by the success of science. As traditional accounts of astronomy, physics, and anatomy were radically replaced by understandings established by new scientific studies, reason appeared able to unlock the secrets of nature. Secular rationality also promised to disclose a common morality. This promise was embraced in reaction to the religious wars of the 16th and 17th centuries. The modern moral philosophical project renewed one of the philosophical promises of the

Western Middle Ages: a rationally grounded account of morality. But this time, this rational account would be divorced from faith and the passions of religious controversy. This historical experience ushered in a profound secularization of moral thought. Secular morality not only displaced religious moral reflection, it also promised what religious morality had failed to provide: even if religious morality were plural, secular morality could be one.

The fragmentation of the Western medieval moral consciousness into numerous competing religious moral self-understandings (and bioethics) led to the third rupture from its religious past (this first being the separation from the Church of the first millennium and the second the Protestant Reformation) through the articulation of a Western European, secular moral consciousness. The modern philosophical project of grounding morality in reason, even when this was a back-handed grounding that undermined the morality and theology of the established religions thus transcending religious diversity, led to the fully secular, moral aspirations of the Enlightenment, and finally to the emergence of contemporary secular bioethics. The next chapter will turn to these in greater detail. Here it is enough to note that these aspirations drew credibility from the religious turmoil that marked the West during the 16th and 17th centuries, and thus in the end gave credibility to secular over religious bioethics. There was on the part of many a moral revulsion at the bloodshed that Western Christianity had engendered. Pierre Bayle (1647-1706), in a book first published in 1686, observes that

> [F]or my part, I'm amaz'd that we have not more of this sort [i.e., Free-Thinkers and Deists] among us, considering the havock which Religion has made in the World, and the Extinction, by an almost unavoidable Consequence, of all Vertue; by its authorizing, for the sake of a temporal Prosperity, all the Crimes imaginable, Murder, Robbery, Banishment, Rapes, &c. which produce infinite other Abominations, Hypocrisy, sacrilegious Profanation of Sacraments, &c.[80]

Against the backdrop of the bloodshed of the religious wars of the 17th century, Enlightenment philosophers promised a universally accessible secular basis for human community justifiable without appeal to particular religious, cultural, or traditional moral commitments or insights, and which could rely on an immanent authority (e.g., human reason, human sympathies, human sentiments, etc.) rather than a transcendent one (i.e., God's). The end of the 17th century involved a profound change in Western European thought. There was the forthright emergence of a secular culture. As Butterfield observes,

> The closing decades of the seventeenth century see the greatest transition in the history of civilization that has been witnessed in our part of the globe since the rise of Christianity. It was the period of the Great Secularization in thought. ...[81]

This secularization marked the beginning of the end of Christendom, the end of Christianity's establishment.

The Enlightenment sought a morality equivalent in general substance to that of Christianity but without the illiberal constraints of Christian history, belief, and ritual. Christ and Christianity could be recast in rational moral terms (as Kant attempted in *Religion innerhalb der Grenzen der blossen Vernunft* [1792]). One could have a revised Christianity without Jesus with His crucial historical and metaphysical claims. Christ was no longer regarded as the Messiah of Israel and the Son of God Who rose from the dead, but at best as a world historical figure whose exemplary virtue had been decisive for human history. Theological and ritual concerns were if possible to be translated into a moral significance or to disappear so that within a religion of morality one could have progress without religious conflicts. Against the background of religious division, one could affirm the unity of humanity in a common morality: all could with Kant aspire to a universal secular recognition of human rights.[82] This imperative provided the basis for the secular hopes for bioethics in the 1970s. Secular moral rationality supported the critical reassessment of Christian bioethics, as had occurred for moral theology in the mid-1960s and afterwards. Christian bioethics in the mid-1970s and afterwards was reshaped in terms of the secular heritage.

The secular medical ethics or bioethics of the 1960s and 1970s drew confidence from the modern philosophical and Enlightenment projects of accounting for morality without an appeal to a particular religious faith[83] (i.e., Christianity) or even a particular cultural perspective (i.e., Greece or the West).[84] On the one hand, bioethics could draw from an Enlightenment goal of establishing a universally valid moral perspective (even when this validity could only be articulated in negative terms, as a freedom from the illiberal hand of traditional tyrannies), which undoubtedly had its best articulation in the work and thought of Immanuel Kant (1724-1804), but which also had expression in the French Revolution's August 26, 1789, Declaration of the Rights of Man. On the other hand, it could draw from those dimensions of the Enlightenment that sought to establish human self-government not through a systematic philosophy, but through both a fundamental, usually non-rational recasting of the foundations of morality and a critique of the clerical constraints of traditional Christianity (e.g., this found a particularly powerful expression in the anti-religious sentiments of David Hume [1711-1776]). This complex set of intellectual concerns gave birth to the assumption that one could articulate a secular account of morality understandable outside of any particular religious or cultural tradition.

The Enlightenment and its Dirty Hands

The first fruits of the Enlightenment aspiration to a polity grounded in a secular recognition of human rights included not just the secular American Republic, but the bloodshed of France's First Republic. The intellectual project of resituating moral understandings outside the constraints of traditional Christianity and its churches issued in one of the most decisive moments in the further secularization of Western Christendom: the French Revolution[85] and its carnage. The Reign of Terror was followed by Napoleon (1769-1821),[86] who brought further dramatic changes in the moral, legal, and political character of Europe through large-scale warfare. Even the character of warfare changed with a novel commitment to the total mobilization of all citizens. The cultural face of Europe was transformed. The slaughterheaps of the Napoleonic wars produced a substantial secularization of European Christendom,[87] of which the central European Secularization of 1803[88] was only one, although a very important, event. Despite, if not because of, all these developments, European society embraced the 19th century with a confidence in secular progress and an abiding expectation of a peace that would bind all in a common secular faith. Hegel, who has been insightfully characterized as the Protestant equivalent of Thomas Aquinas,[89] followed Kant, by relocating Protestant Christianity in a rationality that no longer acknowledged the particularity of Christian history. Christian history was rationally recast as world history leading to the liberal societies of early 19th century Europe and various genre of millennial hopes in addition to those of Karl Marx (1818-1883) and Friedrich Engels (1820-1895).[90] The result was further secular reinterpretation of Western Christian sentiments along with the final collapse of the papal states in 1870. There was as well the emergence of a secular moral consciousness even further disconnected from traditional Christianity, a consciousness that still lies at the roots of much of contemporary bioethics.

A yet further rupture came with the 20th century. First, the secular hope for a perpetual peace grounded in a secular rationality was buried in the trenches of the First World War. The Southern novelist Walker Percy put this well.

> What theorists of the old modern age had to confront were the altogether unexpected disasters of the twentieth century: that after three hundred years of the scientific revolution and in the emergence of rational ethics in European Christendom, Western man in the twentieth century elected instead of an era of peace and freedom an orgy of wars, tortures, genocide, suicide, murder, and rapine unparalleled in history.
> The old modern age ended in 1914.[91]

World War I was followed by the October Revolution, which like the French Revolution sought through terror and blood to purge humanity of Christianity so as to establish the final reign of justice, humanity, and peace. This was followed by the show trials of Stalin, International Socialism, the concentration camps of National Socialism, the prison camps of Maoist China, and the killing fields of Pol Pot. Tens of millions died on behalf of a new and supposedly better secular future in the name of justice, fairness, and workers' rights, or in the recapturing of a pagan past in a new post-Christian future. Medical morality was misshapen to conform with new state interests. New medical moralities were produced to guide physicians in the commission of state-directed moral atrocities. All of this occurred under the umbrella of the two grand anti-Christian attempts to bring heaven to earth and to make meaning merely human: National Socialism and communism. Each in its own way promised to bring paradise to earth by force. Secular moralities were involved in more carnage in absolute terms than had ever been experienced in religious Western Europe.

It was not just that Western Europe and the world were confronted with the 20th century experience of bloodshed in the name of numerous competing secular moralities. It also was becoming clear that secular rationality via sound rational argument alone could not transcend the diversity of moral visions with their pluralities of bioethics. As Max Horkheimer observes, "Reason has liquidated itself as an agency of ethical, moral, and religious insight."[92] At the beginning of the 21st century, Western moral reflection is returned to the polytheism of the ancient world. Despite the carnage of the 20th century, the aspirations of the Enlightenment are desperately affirmed, at least in the aspiration to a universal sense of justice and fairness, in the hope of establishing a global cosmopolitan ethics.

Contemporary secular moral thought, along with its bioethics, are framed against the background of a twofold failure to sustain a universal moral narrative. First, there is the failure of the medieval Western Christian moral narrative to sustain itself as a universal moral narrative. Second, there is the equally defining failure of secular morality to achieve a moral unity comparable to that of the Middle Ages.[93] Real and substantive disagreements about the character of morality remain in the face of a hope for a liberal cosmopolitan world ethic. When Lyotard notes the non-availability of a universal moral narrative,[94] we must recognize the dual failure of the aspirations to a universal moral account: that of Western Christian and that of Western secular universalism. Against and despite the background of these failures, we are witnessing the self-conscious emergence of internationally diverse approaches to bioethics, just as a liberal cosmopolitan ethic seeks to be dominant. Considering the differences separating Asian versus Western understandings of bioethical probity, one must now ask: whose moral traditions? which bioethics?[95] The experience of post-modernity is the recognition that by reason alone secular morality cannot establish a content-full morality equivalent to the Christian morality that fragmented with the Reformation. After the fragmentation of the Reformation and the secularization of the Enlightenment, there is the moral diversity of post-modernity. This moral diversity defines the context for contemporary bioethics. Despite this diversity, contemporary secular bioethics has gathered strength in reaction to the diversity of Christian bioethics. In the pursuit of a common canonical moral vision, bioethics has recapitulated in a short period the Enlightenment's response to religious diversity.

The post-World War II reaction to the bloodshed born of national and international socialism was not to affirm substantive moral diversity, nor to create space for a foundational plurality of moral communities, but nevertheless to search for a content-full, global, secular morality. The hope of discursively justifying a universal content-full morality has not died. After Vatican II such hopes combined with the post-traditional movements of the late 1960s, resulting in a significant turn to secular morality. At the same time, Western Europe was further distancing itself from its previous monotheistic, monocultural, Christian vision of values and reality. The Western Christian vision, which had emerged as the West's dominant self-understanding over against the Christianity of the Mediterranean littoral prior to the time of Charles the Great (742-814),[96] and which had remained intact until the Reformation and to some extent despite the Enlightenment, was now in substantial disarray. Europe was perhaps not in danger of becoming non-Eurocentric.[97] It was in any event nurturing the ancient pagan European cultural resources that had re-emerged with vigor in the Renaissance and the Enlightenment,[98] in the hope of still locating them within a common secular moral rationality. The result was the emergence of both a secular medical morality as well as new interest in the humanities.

Faith in Secular Rationality Unshaken: Secular Medical Ethics and the Medical Humanities

In the wake of the Enlightenment, it seemed necessary explicitly to articulate a medical ethics not reliant on traditional Christian morality or its various expressions in informal codes of gentlemanly behavior.[99] At the end of the 18th and the beginning of the 19th century medical ethical treatises of a secular nature became salient. Much of this occurred as codes of medical ethics or etiquette were crafted for the medical professions. There was the perceived need formally and secularly to determine the nature of proper medical behavior.[100] As one entered the 20th century, there was a heightened recognition that old traditions could not guide and that a new medical morality was needed.[101] For example, a British secular medical ethics text published in 1902 acknowledges that "It is not sufficient to say, as some people do, that medical ethics may be summed up in the Golden Rule, or that a man has only to behave like a gentleman."[102] The author recognizes that the guiding mores were changing so that "what was regarded as customary and even proper some years ago, has often come to be universally condemned."[103] It is as if the author protested too much in denying that "our conception of Christianity and chivalry has undergone a complete revolution within the same period."[104] Cultural, religious, scientific, technological, and economic developments were recasting the landscape of medical practice.

Philosophy promised for health care in the 1960s, 1970s and 1980s what it had offered European societies in the 17th and 18th centuries: a rationally defensible ethics that can bind humans as such and justify in secular terms a content-rich account of human rights, duties, proper character, virtue, sentiments of care, etc.[105] The medical humanities in the 1960s and 1970s recaptured the aspirations of the first, second, and third humanisms.[106] The first humanism in the late 15th and the 16th centuries claimed a basis for human unity over against the emerging Christian religious divisions of the time. At the same time, it reaffirmed classical Greek and Roman pagan ideals of *paideia*, *philanthropia*, and *humanitas*. The second humanism at the end of the 18th and beginning of the 19th centuries[107] continued Enlightenment themes in promising a cultivation proper to humans as such. The third humanism and so-called New Humanism, which surfaced at the end of the 19th and beginning of the 20th centuries,[108] anticipated the medical humanities movement of the 1960s and 1970s. The humanities were invoked to place the new sciences and technologies within the context of immanent human values and to provide a moral unity for an increasingly secular culture.[109] The medical humanities in the 1960s and later bioethics were engaged with similar expectations: to disclose the values and goals proper to humans, so as to bind all in a coherent and well-directed technological culture.

There was an additional claim: medicine and the humanities were recognized as mutually supporting. Medicine as a project of human caring was itself construed as one of the humanities. Its fully self-conscious appreciation was sought in the humanities. On the other hand, the traditional humanities found a concrete bond to the human condition through their contact with medicine. Medicine could inspire, invigorate, and revivify the humanities. The humanities could strengthen the tie between medicine and human values. Medicine, for its part, could reconnect the humanities with the human condition, saving them from being isolated scholarly pursuits. This vision of medicine

and the humanities found its epiphany in Edmund Pellegrino's perceptive and provoc-
ative rallying cry: "Medicine is the most humane of sciences, the most empiric of arts,
and the most scientific of humanities."[110] The humanities, rejuvenated from contact
with medicine, were not just to be an academic undertaking or a cultural achievement.
According to Pellegrino, they were also to constitute a personal moral calling.

> The humanist must also be "authentic." The medical setting requires that
> the humanist incorporate the values he or she professes and the character
> traits that are embodiments of the liberal arts teachings, to be human if
> not humane ... truly, the humanist must be "holier than thou."[111]

The "holiness" sought was not a Christian holiness. It was a secular "wholeness": a
secular realization of deep authenticity, sensitivity, and moral integration understood
in terms of immanent values.

A secular morality and bioethics were needed to meet the needs of a society that was
to be both secular and pluralist. The moral pluralism of society that was originally
rooted in religious diversity had already taken on secular expressions. A secular moral
education was necessary to provide a common *paideia*, schooling in a common sense of
moral appropriateness. Again Pellegrino notes that:

> So far as ethics and the humanities go, they undoubtedly raise the sensitiv-
> ity of students and faculty to ethical and values questions. ... Almost
> everywhere, as a result, patients are better apprised of their part in clinical
> decisions, and of the value and moral issues woven into their relationships
> with the physician. This is a result to be desired in a society that is
> democratic, educated and pluralistic in its value systems. Whatever per-
> sonalizes and particularizes healing will make it more humane.[112]

The particularizing of the healing act was not to be rooted in the morality of a religious
community. Instead, the particularity was personalized in the sense of addressing individual idiosyncrasy on the level of personal response.

The turn to philosophy in the mid-1970s was vigorous but ahistorical. Bioethics
and the philosophy of medicine were engaged as if the field had sprung like Athena
from the head of Zeus.[113] Almost no reference was made to or account taken of the
prior history of sustained analysis and investigation. Scholars turned to the task of
fashioning a bioethics, largely ignoring if not cavalierly dismissing distinctions framed
in theological reflections with centuries of tradition.[114] The significant history of
philosophical reflections concerning medicine[115] was also generally under-appreciat-
ed. There was even a secondary literature on the history of the philosophy of medicine,
which received scant attention.[116] The new bioethics and philosophy of medicine were
embraced as a response to novel cultural, religious, scientific, and technological challenges. They were regarded as of one fabric with the endeavor to disclose and sustain a
core set of commitments proper to a humanity that had emerged at the end of the
Second World War and found itself directed to a common global future. Secular bioethics claimed that a universal human moral community could be recognized and justified
around a set of moral commitments proper to humans as such. Given the considerable

variety of Christian bioethics, given the internal theological disputes into which the Christian religions were falling, and given the pressing need to frame policy regarding the proper approach to issues such as organ transplantation, third-party-assisted reproduction, and the withholding of life-saving treatment, secular philosophical bioethics offered what was wanted: a morality promising to unite all around a set of fundamental moral commitments.

The development of an official bureaucratic or governmental bioethics in the 1970s gave credibility to the claims of secular bioethics: secular bioethics had secured a common moral vision to bind all. In the United States, the National Commission for the Protection of Human Subjects of Biomedical and Behavioral Research (established in 1972) fashioned recommendations to govern research involving humans ranging from the use of fetuses to psychosurgery.[117] The recommendations claimed justification in the Commission's trinity of ethical principles: autonomy, beneficence, and justice.[118] These principles went far beyond a permission-based ethic's elaboration of the limits of authority in forbearance rights, rights not to be touched without permission. The field of secular bioethics gained impetus from the seeming success of the National Commission in bridging moral differences. Their success suggested a content-full background morality on which all could draw. Public bioethical reflection produced the secular equivalent of a content-full moral theology, which delivered secular guidelines for a secular pastoral ethics (a bioethics that could guide secular "ethicists" in giving advice regarding particular cases), along with a kind of secular canon law (e.g., secularly morally justified regulations for research involving human subjects). This accomplishment bolstered the Enlightenment hope of discovering a foundational secular moral communality bound by a common human morality.

Secular bioethics was further buttressed by the publication of Beauchamp and Childress's *The Principles of Biomedical Ethics* with its apparent ability effectively to guide moral choice through its four principles: autonomy, beneficence, non-maleficence, and justice.[119] The authors of *The Principles* and many who applied them secured common decisions when they approached diverse clinical cases, despite divergent theoretical commitments. While religious bioethics remained plural, secular bioethics seemed united at least practically around a common set of bioethical principles. The academy had produced principles that could guide public policy and direct clinical bioethics decision-making. However partial and incomplete, this framework produced individuals who claimed to be experts in bioethics able to guide physicians and patients to morally appropriate health care decisions. The shift from a religious bioethics to a secular bioethics appeared fully vindicated: a neutral, but still content-full, vision of proper moral deportment was at hand. It claimed governance for humans as such. On the basis of this success, the practitioners of bioethics, now titled "ethicists", could function as secular priests. As secular moral theologians, they could guide secular society. Despite the difficulties of the Enlightenment's heritage, secular rationality appeared to have secured for bioethics what Christian bioethics could not offer: a unity of moral understanding open to all through reason able to guide public policy.

Why a Canonical, Content-full Secular Bioethics Cannot be Justified in General Secular Terms: Content Requires Assumptions

The apparent triumph of secular bioethics is hollow. There are as many secular under-standings as well as accounts of morality, justice, and fairness as there are religions. There is no canonical sense or account of justice for the allocation of health care resources that is universally accepted or definitively justified. There is no settled gener-al secular view of, or consensus regarding, the morality of abortion, health care alloca-tion, and euthanasia. There is deep disagreement about the propriety of many forms of third-party-assisted reproduction, indeed even of whether it is ever appropriate to provide medical treatment for individuals wishing to have sexual intercourse outside of the marriage of a man and a woman (e.g., to correct impotence). More significantly, there is no content-full, generally accepted understanding of the good life and of proper conduct. There is also no agreement about how one should proceed to remedy this difficulty and establish a canonical content-full ethics with its appropriate bioeth-ics. Again, it is for this reason that bioethicists face a challenge in giving reliable advice. Depending on the ethics and the bioethics chosen as normative, dramatically different recommendations will be endorsed. The apparent moral unanimity found in the recom-mendations of some bioethics commissions is at best a political construction. One might in particular consider the apparent success of the already mentioned National Commission for the Protection of Human Subjects of Biomedical and Behavioral Re-search, which seemed able both to disclose a set of basic moral principles as well as to fashion generally acceptable health care policy. Actual public policy debates and polit-ical campaigns, not to mention continuing bioethical disputes at the level of both theory and practice, reveal a significant range of conflicting moral visions reaching beyond that encompassed by most bioethics commissions across the world. Even the legitimacy of taxation on behalf of governmentally supported research is far from uncontroversial.

The field of bioethics proceeds as if there were a common background morality ac-cepted by all.[120] In an age that celebrates cultural diversity, there is little recognition of substantive moral diversity.[121] The strategy is instead either (1) to deny or discount the significance of the disagreement (e.g., to hold that the disagreement can be interpreted so as not to lead to the affirmation of radically different health care policies), or (2) to discount or marginalize those who disagree (e.g., to dismiss their moral perspectives as non-mainstream, marginal, or extreme), rather than (3) to allow space for the parallel pursuit of different moral visions (e.g., the establishment of parallel health care systems constituted around different understandings of morality and human flourishing). The failure to acknowledge moral diversity and provide social space for the pursuit of differ-ent understandings of morality, justice, and human flourishing (e.g., once again, one might think here of parallel health care systems informed by different understandings of morally appropriate health care) is especially puzzling, given the history of the last cen-tury. Millions died in the 20th century in disputes about the nature of justice, fairness, equality, human rights, and the character of the good life. The clash of secular moralities produced carnage unparalleled in absolute numbers in human history. Secular philoso-phy even gave terror a recognized place. Consider Merleau-Ponty's exegesis of the role of terror as an instrument for achieving a more humane future:

> It is certain that neither Bukharin nor Trotsky nor Stalin regarded Terror as intrinsically valuable. Each one imagined he was using it to realize a genuinely human history which had not yet started but which provides the justification for revolutionary violence. In other words, as Marxists, all three confess that there is a meaning to such violence – that it is possible to understand it, to read into it a rational development and to draw from it a humane future.[122]

The history of the acceptance of terror and torture shows that there is a polymorphism of human inclinations and intentions regarding moral issues: different persons have different dispositions to give different rankings to important moral values and principles. If one were to regard the phenomenon of moral pluralism in socio-biological terms, one would suspect that this diversity is the result of selective pressure in different environments, and that this polymorphism of behavioral inclinations conveys individual and inclusive fitness in particular circumstances.

The contemporary denial of or failure to observe this obvious diversity of moralities need not be attributed to any disingenuous motive or conscious choice. It likely reflects a strong, albeit unconscious, insufficiently examined desire to justify a particular content-full background morality so as to provide moral authority for the public policy one wishes to have dominate. The result is the establishment of a particular bioethics as an ideology, a false consciousness: a claim of a secular moral consensus so as to legitimate the public policy and clinical roles of bioethicists despite real and persistent moral disagreement. The false consciousness is designed to hide the manifest moral diversity that besets bioethics and health care policy, such as different understandings of the nature and moral importance of equality, freedom, life, and death. Such differences have to be denied so that the conclusions endorsed by governmental ethics commissions can be claimed to follow from a common morality held to be recognized by all humans, the so-called moral consensus.[123] If this diversity were acknowledged, then secular bioethics would need to be recognized as marked by a plurality as profound as that besetting Christian bioethics. Since it is impossible to deny that philosophers dispute regarding the nature of morality, an inviting tactic has been to hold that, though theories differ, the background morality addressed by the theories is the same. If there were a single secularly disclosable canonical content-full morality, then one could construct middle-level principles to guide, despite theoretical moral disagreements. A normative consensus could then be invoked, which would accord with the morality proper to humans. Or if such a consensus did not exist, the appropriate consensus could be claimed to be sufficiently congruent or overlapping so that there would be enough of a commonality to count as a common background morality.[124] The success of commissions in fashioning health care policy and principles in guiding clinical decision-making can then be taken as evidence of a common morality.

Such claims are at many levels implausible. First, one should anticipate that, when impaneling a commission to reach concrete moral conclusions regarding substantive issues of public policy, one would avoid appointing members with truly divergent moral views. One would expect that libertarians would not be appointed together with socialists to a panel charged with developing policy for health care reform. Such persons would differ not only in their theories, but in their deep moral commitments.

One can only imagine how different the discussions of the National Commission for the Protection of Human Subjects in Biomedical and Behavioral Research would have been, had the Commission when discussing fetal research included a representative from the pope of Rome, an atheist feminist, a fundamentalist Baptist, a Maoist communist, a libertarian, and an advocate of unhindered choice in the matter of abortions.[125] A better political strategy would be what in fact appears to have been followed, namely, to appoint individuals with similar background moral commitments, but with some theoretical disagreements.[126] In that fashion, those who establish such commissions, as well as those who participate in them, will be edified by being further convinced of the generality of their morality because analysis and dialogue will secure substantive conclusions despite theoretical differences.

Support for the existence of a common background morality knowable through secular moral reflection, and for the view that actual moral divergence is rooted in diverse theoretical reconstructions of that morality, can also be secured if two authors with similar ideological viewpoints, but with different theoretical perspectives, explore the same bioethical problems. They will discover that, though they start from different theoretical approaches, they will come to manageably similar resolutions of controversies. This is the case as long as their theoretical understandings do not carry with them particular and divergent moral commitments. That is, a rule utilitarian and a deontologist who share the same antecedent views of the content of morality can reconstruct their common morality within their divergent theoretical frameworks to nearly the same effect. One (the utilitarian) will express the lineaments of their common morality in consequence-grounded rules for action. The other (the deontologist) will express the same lineaments in a set of right- and wrong-making conditions grounded in a particular understanding of moral rationality. Only in certain borderline cases that depend on the understanding of exceptional cases may there be any differences. For example, the rule utilitarian will hold that, as a rule grounded in a concern for consequences, one should not violate rules for proper conduct, even when making a particular exception may avoid considerable adverse consequences. For instance, even though telling the truth may have considerable adverse consequences in a particular instance, the rule utilitarian will hold that in the long run the best balance of positive over adverse consequences will be achieved by always telling the truth.

As a result, persons with a common morality but with different moral theoretical commitments will be able to elaborate middle-level principles that can guide them to common solutions of moral and public policy questions. One can hypothesize that something of this sort occurred with Beauchamp and Childress's *Principles of Bioethics*: their volume illustrates this phenomenon.[127] Since the authors had similar background understandings of justice, they could invoke a middle-level principle of justice and come to similar conclusions regarding problems in health care allocation. Had they held substantively different moralities (e.g., if one were socialist and the other libertarian), their invocation of a middle-level principle of justice would have revealed the depth of their disagreement, rather than their background concurrence. The very meaning of the principles would have then changed – they would serve as heuristics for disclosing moral disagreement. In addition, theoretical perspectives can involve unbridgeable differences. They can carry with them fundamentally different moralities, not just different accounts of morality. If the deontologist reconstructing a background morality is a committed Kantian, then that person will understand promise-breaking as wrong without exception, while such will not be the case for act utilitarians (in any event, not on principle). Though in some circumstances Kantians and act utilitarians may agree about the keeping of a promise, those areas of agreement will be bad predictors of whether promises will be held to bind when the costs of commitment are high. Moralities and bioethics (e.g., socialist vs. libertarian, pro-life vs. pro-choice) are plural in their content (e.g., diverse in their ranking of moral principles and/or values) as well as plural in their moral rationalities (e.g., deontological or teleological). The morality of a Kantian is not the morality of an act utilitarian. For example, Kantians and utilitarians will approach the preservation of patient-physician confidentiality in quite different ways. There are numerous moral rationalities, each with its own account of the proper balancing of the right and the good, of non-agent-relative and agent-relative accounts of morality.

Tom Beauchamp provides an excellent example of a person who seriously holds that there is a common morality shared by all. This claim is tantamount to claiming that there is a moral consensus in this regard. To make out his case, he conflates (1) the ordinary notion of morality as either a "doctrine or system concerned with conduct and duty; moral science" or "moral conduct; usually, good moral conduct; behaviour conformed to the moral law; moral virtue"[128] with (2) the notion of an open-ended list of moral considerations that different persons in different communities may rank differently. The latter cannot provide any moral guidance. However, morals are in their ordinary sense concerned with precisely this: giving moral guidance. They bear on "the distinction between right and wrong, or good and evil, in relation to the actions, volitions, or character of responsible beings".[129] When this volume speaks of a morality, it identifies a moral practice that can give guidance. To make out his case, Beauchamp distinguishes between morality in the narrow sense and morality in the broad sense. Morality in the narrow sense for Beauchamp is not a philosophical ethical theory, but a group of principles, rules, or rights. He tries to make this case by listing fourteen rules he holds to be universal, such as "1) Tell the truth. 2) Respect the privacy of others. ... 6) Do not kill."[130] He then without sufficient acknowledgement takes back most of what he has given by admitting "No rule on this list is absolute, and no rule is arranged or lexically ordered to override other rules in cases of conflict."[131] His claim boils down to the assertion that morality in the narrow sense is focused on a list of considerations that turns out to be open-ended. As he admits, his list "does not exhaust morality in the narrow sense."[132] The difficulty lies in the circumstance that determining what is moral or immoral depends on the moral considerations one acknowledges (i.e., what additional rules one may add) and how one ranks them. Beauchamp, for example, also includes the following two rules: "10) Do not deprive of goods. ... 14) Help persons with disabilities."[133] Such rankings also determine when it is allowable to kill and when it is immoral to kill. Consider, for example, the Elder Eddas, a collection of ancient Icelandic texts compiled by Saemund Sigfusson in the late 11th or early 12th century. In "The High One's Lay", attributed to the Norse pagan god Odin, the following moral advice is given. "58. He should early rise, who another's property or life desires to have. Seldom a sluggish wolf gets prey, or a sleeping man victory."[134] Taken at face value, Beauchamp's claim concerning the universality of morality in the normal sense becomes materially equivalent to the claim

that Quakers and Vikings shared the same morality, since both advanced considerations regarding the propriety of killing, though in the case of Quakers they were
committed to pacifism, and in the case of Vikings they recognized that, all else being
equal, it was a good thing to go pillaging and murdering, as long as it took place in
some other country. [135]

If one begins with different rankings of important human values or right-making
conditions, one will not share a common morality. If one does not have the same moral
premises as well as rules of evidence and inference, one will not be able to resolve
moral controversies by sound rational argument.[136] In order to choose one ranking of
values or moral principles over another, one must already possess a background moral
sense or thin theory of the good. But to choose the right background moral sense or
thin theory of the good, one must have yet another moral sense or thin theory even
further in the background. One cannot appeal to intuitions unless one has a background intuition to guide the choice of the right intuitions. To secure the correct
background intuition, one needs a guiding intuition even further in the background. A
similar challenge confronts any appeal to consequences in order to resolve a dispute
about the proper moral understanding to follow. If one has a pluralism of goods or
consequences, one must know apart from the consequences how to rank those goods.
One must already have an independent basis to know the bases for the moral understanding one ought to affirm. So, too, any translation of different genre of consequences into a common measure requires already having an understanding of values that
allows one to rank the different genre of values. To choose the right background moral
sense for this task, one will need another moral sense even further in the background.
This difficulty is not escaped by retreating to a preference utilitarianism that eschews
correcting preferences (after all, one cannot correct preferences to avoid utility mon-
sters unless one already has a background morality more fundamental than the satisfaction of preferences). One must in any case know which discount rate to choose for
preferences. Nor is it possible to resolve moral controversies through an appeal to
moral rationality without already knowing what content that moral rationality should
incorporate.

The same is the case with attempts to develop a casuistry for guiding moral judgment; they presuppose what they hope to provide.[137] Casuistry can only function
successfully if one already knows which cases should count as exemplar cases for what
and in which way. One must already be able to place cases within a functioning moral
perspective within an intact moral institution. The Roman Catholic practice of casuistry guided particular penitents in resolving their moral concerns because it could
presuppose background moral, metaphysical, and institutional assumptions, which
establish certain persons as moral experts (e.g., moral theologians), as well as other
persons as in moral authority (e.g., confessors), able to make binding moral determinations. The cases examined and used for guidance were nested in an institution that was
not itself ever brought into question by those seeking casuistic guidance. It was clear
what morality to apply and particular persons were in authority (confessors) to apply
that morality to specific cases. Moreover, they possessed a well-developed literature of
moral manuals to guide them. To borrow a metaphor from Thomas Kuhn, Roman
Catholic uses of casuistry are examples of normal casuistry,[138] while those of the
contemporary West involve crisis casuistry in which there is not only unclarity and

dispute about how to proceed in a particular case, but also controversy about the appropriate framework of analysis.[139] It is both unclear what morality to apply (including what understanding of casuistry), as well as how to apply the morality chosen to a particular case.

Various forms of pluralistic casuistry fare no better; in order to balance different moral appeals in the analysis of particular cases, one must already have in hand a moral guide to determine when one achieves a proper balance. Of course, this sort of guidance is exactly what is at question.[140] Again, to deliver reliable moral guidance, one must first concede its nature: one must agree to a particular understanding of morality. Nor will it do in secular morality to assert that humans possess a faculty that will allow them appropriately to weigh, balance, or give appropriate consideration to appeals to various moral claims or considerations, or to discern what is moral.

> To a large degree, our fundamental moral intuitions about particular actions, agents, and institutions are forced upon us by our moral cognitive faculties. To the extent that this is so, there are constraints on our intuitive judgments and it is not the case that "anything goes." However unsatisfactory our understandings of these notions and however much that means that we have no rules for evaluating choices, the individual, in making these choices, finds many forced upon him by his cognitive makeup.[141]

Given the pleomorphic character of humans, their capacities, functions, and inclinations, one will always need independent moral guidance to determine when such a faculty for weighing, balancing, or judging appeals or discerning the moral is functioning properly and when it should be morally corrected. To affirm a particular, content-full moral perspective or to endorse a particular balancing of moral appeals is already silently to have assumed particular moral commitments as canonical. One must already possess a canonical moral scale, standard, or understanding in order to know when one is appropriately weighing, balancing, or considering different moral values, principles, interests, appeals, etc.

There is no standpoint from which canonically to balance moral claims or to determine which tradition or version of moral inquiry is more complete without begging the central question at issue: whose morality should govern?[142] Within the sphere of immanence, the choice remains arbitrary until truth itself breaks through. Nor will one escape this difficulty by holding that (1) humans have a "fundamental cognitive capacity which enables us to recognize the moral value of individuals, actions, and social arrangements"[143] and that (2) a theory can systematize these intuitions, explain them, and give guidance where we have no intuitions, as for example through (3) a pluralistic theory expressed in a casuistry using a model of conflicting values. For the theory to be a normative theory, it must already canonize a particular moral understanding as to when human moral intuitions are right or wrong, as to when the "fundamental cognitive capacity" is functioning well or poorly. What turns out to be crucial for moralists is not the theory but this background moral commitment on which everything else depends.

So, too, appeals to human inclinations or human sentiments will reveal moral diversity, not agreement. To find moral guidance, one will need to endorse a particular ordering of inclinations and sentiments, as well as a judgment regarding which inclina-tions are appropriate and which morally misdirected. Selecting the right ordering and the correct judgment will require a further background morality. An appeal to human nature will also fail to provide canonical normative guidance in this matter, if one does not already possess a background normative vision. After Darwin, the problem of identifying the "normative" human nature becomes even more salient, although the fundamental difficulty of knowing how to discern true versus perverted human nature has always challenged any attempt at a natural law account of ethics. One must already have a guiding normative view. Human inclinations and sympathies as natural phe-nomena are the result of the morally blind forces of spontaneous mutation, particular selective pressures, and genetic drift, among other factors. These mortal traits or pro-clivities have evolved in environments where humans once, but no longer, lived. If one turns to human sentiments, this side of Darwin and the recognition of human polymor-phism one is again confronted with a diversity of possible "ideal" human moral types. Different clusters of moral intuitions, sympathies, and inclinations will in different environments be well or poorly adapted to maximizing either individual or inclusive fitness. Different balances of different moral intuitions, sympathies, and inclinations will in different environments provide different advantages. To determine which is the normative or ideal human type, one must determine which moral sentiments, in which order, and in which circumstances (i.e., environment) should govern and why.

The cardinal problem is this: the character of human moral (and immoral) inclina-tions as biologically grounded phenomena is a fact of the matter that could be other-wise and that is likely polymorphic. Inclusive fitness is likely maximized in different ecological niches by different balances of inclinations to kill or be pacific, to tell the truth or cleverly deceive, to be faithful or craftily adulterous.[144] Different strategies of surface (e.g., hypocritical or sham) and substantive collaboration will in different environments lead to different outcomes with regard to individual or inclusive fitness. Since no biological species is necessarily eternal, and given that there may be goods valued more highly than the extended survival of the human species, one must also determine to what extent, why, and under what conditions the survival of the human species should be an overriding good or the object of an absolute moral obligation. To derive a moral lesson from nature, one must already possess a moral understanding so that one can sort moral information from a swarm of biological facts.

One cannot without prior guidance turn to nature to discover criteria for appropri-ate human behavior or guidance in fashioning a bioethics. In a post-Darwinian world one must decide what adaptation, for which goals, in what environments should define biological success, health, and normality. In such circumstances, there are grounds to hold that there will not be a harmony among human moral dispositions, given the success that can be garnered by pursuing different goals in different environments. That is, in a post-Darwinian world that appreciates how environmental differences and multiform selective pressures produce biodiversity, a diversity of moral inclinations should not be unanticipated. One would even expect a biological basis for this diversity of moral sentiments, as well as what many would recognize as immoral inclinations, which in particular ecological niches will support inclusive fitness.[145] There will then be alternative human moral types, but no ideal "natural" type that can be accepted as morally normative for human sympathies and inclinations, not to mention actions.

To identify an account as normative, one must already possess a view of what is morally relevant in any appeal to facts, to nature, to human sensibilities, to human sympathies, or to human moral rationality. One must know how to sort moral information from noise. To discover a moral framework one can share with others, one must already share a basic background moral understanding. One must already possess a guiding moral sense, understanding, or narrative. To bring a moral controversy to a particular conclusion, one must already have in common a cardinal value content. The question is always, which value content? The babble of post-modernity besets us not simply as a de facto socio-historical catastrophe, but as an epistemological condition from which secular moral reason cannot liberate us. It is not just that any particular, content-full morality is controversial. More importantly, its content cannot in principle be established as canonical, as has just been shown. To know how to rank values and moral principles, one must already have a moral or value standard in hand. To resolve moral controversies between individuals who do not share the same moral premises, or who do not acknowledge certain persons as being in moral authority, one must then either beg the question or invoke an infinite regress in order to provide a foundational justification for endorsing one among the many competing views of the secular morality appropriate for humans.[146] The content of any particular morality and its bioethics could always have been otherwise unless one can establish a particular moral rationality as content-fully canonical and transcending history.

This circumstance of contingency has been boldly appreciated by Richard Rorty. Rorty, by forthrightly foregoing any deep grounding for morality, offers a groundless grounding for morality and bioethics. One accepts morality without any scent of transcendence or glimmer of deep meaning. Those who accept the developmental contingency of morality's content as defining the human moral condition will have "a sense of the contingency of their language of moral deliberation, and thus of their consciences, and thus of their community."[147] Morality is then reinterpreted as not requiring a foundation in either God or reason. In this fashion, Rorty seeks further to distance secular morality (and consequently bioethics) from the aspirations of either Christian morality or those Enlightenment reinterpretations of that morality, which maintained a sense of the transcendent.

> We can keep the notion of "morality" just insofar as we can cease to think of morality as the voice of the divine part of ourselves and instead think of it as the voice of ourselves as members of a community, speakers of a common language. We can keep the morality-prudence distinction if we think of it not as the difference between an appeal to the unconditioned and an appeal to the conditioned but as the difference between an appeal to the interests of our community and the appeal to our own, possibly conflicting, private interests. The importance of this shift is that it makes it impossible to ask the question "Is ours a moral society?"[148]

Morality in general and bioethics in particular become grounded in the contingencies of history, place, and perspective: morality and bioethics are the way they are, though they could have been otherwise. Indeed, they are otherwise, as the persistence of moral diversity attests.

The contingencies of history cannot with necessity set this plurality of visions aside. *Pace* Rorty, despite the circumstance that affirming democracy is in political fashion, not all mean the same thing by democracy. The democracy of the United States is not the democracy of Singapore or Iran, such that one can with confidence claim: "I have been urging that the democracies are now in a position to throw away some of the ladders used in their own construction."[149] The contingencies of history will not anoint for all times and all places a particular set of moral prejudices or perspectives. When the good to be achieved by restraining democracy is significant (consider how Chinese politicians might decide to limit democratic choice in order to maintain the stability necessary to provide, among other things, varying levels of health care across areas of their country marked by dramatically different levels of development), much of democracy and democratic health care policy may appear less than inviting. The levels of crime and drug use in many liberal democracies may also make liberal democracy highly uninviting for many. So, too, may the difficulties faced by democratic polities in undertaking health care reform.

One might attempt to escape moral rationality's failure to resolve controversies through sound argument and its inability to give reliable moral guidance (i.e., not be subject to providing radically different injunctions regarding life and death situations) by turning instead to emotions, affections, and moral sensibilities. One might even place this turn under the name of an ethics of care. However, the old problems will recur: there is not one way to care, nor one way to rank or order human emotions and affections. For instance, does one show care better by providing welfare or by allowing people to become skilled by the pedagogy of necessity? To establish an answer, one must already possess a basis for ranking of costs, benefits, and moral principles. Is it caring to provide physician-assisted suicide and euthanasia, or to refuse to do so? The answer will depend on differing understandings of costs and benefits, human flourishing, and right- and wrong-making conditions. Caring as well as moral emotions and sensibilities are embedded in particular moral narratives. It is only within particular narratives and communities that one learns which emotions and sensibilities should have priority and under what circumstances. An ethic of care or an emphasis on moral sensibilities will only recapture the problem of moral diversity in a different context.

In short, there is no way to establish a canonical content-full moral vision without begging the question or engaging in an infinite regress. Given a diversity of moral intuitions, moral senses, and rationalities, and since humans are embedded in biological, evolutionary, and social histories that are morally ambiguous, the human condition is defined by irresolvable moral diversity, ambiguity, and controversy. To resolve controversies regarding the ranking of goods or right-making principles in a principled fashion, one must already possess a standard for choosing a particular content-full moral position. The difficulty is that the character of the standard one should use in so determining the content of morality is exactly what is at issue. Without a prior canonical understanding regarding moral standards, one only begs the question as to which moral standards to use in resolving bioethical controversies. One must already have an answer before one begins.

Nor can one escape this difficulty through simply applying principles or appealing to casuistry while abandoning theory. It is not just that one must identify the principles that must guide or the cases that are paradigmatic. In addition, one must determine how to apply principles or paradigmatic cases to actual cases. One must have a principle of specification. The question is which one. *Pace* Richardson, DeGrazia, Strong, and other defenders of specified principlism and casuistry, one cannot specify principles so as to apply them to particular cases, or know how to use paradigmatic cases in a casuistic account, unless one already has a canonical moral account that can provide guidance.[150] Nor will it do to appeal to pragmatic criteria, claiming that one can eschew a theoretical justification because the advice one gives "works" in the sense of resolving the difficulties for those seeking the advice of the ethicist or bioethicist. Such pragmatic appeals to "what works" fail to notice that advice is helpful only as long as the ethicist and those who consult the ethicist are on the same side of the battles in the culture wars. Pragmatic success, usefulness, "that which works" must be specified in terms of a particular community and its moral assumptions.

The resolution of content-rich controversies about values, as occur in bioethics, is thus freighted with the requirement that one concede certain premises at the outset. Logical systems can be accepted or rejected, depending on their ability to preserve truth and avoid internal contradiction. They need not be regarded as reflecting an independent or "objective" logical reality. Empirical accounts can be accepted or rejected, depending on their ability successfully to make predictions or retrodictions. They need not be regarded as disclosing reality as it is in itself. In each case, there is an internal standard that the participants in a controversy can acknowledge for the resolution of a controversy. The standard for the resolution comes with the controversy: one selects those logical systems allowing reasoning of a particular sort, those forms of investigation producing reliable predictions. By identifying a restricted area of reasoning or practice for engaging the world, one can select goals and pursue the useful while eschewing questions about what should count as the good or the true. Similarly, in morality (including bioethics and health care policy), the resolution of controversies depends on the acceptance of one particular ranking or ordering of moral values or moral principles over other possible rankings or orderings. One must select a particular discount rate for preferences over time, a particular normative moral intuition, etc. At stake is the question of which standard to use.

Individuals need not possess starkly different moral views in order to have different moralities. For example, individuals need only assign different orderings of the moral significance of cardinal goods such as liberty, equality, prosperity, and security. Different orderings of their significance will sustain different moralities with different appreciations of what should count as proper social and political structures (e.g., egalitarian vs. libertarian). It will not be as if individuals with the different orderings will not understand each other. Quite to the contrary, they will likely understand only too well the depth of their disagreements. Different understandings of how life or free choice can be a good can undergird substantively different moral appreciations of abortion, social justice, and euthanasia without the values that the different parties hold being mutually opaque. Moral strangers need not be morally opaque to each other. They may be mutually fully acquainted with each other's position, while in disagreement so as not to be able to resolve controversies either by sound rational argument or appeal to moral authority. Moral acquaintances can be moral strangers.[153]

This diversity, this polytheism of moral narratives, visions, and understandings, emerges against the background of a millennial hegemony of Western Christian moral-

ity (as well as the Enlightenment's attempt to substitute for it a general secular morality). Against this history of an assumed unity of moral narrative, understanding, or
perspective, this diversity constitutes post-modernity. This experience of the loss of a
dominant moral account or a generally accepted moral narrative can only be appreciated against the backdrop of Western Christian universalism and its synthesis of faith
and reason. As Lyotard observes,

> In contemporary society and culture – postindustrial society, postmodern
> culture – the question of the legitimation of knowledge is formulated in
> different terms. The grand narrative has lost its credibility, regardless of
> what mode of unification it uses, regardless of whether it is a speculative
> narrative or a narrative of emancipation.[152]

There is no single, generally accepted moral narrative within which to locate society.
Nor is there a single, generally accepted account of morality by which large-scale
societies can plausibly place their members within one moral community. This is not to
claim that communication across moral communities is impossible. Again, people may
differ only in the circumstance that they differently rank cardinal values. Even if one is
fully committed to a particular, content-full moral vision, one can still understand
those whom one acknowledges as morally strange, in part through identifying what
one takes to be the strangeness in their ordering of values and moral principles. One
can communicate and collaborate with moral strangers in those procedural undertakings that do not require the affirmation of a particular moral content or vision. For
instance, Hassidic Jews, Amish, and atheists can meet and trade in the same market,
though they remain separated in different moral communities with different moral
understandings of the market. In areas outside of the market, their moral differences
will become apparent, as for example regarding abortion and physician-assisted suicide.

The challenge of providing a secular foundation for bioethics can be seen as defined
historically against three fundamental Western experiences of fracture and rupture: (1)
the Reformation with its consequent fragmentation of Western Christendom into a
plurality of Christianities and Christendoms, (2) the Enlightenment with its formation
of a secular, intellectual culture, which aspired to transcend this diversity, and (3) post-
modernity with its recognition that we are returned to this diversity, given the Enlightenment's failure to justify a single, canonical, content-full morality by discursive reason
alone.[153] These experiences frame the moral geography for current debates regarding
bioethics. They establish taken-for-granted expectations regarding moral diversity, the
role of secular morality in spanning religious moral difference, and the contemporary
experience of post-modernity. They account as well for a kind of nostalgia felt for the
moral unity of the Western Middle Ages[154] expressed in various hopes to see humans
bound in a universal moral community governed by a global bioethics enforced legally
across the world and in a persistent faith that discursive moral rationality can establish
a universal ethic, despite its many failures.

This is not to take the position of a metaphysical skeptic regarding moral truths.
Even if one concedes the existence of objective moral truth, one must be able to know
how to know who really knows the truth. Although there are moral truths, and even if

some know them, one must still gain access to a standard independent of the positions of the controversialists to identify those who truly know that they know the moral truth, so as to determine in whose favor moral controversies should be decided. With different standards, there is no encounter with an external moral world that can falsify particular moral claims. No matter how we clothe reality with theories and values, it imposes constraints on empirical claims in a way in which it does not place burdens on particular, purely moral claims. There are for moral controversies no similar constraints imposed by reality that give data such that it becomes highly improbable that real associations, not chance, are binding certain occurrences. Again, imagine attempting to compare outcomes so as to resolve a controversy regarding the proper structure for a health care system when those in disagreement rank differently the moral significance of liberty, equality, prosperity, and security. The participants will differently weigh the same outcomes. For the different parties, the outcomes will be different. For example, there is no independent, non-noetic access to moral reality so as to force the choice of equality over freedom (or freedom over equality) in the framing of health care policy. A different moral vision leads to a different appreciation of moral costs without reality's imposing costs, as occurs, for example, when one denies an element of physical reality (e.g., denying the germ theory's account of contagious diseases). Value interpretations depend on a standard of values. Which standard to choose is what is at issue.

The question is how third parties can know whether those who claim to know moral (including bioethical) truths, for example, those who claim to intuit a particular moral truth regarding the importance of equality in health care, or be good judges in balancing moral claims (e.g., a claim that confidentiality should be maintained versus a claim that confidentiality should be waived for the greater good in a particular case), can be judged to have made a true claim. Since they cannot appeal to better predictions regarding empirical findings, how can anyone assess such value claims, save in terms of a particular standard of values? But which standard should be employed? By default persons become the source of secular moral authority. They must agree as to what standards they will use in their collaboration, as for example in the delivery of health care. The question becomes which individuals have agreed to do what with whom. Once this grounding for secular ethics and bioethics is conceded, one can approach the project of a secular bioethics anew. The character of secular moral understanding is recast in terms of the grounding in permission as the source of secular moral authority. From this vantagepoint, many problems can be recognized as pseudo-problems (e.g., the challenge of "discovering" the correct level of resources to allocate to health care becomes the challenge of agreeing to a level of allocation from commonly owned resources). Many problems can be recognized as having a straightforward solution (e.g., the secular moral question of whether one may provide lifesaving treatment to a competent patient is answered by determining what the patient will allow). There will still be controversies and disputes. There will, however, be an Ariadne's thread one can follow in the direction of possible solutions by looking to the facts of the matter regarding who has really agreed to do what with whom. In the process, one will also have to agree as to how one will resolve controversies of particular sorts: one will need to create procedures for controversy resolution. The focus will be on creating accommodations, not discovering a content-rich moral truth. Answers in such circumstances are always particular, historical, and fashioned through agreement. They will depend on how particular groups of individuals frame agreements to undertake particular projects. The only alternative for the derivation of general moral authority in purely secular terms, given the failure to secure that authority from an appeal to sound rational argument, is to derive the authority from the agreement of those participating. A generally defensible secular bioethics is by default a libertarian bioethics, one grounded in the authority of individuals as the source of permission.[155] Though this libertarian moral framework is by no means a Christian ethic, it makes space for such an ethic.[156]

From a Libertarian to a Liberal Cosmopolitan: The Background of Post-Traditional Christianity

The derivation of moral authority from the consent of collaborators can be illustrated by the readers of this book imagining themselves the only survivors of a world-wide disaster that kills all other humans. The survivors discover themselves assembled in one place, but divided by substantively different religious, philosophical, and moral understandings. They possess different moral standards. In determining what morality they can use in collaborating with each other and in justifying the authority of common undertakings, they will not be able to appeal to a common acknowledgement of God's authority to justify a particular way of common collaboration. Nor will they be able to advance sound rational arguments to establish conclusively one notion of appropriate collaboration over another. Insofar as they wish for whatever reason or motivation to act together without an invocation of force that other participants cannot understand as morally authoritative, they can decide to act together with the common consent of those who collaborate. The authority of their common actions will be derived neither from God nor from reason but from their own agreement. Agreement or permission will be the ground or source of the moral justification of their collaboration. They need not agree regarding any background ranking of values or moral principles. The bioethics secured will give accent to free and informed consent, advance directives, and the contracts binding health care providers and receivers. Its focus will be on procedures for consent and the examination of prior agreements.

Those who wish can even establish and justify a limited *res publica* through this procedural morality. Its secular moral authority can be generally understood as drawn from the permission of those who join in that endeavor. Some participants might consider this solution as also involving divine providence and/or the authority of God. But they will not be able to share this insight with others holding different religious and philosophical premises. It will be enough to ground the moral authority of their common endeavors in the consent of those who participate.[157] The moral authority of common endeavors, including that of states, will be limited, given the diversity of the moral visions of its participants. Such limited democracies will of necessity incorporate the moral equivalent of robust rights to privacy, areas untouched by common authority where individuals are at liberty to do with themselves and consenting others as they agree, because they have not by giving permission transferred to others the authority to control such matters. For the traditional Christian, the focus on individuals as the source of an authority garnered from permission will be far from satisfactory. It will not only ignore significant areas of moral concern. The traditional Christian will also recognize that this approach seriously distorts moral matters. There is much more to the moral life than can be captured by this grounding in permission. Further, many of the autonomous undertakings of consenting individuals will be immoral, perverted, and blasphemous. Much that citizens of a limited democracy will be at liberty to do, traditional Christians will recognize to be gravely wrong, ranging from abortion to physician-assisted suicide.

Since market transactions draw authority from the consent of the participants, a market economy will also be central to such societies. For many, this will lead to the improper commodification of important areas of life. In such circumstances, the remedy will be not to enter such markets. Those who wish to affirm a content-rich secular ethic will find that this sparse morality cannot address many core moral concerns. However, the price of universality is content. A universal secular bioethics able to span persons who do not share a particular moral understanding can only draw its authority from the consent of individuals. It is individuals who have moral controversies. As moral strangers, it is they who can by agreement create a domain of common moral authority. In short, the framing morality will be procedural; moral authority will be secured from permission. Such a morality will justify, sustain, and explain procedurally based moral practices such as forbearance rights and contracts, including contracts for health care services.

All of this will be able to be undertaken without any commitment to a particular understanding of the good, a particular ranking of moral principles, or a particular moral narrative. The principle of permission will have centrality not because it is valued, but because the permission of persons is the only source available for secular authority. In the absence of a canonical content-full ethics, the bioethics of such a society, as already observed, will give priority to practices such as informed consent, rights to refuse treatment, the development of contracts for health care services, and the right to do with oneself and consenting others as mutually agreed (e.g., physician-assisted suicide and euthanasia). Again, as a result, people will have a secular moral right (i.e., others will not have secular moral authority to interfere) to do what many may by special insight know to be very wrong. In secular terms, those with special moral insights will be secularly morally obliged to tolerate (suffer) many choices that they recognize as grievously wrong. The focus of general secular bioethical discussions will not be on the meaning of life, reproduction, suffering, and death. Instead, the focus will be on the basis for individuals collaborating with others or ignoring others in the free pursuit of their own views of proper conduct.

This libertarian understanding of secular bioethics, which is advanced in default of the ability to discover a canonical secular morality, reconstructs a good proportion of contemporary bioethical practices. At least, it reconstructs those through which persons can collaborate in the face of substantial moral disagreement. It grounds bioethical analyses that address chains of permission, authorization, or consent, as well as the withholding of permission and authorization. It gives centrality to contracts or agreements among individuals in their pursuit of care, cure, and the amelioration of suffering. It recognizes the centrality of toleration (i.e., eschewing coercion against the consensual evil actions of others) in secular pluralist societies. This account does not need to assume that individuals share an overlapping moral consensus in order to collaborate. Rather, in the flow of moral discussions, negotiations, compromises, and agreements, particular orderings of values and rights will be accepted in different institutions through different agreements, moved by different motivations. Rankings of values and of rights will be authorized for particular practices and circumstances through the generation of various spontaneous orders such as those that characterize the market's establishment of prices. Again, there will be some individuals who will hold certain things to be priceless, and therefore beyond negotiation and compromise in the market or elsewhere. In such cases, they will invoke their secular moral rights to privacy (i.e., where those "rights" announce the limits of the secular rights of others). The point is that one can easily recognize the emergence of regional rankings of values and principles without appealing either to a background moral sense, to a canonical overlapping of consensuses, or to a particular set of motivations. It is enough to recognize how permission is given as negotiations are undertaken, compromises made, and agreements completed. Secular morality is procedural.

This libertarian cosmopolitan moral understanding can compass divergent moral visions, moral communities, and fragments of moral communities. Although it must allow much to take place which is immoral, it affirms a space for traditional Christians to live as they wish. Orthodox Jews, Orthodox Christians, Amish, Parsi, and all who are willing to live peaceably with others can pursue with co-religionists their full understanding of the struggle to salvation. The libertarian cosmopolitan moral understanding provides a *modus vivendi* with moral force but without content for a world marked by a plurality of moral visions. In this sense it is cosmopolitan. Because it is a procedural morality, it does not offer content for a content-full view of the significance of reproduction, birth, suffering, dying, and death, nor does it have content to support non-procedurally directed understandings of character and virtue. It cannot even provide the substance for a morally coherent biography, or at least a biography that is not morally vacuous. The libertarian ethic is a moral point of view that lacks a vision of the good moral life. Yet, surrogates for moral excellence can emerge in the course of secular moral activities. For example, the spontaneous order of the market moved by a diversity of motivations can create particular understandings of honesty and fraud. Agreements will explicitly or implicitly take shape regarding the areas in which one must be truthful and in what way (consider, for example, the kinds of deception allowed and disallowed within the card game poker). Understandings will form through a multitude of implicit and explicit agreements regarding how one must be honest, and what it means to be honest, as well as regarding the areas in which one can advertise with little or no concern for accuracy. Such practices create content for particular understandings of the honest person.

Similar understandings are generated in clinical contexts. When performing physical examinations, physicians usually do not ask permission for each of the steps. Rather, various bodily movements develop a web of consent so that both parties can understand how far the range of permission extends. One need not affirm any background ranking of values to explain what is taking place. Instead, one need only recognize the development of implicit agreements over time. Such understandings need not be rooted in any substantive understanding of virtue, much less common views of the meaning of human life. They are grounded in the permission of those who participate, a practice that by default has moral salience in the absence of a common, content-full moral vision. The result is that, in the absence of any other moral foundation to bind moral strangers, a libertarian cosmopolitanism claims centrality. Individuals of whatever sex, race, religion, or culture anywhere across the cosmos can agree to collaborate, binding themselves by the authority of their mutual consent.

This libertarian cosmopolitanism is libertarian in drawing authority from the permission of those who collaborate, and not from any particular valued state of affairs, much less from a lexical priority or value given to freedom or liberty. It is cosmopolitan in the sense of providing a framework that can be invoked outside of any particular socio-historical context, tradition, or moral community by drawing simply on the consent of those willing to be involved. Such a sparse moral foundation may be endurable only if the individuals who collaborate primarily place their own lives within functional moral communities where they confront others as moral friends, persons with whom they share a content-full moral vision, and where they share an understanding of the human condition and the meaning of the passages of life. Because increasingly people do not find themselves in such communities, and because they often find themselves hungering for community, value, and meaning, the default position becomes, not as a matter of strict necessity, but as a matter of moral desire, a liberal cosmopolitanism. Because of a search for meaning in a fully secular context, a liberal cosmopolitanism is embraced, which assigns lexical priority to liberty and then to equality of opportunity. Persons without anything to value beyond themselves come to value first the opportunity to shape their own lives. If they cannot discover the deep purpose of life, they will at least give special value to creating with others a life of meaning.

This shift from a libertarian cosmopolitanism to a liberal cosmopolitanism involves a radical change of moral and metaphysical perspective. It establishes a fundamentally different context for a bioethics. A libertarian cosmopolitanism advances no criticism of particular moral communities, as long as those who participate can from the outside be seen as giving their permission, even if those within that moral life experience themselves as submitting in the face of a compelling reality. A libertarian cosmopolitanism provides the philosophical foundation for a procedure, for a general secular structure for the morally authoritative collaboration of moral strangers. It constitutes the moral point of view of moral strangers. It involves no particular ranking of values. It does not offer a content-full vision of human flourishing or the good life. In this sense, the libertarian cosmopolitan moral perspective eschews moral imperialism. This is in contrast to a liberal cosmopolitanism, which assigns a cardinal value to a particular understanding of autonomous choice and holds that all persons should likewise. The liberal cosmopolitan ethos requires that people decide to be autonomous, self-determining individuals. The failure to pursue this ethos of autonomy becomes an indication of a false consciousness. Liberal cosmopolitanism does not simply recognize permission as central to a morality able to convey moral authority in the face of deep moral disagreement. In addition, liberal cosmopolitanism locates self-determination centrally in its account of human flourishing. In the absence of a transcendent moral truth, the focal point of the moral life becomes autonomous self-determination. The good life is not found in submitting to and being determined by the good and the true. Autonomy instead becomes integral to the good.

Liberal cosmopolitanism also seeks to liberate morality in general and bioethics in particular from the dead hand of tradition. Religious and cultural understandings that endorse humility, submission, and hierarchies of authority become objects for reeducation, liberation, and the dispelling of false consciousness. The liberal ethos is cosmopolitan in seeking to provide for all a content-rich moral vision, which should bind individuals across the world as they free themselves from the superstitions and illiberal constraints of the past. Liberal cosmopolitanism is not cosmopolitan in being open to all as they reach out in their own terms to collaborate with moral strangers, while allowing all peaceably to pursue their own moral understanding in their own moral communities (i.e., as does the libertarian cosmopolitan ethos). It is rather cosmopolitan in the robust sense of aspiring to be the global morality that should bind persons as they shed their particular bonds to ethnic roots, cultural traditions, and religious constraints. While the libertarian cosmopolitan presupposes a distinction between society and community (i.e., between [1] the space afforded in civil society for persons and communities of diverse moral commitments to meet and interact, and [2] the highly morally constituted space of particular moral communities), the liberal cosmopolitan seeks to constitute the state and the society it encompasses as a particular moral community, one structured by the liberal cosmopolitan ethos and its particular understandings of the value of liberty and equality. As in Germany after the First World War, in the face of an intractable pluralism there is a hunger for consensus, community, a politics of meaning, and a purpose for life realized through the power of the State.[158] The liberal cosmopolitan ethos grounds a bioethics that in its roots is at odds with a traditional Christian bioethics and seeks to impose its own vision through a political structure that is far from being a limited democracy. The ethos imposed is one of society after the end of the Christian establishment, after the end of Christendom.[159] In chapter 3 we will further examine the liberal cosmopolitan ethic and its relationship to contemporary secular bioethics. Here it is enough to recognize the liberal cosmopolitan ethos as a development out of the attempt to render Christian morality into a universal morality that could be freely affirmed by all guided by right reason.

Christian Bioethics Reconsidered

Christian bioethics, especially one with traditional content, is implausible, if not morally outrageous. Secular bioethics gained significant plausibility from (1) the Western Christian moral theological affirmation of reason's capacity to disclose the substance of the good moral life, (2) the theological crisis engendered by the post-Reformation Western Christian fragmentation into numerous religions each with its own ethics and in the end its own bioethics, (3) the history of bloodshed that marked these religious differences, (4) the allure of the Enlightenment's promise to set this plurality aside in a unitary moral understanding justifiable in general human terms, (5) the crisis of self-identity that has marked Western Christian religions particularly since the 1960s, making it difficult for them to articulate an unambiguous bioethics, and (6) the reaction after the 1960s against the hierarchical and patriarchal character of traditional Christianity. The emerging liberal cosmopolitan culture and its post-traditional character made traditional Christian morality appear divisive, dangerous, sexist, homophobic, inappropriately absolutist, and/or irrelevant. Traditional Christian morality and bioethics are in conflict with the moral rationality of the liberal cosmopolitan worldview. The moral-theological attractiveness of rendering Christian moral theology materially equivalent to secular morality has only reinforced the unattractiveness of those traditional Christian moral commitments that cannot be anchored in secular moral arguments. In contrast, the sought-after material equivalence of Christian moral theological commitments and those of the surrounding secular culture promises ecumenical force and a pacific character for Christian moral reflection. Yet, the realization of this equivalence would deprive Christian ethics, and therefore Christian bioethics, of a moral difference that would allow it to make a contribution of its own.

The expectation that through reason one can justify a canonical, content-full morality and thus secure a canonical secular bioethics is deeply embedded in the history of Western Christianity and its synthesis of faith and reason. To explore the possibility of a Christian bioethics requires examining this history and its discontents. As will become clearer in the next chapter, neither a secular bioethics nor a liberal cosmopolitan Christian bioethics can deliver what traditional Christian morality promised: a morality that can unite the right and the good, as well as the motivation and the justification of morality, within a canonical, content-full moral vision. If there is a way out of what appear to be irresolvable difficulties at the core of contemporary secular and Western Christian morality, this must lie in a radically different approach to acquiring content and unity for ethics. It cannot lie where the Western Middle Ages led us to expect: in discursive argument.

Notes

1. As Baruch Brody has clearly shown with respect to abortion, the bioethical obligations of Jews may be dramatically different from those of Gentiles (i.e., for bnai Noah).

   Abortion has suddenly become for bnai Noah a capital offense. No reason (except for the exegetical analysis) is given. Still, the law remains. What does this mean for the permissibility of abortions, before the fetus has emerged, to save the life of a mother? The question is raised by the commentary of Tosafot who says (59a s.v. leka):
   We have learnt that before the head emerges, one can dismember the embryo, limb by limb, and bring it out in order to save the mother, but such a procedure would be prohibited for a ben Noah since they are commanded against destroying embryos ... but perhaps it would be permissible even in the case of a ben Noah.
   Brody, "Halakhic Material in Medical Ethics Discussions," *Journal of Medicine and Philosophy* 8 (August 1983), 327.

2. The term secular is ambiguous. Secular, secularization, and related terms compass at least seven principal clusters of usages: worldly, not belonging to a religious order, the process of losing the special obligations of membership in a religious order while remaining a priest, removing property from the possession of the church, hostile to established religion, the beliefs of a particular philosophical sect, and purged of, or neutral to, religious significance. See H. T. Engelhardt, Jr., *Bioethics and Secular Humanism: The Search for a Common Morality* (Philadelphia: Trinity Press International, 1991), esp. pp. 22-31. Secular in this volume will be used, unless otherwise noted, to identify those moral frameworks that are neutral with respect to religious, including particular, quasi-religious cultural viewpoints. A viewpoint is secular in the sense of not being the morality of a religious or particular worldview, but of humans as such. Secular in this sense aspires to Enlightenment hope, at least as a regulative ideal, of a viewpoint grounded in the human as such unenlightened by any particular religious understanding.

3. Franco's Spain and Salazar's Portugal, both of which guided their religious life in terms of concordats with the Vatican, were never as Christian as 20th-century Saudi Arabia was Mohammedan. However, Roman Catholicism had a special place in both. See, for example, the following study of Salazar's Portugal, which praises his Catholicism. Michael Derrick, *The Portugal of Salazar* (New York: Campion Books, 1939). To have a sense of the way in which proper church-state relations were understood from the perspective of Roman Catholicism in the early part of the 20th century, consider the following:

All that is essentially comprised in the union of Church and State can be thus formulated: The State should officially recognize the Catholic religion as the religion of the commonwealth; accordingly it should invite the blessing and the ceremonial participation of the Church for certain important public functions, as the opening of legislative sessions, the erection of public buildings, etc., and delegate its officials to attend certain of the more important festival celebrations of the Church; it should recognize and sanction the laws of the Church; and it should protect the rights of the Church, and the religious as well as the other rights of the Church's members.
John A. Ryan and Francis J. Boland, *Catholic Principles of Politics* (New York: Macmillan, 1940), p. 316.

4. The difficulties of justifying a content-full secular ethics, and in particular a content-full secular bioethics, have been explored at length in H. T. Engelhardt, Jr., *The Foundations of Bioethics*, 2nd ed. (New York: Oxford University Press, 1996). They will be reviewed only briefly in this chapter.
5. Alasdair MacIntyre, *Whose Justice, Which Rationality?* (Notre Dame, IN: University of Notre Dame Press, 1988).
6. The terms "moral stranger" and "morally strange" are not used to indicate an opaque other whose actions are not understandable. As already indicated, the terms are employed to identify circumstances in which persons do not share either (1) common moral premises, rules of evidence, and rules of inference so that their moral controversies can be settled by sound rational argument, or (2) a common understanding of who is in moral authority, so that their moral controversies can be settled by a definitive ruling or process.
7. The term "content-full" is used to identify moral or evaluational accounts that supply a particular normative ranking or ordering of moral values, goods, or principles. Such rankings can be either thick or thin with respect to the extent to which there is an all-encompassing ranking of values and moral principles. For an example of a thin account, see John Rawls, *A Theory of Justice* (Cambridge, MA: Harvard University Press, 1971), esp. pp. 395ff.
8. For Rorty, the contemporary Western moral perspective is grounded in sentiments given to us by the contingency of our history. For Rorty, these are the liberal democratic commitments of "'we twentieth-century liberals' or 'we heirs to the historical contingencies which have created more and more cosmopolitan, more and more democratic political institutions.'" Richard Rorty, *Contingency, Irony, and Solidarity* (Cambridge: Cambridge University Press, 1989), p. 196.
9. The 20th century witnessed the salience of "internationalized languages of modernity" (p. 384), the linguistic home of a "rootless cosmopolitanism, [which is] the condition of those who aspir[e] to be at home anywhere – except that is, of course, in what they regard as the backward, outmoded, undeveloped cultures of traditions" (p. 388). For such "citizens of nowhere", it is difficult to understand what it would be to have a morality appropriately conditioned by history and place. MacIntyre, *Whose Justice? Which Rationality?*
10. The 16th and 17th centuries witnessed a blossoming of interest in medicine on the part of moral theologians such as Francisco de Vitoria (1480-1546), Dominic Soto (1494-1560), Gregory Sayrus (†1602), Domingo Bañez (1528-1604), Thomas Sanchez (1550-1610), Francisco Suarez (1548-1617), Paul Laymann (1574-1635), and John Cardinal de Lugo (1583-1660).

11. As noted in the preface, the term "bioethics" was likely coined by Van Rensselaer Potter in 1971 and then in the same year radically recast by André Hellegers to identify the new and developing academic field of biomedical ethics, which was independent of the health care professions. Bioethics reflected and contributed to the deprofessionalization of medicine.

12. The notion of the Enlightenment as a period in Western history or as a movement in Western culture is not without controversy. After all, one is giving a single name to complex developments in different countries, which involved not only philosophers but cultural critics, essayists, and playwrights. In Germany it went by the term *Aufklärung* and in France it found itself generally under the term *siècle des lumières*. There was no international term or sense of an organized movement. In retrospect, one can recognize the period as one of markedly increased and widespread secular, discursive, rational criticism of Western Christianity, and in particular its role in directing moral development and in encouraging "superstitious practices." There is much to argue for the position that the Enlightenment, guided by its *philosophes*, counts as one historical phenomenon. This interpretation is eloquently defended by Peter Gay.

There were many philosophes in the eighteenth century, but there was only one Enlightenment. A loose, informal, wholly unorganized coalition of cultural critics, religious skeptics, and political reformers from Edinburgh to Naples, Paris to Berlin, Boston to Philadelphia. ... The men of the Enlightenment united on a vastly ambitious program, a program of secularism, humanity, cosmopolitanism, and freedom, above all, freedom in its many forms – freedom from arbitrary power, freedom of speech, freedom of trade, freedom to realize one's talents, freedom of aesthetic response, freedom, in a word, of moral man to make his own way in the world.
Peter Gay, *The Enlightenment: An Interpretation* (New York: W.W. Norton, 1995), p. 3.

The Enlightenment sought to set aside spiritual fathers in favor of *philosophes*, who, according to Denis Diderot (1713-1784), were to be the new preceptors of mankind. Although many wished to retain Christianity transformed by the light of philosophical inquiry, all hoped to have it at least reformed by the light of critical examination. The Enlightenment in its various forms and locales stood against superstition and obscurantism, and in favor of science and critical inquiry. The *philosophes* and Enlightenment intellectuals generally were of a part with Socrates, who with the Sophists and physicians effected the secularization of Athens. The Sophists insisted on bringing all to the bar of critical examination. For example, Socrates, like Kant, attempted to direct energies from the divine to the human and from the metaphysical to the moral. "In the first place, he would inquire, did these thinkers suppose that their knowledge of human affairs was so complete that they must seek these new fields for the exercise of their brains; or that it was their duty to neglect human affairs and consider only things divine?" Xenophon, "Memorabilia," in *Xenophon*, trans. E.C. Marchant (Cambridge, MA: Harvard University Press, 1997), I.i.12, p. 9. This moral agenda is well captured by Immanuel Kant's (1724-1804) account of the Enlightenment in his invitation to dare to use one's own intelligence without another's guidance. See, for example, Kant, *Beantwortung der Frage: Was ist Aufklärung?* [1784]. The forces Kant held likely to impede the use of one's critical faculties are first and foremost religious and then political. For Kant, the age of Enlightenment is marked by moral emancipation, free thought, self-governance, toleration, progress, and an emerging society of world citizens. This Enlightenment for Kant is to bring a new Reformation, placing religion before the tribunal of the same rationality that judges and governs secular moral inquiry. An enlightened Christianity may not be governed by claims of insights that transcend the discursive rationality of secular thought. Nor may it be guided by clairvoyant elders or those who claim a special grace.

Schneewind stresses that all of this does not involve the Enlightenment in a crusade for a "fully secular morality". According to Schneewind, the Enlightenment did not by and large seek a secular ethic in that so many of its participants held that (1) God exists, and (2) the idea of God is essential for morality. What Schneewind does not acknowledge is that these Enlightenment figures were pleading for a religion on their terms, not on the terms of traditional Christianity. The morality they were seeking was from the perspective of traditional Christianity a secularized morality, and the society they hoped to establish was from that perspective at best a robustly deChristianized society that might nevertheless acknowledge God. Given these qualifications, Schneewind is correct in arguing that the Enlightenment did not involve a renunciation of religion or a rejection of the importance of the idea of God.

What I have called conceptions of morality as self-governance are often thought to result from a major effort by Enlightenment thinkers to bring about a secularized society. It is assumed that there was an "Enlightenment project" to show that morality had no need of religion because it had its own, wholly rational, foundations. Modern views of morality are then assumed to have been thought out as part of this effort. I find the assumptions questionable in several respects.
J.B. Schneewind, *The Invention of Autonomy* (New York: Cambridge University Press, 1998), p. 8.

In part, Schneewind grants the point that the Enlightenment needed to reform the very idea of God in order to have a morality and society it could find acceptable.

Indeed, if I were forced to identify something or other as "the Enlightenment project" for morality, I should say that it was the effort to limit God's control over earthly life while keeping him essential to morality. Naturally this effort took different forms, depending on how the relations between God and morality were conceived. *Ibid.*

For a somewhat different perspective on the Enlightenment and its relationship to the Western European understanding of its religion, consider the observation of Peter Gay. "I see the *philosophes*' rebellion succeeding in both of its aims: theirs was a paganism directed against their Christian inheritance and dependent upon the paganism of classical antiquity, but it was also a modern paganism, emancipated from classical thought as much as from Christian dogma." Gay, *The Enlightenment: An Interpretation*, p. xi.

13. "Noetic experience" is used to identify the experience of the energies of God that apodictically give knowledge. This understanding of knowledge will be progressively addressed in the course of this work.

14. Of course, there were not only the schisms engendered by the Nestorians after the Council of Ephesus (A.D. 431) and by the so-called monophysites after the Council of Chalcedon (A.D. 451), but numerous other divisions and separations, from the Arians, Docetists, Donatists, and Gnostics in the first centuries to the schism of the Old Believers under Patriarch Nikon (1605-1682) in the 17th century. These admittedly important disputes and divisions did not in the end have the same significance for the Church of the Seven Ecumenical Councils as the Protestant Reformation achieved for Western Europe. For the Church of the Seven Councils (which is in fact the Church of nine Ecumenical Councils, the eighth being held in Constantinople in 879-882 [the Council in the Temple of Holy Wisdom], and the ninth also in Constantinople in 1341, 1347, and 1351), there was a sense of undisturbed integrity spanning well over a millennium. Moreover, the schisms in the East largely did not set aside an integrity of worship and asceticism so that Nestorians, so-called monophysites, and Old Believers with priests remained bound to Orthodoxy by a unity of liturgical and ascetic understandings. In contrast, the Protestant Reformation gave to the West both its sense for revolution (see, for example, Melvin J. Lasky, *Utopia and Revolution* [Chicago: University of Chicago Press, 1976], esp. pp. 220-259) and its acquiescence in a liberal polity, given the impossibility in many countries of imposing a uniform religious understanding (see, for example, G.W.F. Hegel, *Philosophy of Right*, § 270). Finally, it must be noted that the

Nestorians and so-called monophysites were seen to be so close to Orthodoxy that they could be converted by mere profession of faith, without either baptism or chrismation. See Canon XCV of the 102 Canons of the Quinisext Council (A.D. 691-692) in Sts. Nicodemus and Agapius, *The Rudder of the Orthodox Catholic Church* (Chicago: Orthodox Christian Educational Society, 1957), pp. 400-401. It is surely for this reason that the so-called non-Chalcedonians were able to affirm that the Orthodox Church's interpretation of the 4th, 5th, and 6th Ecumenical Councils was and always had been the same as theirs. Thomas Fitzgerald, "Toward the Reestablishment of Full Communion: The Orthodox-Orthodox Oriental Dialogue," *Greek Orthodox Theological Review* 36 (Summer 1991), 169-182.

15. In this volume, "Western Christianity" identifies the cluster of religions that emerged in the West from the 9th century onward. These compass the Roman Catholic church and its various schismatic offspring (e.g., the Old Catholics), along with the thousands of Protestant groups, which have in multiple ways dialectically determined each other, with the result that those religions are closer to each other than to the traditional Christianity from which they sprang. These Christianities are marked in various measures by a confidence in discursive reasoning or an emphasis on individual spiritual judgment isolated from a community of Christians, which experiences itself as one with the Church of the Councils. On the one hand, the content of tradition is evacuated by rationality; on the other hand, tradition is abandoned to individual choice. In this volume, "traditional Christianity" in the strict sense identifies Christianity that is at one with the Church of the first millennium and that recognizes itself united over the centuries by the Holy Spirit in right worship and right belief. Traditional Christianity in this sense is materially equivalent to the Orthodox Church. "Traditional Christian", *grosso modo*, identifies any Christian position or activity in concert with the beliefs of the Church of the Councils. Michael Buckley recognizes that Western Christianity developed from a turn towards a rational grounding of faith. Michael Buckley, S.J., *At the Origins of Modern Atheism* (New Haven: Yale University Press, 1987).

16. In talking of the culture wars, I use a phrase made popular by James Davison Hunter in *Culture Wars: The Struggle to Define America* (New York: Basic Books, 1991). The term identifies conflicting moral and religious understandings of the meaning of life, the nature of human flourishing, and the character of proper conduct.

17. The *Didache* records the early Christian proscription of abortion and infanticide. "Thou shalt do no murder; thou shalt not commit adultery; thou shalt not commit sodomy; thou shalt not commit fornication; thou shalt not steal; thou shalt not use magic; thou shalt not use philtres; thou shalt not procure abortion, or commit infanticide" (*Apostolic Fathers*, vol. 1, trans. Kirsopp Lake [Cambridge, Mass.: Harvard University Press, 1965], II 2). Similar proscriptions are found in the Epistle of Barnabas: "Thou shalt not procure abortion, thou shalt not commit infanticide" (*Apostolic Fathers*, vol. 1, trans. Kirsopp Lake [Cambridge, Mass.: Harvard University Press, 1965], XIX 5).

18. Daniel A. Cronin reviews nearly five hundred years of Roman Catholic bioethical reflections in *The Moral Law in Regard to the Ordinary and Extraordinary Means of Conserving Life* (Rome: Typis Pontificiae Universitatis Gregorianiae, 1958).

19. "The unexpected death of the famous philosopher [René Descartes] at the relatively early age of 54 attracted wide attention in wide circles, the more so as it was generally known that it had been his cherished desire to prolong not only the life of mankind by promoting scientific medicine, but also his own life by appropriate measures. ... In a Belgian journal it was reported, some months after his death, that in Sweden a fool had died who had claimed to be able to live as long as he liked." G.A. Lindeboom, *Descartes and Medicine* (Amsterdam: Rodopi, 1979), pp. 93, 94.

20. Andreas Vesalius was to medicine what Nikolaus Copernicus was to astronomy. In the same year that Copernicus published *De Revolutionibus orbium coelestium* (Norimbergae: Johan-

nes Petrium, 1543), Vesalius published *De humani corporis fabrica* (Basel: A. Operinus, 1543), which took European medicine away from its roots in Galenic anatomy. Vesalius, a man of Renaissance passions, wrote his book in Ciceronian Latin, rendering it inaccessible to many of his less educated colleagues. See Ludwig Edelstein, "Andreas Vesalius, the Humanist," *Bulletin of the History of Medicine* 14 (December 1943), 547-561.

21. William Harvey's 1628 (1578-1657) publication of *Exercitatio anatomica de motu cordis et sanguinis* (Frankfurt/Main: Sumptibus G. Fitzeri, 1628) was a further step away from the physiology and anatomy of Galen toward the physiology and anatomy of modernity.

22. Though anticipated in important respects by Theophil Bonet (1620-1689) in *Sepulchretum sive anatomica practica ex cadaveribus morbo denatis* (Geneva: L. Chouet, 1679), Giovanni Morgagni (1786-1771) in *De sedibus et causis morborum per anatomen indagatis* (Venice: Ex Typographis Remondiniana, 1761) gave impetus to the medical scientific revolution, which led to clinical observations being reinterpreted in terms of anatomical findings.

23. Michel Foucault gives centrality to Xavier Bichat (1771-1802) in his account of the emergence of the new science of medicine. Foucault fails adequately to appreciate the full character of the shift in focus from the clinic to the basic sciences that occurred at the end of the 18th and the beginning of the 19th century. See *Naissance de la clinique* (Paris: Presses Universitaires de France, 1963); *The Birth of the Clinic*, trans. A. M. Sheridan Smith (New York: Random House, 1973). The significance of clinical observation, knowledge, and practice was recast in favor of the basic sciences. It was their birth that transformed medicine: the birth of the basic medical sciences and the medical laboratory. The clinic became grounded in the basic sciences.

24. Rudolf Virchow (1821-1902) secured the connection of the new basic sciences and clinical medicine at the level of cellular investigation, further extending the scientific revolution that tied the clinical practice of medicine to basic sciences such as anatomy, physiology, and pathology.

25. Distinctions between what counts as superficial and what counts as fundamental changes depend on background understandings of the integrity, character, and goals of a practice or institution. With regard to general scientific research programs or paradigms, they may be held to remain intact despite superficial changes, as long as what counts as knowing (i.e., research, investigation, experimentation, such as clinical observation versus anatomical study), appropriate objects of knowledge (i.e., the objects of scientific investigation, such as the reports of patients or findings from bacteriological cultures), as well as exemplar knowledge and knowers (e.g., clinicians or pathologists) remain unchanged. In short, as long as scientists do not bring into question what it is to do exemplar scientific work in their field, what it is that they should be studying, or who should count as exemplar competent investigators, the disputes they have can be placed with what Thomas Kuhn termed normal science. *The Structure of Scientific Revolutions* (Chicago: University of Chicago Press, 1962; 2nd ed. 1970). I employ Kuhn's notion of "normal science" to identify those periods of study when fundamental understandings of investigation and ways of resolving controversies are not brought into question. In "normal science", accepted fundamental understandings are applied to problems to achieve answers without questioning the basic methodology, much less its background commitments. During a period of crisis science, it is not clear which method should be used or what examples of appropriate controversy resolution should guide. Crises emerge as scientists rethink what it is to do science, what is it that science investigates, and who should count as exemplar scientists. With regard to the Christian religion and with respect to Roman Catholic moral theology in particular, one could make similar observations about the history of its approach to moral theology. As long as theologians do not bring into question what it is to do moral theology, what the objects of moral theological knowing are, or who should count as competent moral theologians, there is similarly no crisis in the field.

Theological disputes can then be understood within the metaphor of normal moral theological investigation. Since Roman Catholic moral theology exists within a large institutional framework, its investigation of theological issues must be placed within a broad context of ecclesial structures, liturgical practices, and theological concerns. Roman Catholic moral theologians, unlike scientists, confront not just individuals who claim to be authorities in the sense of expert knowers of the truth, but also individuals who claim to be in authority, as a presiding judge is in authority to determine what evidence can be admitted into consideration and with respect to who should be given a voice in court. Therefore, the ecclesial structure (i.e., the authority of the Pope of Rome and bishops) has claimed a legitimate control over the practice of Roman Catholic moral theology in ways that would be egregious if transferred to secular science so as to allow judges and government officials to resolve scientific controversies. Unlike secular science, moral theology is practiced within a community directed to worshipping God. Since there is a relation of dogma to the character of a religion as a whole, the character of worship will be influenced by dogma (used in the broad sense to include beliefs concerning moral theological matters) and ecclesial structure, just as the character of worship will influence ecclesiology and belief.

26. Bernard of Clairvaux (1090-1153) was the last major Western theologian whose writings had a character at one with that of the unbroken Church. See Chrysostom Frank, "St. Bernard of Clairvaux and the Eastern Christian Tradition," *St. Vladimir's Theological Quarterly* 36, 4 (1992), 315-328.

27. See, for example, Michael Boudewyns, *Ventilabrum medico-theologicum quo omnes casus, tum medicos, cum aegros, aliosque concernentes eventilantur, et quod S.S. P.P. conformius, scholasticis probabilius, et in conscientia tutius est, fecernitur: Opus cum theologis et confessariis, tum maxime medicis perquam necessarium* (Antwerp: Cornelius Woons, 1666); M. A. Alberti, *De convenientia medicinae ad theologiam practicam* (1732); and Francesco Emanuello Cangiamila, *Sacra embryologia sive de officio sacerdotum, medicorum, et aliorum circa aeternam parvulorum in utero existentium salutem* (Ieper: Thomas F. Walwein, 1775).

28. The Council of Trent (1545-1563) set into motion forces that in great measure, for some four centuries, solidified Roman Catholic ecclesial structure, liturgical practice, and the character of theological investigation. It brought into focus developments in the early 16th century and earlier. These structures and understandings remained largely intact until Vatican II, despite debates among probablists, Jansenists, modernists, etc. As a consequence, one could invoke in the 1950s as immediately relevant authorities a long list of contributors to moral theological reflections, many of whom predated Trent, including Thomas Aquinas (1225-1274), Thomas de Vio Cajetan (1469-1534), Francisco de Vitoria (1480-1546), Dominic Soto (1494-1560), Domingo Bañez (1528-1604), Francisco Suarez (1548-1617), John Cardinal de Lugo (1583-1660), and Alphonsus Liguori (1696-1787). Though different schools of theology in different periods gained ascendancy or declined in their influence, the general framework of analysis remained the same and was reaffirmed by Pope Leo XIII in *Aeterni Patris*, August 4, 1879. In the mid-1960s, theology, ecclesial structure, and liturgical practice were all brought into question. Many who engaged in Christian moral reflection in general and Christian bioethics in particular ceased to regard themselves as simply developing the solutions provided by the tradition. There was a sense of radical "renewal".

29. Thomas Kuhn is quite clear in restricting to the natural sciences his use of paradigm, a term introduced to identify a cluster of conceptual, theoretical, instrumental, and methodological commitments. *The Structure of Scientific Revolutions* (Chicago: University of Chicago Press, 1962; 2nd ed. 1970). First, it must be observed that Kuhn's work has an indebtedness to that of Ludwig Fleck, which addressed medicine: *Entstehung und Entwicklung einer wissenschaftlichen Tatsache* (Basel: Benno Schwabe, 1935); *Genesis and Development of a Scientific Fact*, ed. T. J. Trenn and R. K. Merton, trans. F. Bradley and T. J. Trenn (Chicago:

University of Chicago Press, 1979). Second, the ambiguity of Kuhn's use of paradigm must also be acknowledged. As Margaret Masterman has shown, Kuhn employs the term in at least 21 different ways. "The Nature of a Paradigm," in *Criticism and the Growth of Knowledge*, eds. Imre Lakatos and Alan Musgrave (London: Cambridge University Press, 1970), pp. 59-89. The term paradigm is employed in this investigation of Christian bioethics without accepting Kuhn's underlying theory of knowledge. The term is used to identify a cluster of understandings of knowledge claims regarding who is in authority to resolve controversies, of examples of authoritative resolutions of controversies, as well as of background metaphysical commitments. "Paradigm" identifies the thought style of a community of investigators. I here use paradigm to identify the clusters of framing epistemological, metaphysical, and axiological presuppositions that direct the investigations of moral theologians. In this sense, Vatican II marked for Roman Catholic bioethics the abandonment of one paradigm of investigation and of the religious life and the beginning of crisis theology. To take a term from Ludwig Fleck, the "thought-style" changed.

30. For a thorough overview of the development of Roman Catholic moral theological reflections on medicine leading up to and following Trent, see David F. Kelly, *The Emergence of Roman Catholic Medical Ethics in North America* (New York: Edwin Mellen Press, 1979).

31. John Berkman, "How Important is the Doctrine of Double Effect for Moral Theology? Contextualizing the Controversy," *Christian Bioethics* 3 (1997), 91.

32. See, for example, A[lphonsus] Bonnar, *The Catholic Doctor* (London: Burns Oates & Washbourne, 1944). T[imothy] Lincoln Bouscaren, *Ethics of Ectopic Operations* (Chicago: Loyola University Press, 1933). C[arl Franz Nicolaus] Capellmann, *Pastoral Medicine*, trans. William Dassel (New York: F. Pustet, 1882; orig. 1877). Charles Coppens, *Moral Principles and Medical Practice*, 3rd ed. (New York: Benziger Brothers, 1897). Bernard J. Ficarra, *Newer Ethical Problems in Medicine and Surgery* (Westminster, MD: Newman Press, 1951). Patrick A. Finney, *Moral Problems in Hospital Practice*, 2nd ed. (St. Louis: B. Herder, 1922). Peter Flood, *New Problems in Medical Ethics*, trans. Malachy Gerard Carroll (Westminster, MD: Newman Press, 1953-4), 2 vols. Edward Hayes, Paul Hayes, Dorothy Kelly, *Moral Principles of Nursing* (New York: Macmillan, 1964). Edwin F. Healy, *Medical Ethics* (Chicago: Loyola University Press, 1956). Gerald Kelly, *Medico-Moral Problems* (St. Louis: Catholic Hospital Association, 1958). John P. Kenny, *Principles of Medical Ethics* (Westminster, MD: Newman Press, 1952). S[tanislaus] A. La Rochelle and C[harles] T. Fink, *Handbook of Medical Ethics*, trans. M.E. Poupore (Westminster, MD: Newman Book Shop, 1944). Charles J. McFadden, *Medical Ethics for Nurses* (Philadelphia: Davis, 1946) and *Medical Ethics* (Philadelphia: Davis, 1946). Thomas J. O'Donnell, *Morals in Medicine* (Westminster, MD: Newman Press, 1956). Alexander Sanford, *Pastoral Medicine: A Handbook for the Catholic Clergy* (New York: Joseph Wagner, 1905).

33. The 18th and 19th centuries saw the emergence in the West of a cluster of religious viewpoints, which was to a great extent purged of belief in Christ. This came to be expressed in a non-Christian deism. See, e.g., Anthony Collins, *A Discourse of Free-thinking* (London, 1713), as well as Thomas Paine's *Age of Reason* and the Baron Paul Henri Thiry d' Holbach's (1723-1789) *Histoire critique de Jésus-Christ* (London: D.I. Eaton, 1813). Deist concerns blended with the emergence of a post-Christian unitarianism, which emphasized the bond between progress, science, and religion. It distanced itself from revelation, but most particularly from traditional Christianity. Its proponents incorporated a faith in the future directed to the secular realization of peace and progress. "Brothers and sisters, we want to work for humanity. We have a new gospel to proclaim – the gospel of religion and science, two in one – the gospel of faith in man carried out to its extremest consequences ... We have a new gospel of good news, a radical gospel, the gospel of the 'enthusiasm of humanity.' God grant us ... a new Pentecostal outpouring of courage and fidelity to truth!" Francis Abbot, *Report of*

Addresses at a Meeting Held in Boston, May 30, 1867, to Consider the Conditions, Wants, and Prospects of Free Religion in America (Boston: Adams & Co., 1867), pp. 37-40, quoted in Stow Persons, *Free Religion* (New Haven: Yale University Press, 1947), pp. 47-48. In Germany, deism gave way to pantheism, which provided the roots for some of the contemporary German passion for deep ecology. As Heinrich Heine observed, "pantheism is the open secret of Germany. We have, in fact, outgrown deism." *Religion and Philosophy in Germany*, trans. John Snodgrass (Boston: Beacon Press, 1959), p. 79.

34. Rabbinical reflections had for centuries developed and sustained substantive explorations of the proper use of health care. For the most part, these reflections were conducted within the Jewish community and only came into prominent dialogue with others in the 1950s, 60s, and 1970s.

35. Joseph Fletcher, *Morals and Medicine* (Princeton, NJ: Princeton University Press, 1954). Isaac Jakobowits, *Jewish Medical Ethics* (New York: Bloch, 1959). Paul Ramsey, *Fabricated Man* (New Haven: Yale University Press, 1970) and *The Patient as Person* (New Haven: Yale University Press, 1970). Harmon Smith, *Ethics and the New Medicine* (Nashville: Abingdon Press, 1970). Kenneth Vaux, *To Create a Different Future* (New York: Friend Press, 1972) and *Will to Live – Will to Die* (Minneapolis: Augsburg, 1978).

36. In the period immediately after Vatican II, commentators could still regard Roman Catholic moral theology as a moral science. For example, in 1966 Richard McCormick opined, "The Council insisted that renewal in moral theology must not be equated with abandonment of its scientific character." *Notes on Moral Theology, 1965 Through 1980* (Washington, DC: University Press of America, 1981), p. 70. By 1973, his tone reflects the emerging foundational controversy. "The Second Vatican Council, after speaking of the renewal of theological disciplines through livelier contact with the mystery of Christ and the history of salvation, remarked simply: 'special attention needs to be given to the development of moral theology.' During the past six or seven years moral theology has experienced this special attention so unremittingly, some would say, that the Christianity has been crushed right out of it." *Ibid.*, p. 423. It was not just conservatives who saw Vatican II as a watershed of religious understanding. The depth of this change was also appreciated by those often characterized as dissidents in the debates that followed. Charles Curran captures this sense of change in an overview of the new developments in moral theology, as well as in an acknowledgement that the change had been supported by a kind of Vatican palace coup. "In the light of the Second Vatican Council, the self-understanding of Catholic theology itself changed. The manualistic neoscholasticism, which was in vogue immediately before the Second Vatican Council, tended to see theology as an extension of the teaching role of the pope and bishops with the need to explain and confirm this teaching. However, the general theological shift at Vatican II, especially the acceptance of historical consciousness, made theology conscious of a role that did not involve merely the repetition, explanation, and defense of church teachings. The very historical process that was the experience of the Second Vatican Council showed the creative role of theology and the need for theology to constantly probe the meaning of faith in the contemporary cultural and historical circumstances. The theologians who had the greatest effect on the council had been disciplined and suspect before the council itself. Theology is called to have an important role in bringing about change in Catholic thought and life." "Academic Freedom and Catholic Institutions of Higher Learning," in *Readings in Moral Theology No. 6: Dissent in the Church*, eds. Charles Curran and Richard McCormick (New York: Paulist Press, 1988), p. 257. With Vatican II, the very sense of who is in authority changed for Roman Catholic moral theology and therefore for Roman Catholic bioethics. The sense and meaning of magisterium changed as well. "The pre-Vatican II model divided the Church into the teachers – the Pope and the bishops – and the learners – the rest of us. The teacher was presumed to possess the truth and his basic role was to pass on that teaching

to the learners, whose principal task was to receive it docilely. Learning was interpreted virtually as an exercise of obedience. The emphasis was on acceptance of what was taught. That was why public dissent from the Church's teaching authority, the magisterium, was seen as open rejection of it, and was thus unthinkable. ...When the bishops met for Vatican II, almost the first thing they did was to reject this juridical and hierarchical model of the Church as determinative." Kevin Kelly, "Comments on the Curran Case: PRO," in *Readings in Moral Theology No. 6: Dissent in the Church*, pp. 473-4. From Vatican I into the post-Vatican II period, the understanding of who is in authority to resolve controversies in Roman Catholic moral theology has undergone significant change or development. The notion of authentic teaching authority or magisterium took on a different character as it moved from Vatican I's prime focus on the authority of the Pope of Rome to a post-Vatican II focus on numerous centers of authority, including not just the Pope and the bishops, but academic theologians as well as the spiritual experience of the masses.

37. John XXIII, *Ad Petri Cathedram*, 29 June 1959.

38. In anticipation of the Second Vatican Council, Hans Küng captures the desire on the part of some to recast established church discipline. Küng offers a distinction between revolution and reform. Even if the reform proposed is not to be regarded as revolutionary, it is meant to redirect the focus of the church from bringing the world into conformity with the truth that Tradition offers, to having Tradition, now construed as a special genre of historically and socially conditioned custom and oral history, reshaped to conform to contemporary social realities. "Reform as envisaged with reference to the coming Council is to be a renewal of the Church, an adaptation of the Church and her discipline to the demands of the present day" (*The Council, Reform and Reunion*, p. 52). The transformation of Roman Catholicism in the wake of Vatican II was complex. As with all significant historical events, any explanation is always infected by the judgments one brings to interpreting the changes. At the very least, there was an interplay among a number of factors, including (1) the understanding of theology as an intellectual endeavor, (2) the understanding of ecclesiology or the proper structure of the church, and (3) the understanding of pious practices such as the liturgy and fasting. In the half decade after Vatican II with the theological and ecclesiological changes it engendered, the so-called Tridentine Mass was for all intents and purposes radically marginalized. The Tridentine form of the Western liturgy represented Pope Pius V's (1566-1572) attempt to set aside medieval variants in the Western rite and to establish a form that in great measure had its roots in the first millennium of the church. Variants less than 200 years old were abolished. This Western rite endorsed by Pius V's Bull *Quo Primum* of 14 July 1570 was celebrated as the dominant rite for nearly 400 years. The change in Western liturgy after 1969 was associated with the so-called schism of Archbishop Lefevre and his followers, as well as with a significant decrease in the number of Roman Catholic priests. The number fell in the 7 years after the establishment of the new liturgy from 410,000 to about 245,000. During this period, there was also a decline in Sunday Mass attendance. In the period from 1965 to 1974, Roman Catholic attendance in Canada, for example, dropped 29% compared with a drop of only 19% among Protestants. *Index to International Public Opinion, 1978-1979* (Westport, CN: Greenwood Press, 1980). The percentage of Roman Catholics attending Mass weekly began a significant downward trajectory from 74% in 1958 to 26.6% in 1994. Ken Jones, "The Index of Leading Catholic Indicators," *The Latin Mass* 9 (Winter 2000), 93. In Amsterdam between 1973 and 1989, the number of churchgoers decreased from 45,000 to 10,000. Siggi Weidemann, "Altäre unter dem Hammer," *Süddeutsche Zeitung* (18 April 1989). One is confronted with a remarkable change, a "'one shot' decline in church practice in the late sixties and the early seventies," which is most plausibly related to these changes in the liturgy. Andrew M. Greeley, *The Catholic Myth* (New York: Scribner's Sons, 1990). For a study of some of the roots of these changes, see Louis Bouyer, *Der Verfall*

des Katholizismus (Munich: Kösel, 1970). The number of U.S. diocesan and religious semi-narians in 1965 versus 1995 decreased from 5.86/100,000 to 0.59/100,000 Roman Catholics for the former, and from 4.87/100,000 to 0.26/100,000 for the latter. See Kenneth Jones, "Index of Leading Catholic Indicators II," *The Latin Mass* (Summer 1996), 43-46; and "Three Decades of Renewal," *The Latin Mass* (Winter 1996), 32-35. See also R. Bowker (ed.), *Official Catholic Directory* (New Providence, NJ: Reed Reference Publishing, 1995).

39. Alexander Schmemann, *Liturgy and Tradition*, ed. Thomas Fisch (New York: St. Vladimir's Seminary Press, 1990), p. 28.

40. Gabriel Motzkin, *Time and Transcendence: Secular History, the Catholic Reaction, and the Rediscovery of the Future* (Dordrecht: Kluwer, 1992).

41. Hans Küng, *The Council, Reform and Reunion* (New York: Sheed and Ward, 1961).

42. By the 1980s, Anglican Britain had become robustly secularized. Alan D. Gilbert, *The Making of Post-Christian Britain* (London: Longman, 1980). "Membership of the Protestant denominations – which until recently represented the vast bulk of British Christianity – fell from 22 per cent of the adult population in 1900 to just 7 per cent in 1990." Steve Bruce, *Religion in the Modern World* (New York: Oxford University Press, 1996), p. 29.

43. John Paul II, *Veritatis Splendor* (Vatican City: Libreria Editrice Vaticana, 1993), § 106, p. 158.

44. Edward Schillebeeckx, "Silence and Speaking About God in a Secularized World," in *Christian Secularity*, ed. Albert Schlitzer (Notre Dame, IN: University of Notre Dame Press, 1969), p. 156.

45 Steve Bruce, *Religion in the Modern World* (New York: Oxford University Press, 1996), p. 36.

46. Peter Berger, *The Social Reality of Religion* (London: Penguin, 1969), p. 130.

47. Peter Berger, "The Descularization of the World: An Overview," in *The Desecularization of the World* (Washington, DC: Ethics and Public Policy Center, 1999), p. 6. Berger concedes that secularization continues apace in Western Europe, even if it may not characterize religious developments elsewhere in the world.

> In Western Europe, if nowhere else, the old secularization theory would seem to hold. With increasing modernization there has been an increase in key indicators of secularization, both on the level of expressed beliefs (especially those that could be called orthodox in Protestant or Catholic terms) and, dramatically, on the level of church-related behavior – attendance at services of worship, adherence to church-dictated codes of personal behavior (especially with regard to sexuality, reproduction, and marriage), recruitment to the clergy. *Ibid.*, pp. 10-11.

48. For an account of the supposedly unstoppable force of urbanization and industrialization on traditional societies, see Daniel Lerner, *The Passing of Traditional Society* (Glencoe, IL: Free Press of Glencoe, 1962). In noting that Islam has not fulfilled such predictions, one should distinguish the Islamic religious revival of recent decades from the political coercion frequently involved. One need not conclude that the Islamic revival would not have occurred if it had eschewed coercive policies.

49. Joseph Fletcher, *Morals and Medicine* (Princeton, NJ: Princeton University Press, 1954). Fletcher reflected many of the major moral challenges of the time. See also Joseph Fletcher, *Situation Ethics* (Philadelphia: Westminster, 1966). Fletcher spoke to what appeared to be the unraveling of traditional religious conviction. In an address on September 18, 1952, Pope Pius XII raises concerns regarding the situation ethics of which Fletcher became the champion by criticizing "what has otherwise been called 'Situationsethik,' or 'morality according to situations.'" *The Major Addresses of Pope Pius XII*, ed. Vincent Yzermans (St. Paul, MN: North Central Publishing Company, 1961), vol. 1, p. 209.

50. Harvey Cox, *The Secular City* (New York: Macmillan, 1966). Joseph Fletcher and Thomas Wassmer, *Hello, Lovers* (Washington: Corpus Books, 1970). Alan D. Gilbert, *The Making of*

Post-Christian Britain (London: Longman, 1980). R. J. Lawrence, Jr., *The Poisoning of Eros* (New York: Augustine Moore, 1989). David Lerner, *The Passing of Traditional Society* (Glencoe, IL: Free Press, 1962). Douglas Rhymes, *No New Morality* (Indianapolis: Bobbs-Merrill, 1965). John A. T. Robinson, *Christian Morals Today* (Philadelphia: Westminster, 1964). J. S. Spong, *Living in Sin?* (San Francisco: Harper & Row, 1988). W. Stringfellow and A. Towne, *The Bishop Pike Affair* (New York: Harper & Row, 1967).

51. Jeffrey Stout, *Ethics After Babel* (Boston: Beacon Press, 1988), p. 171.

52. The roots of Protestant secularization go deep into the 19th century and indeed into the 18th century and Immanuel Kant's *Die Religion innerhalb der Grenzen der blossen Vernunft* (1792). Von Hartmann at the end of the 19th century observed: "Liberal Protestantism has necessarily become an irreligious phenomenon of history, because Protestantism has taken the interest of modern culture to be the criterion." Eduard von Hartmann, *Die Selbstzersetzung des Christenthums* (Berlin: Duncker's, 1874), p. 87.

53. Jeffrey Stout, *Ethics After Babel*, p. 182.

54. Recently, evangelical and other Protestants have turned to bioethics. This growing literature includes Franklin E. Payne, Jr., *Biblical/Medical Ethics: The Christian and the Practice of Medicine* (Milford, MI: Mott Media, 1985); Hessel Bouma III *et al.*, *Christian Faith, Health, and Medical Practice* (Grand Rapids, MI: W.B. Eerdmans, 1989); John Kilner, Nigel Cameron, and David Schiedermayer (eds.), *Bioethics and the Future of Medicine* (Grand Rapids, MI: W.B. Eerdmans, 1995); Gilbert Meilaender, *Body, Soul, and Bioethics* (Notre Dame, IN: University of Notre Dame Press, 1995); Stephen E. Lammers and Allen Verhey (eds.), *On Moral Medicine: Theological Perspectives in Medical Ethics* (Grand Rapids, MI: W.B. Eerdmans, 1998); J.P. Moreland and Scott B. Rae, *Body and Soul* (Downers Grove, IL: InterVarsity Press, 1999) and Scott Rae and David Cox, *Bioethics: A Christian Approach in a Pluralistic Age* (Grand Rapids, MI: W.B. Eerdmans, 1999). This literature is set within a substantive Christian moral theological literature, addressing underlying issues foundational to bioethics. See, for example, Alvin Plantings and Nicholas Wolterstorff (eds.), *Faith and Rationality* (Notre Dame, IN: University of Notre Dame Press, 1983); Richard J. Mouw, *The God Who Commands* (Notre Dame, IN: University of Notre Dame Press, 1990); L. Gregory Jones, *Transformed Judgment* (Notre Dame, IN: University of Notre Dame Press, 1990); Nicholas Wolterstorff, *Divine Discourse* (New York: Cambridge University Press, 1995); and Robert Audi and Nicholas Wolterstorff, *Religion in the Public Square* (Lanham, MD: Rowman and Littlefield, 1997). It is interesting that Mouw in his volume has drawn upon material he originally published in the *Journal of Medicine and Philosophy*.

55. Paul Ramsey, *Fabricated Man* (New Haven: Yale University Press, 1970) and *The Patient as Person* (New Haven: Yale University Press, 1970). Stanley Hauerwas, *Vision and Virtue* (Notre Dame, IN: Fides Publishers, 1974) and *Truthfulness and Tragedy* (Notre Dame, IN: University of Notre Dame Press, 1977).

56. Stanley Hauerwas, "How Christian Ethics Became Medical Ethics: The Case of Paul Ramsey," *Christian Bioethics* 1 (1995), 11-28.

57. Joseph Fuchs, "Is There a Christian Morality?" in *Readings in Moral Theology No. 2: The Distinctiveness of Christian Ethics*, eds. Charles Curran and Richard McCormick (New York: Paulist Press, 1980), p. 11.

58. James Walter, "Christian Ethics: Distinctive and Specific?" in *Readings in Moral Theology No. 2*, p. 107.

59. The natural law accounts of morality that developed out of Western Christianity came to hold that even without knowledge of Christianity one could in principle determine how one ought to act. For example, with regard to bioethical issues, it was argued:

All men, then, are called upon to obey the natural law. Hence it matters not whether one be a Roman Catholic, a Protestant, a Jew, a pagan, or a person who has no religious affiliations whatsoever; he is

nevertheless obliged to become acquainted with and to observe the teachings of the law of nature. In the present volume all the obligations which are mentioned flow from the natural law, unless the contrary is evident from the context.
Edwin F. Healy, *Medical Ethics* (Chicago: Loyola University Press, 1956), p. 7.

60. Charles E. Curran, *Catholic Moral Theology in Dialogue* (Notre Dame, IN: University of Notre Dame Press, 1976) p. 20.

61. J.-M. Aubert, "La spécificité de la morale chrétienne selon saint Thomas," *Supplément* 92 (1970), 55-73; F. Böckle, "Was ist das Proprium einer christlichen Ethik?" *Heythrop Journal* 13 (1972), 27-43; James F. Bresnahan, S.J., "Rahner's Christian Ethics," *America* 23 (1970), 351-54; Joseph Fuchs, S.J., "Gibt es eine spezifisch christliche Moral?" *Stimmen der Zeit* 185 (1970), 99-112; John Macquarrie, *Three Issues in Ethics* (New York: Harper & Row, 1970); R. Simon, "Spécificité de l'éthique chrétienne," *Supplément* 92 (1970), 74-104. The appreciation of Christian moral theology as materially equivalent to secular moral reflection was in great measure a fulfillment of a significant tendency within Roman Catholic moral theology, namely, to ground itself in natural law and a rational account of morality. Such accounts of Christian morality were resisted by Protestant moral theologians. They were opposed on principle by such as Karl Barth. In the 1960s, theologians associated with bioethics such as James M. Gustafson took a stand somewhat analogous to Barth's rejection of the reduction of Christian morality to philosophical morality; see *Christ and the Moral Life* (New York: Harper & Row, 1968). This reduction was also resisted by Roman Catholic moral theologians such as Bernard Häring, who argued that "Some people, including certain Catholic theologians, still have the incredible idea that the moral teaching of the New Testament adds no new content to the natural law, that it only offers new motives. This is actually worse than the moral doctrine of Pelagius ..." (*Road to Relevance* [New York: Alba, 1970], p. 66). Nevertheless, James Gustafson for his part developed a post-traditional Christian theology, arguing against God's omniscience and omnipotence, against the view that "God has intelligence, like but superior to our own, and that God has a will, a capacity to control events comparable to the more radical claims made for human beings..." (*Ethics from a Theocentric Perspective* [Chicago: University of Chicago Press, 1981, 1984], vol. 1, p. 270). Moreover, his Christology is not one that affirms the traditional Christian centrality of Christ's Resurrection or the resurrection of the body. Bernard Häring has also recently called for a restructuring of the Roman church in ways that would importantly recast traditional Roman Catholic beliefs. See, for example, Bernard Häring, *My Witness for the Church*, trans. Leonard Swidler (Mahwah, NJ: Paulist Press, 1992).

62. Richard McCormick, *Notes on Moral Theology, 1965 through 1980* (Washington, DC: University Press of America, 1981), pp. 296-303, 428-432.

63. J.-M. Aubert, "La spécificité de la morale chrétienne selon saint Thomas," *Supplément* 92 (1970), 55-73.

64. The account of Christian moral theology advanced by many in the 20th century, who discern no material difference between what moral theology can offer and what secular morality can justify, contrasts somewhat with the traditional view of the Roman church. For example, the 1913 edition of the *Catholic Encyclopedia* states: "Moral theology, correctly understood, means the science of supernaturally revealed morals. ... It is also plain that although this Supreme lawgiver can be known by natural reason, neither He nor His law can be sufficiently known without a revelation on His part. Hence it is that moral theology, the study of this Divine law, is actually cultivated only by those who faithfully cling to a Divine Revelation, and by the sects which sever their connexion with the Church, only as long as they retain the belief in a supernatural Revelation through Jesus Christ" ([New York: Encyclopedia Press, 1914], vol. 14, p. 604). This view continued to be held by certain traditional Roman Catholic thinkers, such as Jacques Maritain.

The rules of human life are taught from on high. The knowledge of them is brought to us by faith, not by reason. It is a revealed knowledge, even the knowledge of the moral rules which are otherwise naturally knowable by the human intelligence and are, in a more or less obscure, imperfect or warped way, spontaneously perceived by human intelligence (the precepts of the Decalogue) are essentially a revealed formulation of the principles of natural law.

Humanity finds itself in the presence of a revealed ethics, an essentially religious ethics.
Jacques Maritain, *Moral Philosophy* (New York: Charles Scribner's Sons, 1964), p. 87.

In this account, morality is only fully understood within the context of right worship and belief. True morality is Christian morality.

65. There has not yet been a sufficient assessment of what would have better protected German medicine from its moral corruption during the 1930s and 1940s at the hands of National Socialism. It is to be noted that immediately prior to Hitler's ascendancy the Germans enacted an impressive set of legal protections for human subjects in research. Hans-Martin Sass, "Reichsrundschreiben 1931: Pre-Nuremberg German Regulations Concerning New Therapy and Human Experimentation," *Journal of Medicine and Philosophy* 8 (May 1983), 99-111. There was also a rich history of German regulations protecting prisoners and patients from unconsented-to research, reaching back to the end of the 19th century.

66. See, for example, such decisions as *Canterbury v. Spence*, 464 F. 2d 772, 789 (D.C. Cir. 1972); *Cobbs v. Grant*, 8 Cal. 3.d 229, 246; 502 P.2d 1, 12; 104 Cal. Rptr. 505, 516 (Calif. 1972); and *Sard v. Hardy*, 397 A. 2d 1014, 1020 (Md. 1977).

67. *The United States of America, Appellants, v. The American Medical Association, A Corporation; The Medical Society of the District of Columbia, A Corporation; et al.*, 317 U.S. 519 (1943).

68. *American Medical Assoc. v. Federal Trade Comm'n*, 638 F.2d 443 (2d Cir. 1980).

69. See, for example, Council on Ethical and Judicial Affairs of American Medical Association, *Code of Medical Ethics* (Chicago: AMA, 1997).

70. The Flexner report marked the triumph of the scientific model over American medicine so that orthodox medical education was seen to require a substantial foundation in the sciences that had now been able to transform themselves into basic sciences, the sciences foundational to the very conduct of contemporary medicine. See Abraham Flexner, *Medical Education in the United States and Canada, A Report to the Carnegie Foundation for the Advancement of Teaching, Bulletin No. 4* (New York: Carnegie Foundation, 1910). For an interesting retrospective on the transformation by managed care of the ethos of contemporary medicine, see Frank Davidoff, "Medicine and Commerce. 1: Is Managed Care a 'Monstrous Hybrid'?" *Annals of Internal Medicine* 128 (1998), 496-499, and "Medicine and Commerce. 2: The Gift," *Annals of Internal Medicine* 128 (1998), 572-575.

71. Vatican I reflected the Roman church's attempt to strengthen the tradition it had developed over the previous millennium by robustly endorsing the role of natural reason. It became a matter of faith that one can know the existence of God without faith, that is, by natural reason alone. "The same holy mother church holds and teaches that God, the source and end of all things, can be known with certainty from the consideration of created things, by the natural power of human reason: ever since the creation of the world, his invisible nature has been clearly perceived in the things that have been made." "Dogmatic constitution on the catholic faith" in "First Vatican Council – 1869-1870," in Norman Tanner, S.J. (ed.), *Decrees of the Ecumenical Councils* (Washington, DC: Georgetown University Press, 1990), vol. 2, p. 806. Out of this confidence in reason, John Paul II encourages philosophers "to trust in the power of human reason and not to set themselves goals that are too modest in their philosophizing." *Fides et Ratio* (Vatican City: Libreria Editrice Vaticana, 1998), § 56, p. 86.

72. On the basis of Stoic moral and legal reasoning, Gaius asserts in his 2nd-century *Institutes* that "the law that natural reason established among all mankind is followed by all people

alike, and is called ius gentium [law of nations or law of the world] as being the law observed
   by all mankind." *Institutes of Gaius*, trans. Francis De Zulueta (London: Oxford University
   Press, 1976), vol. 1, p. 3.
73. See, for example, Thomas Aquinas, *Summa Theologica*, I-II Q. 94, art. 6.
74. Thomas Aquinas argues that grace plays a role in all human knowledge. See *Treatise on
   Grace*, Q 109, Art 1.
75. Gerald Kelly, *Medico-Moral Problems* (St. Louis, MO: Catholic Hospital Association, 1958),
   p. 34.
76. Western medieval Christianity responded to the threat of moral diversity with deadly force,
   suppressing it through military and police action. The Fourth Lateran Council, for example,
   to encourage the suppression of heresy, provided the same indulgences to those who extermi-
   nated heretics as to those who went on Crusades. "Catholics who take the cross and gird
   themselves up for the expulsion of heretics shall enjoy the same indulgence, and be strengthened by the same holy privilege, as is granted to those who go to the aid of the holy Land."
   "Constitutions: 3. On heretics" in "Fourth Lateran Council – 1215", in Norman Tanner, S.J.
   (ed.), *Decrees of the Ecumenical Councils* (Washington, DC: Georgetown University Press,
   1990), vol. 1, p. 234. The same constitution declared:

   We condemn all heretics, whatever names they may go under. They have different faces indeed but their
   tails are tied together inasmuch as they are alike in their pride. Let those condemned be handed over to
   the secular authorities present, or to their bailiffs, for due punishment. ... Let secular authorities,
   whatever offices they may be discharging, be advised and urged and if necessary be compelled by
   ecclesiastical censure, if they wish to be reputed and held to be faithful, to take publicly an oath for the
   defence of the faith to the effect that they will seek, in so far as they can, to expel from the lands subject
   to their jurisdiction all heretics designated by the church in good faith.
   "Fourth Lateran Council", p. 233.

   With this endorsement of force by an ecumenical council of the Western church, the Inquisition began to take shape. In 1232 Conrad of Marburg was established as the first *Inquisitor
   haereticae praevitatis*. In 1252 with the bull Ad extirpanda, Innocent IV officially inaugurat-
   ed the Inquisition, in 1253 Peter of Verona was canonized as the patron saint of inquisitors,
   and in 1254 Italy was divided into two inquisitorial territories, one assigned to the Domini-
   cans and the other to the Franciscans. In this period, Thomas Aquinas helped to provide
   theological support for the Inquisition by defending the death penalty for recalcitrant heretics. "I answer that with regard to heretics ... on their own side there is the sin, whereby they
   deserve not only to be separated from the Church by excommunication, but also to be
   severed from the world by death. For it is a much graver matter to corrupt the faith which
   quickens the soul, than to forge money, which supports temporal life. Wherefore if forgers of
   money and other evildoers are forthwith condemned to death by the secular authority, much
   more reason is there for heretics, as soon as they are convicted of heresy, to be not only
   excommunicated but even put to death." *Summa Theologica of St. Thomas Aquinas* (Westminster, MD: Christian Classics, 1948), vol. 3, p. 220; II-II, Q. 11, art. 3. This commitment
   of Thomas Aquinas led to centuries of concerted attempts to suppress moral and religious
   diversity. In the time of the Inquisition, this was expressed in the Act of Faith, the auto-da-fé.
   It was so called because those present at the burning of the heretics, in particular the rulers,
   would swear that they would use all their power to defend the church of Rome and to aid the
   Holy Inquisition in its efforts to extirpate heretics. Those executed met their end under the
   standard of the Inquisition, a flag of crimson damask on which was emblazoned the white
   and black escutcheon of the order of Dominic, the Order of Preachers, the order of Thomas
   Aquinas. On the ends of the flag there were the words *Exurge, Domine, et judica causam
   tuam*. See William Thomas Walsh, *Characters of the Inquisition* (New York: P.J. Kenedy,
   1940), p. 228. The following eyewitness description from 1690 conveys the character of the
   event.

> At the place of execution there are so many stakes set as there are prisoners ..., a large quantity of dry furze being set about them. The stakes of the Protestants ... are about four yards high, and have each a small board, whereon the prisoner is seated within half a yard of the top. The professed then go up a ladder betwixt two priests, who attend them the whole day of execution. ... [T]he priests spend near a quarter of an hour in exhorting them to be reconciled ... [with] Rome. On their refusing, the priests come down, and the executioner ascending, turns the professed from off the ladder upon the seat, chains their bodies close to the stakes, and leaves them. Then the priests go up a second time ...; and if they find them ineffectual, usually tell them at parting, that 'they leave them to the Devil, who is standing at their elbow ready to receive their souls, and carry them with him into the flames of hell-fire, as soon as they are out of their bodies'. A general shout is then raised, and when the priests get off the ladder, the universal cry is: 'Let the dogs' beards be made!' ([i.e.], singe their beards). This is ... performed by ... flaming furzes, thrust against their faces with long poles. This barbarity is repeated till their faces are burnt, and is accompanied with loud acclamations. Fire is then set to the furzes, and the criminals are consumed.
> Edward Burman, *The Inquisition: Hammer of Heresy* (New York: Dorset, 1992), pp. 154-155.

77. The coronation of Charles the Great by Pope Leo III after the third Mass on Christmas, 800, was one of those few individual acts that dramatically changes all human history. From this event, the West took on a new and independent identity. Beginning in 781, the Roman popes had ceased to date their Acta with the reign of the emperor of Constantinople. In 800, they dated them from the reign of Charles the Great. A new age had dawned. See, in particular, chapter 2 of Yves Congar, *After Nine Hundred Years* (New York: Fordham University Press, 1959). "The coronation of Charles is not only the central event of the Middle Ages, it is also one of those very few events of which, taking them singly, it may be said that if they had not happened, the history of the world would have been different." James Bryce, "The Coronation as a Revival of the Roman Empire in the West," in *The Coronation of Charlemagne*, ed. Richard E. Sullivan (Boston: D.C. Heath, 1959), p. 41. See also Donald A. Bullough, *The Age of Charlemagne* (London: Paul Elek, 1973); Robert Folz, *Le couronnement impérial de Charlemagne* (Paris: Gallimard, 1964); and François Ganshof, *The Imperial Coronation of Charlemagne* (Glasgow: Jackson, 1949).

78. The Western Middle Ages produced a new view concerning what it is to know God and to be a theologian; the theologian became the academic. This point will be developed at greater length in Chapters 2 and 4. Here it is enough to note that this contrasts with the Church of the first millennium, a contrast that continues to define the differences between Orthodox and non-Orthodox Christianity. For example, with regard to theology in general,

> to a degree larger than in the West, the Byzantine Church sees in the saint or in the mystic monk the guardian of the faith and trusts him more than any permanent institution. And we must always keep in mind that in Byzantine society as well, as in modern secular societies of Eastern Europe, the greatest saints and theologians were and are men of prayer and monastic spirituality, devotees to the Eucharistic Liturgy, with its free experience of the heavenly and of the Spirit, this Liturgy being a mystical unfolding of the full abundance of divine acts of redemption and divinely revealed truths.
> Constantine Tsirpanlis, *Introduction to Eastern Patristic Thought and Orthodox Theology* (Collegeville, MN: Liturgical Press, 1991), p. 89.

This understanding of what it is to know God separates the Western churches from the Church of the first millennium, the Orthodox Church.

> The Councils of Constantinople of 1341, 1351 and 1368 affirm, among other things, that God lives absolutely inaccessible insofar as His essence is concerned, which cannot be the object of knowledge or vision even for the blessed and the angels, to whom the Divine Being is revealed and has become knowable in His uncreated and deifying energies. In Rome, or rather in Avignon, the question of the beatific vision was raised in a different way. It simply involved the question whether the elect could enjoy the vision of the divine essence after death and before the last judgment, or whether this bliss was reserved for the state of final beatitude after the resurrection. Pope Benedict XII, in his constitu-

tion Benedictus Deus of January 29, 1336, censuring the opinion of his predecessor John XXII, according to whom the face to face vision of God would take place only after the resurrection, has this to say among other things: "...after the passion and death of our Lord Jesus Christ, they (the elect) will see and do see the divine essence in an intuitive and face to face vision, without any created intermediary which would interpose itself as an object of vision, the divine essence appearing to them immediately, without a veil (nude), clearly and openly; so that in this vision they might enjoy the divine essence itself." Five years later, in 1341, the same Benedict XII, examining the doctrine of the Armenians who were seeking union with the Church of Rome, reproached them – among other erroneous opinions – for having denied to the blessed the intuitive vision of the essence of God. Vladimir Lossky, *The Vision of God* (Crestwood, NY: St. Vladimir's Seminary Press, 1983), pp. 12-13.

Through these various steps the West came to think of theology in a new light, one that was primarily academic and one that no longer recognized God as fully transcendent. God's essence came to be the object of academic theological investigation. Theology was no longer the experience of God but the study of God. As a result, the West has suffered from a caesaro papism of scholars who attempted to seize the authority of the living and unchanging revelation of the Holy Spirit. See Lossky, pp. 71-72.

79. It is important to note that the product of the Western Middle Ages was not simply moral diversity, but a political and cultural diversity no longer united in principle under the pope of Rome and the Western emperor.

80. Pierre Bayle, *A Philosophical Commentary on These Words of the Gospel, Luke XIV.23* (London: F. Darby, 1708), vol. 1, p. 42.

81. Herbert Butterfield, *Christianity in European History* (London: Collins, 1952), p. 35.

82. A paradigm exemplar of the Enlightenment hope of progress, unity, and peace is offered by Kant's *Zum ewigen Frieden* [1795].

83. John Rawls characterizes the Enlightenment project as the program of finding "a philosophical secular doctrine, one founded on reason and yet comprehensive. It would then be suitable to the modern world, so it was thought, now that the religious authority and the faith of Christian ages was alleged to be no longer dominant." *Political Liberalism* (New York: Columbia University Press, 1993), p. xviii.

84. The penchant to free morality from a bondage to its Western cultural origins has roots that can be traced to the Enlightenment aspiration of Kant to provide a morality for persons as such. His kingdom of ends is a realm that binds not merely humans but all moral agents.

It follows incontestably that every rational being must be able to regard himself as an end in himself with reference to all laws to which he may be subject, whatever they may be, and thus as giving universal laws. For it is just the fitness of his maxims to a universal legislation that indicates that he is an end in himself. It also follows that his dignity (his prerogative) over all merely natural beings entails that he must take his maxims from the point of view which regards himself, and hence also every other rational being, as legislative. (The rational beings are, on this account, called persons.) In this way, a world of rational beings (mundus intelligibilis) is possible as a realm of ends, because of the legislation belonging to all persons as members. Immanuel Kant, *Foundations of the Metaphysics of Morals*, trans. Lewis White Beck (Indianapolis: Bobbs-Merrill, 1959), AK IV.438-9, pp. 56-7.

Because of these foundations of his metaphysics of morals, Kant is able to conceive of his *Idea for a Universal History with a Cosmopolitan Purpose* (published in 1784, two years before the *Foundations*), in which he concludes with the following proposition: "A philosophical attempt to work out a universal history of the world in accordance with a plan of nature aimed at a perfect civil union of mankind, must be regarded as possible and even as capable of furthering the purpose of nature itself." *Kant's Political Writings*, ed. Hans Reiss, trans. H. B. Nisbet (New York: Cambridge University Press, 1970), AK VIII.29, p. 51. See also Kant's *Zum ewigen Frieden* (1795).

85. The French Revolution understood itself as a rupture in European history and a radical break from the Christian past. It brought a new calendar, a new division of the hours of the day, new laws, and a new religion. The non-Christian nature of the Republic was celebrated in the official Cult of Reason in the autumn of 1793 in the ceremonies of the Feast of Reason held in the Notre Dame cathedral (November 9), as well as elsewhere. The Christian past was to be transformed where it could not be fully abolished. Albert Mathiez, *Les Origines des cultes révolutionnaires* (Geneva: Slatkine, 1977; 1st ed. 1904); André Latreille, *L'Église catholique et la révolution française* (Paris: Hachette, 1948), 2 vols.

86. From the First Republic to Napoleon, there were two notorious abductions of the pope of Rome. A year after the French arranged the proclamation of a Roman republic in February, 1798, Pope Pius VI was taken to France, where he then died. Napoleon, for his part, induced the successor, Pius VII, to come to Paris to crown him emperor. Napoleon then rebuffed the pope and crowned himself on December 2, 1804. After the Papal States were assimilated into the French Empire, the pope's apartment was forcibly entered on July 5, 1809, and the pope was again taken as a prisoner to France.

87. The 19th century continued the deChristianization of Europe. This was often pursued through an anti-clericism and a concern to secularize or laicize society. An instance of this drive to remove Christianity from the center of culture and society is found in the attempt to laicize French schools in which Jules Ferry (1832-1893) played a significant role. Maurice Reclus, *Jules Ferry* (Paris: Flammarion, 1947).

88. The incursions by Napoleon into the old Holy Roman Empire made attractive seizing Roman Catholic church property as compensation to, as well as spoils for, German sovereigns after the Peace of Lunéville in 1801. An extraordinary Reichsdeputation, which assembled on August 24, 1802, dissolved the remaining episcopal principalities to produce the needed resources. This occurred in 1803. See "Der Reichsdeputationshauptschluss," in *Quellen zum Verfassungsorganismus des heiligen römischen Reiches deutscher Nation*, ed. H. H. Hofmann (Darmstadt: Wissenschaftliche Buchgesellschaft, 1976), pp. 329-358. There followed an iconoclasm, a *Bildersturz* during which priceless works of art were damaged and libraries wasted. Most significantly, a traditional religious source for education and welfare, independent of the secular state, was abolished: the institutions of the Roman church. The provision of welfare for the poor passed from the charge of the church to that of the police, a circumstance lamented by the Silesian German poet Eichendorff. Joseph Freiherr von Eichendorff, "Über die Folgen von der Aufhebung der Landeshoheit der Bischöfe und der Klöster in Deutschland," in *Werke und Schriften* (Stuttgart: Cottasche, 1958), vol. 4, pp. 1133-1184.

89. "And we may rely on Karl Barth's apt formulation that Hegel seeks to do for the modern Protestant world what St. Thomas Aquinas has done for the Catholic Middle Ages." Emil Fackenheim, *The Religious Dimension in Hegel's Thought* (Bloomington: Indiana University Press, 1967), p. 10.

90. For an example of the argument that spirit must enter into history and change it, see August von Cieszkowski, *Prolegomena zur Historiosophie* (Berlin: Veit, 1838). For a study of the significance of Cieszkowski, see Walter Kühne, *Graf August Cieszkowski: ein Schüler Hegels und des deutschen Geistes* (Liechtenstein: Kraus, 1968). Also see Klaus Hartmann, *Die marxsche Theorie* (Berlin: de Gruyter, 1970), pp. 13-68.

91. Walker Percy, *The Message in the Bottle* (New York: Farrar, Straus and Giroux, 1987), p. 27.

92. Max Horkheimer, *Eclipse of Reason* (New York: Continuum, 1974), p. 18.

93. Despite all of the contentions of the Western Christian Middle Ages, there was the presumption that, in principle, arguments regarding natural law obligations could be resolved by sound rational argument and that the pope of Rome was in authority to bring appropri-

ate closure to debates. After the Reformation, no such institutional moral ideal could bind the societies of the West.

94. Jean-François Lyotard, *The Postmodern Condition*, trans. G. Bennington and B. Massumi (Manchester: Manchester University Press, 1984), p. 37.

95. The emerging recognition of the diversity of American, European, and Japanese bioethics is presented in Kazumasa Hoshino (ed.), *Japanese and Western Bioethics* (Dordrecht: Kluwer, 1997).

96. John S. Romanides, *Franks, Romans, Feudalism, and Doctrine* (Brookline, MA: Holy Cross Orthodox Press, 1981).

97. There is merit to the contention that European culture is losing its European character. Consider the reflections of Harold Rosenberg regarding the intrusion of non-European art into European aesthetics. "Under the slogan, FOR A NEW ART, FOR A NEW REALITY, the most ancient superstitions have been exhumed, the most primitive rites re-enacted: the rummage for generative forces has set African demon-masks in the temple of the Muses and introduced the fables of Zen and Hasidism into the dialogue of philosophy. Through such dislocations of time and geography the first truly universal tradition has come to light, with world history as its past and requiring a world stage on which to flourish." *The Tradition of the New* (London: Thames and Hudson, 1962). When assessing Rosenberg's suggestion, one must observe that the emerging global culture is an outgrowth of the European Enlightenment, even when it reflects post-modernism, the West's deconstruction of its Enlightenment. World culture as universal culture turns out paradoxically to be particular when expressed as liberal cosmopolitanism, carrying with it its own ranking of values (e.g., of liberty, equality, prosperity, and security). World culture thus remains framed by and within European anthropological assumptions. Moreover, its engagement in the different and the exotic resonates with similar engagements by European pagan culture during the first three centuries of the Christian era.

98. One finds interesting indications of the resurgence of European paganism: "Perhaps if we are patient enough, if we listen closely enough to the moods, emotions, unusual behaviors, dreams, and fantasies of ourselves and our societies, we may hear some songs that are very old, now coming once again from the severed head of Orpheus that floats in every sea just off every isle of Lesbos. The songs, their narratives and their dramas, are those of the Gods and Goddesses announcing an expanding consciousness, a new sensibility, a new polytheism, a remythologization of life." David L. Miller, *The New Polytheism: Rebirth of the Gods and Goddesses* (New York: Harper & Row, 1974), p. 83.

99. One must note that gentlemanly virtues were still held to be essential for the proper moral formation of physicians. Into the 20th century, at least in the United States, the virtuous physician was one who had the moral resources of the Christian gentleman. Chester R. Burns, "American Medical Ethics: Some Historical Roots," in *Philosophical Medical Ethics*, eds. S. F. Spicker and H. T. Engelhardt, Jr. (Dordrecht: D. Reidel, 1977), pp. 21-26. For an account of the integration of rationalist concerns and Christian sentiments on the Continent, see Dietrich von Engelhardt, "Virtue and Medicine During the Enlightenment in Germany," in *Virtue and Medicine*, ed. Earl E. Shelp (Dordrecht: D. Reidel, 1985), pp. 63-79.

100. See, for example, John Gregory, *Observations on the Duties and Offices of a Physician* (London: Strahan, 1770), and Thomas Percival, *Medical Ethics* (Manchester: Russell, 1803). Scotland was a source of substantial interest in codes of medical ethics; for an overview, see Jacqueline Jenkinson, *Scottish Medical Societies 1731-1939* (Edinburgh: Edinburgh University Press, 1993), especially pp. 53-67. For a study of John Gregory's work, see Laurence B. McCullough, *John Gregory and the Intention of Professional Medical Ethics and the Profession of Medicine* (Dordrecht: Kluwer, 1998). Also, a critical

edition of Gregory's work is provided by Laurence B. McCullough (ed.), *John Gregory's Writings on Medical Ethics and Philosophy of Medicine* (Dordrecht: Kluwer, 1998).

In the early 19th century in the United States there was a flourishing of codes of medical etiquette or ethics designed to give guidance to physicians and moral standing to the profession. See, for example, Samuel A. Cartwright, "Synopsis of Medical Etiquette," *New Orleans Medical and Surgical Journal* 1, no. 2 (1844), 101-4. Medical Association of North Eastern Kentucky, *A System of Medical Etiquette* (Maysville, KY: Maysville Eagle, 1839). *Code of Medical Ethics Adopted by the American Medical Association at Philadelphia in May, 1847, and by the New York Academy of Medicine in October, 1847* (New York: H. Ludwig, 1848). Donald E. Konold, *A History of American Medical Ethics, 1847-1912* (Madison: State Historical Society of Wisconsin, 1962). These developments grew from a long history of reflections, which though initially Christian in character, slowly took on a more secular idiom. See Carlo Cipolla, *Public Health and the Medical Profession in Renaissance Italy* (New York: Cambridge University Press, 1976). Although the interest initially maintained a Christian character, it soon took on a more secular idiom. Important in this period of transition were Giovanni Codronchi, *De Christiana ac tuta medendi ratione libri duo* (Ferrara, 1591) and Rodericus Castro, *Medicus-Politicus: sive de officiis medicopoliticis tractatus* (Hamburg: Frobeniano, 1614). Concerns with community health in the 18th century were placed under the rubric medical police, a term coined by Wolfgang Thomas Rau (1721-1772) in *Gedanken von dem Nutzen und der Nothwendigkeit einer medicinischen Policeyordnung in einem Staat* (Ulm: Stettin, 1764). The most famous synthesis of this movement was provided by Johann Peter Frank (1745-1821) in *System einer vollständigen medicinischen Polizey* (Mannheim: C.F. Schwan, 1779). For an English translation, see Johann Frank, *A System of Complete Medical Police*, trans. E. Wilim (Baltimore: Johns Hopkins University Press, 1976). George Rosen has provided an excellent overview of these developments and their impact on contemporary medicine in *From Medical Police to Social Medicine: Essays on the History of Health Care* (New York: Science History Publications, 1974).

101. In the preface to his treatise on medical ethics, Saundby indicates that lectures on medical deontology had become part of French medical education before the end of the 19th century. R. Saundby, *Medical Ethics: A Guide to Professional Conduct* (Bristol: Wright, 1902), p. v.

102. *Ibid.*, p. 2.

103. *Ibid.*, pp. 2-3.

104. *Ibid.*, p. 3.

105. Faith in the ability of reason to establish a universally valid morality is presented by one of the contributors to bioethics, Bernard Gert, in his account of morality: "A justified moral system is one that all impartial rational persons, using only those beliefs that are shared by all rational persons, would advocate adopting as a public system that applies to all rational persons. I believe that any system that satisfies the definition of morality will be a justified moral system. I also believe that there is only one such system, viz., the one described in this book." *Morality: A New Justification of the Moral Rules* (New York: Oxford University Press, 1988), pp. 282-283. As Robert Veatch recognizes, in the shadow of Western rationalist aspirations, these hopes from discursive argument are ubiquitous.

> Most people, even those functioning within a sectarian framework, tend to hold that the important questions – in the realm of science or in the realm of values – are ones which, in principle, we should all be able to agree upon. Such issues are viewed as questions of truth or, at least, questions about which reasonable people ought to be able to agree. It may turn out that we are unable to reach such an agreement so that we have to return to more sectarian, smaller groups. It is worth trying for a more universal foundation of morality, however.

> Veatch, *A Theory of Medical Ethics* (New York: Basic Books, 1981), p. 112.

106. The term humanism encompasses at least four major and quite different clusters of undertakings: (1) humanism as refinement, (2) humanism as a body of learning, (3) humanism as concern for others, and (4) humanism as a particular school of philosophical and moral theory. Engelhardt, *Bioethics and Secular Humanism*, pp. 43-52.

107. Friedrich I. Niethammer, *Der Streit des Humanismus und Philanthropismus in der Theorie des Erziehungsunterrichts unserer Zeit* (Jena, 1808).

108. J. D. Hoeveler, Jr, *The New Humanism* (Charlottesville: University Press of Virginia, 1977). Horst Rüdiger, *Wesen und Wandlung des Humanismus* (Hamburg: Hoffmann & Campe, 1937).

109. In the 1960s, medical educators began to embrace the humanities in a fashion reminiscent of Abraham Flexner, a major author of the American medical educational reforms at the beginning of the 20th century. *Medical Education in the United States and Canada, A Report to the Carnegie Foundation for the Advancement of Teaching*, Bulletin No. 4 (New York: Carnegie Foundation, 1910). Flexner spoke in the spirit of the third humanism, endorsing the importance of the humanities in sustaining human values. *The Burden of Humanism* (Oxford: Clarendon Press, 1928).

110. Edmund D. Pellegrino, *Humanism and the Physician* (Knoxville: University of Tennessee Press, 1979), p. 17.

111. Edmund D. Pellegrino and Thomas McElhinney, *Teaching Ethics, the Humanities, and Human Values in Medical Schools* (Washington, DC: Society for Health and Human Values, 1982), p. 26. Pellegrino's connection of medicine with the humanities recalls the Hippocratic corpus, which likens to a god a physician who is also a philosopher. "For a physician who is a lover of wisdom is the equal of a god. Between wisdom and medicine there is no gulf fixed; in fact medicine possesses all the qualities that make for wisdom." Hippocrates, "Decorum" V in *Hippocrates*, trans. W. H. S. Jones (Cambridge, MA: Harvard University Press, 1959), vol. 2, p. 287.

112. Pellegrino & McElhinney, p. 51.

113. For reflections at the beginning of the recent concern for the philosophy of medicine, see H. T. Engelhardt, Jr., and Stuart F. Spicker (eds.), *Evaluation and Explanation in the Biomedical Sciences* (Dordrecht: Reidel, 1975).

114. Little attention was given in the secular literature to the rich distinctions that had been drawn regarding limiting treatment in the previous four centuries of Roman Catholic medical ethics, though they could have been recast in secular terms. See Daniel A. Cronin, *The Moral Law in Regard to the Ordinary and Extraordinary Means of Conserving Life* (Rome: Typis Pontificiae Universitatis Gregorianiae, 1958). These did come to have some influence of secular health care policy. See, for example, *Satz v. Perlmutter*, Fla. App. 362 So 2d 160 (1978). See also *Eichner v. Dillon*, 420 N.E. 2d 64 (N.Y. Ct. App. 1981).

115. For examples of literature in the philosophy of medicine, see Elisha Bartlett, *Essay on the Philosophy of Medical Science* (Philadelphia: Lee and Blanchard, 1844). Francesco Berlinghieri, *La Filosofia della Medicina* (Lucca: aux frais de l'auteur, 1801). W. Bieganski, *Logika Medyzyny* (Warsaw: Kowalewski, 1894). Gilbert Blane, *Elements of Medical Logic* (London: T and G Underwood, 1819). Jean Bouillauds, *Essai sur la philosophie medicale et sur les généralités de la clinique medicale* (Paris: J. Rouvier et E. le Bouvier, 1836). F. Osterlen, *Medical Logic*, ed. and trans. G. Whitney (London: Sydenham Society, 1855).

116. W. Szumowski, "La Philosophie de la médecine, son histoire, son essence, sa dénomination et sa définition," *Archives Internationales d'Histoire des Sciences* 9 (1949), 1138.

117. National Commission for the Protection of Human Subjects of Biomedical and Behavioral Research, *Research on the Fetus* (Washington, DC: HEW, 1975); *Research Involving Prisoners* (Washington, DC: HEW, 1976); *Report and Recommendations on Psychosurgery*

(Washington, DC: HEW, 1977); *Psychosurgery* (Appendix) (Washington, DC: HEW, 1977); *Research Involving Children* (Washington, DC: HEW, 1977); *Research Involving Those Institutionalized as Mentally Infirm* (Washington, DC: HEW, 1978).

118. National Commission for the Protection of Human Subjects of Biomedical and Behavioral Research, *The Belmont Report: Ethical Principles and Guidelines for the Protection of Human Subjects of Research* (Washington, DC: HEW, 1978). The author of this book must confess the sins of his youth, which include a contribution to the salience of principlism. Albert Jonsen, in his account of the development of the Belmont principles, recalls that Joseph V. Brady, a fellow member of the National Commission,

> professed that he was attracted to three principles only: beneficence, freedom, and justice. I seconded Brady's point because these three principles seemed to do what ethical principles should do – namely, serve as rational justification for decisions and policies. We also had in our dossier of philosophical essays H. Tristram Engelhardt's paper which had suggested three basic principles: "respect for persons as free moral agents, concern to support the best interests of human subjects in research, intent in assuring that the use of human subjects of experimentation will on the sum redound to the benefit of society." Tom Beauchamp had also contributed a paper entitled "Distributive justice and morally relevant differences." After much discussion, the commissioners took Engelhardt's first two principles and Beauchamp's principle of distributive justice and crafted "crisp" principles: respect for persons, beneficence, and justice. Stephen Toulmin was directed to redraft the report for presentation at the March meeting.
>
> Albert Jonsen, *The Birth of Bioethics* (New York: Oxford University Press, 1998), p. 103.

However, somewhat in exculpation, Engelhardt's first principle was not equivalent to the principle of autonomy. Moreover, his goal had been to reconstruct the dominant moral visions of the time. Engelhardt, "Basic Ethical Principles in the Conduct of Biomedical and Behavioral Research Involving Human Subjects," *The Belmont Report*, Appendix vol. 1 (Washington, DC: Department of Health, Education, and Welfare, 1978), publication # (12) 78-0013, section 8, pp. 1-45. This article was reprinted in *Texas Reports on Biology and Medicine* 38 (1979), 132-168.

119. Tom L. Beauchamp and James F. Childress, *Principles of Biomedical Ethics* (New York: Oxford University Press, 1979). For their response to reflections on their principlism, see Tom L. Beauchamp, "Principlism and Its Alleged Competitors," *Kennedy Institute of Ethics Journal* 5 (1995), 181-198.

120. The reader may wish to consult my reflections in footnote 2 of the Preface concerning the position taken by Tom L. Beauchamp regarding background morality "in the broad sense". See also Beauchamp, "Comparative Studies: Japan and America," in *Japanese and Western Bioethics*, ed. Kazumasa Hoshino (Dordrecht: Kluwer, 1997), pp. 25-47. A distinction must be drawn between the assertion that there is a common background morality and the assertion that we enjoy a consensus regarding that morality. That is, theoretical reflections might obscure or distort a pre-theoretical moral understanding. See Stephen Toulmin, "How Medicine Saved the Life of Ethics," in *New Directions in Ethics*, eds. J. P. DeMarco and R. M. Fox (New York: Routledge and Kegan Paul, 1986), pp. 270-281. Given the collective character of health care policy, there is a pressing need for uniform medical decision-making. See Peter Caws, "Committees and Consensus: How Many Heads are Better than One?" *Journal of Medicine and Philosophy* 16 (1991), 375-391. This point is made as well in Bruce Jennings, "Possibilities of Consensus: Toward Democratic Moral Discourse," *Journal of Medicine and Philosophy* 16 (1991), 447-463 and Jonathan D. Moreno, "Consensus, Contracts, and Committees," *Journal of Medicine and Philosophy* 16 (1991), 393-408. As Henk ten Have and Hans-Martin Sass aptly put the matter, "Moral agents need to construct consensus because there is no other basis available for the author-ity of moral claims." "Introduction," in *Consensus Formation in Healthcare Ethics*, eds.

Henk ten Have and Hans-Martin Sass (Dordrecht: Kluwer, 1998), p. 6. Given pressing political and public policy agendas, there is a significant incentive to create the appearance of agreement on important moral issues so as to guide action and provide advice that will generally be accepted as reliable. For an interesting exploration of some of these issues, see J. Braaten, "Rational Consensual Procedure: Argumentation or Weighted Averaging?" *Synthese* 71 (1987), 347-354. See also Kurt Bayertz (ed.), *The Concept of Moral Consensus* (Dordrecht: Kluwer, 1994). In all discussions of consensus, one must distinguish between (1) agreements to act in concert and (2) agreements to a common moral understanding. The first is grounded in permission; the second requires at least that the moral matters at stake be viewed as (1) open to compromise, and (2) in part disclosable by communal examination and reflection. The first is possible when one allows the politically useful to trump considerations regarding the morally true. The first is possible as well when the pursuit of particular non-moral values is seen to be more significant than a fastidious pursuit of the morally true.

121. It is remarkable how the commitment to broad consensus and moral rationalism can lead even Christian thinkers to celebrate a medical-moral tradition independent of the truth of Christianity. Nigel Cameron, for example, speaks of a Christian-Hippocratic consensus as that which constitutes the medical tradition and "is no mere tradition, but that which encapsulates the Christian stake in medicine." "The Christian Stake in Bioethics: The State of the Question," in *Bioethics and the Future of Medicine*, eds. John Kilner, Nigel Cameron, and David Schiedermayer (Grand Rapids, MI: Eerdmans, 1995), p. 4. Aside from the view that apparently locates Christian biomedical concerns in terms of medicine rather than medicine in terms of Christianity, there is a failure to explore how it could be that the Hippocratic paganism he endorses turns out to be so congenial to a Christian account of medicine. The values appear to be generated from a special conjunction of value and technique. "The marriage of value and technique which gave birth, first, to Hippocratic paganism and, in due course, which matured into the enduring Christian-Hippocratic consensus," seems to provide a truth independent of the Judeo-Christian revelation celebrated by the author. It is interesting to note that some Christians of the 17th century solved this problem by concluding that Pythagoras was in fact Jewish. For an exploration of "the Pythagoras story" see J. B. Schneewind, *The Invention of Autonomy* (New York: Cambridge University Press, 1998), pp. 536-543. See also Scipion Dupleix, *L'Ethique ou philosophie morale* ([1610] Paris: Fayard, 1994). More clearly than Cameron, T.S. Eliot understood it is Christianity that encapsulates and gives final orienting place to the medical tradition. For him, being a Christian, indeed being a Catholic in the broad sense, was the central concern and the source of meaning for being a physician. Consider the following account given by Roger Bulger of a discussion with Eliot.

During the course of this animated conversation he found out that I was a Roman Catholic and later, after I had expressed some ambivalence about going to medical school, he said in a way I have never forgotten, "The world needs good Catholic doctors." Many times since I have recalled those words, which still seem to thunder down at me from some mountaintop oracle. He could just as easily have said, "The world needs good agnostic doctors" or "good atheist doctors" or "good Buddhist doctors," because what he was telling me was that the world needed good doctors and he thought I had the stuff to be one. That thought of Mr. Eliot's and his confidence in me have been very important in sustaining me through low periods in medical school and ever since.
Roger J. Bulger, "The Search for a New Ideal," in *In Search of the Modern Hippocrates*, ed. Roger J. Bulger (Iowa City: University of Iowa Press, 1987), p. 19.

122. Maurice Merleau-Ponty, *Humanism and Terror*, trans. John O'Neill (Boston: Beacon Press, 1969), p. 97.

123. The moral assumptions that guided the National Commission and similar undertakings are ideological in the Marxist sense of engaging a false consciousness in the service of political power: the canonization of a particular morality as if it were the common morality of humans as such, and therefore normative without question and able to legitimate the public policy in question. It is easier to have people submit to a policy if they believe it is morally appropriate. One might also consider Marx and Engels' understanding of the role thinkers play in giving legitimacy to a ruling class: here, a class that wishes to impose a particular health care policy. Bioethicists under such circumstances play the role of "conceptive ideologists, who make the perfecting of the illusion of the class about itself their chief source of livelihood". Karl Marx and Friedrich Engels, *The German Ideology* (New York: International Publishers, 1960), p. 40.

124. Consider John Rawls' invocation of an overlapping consensus, such that there will be a sufficient overlap among diverse moral visions and philosophical approaches, so as to justify a particular political, if not moral, understanding. "We hope that this political conception of justice may at least be supported by what we may call an 'overlapping consensus,' that is, by a consensus that includes all the opposing philosophical and religious doctrines likely to persist and to gain adherents in a more or less just constitutional democratic society." "Justice as Fairness: Political Not Metaphysical," *Philosophy and Public Affairs* 14 (Summer 1985), 223-51. To identify the right overlapping consensus, Rawls must qualify this collage as (1) that consensus formed from those opposing philosophical and religious doctrines he believes will likely persist and gain adherents and (2) that compatible with his view of a "more or less just constitutional democratic society". He engages this understanding of a canonical overlapping consensus in *Political Liberalism* (New York: Columbia University Press, 1993).

125. For this illustration, I am in debt to my discussions with Kevin Wm. Wildes, S.J., in which we together explored these issues at length. For his views on this matter see Kevin Wm. Wildes, S.J., *Moral Acquaintances* (Notre Dame, IN: University of Notre Dame Press, 2000).

126. To assure that a bioethics commission will not become a philosophical seminar in which issues can be vigorously and exhaustively debated without a conclusion in sight, one will be best advised to establish an agenda and appoint a determined, like-minded person to chair the commission.

127. Tom L. Beauchamp and James F. Childress, *Principles of Biomedical Ethics* (New York: Oxford University Press, 1979).

128. *Oxford English Dictionary* [1933], VI.655.

129. OED VI.653.

130. Beauchamp, "Comparative Studies: Japan and America," in *Japanese and Western Bioethics*, ed. Kazumasa Hoshino (Dordrecht: Kluwer, 1997), p. 26.

131. *Ibid.*

132. *Ibid.*

133. *Ibid.* For a slightly different text and account, see Bernard Gert, Charles M. Culver, and K. Danner Clouser, *Bioethics: A Return to Fundamentals* (New York: Oxford, 1997), esp. p. 34f.

134. Saemund Sigfusson, *The Elder Eddas*, trans. Benjamin Thorpe (New York: Norrœna Society, 1906), p. 35.

135. Consider the following poem, which describes a foray some time between 985 and 988 by Olaf Trygvason, king of Norway, and conveys the spirit of the moral view of "The High One's Lay".

Death through Northumberland is spread
From battleaxe and broad spearhead.
Through Scotland with his spears he rides;
To Man his glancing ships he guides:
Feeding the wolves where'er he came,
The young king drove a bloody game.
The gallant bowmen in the isles
Slew foemen, who lay heaped in piles.
The Irish fled at Olaf's name –
Fled from a young king seeking fame.
In Bretland, and in Cumberland,
People against him could not stand:
Thick on the fields their corpses lay,
To ravens and howling wolves a prey.
Alfred Vandredaskald, "King Olaf Trygvason's Saga" in Snorre Sturlason, *The Heimskringla*, trans.
Samuel Laing (New York: Norrœna Society, 1906), vol. 1, p. 151.

136. For a critical response to Tom Beauchamp, see Ruiping Fan, "Three Levels of Problems in Cross-Cultural Explorations of Bioethics" in *Japanese and Western Bioethics*, ed. Kazuma-sa Hoshino (Dordrecht: Kluwer, 1997), pp. 189-199.

137. For a study of the difficulties of resolving policy disputes that involve an evaluational overlay, see H. T. Engelhardt, Jr., and Arthur Caplan (eds.), *Scientific Controversies* (New York: Cambridge University Press, 1987).

138. See, for example, Albert Jonsen and Stephen Toulmin, *The Abuse of Casuistry* (Berkeley: University of California Press, 1988). A critique of Jonsen and Toulmin's approach is provided by Kevin Wm. Wildes, S.J., *Moral Acquaintances* (Notre Dame, IN: University of Notre Dame Press, 2000).

139. Consider the following case in which those in authority are invoked (i.e., the Holy Office), as well as background understandings of a metaphysical sort bearing on salvation.

XXXVIII. What to do if a Non-Catholic Sponsorship Seems Unavoidable.
Case. The Protestant Titus, whose wife is Catholic, comes to the Catholic priest to ask if he will baptize his first-born; remarking, by the way, that the godfather will be a Protestant friend. Upon being told by the priest that the Catholic Church does not permit non-Catholic sponsors, Titus replies that unfortunately it cannot be helped in this case. The promise has already been given and he could not afford to offend the sponsor as the latter was fairly well to do, and could later on be of substantial assistance to his child. The priest knows well that if he insists on refusing the Protestant sponsor, the Protestant father will have the child baptized by his minister, and therefore he performs the Baptism with the non-Catholic sponsor in order to make sure of the child's Catholic baptism, and, no doubt, he acts correctly on his part.
Question. What may the priest do, so that, despite this irregular sponsorship, he may not break the canonical rules?
Solution. The way out of this difficulty is to let the Protestant sponsor act merely as a witness to the Baptism, as honorary sponsor, but not as real sponsor. In our case this is no doubt allowable, and is not in opposition to the decree of the Holy Office, of May 3rd, 1893, which decrees that Baptism should rather be administered without any sponsors if otherwise a non-Catholic godfather is unavoidable, meaning a sponsorship in the Catholic sense. Since, now, a merely honorary sponsorship is a purely external thing, without any of the obligations towards the child, it is certainly allowed, even if the person is non-Catholic, in a case of necessity. Of course the Protestant sponsor, be it distinctly understood, must not perform any of the functions of a Catholic sponsor, such as making the act of faith or holding the infant during the ceremony; this should be done by some one else present, the nurse for instance, or the sexton. The Protestant may be told that as a Protestant he will not be expected to affirm the Catholic creed. The non-Catholic honorary sponsor is to be entered upon the books merely as witness, not as sponsor.
J. A. McHugh (ed.), *The Casuist* (New York: Joseph Wagner, 1917), vol. 5, pp. 102-103.

For another example of literature in this vein, see Thomas Slater, *Cases of Conscience for English-Speaking Countries* (New York: Benziger Brothers, 1911), 2 vols.

140. In his account of the history of science, Thomas Kuhn distinguishes between "normal science", which acts within the general presuppositions of a particular scientific paradigm, and "crisis science", which brings a paradigm into question. See Kuhn, *The Structure of Scientific Revolutions* (Chicago: University of Chicago Press, 1962; 2nd ed., enlarged, 1970). Roman Catholic casuistry provided an example of normal moral reasoning, as well as normal casuistry. Contemporary morality, in disputing about what kind of moral assumptions should govern and guide, provides an example of crisis morality in which only crisis casuistry is possible. Crisis casuistry, to develop this metaphor, would involve cases that raise questions that lead to an unclarity as to how one might resolve the disputes at hand. It is instructive to note that, given the foundational questions in moral theology engendered by Roman Catholic Vatican II, its casuistry has fallen into desuetude.

141. Baruch A. Brody, "Intuitions and Objective Moral Knowledge," *The Monist* 62 (October 1979), 455. For an example of a very interesting and sophisticated form of casuistic intuitionism, which attempts to resolve moral controversies by balancing moral appeals, see Baruch A. Brody, *Life and Death Decision Making* (New York: Oxford University Press, 1988).

142. It is not simply that, as Alasdair MacIntyre argues, "the fate of contemporary applied ethics confirms rather than disconfirms the thesis that moral enquiry without some kind of presupposed prior agreements is barren," but more fundamentally that applied ethics cannot be morally reliable, for it delivers contrary advice about issues of great moment. MacIntyre, *Three Rival Versions of Moral Enquiry* (Notre Dame, IN: University of Notre Dame Press, 1990), p. 227.

143. Baruch Brody, *Life and Death Decision Making* (New York: Oxford University Press, 1988), p. 12.

144. For an exploration of how immoral behavior may have guided the evolution of human dispositions, see, for instance, Christian Vogel, *Vom Töten zum Mord* (Munich: Hanser Verlag, 1989). Donald Symons provides an evolutionary explanation for the development of human sexuality in terms of the differential adultery strategies of men and women. See *The Evolution of Human Sexuality* (New York: Oxford University Press, 1979), especially pp. 144-158.

145. For a general account of the biological basis of moral inclinations, see Richard Alexander, *The Biology of Moral Systems* (Hawthorne, NY: de Kruyter, 1987). For a classical study of this issue, see George C. Williams, *Adaptation and Natural Selection* (Princeton, NJ: Princeton University Press, 1966) and Edward O. Wilson, *Sociobiology* (Cambridge, MA: Harvard University Press, 1975).

146. The arguments sketched in this section are developed at greater length in H. T. Engelhardt, Jr., *The Foundations of Bioethics*, 2nd ed., chapter 2.

147. Richard Rorty, *Contingency, Irony, and Solidarity* (Cambridge: Cambridge University Press, 1989), p. 61.

148. *Ibid.*, p. 59.

149. *Ibid.*, p. 194.

150. There have been numerous attempts to justify the role of bioethicists in giving advice in the absence of a general agreement about a canonical moral theory or a canonical content-full morality. See, for example, David DeGrazia, "Moving Forward in Bioethical Theory: Theories, Cases, and Specified Principlism," *The Journal of Medicine and Philosophy* 17 (1992), 511-539; H. S. Richardson, "Specifying Norms as a Way to Resolve Concrete Ethical Problems," *Philosophy and Public Affairs* 19 (1990), 279-310; and Carson Strong, *Ethics in Reproductive and Perinatal Medicine: A New Framework* (New Haven, CN: Yale University Press, 1997). For a recent review of these issues, see the articles by these authors, along with the piece by Bernard Gert, Charles Culver, and K. Danner Clouser,

"Common Morality Versus Specified Principlism: Reply to Richardson," in the third issue of *The Journal of Medicine and Philosophy* 25 (June, 2000), 308-322.

151. Here I am in disagreement with the gloss given to this point by Kevin Wm. Wildes in "Engelhardt's Communitarian Ethics: The Hidden Assumptions," in *Reading Engelhardt*, eds. Brendan Minogue, Gabriel Palmer-Fernández, and James Reagan (Dordrecht: Kluwer, 1997), pp. 90-91.

152. Jean-François Lyotard, *The Postmodern Condition*, trans. G. Bennington and B. Massumi (Manchester: Manchester University Press, 1984), p. 37.

153. It must surely be acknowledged that the Enlightenment and its understandings of reason were not uniform or homogeneous. Yet in most cases, a secular, and indeed immanent understanding of reason was sought. For the purposes of this volume, Kant's moral and epistemic accounts are accepted as paradigmatic, not simply because they are the most systematic, but also because Kant's work at the end of the Enlightenment came to be so influential for Western Europe and philosophy generally. Through Locke and Hume the Enlightenment in the island off the coast of France had its impact more on the United States and Texas.

154. No doubt, Western medieval Christendom compassed diverse cultures, countries, and languages. However, *pace* the fracturing of Western Christianity by various schisms and by popes resident in Rome, Avignon, and Pisa, there was at least a theoretical presupposition that moral controversies could in principle be resolvable by appeal to the papacy (if one could find the right pope) and by a tradition of philosophical moral reflection robustly rooted in assumptions regarding the universal claims of natural law. In addition, the intelligentsia of this culture were bound together in one language, Latin, and a single understanding of canon law.

155. An extensive account of the grounding of secular morality and of bioethics in permission is given in Engelhardt, *The Foundations of Bioethics*, 2nd ed.

156. A libertarian cosmopolitan ethic will not impose a particular moral vision, but allow communities to pursue with consenting collaborators their own understanding of human flourishing. Thus, traditional Christian communities would be free to regulate themselves and to pursue freely and peaceably their understanding of salvation.

157. Deriving authority from the permission of those who collaborate in a project is a special form of appeal to authority, namely, to persons as the source of authority for their consensual actions.

158. For an excellent account of contemporary dissatisfactions with the moral neutrality of liberal democracy, see Ezekiel Emanuel, *Ends of Human Life* (Cambridge, MA: Harvard University Press, 1991).

159. In the United States, Christianity as Protestant Christianity was the generally established religious faith not only de facto but indeed *de jure*. See, for example, *United States v. Macintosh*, 283 US 605 (1931). It was only later, especially in the 1950s, that this Christian character of America was set aside in favor of a frankly secular society. See, for example, *Tessim Zorach v. Andrew G. Clauson et al.*, 343 US 306, 96 L ed 954, 72 S Ct 679 (1951); *Roy R. Torcaso v. Clayton K. Watkins*, 367 US 488, 6 L ed 2d 982, 81 S Ct 1680 (1961); and *School District of Abington Township v. Edward L. Schempp et al., William J. Murray et al. v. John N. Curlett et al.*, 374 US 203, 10 L ed 2d 844, 83 S Ct 1560 (1963).

2 At the Roots of Bioethics: Reason, Faith, and the Unity of Morality

Religious and Secular Ethics: Rethinking the Project of Morality

Western Christianity is a source of post-modernity. Western Christianity promised a rational demonstration of the existence of God, as well as a universal morality generally disclosable by reason. Instead, discursive rational or speculative proofs for the existence of God go aground on the difficulty of inferring from the finite the existence of the infinite.[1] It also provided religious moralities grounded in different moral rationalities, some speculative and others biblical. It engendered what proved to be unfulfillable expectations regarding morality, as well as substantive and sometimes bloody divisions separating religious communities. Because of the fragmentation of Christian ethics, secular morality is invoked to secure what Western Christian morality promised: a coherent universal ethic. Secular thought is to supply a rationally justifiable, canonical, content-full morality that can reconcile the claims of the right and the good as well as bring into harmony the justification for morality and the motivation to be moral. As Kant understood, such a task can only be achieved by a morality that, among other things, can guarantee the congeniality of morality and reality.[2] Secular morality has shown itself to be diverse, sundered, and unable to prevent profound tensions between the right and the good, between worthiness to be happy and happiness, between morality and reality. Secular morality cannot show that the morally righteous life will not, at least in some circumstances, be a miserable life, at least in this world. In a world that rewards cunning, not virtue, the price of living morally can be high. Finally, secular morality cannot deliver an unambiguously binding, unique, and rationally justified content for morality.

In terms of deep justification, secular morality cannot substitute for the morality religious ethics failed to maintain. It cannot produce a canonical secular bioethics or show that acting rightly will not at times have ultimately adverse consequences for at least some who act rightly, if not for all persons. In pre-Christian times, the failure to establish a unique and integrated morality would not have cut as deeply. The ancient world experienced itself as naturally polytheistic, pluralistic, and subject to tragedy. In contrast, contemporary moral pluralism is experienced against medieval and early modern Europe's expectation of a deep integrity of being and morality. The contemporary sense of moral fragmentation and the passion for a consensus to bridge that fragmentation can only be fully appreciated against an understanding that once took for granted morality as deeply whole, integrated, and complete. The limitations of a secular ethic are culturally disturbing because they are seen against what Western Christianity had once promised.

This chapter probes Western Christianity's connections among rationality, canonical moral content, faith, and God. The goal is to gauge the extent to which an appeal to a grounding in God can deliver bioethics from the challenges currently facing both Christian and secular morality. First, there is a tension between the right and the good when morality is not grounded in a personal, loving, omniscient, and omnipotent God. Doing what is right does not seem necessarily to maximize the good. This tension is, for example, the source of bioethical conflicts between patients' rights and patients' best interests, to name only one fault-line of controversy. Second, the whole project of ethics finds itself lodged in a "polytheism" of possible moral perspectives. The recent history of philosophy shows the roots of these difficulties. As a philosophical case study of an attempt to resolve this tension and to restore unity, Immanuel Kant (1724-1804) is given special attention. Unlike Enlightenment figures such as David Hume (1711-1776) and Jean-Jacques Rousseau (1712-1778), Kant wishes to find a place for a rationally transformed Christianity within a philosophical account of morality. Kant exemplifies the Enlightenment aspiration to a comprehensive secular morality able to substitute for Western Christian morality, but he in particular seeks to shape belief in rational terms and turn the Christian God into a philosophical principle. To accomplish this task, Kant realized he would have to integrate the dimensions of morality, in particular, the right and the good, and the justification for morality and the motivation for being moral. Kant sought to ground in reason both the unity of morality and the necessity of its content. He failed. The content of morality is unavoidably contingent and the gulf unclosed between the right and the good, as well as between the justification of morality and the motivation to act morally.

The chapter next probes the character of morality's contingency by a study of G.W.F. Hegel (1770-1831) and Søren Kierkegaard (1813-1855). Hegel's post-Enlightenment philosophy provides a rationale for morality that accommodates the irreducible contingency and diversity of moral standpoints. It provides the theoretical justification both for Christian bioethics to contribute content-full ethical guidance to particular Christian health care networks, and for secular bioethics to guide state health care policy. Hegel's state is ideally a constitutional monarchy where religion has been transformed into a cultural achievement expressing the moral commitments of a people. The difficulty for traditional Christianity is that Christianity's particular content is thus rendered socio-historically contingent and its universal significance made but a presentation of a deeper philosophical, not religious, truth.

Kierkegaard attempts to recapture something of traditional Christianity from this established cultural Christianity. He rejects Hegel's categorially domesticated Christianity by mooring the contingency of Christian belief in an existential experience of the necessity of faith. Kierkegaard sets the passion of the individual against the rationality of the universal. In protesting against a reduction of Christianity to philosophical rationality, Kierkegaard grounds Christianity in an individual turn to inwardness. Kierkegaard's response to Hegel engages a dialectic between faith and reason: between discursive reason as the ground of moral content, and faith as the ground of the Christian life. Given his understanding of faith as passionate inwardness and given his failure to see the Incarnation as securing the possibility of union with God in this world, Kierkegaard can provide little content-full guidance for bioethics. His faith does not lead to knowledge. Still, he can offer an important warning: a Christian bioethics should never be simply a matter of academic erudition. Christian ethics must be lived.

Neither discursive rationality nor passionate faith without experience of God can secure a connection to traditional Christian morality as a basis for bioethics. The turn to secular rationality recasts Christian morality in secular terms. The turn to passionate faith provides existential force without necessary moral content. As Kant and Hegel realize, by nesting Christian moral concerns within secular moral assumptions Christian morality is reshaped in terms of secular moral understandings. In this view, truly Christian morality has a proper content only if it is in accord with the truly secularly rational. For Kant, Christianity's moral rationality must be governed by the necessity of practical reason. For Hegel, Christianity's moral rationality is crucially shaped by a history that discloses the truth of Protestant Christianity as freedom: "This is the essence of the Reformation: Man is in his very nature destined to be free."[3] For both Kant and Hegel, Christianity must be recast within the requirements of a liberal cosmopolitan ethos. For Kant, the child of the Enlightenment, Christianity must be freed from the surd burdens of tradition and rendered rationally transparent. For Hegel, a contemporary of Napoleon (1769-1821), Christianity must be understood in philosophical terms and located within the larger concerns of world history aimed at liberation. Only in secular rationality, which serves as an absolute point of reference, can all human undertakings be given their proper place. It is in this sense that Hegel can appreciate philosophy as the higher truth of religion. Against this global reinterpretation of Christianity within Western liberal secular aspirations, Kierkegaard stands defiantly, but in the end impotently, as an aristocratic warrior of inwardness, ignorant of a grace that can give true knowledge.

Pluralism and Conflict in Ethics and Bioethics: The Right, the Good, the Particular, and God

The plurality of moral visions constituting post-modernity is only one aspect of the challenge to contemporary morality. The elements or dimensions of morality cannot be fully integrated in a secular moral vision. One cannot bring into harmony (1) the right and the good,[4] (2) the claims of a universal moral perspective and particular moral commitments,[5] (3) the justification of morality and the motivation to be moral,[6] or even (4) justify the content of morality. Secular morality and with it secular bioethics sunder into only partially reintegratable deontological and teleological moralities. Unlike a religious moral vision grounded in the revelation of a personal, loving, omniscient, and omnipotent God, a secular morality must be grounded in some generally accessible feature of immanent reality such as the character of human reason, sympathies, inclinations, or nature. In such circumstances, tensions emerge setting the right against the good, as well as general moral interests against the good of particular communities and individuals. The moral rationalities directed to acting rightly and to achieving the good will not be in full harmony unless one can reduce all concerns regarding right-making conditions to the pursuit of the good. Even in that case, the pursuit of the good can be understood unambiguously only if all goods (e.g., the avoidance of an early death and the avoidance of suffering) are commensurable. For example, in fashioning health care policy how should one compare the goods of liberty, equality, prosperity, and security? It will depend on the standard chosen for comparison. Moreover, the pursuit of one good may be in tension with the pursuit of a different good. For example, the liberty interests of patients in making all their own health care choices may collide with their security interests in always receiving that health care most likely to postpone death and preserve health.

If there is a sense of the right not reducible to the good, the right and the good need not be in harmony. If the right is independent of the good, then acting rightly may diminish the amount of the good, such as the amount of happiness for everyone. The tension between the right and the good is especially pronounced when the happiness or good of the greatest number collides with the right so that doing what is right has significant costs for most persons. For example, even if it is wrong to use persons in research without their full consent, some shortcuts may nevertheless maximize the greatest good for the greatest number by achieving very important medical progress. May one under such circumstances give short shrift to a few rights in health care policy in order to achieve much good?

To appreciate further such conflicts of moral rationalities, sympathies, and intuitions, one might conjure up circumstances in which the spread of a highly lethal and very contagious disease threatening most of the world population can only be avoided by preemptively killing some innocent persons who will likely become infected and carry the infection to others (i.e., something like creating a firebreak). Or, to choose an even clearer example, imagine a circumstance in which using some against their will as experimental subjects will save the lives of millions. When violating the rights of a few will achieve significant good for nearly all, it is not merely that one has a temptation to act against the right. One confronts a deep tension between the moral rationality of acting rightly and the moral rationality of achieving the good. It is clear that Immanuel Kant's moral intuitions and arguments are all in favor of honoring the right, whatever the consequences. On the other hand, G.W.F. Hegel's moral judgments are to the contrary.[7] In either event, the conflict remains. In some cases, radically doing what is wrong may maximize the good or preserve very important human interests. In all of life, most people seem to take morality with at least a grain of salt: they are committed to doing that which is right as long as it does not cost them too much. Moral zealotry may be righteous, but it appears to most as unreasonable.

To take a different example, if treating competent patients without their consent is a wrong-making condition, this may be at tension with the health and likely future wishes of some patients. Consider how a physician might overaccentuate (but still nevertheless thereby falsely portray) the risks of non-compliance when attempting to gain the full attention and collaboration of an 18-year-old diabetic who is unconcerned with adopting a diet recommended as a way of postponing and ameliorating future health risks. A physician may feel confident that the now 18-year-old patient when 35 will wish to have been overborne by the physician's statements. However, now the patient will not respond in the absence of some modicum of deception. Moreover, the patient at 18 will abhor any deception. In this circumstance, the good of the patient collides with the rights of the patient. May a physician act to save a patient (e.g., a patient will very likely refuse a needed operation if told about a very unlikely risk), although this violates the patient's rights (e.g., the physician knows the patient deeply fears this risk and the patient has clearly and emphatically asked to be informed about such risks)? If the physician "may" omit the information, what is the moral force of "may"? One encounters a contrast of different moral and value rationalities.

Or one might consider cases in which the good from a general moral point of view (i.e., the realization of the good, disinterestedly considered) is not decisive for a particular moral agent, who instead acts to achieve the good of those whom the agent loves, those for whom the agent has a special interest. Consider a physician who is confronted with confidential information regarding a person which is important for the welfare of a member of the physician's family. How should one consider the physician who acts to preserve the good of some persons (e.g., violating confidentiality to protect the interests of a family member), even if this also risks the good derived from the practice of confidentiality and violates a right-making condition considered integral to medical practice? How does one balance anonymous general moral commitments with moral commitments directed to particular personal obligations? In such circumstances, there is a tension between moral action as justified in terms of universal right-making conditions, and the realization of the good of a particular community or a person for whom the agent has special concern.[8] A particular moral point of view advances its claims against the generality of a perspective that considers all.

If there were no view from eternity, if there were no God, why should universal interests, interests considered from a Godlike perspective, always trump particular concerns for particular communities or persons? If all in the end will in any event be dead, why should not particular moral commitments defeat general rights? In the absence of a canonical content-full moral perspective, there is no final binding ranking of the various goods humans pursue, including local, community-relative goods and those goods that are articulable only in anonymous, universal terms. Put more starkly, how does one justify as the moral point of view the choice of a universal, Godlike moral perspective over one bound to the intimacy of community-directed moral sentiments? What good or right-making character does universality have that should trump the bonds of community-directed sympathies? Indeed, cannot the concern for a particular community or set of persons be advanced by appeal to intuitions about special, community-directed, right- and wrong-making conditions? For example, the practice of acting first to honor the claims of one's own community rather than the claims of an anonymous moral perspective can be justified by an overriding concern for the welfare of those with whom one most closely identifies. It is these who exert the strongest claims of sympathy and therefore ought to prevail over an anonymous, universal perspective that in the end cannot prevail. Consider the physician whose family will die of an infection unless the physician purloins vaccine that is in short supply. If there were in fact no eternal perspective, why must one view matters *sub specie aeternitatis*? The claims of a family member to protection against harm could then trump claims of confidentiality and property rights articulated from an anonymous moral perspective. At the very least, such contrary moral perspectives will collide without a definite point of resolution unless an anonymous moral perspective can be shown to be that which accords with the demands of reason and the character of reality. There will not be a resolution justifiable by sound rational argument in the absence of a canonical, content-full moral vision that is, unfortunately, unavailable (as we saw in chapter 1).

The tension between the good and the right, among competing moral perspectives, and among various important goods, discloses the gulf between the justification of morality and the motivation to be moral. For example, Soviet physicians are judged to have acted wrongly in treating political dissidents for "sluggish schizophrenia" as a means of stifling protest.[9] Still, one must recognize the significant personal costs of refusing collaboration in some contexts. In such circumstances, the value rationality of the individual conflicts with moral rationality understood from a disinterested moral point of view, a sort of secular equivalent of God's point of view (i.e., the view of how one ought to discharge one's duties disinterestedly, do what is right, and/or achieve the greatest good for the greatest number). Such a secular perspective does not have the same force as that of God's viewpoint, which leads to final, indeed eternal, judgment. Even when morality is grounded in a fact of reason or in the constraints of universalizability, individual costs attendant to acting morally can make it "rational" to act against universal human moral reason and in favor of important individual and local interests. If the costs to the individual's commitments or family are considerable (e.g., one's family will be killed if one does not violate important right-making conditions), it may not just be "understandable", but in some sense "rational" to accept being found morally blameworthy in order to discharge special obligations to one's family.[10] Indeed, if the universe were without enduring personal meaning, how could significant personal sacrifice be required, much less expected?[11] What is at stake is not only the tension between a categorical moral obligation and a powerful teleological or hypothetical concern, but a tension at the very core of moral rationality itself. That is, from what perspective of rationality does one know that it is rational always to favor the right over the good, the universal moral perspective over the particular, whatever the consequences?

For the traditional Christian, any seeming tension between the right and the good, as well as among goods, can ultimately be discounted. In the end, each person will receive appropriate eternal rewards or punishments. Pursuing the righteousness of God will be rewarded by good without measure. In the long run, there will not be a tension between the right and the good, between moral obligations generally considered and obligations to community and family. In the long run the true good of any person is to be achieved by loving God and others as oneself. Acting rightly will secure the most good possible for oneself and for those whom one loves. Immediate, voluntary, and direct involvement in evil is to be avoided at whatever costs, even that of martyrdom (e.g., the physician asked to do the immoral bidding of the National Socialist or Soviet state must refuse even at the cost of death, including that of the physician's family). But without a deep harmony between the right and the good, and among the various goods of life, doing what is morally required may involve significant costs to oneself or to those for whom one has a special concern or commitment, all without any final compensation to those injured for one's having acted "rightly" and in the service of the greatest good.

In favoring the good or even a particular moral perspective over the right, one may still regard oneself as acting morally. One may do that which one holds all should do when similarly situated, namely, (1) realize a great good for those to whom one is closely committed, even if this involves acting wrongly, or (2) fulfill important obligations to family and community, even if this involves violating obligations as these would be understood from a general moral perspective. What then of the action one knows and holds to be morally improper but highly personally advantageous? If the benefit to oneself is very considerable, the likelihood of being identified as the malefactor extremely remote, and the evil of the act not that great (e.g., one finds a rich man's wallet with ten thousand dollars in cash and can remove the money without being detected), one may not discern a sufficient reason to act morally. It is not just that one may have a weakness of will. One may ask why in the absence of a Final Judgment one should always assume a universalist position. When all will be dead in the long run, one questions whether it is rational always to act morally. One comes legitimately to ask how to compare the good of morality with other goods.

A deep harmony of the right and the good, of the universal and the particular moral perspective, and of justification and motivation of morality, cannot be secured in general secular terms. Secular morality cannot promise for each individual the final cosmic harmony of the right and the good as can traditional Christian thought. When morality is drawn from the encounter with an omnipotent, omniscient, loving, personal God, then the justification and motivation for morality can be grounded in the being of God Himself, Who is the Source of all being. When the justification of morality is rooted in the source of all being and rationality, God through His omnipotence guarantees that happiness will come to those worthy to be happy. When reality is regarded as not necessarily directed to human interests or morality, the cleft between the justification of morality and the motivation of moral action opens wide. If reality is indifferent to human moral concerns, the moral agent must expect to be confronted with tensions within the moral life between the right and the good, and between general moral rationality and the value rationality of actions oriented to particular value interests (e.g., saving the life or health of a family member even when this violates the good or rights of others outside one's family, or one's duties as a physician). As one encounters different possible accounts of how one ought to balance the right and the good, as well as competing senses of moral rationality, one also faces an irreducible plurality of moral foundations. The secular moral condition framing the context of contemporary health care policy is characterized by incompatibilities (1) between the right and the good, (2) between the moral rationality of realizing the right or the good from a universal moral point of view, and the rationality of realizing the right or the good from the perspective of a particular moral community or with respect to specially relevant others (not to mention tensions among competing content-full understandings of morality), and (3) between the justification of morality and the motivation to act morally.

With the secularization of morality, a new gulf emerges between the ideals of moral action and the broken character of the world. The physical world is deaf to human suffering, and tragedy is unredeemed. The universe is suffused with suffering, human and animal. Death and suffering shatter the lives of individuals, spouses, parents, children, families, and communities. The physical world is unresponsive to the ideals of the right and the good. Ours is a cosmos that breaks projects, hopes, interests, and strivings. Worse yet, the struggle for survival, out of which all life is seen to have evolved, is characterized by suffering, death, and the frustration of the deepest yearnings of both humans and animals. Without the metaphysical force of Christian redemption, the world apart from God is unredeemed from non-moral as well as moral evil. After all, in the long run, without God all is obliterated.[12] This unredeemed brokenness makes implausible striving at all costs for the right and the good, if this goes contrary to intimate bonds and sympathies. If nothing endures in the long run, why should one struggle courageously for the right and the good, especially in those circumstances when this will be at the expense of kith and kin? Without God and immortality, why should one sacrifice those whom one loves on behalf of abstract commitments to the right and the good?[13]

Kant recognizes this difficulty. However, Kant only in part acknowledges the depth of the tension between morality and reality, which Christianity had healed in the face of the ancient world's pagan stoicism. In the shadow of the loss of the traditional Christian metaphysical perspective, the cosmos is manifestly deaf to the right and the good. Moral ideals that had been nurtured in the expectation of eternity are now placed in an indifferent if not hostile cosmos. In profound contrast, traditional Christianity recognizes that the broken character of the universe, rooted in the free choice of Adam and Eve, finds its restoration through the free choice of a second Eve and a second Adam. The second Eve submits and gives birth to the second Adam, Christ, Who as God and man reconciles the cosmos with God, guaranteeing full reward for human moral striving.[14] All of morality and human history are embedded in a narrative defined both by human freedom and God's infinite power. Human choice and its consequences are real, including the free choices of the God-man Christ in conformity with the will of the Father and in the Holy Spirit. In this cosmic narrative in which God plays the cardinal role, the right and the good are in the end fully integrated, the various goods placed in concert, and the motivation for justified moral action secured (e.g., through eternal punishments and rewards). Tragedy is real, though redeemed. Against such expectations, secular morality is at best broken and incomplete.

Immanuel Kant and his As-If God

In assessing the prospects for a secular morality, Immanuel Kant recognizes the tensions at its core. He addresses the tension between the good and the right, as well as between the motivation and the justification of morality. He also acknowledges the challenge of justifying canonical moral content. Still, he is confident that he can meet these challenges through a systematic account of knowledge and moral action which he develops and lays out in the *Critique of Pure Reason* (the first Critique appeared in 1781, a second edition in 1787), the *Critique of Practical Reason* (1788), and the *Critique of Judgment* (1790) and completes in *Religion Within the Limits of Reason Alone* (1792) and *Metaphysics of Morals* (1797). He grounds his account in the character of human knowledge, human judgment, and the nature of moral choice. On the one hand, Kant abandons the aspiration to know truly the nature of being. Kant embraces a metaphysical epistemological skepticism: he acknowledges that human discursive reason cannot theoretically establish the nature of being, the existence of God, the freedom of the will, or the prospects for immorality. Human knowledge, at least human theoretical knowledge, is limited to the world as it appears to us, the domain of discursive, spatio-temporal sensible experience. Human understanding can succeed in such ventures as Isaac Newton's *Philosophiae naturalis principia mathematica* (1687), because it is understanding that constitutes the structure of phenomenal reality. Humans remain ignorant of reality as it is in itself, the world of the noumenon.

Contemporary morality, at least in the West, finds itself lodged within the horizon of immanence. All appears only too thisworldly. To begin with, contemporary science and morality are at their roots sealed off from transcendence. Kant sees this clearly. Even where Kant is not explicitly embraced, it is he who appreciated the watershed turn from transcendence to immanence. Though many in the Enlightenment recognized the limited, immanent character of the human sciences and morality, no one addressed these limitations as systematically as did Immanuel Kant. Others, such as David Hume, had a significant influence through the Enlightenment on our contemporary world. Yet it is Kant who sought to harmonize the right and the good, as well as the motivation and the justification for moral action. Kant showed how radically to recast metaphysics, science, and morality in terms of a foundational insight: science and morality can be dislodged from any metaphysical grounding and understood instead as unavoidable practices, or at least unavoidable practices for finite persons.[15] They need have no deep or metaphysical justification.[16] The grammar for the coherence of these practices can be found in our character as knowers and agents. Transcendental knowledge for Kant is not knowledge of the transcendent, but a recognition of the framing and inescapable character of our immanence.[17]

Kant rightly knew this shift in focus from object to subject to be revolutionary. He recognized that Western culture had changed its point of focus. It had turned away from seeking God and scrying the depths of being to seeking the realization of humanity and its immanent aspirations. The focus shifted from the transcendent object to the human subject. In explicitly confronting this, Kant gives the first systematic account of contemporary Western culture as it turns away from God toward grounding science and morality. It is in agreement with Protagoras of Abdera, the Sophist, who taught that "man is the measure of all things, of things that are that they are, and of things that are not that they are not."[18] More precisely,

> ... hitherto it has been assumed that all our knowledge must conform to objects. But all attempts to extend our knowledge of objects by establishing something in regard to them a priori, by means of concepts, have, on this assumption, ended in failure. We must therefore make trial whether we may not have more success in the tasks of metaphysics, if we suppose that objects must conform to our knowledge.[19]

Kant's Copernican Revolution involved understanding the known in terms of the knower, the object in terms of its constitution by the subject. Kant's Copernican revolution involved moving from an account of knowledge directed to the transcendent and instead anchoring knowledge in the immanence of finite knowers. The finite subject, not the object or God, became the foundation of knowledge. *The Critique of Pure Reason* (1781) reconceptualized knowledge in secular and immanent terms. Kant offered an integrated account of knowledge, morality, and religion, and thus a basis for a bioethics that has no need for a transcendent God.

Natural philosophy and the science of morality were once engaged to plumb the core of reality: to know things as they are in themselves. Philosophy was once thought able to determine if fetuses have souls and if so whether these souls are nutritive, sensitive, or intellectual, as well as when they might be infused.[20] Philosophy addressed reality with the assumption that human reason could disclose the rational structure of reality, so that a bioethics grounded in such a philosophical metaphysics could give detailed metaphysical answers. The presumption was that philosophical inquiry could gauge reality's depths and answer questions such as:

> How can we by rational investigation discover the canonical, content-full morality that should guide bioethics?
> How can we by rational investigation discover the deep being of reality, so as to answer the ontological questions posed by bioethics (e.g., are fetuses persons)?

Without at the onset conceding the needed premises, it is not possible to establish answers to these questions by sound rational argument.

Kant recognized that such questions cannot be answered in the terms they were asked and that much can be accomplished if such deep questions are avoided. Questions concerning the deep structure of being and the nature of canonical moral standards can give place to more modest inquiries.

> How can we act with common moral authority in framing health care policy in the face of moral diversity?
> How can we intersubjectively investigate the character of phenomenal reality (determining, among other things, whether zygotes are persons), despite the persistence of metaphysical disagreements?

Such retreats from transcendent reality to immanent experience recognize the limits set by the human predicament and define a context for contemporary bioethics, both secular and Christian.

God as transcendent becomes irrelevant to the tasks of human knowers, who must investigate reality within the bounds of possible human experience. Before Kant, God served an epistemological role for philosophy. Epistemology was theocentric. God offered the perspective with reference to which one could talk about true knowledge of reality, knowledge of reality as it is in itself. God's perspective provided the gold standard, the final and cardinal point of epistemic reference. Kant disengaged his account of human knowledge from this divine point of reference. Kant's bold proposal was systematically to bring the sphere of scientific investigation and epistemological reflection within the bounds of possible experience. Knowledge in general and science in particular were resituated in terms of the necessary conditions for the possibility of the coherent experience of finite sensible discursive knowers. Objectivity as correspondence with the object as it is in itself could be replaced by objectivity as intersubjectivity. Scientific objectivity became the coherence that can be shared by spatio-temporal sensible discursive knowers.

In this fashion, Kant brings this solution to the issue of free will versus determinism (i.e., Kant's third antinomy).[21] Science (i.e., empirical knowing) and morality become the standpoints of two unavoidable practices into which one must enter.[22] There is the practice of empirical science in which we experience ourselves, empirically study ourselves, and regard ourselves as determined, and another practice, morality, in which we think of ourselves as free.[23] Morality for its part (including the lineaments of a general secular bioethics) is secured in terms of the grammar of responsible choice, imputable action, and the moral law as a fact of reason.[24] Morality is the framework within which we can think of ourselves as agents who can be blameworthy or praiseworthy, although we never know this as a metaphysical truth.[25] Kant's morality and the bioethics it would support are shorn of metaphysical depth.

Kant's proposal not to ground human morality and science in a transcendent reality, but to recognize human morality and science as unavoidable practices, secures them in circles large enough so as not to be vicious. They are nearly uneschewable spheres of meaning. The invitation is then: take it or leave it. However, eschewing these practices involves retreating into a form of epistemic or moral autism in which one can no longer share a common world with metaphysical or moral strangers. If one is intersubjectively to resolve empirical disputes with metaphysical strangers, then one is committed to a minimal grammar of coherence. The particular observations of any scientist have standing only insofar as they can be placed within a framework of coherence encompassing observations by other scientists. Investigators can compensate for observer bias and resolve controversies without ever introducing claims as to what reality is in itself. It is enough to focus on objectivity as intersubjectivity: empirical findings as falsifiable data are set within accepted *ceteris paribus* conditions whereby observations can be assessed and compared.

After establishing a principled epistemic agnosticism regarding God, freedom, and immortality, and after restricting true knowledge to the world of empirical experience, Kant attempts to ground morality in the practice of accountable choice. The fact of reason's ability to appreciate moral agents as blameworthy or praiseworthy identifies a domain of reality into which persons can think themselves, even if they cannot experience themselves. Thus, while all of reality, including humans, must be understood empirically as causally determined, moral agents must think of themselves as free. Kant embeds human morality and free choice in a rational will. It is from this rational will that he develops his account of moral action, namely, that moral action is autonomous in the sense of being determined by the requirements of reason so that one can prescind from causal influences. In this way, Kant hopes to treat persons as both free and determined: free as moral agents and determined as beings de facto incarnate in a phenomenal world. Given this accent on rationality, to act freely for Kant is not to choose what one wants but what reason requires. The content of what reason requires is determined by appealing to a standpoint of anonymous, rational, universal choice as a categorical requirement or imperative. Kant holds that if one acts so as to treat oneself and all other moral agents as bound by these conditions, while willing as if one were by one's own choices making universal laws and acting as a universal legislator and treating all persons as ends in themselves, then one will have acted so as to be worthy of happiness. From rationality and universality Kant hopes to derive content for the moral life. As we will see, he adds other constraints in order to acquire the moral content he wants. In this way, Kant hopes to have disclosed a universal rational morality binding all persons, including God.

To act rightly for Kant is to act in accord with these rational constraints, whatever the costs may be. One must as a rational agent recognize that morality is nested in the very character of rationality, so that moral agents must do as this rational account of morality requires, even if this involves great loss, death, and destruction. Yet, the first edition of the *Critique of Pure Reason* (1781) concedes the difficulty of showing the rationality of individuals subjecting themselves or others, especially those whom they hold dear, to great loss, or painful deaths in the service of duty, without a quasi-religious account of the harmony between happiness and worthiness of happiness.

The morality that Kant offers is in its general content that of Western Christianity, albeit grounded and restructured within discursive rationality. All particularity is supposedly set aside and only the universal requirements of philosophical rationality remain. In this sense, Kant completes the rationalistic aspirations of Medieval Western Christianity by embedding Christian morality in his natural law account of moral obligations. Indeed, Kant's bold rationalist conception of natural law carries the Western Christian tradition a radical step further than even the Thomists of the "Second Scholastic", such as the school of Salamanca's Francisco de Vitoria (1486?-1546). These strove to establish through scholastic arguments that all persons, even the Indians of the New World subjected to the conquest by Spain, possess basic human rights, including property rights.[26] Like Vitoria, Kant hopes for a world in which nations will not act against the universal obligations binding all men. The difference between Kant and the school of Salamanca lies in Kant's radical relocation of the history of moral progress and hope, not in a Christian faith and its eschatological expectations, but in the requirements of rationality and morality. The Christian eschatological account remains only as a myth to inspire and at times direct rational action. Kant looks to the future and makes moral judgments regarding the present in terms of frankly secular cosmopolitan expectations[27] that are more liberal than libertarian. In order universally to guarantee human rights and to abolish imperialism as well as colonialism, Kant lays out the project of a league of nations leading to perpetual peace.[28] This is not to suggest that Western Christians ever lacked some sense of universal human rights.[29] Kant embeds human rights in a Christianity transformed by the Enlightenment and freed of its particularity. Indeed, Kant, Hegel, and Kierkegaard provide contrasting case studies of the attempt to secure the content of a Christian ethics in an increasingly post-Christian culture.

Kant attempts to dispel the tensions between the justification of morality and the rational motivation to be moral, as well as between the right and the good, by holding that one should act AS IF there were a God and immortality, so that one can then act AS IF there were a deep harmony between the right and the good. As Kant already acknowledges in the first edition of the first Critique (1781):

> Since, therefore, the moral precept is at the same time my maxim (reason prescribing that it should be so), I inevitably believe in the existence of God and in a future life, and I am certain that nothing can shake this belief, since my moral principles would thereby be themselves overthrown, and I cannot disclaim them without becoming abhorrent in my own eyes.[30]

Kant recognizes a difficulty at the root of the moral project if one is asked to sacrifice all for right action when this will require great suffering for oneself.

> Without a God and without a world invisible to us now but hoped for, the glorious ideas of morality are indeed objects of approval and admiration, but not springs of purpose and action.[31]

There is a deep tension between the right and the good, unless one assumes a harmony between the kingdom of nature and the kingdom of grace grounded in God.[32]

Though he cannot prove His existence, Kant invokes God as a moral necessity to secure the needed wholeness or integral rationality of morality. As he argues in the *Critique of Practical Reason* (1788):

> The *summum bonum*, then, practically is only possible on the supposition of the immortality of the soul; consequently this immortality, being inseparably connected with the moral law, is a postulate of pure practical reason (by which I mean a *theoretical* proposition, not demonstrable as such, but which is an inseparable result of an unconditional *a priori practical* law).
>
> This principle of the moral destination of our nature, namely, that it is only in an endless progress that we can attain perfect accordance with the moral law, is of the greatest use, not merely for the present purpose of supplementing the impotence of speculative reason, but also with respect to religion. In default of it, either the moral law is quite degraded from its *holiness*, being made out to be *indulgent*, and conformable to our convenience, or else men strain their notions of their vocation and their expectation to an unattainable goal, hoping to acquire complete holiness of will, and so they lose themselves in fantastical *theosophic* dreams, which wholly contradict self-knowledge. In both cases the unceasing *effort* to obey punctually and thoroughly a strict and inflexible command of reason which yet is not ideal but real, is only hindered. For a rational but finite being, the only thing possible is an endless progress from the lower to higher degrees of moral perfection.[33]

God and immortality are accepted for the sake of the coherence of morality. In the first *Critique* (1781) he sees that a necessary connection between happiness and worthiness of happiness is possible only if there is a Supreme Reason that governs both moral rules and nature. In confronting the tension between the intelligible world of morality in which we must understand ourselves and the world of the senses in which we find ourselves, he concludes that

> Now since we are necessarily constrained by reason to represent ourselves as belonging to such a world, while the senses present to us nothing but a world of appearances, we must assume that moral world to be a consequence of our conduct in the world of sense (in which no such connection between worthiness and happiness is exhibited), and therefore to be for us

a future world. Thus God and a future life are two postulates which, according to the principles of pure reason, are inseparable from the obligation which that same reason imposes upon us.[34]

One acts AS IF in the long run there will be a coincidence between worthiness of happiness and happiness.[35]

Because of his concern not to introduce an element of heteronomy (i.e., a ground for acting other than out of regard of the moral law, such as happiness, even if it is happiness in proportion to what one deserves) into moral choice (i.e., the decision to act because of the requirements of morality), Kant carefully construes his solution as preserving the rationality of morality rather than as establishing a reward that would justify right-regarding action.[36] Towards this end, Kant engages Christianity as offering an insight regarding this grounding of the rationality of his morality (and by implication bioethics), if only in a backhanded fashion.

> Christian ethics supplies ... [an] indispensable component of the highest good by presenting a world wherein reasonable beings single-mindedly devote themselves to the moral law; this is the Kingdom of God, in which nature and morality come into a harmony, which is foreign to each as such, through a holy Author of the world, who makes possible the derived highest good. ... Therefore, morals is not really the doctrine of how to make ourselves happy but of how we are to be *worthy* of happiness. Only if religion is added to it can the hope arise of someday participating in happiness in proportion as we endeavored not to be unworthy of it.[37]

For Kant, the truth of Christianity is the support and direction it gives to moral action. Christianity provides a story of moral progress. The Christian narrative finds its true significance in encouraging the moral life, not in sustaining a particular religious understanding of salvation.

In the full strength of the Enlightenment, and one year before the revolutionaries' celebration of the Feast of Reason in Notre Dame de Paris on November 9, 1793, Kant proclaimed a religion grounded in reason alone.[38] This religion, despite an attempt to relocate and preserve remnants of Christianity, is a secular philosophical religion whose truth is found in the morality it sustains. Such a religion does not require faith as it has traditionally been understood in the West. It requires no experience of God. It requires only good arguments to sustain it. In the Enlightenment, reason supplants faith and morality becomes the only truth of dogma. Kant's religion, the religion of the Enlightenment, depends neither on history nor on grace. Above all, it avoids any claim of mystical insight or "communion with God", which Kant denominates as religious fanaticism and condemns in the strongest terms. "...[S]triving for what is supposed to be communion with God is religious *fanaticism*. ... The fanatical religious illusion ... is the moral death of reason; for without reason, after all, no religion is possible, since, like all morality in general, it must be established upon basic principles".[39] Because of his emphasis on individual choice and autonomy, Kant also condemns the role of spiritual fathers.[40]

Kant's religion is true, and known to be true, because it is reasonable. Yet even Kant recognizes the socio-psychological need for some of the trappings of religion.

> *Pure religious faith* alone can found a universal church; for only [such]
> rational faith can be believed in and shared by everyone, whereas an
> historical faith grounded solely on facts, can extend its influence no fur-
> ther than tidings of it can reach, subject to circumstances of time and
> place and dependent upon the capacity [of men] to judge the credibility of
> such tidings. Yet, by reason of a peculiar weakness of human nature, pure
> faith can never be relied on as much as it deserves, that is, a church cannot
> be established on it alone.[41]

Kant's concession to those supports of religion that fall beyond the immediate requirements of reason are few. Many a Protestant would be sympathetic with Kant's denun-
ciation of clericism, ritual, and monasticism. However, Kant condemns not only dogma but also worship, characterizing the latter as the "...superstitious belief of divine
worship".[42] Hegel, however, seeks to disclose the categorial truth of the religion he
finds.

Like Moses Mendelsohn (1729-1786), who influenced Kant and regarded the Enlightenment's deism as both the universal religion and identical with the truth of
Judaism, Kant affirms the same with regard to Christianity.[43] Kant offers a further
rationalized form of a *religio catholica* and anticipates the "Catholic Christians" of
early 19th century America, who sought to bring Christianity into accord with the
progressive hopes of the age. Kant endorses a deconstruction of religious ceremonies
and rituals so that they serve the purposes of morality. Religion is no longer a way of
salvation, but a way of moral improvement. Kant's religious gatherings would be
restrained feasts of reason, where ritual is fully transformed into encouragement in the
moral life and where references to Christ are transmuted into endorsements of a human
moral ideal. There is much that Kant would need to reform in the Protestantism of his
day. In contrast, Hegel could enter easily into any Lutheran church and feel in its
services the truths that he knows as a philosopher.

Like many of the Roman Catholic moral theologians reviewed in the last chapter,
so, too, for Kant Christianity does not offer moral content, only appropriate moral
inspiration.

> [T]he sacred narrative, which is employed solely on behalf of ecclesiastical
> faith, can have and, taken by itself, ought to have absolutely no influence
> upon the adoption of moral maxims, and since it is given to ecclesiastical
> faith only for the vivid presentation of its true object (virtue striving
> toward holiness), it follows that this narrative must at all times be taught
> and expounded in the interest of morality; and yet (because the common
> man especially has an enduring propensity within him to sink into passive
> belief) it must be inculcated painstakingly and repeatedly that true reli-
> gion is to consist not in the knowing or considering of what God does or
> has done for our salvation but in what we must do to become worthy of
> it.[44]

Once Christianity is recast in terms of an immanent, rational morality, the elements of
Christ's life, which show Him as God,[45] especially accounts of His miracles,[46] are

reinterpreted as morally edifying, not as encounters with the energies of the transcendent God. For Kant, Christianity provides morally directing images and symbols[47] such that Christ is the cardinal symbol[48] and the Bible a good text for moral education.[49] Kant completes the Enlightenment project of recasting Christianity in secular terms. His approach would fully endorse the reduction of a Christian bioethics to the general constraints of a liberal secular bioethics. Christ is no longer recognized as the Messiah of Israel – much less as the Son of God in a robustly metaphysical sense. Instead, he is the archetype of moral perfection, the exemplar of human moral striving.

> This ideal of a humanity pleasing to God (hence of such moral perfection as is possible to an earthly being who is subject to wants and inclinations) we can represent to ourselves only as the idea of a person who would be willing not merely to discharge all human duties himself and to spread about him goodness as widely as possible by precept and example, but even, though tempted by the greatest allurements, to take upon himself every affliction, up to the most ignominious death, for the good of the world and even for his enemies.[50]

What is offered is an account of Christianity as a religion of morality whose full truth is revealed only in the Enlightenment. For Kant, the truth of Christianity is its morality, not its dogmas or metaphysics.

> And since this faith which, on behalf of religion in general, has cleansed the moral relation of men to the Supreme Being from harmful anthropomorphism, and has harmonized it with the genuine morality of a people of God, was first set forth in a particular (the Christian) body of doctrine and only therein made public to the world, we can call the promulgation of these doctrines a revelation of the faith which had hitherto remained hidden from men through their own fault.[51]

According to Kant, what must be revealed are the requirements of the moral law, a disclosure not fully possible at the time of Christ, but only in the Enlightenment.

Christianity secularly recast supplies a theological-philosophical myth, an as-if unity for a morality significantly disunited into concerns with the right and the good, and for the gulf between the motivation for and justification of moral action. It offers a story of human moral progress not as a factual or a metaphysical claim, but as a morally orienting account that directs us to our rational, moral commitments. Moreover and most importantly, Christianity as a mystical, ascetic religion is dismissed out of hand. In this respect, the Enlightenment completes the work of the Protestant Reformation. Kant considers with particular horror how

> the mystical fanaticism in the lives of hermits and monks, and the glorification of the holiness of celibacy, rendered great masses of people useless to the world; how alleged miracles accompanying all this weighed down the people with heavy chains under a blind superstition; how, with a hierarchy forcing itself upon free men, the dreadful voice of orthodoxy

was raised, out of the mouths of presumptuous, exclusively "called," Scriptural expositors, and divided the Christian world into embittered parties over credal opinions on matters of faith (upon which absolutely no general agreement can be reached without appeal to pure reason as the expositor).[52]

The remedy for religious fanaticism and the real significance of religion are the same: religion is to be regarded as an initiation into morality. The metaphysical significance of religion must be reconstrued in moral terms. Religion must be secularized. Kant's as-if account of God and immortality aided in the secularization of Christianity more than it brought harmony to the deontological and teleological elements of morality.

Kant hoped to have justified a universal morality recast. His hopes were unjustified. He was unable to pull the rabbit of a canonical, content-full morality out of the magical hat of philosophical arguments. As the first chapter showed, such is not possible: one cannot by sound rational argument alone specify and justify a canonical, content-full moral vision.[53] The appeal to the universality of law or legislation, or the appeal to treat persons as ends in themselves, will not provide guidance beyond considerations of strict contradiction, unless one already knows what to universalize, or how persons should deport themselves as ends in themselves (i.e., the formulation of the categorical imperative). [54] At best, one can show what is involved in a practice: one cannot demand that a particular practice of morality prevail while at the same time violating that particular practice. For example, one cannot coherently demand that one always be told the truth and at the same time lie. Kant imports content into his considerations when his appeals to what he holds cannot de facto be universalized as a law of nature[55] or cannot be universalized without a contradiction in will.[56] Further, Kant's integration of the right and the good in terms of an as-if account of God and immortality requires moral belief in the face of theoretical agnosticism: an intellectual schizophrenia at best religiously unsatisfying and at worst, for his purposes, morally insufficient.[57]

Kant's Enlightenment myth does not speak to existential concerns and questions regarding the meaning of suffering and death, which arise as many patients confront their own illness and death. Kant's systematic integration of theoretical knowledge, morality, and aesthetics cannot include a personal theodicy. The anonymous perspective of moral rationality does not touch the concerns with meaning that surface as patients confront their finitude in disability, dysfunction, suffering, and death. Kant attempts a final, as-if harmony of the morally right and the good in an as-if afterlife, but he does not attempt to account for the existence of the non-moral evils of suffering and death in this life. That would require a secular equivalent of an account of the Fall. Such a personal theodicy lies beyond Kant's and the Enlightenment's anonymous God: such a theodicy requires not only an appreciation of the cosmic force of human choice in Adam's sin, but also the redemptive response to that sin by a personal, loving, omniscient, and omnipotent God, Who is the Master of history and eternity. Only from such a God can individual patients expect to receive a loving attention concerned with even the hairs of their head.[58] Kant's approach cannot directly address the individual patient who in the face of overwhelming illness asks, "Why is this happening to me?" and hopes to be answered personally, not just in principle.

Kant offers the results of an experiment in rationally reconstructing Christian morality. The very scope and ambition of his project, even when it fails, provides an insight into the gulf between a secular morality and a traditional Christian morality, between a secular bioethics and a traditional Christian bioethics. A rational reconstruction in secular terms of the aspirations of Christian morality will not only fall short of securing either a canonical, content-full morality or a justified harmony of the right and the good. It will also fail to reach to the person of sufferers in their own particular context, as is the aspiration of Christianity. Kant's project fails thrice over. First, his post-traditional Christian morality is in its very nature disunited into different moral rationalities. It cannot achieve the unity to which Western Christian morality once aspired, without an at least backhanded invocation of God. Nor can it provide a Christian bioethics with such an integration. The failure of Kant's project shows the cardinal place of God in uniting the fragmented elements of morality and thus bioethics. Second, an appeal to reason alone will not deliver canonical moral content. Finally, the personal, loving concern of a God with the suffering of individual patients (and the possibility of placing these within a theodicy) falls beyond the power of secular moral thought. Each of these points of failure indicates the distance between the thick fabric of a traditional Christian moral account and what is feasible through a secular moral reconstruction of its aspiration.

Disbelief in his solution leaves us with the parts of what once was a whole, but without the resources for a fully integrated secular bioethics. Belief in Kant's solution requires embracing an ontologically and epistemologically fractured worldview united in an as-if commitment to freedom, God, and immortality. Kant's world is fractured into phenomenal and noumenal reality, theoretical and practical knowledge, a determinist self-understanding and one that construes humans as free, a theoretically agnostic account of God and a practical account that requires acting as if God exists. All of this is required without being able to secure a canonical, content-full morality.

The Necessity of Contingency: Hegel and the Justification of Moral Particularity

At the end of the Christian age, how can one secure a normative content for morality and especially for bioethics? How can one find a source for morality that is not contingent and thus not hostage for its content to the happenstance of history? In particular, can a further revision of what the West has inherited from Christianity disclose a way out of the blind alleys of secular moral thought, so as to unite its dimensions and secure a canonical content? Can such an account provide a Christian bioethics not rent by diversity of content, or marked by the tensions between the right and the good that characterize secular bioethics? Can one again realize an integrated morality whole in its account of the right and the good, as well as of motivation and justification? In the post-Enlightenment West, contemporary moral reflection has ceased generally to attempt to ground secular moral thought in an as-if appeal to deity. Nor does it include pious but restrained acknowledgements of the deist's God. Nor would such an appeal provide the needed normative content. Absent a special revelation, any particular ordering of moral content remains contingent, as shown in Chapter I. If one turns inward to human rationality, one will not find a canonical normative ranking of moral content, as Kant assumes. One is left with begging the question or engaging in an infinite regress in order to establish as canonical any particular ranking of values or content-full moral principles. Again, if the ground of moral content is located in the mere contingency of human history, the gulf between the right and the good as well as between moral obligation and individual long-run advantage can be considerable.

The contingency of content that characterizes any particular moral interpretation has transformed the contemporary experience of Christianity, with dramatic implications for Christian bioethics. Many who recognize that a divine revelation occurred 2000 years ago find that revelation only in Scriptures, oral traditions, and historical records embedded in the socio-historical idiosyncrasies of the particular times and places of their composition. Any record is always socio-historically conditioned. As a consequence, divine Scriptures, oral traditions, and traditional Christian morality become available for immanent re-interpretation. Their particular character, the mode of their expression, could possibly have been otherwise under different socio-historical influences. Even if one were to concede the uniqueness of a previous Christian revelation and its morality, the uniqueness is lost in the contingency of particular socio-historical assessments and re-imagings. The Absolute in history is still lost in history, if it is not always present beyond history. That which is in history, as being in history, is contingent.

This state of affairs for secular morality and Christian experience was understood by Hegel, who serves as a singular bridge between the Enlightenment and post-modernity. Hegel recognizes the contingent character of content-full morality as well as the necessity of particular content. In his criticism of Immanuel Kant, Hegel argues that the invocation of universality does not provide moral content. "Kant's further formulation, the possibility of visualizing an action as a universal maxim, does lead to the more concrete visualization of a situation, but in itself it contains no principle beyond abstract identity and the 'absence of contradiction'."[59] Hegel thus accepts the shipwreck of the hopes of abstract thought and the distance of the contemporary world from the Enlightenment. Its universalistic hopes cannot be achieved. In particular, the "abstract universality of its [*Moralitäts*] goodness"[60] is not enough to guide concrete moral behavior, because it does not sufficiently specify duty. Kant's morality (i.e., *Moralität*) is inadequate for the moral life and therefore for bioethics. The turn inward to reason to find canonical content fails. "Here we at once come back to the lack of content. ... The universal, the non-contradiction of self, is without content."[61]

Morality finds itself, along with bioethics, at an impasse. Moral content is necessary. However, reason by itself cannot establish any particular content as necessary for morality.

> Because every action explicitly calls for a particular content and a specific end, while duty as an abstraction entails nothing of the kind, the question arises: what is my duty? As an answer nothing is so far available except: (a) to do the right, and (b) to strive after welfare, one's own welfare, and welfare in universal terms, the welfare of others.[62]

The challenge is then to understand, which concrete understanding of the right should govern? What construal of welfare should guide? To act, one needs answers and direction. The moral life and health care policy require precisely what moral rationality by itself cannot secure. Hegel advances a revolutionary solution. He offers for morality what is tantamount to a rational argument for the necessity of contingent moral content. In turning from *Moralität* [universalist morality grounded in the rational interiority of the agent] to *Sittlichkeit* [customary or social ethics], Hegel turns from what moral rationality can provide to what custom has established: the moral understandings that one acquires through being embedded in the thick socio-historical content of a particular community. "In an ethical community [*in einem sittlichen Gemeinwesen*], it is easy to say what man must do, what are the duties he has to fulfil in order to be virtuous: he has simply to follow the well-known and explicit rules of his own situation."[63] Hegel then embeds the experience of individuals in ethical communities, most particularly families with their immediate pieties (*Philosophy of Right* §163), within the open space of civil society and the framework of a state that compasses numerous moral communities (and possibly numerous bioethics).

Within this sociopolitical space, unlike for Marx, the universal class is composed not of workers, but of civil servants. The universal class is the bureaucrats who can bridge a diversity of moral visions and class interests through their function in a political unity that is not a particular community. This solution anticipates the procedural character of much of contemporary secular bioethics.[64] Hegel sketches the socio-moral geography within which contemporary bioethics and health care policy are articulated and which the moral world of limited democracies framed.

Hegel both anticipates and goes beyond Richard Rorty's understanding of the bond between contingency and the content of morality. On the one hand, Hegel recognizes the contingency of moral content. On the other, his arguments commit him to distinguishing community, society, and state.[65] Civil society and the state are social categories different in content and function from those of community and family. They do not directly provide content-full moral guidance, but instead a categorial framework for uniting diverse individuals and different communities.[66] Hegel's account of civil society and state is in principle explicitly pluralist. The state can give place for its citizens to pursue their own views of the concrete moral life within a framing context that creates space for diversity, including bioethical diversity.[67] Hegel also anticipates the moral pluralism of post-modernity: he recognizes and accommodates to a possible diversity of moral content. "In consequence of the indeterminate determinism of the good, there are always several sorts of good and many kinds of duties, the variety of which is a dialectic of one against another and brings them into collision."[68] His understanding of social and political life is framed in recognition of this pluralism. The state should be a category that can compass a diversity of moral communities (with possibly different health care systems) in a social space that places this "collision" within a liberal framework of civil rights providing a categorially principled space for a peaceable plurality of moral understandings. In this fashion, Hegel takes a bold step away from the Aristotelian morally monolithic vision of the state, which conflated community, society, and state.

Aristotle's ideal polity was well-ordered in part because it was composed of no more than one hundred thousand free citizens of similar background and moral convictions.[69] The ideal society for Aristotle was clearly not pluralist.

... if the citizens of a state are to judge and to distribute offices according to merit, then they must know each other's characters; where they do not possess this knowledge, both the election to offices and the decision of lawsuits will go wrong. When the population is very large they are manifestly settled at haphazard, which clearly ought not to be. Besides, in an over-populous state foreigners and resident aliens will readily acquire the rights of citizens, for who will find them out?[70]

Ironically, a new world was emerging just as Aristotle turned nostalgically to the political life of small and isolated Greek city-states to provide a paradigm of a good polity. Aristotle's pupil, Alexander the Great, was through his empire to fashion a large-scale state compassing a truly multi-cultural, morally diverse society, fully at odds with Aristotle's vision of a homogeneous, contained polis. Nevertheless, Aristotle's vision, which looked backwards to an idealized view of the polis bound by a thick moral understanding, took deep root and directed subsequent interpretations of society and state, communal moral diversity to the contrary notwithstanding.

The Christendom of medieval Western Europe aspired to being a polis on a large scale: all would be united in one faith, guided by right reason (and presumably by one bioethics). After the Reformation, the formula of subjects taking the religion of their sovereign, *"cuius regio, eius religio"*, over the long run did not succeed in providing a unifying belief for each polity. The reaction to the bloodshed engendered by the wars that followed was the Enlightenment's attempt to discover, justify, and impose a content-full moral unity that could transcend religious and political boundaries. As the Christian Western Middle Ages sought to re-invent the Aristotelian polis as a Christian empire justified in God and in reason, the Enlightenment attempted to realize the aspirations of the Aristotelian city-state as a universal community of all united in a rationally justifiable morality and polity. Neither the Middle Ages nor the Enlightenment had much place for substantive moral diversity. Still, the former gave greater place for parallel systems of law than did the latter. [71] Each grounded its unity at least in part in discursive rationality. Medieval Christendom presumed a twin disclosure of moral content from faith and reason. Modernity in contrast presumed a disclosure under reason's guidance alone, including the scientific study of the human condition. Such investigations were to justify a canonical moral content. When this project of justifying canonical content for a universal secular morality failed, with it collapsed as well the justification for a large-scale secular polis grounded in such a universal narrative. Western culture was returned to a context of moral pluralism and skepticism. It was returned to an engagement in the world such as that which marked the pagan culture that characterized the Mediterranean littoral after Alexander the Great. We are left with a multiplicity of bioethics, rather than the fulfillment of the traditional Western aspiration for a single canonical ethics and therefore a single canonical bioethics. Yet there is still a hunger for that unity.

Hegel's moral and political insight reaffirms the ancient world's diversity. This time it is expressed in a unity clothed in metaphors taken from Protestant Christianity. Hegel's development of a highly secularized moral religion out of Protestant Christianity could draw on resources inherent in Protestantism even at the beginning of the 17th century. J.V. Andreae (1596-1654) in his *Christianopolis* (1619) had begun to argue that true

Christianity is to be expressed in a *praxis pietatis*, which included the dissemination of scientific knowledge, education of the young, and social reform.[72] This second Reformation[73] was to transform the moral character of Protestant society and its institutions. If these movements constituted a second Reformation, the Protestant Kant helped to shape the third Reformation: his Enlightenment reformation and transformation of Christian morality into a universal religion.[74] Hegel takes this Reformation for granted and seeks to complete it. It is for this reason that Walsh describes Hegelianism as "secularized theology".[75] Hegel recognizes the necessity of a relatively neutral, political structure compassing various communities of different belief within a political unity that still supports religious faith. "The state should even require all its citizens to belong to a church – a church is all that can be said, because since the content of a man's faith depends on his private ideas, the state cannot interfere with it."[76] Still, the standing of a citizen is to be bound neither to race nor to religion. "A man counts as a man in virtue of his manhood alone, not because he is a Jew, Catholic, Protestant, German, Italian, &c."[77] Hegel articulates an appreciation of human rights as well as human diversity. Hegel continues Kant's project of providing a rationally sanitized version of Christianity: a Christianity that affirms the moral truth of the freedom of all. However, insofar as Christianity is not understood and justified notionally, the particular content of Christian morality (and therefore of Christian bioethics) becomes in principle one among other possible philosophically justified moral contents.

The moral cement of the state must be recognized in a liberal political structure able to compass numerous different moral perspectives. As a consequence, the liberal state is, according to Hegel, the product of the Reformation despite itself and the religious disunity it unintentionally engendered.

> This distinction [i.e., between the moral sphere of the state and that of religion and faith] emerges only in so far as the church is subjected to inward divisions. It is only thereafter that the state, in contrast with the particular sects, has attained to universality of thought – its formal principle – and is bringing this universality into existence. (In order to understand this, it is necessary to know not only what universality is in itself, but also what its existence is.) Hence so far from its being or its having been a misfortune for the state that the church is disunited, it is only as a result of that disunion that the state has been able to reach its appointed end as a self-consciously rational and ethical organization. Moreover, this disunion is the best piece of good fortune which could have befallen either the church or thought so far as the freedom and rationality there is concerned.[78]

Out of this complex historical-moral appreciation of the Reformation, Hegel gives central place in the development of morality and liberal polity to Christianity, in particular Protestant Christianity. As with Kant, those elements of Christianity that cannot be rationally assumed are not categorially redeemed. They are not preserved within the structures of dialectical, rational necessity.

Hegel does not directly provide a content-full morality. Instead, he offers a categorial account of the tension among different moral rationalities. Moral tensions (e.g., between the right and the good) become the unavoidable but sublateable results of the diversity integral to moral rationality. Hegelian ethics, and therefore bioethics, need not be as concerned as Kantian bioethics with truth-telling and promise-keeping, with the realization of a particular morality, but instead with the realization of the moral space within which various moral understandings can flourish. The focus is on categories of moral concern, rather than on particular moral content. Thus, Hegel's polis is a large-scale state which finds the unity of its moral diversity in law. The state sustains the space of civil society within which individuals from diverse communities can interact, trade, contract, and establish diverse institutions for health care. Hegel's categorial analysis of morality provides a place for both the bioethics of diverse particular moral communities as well as the governmental bioethics that guides the state's civil servants. There can be both moralities for persons as members of various Christian religions, and a morality for persons as citizens, though the first for Hegel, as well as for all the descendents of the Enlightenment, must be located within the place and constraints of the second. The first as the ethics, *Sittlichkeit*, or customs of a particular community may be robustly Christian. The second, in realizing the categorial "higher truth" of Christianity, provides the moral cement of a liberal polity, including a constitutional monarchy with a market economy, and an establishment of religion.

Hegel's multi-level appreciation of morality and social structures can even be regarded as committed to the articulation of a liberal state sufficiently neutral to compass numerous non-geographically located communities. Each could preserve its own bioethics within its own health care system.[79] Within this paradigm, one could imagine (although Hegel does not explicitly entertain such images) parallel Lutheran, Roman Catholic, New Age, agnostic, atheist, Shiite Mohammedan, Baptist, and Orthodox Jewish health care networks, each shaped by its own special regulations grounded in its own bioethics, each perhaps even sustaining special civil and criminal law for its own institutions and communities. The provision of abortion or euthanasia in Roman Catholic hospitals could be a criminal, indeed capital, offense. All of this would have to be placed within the general commitments of the state and the general protections guaranteed to citizens.[80] Hegel's state in principle provides a significant space for moral pluralism.

However, the pluralism is radically muted. Since Hegel addresses primarily categorially normative issues, morally normative concerns become relocated in terms of conceptual or categorial relationships (e.g., religion is explained in terms of its relationship to art and philosophy or absolute spirit). As a consequence, there is a kind of domestication of belief, morality, and bioethics incompatible with the zeal associated with the faith of early Christians. Hegel recognizes a categorial place for both Christian morality and its religious feelings, particularities, and images, indeed for limited Christian zeal within Christian communities lodged in the embrace of the larger civil society and the constraints of the state. He sees their significance in terms of the relationships between being and thought: their categorial meaning.[81] Religious belief, community, and zeal are given their "higher truth" by philosophy, so that religion has a categorial significance, not a traditional metaphysical significance.

Even in his youth, Hegel understood that religion transformed by the Enlightenment no longer needed a transcendent God.[82] The Enlightenment created a culture predicated on the irrelevance of a living, personal God. The culture was shaped by the death of God, by "the feeling that 'God Himself is dead,' upon which the religion of more recent times rests."[83] Philosophy for Hegel must take this feeling of the loss of God seriously. God must be resurrected by philosophy into the life of philosophical significance.[84] This new philosophical God, though not truly transcendent, must reveal the higher truth of transcendence. In the grace of this safely reconstructed God, philosophy must disclose the truth of religion, in particular the world-historical truth preserved in Protestantism.[85]

> It [the pure concept] must re-establish for philosophy the Idea of absolute freedom and along with it the absolute Passion, the speculative Good Friday in place of the historic Good Friday. Good Friday must be speculatively re-established in the whole truth and harshness of its God-forsakenness. Since the [more] serene, less well grounded, and more individual style of the dogmatic philosophies and of the natural religions must vanish, the highest totality can and must achieve its resurrection solely from this harsh consciousness of loss, encompassing everything, and ascending in all its earnestness and out of its deepest ground to the most serene freedom of its shape.[86]

For Hegel, philosophy, enjoying the coincidence of thought and an immanentized being, can reapproach its tasks, having finally put God in His place, free of true transcendence. Hegel's Christianity has its full categorial significance as a particular conditioned presentation of the highest, universal, notional unity: Hegel's Absolute.[87]

Hegel's categorial architectonic allows two different ways of appreciating the standing of Christian bioethics. True to his affirming "both/and" rather than "either/or", the structure of Hegel's arguments affords the possibility of Christian bioethics being (1) particular and different, as well as (2) equivalent, in its higher truth, to general secular bioethics. On the one hand, Hegel could accept various particular Christian bioethics with their special content having regional or communal governance. As noted, there could be various Christian bioethics for different Christian communities, each perhaps with its own health care system or network. Such Christian bioethics would be different over against any particular secular bioethics. They would also differ among themselves. That there would be numerous senses of Christian and secular bioethics does not present a conceptual challenge for Hegel's account or his polity. Civil society would span this diversity of *Sittlichkeiten*. Large-scale states would not be single moral communities, but social structures spanning real moral diversity. On the other hand, the higher truth of Christian bioethics would in Hegel's terms be captured in the commitment to liberal mutual respect that expresses the moral unity of a large-scale, religiously neutral state. The state is the higher truth, indeed the quasi-libertarian or liberal cosmopolitan truth of Christianity. As a consequence, it can compass not only the various Christianities, but Christian and non-Christian moral communities. For Hegel, it is philosophy that certifies the significance and place of religion as well as of religious bioethics. Finally, since Hegel's Absolute is the perspective of the unity of non-transcendent thought and being, it ignores on principle the reality of a truly transcendent God. After all, the goal of Hegel is to resurrect Protestant Christianity through and within the life of philosophy. The God of Hegel, Hegel's Absolute, is categorial philosophical thought, not the transcendent personal God of the Jews and the Christians.

Rationality, Belief, and Kierkegaard: Being a Christian in the Post-Christian Age

Kant intends to abolish traditional faith, while Hegel sets faith within reason's dialectic so as to disclose speculative reason as the higher truth within which it is sublated, that is, categorially placed. The Christianity of both Kant and Hegel is domesticated, secularized, and rendered integral to the intellectual, cultural, and moral concerns of a post-traditional Europe. Although his influence is widespread, Kant's Enlightenment Protestant legacy to organized religion is probably most directly felt in Reform Judaism.[88] Hegel sets the tone for Protestant higher criticism's changing the character of Western Christianity. For both Hegel and Kant, Christianity appropriately transformed becomes the root of liberal morality and polity. Each sees morality and governance protecting appropriate free choice. Where Kant focuses on demythologizing Christianity in the service of producing a rational religion serving an autonomy-oriented morality, Hegel, to use Charles Taylor's characterization, de-theologizes Christianity in the service of preserving its truth as the absolute religion. As such, it is the best imaginable presentation, *Vorstellung,* of a purely categorial Absolute Truth, which accounts for the liberal polity within which all men are free.[89] For Hegel, God has become the highest achievement of culture: philosophy, within which all men can be appreciated as free. This categorial standpoint is the reflective self-consciousness that puts everything, including moral action, in its place. Since only discursive reason can answer discursive rational questions, it is the standpoint of discursive rationality addressing itself that has the last word about everything. This is the Absolute, this is the secular culture's God, the God of Hegel.[90] It is the speculative life of the philosopher gained by a "second birth" in absolute consciousness that renders the transcendent immanent. Philosophy thus became the very Absolute, the true God, so that Hegel's followers could compare Hegel with Jesus. In a letter to Hegel, the Hegelian Christian Kapp (1780-1874) in all seriousness asserts in 1823, "Only in the system itself can salvation be found."[91]

Kierkegaard directs his entire life against this rational reformation of Protestantism. He wants, insofar as he understands it, to be a traditional Christian.[92] He recognizes that the established Protestant churches of northern Europe are (1) being reshaped in the image and likeness of Kantian and Hegelian rationality, while (2) the community of Christians is being reinterpreted in conformity with the kingdom of ends or the society of citizens in a liberal constitutional monarchy. He appreciates that these developments are uncongenial to traditional Christianity, and he protests. However, he finds himself in a religious and cultural context, within which (1) the manifest divinity of Christ appears implausible, not to mention (2) the presence of the miraculous, or (3) access to noetic knowledge, knowledge from an intimate union with God. [93] The result is that he can at best consider himself a member of (1) a virtual community of sincere protestors against the reformation of traditional Christianity, but never (2) lodged securely within a living community of saints actually available spanning space and time. As a further consequence, Kierkegaard undertakes his struggle as a Christian individual rather than as a believer thickly bound within a manifest community of saints. His Christianity is marked by a certain religious anomie; he cannot discern the manifest presence of the Incarnate Christ in the Church, which is His Body.

From this vantagepoint, Kierkegaard recognizes Hegel's, not to mention Kant's, domesticated and secularized account of Christianity as violating traditional Christian understandings of a personal and fully transcendent God. Kierkegaard is a prophet decrying a Christian faith lived without struggle and in conformity with a rationally ordered system of morality and/or taken-for-granted external pieties. Kierkegaard rightly criticizes the view that Christian faith could consist of everyday bourgeois conformity to a world of secularized Christian conventions without an inward passion or subjective engagement.[94] Christianity is not the rationally obvious morality of Kant, nor Hegel's enveloping *Sittlichkeit* or customary morality, nor even his quasi-pictorial presentation of the Absolute. Kierkegaard reacts against the transformation of this secularized Christianity through a dialectic of doubt rather than an ascetic struggle. Within a post-Enlightenment society in which the miracles of Christ are no longer believable, he articulates his plea for faith over against Hegel's system and the established church of Denmark. In response to all of this and more, Kierkegaard grounds the substance of Christianity (and thereby of Christian ethics and bioethics) in the inwardness of the subjective by means of an orientation to belief undertaken in inward passion.[95] Faith is not replaced by reason. Faith is framed by uncertainty and unguided by objective criteria. Belief finds its necessary grounding in an inward Christian act of faith, not in independent rational considerations. Christianity is never to become a merely scientific or philosophical truth;[96] Kierkegaard seeks above all to show the falsehood of Hegel's claim to being the highest form of Christianity.[97]

The focus shifts from rational argument to obedient religious commitment. Where Hegel embeds the content of morality in the necessity of a categorial framework, Kierkegaard attempts to embed the content of the Christian life in the inward necessity of an existential subjectivity. In the absence of a discursive justification of Christianity, Kierkegaard in his *Concluding Unscientific Postscript* (1846) attempts to ground faith in a critical inwardness of the will.

> Faith is the objective uncertainty with the repulsion of the absurd, held fast in the passion of inwardness, which is the relation of inwardness intensified to its highest. This formula fits only the one who has faith, no one else, not even a lover, or an enthusiast, or a thinker, but solely and only the one who has faith, who relates himself to the absolute paradox.[98]

Where Hegel invokes a dialectic of rationality, Kierkegaard invokes a dialectic of the will.[99] Where Hegel grants religion various levels of political and philosophical legitimacy, Kierkegaard inveighs against the corruption of established religion and the blasphemy of arguing that Christianity secures its higher truth in philosophy. Finally, where Kant and Hegel look to political structures, Kierkegaard publishes pamphlets campaigning against the state church (one might ponder what Kierkegaard's view would have been regarding a state-established bioethics) and dies refusing communion because it comes at the hands of a minister paid by the crown.[100] Kierkegaard is a rebel

against the official order while Hegel and Kant are its critical, but still loyal, supporters. Kierkegaard's position is anti-establishment, inward, and passionate.

For Kierkegaard, Christianity should not be justified in terms of the good it might
produce. It is not just that Christian faith is not secured by Scholastic, Kantian, Hegelian, or other rationalistic projects of providing a support for or a justification of faith.
As Kierkegaard recognizes, such supports are not only useless but distort our relationship to the object of belief, because such frameworks of argument are immanent in
orientation, while God is transcendent. Belief for Kierkegaard is more than an affirmation of revelation as if it were true, that is, without the justification of discursive
rationality. At times, Kierkegaard's understanding of belief goes so far as to make belief
not merely assent to the truth of revelation, but an understanding that this revelation is
true. For Kierkegaard, faith brings knowledge. It is a knowledge garnered out of
obedience in the Christian life. It is also a knowledge that carries us beyond ourselves.
Kierkegaard recognizes the infinite gulf between time and eternity, finite human existence and the absoluteness of God. Still, if this gulf is taken seriously without recognizing God as giving knowledge through uniting Himself directly with His creatures, then
the Christian remains within the horizon of the immanent, even when changed through
a personal relationship with God. God through various forms of created grace, through
various ways of being the evocative teacher of man, can bring humans to repentance
and to affirming the revelation of Christ. All that is secured appears this side of the
horizon of the finite. Though faith is evoked by the infinite, and though his experience
of God surely involves an encounter with God, it does not involve knowledge through
union with the radical otherness of God. The distance between the temporal and the
eternal, the finite and the infinite is for Kierkegaard a theological problematic that is
never definitely solved by closure through illumination and immediate contact with
God. Kierkegaard's account goes awry in a view of the Incarnation that does not
permit Kierkegaard to recognize how Christ as the humble one manifests the power of
God.

Faith for Kierkegaard is encountered as a change in the character, indeed in the
psychology of the believer, not as a radical connection with the infinite as transcendent.
Such a connection would not only set aside all doubt, but constitute for others an
occasion for experiencing the immediate power of God. C. Stephen Evans in this regard
gives a helpful summary of Kierkegaard's account of faith.

> One way to think about Kierkegaard's claims about subjectivity is to see
> them as claims about the character of the ground of religious beliefs. The
> specifically Christian beliefs he is discussing, for example, can be under-
> stood as beliefs that require a particular set of emotions (or 'passions' in
> Kierkegaard's language). A person cannot come to believe in Christ with-
> out a strong sense of sinfulness and a desperate desire for God's forgive-
> ness. Those are the factors that provide the beliefs. When they are present,
> the evidence is always sufficient; when they are lacking, no amount of
> evidence is enough. ... faith is a transforming passion of trust that enables
> the individual to grasp truths that would otherwise be opaque or even
> appear absurd.[101]

As philosophers have provided rational psychologies, Kierkegaard offers a theological psychology of faith in which he accounts for the transformation of the Christian in the absence of an immediate encounter with divinity. Kierkegaard can gesture to the transcendent but not go beyond the horizon of immanence to union with the transcendent.

Kierkegaard seeks in his relationship to God "an absolute relationship to the absolute".[102] This relationship is crucially conditioned by Kierkegaard's reaction to claims of the immediate manifestation of God. Kierkegaard insists not only on divine transcendence and the inaccessibility of God's nature, but on His very invisibility. Even God Incarnate does not show Himself as God.

> What, then, is the absurd? The absurd is that the eternal truth has come into existence in time, that God has come into existence, has been born, has grown up, etc., has come into existence exactly as an individual human being, indistinguishable from any other human being, inasmuch as all immediate recognizability is pre-Socratic paganism and from the Jewish point of view is idolatry.[103]

The mystery of the Incarnation through which eternity takes on time and the infinite becomes embodied in the finite is for Kierkegaard the absurd. Moreover, for him the Incarnation is hidden. Christ as God in His Incarnation remains hidden. Though once present in history, He is now silent and separated from us by centuries. For Kierkegaard,

> the speaker is the abased one, just as the words historically were not spoken yesterday or the day before yesterday but 1,800 years ago, when the abased one was not lifted up. ... As far as Christ's life is concerned, this information is easy to find, for his loftiness does not begin until his ascension to heaven, and since that time not one single word has been heard from him – thus every word he said was said in his abasement.[104]

Christ gives no hint of His divinity but appears fully within the horizon of immanence. If it were not otherwise, the circumstances of Christ's divinity for Kierkegaard would have the character of paganism.

Christ's divinity must be experienced as a second immediacy which sets aside the pagan immediate experience of God. Only through such struggle can one in faith regain an immediacy with God. Kierkegaard requires this struggle in order to distinguish authentic faith from both the immediacy of pagan spirituality, as well as the domesticated comfort of establishment Christianity. It is for this reason that Kierkegaard insists that "indeed, he [God] is so far from being remarkable that he is invisible."[105] We can turn to God, but Kierkegaard cannot provide an adequate account of how we can experience Him when He turns to us. This is not to deny that Kierkegaard attempts to provide an account of God's evoking and transforming grace. He portrays the interaction between God and the believer as a dialectic that by grace transcends the Socratic standpoint.

> But one who not only gives the learner the truth but provides the condition is not a teacher. Ultimately, all instruction depends upon the presence of the condition; if it is lacking, then a teacher is capable of nothing, because in the second case, the teacher, before beginning to teach, must transform, not reform, the learner. But no human being is capable of doing this; if it is to take place, it must be done by the god himself.[106]

God interacts with man to bring him through repentance to God.[107] Kierkegaard seeks, and considers himself experiencing, a personal relationship with a personal God. The interaction between God and man is deeply felt by Kierkegaard. Anticlimacus, in Kierkegaard's *Training in Christianity* (1850), employs the moving refrain, "He will draw all unto Himself." Kierkegaard experiences a deep joy from his encounter with Christ.

The puzzle is again to understand how for Kierkegaard God draws us to Him and how exactly Kierkegaard understands us as entering into His presence. The challenge is to make out the character of this personal relationship, since a sense of immediate relationship to God must for Kierkegaard be brought into question. "All paganism consists in this, that God is related directly to a human being, as the remarkably striking to the amazed."[108] Faith for Kierkegaard requires a prior interruption of such a relationship to God, characterized by a recognition of the inaccessibility of God.

> But the spiritual relationship with God in truth, that is, inwardness, is first conditioned by the actual breakthrough of inward deepening that corresponds to the divine cunning that God has nothing remarkable, nothing at all remarkable, about him – indeed, he is so far from being remarkable that he is invisible.[109]

Kierkegaard's point is that a naive direct relationship to God unmarked by both inwardness and risk will not suffice as faith. For Kierkegaard, "In paganism, the direct relation is idolatry; in Christianity, everyone indeed knows that God cannot manifest himself in this way."[110] The further consequence of this position, which is a function of his understanding of the Incarnation, is that Kierkegaard by implication describes as pagan what was in fact the Apostles' first experience of Christ as God. A week after Christ promises, "Verily, I say to you, there are standing here some of those who in no wise shall taste of death, until they see the Son of Man coming in His kingdom" (Matt 16:28), He goes to Mount Tabor with Peter, James, and John, where He is transfigured. Christ is not just the humbled One.

> And He was transfigured before them. And His face did shine as the sun, and His garments became white as the light. And behold, Moses and Elias appeared to them, talking together with Him. ... While he yet spoke, a bright cloud overshadowed them. And behold, there came to be a voice out of the cloud, saying, "This is My Son, the Beloved, in Whom I am well pleased; be hearing Him!" And after the disciples heard it, they fell on their face, and were exceedingly afraid (Matt 17: 2-3, 5-6).

The testimony of the Gospels, not to mention the mystics, is that they immediately experience God. In contrast, Kierkegaard holds that "With regard to the essential truth, a direct relation between spirit and spirit is unthinkable."[111] Yet, this is indeed what occurs at Pentecost when the Holy Spirit descends and the Apostles finally speak with conviction out of an immediate experience of the Spirit (Acts 2:1-41).

Kierkegaard's critique of immediate experiences of God results in a foundational contrast between his portrayal of the invisibility of Christ as God and the Gospel's portrayal of the visibility of Christ's power. Granted, one only comes to the knowledge of the Divinity of Christ through the grace of God (Matt 16:17). Still, Christ discloses His uniqueness as an invitation to turn in the heart, to see Him as the Messiah and then ultimately as God.[112] As St. John the Theologian records, Christ declares to the Apostle Philip: "The one who hath seen Me hath seen the Father" (John 14:9). In the Gospels, Christ manifests the radical presence of divine power. Christ raises the dead (Matt 9:18-26) and *en passant* is recognized by the woman with the issue of blood as possessing energies that will heal her if she can but touch Him. Christ calms the seas (Mark 4:35-41), feeds five thousand (Matt 14:13-21), and walks on water (Matt 14:22-31). Even if one grants Kierkegaard's point that only those who have faith will understand the meaning of a miracle, before the descent of the Holy Spirit at Pentecost the Apostles know that they are dealing with an individual who is more than a humble man. As the Gospel reports, they are terrified by what Christ can do (Mark 4:41). Being a contemporary of Christ, a disciple at first hand, counts for a lot. *Pace* Kierkegaard, this is the case not just because the contemporary, the disciple at first hand, sees wonders, but because the contemporary can touch Christ. The radical character of the incarnation of God in man is then carried forward in the Apostles who have taken on Christ so that in each generation there are disciples at first hand. Indeed, Christ in the epilogue to Mark's Gospel promises that His Church will do wonders as signs of its authenticity (Mark 16:17-18).[113] Peter's shadow has power (Acts 5:15) and handkerchiefs and aprons touched to Paul cure the sick (Acts 19:11). There is in the Scriptures a presentation of the manifest incarnation of holiness, of the presence of God in His saints.[114] Kierkegaard's account cannot adequately come to terms with the immediate power of God to bring faith and transform, as with St. Paul who by the grace of God becomes at once a new man certain in his new faith.

Kierkegaard's attitude to the miraculous is defined by the post-Enlightenment culture against which he struggles. He is left estranged from the radically miraculous character of holiness and its manifest continuity in the saints. He cannot recognize how the horizon of the immanent is broken by Christ and His saints. Kierkegaard is a want-to-be traditional Christian who has lost continuity with the Tradition. He is a latter-day Protestant attempting once more to reform the Reformation, as if in Western Europe one could always begin Christianity anew without an obligation to achieve continuity with the community of Christians over the centuries. Among other things, Denmark's reforming protestor has no concern about what the Church unbroken in Palestine might have to teach. His struggle of faith has a character that is a part of his age and apart from traditional Christianity. His are the doubts of a man who has seen Hegelianism face-to-face, along with the higher criticism it spawned, and then strives to live as a Christian outside of the continuity of the Christian community.

Kierkegaard's account of the Incarnation predestines his ecclesiology. Just as Christ's divinity is invisible, so, too, His action upon the Christian is also invisible. In this interaction, we never encounter the manifest immediacy of God. Instead, Kierkegaard in his phenomenology of belief always interposes a mediacy. There is personal change without transcendence. The difficulty is that, despite his best intentions in the matter, because of his qualifications regarding the hidden character of Christ's Divinity in His Incarnation, Kierkegaard's intimations of the transcendent are always located within the domain of the finite. The grace Kierkegaard acknowledges is a created energy, a force that is never that of the uncreated energies of an unquestionably manifest transcendent God. His account of the Incarnation commits Kierkegaard to a portrayal of Christian community (including the communion of saints) which suggests that the enduring Christian community should be as clandestine as Christ's divinity is invisible. True to themes within both the Reformation and the religious anomie of his context, Kierkegaard finds himself as an individual alienated from his community of Christians and ignorant of analogues of the Apostles who have taken on Christ and in so doing continued to manifest the power of His uncreated energies. Consider, for example, Kierkegaard's suggestion that

> Even if the contemporary generation had not left anything behind except these words, "We have believed that in such and such a year the god appeared in the humble form of a servant, lived and taught among us, and then died" – this is more than enough. The contemporary generation would have done what is needful.[115]

As one would expect for Kierkegaard, the continuity of the community resides in the report of a revelation, rather than in a grace that transcends the horizon of the finite, uniting the Church across history. The passage, following the divine commission, "And behold, I am with you all the days until the completion of the age" (Matt 28:20), must be construed as promising that Christ the humbled One, not Christ the exalted One, will be with His Church, a united community of Christians.

It is difficult within the context of Western theological reflection to recognize how starkly Kierkegaard's position remains within the confines of his theological psychology and the horizon of the immanent. His spiritual struggles focus on gathering his passions, so as effectively to will only God and thus be able to see God's revelation. Though he perceives the response of God's love, he does not (insofar as his work attests) experience the transforming force of God's uncreated energies. If Kierkegaard had, he would have recognized the miraculous as betokening the transforming power of the holy and have understood the possibility of an immediate Christian experience of the Divine. As significantly, he would have understood this holiness as sustaining the community of Christians unbroken by death or history. His failure to acknowledge this community is again a function of Kierkegaard's understanding of the Incarnation. He cannot see in the Church the living organism of the Body of Christ (Eph 5:23, 30). The result is an ecclesial anomie that always relocates Kierkegaard as an individual abandoned within the horizon of the immanent.

Consider in contrast the following account by Geronda Ephraim of his journey to Mount Athos. The story, which lives in the immediacy of the Church as the Communion of Saints, presents without any self-consciousness that the monk waiting for Geronda Ephraim had been alerted to his arrival by St. John the Baptist.

> When the time finally came – September 26, 1947 – a small boat brought us slowly one morning from the world to the Holy Mountain as if from the shores of the ephemeral to the other side of eternity.
> At the dock of St. Anne's, a venerable old man, Geronda Arsenios, was waiting for me.
> "Aren't you Johnny from Volos?" he asked.
> "Yes," I replied, "but how do you know me?"
> "Oh," he said, "the Honorable Forerunner appeared to Elder Joseph last night and said to him, 'I am bringing you a little lamb. Put it in your sheepfold.'"
> My thoughts were fixed on the Honorable Forerunner, my patron saint, on whose birthday I was born. I was very grateful to him for looking out for me in this way.[116]

Geronda Ephraim was on his way to become the spiritual child of Elder Joseph the Hesychast (†1959), who would describe vividly his experience of God.

> He is illumined. Everything is open to him. He is filled with wisdom, and like a son he possesses his Father's belongings. He knows that he is nothing – made of clay – but also a son of the King. He owns nothing, but possesses everything. He is filled with theology. He cries out insatiably, confessing with full awareness that his existence is nothing. His origin is clay, but his vital force is the breath of God – his soul. Immediately his soul flies to heaven! – "I am the inbreathing, the breath of God! Everything has dissolved and remained on earth, out of which it was taken. I am a son of the eternal King! I am a god by grace! I am immortal and eternal! In a moment I am beside my heavenly Father!"[117]

There is surely the sense that Kierkegaard is struggling to go where Elder Joseph went, but also the clear sense, at least in terms of his writings, that he never arrived. Kierkegaard is this side of the infinite gulf between the immanent and the transcendent. His genre of reflection is more a part of the genre of the European Romantic than the Christian ascetic. Kierkegaard cannot secure the standpoint that would radically set aside the post-Enlightenment's culture of immanence.

It is because of his understanding of the Incarnation and Christ's community with Christians that Kierkegaard sides with the Christian of hidden, inward passion and against the monasticism exemplified by St. John of the Ladder.[118] The monk in securing through ascetic struggle a knowledge gained through divine illumination possesses a theological standpoint beyond the discursive rationality that Kierkegaard decries or the subjectivity he affirms.[119] Kierkegaard's failure to appreciate the possibility of knowledge through union with God is magnified in Kierkegaard's understanding of the Incarnation, which must discount monasticism because he presupposes an invisibility of both Christ and the Christian. Given Kierkegaard's account of the Incarnation, the monk, in being clearly, externally, and visibly a monk, is judged to have lost his inwardness in mere outwardness. In some measure, Kierkegaard's account of monasticism is to be expected. Kierkegaard's paradigm of monasticism is drawn from the Western Middle Ages rather than from the first millennium when monastics provided a critical spiritual force over and against the official hierarchy of the Church. Kierkegaard's criticism of monasticism fails to recognize a parallel between his pamphleteering and the critical public role of the monk. Where Kierkegaard's pamphleteering was a rebuke to the restrained Christianity of the established church, the monk is a rebuke to life lived comfortably in the world. True monasticism constitutes a kind of perpetual pamphleteering and criticism of the world as well as the established Church.

Kierkegaard and St. John Climacus disclose two quite different Christianities. For Kierkegaard, the struggle of faith is against a philosophically grounded reason and an objectified Christianity, as well as against disbelief and the failure to assume risk. The demons against which Kierkegaard contends are not spirits but systems of ideas, Kantian and Hegelian, as well as approaches to the faith that would reduce the Bible to a worldly text. One might think of David Strauss [1808-1874] and his followers, who rejected the historical authenticity of the Gospels as immediate witnesses to Christ, along with discounting any divine or supernatural claims for Jesus. For St. John, the struggle of faith is not against objective uncertainty, but against personal powers. St. John's struggle is with himself (e.g., his passions, as is also the case for Kierkegaard) and other persons (i.e., the demons) who would cloud his soul and make experience and knowledge of the Persons of the Trinity impossible. St. John Climacus' faith is directed against temptations and towards an experience of God that gives knowledge of the transcendent. Kierkegaard's faith is perfected in the subjectivity of a passion of inwardness expressed in his imitation of Christ, about which he cannot say more without turning to either the mysticism of the early Church or the rationalism of the post-Enlightenment.[120] St. John Climacus' faith is perfected in an ascetic struggle towards union with God, knowing that other Christians are also struggling towards this goal. St. John, even in solitude, possesses a community of faith. In contrast to the dark night of Kierkegaard's encounter with the Incarnation as the absurd, St. John Climacus in the spirit of Christ invites the Christian to ascend through faith to a transforming illumination by God. These differences are to be expected, given the history of ideas within which Kierkegaard finds himself entrapped. For Kierkegaard, Christian faith does not lead to illumination; it does not effectively bridge the horizon of the immanent.[121] Such an availability of knowledge of the divine is for Kierkegaard regarded as heathen.

Unlike St. John Climacus, Kierkegaard does not recognize that the power of God, which transformed Paul into a living holy relic, can immediately bring union with God. Because for Kierkegaard there is no noetic knowledge through faith,[122] Kierkegaard cannot acknowledge the experience of God presupposed by St. John of the Ladder, whose name he employs in antithesis for the authorship of *Concluding Unscientific Postscript*.[123] Kierkegaard's dialectic between Climacus and Anticlimacus is thus deeply revelatory: Kierkegaard has no recognition of the truth that St. John Climacus knows through faith to be the transforming uncreated energies of God. Kierkegaard's dialectic of faith and the absurd, of faith and objective uncertainty, of faith and risk, reflects the struggle he finds between anonymous rational objectivity and the inward subjective passion of faith. This dialectic of objectivity and subjectivity, which defines Kierkegaard's faith, is not that which defines the struggle of St. John Climacus. Separating Kierkegaard and St. John Climacus are fundamentally different understandings of the Incarnation and Christian community. For St. John of the Ladder, the Christian is called to ascend to a "unity of faith and of the knowledge of God."

Kierkegaard despite himself is dialectically bound to discursive rationality: what rationality cannot establish remains in an objective uncertainty that defines the journey of faith. Uncertainty is also that which defines risk, which for Kierkegaard also frames faith.

> Faith is the contradiction between the infinite passion of inwardness and the objective uncertainty. If I am able to apprehend God objectively, I do not have faith; but because I cannot do this, I must have faith. If I want to keep myself in faith, I must continually see to it that I hold fast the objective uncertainty, see to it that in the objective uncertainty I am "out on 70,000 fathoms of water" and still have faith.[124]

The ethics and the bioethics of the Christian would need to avoid not only all marks of triumphalism, but also any immediate disclosure of the transcendent. Here, again, one must remember in contrast the remarkable presence of God's energies not only in St. Paul, but in objects that touch St. Paul (Acts 19:12). The Incarnation brings Christ as God radically into His saints who manifest His power. The incarnational ethics of the early Church saw the Christian way of life as able to transform its members into people such as St. Paul. Most particularly, this incarnational ethics was focused on the irruption of the transcendent into the immanent, not just as a psychological event, but as a miraculous transformation, even of the bodies of the saints. This is too much for the post-Enlightenment, Protestant Kierkegaard, who needs more distance from God in order to avoid what he takes to be the immediacy of paganism. As a consequence, Kierkegaard would not see ethics (and bioethics) as primarily spiritually therapeutic, as leading to a transformation of the person as St. Paul was transformed, as leading to a purity of heart in which one can see God, experience God immediately even in this life (Matt 5:8). That is, Kierkegaard cannot find in morality what St. John Climacus experienced: a way to approach God by ascetically purifying one's heart.[125]

In summary, Kierkegaard fails to elude the Enlightenment's resituation of humanity within a taken-for-granted horizon of immanence. One is brought to a precipice across which one can leap, rather than be conducted by the sure hand of God. For Kierkegaard, in the journey to salvation there is no intimate synergy between the will of man and the power of God. For this reason, his phenomenology of faith is characterized by a struggle with doubt tied to the metaphor of the leap.[126] Kierkegaard's religious life is shaped by his perception of the risk of belief, his distance from the possibility of the miraculous, his isolation from a manifest community of saints, and the absence of noetic theological knowledge. All of this, particularly his ecclesiology, is rooted in his incarnational theology, which stresses the invisibility of Christ as God. Kierkegaard produces an account that is one-sidedly inward and lacking in an anchor in the enduring community of Christians. Because that community is the Body of Christ (Eph 5:23, 30), Kierkegaard fails to ground his belief adequately in the incarnate Christian God, at least as He was understood by the Church of the first millennium. His intentions to the contrary notwithstanding, Kierkegaard places himself within a nearly millennium old Western dialectic of the objective and subjective expressed as a dialectic of discursive reason and romantic passion. This dialectic is inevitable. On the one hand, there is the impersonal, discursive, philosophical edifice of Western moral scholasticism, as well as Kant's rational morality and Hegel's system to which Kierkegaard reacts. On the other hand, there is the passion of inwardness, which has traditionally marked Western religious renewals, pietism, and the Romantic critique of rationalism. With Kierkegaard, there is a passion of inwardness, a dark night of the soul without the dawn of illumination.

Perhaps here lies the explanation of why this 19th-century literary figure succeeded so well in the mid-20th century. Kierkegaard captures the texture and feeling of the mid-20th century religious agony of separation from a once taken-for-granted personal presence of God and from an enduring experience of community. There is a yearning for a transcendence that is never achieved, a hope for ultimate meaning despite a perceived silence of God, an inward passion for spirituality that never culminates in a final revelation and a search for community that is never fully realized. Kierkegaard's passionate individualism has a deep consanguinity with the lived experience of the post-modern denizens of the 20th century. Kierkegaard offers the sense that one can at least cry out to the absurd, to God. Consider, for example, how Ingmar Bergman in his portrayal of the cancer patient Agnes in *Cries and Whispers* articulates this deep sense of abandonment, doubt, and agony. In the final part of the prayer, the chaplain addresses to Agnes his own anguish in the form of a request for her to make to God after her death.

> If it is so that you have gathered our suffering in your poor body, if it is so that you have borne it with you through death, if it is so that you meet God over there in the other land, if it is so that He turns His face toward you, if it is so that you can then speak the language that this God understands, if it is so that you can then speak to this God, if it is so, pray for us. Agnes, my dear little child, listen to what I am now telling you. Pray for us who are left here on the dark, dirty earth under an empty and cruel Heaven. Lay your burden of suffering at God's feet and ask Him to pardon us. Ask Him to free us at last from our anxiety, our weariness, and our deep doubt. Ask Him for a meaning to our lives. Agnes, you who have suffered so unimaginably and so long, you must be worthy to plead our cause.[127]

One may believe but yet never find union with the object of belief, opening a gulf marked by an unfulfilled yearning for union with ultimate meaning. The agony of the absurd becomes celebrated in its own right.

Kierkegaard gained influence and was "discovered" in the 20th century. He engages us despite the circumstance that the critical passions of his pamphleteering were primarily directed against the established church of 19th-century Denmark, an established church that, as most established Western churches, has subsequently fallen into even more significant decay. He lived passionately up against the absurdity of the Christianity of the high secular culture of his time, which culture underlies the general secular culture of much of the 20th century and the new millennium. Kierkegaard recognized that he was witnessing the scholarly deconstruction of the Christian Scriptures, a process that dissociated many intellectual Christians from a traditional view of the Scriptures and Jesus. He accepted that philosophy could not prove the existence of the God he wished to worship. Yet Kierkegaard was determined to believe against all odds. Most significantly, he recognized that life was more than rationality or a philosophical system can grasp. Kierkegaard's faith takes on the character of a protest, an inward passion of assertion, without a developed content. It lives in an agony of God's hiddenness, which in the 20th century is expressed as God's silence.

Through his theology of God's elusiveness, Kierkegaard cannot provide substantive guidance for bioethics or health care policy or a substantive response to the crisis of faith in post-modernity. Rather, the pain of Kierkegaard's belief displays with lyric eloquence the struggle of a faith lived in uncertainty towards an object of belief experienced as absurd. Kierkegaard's account does not show how to justify a particular canonical content for bioethics. It does offer an important reminder: Christianity, including Christian bioethics, is a matter of personal transformation, not disengaged erudition. Christianity for Kierkegaard, as he makes plain in *Judge for Yourself!* (1851), is a matter of the imitation of Christ as "the prototype".[128] Because Kierkegaard fails to recognize that Christian doctrine serves to guide the Christian in the imitation of Christ, he articulates an either/or between doctrine and the Christian life, leaving the Christian life without objective guidance.[129] The moral force of Kierkegaard's account of faith is that a Christian ethics (and therefore a Christian bioethics) should not primarily be an exercise in erudition, nor a merely discursive account of rules, nor a rational morality. Because he cannot supply guidance sufficient for this task, Kierkegaard confronts us with the question: What kind of faith can legitimately underlie a Christian bioethics in a post-Christian age? He also confronts us with the challenge that, whatever this faith is, it must be lived with full engagement: Christian bioethics should never be understood as only a scholarly field. The truth of Christian bioethics cannot adequately be portrayed simply as a set of objective prescriptions and proscriptions, or even commitments to virtue and character. A Christian ethics and bioethics should instead be grounded in a passionate inward engagement in faith. Kierkegaard's position would move Christian bioethics away from an academic account of moral conduct to an inward engagement through a Christian bioethics embedded in the imitation of Christ. In summary, Kierkegaard provides an important warning for Christian bioethics: produce a bioethics that is lived.

If a Christian bioethics must be lived with full engagement, it will never be fully accessible to uncommitted Christians, misguided Christians, not to mention non-Christians. Kierkegaard's approach has robustly non-ecumenical implications for the field of religious bioethics. To the traditional Christian, this can only be positive. The disappointment lies in the failure of Kierkegaard to show unambiguously the way out of the horizon of the immanent to union with God. This failure leaves the struggling Christian in doubt and unclarity, which Kierkegaard felt so acutely in his own religious journey. Worse yet, Kierkegaard's protest against the established Protestantism of his day leaves him alienated from both his society and his religious community. Where Kant collapsed society in to the bounds of rational community, and Hegel sought a distance between society and community in the contingent particularity of *Sittlichkeit*, Kierkegaard addressed the Christian individual outside of the concrete, often miraculous manifestations of the community of saints. Disaffected from society and community, as well as from the miraculous force of grace uniting individuals in a Church across the centuries, Kierkegaard becomes the harbinger of post-modernity. Kierkegaard stands alone.

Reason, Faith, and Bioethics

Not all will consider Kierkegaard justified in his attempt to wrest Christianity from its secularization. Not all will judge Kant and Hegel wrongheaded in their attempt to provide a secularly transformed Christianity. Many will find in Kierkegaard at best an engaging form of sectarianism. Kierkegaard's morality is not the morality that can guide our contemporary societies. It is to this that Kant and Hegel aspire. Kant and Hegel offer the foundations of a liberal cosmopolitan Christianity in affirming liberty and the secular transformation of Christianity. Kant's Christianity is free of inward passion precisely so that it can guide the moral life of all reasonable persons. Hegel's Christianity lacks transcendent metaphysical depth precisely so that religious passion can be relocated in philosophical terms. The Christianity of Kant and Hegel, unlike that of Kierkegaard, is open to Christian and non-Christian alike. On the other hand, the Christianity of Kierkegaard is for Christians only. It provokes and divides. The cleft between Kant and Hegel on the one side and Kierkegaard on the other separates those who would understand Christianity in the universal terms of secular reason from those who would understand Christianity in terms of the particularities of Christianity. Kierkegaard risks becoming one of the many rootless voices telling his own moral narrative in a cosmopolitan culture where the particularities of societal and communal claims have lost their force.

We are returned to where this chapter began: the challenge posed by traditional Christianity to the peace of a tolerant pluralist polity, as well as the challenge posed by the post-Christian era to the project of taking traditional Christianity seriously. These provocations can now be regarded within a developed dialectic of faith and reason. Reason, on the one hand, by offering discursive justification domesticates and secularizes faith. Faith, on the other hand, by evoking passion unleashes religious zeal and challenges secular accommodations. Yet reason fails to secure the canonical justification for the content many want it to justify. So, too, faith as passionate can provide motivation but no justified content. In either case, content is lost, whether through the failure of arguments or in the passion of an insufficiently illumined faith. Neither erudition nor passion can secure a canonical moral content. One confronts as well the uninviting choice of objectivity without engagement, or subjective engagement without substance.

Under such circumstances, how is a Christian bioethics possible? At the end of the Christian age, how should one proceed? Christians were once persecuted and had flourished in a pre-Christian age, an age before the establishment of Christianity or the fashioning of a scholastic Christian philosophy. Christians then flourished and persecuted in the West in an age that gave birth to high rational hopes for theology.[130] Just as Christendom nearly compassed the world, Western Christianity spawned the Renaissance and modern concerns with technology, science, medicine, and imperial expansion. As a seemingly triumphant and imperial Western Christendom expanded across the world under Emperor Charles V (1500-1556), who embraced the globe from Texas to the Philippines, everything fractured. In reaction to the bloody consequences of this fragmentation, Western culture took steps towards rearticulating its morality in terms of secular rational foundations. Western Christendom then faded in the brilliance of the Enlightenment and the secular forces it unleashed and nourished. The quandaries and discontents of Christianity are now defined within a post-Christian, discursively successful world. That world has developed political, scientific, and intellectual resources apparently sufficient to trivialize and domesticate, if not deconstruct, traditional Christian morality.

If neither discursive reason nor subjective faith can dispel the difficulties that confront a Christian bioethics, we will need to look elsewhere. A reexamination of Christian bioethics brings us once more to the task of reassessing the epistemological assumptions needed to sustain a Christian bioethics. Can the claims of a Christian bioethics be secured without their devolving into a latter-day scholasticism that will either beg the question or argue in a circle? Can one speak of the discursive rationale of Christian knowledge without falling into the arms of another Kant or Hegel? What should the object of belief be, if it is not to remain the inaccessible absurd of Kierkegaard's apophatic theology or a socio-historically conditioned object easily deconstructed? Were a Christian ethics fashioned to sustain a Christian bioethics, what would be the character of its axiological commitments and the character of moral experts? Would its experts be the academicians of a new scholasticism, or would they be the preachers of jeremiads, such as Kierkegaard? Or is there a tertium quid?

The next chapter examines the possibilities for a Christian bioethics within a Christianity that conforms to our post-traditional, post-modern world. The Christianity it addresses is a post-Enlightenment, cosmopolitan Christianity set within the bounds of immanent experience and the limits of reason. The chapter begins with the one general ground for justifying a morality among moral strangers once it is recognized that one cannot by sound rational argument discover the canonical content of a secular morality: permission. This Christianity is first approached within a libertarian cosmopolitan perspective in the sense of being grounded in permission and being available to anyone. This perspective can take traditional Christianity seriously or provide the basis for a thoroughly immanentized Christianity grounded in human choice. In the shadow of the Enlightenment and in the ruins of post-modernity, the focus is first on the latter. Because this Christianity is too sparse for anyone but a libertarian ascetic of the secular, chapter three then turns to a Christianity and Christian bioethics embedded in liberal cosmopolitan assumptions: a secularized Christianity that not only regards humans as the source of common moral authority when they meet as moral strangers, but also finds in self-chosen life-projects a cardinal source of meaning. This Christianity, this grandchild of the Enlightenment, renders immanent both the metaphysics and ethics of traditional Christianity in its celebration of autonomy and equality. It is the cul-de-sac of Western Christianity. Once here, it is clear that one must return to where Christianity began: the Christianity of the first millennium.

Notes

1. Can only the infinite be the sufficient cause of the finite? Is the universe absurd in its meaninglessness unless there be an infinite Person to convey a meaning and purpose? These are questions that can open the heart and turn one to God, though they cannot prove the existence of God, for from the finite one cannot ever conclude to the infinite. In strictly logical terms the gulf is infinite. This gulf can only be bridged by God, Who responds to the heart that turns to Him in prayer.

2. In the first *Critique*, Immanuel Kant recognizes the rational need to bring into harmony worthiness of happiness and happiness in order to avoid a tension at the very heart of morality.

    > I maintain that just as the moral principles are necessary according to reason in its practical employ-
    > ment, it is in the view of reason, in the field of its theoretical employment, no less necessary to assume
    > that everyone has ground to hope for happiness in the measure in which he has rendered himself by his
    > conduct worthy of it, and that the system of morality is therefore inseparably – though only in the idea
    > of pure reason – bound up with that of happiness.
    > *Immanuel Kant's Critique of Pure Reason*, trans. Norman Kemp Smith (London: Macmillan, 1964), p.
    > 638, A809=B837.

3. G.W.F. Hegel, *The Philosophy of History*, trans. J. Sibree (New York: Dover, 1956), p. 417.

4. The conflict of the right and the good springs from a lack of necessary harmony between (1) those elements of morality that are intrinsically right- or wrong-making, irrespective of their consequences, and (2) those that have moral significance because of the good they achieve or preserve. If secular moral authority is derived from the permission of those who collaborate, the constraining of persons without their consent is wrong, no matter the consequences.

5. At stake is a moral rationality that enshrines as the moral point of view an anonymous perspective, thereby discounting as non-moral any would-be moral rationality that would enshrine as the moral point of view a community-directed perspective that takes persons and their special obligations seriously. Yet, one can assert universally that one should give precedence to particular obligations, thus discounting aid to strangers in favor of aid to kith and kin.

6. The justification of a morality accounts for why its particular moral claims (e.g., never treat competent adult patients without their consent) should be morally obligatory for all created persons, or at least all humans (i.e., the justification of a morality answers questions such as, "Why ought one to recognize a particular set of rights and duties as binding?"). For example, rational argument gives an internal consideration in favor of acting morally. Moral behavior is the rational thing to do so that to reject morality is to reject rationality. In this sense, immorality involves the rejection of one system or cluster of rational considerations: coherent answers about how to achieve the greatest amount of the good or how to act so as to be praiseworthy or worthy of happiness. Yet there may be good non-moral reasons to act immorally. It can in some sense in some circumstances be irrational to act morally. Morality of itself may provide a reason to be moral, but surely not always a sufficient reason, at least for many persons in many circumstances. Thus, there is a gulf between the justification of morality and the motivation to act morally. The motivation for being moral accounts for why one should do what one acknowledges to be obligatory (i.e., the motivation for being moral answers the question, "Why should I do what I ought to do?") from a universalizable perspective. Motivation is used here to identify not just inclinations or drives to action, but grounds for wanting to do that which one ought to do from a particular account of moral probity. The question at issue is whether it is rational always to judge actions from the standpoint of what is universally obligatory. If in the end the cosmos is without meaning and human ideals are doomed to

extinction with the human race, then can one justify sacrificing the lives of those one loves for abstract moral ideas? At stake are competing visions of probity.

7. Hegel remarks regarding the putatively absolute claims of the right over against the good that "Welfare without right is not a good. Similarly, right without welfare is not the good; *fiat justitia* should not be followed by *pereat mundus*." G.W.F. Hegel, *Hegel's Philosophy of Right*, trans. T. M. Knox (Oxford: Clarendon Press, 1965), p. 87, §130. This view has important implications for the tensions among deontological and teleological concerns in bioethics. The claim of neither genre of moral rationality is absolute.

8. Balancing the claims between a universal and a particular moral perspective involves ordering one's moral relationships and obligations to persons in terms of the force of their claim on the agent: the claim of a nuclear family member, the claim of an extended family member, the claim of a patient, the claim of an anonymous individual.

9. A. Koryagin, "Unwilling Patients," *Lancet* 1 (1981): 821; Harold Mersky, "Variable Meanings for the Definition of Disease," *Journal of Medicine and Philosophy* 11 (Aug. 1986): 215-32.

10. For an assessment of the dependence of Immanuel Kant's moral account on a commitment to religious belief so as to make rational the discharge of moral obligations in the face of severe personal costs, see Alasdair MacIntyre, "Can Medicine Dispense with a Theological Perspective on Human Natures," pp. 119-138, and Paul Ramsey, "Kant's Moral Theology or a Religion Ethic?" pp. 139-170, and MacIntyre, "A Rejoinder to a Rejoinder," pp. 171-174, in *The Roots of Ethics*, eds. Daniel Callahan and H. T. Engelhardt, Jr. (New York: Plenum Press, 1981).

11. For a study of the "absurd" choice to act on behalf of the good despite significant personal risks and in the face of a universe taken to be meaningless, see Albert Camus, *The Plague* (1948).

12. For example, Camus recognizes how one must consider the future once one regards reality in the absence of God. "The absurd enlightens me on this point: there is no future." Albert Camus, *The Myth of Sisyphus*, trans. Justin O'Brien (New York: Alfred A. Knopf, 1961), p. 58.

13. If there were no God and no immortality, could one justify failing to collaborate with a totalitarian government, if the price of resistance were the painful death of one's family and friends? How could one let those one loves suffer on behalf of abstract ideals? What could the reasonable claim of moral ideals be if the universe were absent of ultimate meaning?

14. Christianity recognizes that with the second coming of the Messiah all will be restored: "Now I saw a new heaven and a new earth, for the first heaven and the first earth had passed away. Also there was no more sea. Then I, John, saw the holy city, New Jerusalem, coming down out of heaven from God, prepared as a bride adorned for her husband. And I heard a loud voice from heaven saying, 'Behold, the tabernacle of God is with men, and He will dwell with them, and they shall be His people. God Himself will be with them and be their God. And God will wipe away every tear from their eyes; there shall be no more death, nor sorrow, nor crying. There shall be no more pain, for the former things have passed away'" (Rev 21:1-4).

15. It is persons of a certain sort, not merely humans, who are central to Kant's as well as this book's account of finite human knowledge and secular morality. This issue is explored at greater length in Engelhardt, *The Foundations of Bioethics*, 2nd ed. (New York: Oxford University Press, 1996), especially pp. 135-154. See, also, the contrast between *humanitas* and *personitas* in Engelhardt, *Bioethics and Secular Humanism: The Search for a Common Morality* (Philadelphia: Trinity Press International, 1991), p. 125.

16. To be fair to Kant, some qualifications are needed. First, Kant understands himself as providing the necessary conditions for the possibility of spatio-temporal, sensible, discursive experience. He directs his epistemological focus only to beings who experience the world

through one temporal and three spatial dimensions. Kant does not exclude the possibility of beings who might otherwise experience reality. One might consider, for example, the possibility of beings who have sensible experience in six temporal and six thousand spatial dimensions (i.e., somewhat like the six-winged, many-eyed cherubim). Kant's position is that "This [our] mode of intuiting in space and time need not be limited to human sensibility. It may be that all finite, thinking beings necessarily agree with man in this respect, although we are not in the position to judge whether this is actually so. But however universal this mode of sensibility may be, it does not therefore cease to be sensibility." *Critique of Pure Reason*, p. 90, B72. Kant restricts his empirical focus to sensible rather than to intellectual knowledge. Sensible experience for Kant is contrasted with intellectual intuition, through which God would know things immediately from the inside out. Kant's account of knowledge is not justified in human nature but more broadly in the character of sensible spatio-temporal discursive knowers. Kant justifies knowledge within the sphere of possible experience, the world of immanence that defines the context and condition of humans. Knowledge is not understood from the perspective of God.

More substantive qualifications must be introduced regarding Kant's account of morality. His morality is for persons as such, not just embodied persons, much less only humans. His morality is embedded in a fact of reason that marks moral agency and would apply to angels. Moral agents can recognize themselves as acting under a moral law so that "the maxim of your will could always hold at the same time as a principle establishing universal law." *Critique of Practical Reason*, trans. Lewis White Beck (Indianapolis: Bobbs-Merrill, 1956), p. 30, AK V, 30. Within his Second Critique, this possibility is for Kant a fact of reason. "The consciousness of this fundamental law may be called a fact of reason, since one cannot ferret it out from antecedent data of reason, such as the consciousness of freedom." *Ibid.*, p. 31, AK V, 31. Kant's account of morality is defined without requiring the actual existence of a transcendent God and focuses on the predicament of finite agents locked in the sphere of immanence. Kant does not as clearly subject his account of morality to the consequences of his Copernican revolution, as he does human knowledge. Morality for moral strangers is not seen to be grounded in an intersubjectivity of the will as knowledge for metaphysical strangers is seen to be grounded in an intersubjectivity of empirical understanding. Kant does not recognize that the universality of the will cannot be found in a particular vision of rationality and must instead be found in the will itself and its ability to recognize universal obligations (e.g., never use moral agents as mere means).

17. "I entitle *transcendental* all knowledge which is occupied not so much with objects as with the mode of our knowledge of objects in so far as this mode of knowledge is to be possible *a priori.*" *Critique of Pure Reason*, p. 59, A11=B25. The categories in Kant's account function as the cardinal points of this grammar of coherence. "The principle of the analogies is: Experience is possible only through the representation of a necessary connection of perceptions." p. 208, A176=B218. Or as Kant also puts it, "The conditions of the *possibility of experience* in general are likewise conditions of the *possibility of the objects of experience.*" p. 194, A158=B197.

18. Diogenes Laertius, *Protagoras* IX, 51, in *Lives of Eminent Philosophers*, trans. R. D. Hicks (Cambridge, MA: Harvard, 1979), vol. 2, pp. 463, 465. Protagoras' views regarding the centrality of the human perspective had an epistemological grounding different from that developed by Immanuel Kant. "Protagoras was the first to maintain that there are two sides to every question, opposed to each other, and he even argued in this fashion, being the first to do so." Diogenes Laertius, *ibid.* IX, 51, vol. 2, p. 463.

19. Kant, *Critique of Pure Reason*, p. 22, Bxvi.

20. Thomas Aquinas' account of the infusion of the soul is complex. See, for example, Thomas Aquinas, *Summa Theologica*, 1, Q. 118, art. 2, reply to objection 2. His views led Aquinas to

be indulgent of Aristotle's support for early abortions prior to "animation". Aquinas did not consider such to be murder, the taking of the life of a person, although he on independent grounds held early abortion to be gravely sinful. See *Aristoteles Stagiritae: Politicorum seu de Rebus Civilibus*, Book VII, Lectio XII, in *Opera Omnia* (Paris: Vives, 1875), vol. 26, p. 484. Roman Catholic canon law drew from Aristotle the position that a male fetus was not rationally ensouled until 40 days, and a female fetus until 80 or 90 days. *De Generatione Animalium* 2.3.736a-b and *Historia Animalium*, 7.3.583b. Roman Catholic canon law built on a particular case from the 12th century that accepted these biological/metaphysical premises. See *Corpus Juris Canonici Emendatum et Notis Illustratum cum Glossae: decretalium d. Gregorii Papae Noni Compilatio* (Rome, 1585), *Glossa ordinaria* at bk. 5, title 12, chap. 20, p. 1713. These reflections led to the Roman church from 1234 until 1869 not to regard early abortions as murder, save for the 3-year period from 1588 to 1591. See Pope Sextus V, *Contra procurantes, Consulentes, et Consentientes, quorunque modo Abortum Constitutio* (Florence: Georgius Marescottus, 1588).

21. Kant, *Critique of Pure Reason*. See, in particular, A532=B560 through A558=B586 for Kant's account of the compatibility of the practices of empirical knowing and of morality.

22. "For this reason a rational being must regard himself as intelligence (and not from the side of his lower powers), as belonging to the world of understanding and not to that of the senses. Thus he has two standpoints from which he can consider himself and recognize the laws of the employment of his powers and consequently of all his actions: first, as belonging to the world of sense under laws of nature (heteronomy), and, second, as belonging to the intelligible world under laws which, independent of nature, are not empirical but founded only on reason." Kant, *Foundations of the Metaphysics of Morals*, trans. Lewis White Beck (Indianapolis: Bobbs-Merrill, 1959), p. 71, AK IV, 453. It is important to note that Kant denies the possibility of intellectual intuition (what the 4th chapter will introduce under the rubric of noetic knowledge). See *Critique of Pure Reason*, B307.

23. "We have finally reduced the definite concept of morality to the idea of freedom, but we could not prove freedom to be real in ourselves and in human nature. We saw only that we must presuppose it if we would think of a being as rational and conscious of his causality with respect to actions, that is, as endowed with a will; and so we find that on the very same grounds we must ascribe to each being endowed with reason and will the property of determining himself to action under the idea of freedom." Kant, *Foundations of the Metaphysics of Morals*, trans. Lewis White Beck (Indianapolis: Bobbs-Merrill, 1959), p. 67, AK IV, 448-9.

24. In *Prolegomena to Any Future Metaphysics*, Kant identifies the necessary conditions for the possibility of knowledge with the elements of a grammar, the "Elemente zu einer Grammatik". Here, Kant heuristically employs the metaphor of grammar to indicate the conditions for the possible coherence of a domain of human experience. *Prolegomena zu einer jeden künftigen Metaphysik*, AK VI, 323. Wittgenstein picks up a similar point in noting that "Essence is expressed by grammar." *Philosophical Investigations*, trans. G. E. M. Anscombe (Oxford: Basil Blackwell, 1963), §371. Also, "Grammar tells us what kind of an object anything is." §373. Stanley Cavell underscores the tie between Wittgenstein's use of grammar and Kant's use of transcendental in "Availability of Wittgenstein's Later Philosophy," in George Pitcher (ed.), *Wittgenstein: The Philosophical Investigations* (New York: Doubleday, 1966), pp. 151-85.

25. Kant distinguishes his account of morality from those accounts directed to or dependent on the realization of particular values, goals, or goods. Kant's position is that "morals is not really the doctrine of how to make ourselves happy but of how we are to be worthy of happiness." *Critique of Practical Reason*, trans. L. W. Beck (Indianapolis: Library of Liberal Arts, 1956), p. 134, AK V, 130.

26. As an example of such a defense of universal human rights, one might think of "Reflection of the Very Reverend Father Friar Francisco de Vitoria, Master of Theology and Most Worthy Prime Professor at the University of Salamanca, Delivered in the Said University, A.D. 1539." Francisco de Vitoria (1486?-1546) was not alone in his bold attempt to reconsider Scholasticism so as not only to establish universal human rights, including rights to property, but also to make place for markets and the charging of interest, thus escaping the Western Christian proscriptions on usury, even by laymen. Vitoria was followed by such associates and students as Domingo de Soto (1494-1560), Luis de Molina (1535-1600) and Francisco Suárez (1548-1617).

27. See Kant's "Idea for a Universal History with a Cosmopolitan Purpose," which appeared in 1784 as *Idee zu einer allgemeinen Geschichte in weltbürgerlicher Absicht.*

28. See, for example, Kant, *Zum ewigen Frieden* (1795).

29. As an example of the Spanish concern to avoid unjustly seizing the property and taking the lives of the inhabitants of the New World, one might consider the remarkable manifesto or Requirement that was read to Indians prior to their being attacked. If opportunity allowed, the fact of its reading was notarized, necessitating the presence of notaries on such expeditions. The first recorded instance of the Requirement being read was June 14, 1514. The Requirement included a brief history of the world from creation to the conquest of the Americas, including an account of the authority of the papacy. This incorporated an account of Pope Alexander VI's donation of "these isles and Tierra Firme" to the kings of Spain. The document requires that the Indians who hear it (1) acknowledge the Roman Catholic Church and the Pope as the ruler of the world and (2) allow Roman Catholicism to be preached in their territories. The document guarantees that if the Indians accede to these points, there will be no hostilities. However, if they fail immediately to concede these points, the document contains the following warning:

> We shall take you and your wives and your children, and shall make slaves of them, and as such shall sell and dispose of them as their Highnesses may command; and we shall take away your goods, and shall do all the harm and damage that we can, as to vassals who do not obey, and refuse to receive their lord, and resist and contradict him; and we protest that the deaths and losses which shall accrue from this are your fault, and not that of their Highnesses, or ours, nor of these cavaliers who come with us. And that we have said this to you and made this Requirement, we request the notary here present to give us his testimony in writing, and we ask the rest who are present that they should be witnesses of this Requirement.
> Lewis Hanke, *The Spanish Struggle for Justice in the Conquest of America* (Philadelphia: University of Pennsylvania Press, 1949), p. 33.

In June, 1514, after the Spanish landed and read the Requirement, there were no Indians in sight. As a consequence, Gonzalo Fernández de Oviedo, the new governor, declared in the presence of his men: "My Lords, it appears to me that these Indians will not listen to the theology of this Requirement, and that you have no one who can make them understand it; would Your Honor be pleased to keep it until we have some one of these Indians in a cage, in order that he may learn it at his leisure and my Lord Bishop may explain it to him." *Ibid.,* pp. 33-34. For a further study of some of these issues, see Anthony Pagden, *The Fall of Natural Man: The American Indian and the Origins of Comparative Ethnology* (Cambridge: Cambridge University Press, 1982).

30. *Critique of Pure Reason,* p. 650, A828=B856.

31. *Ibid.,* p. 640, A813=B841.

32. Kant frequently construes the tension between the good and the right as one between nature and freedom. The issue is whether the structure of reality is congenial to human moral freedom such that, when persons freely act to be worthy of happiness, they will be commensurably happy. *Critique of Pure Reason,* A815=B844.

33. Kant, *Critique of Practical Reason*, trans. Thomas Abbott (London: Longmans, 1967), p. 219, AK V, 122-123.

34. *Critique of Pure Reason*, p. 639, A811=B829.

35. In his *Opus Postumum* Kant abandons this invocation of God and immortality because of its threat to non-heteronomous moral choice.

36. Kant insists that one may not have as a ground for acting according to the moral law the reward of happiness being in proportion to one's worthiness for happiness. "One must never consider morals itself as a doctrine of happiness, i.e., as an instruction in how to acquire happiness." *Critique of Practical Reason*, trans. Lewis White Beck (Chicago: University of Chicago Press, 1949), p. 233, AK V, 130.

37. *Critique of Practical Reason*, trans. Beck, pp. 133-134, AK V, 129, 130. Kant's appeal to Christian ethics and religion is explicitly secular: their religious significance has been transformed into their role in his account of morality.

38. Kant, *Die Religion innerhalb der Grenzen der bloßen Vernunft*.

39. Kant, *Religion Within the Limits of Reason Alone,* trans. T. M. Greene and H. H. Hudson (New York: Harper, 1960), p. 162, 163, AK VI, 174, 175.

40. *Ibid.*, AK VI, 175.

41. *Ibid.*, p. 94, AK VI, 102-3.

42. *Ibid.*, p. 118, AK VI, 109. Kant indeed is critical of the idea that worship, turning to God other than simply by discharging one's moral duties, is anything but superstitious. "The illusion of being able to accomplish anything in the way of justifying ourselves before God through religious acts of worship is religious *superstition*...." *Ibid.*, p. 162, AK VI, 174.

43. For an influential account of the relationship that Moses Mendelsohn saw between the religion of reason and the Jewish religion and its expression in Jewish law, see Hermann Cohen, *Religion of Reason*, trans. Simon Kaplan, 2nd ed. (Atlanta: Scholars Press, 1995 [*Religion der Vernunft aus den Quellen des Judentums*, Leipzig, 1919]), pp. 357-58.

44. Immanuel Kant, *Religion Within the Limits of Reason Alone*, trans. T.M. Greene and H.H. Hudson (New York: Harper, 1960), p. 123, AK VI, 132f.

45. "The more secret records, added as a sequel, of his resurrection and ascension, which took place before the eyes only of his intimates, cannot be used in the interest of religion within the limits of reason alone without doing violence to their historical valuation." Kant, *Religion Within the Limits of Reason Alone*, p. 119, fn., AK VI, 128.

46. "Were it a question of *historical belief* concerning the derivation and the rank, possibly supermundane, of his person, this doctrine would indeed stand in need of verification through miracles; although, as merely belonging to moral soul-improving faith, it can dispense with all such proofs of its truth." Kant, *Religion Within the Limits of Reason Alone*, p. 120, AK VI, 129.

47. "This [Christian] sketch of a history of after-ages [reward and punishment following the Final Judgment], which themselves are not yet history, presents a beautiful ideal of the moral world-epoch, brought about by the introduction of true universal religion and in faith *foreseen* even to its culmination – which we cannot *conceive* as a culmination in experience, but can merely *anticipate*, i.e., prepare for, in continual progress and approximation toward the highest good possible on earth (and in all of this there is nothing mystical, but everything moves quite naturally in a moral fashion)." Kant, *Religion Within the Limits of Reason Alone*, p. 126, AK VI, 135f.

48. "The Teacher [Christ] of the Gospel revealed to his disciples the kingdom of God on earth only in its glorious, soul-elevating moral aspect, namely, in terms of the value of citizenship in a divine state, and to this end he informed them of what they had to do, not only to achieve it themselves but to unite with all others of the same mind and, so far as possible, with the entire human race." Kant, *Religion Within the Limits of Reason Alone*, p. 125, AK

VI, 134. Christian bioethics for Kant would not properly have content beyond that possessed by secular bioethics.

49. Regarding the Bible, Kant follows "the principle of reasonable *modesty* in pronouncements regarding all that goes by the name of revelation. For no one can deny the *possibility* that a scripture which, in practical content, contains much that is godly, may (with respect to what is historical in it) be regarded as a genuinely divine revelation. It is also possible that the union of men into one religion cannot feasibly be brought about or made abiding without a holy book and an ecclesiastical faith based upon it. Moreover, the contemporary state of human insight being what it is, one can hardly expect a new revelation, ushered in with new miracles. Hence the most intelligent and most reasonable thing to do is from now on to use the book [Bible] already at hand as the basis for ecclesiastical instruction and not to lessen its value through useless or mischievous attacks." Kant, *Religion Within the Limits of Reason Alone*, pp. 122-23, AK VI, 132.

50. Kant, *Religion Within the Limits of Reason Alone*, p. 55, AK VI, 61.

51. *Ibid.*, p. 132, AK VI, 141.

52. *Ibid.*, p. 121, AK VI, 130.

53. For a full development of these points, see Engelhardt, *The Foundations of Bioethics*, 2nd ed., chapters 1-3.

54. That is, one cannot derive content for morality by appealing to any or all of the formulations of Kant's categorical imperative.

55. For example, in order to condemn suicide, Kant develops a number of arguments that invoke the principle of avoiding a contradiction. Among these is his contention that to commit suicide out of self-love requires the perversion of a feeling that should lead to self-improvement, not self-destruction. Therefore, in committing suicide one would universalize an impulse, self-love, in a way that would lead to the destruction of life, self-destruction. "One immediately sees a contradiction in a system of nature whose law would be to destroy life by the feeling whose special office is to impel the improvement of life. In this case it would not exist as nature; hence that maxim cannot obtain as a law of nature, and thus it wholly contradicts the supreme principle of all duty." Immanuel Kant, *Foundations of the Metaphysics of Morals*, trans. Lewis White Beck (Indianapolis: Bobbs-Merrill, 1959), p. 40, AK IV, 422. In his *Metaphysical Principles of Virtue*, Kant adds other arguments, including the contention that to will to commit suicide is to will to obliterate moral agents from the universe. "To destroy the subject of morality in his own person is tantamount to obliterating from the world, as far as he can, the very existence of morality itself; but morality is, nevertheless, an end in itself." Kant, *Metaphysical Principles of Virtue*, trans. James Ellington (Indianapolis: Bobbs-Merrill, 1964), p. 83f, AK VI, 423. However, in order to avoid a strictly logical contradiction, one need only specify matters carefully: "I affirm all moral agents should recognize their finitude and end their lives when (1) it is very likely that they will in any event die within six months, and (2) the remaining life would be incompatible with their understanding of a dignified, rational life." This maxim involves no contradiction. Moreover, if the impulse of self-love is to maintain one's self as worthy of one's self-regard, there may also be no contradiction.

56. In order to import moral content, Kant appeals not only to a logical contradiction, but also to what he claims cannot be willed consistently by a person. In this way, for example, he claims to establish obligations of charity. Although one could consistently will neither to give nor to require charity, Kant holds one would still hope for charity if in need. See *Grundlegung zur Metaphysik der Sitten*, AK IV 423-424.

57. Kant requires AS-IF belief in God to remedy what was, at least until the latter years of his life, a morally unacceptable conclusion: that the harmony of reward and righteousness could not be guaranteed. At the end of his life Kant steps away from his argument that one is

required by practical reason to act as if there were God and immortality in order to guarantee harmony between moral obligation and the *summum bonum*. Apparently between 1800 and 1803 Kant begins to view this role of God as introducing an element of heteronomy. In the *Opus Postumum* Kant approaches the existence of God anew. As Norman Kemp Smith observes, he does this in three ways: (1) God's reality is shown through the categorical imperative, which can be understood as a divine command; (2) the idea of God is central to understanding duties as divine commands; and (3) God as a transsubjective being is immanent in the human spirit. In short, in comparison to the *Critique of Pure Reason*, "God is no longer viewed as a Being who must be postulated in order to make possible the coincidence of virtue with happiness. God speaks with the voice of the categorical imperative, and thereby reveals Himself in a direct manner." Norman Kemp Smith, *A Commentary to Kant's 'Critique of Pure Reason'* (London: Macmillan, 1979), 2nd ed., pp. 640-1.

58. "Are not two sparrows sold for a penny? Yet not one of them will fall to the ground apart from the will of your Father. And even the very hairs of your head are all numbered. So don't be afraid; you are worth more than many sparrows." Matt 10:29-31.

59. G.W.F. Hegel, *Hegel's Philosophy of Right*, trans. T.M. Knox (Oxford: Clarendon Press, 1965), p. 90, §135.

60. G.W.F. Hegel, *Hegel's Philosophy of Mind*, trans. A.V. Miller (Oxford: Clarendon Press, 1971), p. 253, §513.

61. G.W.F. Hegel, *The Philosophy of History*, trans. J. Sibree (New York: Dover, 1956), p. 460.

62. Hegel, *Hegel's Philosophy of Right*, p. 89, §134.

63. *Ibid.*, p. 107, §150.

64. *Philosophy of Right*, §303.

65. Hegel's criticism of the anti-Semites of the early 18th century provides a further basis for holding that Hegel's state need not impose a particular religion but could in this sense be pluralist. *Philosophy of Right*, §209. See also §270.

66. For a further development of this interpretation of Hegel, see H. Tristram Engelhardt, Jr., "Sittlichkeit and Post-Modernity: An Hegelian Reconsideration of the State," in *Hegel Reconsidered*, eds. H. T. Engelhardt, Jr., and T. Pinkard (Dordrecht: Kluwer, 1994), pp. 211-224.

67. To appreciate Hegel's commitment to a possible plurality of moral visions, compare Hegel's statement regarding fulfillment in a particular moral community with his insistence that citizenship should span religious and cultural identities. On the one hand, Hegel holds:

> The right of individuals to be subjectively destined to freedom is fulfilled when they belong to an actual ethical order, because their conviction of their freedom finds its truth in such an objective order, and it is in an ethical order that they are actually in possession of their own essence or their own inner universality. *Hegel's Philosophy of Right*, p. 109, §153.

On the other hand, Hegel insists that the state provides a moral unity that transcends moral pluralism. As noted in the text of this chapter, "A man counts as a man in virtue of his manhood alone, not because he is a Jew, Catholic, Protestant, German, Italian, &c." *Hegel's Philosophy of Right*, p. 134, §209. Hegel's state provides the political space for a diversity of moral communities and a diversity of bioethics.

68. *Hegel's Philosophy of Mind*, p. 251, §508.

69. Aristotle, *Nichomachaean Ethics* IX.10.1170b.

70. Aristotle, *Politics* VII 4.1326b, in *The Complete Works of Aristotle*, ed. Jonathan Barnes (Princeton, NJ: Princeton University Press, 1984), vol. 2, page 2105.

71. Despite its persecutions of Jews, medieval European society provided a special place for Jewish law and was in this narrow sense pluralist. See Jacob Katz, *Tradition and Crisis: Jewish Society at the End of the Middle Ages*, trans. Bernard Cooperman (New York: Schocken Books, 1993).

72. Important also in the later development of the Enlightenment was Philipp Jakob Spener (1635-1705), who founded pietism which, despite the original intentions of the pietists, led in its final secularized versions to a kind of democratic immanentism. Spener and the devout pietists sought to realize the kingdom of God on earth. Once this pietism was deprived of its supernatural orientation, it could easily provide energies for a kind of social gospel, as one finds in that child of pietism, Immanuel Kant. Among other things pietism supported (1) a larger role of the laity in church governance, (2) a friendlier response to heretics, (3) a more individualistic attitude, (4) a greater emphasis on the practical side of religion, and (5) an opposition to narrow dogmatic concerns. For an overview of the religious background framing Hegel's thought, see Laurence Dickey, *Hegel: Religion, Economics, and the Politics of Spirit, 1770-1807* (Cambridge: Cambridge University Press, 1987), especially pp. 1-179.

73. It can be heuristic to consider how many reformations or restructurings of Christianity have taken place. Generally, one takes for granted that the Protestant Reformation of the 16th century marks the first profound discontinuity in the history of Christianity. However, the emergence of the papacy of old Rome under the new empire of Charles the Great (742-814) and the contentions of Nicholas I (858-867) mark the birth of the West and its Christian religions as a separate cultural endeavor. There is surely a further dramatic reformulation of this religion as the result of the labors of Hildebrand, Pope Gregory VII (1020?-1085, pope 1073-1085), who sought to establish the temporal power of the pope over the Western emperor (he not only excommunicated emperor Henry IV but also absolved his subjects of their obligation to show allegiance to him), centralized the administration of the Western church, and, most significantly for the abuses that fueled the Protestant Reformation, forbade a married clergy, provoking outbursts in Germany. This administrative, ecclesiological centralization was then followed by the dramatic rationalistic transformation of Western Christianity by the Scholasticism of the 13th century. Each of these constituted a reformulation as well as a reformation of the character of Western Christianity. The latter proved so influential that Protestantism despite itself returned again and again to the embrace of secular discursive concerns, which in the 18th and 19th centuries dramatically transformed its character.

74. This third Reformation of Protestantism constituted its reshaping in robustly secular and discursive rational terms. Protestantism, which had in great measure rejected faith in favor of reason, was in the end recaptured by the reason of the Enlightenment and transformed.

75. W. H. Walsh, "The Origins of Hegelianism," in *Hegel*, ed. Michael Inwood (Oxford: Oxford University Press, 1985), p. 29.

76. *Hegel's Philosophy of Right*, p. 168, §270.

77. *Ibid.*, p. 134, §209.

78. *Ibid.*, pp. 173-174, §270.

79. For an account of parallel health care systems within a state, see Engelhardt, *The Foundations of Bioethics*, 2nd ed., especially pp. 175-177, 398-402.

80. Although not explicitly addressed by Hegel, his state allows space for moral difference so that one can envisage a legal system within which the violation of the bioethics of particular institutions would give grounds for civil recovery, as well as for being charged with misdemeanor, perhaps even felony criminal, indeed capital, offenses. Those receiving care within such institutions might be required to submit to trial by special institutional or ecclesiastical courts. Certain general legal safeguards as well as rights to appeal to general secular courts could be preserved. Within such a framework, Roman Catholic hospitals could forbid the provision of abortion on their premises and could enforce this through civil and criminal penalties. This topic will be discussed further in Chapter 7.

81. For an introduction to the categorial, non-metaphysical reading of Hegel that frames these analyses, see Klaus Hartmann, "Towards a New Systematic Reading of Hegel's Philosophy

of Right," in Z. A. Pelczynski (ed.), *The State and Civil Society* (Cambridge: Cambridge University Press, 1984), pp. 114-136; and "Hegel: A Non-Metaphysical View," in *Hegel*, ed. Alasdair MacIntyre (Notre Dame, IN: University of Notre Dame Press, 1972), pp. 101-124. See, also, *Die ontologische Option* (Berlin: de Gruyter, 1976), and *Studies in Foundational Philosophy* (Amsterdam: Rodopi, 1988).

82. In 1795, Hegel anticipated David Friedrich Strauss (1808-1874) and his *Das Leben Jesu kritisch bearbeitet* (1835-36) with his own *Das Leben Jesu* ("The Life of Jesus" in *Three Essays, 1793-1795*, ed. & trans. Peter Fuss and John Dobbins [Notre Dame, IN: University of Notre Dame Press, 1984], pp. 104-165).

83. G.W.F. Hegel, *Faith & Knowledge*, trans. Walter Cerf and H.S. Harris (Albany: State University of New York Press, 1977),p. 190.

84. For an overview of Hegel's *Philosophy of Religion*, see Karl Rosenkranz, *Kritische Erläuterungen des Hegel'schen Systems* (Hildesheim: Georg Olms, 1963), pp. 217-251. This is a photographic reprint of the Königsberg edition from 1840.

85. The Hegelian philosophy is Protestant. "I term Protestantism that form of religion that grounds the reconciliation of God and humanity through the certainty that the essence of human self-consciousness has as its content the divine self-consciousness and therefore has freedom as its form." Karl Rosenkranz, *Georg Wilhelm Friedrich Hegels Leben* (Darmstadt: Wissenschaftliche Buchgesellschaft, 1971), p. xxxiii.

86. Hegel, *Faith & Knowledge*, trans. Walter Cerf and H.S. Harris (Albany: State University of New York Press, 1977), p. 191. Walter Kaufmann stresses the importance of this passage as a key to understanding Hegel's affirmation of the philosophical perspective gained at the end of the *Phenomenology of Spirit*, which provides the basis for his systematic account of philosophy in his *Encyclopedia*. "Thus Hegel's essay ends, in German, with the words: *auferstehen kann und muss*, can and must be resurrected, or can and must rise again. As we shall see, the *Phenomenology* ends with a comparable image: there the famous 'speculative Good Friday' is replaced by a vision of Golgotha." Walter Kaufmann, *Hegel: A Reinterpretation* (Garden City, NY: Doubleday Anchor, 1966), p. 78.

87. Rosenkranz provides an account of the Hegelian construal of the higher truth of religion, in particular Christianity, indeed most especially Protestantism, as philosophy and the state. Although Christianity may appear to be on the brink of collapse, it is indeed resurrected in a philosophically mediated culture. "Protestantism, and with it Christendom, are now raising themselves again to a purer, higher form. The ferment of this progress makes Protestantism, indeed Christendom, appear to have instantaneously collapsed. Protestantism, however, is only able to free itself from its finished, indeed dead forms, thereby winning for the dead who want to remain dead, and for those who are proud of the changelessness of their faith, the appearance of being unprincipled. ... The strength of Protestantism is that it is only apparently threatened by the dissolution of its confessional differences, because it contains an adequate concept of the spirit, being itself the living unity of truth and its certainty." Rosenkranz, *Georg Wilhelm Friedrich Hegels Leben*, pp. xxxvi, xxxvii [author's translation]. It is worth noting that Rosenkranz anticipates 20th century German Protestantism's involvement with National Socialism by regarding the truth of the Protestant religion as realized in the culture of the German Volk.

88. Baruch Spinoza's (1632-1677) critical scriptural studies anticipate some of Kant's deconstruction of the New Testament. For an exploration of Spinoza's scholarship in this area, see Leo Strauss, *Die Religionskritik Spinozas als Grundlage seiner Bibelwissenschaft* (Hildesheim: Georg Olms, 1981), esp. pp. 247-264. Immanuel Kant had a complex influence on Reform or liberal Judaism, especially through Hermann Cohen (1842-1918). See, for example, Cohen, *Religion of Reason*. Cohen recognized the centrality of Kant to modern appreciations of culture and morality.

Modernity as such, with its general philosophy, stimulated deep reforms in all spheres of the mind. Only scholastic philosophy remained tied to the past, particularly with regard to ethical problems. In its arrangements and applications of these, it stuck fast to its connections with theology and the disciplines of law. ... This ethics, which was conceived as independent and pure philosophy ... in its innermost spirit related to the new religiosity of the Reformation, as well as to the Pietists. On the other hand, it was influenced by Rousseau, and thus animated by the social problems and the political ideas of the betterment of the general condition of the world. Thus, Kant's ethics breathes the spirit of mankind. Cohen, *Religion of Reason*, pp. 240-41.

"The more recent development of Judaism only begins, significantly enough, in the age of the German enlightenment; it comes about in connection with changes in the attitude toward the ceremonial law." *Ibid.*, p. 375. The influence of Kant was so pervasive that Martin Buber (1878-1965) offered for Reform or liberal Jewish sentiments what is tantamount to a Jewish humanism. For Buber, humanism was central. He endorsed what he termed a "'faithful humanism' which differed from the humanism of Erasmus's day. Today, he said, humanity and faith no longer appear as two separate spheres." Audrey Hodes, *Martin Buber* (New York: Viking Press, 1971), pp. 214-15. Buber aspired to a religious humanism without Kantian constraints. As Franz Rosenzweig (1886-1929) remarked in a letter to Buber, "Earlier centuries had already reduced the teachings to a genteel poverty, to a few fundamental concepts; it remained for the nineteenth to pursue this as a consistent method, with the utmost seriousness. You have liberated the teaching from this circumscribed sphere and, in so doing, removed us from the imminent danger of making our spiritual Judaism depend on whether or not it was possible for us to be followers of Kant." Rosenzweig, *On Jewish Learning*, ed. N. N. Glatzer (New York: Schocken Books, 1965), pp. 76-77. Despite Rosenzweig's remarks, Buber's views resonated with and had roots in Kant's Enlightenment hopes for a religion of morality, justice, and perpetual peace, which would break free of the constraints of tradition. Buber perceptively saw himself at one with these aspirations, as he saw himself at one with the post-traditional spirit of Vatican II and Pope John XXIII.

"We have radically altered the circumstances of our lives," he said to me. "We have our own state, for the first time in nineteen centuries. And yet no Chief Rabbi of Israel has found the courage to say, 'Come, let us acknowledge this revolutionary alteration of our situation and institute the reforms which must flow from it.' We need someone who would do for Judaism what Pope John XXIII has done for the Catholic Church." (This was during the Second Vatican Council.) "Perhaps we need a Sanhedrin: an assembly of religious leaders from all over the world. A kind of World Jewish Council, which would bring the laws up to date and would discuss such vital issues as war and poverty, on which our organized religion is almost silent.
"But if a religion is to stay fresh and spontaneous, the only way is for it to change itself constantly, to renew itself in each generation, from the inside. Else it will harden and die, even though it might not be aware of its approaching death." Hodes, *Martin Buber*, p. 74.

Buber's influence was far greater on Christians of a liberal cosmopolitan commitment than on believing observant Jews. See *ibid.*, pp. 176-189.

89. Taylor provides a very useful characterization of Hegel's recasting of religion, and in particular of Christianity.

Thus the Hegelian ontology itself in which everything can be grasped by reason because everything is founded on rational necessity is ultimately incompatible with Christian faith. ...Hegel himself was the first 'death of God' theologian. For we have seen that Christ's death plays a crucial and necessary role as the indispensable basis for the coming of the Spirit and hence the Spiritualization of God's presence, which is the same as the building of this presence into the life of the community. Men must first of all see God concentrated in a single man. But this point of concentration has to disappear, if the fuller truth is to emerge that men carry God as a community, that God is in each and beyond each. God is like a flame which passes from mortal candle to mortal candle, each destined to light and go out, but the flame to be eternal.
Charles Taylor, *Hegel* (Cambridge: Cambridge University Press, 1975), p. 494.

90. This account of Hegel and his understanding of religion and God presupposes a non-meta-physical reading of his work. See, for example, Engelhardt and Pinkard (eds.), *Hegel Reconsidered*. This approach allows one to address realities not in terms of their existence as particular beings, but rather in terms of their categorial significance. For an example of such an account, see especially chapter 4 in H. T. Engelhardt, Jr., *Mind-Body: A Categorial Relation* (The Hague: Martinus Nijhoff, 1973).

Given the difficult character of much of Hegel's argument, his non-metaphysical position has often been difficult to discern. Heinrich Heine (1797-1856) gives a clear and somewhat cynical presentation of Hegel's views in this matter with regard to God and religion. As Walter Kaufmann notes, Heine's conversations with Hegel left him convinced that Hegel was a humanist opposed to traditional Christianity and theism.

> One beautiful starry-skied evening, we two stood next to each other at a window, and I, a young man of twenty-two who had just eaten well and had good coffee, enthused about the stars and called them the abode of the blessed. But the master grumbled to himself: "The stars, hum! hum! the stars are only a gleaming leprosy in the sky." For God's sake, I shouted, then there is no happy locality up there to reward virtue after death? But he, staring at me with his pale eyes, said cuttingly: "So you want to get a tip for having nursed your sick mother and for not having poisoned your dear brother?" – Saying that, he looked around anxiously, but he immediately seemed reassured when he saw that it was only Heinrich Beer, who had approached to invite him to play whist. ... I was young and proud, and it pleased my vanity when I learned from Hegel that it was not the dear God who lived in heaven that was God, as my grandmother supposed, but I myself here on earth. This foolish pride did not by any means have a corrupting influence on my feelings; rather it raised them to the level of heroism. At that time I put so much effort into generosity and self-sacrifice that I certainly outshone the most brilliant feats of those good Philistines of virtue who merely acted from a sense of duty and obeyed the moral laws. After all, I myself was now the living moral law and the source of all right and sanctions.
> Quoted in Walter Kaufmann, *Hegel: A Reinterpretation* (New York: Doubleday Anchor, 1966), pp. 366-7 [Heinrich Heine, *Geständnisse*, in *Sämtliche Werke*, XIV (1862), 275-82].

91. J. Hoffmeister (ed.), *Briefe von und an Hegel* (Hamburg: Meiner, 1952-60), III, 29, quoted in John Edward Toews, *Hegelianism* (Cambridge: Cambridge University Press, 1980), p. 90. It is interesting to note that Hegel felt that Kapp had plagiarized from his own lectures. Hegel, *Hegel: The Letters*, trans. Clark Butler and Christiane Seiler (Bloomington: Indiana University Press, 1984), p. 507.

92. Kierkegaard is quite emphatic in his commitment to be true to a Christianity that does not change. He is in this sense opposed to *aggiornamento*.

> Therefore, we insist on a Christianity that can be brought into harmony with all the rest of our life, corresponding to the change that has occurred in the human race through increasing enlightenment and culture and liberation from all unworthy pressures, or at least in what amounts to the main stem of the human race – the cultured public. ... No, Christianity cannot be changed ....
> Kierkegaard, *Judge for Yourself!*, eds. Howard Hong and Edna Hong (Princeton, NJ: Princeton University Press, 1990), p. 155, XII 428-9.

93. Hermann Deuser, "Religious Dialectics and Christology," in *The Cambridge Companion to Kierkegaard*, eds. Alastair Hannay and Gordon Marino (Cambridge: Cambridge University Press, 1998), p. 385f.

94. "Being a Christian in Christendom in plain conformity is as impossible as doing gymnastics in a straitjacket." Søren Kierkegaard, *Papers and Journals*, trans. Alastair Hannay (London: Penguin, 1996), p. 640, 54 XI 2 A 349.

95. "Part of the genius of the Danish philosopher-theologian Søren Kierkegaard (1813-55) was a sure grasp of the idea that faith is not primarily intellectual in nature. In Kierkegaard's language, faith is a passion, and the passions are enduring traits that shape a person's character. ... He maintains, in fact, that faith is something like a skill, a skill which is required if one is to grasp religious truths." C. Stephen Evans, *Faith Beyond Reason* (Grand Rapids, MI: W. Eerdsmans, 1998), p. vii.

96. "And with the professor came scientific scholarship, and with scholarship came doubts, and with scholarship and doubts came the scholarly public, and then came reasons pro and contra...." Kierkegaard, *Judge for Yourself!*, p. 195, XII 462.

97. Merold Westphal, "Kierkegaard and Hegel," in *The Cambridge Companion to Kierkegaard*, p. 111.

98. Kierkegaard, *Concluding Unscientific Postscript*, in *Kierkegaard's Writings* XII.1, eds. and trans. Howard Hong and Edna Hong (Princeton, NJ: Princeton University Press, 1992), vol. 1, p. 611, VII 532.

99. "Christianity, as it is in the New Testament, focuses on man's will; everything turns on that, on transforming the will; all the phrases (renounce the world, deny one's self, die from the world, etc.; similarly, hate oneself, love God, etc.), everything relates to this fundamental idea in Christianity, what makes it what it is: transformation of will." Kierkegaard, *Papers and Journals*, p. 618, 54 XI 2 A 86.

100. "Boesen asked Kierkegaard whether he would like to receive the last rites. 'Yes, indeed,' said Kierkegaard, 'but from a layman, not a priest.' 'That can hardly be done,' said Boesen. 'Then I'll die without.' 'You can't do that!' said Boesen. 'The matter is not in question, I have made up my mind. The priests are royal functionaries, and royal functionaries have nothing to do with Christianity.'" Kierkegaard, *Papers and Journals*, pp. 654-655.

101. C. Stephen Evans, *Faith Beyond Reason* (Grand Rapids, MI: Eerdmans, 1998), pp. 109, 152-153.

102. Kierkegaard, *Fear and Trembling*, eds. and trans. Howard Hong and Edna Hong (Princeton: Princeton University Press, 1983), p. 56, III 106.

103. Kierkegaard, *Concluding Unscientific Postscript*, vol. 1, p. 210, VII 176.

104. Kierkegaard, *Practice in Christianity*, eds. and trans. Howard Hong and Edna Hong (Princeton: Princeton University Press, 1991), pp. 161-162, XII 151.

105. Kierkegaard, *Concluding Unscientific Postscript*, vol. 1, p. 245, VII 206.

106. Kierkegaard, *Philosophical Fragments*, p. 14-15, IV 184.

107. "...God is certainly personal, but whether he wishes to be so in relation to the individual depends upon whether it so pleases God. It is the grace of God that he wishes to be personal in relation to you; if you throw away his grace he punishes you by behaving objectively towards you." Kierkegaard, *The Journals of Kierkegaard*, trans. Alexander Dru (New York: Harper, 1959), p. 250, entry from 1854.

108. Kierkegaard, *Concluding Unscientific Postscript*, vol. 1, p. 245, VII 206.

109. *Ibid.*

110. *Ibid.*, p. 246, VII 207.

111. *Ibid.*, p. 247, VII 208.

112. St. John Climacus, *The Ladder of Divine Ascent*, p. 230.

113. This is not to deny that it is a blessing to believe without having encountered the miraculous (John 20:29).

114. "Saints, according to St. Symeon the New Theologian, are 'those who have acquired the whole Christ within them wholly by work and experience and perception and knowledge and vision of God'. From this witness it seems clear that saintliness does not have an abstract and ethical meaning. Saintliness is participation in the uncreated deifying energy of God, and the person deified is a saint. Saints are those who have experience and knowledge and perception and vision of God. They are not simply the good people."
Hierotheos [Vlachos], *The Mind of the Orthodox Church*, trans. Esther Williams (Levadia, Greece: Birth of the Theotokos Monastery, 1998), p. 136.

115. Kierkegaard, *Philosophical Fragments*, eds. and trans. Howard Hong and Edna Hong (Princeton, NJ: Princeton University Press, 1985), p. 104, IV 266.

116. Elder Joseph the Hesychast, *Monastic Wisdom* (Florence, AZ: St. Anthony's Greek Orthodox Monastery, 1998), pp. 19-20.

117. *Ibid.*, p. 84.

118. Kierkegaard is critically sympathetic to the role of monasticism in the Middle Ages. Though he is critical of its externality and much of its substance, he admires its engagement. "The Middle Ages conceived of Christianity along the lines of action, life, existence-transformation. This is the merit. It is another matter that some of the actions they hit upon were strange, that it could think that in itself fasting was Christianity, that entering the monastery, giving everything to the poor ... was supposed to be true imitation. This was an error." *Judge for Yourself!*, p. 192, XII 460.

119. In *Judge for Yourself!*, Kierkegaard portrays subjectivity as engagement in the imitation of Christ without concern for doctrine.

120. For an exploration by Kierkegaard of the claim of a direct revelation from God, see his study of the case of the Danish priest Adolph Adler, who claimed such a revelation. Kierkegaard, *On Authority and Revelation*, trans. Walter Lowrie (New York: Harper and Row, 1966), pp. 105f.

121. Kierkegaard does not deny claims of the experience of God through faith. After all, he speaks of his conversion experience on May 19, 1838. "There is an indescribable joy that is kindled in us just as inexplicably as the apostle's unmotivated exclamation: 'Rejoice, and again I say, Rejoice'." *Papers and Journals*, p. 97, 10:30 a.m. 19 May 38 II A 228. Such experience does not bring knowledge from immediate union setting aside the horizon of immanence.

122. Chapter 4 will explore that knowledge gained through faith that involves an experience of the transcendent God. This will be characterized as a noetic experience of God, an experience by the created of the uncreated. At stake here is a fundamental issue concerning the nature of grace: for an encounter with God to take man beyond the immanent, it must involve uncreated grace, that is, the very uncreated energies of God Himself. Here it is enough to recognize the possibility of such direct experience of God achieved by a faith that leads through illumination to union with God. Noetic knowledge is the realization in this life of the 6th beatitude – "Blessed are the pure in heart, for they shall see God" (Matt 5:8).

123. Given the actual character of St. John of the Ladder's writings, it is ironic that Kierkegaard attributes his authorship of *Philosophical Fragments, or a Fragment of Philosophy* (1844) and *Concluding Unscientific Postscript to the "Philosophical Fragments"* (1846) to Johannes Climacus while ascribing *Fear and Trembling* (1843) to Johannes de Silentio, and *Either/Or* (1843) to Victor Eremita. The significance of his ascribing *Sickness unto Death* (1849) and *Practice in Christianity* (1850) to Johannes Anticlimacus is even more complex. For a brief discussion of the history of Kierkegaard's use of the pseudonym, see Niels Thulstrup, "Commentary," in *Philosophical Fragments*, trans. David Swenson (Princeton: Princeton University Press, 1974), pp. 148-149. Niels Thulstrup quotes Kierkegaard in this matter: "Hegel is a Johannes Climacus who did not, like the giants, storm heaven by setting mountain upon mountain but entered by means of his syllogisms" (*ibid.*, p. 148). Thulstrup also quotes (p. 149) Kierkegaard's remarks that "the pseudonym [used for *The Sickness unto Death*, which had just been delivered to the printer] is called Johannes Anticlimacus in contrast to Climacus, who declared himself not to be a Christian [*Postscript*, p. 19]. Anticlimacus is the opposite extreme in being a Christian to an extraordinary degree, but I myself manage to be no more than a very ordinary Christian." Suffice it to say that Kierkegaard's account of faith runs counter to that of St. John Climacus (c.523-603), the great hesychast, whose dates may have been as late as c.579-649. St. John Climacus took seriously faith's power to disclose the fruit of asceticism: knowledge of God. His

work, *The Ladder of Divine Ascent*, constitutes one of the classic manuals for monks seeking illumination through God's energies. Unlike Kierkegaard, St. John Climacus understood that faith "can make and create all things." *The Ladder of Divine Ascent*, rev. ed. (Boston: Holy Transfiguration Monastery, 1991), p. 225, Step 30.3.

124. Kierkegaard, *Concluding Unscientific Postscript*, vol. 1, p. 204, VII 171.

125. Kierkegaard's account of purity of heart in his *Edifying Discourses in Various Spirits* (1847), as well as in his *Journals*, portrays little sense of an ascetic struggle to holiness. Nor does his account of willing of one thing, namely, God, transform the person who wills to immediacy of union with God.

126. It must be underscored, as many have observed, that Kierkegaard does not use the phrase "leap of faith". His metaphor of leap must be understood in terms of his reaction against the rationality of Hegel's dialectic. "The leap is the most decisive protest against the inverse operation of the [Hegel's] method." Kierkegaard, *Concluding Unscientific Postscript*, vol. 1, p. 105, VII 85.

127. Ingmar Bergman, "Cries and Whispers" in *Four Stories by Ingmar Bergman* (Garden City, NY: Anchor Doubleday, 1976), p. 75.

128. Kierkegaard, *Judge for Yourself!*, p. 207, XII 473.

129. Kierkegaard considers a focus on doctrine as substantively perverting Christian life. "Through the conceiving of Christianity as doctrine, the situation in Christendom has become utter confusion." *Ibid.*, p. 209, XII 474. He does not recognize doctrine as a guide in the life of the Christian. He would have been better served to have argued that a doctrine that cannot be lived is not a Christian doctrine.

130. Alexandria of the 2nd century and later created a highly influential school of philosophical-theological reflection and study. Yet this school never achieved the central importance of the theologians of the Egyptian desert (i.e., the monks). Neither the philosophical concerns of Alexandria nor those of the Christian Hellenists of Constantinople were able to establish a cardinal importance for discursive theology, as the Schoolmen of the 13th century West did for Western Christianity.

3 Christian Bioethics as a Human Project: Taking Immanence Seriously

The Enlightenment's Bequest

Christian bioethics, indeed Christian ethics, as it has come to be understood is impossible. In its rationalist forms, it aspires to a canonical, content-full morality disclosable by reason. In its biblically oriented forms, it seeks a grounding in records of a two-thousand-years-old revelation. In either case, it pursues a transcendent foundation within the bounds of immanence. Such projects misunderstand the possibilities for both morality and Christianity. By seeking the transcendent within the immanent, Christian morality is reduced to a human morality, a limited project grounded in humans, or at least in finite persons.[1] Christian ethics ceases to recognize that, in the face of the Transcendent, morality is primarily a discipline for turning to God, so as to love Him with one's whole heart, and then to love one's neighbor as oneself. Once morality ceases to be theocentric, it becomes a puzzle as to why David prays in repentance for adultery and murder, "Against Thee only have I sinned and done this evil before Thee" (Ps 50:4, LXX).

The difficulty is that one cannot by sound rational argument establish which content-full morality is canonical without begging the question or engaging in an infinite regress. Similarly, one cannot find in the conditioned character of texts and oral traditions the presence of the transcendent. If, as the Enlightenment claimed, the bounds of immanence cannot be pierced by the energies of God, if there are no miracles and no communion with God, then the horizon of the finite is all-encompassing. Insofar as Christian bioethics is dependent on a revelation available in immanent experience, it finds God absent. If God is available to us only through arguments, texts, and oral traditions, God is obscured by the immanent, the finite, the contingent, and the historically conditioned. Both Kant and Kierkegaard appreciated this point: if all one encounters is phenomenal, socially conditioned reality, God as transcendent is inaccessible. Moreover, an as-if, immanent idea of God cannot guarantee the harmony of the right with the good, or an accord between the justification of morality and the motivation to be moral. The state of affairs confronting a Christian bioethics can be summed up thusly: if Christian bioethics turns to secular moral philosophy for its grounding, it finds diverse foundations and fractures into numerous content-full bioethics. If Christian bioethics attempts to ground its claims in a revelation encountered only in immanent terms, it finds no transcendent grounding. Christian bioethics confronts a plurality of socio-historically grounded accounts of revelation and transcendence. Most importantly, it does not find God. In this very important sense, God has died for Western ethics. He is defined by His inaccessibility. For Western morality, He is silent, inactive, unresponsive, and unreachable.

The difficulties appear insurmountable both for Christian and for secular bioethics. One needs a canonical morality that can declare itself as such. To establish a particular, content-full morality as canonical, one must reach to a truth that transcends any controversy about its standing, so as to avoid begging the question. The difficulty is that access to such truth seems in principle blocked. The Western Scholastic assumption of the congeniality of the knower and the known goes aground on the problem of discursively showing when one knows that one knows the character of the known. One needs to be able to establish when one knows truly without assuming what is at issue. In addition, one needs to know whether there is a personal, omnipotent, omniscient God to unite the dimensions of morality. If one cannot secure access to such transcendence, one is left with a fractured human-centered morality. Both Kant and Hegel in different ways recognize this circumstance: mankind appears surrounded by an impenetrable horizon of immanence. Kierkegaard protests against that immanence but cannot break through to transcendence. Nor, for Kierkegaard, can we recognize when the Transcendent breaks through to us. It is not without accident that Protestantism breaks into a plurality of moral and religious understandings. It lacks either an external force to contain it or an internal power to guide it.

In the face of such challenges, one can embrace objectivity as intersubjectivity, not as correspondence with a reality external to consciousness. Moral truth becomes humanly constituted, if not conventional. The character of the sphere of moral immanence becomes constituted by us. Confronted with an irresolvable moral pluralism, secular bioethics turns to permission and procedural solutions such as free and informed consent, the market, and limited democracy to secure immanent moral authorization for common endeavors. Why should a secularized, post-traditional Christianity not do the same? What other options are open to such a Christianity but to seek the resources for a religious ethics within man himself? Faced with a dialectic between an objectivity reduced to intersubjectivity and a subjectivity unable to break through to transcendence, why not affirm with Hegel that thought and being are one? If one cannot encounter the truly transcendent, one can still embrace as the transcendent that immanent that endures beyond particular knowers: it is the only reality to which finite beings can reach. It may then seem plausible that human life projects can sustain the religious. For those ignorant of the real power of the truly transcendent, the immanent marked with intimations of transcendence may seem sufficiently rich to constitute a full religious life.

What follows is an account of a Christianity, Christian ethics, and Christian bioethics, which cannot be avoided by a post-Enlightenment culture that has closed itself off from the transcendence of God. Neither the theological reflections of the Scholastics nor the investigation of scriptural scholars can disclose the presence or requirements of a transcendent God. Philosophical reflections are undertaken with concepts condign for immanent truths. Scriptures as literature are always socio-historically conditioned and in themselves not presentations of the transcendent.

This circumstance frames the contemporary religious predicament of the West. It sets the condition for a post-traditional Christian bioethics: a bioethics without transcendence. Kant and Hegel, each in his own way, correctly recognize the invisibility of the truly transcendent within the sphere of the immanent. They recognize as well the attractiveness of a cosmopolitan rational religion aimed at supporting a global ethics, or for Hegel the culmination of world history in philosophy as absolute spirit. The Christian ethics and bioethics sketched in this chapter are an epiphany of the consequences of this loss of the transcendent, the loss of an experience of the God Who is personal, Who commands, Who works miracles, and Who is radically other.

Knowledge, Morality, and Religion as Limited Human Projects

Kant was not as bold in rethinking the character of human morality as he was in rethinking the character of human knowledge. He did not recognize that his Copernican revolution can also radically reorient morality, establishing a purely agent-grounded framework for moral coherence. Because Kant attempted to ground freedom in a concrete understanding of rationality and therefore autonomy, he did not recognize the centrality of permission. Different persons may have different rankings of values, though they can still share a common world of moral responsibility, sustained through deriving from permission authority for blame and praise. Secular morality provides a practice within which humans can collaborate in health care with a common moral authority, but without a common, content-full, normative account of human flourishing. Here, Richard Rorty's observations in *Contingency, Irony, and Solidarity* are to the point.[2] We cannot bootstrap ourselves out of our immanent circumstances to a transcendent reality that can order the diversity of religious and particular secular moral visions, much less disclose which one is canonical. We cannot find in our moral reflections, which are bound to our possible empirical experience, a grounding in a guiding transcendent truth beyond the horizon of moral agency.

This immanence of a merely intersubjective reality and morality is not hostile to transcendence. *Sensu stricto*, it is only a *modus vivendi* available when one encounters metaphysical and moral strangers. It also makes space so that persons can collaborate with metaphysical and moral friends and even join in turning to and experiencing the transcendent God. Strictly, this framework of intersubjective reality and morality is neutral to the recognition of transcendent truth. As an element of the Enlightenment's project, this neutrality is culturally transformed from indifference into a commitment against the possibility of recognizing and experiencing the presence of the transcendent. The result is an ethos of immanence, hostile to the metaphysics and morality of transcendence. Kant provides the framework of a metaphysical and moral understanding that in its revolutionary force shows how the Enlightenment project can reach further than Kant is willing. Even though Kant invites us to abandon a theocentric justification of knowledge and morality, he returns again and again to the centrality of at least the idea of God. The regulative and moral functions of the idea of God remain central for Kant,[3] though knowledge, morality, religion, Christianity, and bioethics can be construed in the terms of finite discursive rationality.[4] Moreover, Kant's free choice is guided by a content-rich view of autonomy.

Empirical scientists have been able to step beyond metaphysical disputes by approaching reality within phenomenal experience via commonly agreed-upon *ceteris paribus* conditions, which fix points of reference within an intersubjectively defined domain of objectivity. Within such bounds, one can compare claims regarding reality. One can choose among explanations in terms of which are better at providing falsifiable, empirical predictions. Reference to a deeper reality is not needed beyond that disclosable within the ambit of empirical findings. On the one hand, in the empirical sciences there are agreed-upon basic parameters, which are established by convention. On the other hand, there is an encounter with an external reality that imposes explanatory costs. In default of a common metaphysics, empirical science can make do with the grammar of intersubjective empirical collaboration, eschewing any ontology not grounded in immanence.

The default position available for a secular morality and bioethics is, as we have seen, in important aspects similar. The objectivity of secular morality and bioethics is found in their intersubjectivity. Such a bioethics cannot take account of community-independent moral standards or of the wishes of God. It can appeal only to the agreement of persons disposed to collaborate. The authority of general secular moral undertakings is rooted not in independent moral standards, but in actual moral agreements. Unlike empirical science, however, there is no external moral reality to impose costs on a false moral account as occurs with empirical accounts. Compare, for example, a dispute as to whether the human immunodeficiency virus or some other factor is more important in the etiology of AIDS (acquired immunodeficiency syndrome) with a dispute as to whether liberty or equality is more important for the moral life or for a just health care policy.[5] In the first case, appeals to observed associations between HIV and various factors in the development of AIDS, as well as the finding of intervening pathological changes, make accepting a particular factor (i.e., HIV) as a necessary condition for the appearance for the disease (i.e., AIDS) very difficult to avoid. In the second case, as we have found, depending on the ranking of liberty and equality, the costs one observes in comparing alternative moral approaches to health care policy formation are radically different. There is no particular ranking of liberty and equality favored by external reality, since what is at stake is the evaluation of reality, at least social reality. One cannot discover whether a liberty-promoting or an equality-promoting approach to health care is to be preferred, given their consequences, unless one already knows how to rank or order such values or goals as liberty and equality in order to compare the consequences. The intersubjective morality binding moral strangers is by default grounded for its authority in the permission of the persons who collaborate. They must decide, not discover, how to rank values.

Morality (and therefore bioethics) are by default reinterpreted in terms of the agent. The secular Western culture nurtured by the Enlightenment cannot draw on revealed religion in giving an account of knowledge or the content of morality. It remains restricted within an immanent human-based grounding. Indeed, the Enlightenment portrayed humans as finally coming into possession of their own history and destiny only when they recognize themselves in authority over themselves. Kant's Enlightenment proclaimed the rational self-governance of individuals, their liberation from superstition and the constraints of tradition.

Enlightenment is man's release from his self-incurred tutelage. Tutelage is man's inability to make use of his understanding without direction from another. Self-incurred is his tutelage when its cause lies not in lack of reason but in lack of resolution and courage to use it without direction from another. *Sapere aude*! "Have courage to use your own reason!" – that is the motto of enlightenment.[6]

The result is to recast morality (and by implication bioethics) and religion in fully human terms. As Kant stresses, though actual religions differ, "moral faith is everywhere the same."[7] Religion is understood in terms of morality, and morality is understood in terms of discursive rationality. Through the identification of religion, morality, and discursive rationality, Kant can affirm that human knowers and agents are the keystones of reality which is now immanent. In stepping away from God, the Enlightenment completed the Renaissance project of placing humans centrally. Although Kant's morality is for moral agents as such, it is grounded in terms of the human predicament.

Kant's account of morality offers the possibility of this further development in a direction he does not take. Morality (including bioethics) can be made fully subject to the force of the revolution Kant recognized as unavoidable for a secular account of empirical knowledge and science. Morality can be made fully agent-centered and in the process be freed of the value assumptions that Kant unwittingly incorporated in his moral theory, especially the lexical prior ordering of the value of freedom and rationality, which he implicitly endorses. It is because freedom is given a trumping lexical priority that Kant will not allow one freely to decide not to be free. In this way, Kant seeks to exclude suicide (and thereby physician-assisted suicide and voluntary euthanasia).[8] *Pace* Kant, Kant's morality can be recast in terms of freedom as the source of moral authority. Secular morality can be recognized as a framework for free choice, a nexus of responsible action, by grounding it in permission. So reconceived, it is not the values of the agent or any values supposedly integral to moral agency that sustain the framework of morality, but the agency of the agent: the bare possibility of giving permission. One can then step away from particular rankings of values, as science can step away from metaphysical accounts of the deep structure of reality as well as from commitments to any particular empirical findings. One instead affirms a procedural moral framework grounded in permission as the basis for a bioethics that can compass moral strangers, as modern science allows the collaboration of metaphysical strangers (i.e., persons with irresolveable disagreements regarding the deep structure of reality, such as whether there are immortal souls) who can still resolve empirical controversies as controversies about phenomenal reality. Secular morality (including bioethics) must become, as has science, procedural rather than committed to particular content.[9]

Just as one can collaborate scientifically in a world of metaphysical strangers (i.e., those with whom one has disagreements regarding the metaphysical structure of reality and shares no avenue for resolving such controversies by sound rational agreement or by an appeal to a commonly recognized authority) by affirming a limited, immanent intersubjective understanding of scientific objectivity, so, too, one can collaborate with moral strangers (i.e., those with whom one has disagreements regarding the content of morality and with whom one lacks a way to resolve such controversies by sound rational argument or by an appeal to a commonly recognized moral authority) by entering into a similar, limited world of intersubjective moral collaboration.[10] Just as metaphysical strangers can collaborate in empirical science only as long as they ignore questions of metaphysical significance, moral strangers can collaborate in framing health care policy only insofar as they ignore the particular content-full moral differences that separate them (e.g., differing views as to whether the human genome is unconditionally morally inviolable). They must instead focus on an intersubjective world of common moral authority drawn from the consent of those who participate. Deep metaphysical views of reality are simply not pertinent when one is engaged in the immanent undertakings of empirical science. When one does science with metaphysical strangers, metaphysical insights cannot be shared. Similarly, even if one has an intuition of what a just price might be, this is irrelevant to the practices of a secular health care market. So, too, even if one has an intuition of a deep good or rightness characterizing limited democracies, such moral insights are not directly pertinent to a general secular moral justification of limited democracies. It is sufficient that one acknowledge the role of permission in grounding collaborative endeavors such as free and informed consent, the contracts of physicians and patients, health care markets, and the health care policies of limited democracies. The practices themselves are not grounded in particular values or orderings of moral principles, but in the authorization of persons.

In this way secular morality (including bioethics) becomes a way of resolving controversies intersubjectively. No value standard or ordering is presumed. It is simply that a practice of collaboration is possible, envisaged, and engaged. Within this practice, and the procedures it grounds (e.g., contracts), controversies can be resolved. Outside this practice, without the entrance of a truth accepted by all, moral controversies are irresolvable with a moral authority commonly available to moral strangers. With an appeal to permission, the standard for resolving moral controversies becomes integral to the practice of morality, all without affirming any particular ranking of values or of moral principles. Permission is the keystone of general secular moral authority, which principle cannot be avoided when one turns to collaborate with moral strangers in framing secular health care policy. This approach to morality, when confronted with moral diversity and trapped within immanence, seemingly offers to post-traditional Christian bioethics a way to justify its authority in the sparse conditions for morally authoritative common collaboration.[11] In this fashion, not just secular but also Christian bioethics are to be subjected to the Copernican revolution of grounding all in the subject, not the object of either knowledge or morality. The result is Kant's fully post-traditional Christianity. Christian bioethics can be grounded in the permission of moral agents. Post-traditional Christian morality and bioethics thus radically reconceived become different from anything to which Christianity has traditionally aspired.

Kant's Copernican revolution (i.e., the recognition that, in the absence of an experience of God, humans provide the ground for human knowledge) has been brought to Christianity (i.e., a post-Enlightenment Christianity) and to Christian bioethics. In a post-Enlightenment culture, one moves away from Western Christian questions (i.e., which do not recognize the possibility of the experience of God) such as

> How can one by rational investigation disclose the existence and nature of God as well as the substance of His commandments and His intentions regarding bioethics? and

> How can one by a scholarly investigation of texts and oral tradition discover the substance of God's revelation, so as to give content to a Christian bioethics?

Such questions presuppose a discursive rational access to the transcendent, or a disclosure of the transcendent within the socio-historically conditioned sphere of the immanent. Such questions are replaced by a question that refocuses religious interests within the sphere of the immanent.

> How can people in community investigate, clarify, revise, and renew their religious-moral and metaphysical commitments and narratives and then affirm them in their own right and as a part of the human cultural inheritance, providing, among other things, a Christian bioethics?

Christianity and Christian bioethics are seen to be grounded not in God but in a grammar of consent from human persons who have concerns about the sacred, the holy, and the transcendent. The transcendent is immanentized and articulated within particular clusters of religious narratives. Religious moral claims are domesticated and given their meaning within particular finite provinces of religious experience.

Christianity traditionally understood itself as proclaiming the entry of God Who is transcendent into the immanence of our history: God becoming "man that we might be made God."[12] Indeed, Christianity recognizes that man's isolation in the sphere of immanence is the result of the Fall. After all, before the expulsion, God walked in the Garden with Adam and Eve (Gen. 3:8). A reconceived Christian morality as grounded in human agency and at home in immanence denies the traditional, absolute proclamation of the presence of a transcendent God Who can be experienced and Who works wonders. Instead, such an immanently recast Christianity relocates itself and its bioethics in terms congenial to late Greco-Roman paganism, against which early Christianity stood without compromise. Christianity becomes one among a diversity of religious narratives. Consider the account given of Severus Alexander (A.D. 222-235).

> In the early morning hours he would worship in the sanctuary of his Lares, in which he kept statues of the deified emperors – of whom, however, only the best had been selected – and also of certain holy souls, among them Apollonius, and, according to a contemporary writer, Christ, Abraham, Orpheus, and others of this same character and, besides, the portraits of his ancestors.[13]

Christianity, when understood in these terms, no longer advances its characteristically exclusive moral and metaphysical claims.

When Christianity claims to be the only true faith, rather than accommodating to syncretical pagan understandings, it invites persecution for being intolerant. It was Severus Alexander's antecedent, Septimus Severus (A.D. 193-211), who in A.D. 202 persecuted the Christians and, among other things, brought Clement of Alexandria to flee Egypt. Christianity reconstrued in the terms of Severus Alexander becomes not only tolerant but accepting of other religious views as disclosing alternative perspectives on the human condition. Though few pagans may have believed in their gods, and instead supported their cults only as sources of cultural orientation, still, the traditional Christian view has been that it is better to die confessing the faith than to endorse paganism with even a few grains of incense. After the Copernican revolution of faith, post-traditional Christians and pagans can join in prayer, for both are focused on the truly human rather than the transcendentally divine. They are not oriented to different transcendent truths. This ecumenical reconciliation between post-traditional Christianity and paganism can celebrate the immanent world they share. A Christian bioethics sustained by such a Christianity would have become fundamentally post-Christian.

Three Visions of the Secular Cosmopolis: Living in a World Deaf to God

The Enlightenment's cosmopolitan hope was to overcome the divisive particularities of history, tradition, and social contexts. It aspired to a universal ethics binding all in a rational universal religion of morality, a secular *religio catholica*. It followed the hope that the seemingly interminable wars and conflicts that bloodied mankind's history could be a matter of the past when persons no longer saw themselves as first and foremost members of particular religious communities separated from others by disagreements over the nature of transcendent truth. Instead, all were to regard themselves first as members of a moral community uniting all humans in a common set of moral commitments. This aspiration to a cosmopolitan moral perspective resonates with the universalistic rationalistic character of Roman Catholic Scholastic moral reflections, in particular, with its understanding of natural law. It is more than an accident of history that at the beginning of the 19th century supporters of early Unitarian movements in Boston referred to themselves as Catholic Christians, as many Roman Catholics do today.[14] The secular, cosmopolitan aspirations of the Enlightenment, the French Revolution, and even Napoleon have roots in the rationalism of Western Christianity.

The difficulty with this cosmopolitan universalistic moral perspective is, as we have seen, that it cannot discover a particular, canonical, content-full moral perspective. If this limit on moral rationality is taken seriously, the cosmopolitan moral perspective becomes a libertarian cosmopolitanism. It provides a content-less, procedural moral framework through which individuals and communities can collaborate with each other. Because the religious and secular moral aspiration of the West is to more than a procedure for negotiation among moral strangers, there are strong motivations to regard this procedure for gaining common authority as if it were a flesh-and-bones morality. This involves the category mistake of confusing free choice as a source of authority with liberty as a value. This category mistake becomes the basis for affirming as universal a particular moral vision. This affirmation of liberty invites the development of a morality focused on the cardinal value of autonomous choice, including the conditions for the realization of this liberty. This leads to framing a full-fledged, liberal cosmopolitan moral view.

The libertarian cosmopolis as a framework
If secular moral rationality cannot deliver a justification for a particular content-full moral view, then, as chapter 1 shows, moral authority must be derived from common

consent. While fully recognizing the transcendent God, one can also recognize that others are deaf to Him. With those with whom one shares a social world in which God as transcendent is not recognized, one can without rejecting God, indeed while proclaiming the Gospel, collaborate through consent in common endeavors (of course, invoking one's rights to privacy, one must refuse collaboration in evil). One abandons the project of discursively justifying a canonical content-full morality for all, acknowledging that one cannot establish such a morality without already having the foundation for the morality one seeks. One must already know which moral standard should guide (e.g., which thin theory of the good, which ordering of which guiding moral intuitions, which discount rate for goods or preferences over time, which balancing of intuitions, etc., should be invoked in resolving concrete bioethical disputes?). The default position is instead to ask the question: who has agreed to do what with whom? In this case one derives authority from the agreement of those who participate in an undertaking. One can justify from agreement the moral content of a particular religious community's commitments.

In the case of secular social institutions, one gains by appeals to consent a way of morally justifying the authority of common endeavors without needing to discover an external, canonical, moral standard. For instance, as noted in chapter 1, the moral authority of many widespread contemporary practices and institutions bearing on health care is rooted in permission, such as free and informed consent (i.e., the consensual collaboration of physicians and patients), forbearance rights (i.e., rights to withdraw permission), rights to privacy (i.e., the secular moral right to engage in mutually consented-to projects without the interference of others, such as venerating relics in the hope of a divine cure for a serious disease, though some might find this improper), contracts with others (e.g., the establishment of religiously informed networks of health care), interactions in the market (e.g., the purchase of health care service one finds religiously acceptable), and the creation of limited democracies (i.e., the creation of governments morally neutral in not constraining collaborative undertakings with consenting individuals, even if many hold such actions improper, thus allowing for a range of religiously diverse approaches to health care). These institutions and practices can be recognized as morally authorized not because they are valued, but because they can bind individuals with the common secular moral authority of consent. Persons across the world can be recognized as bound and united by this source of moral authority: they live implicitly in a libertarian cosmopolis.

This procedural framework allows individuals with diverse moral commitments in their own moral communities to act with common moral authority and live peaceably within a larger secular society, as long as they draw common authority from agreement. Such a framework is materially equivalent to a limited democracy with robust rights to privacy not only for individuals, but for communities. A distinction is thus drawn between (1) morally thick communities grounded in the choice of their members to associate in the pursuit of a particular understanding of the good and/or human flourishing versus (2) secular societies that provide a neutral space for individuals on their own or within communities to engage in limited consensual collaboration while the peace of that society is secured by (3) a limited democracy committed to recognizing the difference between community and society. Within such a framework, one can imagine numerous moral communities, including traditional Christians, peaceably pur-

suing their own understandings of the good human life. Such non-geographically located communities can establish their own institutions for the provision not only of
religious services, but of health care and welfare as well. The term "non-geographically
located communities of belief" identifies a phenomenon ubiquitous in North America
and increasingly in Western Europe: there are few areas in which all the inhabitants
belong to one religion. In the West, although there are enclaves of religious uniformity
(e.g., monasteries, communes, or Amish farming communities), these tend to be the
exception and are often lodged within areas of the same polity lacking any or many of
their co-religionists. Religious communities no longer find themselves located in particular geographical areas, but instead maintaining institutions and facilities that exist
side-by-side with institutions and facilities of other religions. This portrayal of religious communities with their own moral understandings and institutions embedded
within a larger secular societal framework should not be regarded as radically different
from the circumstances in which many currently find themselves in the West. Religions
are non-politically empowered, limited, non-geographically located communities: the
institutions of the various religions can and do exist side by side. Roman Catholics,
Jews, Mohammedans, Baptists, and Hindus can live together in areas, even neighbor-
hoods, administered by no particular religion with no religious body directly claiming
a monopoly on force, as do secular states. In a particular neighborhood, there can then
be numerous different religions "ministering" to the spiritual and moral needs of their
members who may be living next to each other but not constituting one moral community.

The point in all of this is to recognize that non-geographically located communities
of belief can maintain the social fabric of their moral commitments without functioning as do large-scale states, which directly impose their authority on all within their
geographical area of governance. This appeal to the vision of a neutral state compassing numerous non-geographically-based moral communities does not deny that in non-
limited democracies religions with significant influence at times do impose their will
through the democratic process. So, too, particular secular moral understandings are
imposed. For example, physicians who find particular medical interventions so unacceptable on religious grounds that they may not even refer patients to providers of
those services currently may find themselves legally obliged to do so or face civil suit.
This may occur with respect to abortion when a physician on religious grounds will not
(and for that matter morally should not) even refer a patient wanting an abortion to a
provider. In principle, such legal abuse of the consciences of physicians should not
occur. In a sufficiently limited constitutional democracy, such impositions on physicians would never occur.[15]

The structure of a truly limited democracy should give sufficient space for communities and individuals peaceably to act on their own view of morality and religion with
their consenting members. From the outside, religious communities can be regarded as
deriving their moral authority from the consent of those who participate. Indeed, this
is how one should gauge the moral authority of a church body when one does not
consider it as acting with the authority of God. For example, John Locke accents the
voluntary nature of ecclesial bodies. "A church then I take to be a voluntary society of
men, joining themselves together of their own accord... "[16] Under this model, as we
will see in chapter 7, non-geographically located religious communities could offer the

possibility of numerous parallel, even international, religious health care networks, each with its own bioethics. Religious and other communities could maintain their own moralities in their various religious, educational, and health care institutions, although they would need to authorize and sustain facilities in different locations, independently of overarching political structures. From the outside, their authority must be regarded as legitimate through the consent of the members of these communities. That is, non-geographically located religious communities can draw general secular moral authority from the consent of their members, while being constrained to live with moral diversity. After all, they themselves will enjoy the space that such diversity leaves for others. As paradigm cases of such morally thick communities, one might think of Hassidic Jews and the Amish. Being a member of such a community trumps commitments to all other communities, so that such membership becomes radically secondary and qualified. Thus, being a Texan, even a member of the Sons of the Republic of Texas, will not be as important as being Hassidic Jew or Amish. Most individuals, unfortunately, will live in moral communities that are both wrongly directed and morally incoherent. In principle, with the consent of their members, communities should even be free to impose on their members and their institutions their own civil and criminal law. The libertarian cosmopolitan framework offers a universal structure for taking moral diversity, community integrity, and individual authorization seriously. It does not deny the existence or experience of a transcendent God. Instead, it offers a moral perspective for common collaboration when all do not hear God and turn to Him.

The libertarian cosmopolis as a way of life

The libertarian cosmopolitan framework presumes one already has an understanding of morality and human flourishing, which one shares with members of one's own community. After all, one appeals to permission when one wishes to collaborate with moral strangers, persons with whom one does not share a sufficiently thick view of morality so as to be able to resolve controversies by sound rational argument or by invoking a commonly acknowledged moral authority. This strategy for collaborating with moral strangers suggests that one has moral friends: people with whom one does in fact share a substantive understanding of rights, the good, and virtue. But what if this suggestion is false? What if the chaos of the moral life is such that many people possess no coherent understanding of the right, the good, and the virtuous? Thoroughly post-modern persons that not only have no moral narrative to share with others but also no coherent moral account of their own lives are exactly such individuals. Life happens to them, including their passions. They are persons without a moral plot for their own biographies. They have desires, impulses, urges, needs, wants, and concerns, but no moral projects that shape and unite their lives as a whole. In particular, they have no coherent sense of good or evil to structure their life projects. This does not mean that such persons lack coherence to the point of suffering from a moral thought disorder disabling them from acting as moral agents. They can quite coherently and accountably seek satisfaction, fulfillment, and happiness. They simply lack a coherent substantive personal moral narrative. Instead, their life is a sequence of happenings.

Moral issues also tend to be transformed into aesthetic concerns insofar as moral concerns lack normative moral status apart from being chosen. Because rationality cannot establish canonical moral content, morality is grounded in a will unguided by content-full normative constraints. The goal of the agent can range from that of a Nietzschean will to power to the aesthete's will to fulfillment in a life that is beautiful and pleasant. The last has a profound resonance with Greco-Roman pursuit of that which is truly human[17] as, for example, a passage from Marcus Terentius Varro (116-27 B.C.) indicates.

> ... we wish to have a house not merely that we may be under a roof and in a safe place into which necessity has crowded us together, but also that we may be where we may continue to experience the pleasures of life; and we wish to have table-vessels that are not merely suitable to hold our food, but also beautiful in form and shaped by an artist – for one thing is enough for the human animal, and quite another thing satisfies human refinement [*humanitate*]: any cup at all is satisfactory to a man parched with thirst, but any cup is inferior to the demands of refinement [*human-itate*] unless it is artistically beautiful: – but as we have digressed from the matter of utility to that of pleasure, it is a fact that in such a case greater pleasure is often got from difference of appearance than from likeness.[18]

Such aesthetes can tie their biographies together in the pursuit of refined satisfaction. Or, they can simply seek satisfaction of any kind, limited only by the constraint of never using others without their permission. As soon as such persons seek to give to their lives a content drawn from the freedom that is the source of their moral coherence, they cease to be cosmopolitan libertarians and become liberal cosmopolitans.

The liberal cosmopolis as a way of life
If there were no transcendent God to Whom all should in humility submit, then humans could properly treat themselves as the center of moral concern, and not just because they are free and accountable moral agents. They would not only be the source of the permission that conveys moral authority to the collaboration of moral strangers. They and their life projects would be the source of all meaning and the measure of all good. The Enlightenment would be found in this realization of the immanent as the source of value and through liberation from the tyranny of supposed transcendently based authority and knowledge. Religion, insofar as it claims authority from the transcendent, would then be regarded as an illiberal superstition to be set aside by entering into the *siècle des lumières*. If Kant and others of the Enlightenment were right, one would then also find in one's own nature, reason, and/or sympathies the basis for avoiding Smerdyakov's conclusion in Dostoevsky's *The Brothers Karamazov*: "now everything is permitted." One would possess a canonical secular morality. There would be no French Revolution, October Revolution, or Killing Fields of Pol Pot. This morality in its full form, as with Kant, would accent human freedom and autonomy and give grounds for valuing liberty in all areas of life, including moral theology, where the proclamation of an unchanging tradition and of the authority of bishops would not merely be a violation of academic freedom in a narrow sense. It would be an offense against human dignity. The Enlightenment's spirit of open investigation and dispute invites all to bring everything into question, to bring everything to the tribunal of

critical secular reflection. From the Enlightenment's spirit of liberation from the customs, traditions, and habits of the past, there emerges an ethos that celebrates the human and the spirit of liberty. The Enlightenment is a completion of the West's humanistic project to give centrality to human values while avoiding the dominance of transcendent claims.

Once human self-understanding is disconnected from the transcendent God, human authority over nature is not necessarily recognized. Humans no longer have the unique connection with nature that comes from a transcendent creator God Who can bestow the right not only to rule over all life (Gen 1:28-29), but also to have all living creatures as prey (Gen 9:2-3). Humans cease to be the privileged animal who has been given the command through the incarnation of Christ to be united with God. If there is no transcendent point of focus for the cosmos, one cannot even speak of evolution as having a goal, of evolution going anywhere. Instead, evolution just happens. It goes in different directions, driven as much by happenstance and catastrophe as by physical laws, chemical constraints, and selective pressures. One can speak of species being better or worse adapted to maximizing inclusive fitness in particular environments. But, one can no longer speak of higher or lower life forms.

For morality, and for bioethics in particular, this has important implications. Humans are no longer separated from other animals by a unique transcendent destiny and special authority. The moral distance between humans and all life has become closer. Since all life shares the good of sensation and pleasure, these provide a bond uniting humans with all living beings. In particular, the more animals can enjoy conscious sensation and fulfillment, the more humans should be concerned about protecting other life forms out of a commitment to maximize satisfaction and minimize pain, to maximize the common good binding all life. In this circumstance, a living being has its moral status not because of the species to which it belongs, but because of its actual ability to feel and achieve fulfillment. As a result, all else being equal, it is worse to constrain in pens calves that are complex and conscious beings so as to produce veal than to abort human fetuses, who at that stage are sentiently less complex, in order better to realize the life projects of women. The liberal cosmopolitan ethic will thus tend to endorse a pro-choice vegetarianism, or at least an understanding that human life is not to be valued simply because it is human, all without grasping the deep evil of abortion. This bond with all who experience pain and pleasure leads to a heightened concern with animals expressed in a demand for animal liberation.[19] Yet one more hierarchy falls. Even where a vegetarianism is not fully endorsed, there will be a willingness to invest research funds for the care and amenities of animals, thus reducing the resources that can save human lives.[20] This is especially the case with the reticence to use "higher" primates in research that can contribute to human welfare.[21]

The emergence of this cosmopolitan liberal ethos is a global phenomenon. Religious and cultural traditions across the world are required to give a discursive justification of their content and to reassess this content in terms of the cardinal value of autonomous choice. As each tradition discovers, such a justification cannot be produced and, moreover, its commitments generally do not give centrality to individual autonomy. The content of the tradition is then evacuated as rationally unjustified as well as condemned as illiberal. Its religious requirements are transformed into aesthetic possibilities. Ritual observances take on the significance of a bond with history rather than with a transcendent reality. As persons bring their traditions to a rational accounting, they enter into a post-traditional, liberal cosmopolitan culture or ethos.[22] Those who take this critical attitude over against their religion find themselves entering into a world-wide ethos of liberation from the past as from superstition. They find themselves engaged as well in the joys of self-determination and self-fulfillment, which the global consumerist culture enables. This liberation is bloodless, hedonic, and individualistic.

From this focus on the individual as the source of value, and because this value is pursued within a thisworldly life project, there also emerge claims to an equality of opportunity in the realization of one's own values. The individual is not merely a source of authority but also a source of value. It is the autonomous individual and the life of self-determination that are the lynchpins of the liberal cosmopolitan vision of the moral life. The world is better, so this ethos affirms, the more individuals realize their life projects, their visions of the good, in ways compatible with others doing the same. The libertarian focus on freedom as the source of forbearance rights is trans-formed into a focus on claim rights to the opportunity to realize one's own rational life plans, the concrete expressions of one's own free choices. Because of the desire to realize the greatest good held to be achievable in the face of a limited life (i.e., individ-ual autonomous choice in the realization of one's self-fulfillment), there is an affirma-tion of equality in liberty of choice and in the pursuit of satisfaction or fulfillment, which affirmation gives flesh and substance to moral rationality. To assure an accepta-ble distribution of resources, the allocation of resources is understood from the per-spective of an *ab initio*, divine-like distribution of entitlements where each would have grounds to accept as fair that which is provided.[23] The shift is from freedom as a side constraint,[24] from the recognition of permission as a right-making condition when moral strangers meet, to liberty as a value, including liberty as the opportunity to define and then realize one's life projects in order to achieve one's own fulfillment. All of this is set with the guidance of an autonomy- and equality-affirming understanding of moral rationality. In such circumstances, the good of the collaboration of consenting others is found in their mutual autonomous self-realization and mutual affirmation. It is found in the realization of individual life projects and in the affirmation of the provision of similar space and resources to others, rather than in a meaning external to those relationships, projects, and experiences immanently understood. The focus is on fashioning and realizing a life that is mutually personally fulfilling. For health care policy, this will mean establishing an encompassing health care system that includes among its welfare rights those integral to the realization of one's own life projects such as access to third-party-assisted reproduction for homosexual couples, abortion, and physician-assisted suicide.

Liberal cosmopolitanism is a particular, content-full moral vision with a particu-lar understanding of the value of autonomy or liberty set in a particular relationship with other values (e.g., liberty and equality are set in a lexical priority to prosperity). It is liberal in being committed to a particular vision of autonomous self-realization. The moral life of the cosmopolitan involves neither living in accord with the tran-scendent meaning of the universe, nor is it the limited project of the morally author-itative collaboration of moral strangers grounded in consent. Instead, the liberal cosmopolitan vision is committed to living in conformity with a particular concrete, canonical moral understanding that gives centrality to liberty, equality, and personal fulfillment. It is cosmopolitan in being tied to a moral sense at home in an emerging global consumer culture, which frames its understandings beyond the constraints of particular traditions and religious commitments. For the liberal, the virtue of the market is not just its ability to increase wealth as well as to enrich the range of available products and services, and it is surely not its ability to allow persons within diverse moral communities to realize their own non-liberal moral visions, even if these are consensual. Very significantly, the market rewards the pursuit of self-fulfillment and self-satisfaction This reinforcement will tend to support an ethos that considers suspect, if not morally deficient, moral communities that do not recognize autonomous self-determination as the keystone of moral flourishing. As a consequence, this celebration of autonomous self-determination radically brings into question traditional religious, especially ascetic pursuits. Self-fulfillment becomes fully thisworldly.

The consumer culture of global capitalism can thus reinforce liberal cosmopolitanism's concerns with equality of opportunity, paradoxically leading to restrictions on the market. That is, in the absence of robust, functional moral communities, the market may support an ethos directed to the wholehearted pursuit of self-satisfaction and self-fulfillment, leading to an affirmation of different degrees of claims to equality of opportunity in the fulfillment of thisworldly life projects (e.g., ranging from state-supported education and redistributed taxation to affirmative action). In the face of the moral vacuum that emerges in the absence of functioning robust moral communities, and given the attraction of immediate satisfaction through the market, an ethos of guaranteeing to each person an adequate level of satisfaction and fulfillment can become central, even including welfare claims of an equality of opportunity in the pursuit of thisworldly, immanent life projects. In short, the market is no longer morally located and understood as a vehicle for the consensual collaboration of moral strangers. The market becomes not a morally neutral instrument for achieving goals beyond the market, but a way of realizing self-fulfillment and self-satisfaction through increasing the quantity and quality of products and services.[25] This understanding of the market also tends to erode the cultural environment necessary for the market to function freely, that is, without particular ideological constraints.

Liberal cosmopolitanism is an ethos full and entire, affirming liberty, equality of opportunity, self-fulfillment, self-satisfaction, and prosperity. It reinterprets many moral concerns as aesthetic projects (e.g., the choice or determination to live a monogamous heterosexual lifestyle becomes a matter of self-fulfillment as the achievement of a pleasing and satisfying lifestyle rather than a moral challenge, as does the choice of whether to use abortion in family planning). The focus is on freedom from the surd constraints of nature and the traditional authority of others. As such, the liberal cosmopolitan contrasts robustly with traditional Christian concerns with patience in suffering, as well as with humility, submission, and respect of those in authority (e.g., bishops over churches, husbands over wives), in the ascetic pursuit of salvation. As already indicated, this ethos is in conflict with traditional Christian moral judgments regarding reproduction, suffering, dying, and death. For instance, liberal cosmopolitanism finds the significance of sexuality in the free decision with others to achieve common projects of intimacy, satisfaction, fulfillment, and pleasure. This view is often announced in such cliché remarks as "I hope he is happy in this new relationship" or "At least she has found satisfaction in her fourth marriage" or "Do whatever makes you comfortable with consenting others." The focus is not just on permission as a source of moral authority. The focus is first and foremost on autonomous self-fulfillment. Meaning is not sought in submitting freely as man and woman joined in a Mystery leading to union with God. Indeed, the encouragement of submission to transcendent goals collides with the liberal cosmopolitan's thisworldly celebration of individual autonomy.

This emerging cosmopolitan ethos is liberal five ways over[26]: (1) it gives lexical priority to individual self-determination and autonomy insofar as actual free choice is compatible with a social democratic appreciation of the benefits of the market; this ethos is thus liberal in giving priority to a particular understanding of liberty; (2) it is committed to state-realized social justice as the quarantee of the material and social bases for fair equality of opportunity; it is liberal in freeing from material and societal constraints; (3) it encourages liberation from the past through the critical assessment of tradition, as well as public re-education in the emerging cosmopolitan culture; it is thus liberal in seeking liberation from structures claiming special communal authority, whether religious or familial; (4) it frees from "outworn" moral restraints by encouraging the pursuit of self-satisfaction as well as fulfillment in a consumer economy that both evokes desire and fulfills it; it is thus liberal in pursuing the eradication of moral constraints against the consensual satisfaction of desire; and (5) it frees from transcendent or metaphysical commitments; it is thus liberal in setting aside transcendent and therefore democratically non-negotiable sources of obligation. This global, social-democratically constrained consumerism can thus recruit very basic urges for fulfillment and satisfaction in support of the liberal cosmopolitan project of bringing into question all life projects that do not involve liberation from restraints against autonomy. Enlightenment and liberation are thus re-enforced by an economy focused on production and consumption within constraints of social justice. The intellectual commitment to liberation from the constraints of tradition is energized by a consumer economy's provocation of concupiscence in the pursuit of profit. Because sex sells and self-indulgence is appealing, a market ethos can thus favor a liberal cosmopolitan critique of asceticism, Christian tradition, and heterosexist ideals. The general affirmation of consensual sexual gratification becomes the norm. By appealing to immediate and simple gratification, or refined self-satisfaction (admittedly a smaller market niche), the focus becomes robustly thisworldly[27] and openly post-metaphysical. Reality is as one finds it in the sphere of immanence.

This ethos, because of its content-rich understanding of liberty, views negatively commitments to traditional patriarchal, heterosexist family structures (i.e., the husband as the head of the household and primary breadwinner, with the wife chiefly engaged in the raising of the children). Such traditional family structures are open to criticism because they direct energies to nurturing children within traditional, illiberal religious moral understandings (e.g., affirming deference to ecclesial authority, asceticism in the service of giving priority to salvation over self-satisfaction, and sexuality affirmed in exclusively heterosexist terms) rather than pursuing a higher standard of living and moral integration within the liberal cosmopolitan consumerist ethos. From the perspective of the liberal secular cosmopolitan ethos, such traditional religious and family commitments are profoundly impoverished: (1) in financial status, (2) in opportunities for fulfillment and gratification, (3) in their moral commitments (i.e., by the pursuit of illiberal transcendent goals and by being oriented to a heterosexist image of the family rather than being liberally socially aware), and (4) in their metaphysical foundations. In particular, the commitment to traditional family structures is considered seriously morally flawed in failing to liberate women from stereotypical social roles. In contrast, the pursuit of satisfaction frees from tradition and the restraints of the past by ensuring that all enter into the economy (and its cycle of desire, production, and consumption) which becomes a central mode of social liberation. Its immanent character once dissociated from the perspective of a rational tradition brings transcendent commitments into question as much by the allure of its satisfactions as by any appeal to argument. This encompassing cosmopolitan ethos is usually offered as a taken-for-granted moral truth without noting its content-full particularity. Nor are its ties to a global consumerist culture generally well appreciated.

In leading beyond an appeal to moral agency as the source of moral authority (i.e., beyond a libertarian cosmopolitan ethic), the liberal cosmopolitan ethos invites a fundamental abandonment of all hierarchies, not just those of kings over their subjects, imperial powers over their colonies, and men over women, but also of humans over animals. As one moves from permission as the source of authority (which will itself condemn the rule of imperial powers over their colonies in the absence of consent) to the celebration of liberty in all human projects, there is a concern to guarantee equality of opportunity in the pursuit of such projects. As already noted, if liberty is central, the right to be at liberty to pursue one's own life projects becomes central, requiring not merely equality of opportunity and basic welfare rights, but also a liberty of the sexes understood as liberty of men and women as persons, not as embedded in particular traditional roles. As liberty becomes the salient good, so, too, does the goal of the realization of liberty in the lives of all. Because of the centrality of liberty, the state must be given sufficient power and authority not just to redistribute resources to ensure autonomy and equality, but also in order to establish a liberal secular ideology in education, political discourse, and, if possible, family relationships.[28] The liberal cosmopolitan ethos thus leads to advancing a social democratic political agenda that is (1) egalitarian in supporting equality of opportunity, (2) welfarist in seeking to guarantee an adequate package of education, health care, and amenities for all set within (3) constraints and regulations designed to make traditional lifestyles costly and difficult, even when they are not directly forbidden by law, while at the same time (4) encouraging a consumerist market economy designed to evoke desires and then fulfill them, while (5) undermining strong transcendent commitments, (6) encouraging an animus against traditional Christian commitments and community, thus (7) creating a hunger it can never adequately satisfy.[29]

The goal is a cosmopolitan vision where the bond to humanity as a whole is stronger than bonds to family, race, religion, culture, or citizenship. The particularities of family, ethnicity, religion, culture, and nationality are reduced to aesthetic concerns: they become variations on the rich pattern of human culture. Although much is made of diversity within the liberal cosmopolitan ethos, the diversity affirmed is domesticated, transformed, and purged of moral differences that would separate. As a consequence, religious differences are recast primarily as functions of historical happenstance (e.g., as being "traditions" in a weak sense of mere customs) and are shorn of metaphysical depth. Diversity in this sense has a significance somewhat like the culinary variations in ethnic restaurants. They provide a plurality of approaches to cooking, seasoning, serving, and décor, without usually involving matters that can lead to adverse moral judgments (e.g., "You are a fine fellow, but your religion is an idolatrous deception engendered by the devil"). The ethos is cosmopolitan in both (1) liberating from regional and historical particularities, as well as (2) being available anywhere throughout the world via the assumption of a critical attitude to the mere givenness of tradition on behalf of establishing a priority for liberty. This ethos directs moral energies to liberty, equality, and community in the pursuit of self-fulfillment. It possesses a robust and particular vision of social justice, which is perhaps best captured by John Rawls (1921--).[30]

Christianity Transformed: Towards a Christian Bioethics Without Transcendence

If the truth of religion is to be found in morality, and if that morality is liberal cosmopolitan, then the Christianity must be committed to fashioning a theology that is post-traditional: Christian ethics must be reconceived to the benefit of the fundamental commitments of a liberal cosmopolitan moral vision.[31] The rich and historically deep resources of Christian ethics must be purified of patriarchal, sexist, and heterosexist residua. It must be reoriented, reimaged, and relocated within a liberal cosmopolitan ethos directed to social democratic principles. While maintaining the images and narratives of its history, insofar as they are not illiberal, a liberal cosmopolitan Christianity must at the same time recognize itself as one among many religious, cultural resources. Along with a suitably liberated Jesus, there can then be a place also in a Christian's heart for Buddha and the goddess Sophia. Once religion is no longer anchored in a veridical experience of the transcendent truth of God, it becomes a special art form, which can be affirmed as long as it accords with the moral rationality of the liberal cosmopolitan ethos. It is out of this commitment to this very particular understanding of liberty that traditions must be examined and then set aside or revised. It is out of this commitment that religion must be foundationally ecumenical.

The phrase "religious traditions" highlights how the meaning of religion is thus recast as a set of religio-aesthetic concerns, sustained by a web of understandings spanning generations. To regard one's faith as one among a number of traditions is no longer to consider it as *the* bearer of God's revelation, but as one among a number of alternative appreciations of the aesthetic experience of the holy or Divine. As Thomas Scanlon observes, "When people start talking in general terms about 'the value of traditions' they are often on the verge of ceasing to care about their own."[32] Religious faiths as traditions become analogous to special artistic traditions directed to portraying the transcendent and the aesthetic experience of the spiritual. *Pace* Kierkegaard and Hegel, this engagement with transcendence finds its higher truth in aesthetic terms. In this fashion, Christian bioethics becomes post-Christian in not invoking as its ground the uniqueness of the Christian revelation of Christ as God. Christ for a post-traditional Christian bioethics becomes an expression of human culture. This immanentizing of Christian bioethics develops elements of Kierkegaard's insights (his full views in the matter to the contrary notwithstanding) by recognizing with him that immanent human experience is to its very horizon thisworldly. Because God as God is invisible in the world of immanent phenomenal experience, human experience is closed to knowledge of true transcendence, though a hunger for transcendence can give birth to an inward subjective passion for engagement.

The members of different religions can experience their bioethics as possessing complimentary subjective powers, but without a judgment that their moral claims have a unique and universal governance, or that their metaphysical insights require the conversion of others. In this fashion, the various Christian bioethics can celebrate their particular histories without offending or challenging others. As various *Gemeinschaften* within a social democratic polity, they can offer rich, competing religious-moral narratives and bioethical insights. But they cannot justify universal moral claims for their content. Instead, they command a special genre of the aesthetic, arraying cultural and even moral concerns around a sense of holiness and the transcendent. The various post-traditional Christian bioethics can through religious images and understandings convey different senses of the sacred importance of particular important human projects and concerns (e.g., the provision of medical care to the suffering). Considerations of the "sanctity of life" or the "sacredness of human nature" can supervene on moral judgments without adding further moral content. Such considerations sustain a history of experience endorsed by the members of particular communities who have nurtured particular images *as if* they were canonical moral judgments. The images gesture beyond the immanent. By engaging considerations such as "sanctity of life" and "the sacredness of the human genome", religious bioethical discourse reaches beyond strictly secular moral traditions without going beyond the bounds of the immanent. Religious images, accounts, and stories constitute a genre of poetry anointed through history and conveying a special sense of depth to bioethical concerns and decisions.

Christian bioethics becomes a special genre of liberal cosmopolitan morality expressed through ennobling, and if at all possible liberating myths. The "myths" may have a special status as hallowed by generations and accepted as conveying meaning. The historical and metaphysical commitments of Christianity become transformed á la Kant into myths by which to take seriously the sublimity of human life, the tragedy of human sin, suffering, and death, and the transcendence of human aspirations. Theodicy can be recaptured as a religious art form, rather than as a discursive metaphysical task, much less a noetic experience of God's loving, sovereign, governing presence. For example, within this special aesthetic understanding, a chaplain or even a bioethicist can reassure a patient ("your suffering has been a redemptive experience") without believing in a transcendent God. The term "redemptive" would be preferred over "maturing" so as to emphasize that the suffering was not without special personal value. Religious language thus adds a special exclamation mark and an aesthetic appreciation of the spiritual without invoking a grounding in a transcendent God. The content of such bioethics can include images of the transcendent, but they are nested within the immanence of human experience and moral agency, thereby loosing any claim on the outsider for unconditional repentance or conversion. There is only an invitation to recognize the rich aesthetic if not indeed curative powers of a genre of religious or spiritual images. Christian bioethics reinterpreted as secular bioethics augmented or completed within directing and fulfilling images of the sacred and transcendent is fully post-Christian in its grounding and the scope of its governance.

This recasting of Christian bioethics can be welcomed by many. It dissolves the threat of fanaticism associated with true belief. The force of Christian ethics and bioethics would, after all, have been reinterpreted in terms of religious aesthetic meanings: an aesthetic of the spiritual. The powers of spiritual images can be seen not only as offering a special wholeness but also possessing empirically curative force (e.g., spirituality can be regarded as a supplement to therapeutic modality). One can then accept the various Christian bioethics along with other religious and secular bioethics as providing variations in the project of giving spiritual meaning to human birth, suffering, disability, and death, while avoiding any concrete and especially denominational definitions of spirituality. The various Christian bioethics offer alternative narratives framed through images of sanctity, transcendence, and ultimate meaning. The diversity of these narratives conveys the beauty of the mosaic of human experience. The aesthetic relocates the ethical. The very diversity of Christian bioethics is, in this light, positive: it supplies alternative resources not only for conveying moral content to bioethics but for experiencing that content in terms of a sense of a greater meaning. What was a problem (i.e., the multiplicity of Christianities and Christian bioethics) becomes a resource for different strategies for conveying a special significance to all human encounters with finitude. Given its eclectic character, this collage of spirituality has a distinctively neo-pagan character: it resists exclusivist monotheist accounts, especially those tightly bound to traditional Christian understandings. There is an appreciation of a general possibility for human flourishing through identification with images that convey an experience of the sacred and an intimation of transcendence.[33]

A liberal cosmopolitan reconceptualization of Christian bioethics not only discourages what many take to be insensitive metaphysical and religious judgments (e.g., "I respect you, but your religion and its views regarding physician-assisted suicide are wrong, you should repent and convert because otherwise you may go to hell," or "my religion declares that abortion involves the sin of murder and you will act immorally if you have an abortion, even if you do not belong to my religion"). It also discourages considering issues of spirituality in denominational terms (e.g., making such judgments as "miracles outside of true belief and worship are either acts of God's unsearchable mercy, the result of achieving some degree of real union with the one true God, the work of the devil, an empirically explicable phenomenon, a sincere misperception of what occurred, or a fraud"). Instead, it supports a nonjudgmental ecumenism (for example, one is never to say "you should convert to true Christianity, only then will you know what true spirituality involves;" instead, one is to suppose true spirituality is equally available within all religions), one congenial to drawing on the spiritual resources of the various Christian religions as well as non-Christian religions. Spirituality becomes a special therapeutic modality that can enrich the role of Christian bioethics without any claim being made about the transcendent.

A Christian bioethics so reinterpreted can still command its own academic integrity. Christian bioethicists can be experts in lodging the human predicament within particular traditions of moral exegesis. Not only can Christian bioethicists focus on issues of free and informed consent, as can secular bioethicists, but Christian bioethicists, ministers, and chaplains can through their knowledge and expertise regarding special geographies of spiritual concerns locate health care decisions within content-rich contexts of religious values, images, and narratives. They can indicate with what choices members of particular religions may find themselves comfortable. They can indicate the need for special rituals. Where the libertarian bioethicist can as such give little guidance as to what promises one should make in health care (i.e., only that one should keep the promises one makes), and where the liberal cosmopolitan bioethicist can invite in the direction of liberal egalitarianism, the Christian bioethicist can offer substantive but not canonical moral guidance. Thus, a religious bioethics can counsel that a Roman Catholic should consider not agreeing to being a surrogate mother, because this may engender significant moral dissidence within key moral narratives regarding the meaning of reproduction. The Christian bioethicist so understood can be a special resource for patients, their families, and health-care providers who find themselves guided by a particular religious tradition (as, mutatis mutandis, would Jewish, Mohammedan, Hindu, etc. bioethicists).

Religious bioethics, once placed in this light, can guide bioethicists in responding to diverse religious bioethical questions transcending confessional boundaries. Religious bioethicists or chaplains would not need to be of the same religious affiliation as the physicians, nurses, or patients to whom they brought their services. It would be enough to understand how the various religions appreciate the passages of life and respond to the major challenges and controversies of bioethics. Religious bioethics, as well as chaplaincy, would not have to be religion-specific. Religious bioethics and chaplaincy can claim the generic character they have increasingly assumed. Chaplains would not need to maintain a "brand name" integrity. It would not be of great moment whether the bioethicists or chaplains were Baptist, Episcopalian, Roman Catholic, or for that matter Buddhist or Mohammedan.[34] In many circumstances, if not most, bioethical guidance and even spiritual succor could be provided across denominational and religious borders. What would be important would be an appreciation of the different geographies of values, religious narratives, and special religious concerns that structure the experience of different religious groups. Christian bioethicists and chaplains can like travel agents offer different possibilities for moral guidance and spiritual experience. Moreover, they can help resituate religious concerns in terms that accent individual choice and equality, while attempting to set aside traditional patriarchal and heterosexist assumptions.

This liberal cosmopolitan reconceptualization of Christian bioethics is congenial to our times. It is non-judgmental. It blunts zealotry. It is supportive of ecumenism. It places Christian bioethics among other secular health care resources. At the end of modernity and with the emergence of a new post-modern, global liberal cosmopolitan and consumerist culture, human knowledge and morality are recognized as just that: human devices and practices. In such terms, religion in general and Christian bioethics and spirituality in particular become human projects that convey intimations of profound sacredness and transcendent meaning, but have only an immanent significance. All of this is to the benefit of defanging fanaticism, and supporting a cosmopolitanism that can be a vehicle for making available the range of acceptable human resources for religious and spiritual insight. Given this understanding of religion, ecumenism can be pursued unconstrained by the demands of a transcendent God. It can instead concentrate on disclosing the communality of human concerns regarding the divine and on building a religious unity in which most, if not all, can participate.

If religion is a special form of human experience refined through history and articulated in community, then religious diversity and bioethical differences are best understood as variations in the appreciation of the human condition and the experience of
spirituality that do not depend on transcendent truths, but on human creativity. As a
consequence, mutual understanding and collaboration should place differences in perspective within a common peaceable respect for the sacredness of life, the wonder of
existence, a sense of the divine, and a common appreciation of social justice. In this
light, a unified Christian or perhaps even a universal ecumenical religious bioethics is
possible, which compasses in its ecumenism a diversity of traditions.

One can imagine a transformed Roman papacy presiding over a worldwide coalition of believers drawn from all religions. As such, the Roman papacy would offer
leadership to all who turn to the divine, whether Christian, Mohammedan, Hindu,
Buddhist, or New Age – all without claims of universal jurisdiction, much less infallibility. By drawing on its deep commitments to rationality and universality, the Roman
papacy could realize leadership on a worldwide scale. In these terms it would achieve
three ecumenical goals.

> (1) All would be united in one Christian coalition, or perhaps even fashion
> a religious united front compassing the major religions. This coalition
> would be grounded in a common morality, a liberal cosmopolitan reli-
> gious ethos enabling a common pursuit of the divine and a universal
> experience of the spiritual, even if the divine is understood only as an idea
> or ideal, and even though its pursuit is undertaken through a diversity of
> symbols and expressions of belief, somewhat as different rites within an
> all-encompassing church.
> (2) Religion would offer the energies for the pursuit of a liberal cosmopol-
> itan vision of social justice on a global scale.
> (3) Christian bioethics could be lodged in this ecumenical and catholic
> faith.

Such a post-Enlightenment, post-Christian Christianity offers many the hope, if not for
a perpetual peace, then at least for the resources for better mutual understanding and
peaceable collaboration in a thick community of common moral commitments. The
libertarian and the traditional Christian can only regard this moral and political ideal
with horror and foreboding.[35]

Christian Bioethics Reconsidered

The differences between a traditional Christianity and a Christianity directed towards
understanding itself in immanent aesthetic terms are radical. They are separated by
fundamentally different ways of thinking about God, religion, and bioethics. While a
post-traditional Christianity can celebrate the cosmopolitan ecumenical vision just
articulated, traditional Christianity can at best condemn the vision as blasphemy.
Traditional Christianity recognizes that morality, human community, and spirituality
must conform to the demands of a unique and very personal God. In contrast, Christi-

anity understood in the immanent terms of the liberal cosmopolitan ethos appreciates God and religious experience only within the concerns, hopes, and aspirations of humans. Such a religious understanding fulfills Kant's aspiration to a rational morality binding mankind, and the Hegelian project of relocating religion within the higher truth of an absolute philosophy. It is for traditional Christianity an image of the Anti-Christ.

At stake is a clash of moral and metaphysical worlds. Traditional Christianity is anchored in a noetic experience of the transcendent God to Whom all must conform in terms at odds with the morality and sentiments of secularity and modernity. Post-traditional Christianity, in contrast, has deep roots in the Western Christian Scholastic enterprise, which has from the Middle Ages sought to relocate the divine within the concerns of reason and of a natural law that can be understood in secular terms.[36] This Christianity wanted to speak to, participate in, and be understood within the public forum, even when it is secular. The Renaissance's reconnection with the pagan Europe-an celebration of humans as the center and source of value, the modern philosophical project of a rational justification of morality, and the Enlightenment's hope for a universal religion of morality further developed Western Christianity's commitment to discursive rationality. It encouraged the aspiration to a rational and ecumenical *religio catholica*. The catholicity of the Middle Ages joins with the richness of the Renaissance in the rational universalistic aspirations of modern philosophy and the Enlightenment. Catholicity is now explicitly sought in a discursive rational universality. This aspira-tion to universality and the affirmation of the cosmopolitan naturally support the aspirations of ecumenism. This rationalistic, liberal understanding of religion looks to a unity in reason with the divine understood as a general principle or idea giving direction to human aspirations. As the first chapter indicates, this vision underlies the contemporary Roman Catholic claim that Christian morality and therefore Christian bioethics are not different from the morality binding humans as such. Catholicity, humanity, and universality are expressed in an ecumenism of faith become rational and oriented towards the divine, if only as an idea or ideal. Even Kant's Protestantism reformed through the Enlightenment can regard this catholicity as the moral truth of religion. In contrast, traditional Christianity recognizes catholicity not in the universal-ity of an ecumenist rationality, but instead in the wholeness of true worship and belief.[37] In reading catholicity as wholeness, not primarily as universality, traditional Christianity turns not to an idea of the divine, but to the unchanging experience of a personal, transcendent God.

The differences between these two understandings of Christianity, religion, and God underlie the conflicts in the so-called "culture wars", whose battles erupt around bioethical issues. The differences cut deeply. For instance, is artificial insemination from a donor a sin, a form of adultery, even if the husband, wife, and the semen donor all consent to the project of producing a child? Or, is it a form of early adoption? At stake are different views of marriage. If there is no transcendent grounding for mar-riage, and if no harm is done to others, then consent should cure all problems. Difficul-ties arise when an appeal is made to obligations imposed by a transcendent God. So, too, does abortion promise the empowerment of women or the murder of unborn children? Does health care justice promise fairness as equality of opportunity through the guarantee of a basic uniform health care package for all, or does it impose restrictions on bioethical conscientious objection, by mandating through a single-payer system services a traditional Christian will find to be deeply wrong, indeed as temptation to great evils (e.g., prenatal screening and abortion)? Does physician-assisted suicide promise liberation from the tyranny of nature or an opportunity to have others collaborate in one's self-murder? The bioethical issues look quite different depending on whether God is an idea important for unifying morality or is instead a transcendent Trinity of Persons commanding our obedience in very particular ways.

At issue are also different views concerning who are the exemplar experts able to resolve controversies about what Christian bioethics requires (e.g., anyone of good will, learned in the matters at issue, or instead those who have prepared by a special asceticism so as to achieve understanding through holiness). The differences between these paradigms of Christianity and of the bioethics they can sustain are rooted in fundamental disagreements regarding issues of metaphysics, epistemology, axiology, and the sociology of moral knowledge. The stumbling blocks are metaphysical. They are foundational. They lie at the roots of morality. They are religious; they spring not just from the fragmentation of Christianity, but from the emergence of a profoundly post-traditional understanding of God, religion, morality, and spirituality.

The next chapter will turn to the aspirations of traditional Christianity. If they are sustainable, then Christian bioethics will have a moral, ecumenical, and public policy character quite different from the post-Christian Christianity and bioethics just sketched. Where traditional Christianity is committed to a truth beyond negotiation and likely at variance with much of contemporary post-Christian sensibilities, post-traditional Christianity understands itself to be committed to a cluster of developing, intertwining traditions, which are always open to negotiation and change, as long as they support and affirm liberal cosmopolitan moral commitments. Liberal cosmopolitan Christianity understands its task as reading the signs of the times and inspiring the liberation of the human spirit from the bond of illiberal tradition. In this case, theologians par excellence are experts concerning their traditions, analytic philosophers skilled in examining the issues at stake, talented negotiators regarding matters of morality and religion, and visionaries able to reimage Christianity in conformity with the morality of the liberal cosmopolitan ethos. Especially important will be those theologians who can creatively respond to the changing world around them. Traditional Christianity will be at variance with such aspirations, just as it was with the cultivated refinement of the pagan humanism of the early Christian era. In contrast, traditional Christianity recognizes its task as bringing the world to conform to the requirements of a personal God Who is beyond discursive reason. In this case the theologians par excellence are those whom Kant execrated, those who are in communion with God.[38] We are brought to a final set of foundational questions that lead to the challenge of the rest of this book.

> Is it possible to lay out a coherent account of bioethics grounded in a traditional understanding of Christianity?
> What would a Christian bioethics need to be to build on a coherent religious morality oriented to a transcendent God?
> What would be needed for such an ethic to provide canonical moral content, bring into harmony the good and the right, as well as integrate

the motivation and justification of morality, while aiming at a transcendent God Who seems inaccessible within the horizon of our immanence?

Answering such questions requires sketching the epistemological and metaphysical foundations required to secure a traditional Christian bioethics. Such an exploration cannot by itself establish a traditional Christian bioethics. It can, though, examine the conditions necessary and sufficient for its possibility. One must then determine if those sufficient conditions are fulfilled. The next chapter turns to this project, the project of laying out these conditions: the conditions for a traditional Christian bioethics.

Notes

1. Because secular human morality is grounded in the character of persons as finite agents who must make choices within the bounds of an immanent reality, that morality is the morality for more than just humans. It holds for all other similarly situated spatio-temporal discursive moral agents anywhere in the cosmos. It would not in all respects hold for, or in the same way be applicable to, angels, who are personal bodiless powers not moved, for example, by concupiscence, but who stand in the presence of God.
2. Richard Rorty, *Contingency, Irony, and Solidarity* (Cambridge: Cambridge University Press, 1989).
3. There is not only the as-if function of God for the unity of morality, but also the regulative function of the idea of God for knowledge. See Immanuel Kant, *Critique of Pure Reason*, the appendix to the Transcendental Dialectic A642=B670 through A704=B732.
4. This text develops a point only implicit in Kant: secular morality can be regarded as an intersubjective framework that provides for the possibility of blame and praise on an analogy with empirical knowledge, which is grounded in an intersubjective framework that allows for the possibility of empirical experience. Both empirical knowledge and secular morality function without a grounding in transcendent realities, though for Kant, moral agents must be thought of as if they transcended human phenomenal experience. This latter point is complex, touching on Kant's various invocations of the noumenon as well as the transcendental object and the thing-in-itself. For an interesting treatment of some of these issues, see Moltke S. Gram, *The Transcendental Turn* (Gainesville: University of Florida Press, 1984); and John N. Findlay, *Kant and the Transcendental Object* (Oxford: Clarendon Press, 1981).
5. For a brief introduction to some of the controversy regarding the cause of AIDS, see Eileen Baumann, Tom Bethell, Harvey Bialy, *et al.*, "Letter to the Editor," *Science* 267 (Feb. 17, 1995), 945-6; Joseph Palca, "Duesberg Vindicated? Not Yet," *Science* 254 (Oct. 18, 1991), 376.
6. Immanuel Kant, "What is Enlightenment?" in *Foundations of the Metaphysics of Morals*, trans. L.W. Beck (Indianapolis: Bobbs-Merrill, 1976), p. 85, AK VIII, 35.
7. Immanuel Kant, *Religion Within the Limits of Reason Alone* (New York: Harper, 1960), p. 123, AK VI, 132.
8. Kant attempts to ground his moral maxims in what can be universalized without contradiction, or at least without a contradiction in will. *Grundlegung zur Metaphysik der Sitten*, AK IV, 423. With regard to suicide, he wishes to bar the move by which one would freely and rationally choose death by freely deciding no longer to be free and rational. There would be no contradiction in a choice for suicide if freedom and rationality are side constraints defining the practice of morality, rather than capacities valued such that they should be maintained as long as possible. In his lectures on ethics, while not invoking the value of life, Kant

does invoke the special value of being a moral agent. "If he disposes over himself, he treats his value as that of a beast. He who so behaves, who has no respect for human nature and makes a thing of himself, becomes for everyone an object of freewill.... Suicide is not abominable and inadmissible because life should be highly prized ... But the rule of morality does not admit of it under any condition because it degrades human nature below the level of animal nature and so destroys it." *Lectures on Ethics*, trans. L. Infield (Indianapolis: Hackett, 1963), p. 152. For a further summary of Kant's view on suicide, see Engelhardt, *The Foundations of Bioethics*, 2nd ed. (New York: Oxford University Press, 1996), pp. 131-133.

9. Kant regarded his account of science as lodged in a commitment to (and indeed a grounding of) Newtonian physics, even to the point of claiming that the laws of motion and the general character of Newtonian physics were justified in the necessary conditions for the possibility of sensible, spatio-temporal, discursive experience. See, for example, Kant's *Metaphysische Anfangsgründe der Naturwissenschaften* (1786). Kant could have forgone this commitment to a particular account of physics, which is dependent on a particular understanding of causality and substance, and instead appealed to the general conditions for the possibility of the coherence of sensible, spatio-temporal, discursive experience. In so doing, he would have articulated a fully procedural account of science, committed to no particular content-full scientific truths, but only to the general practice or method of intersubjectively resolving controversies regarding the character of empirical reality.

10. To remind the reader once more, the term "moral stranger" is used to identify individuals with whom one cannot resolve moral controversies by sound rational argument (i.e., those who share a controversy but lack sufficient common moral premises, moral rules of evidence, and/or moral rules of inference so as to allow the controversy's closure by sound rational argument) or by an appeal to a mutually recognized moral authority (i.e., those who share a controversy but who do not live in a moral community within which particular persons or groups of persons are recognized as *in* authority to declare a resolution to their moral controversy). "Moral friends" is used to identify individuals with whom one can resolve moral controversies by sound rational argument or by an appeal to a person or persons recognized as in authority. See Engelhardt, *The Foundations of Bioethics*, especially pp. 24-25. See, also, Engelhardt and Arthur Caplan (eds.), *Scientific Controversies* (New York: Cambridge University Press, 1987).

11. Although there are similarities between the procedural, content-less morality that can bind strangers in post-modernity and the morality of Kant, there are also very important differences. The procedural morality sketched in this volume, as well as in *The Foundations of Bioethics*, is grounded in a will to collaborate within a framework sufficient for a common sphere of moral authority. Autonomous choices within a general procedural secular morality would for Kant usually count as heteronomous choices: such choices would not necessarily be determined by Kant's content-rich categorical imperative, but often by the inclinations of particular agents. See Engelhardt, *The Foundations of Bioethics*.

12. St. Athanasius, "De incarnatione verbi dei" §54.3, in NPNF2, vol. 11, p. 65.

13. Aelius Lampridius, "Severus Alexander" xxix, in *The Scriptores Historiae Augustae*, trans. David Magie (Cambridge, MA: Harvard University Press, 1967), vol. 2, p. 235.

14. *Encyclopaedia Britannica*, 11th ed. (1911), vol. 27, p. 596.

15. A limited democracy that draws its authority from the consent of its members will not have the secular moral authority to impose a particular moral understanding, such as the requirement that physicians who have a moral objection to abortion or physician-assisted suicide at least refer patients to those who will perform such services.

16. John Locke, *A Letter Concerning Toleration* (Amherst, NY: Prometheus Books, 1990), p. 22. Locke seems to take seriously the transcendent goal of Christianity, recognizing the pursuit of salvation as the purpose of a church.

17. The ideals of the humanities reflect a celebration of the distinctively human understood in immanent terms.

> Those who have spoken Latin and have used the language correctly do not give to the word *humanitas* the meaning which it is commonly thought to have, namely, what the Greeks call "philanthropia," signifying a kind of friendly spirit and good-feeling towards all men without distinction; but they gave to *humanitas* about the force of the Greek *paedeia*; that is, what we call *eruditionem institutionemque in bonas artes*, or "education and training in the liberal arts." Those who earnestly desire and seek after these are most highly humanized. For the pursuit of that kind of knowledge, and the training given by it, have been granted to man alone of all the animals, and for that reason it is termed *humanitas*, or "humanity."
> John C. Rolfe (trans.), *The Attic Nights of Aulus Gellius* XIII.xvii.1 (Cambridge, MA: Harvard, 1978), vol. 3, p. 457.

18. Varro, *On the Latin Language* VIII, 31, trans. R. G. Kent (Cambridge, MA: Harvard, 1979), vol. 2, p. 395.
19. Peter Singer, *Animal Liberation* (New York: Avon Books, 1990).
20. See, for example, Lynette A. Hart (ed.), *Responsible Conduct with Animals in Research* (New York: Oxford, 1998); and F. Barbara Orlans, Tom Beauchamp, *et al.*, *The Human Use of Animals* (New York: Oxford, 1998).
21. Engelhardt, "Animals: Their Right to be Used," in *The Use of Animals in Medical Research*, eds. Fred D. Miller, Jr., and Jeffrey Paul (New Brunswick, NJ: Transaction Publications, 2000), in press.
22. The term "liberal cosmopolitan ethos" is used generally to identify a way of life, an emerging culture. The term "liberal cosmopolitan ethic" is meant to indicate a particular articulation or statement of this ethos. In general, the two can be seen as materially equivalent.
23. In *A Theory of Justice* (Cambridge, MA: Harvard University Press, 1971), John Rawls introduces the notion of regarding the distribution of social primary goods from the perspective of the original position (see p. 137), which he understands to be an expository device that allows us to understand the appropriate basis for entitlement. According to Rawls, "to see our place in society from the perspective of this position is to see it *sub specie aeternitatis*: it is to regard the human situation not only from all social but also from all temporal points of view. The perspective of eternity is not a perspective from a certain place beyond the world, nor the point of view of a transcendent being; rather it is a certain form of thought and feeling that rational persons can adopt within the world." *Ibid.*, p. 587.
24. Robert Nozick, *Anarchy, State, and Utopia* (New York: Basic Books, 1974), see especially pp. 30-34.
25. A distinction must be recognized between the market as a practice that allows the realization of individual goals and the market as an institution that tends morally to transform individuals and communities due to the constraints imposed on communities by liberal cosmopolitan societies.
26. Already in the 19th century, humanistically transformed Christianities, especially progressive forms of Unitarianism, came to identify themselves with the "gospel of liberalism", the faith that mankind generally could be freed from the superstitions of the past and evolve economically, morally, politically, and spiritually. See, for examples, Joseph Henry Allen, *Our Liberal Movement in Theology* (Boston: Roberts Brothers, 1892), pp. 176-201.
27. One might think here of Bernard Mandeville's (1670-1733) poem, "The Grumbling Hive: or, Knaves turn'd Honest," in which he celebrates the wealth-producing character of an open-market economy that allows lust and greed, placed within constraints, to generate wealth. He observes, "Thus every Part was full of Vice, Yet the whole Mass a Paradise...So Vice is beneficial found, When it's by Justice lopt and bound..." *The Fable of the Bees* (Indianapolis: Liberty Classics, 1988), vol. 1, pp. 24, 37.

28. 19th century Europe witnessed the concerted effort to replace religious with secular education, often with a robustly anti-clerical, if not anti-Christian animus. This was associated in France with laicism or *laicisme* and featured prominently in French cultural debates after 1879, in which Jules Ferry (1832-1893) played a very prominent role. For an overview of some of these issues, see Kurt Galling (ed.), *Die Religion in Geschichte und Gegenwart* (Tübingen: J.C.B. Mohr, 1959), vol. 4; and Maurice Reclus, *Jules Ferry* (Paris: Flammarion, 1947).

29. For two recent reflections on the moral force of the market (including its morally corruptive force) when set within the constraints of a liberal cosmopolitan polity, see Francis Fukuyama, *The End of History and the Last Man* (New York: Free Press, 1992) and John Gray, *False Dawn: The Delusions of Global Capitalism* (New York: New Press, 2000).

30. John Rawls, *A Theory of Justice*.

31. Religion becomes a way of inspiring a commitment to a progressivist, liberal ethos. "The thought of a Divine existence, of an infinite Will, remains, – but only to give lift to imagination, gravity to reflection, reverence to the temper of the soul, and a foundation of gratitude and trust.... It is the task of the Religion of Humanity not simply to recognize the broad field of various beliefs in which the races of mankind have been trained, but, far more, to recognize whatever common spirit of justice, mercy, and truth may be in them all." Joseph Henry Allen, *Our Liberal Movement in Theology* (Boston: Roberts Brothers, 1892), pp. 172, 174.

32. Thomas Scanlon, *What We Owe to Each Other* (Cambridge, MA: Harvard University Press, 1998), p. 336.

33. There is a rich literature of concerns regarding spirituality in health care. See, for example, D. Aldridge, "Is There Evidence for Spiritual Healing?" *Advances* 9 (1993), 4-21; R. Bellingham *et al.*, "Connectedness: Some Skills for Spiritual Health," *American Journal of Health Promotion* 4 (1989), 18-24; E. Braverman, "The Religious Medical Model: Holy Medicine and the Spiritual Behavior Inventory," *Southern Medical Journal* 80(4) (1987), 415-20; S. Cronk, *Dark Night Journey* (Philadelphia: Pendle Hill Publications, 1991); L. Dossey, *Healing Words* (San Francisco: Harper, 1993); B. Douglas-Smith, "An Empirical Study of Religious Mysticism," *British Journal of Psychiatry* 118 (1971), 549-554; J.D. Gartner, D.B. Larson, G. Allen, "Religious Commitment and Mental Health: A Review of the Empirical Literature," *Journal of Psychology and Theology* 19 (1991), 6-25; J. Gerwood *et al.*, "The Purpose-in-life Test and Religious Denomination: Protestant and Catholic Scores in an Elderly Population," *Journal of Clinical Psychology* 54(1) (1998), 49-53; J.E. Haase *et al.*, "Simultaneous Concept Analysis of Spiritual Perspective, Hope Acceptance and Self-transcendence," *IMAGE: Journal of Nursing Scholarship* 24 (1992), 141-147; R. Hatch *et al.*, "The Spiritual Involvement and Beliefs Scale – Development and Testing of a New Instrument," *Journal of Family Practice* 46(6) (1998), 476-86; N. Kehoe and T. Gutheil, "Neglect of Religious Issues in Scale-based Assessment of Suicidal Patients," *Hospital and Community Psychiatry* 45(4) (1994), 366-9; H.G. Koenig, L.K. George, I.C. Sigler, "The Use of Religion and Other Emotion-regulating Coping Strategies among Older Adults," *Gerontologist* 28 (1988), 303-317; M. Leetun, "Wellness Spirituality in the Older Adult. Assessment and Intervention Protocol," *Nurse Practitioner* 21(8) (1996), 60; J.S. Levin, "Esoteric vs. Exoteric Explanations for Findings Linking Spirituality and Health," *Advances* 9 (1993), 54-56; J.S. Levin, "Investigating the Epidemiologic Effects of Religious Experience: Findings, Explanations and Barriers," in *Religion in Aging and Health*, ed. J.S. Levin (Thousand Oaks, CA: Sage, 1994), pp. 3-17; J.S. Levin and Harold Y. Vanderpool, "Is Religion Therapeutically Significant for Hypertension?" *Social Science and Medicine* 29 (1989), 69-78; R. Mathew *et al.*, "Measurement of Materialism and Spiritualism in Substance Abuse Research," *Journal of Studies on Alcohol* 56(4) (1995), 470-5; L. Morris, "A Spiritual Well-being Model: Use with Older Women who Experience Depression," *Issues in Mental Health Nursing* 17(5) (1996),

439-55; E. Raleigh and S. Boehm, "Development of the Multidimensional Hope Scale," *Journal of Nursing Measurement* 2(2) (1994), 155-67; and R. Turner *et al.*, "Religious or Spiritual Problem. A Culturally Sensitive Diagnostic Category in the DSM-IV," *Journal of Nervous and Mental Disease* 183(7) (1995), 435-44.

34. For an exploration of what is morally and spiritually at stake in the use of generic chaplaincy, see a special issue of *Christian Bioethics* (vol. 4, December 1998) dedicated to this topic. It includes the following articles: H.T. Engelhardt, Jr., "Generic Chaplaincy: Providing Spiritual Care in a Post-Christian Age", pp. 231-238; Kurt W. Schmidt and Gisela Egler, "A Christian for the Christians, a Muslim for the Muslims? Reflections on a Protestant View of Pastoral Care for all Religions", pp. 239-256; Joseph J. Kotva, Jr., "Hospital Chaplaincy as Agapeic Intervention", pp. 257-275; Rev. Thomas Joseph, "Secular vs. Orthodox Christianity: Taking the Kingdom of Heaven Seriously", pp. 276-278; V. Rev. Edward Hughes, "Two Contemporary Examples of Christian Love", pp. 279-283; Corinna Delkeskamp-Hayes, "A Christian for the Christians, a Christian for the Muslims? An Attempt at an Argumentum ad Hominem", pp. 284-304; Christopher Tollefsen, "'Meta Ain't Always Betta': Conceptualizing the Generic Chaplaincy Issue", pp. 305-315. This issue of *Christian Bioethics* has appeared in German with some additional material as *(Klinik-) Seelsorge im multireligiösen Kontext*, ed. Kurt Schmidt (Frankfurt: Zentrum für Ethik in der Medizin, 1999).

35. This content-rich vision of a global, liberal cosmopolitan ethos sustaining an ecumenical faith confirms Dostoevsky's powerful insight into the tie between Western Christianity, socialism, and the anti-Christ figure of the Grand Inquisitor. Now, however, the post-modern Grand Inquisitor has a softer and much more seductive character. The Inquisitor still recognizes that the full range of human choice must be constrained in favor of a "true" liberty, for most will "never be capable of using their freedom." Fyodor Dostoevsky, *The Brothers Karamazov*, ed. Ralph Matlaw, trans. Constance Garnett (New York: W.W. Norton, 1976), p. 242. It is the Inquisitor who must establish this range. Similarly, the liberal cosmopolitan must assure that all are liberated from any "false consciousness" that would be a stumbling block to their embrace of the liberal cosmopolitan ethos. The pleasing allures of immanence can control more effectively than the threat of torture. As a result, within an emerging global liberal cosmopolitan culture, "the flock will come together again and will submit once more" (p. 239). The liberal cosmopolitan Inquisitor is able to celebrate a diversity of religious and moral visions directing diverse communities as long as they all unite within a global community, somewhat like the Uniate churches of Rome governed within a set of robust, lexically prior constraints established by the Vatican. In the end, the goal is a global religion as a "unifying expressive activity through which we can…build our common world." Don Cupitt, *After God: The Future of Religion* (New York: Basic Books, 1997), p. 127.

36. Western Christian theology emerged with a deep faith in reason's capacity to disclose truths about God and the moral law. It initially promised proofs for God, freedom, and immortality. When it could not keep these promises, it was as if Western Christianity had evoked a *modus tollens*. This failure brought into question traditional Christianity and belief in a personal God. In this sense, Western Christianity and its faith in reason lie at the very roots of Western atheism. For a discussion of some of these issues, see Michael Buckley, S.J., *At the Origins of Modern Atheism* (New Haven, CN: Yale University Press, 1987).

37. The first known use of "Catholic" by the Church is in St. Ignatius of Antioch's "Letter to the Smyrnaeans" (VIII.2), where he says: "Wherever the bishop appears let the congregation be present; just as wherever Jesus Christ is, there is the Catholic Church." The passage does not concern simply the universality of the church, but the Church as an integral whole. *The Apostolic Fathers*, trans. Kirsopp Lake (Cambridge, MA: Harvard University Press, 1965), vol. 1, p. 261.

38. Kant, *Religion innerhalb der Grenzen der bloßen Vernunft*. See, in particular, AK VI, 174-175.

4 Bioethics and Transcendence: At the Heart of the Culture Wars

Sects, Cults, Fundamentalism, and Traditional Christian Bioethics

There still is heresy. There is especially bioethical heresy. In a world of ecumenical zeal and cosmopolitan aspirations, divisive bioethical religious commitments are disruptive. They go against the grain of the times. They challenge the hunger for consensus. They undermine the hope for a common morality. They call into question the possibility of an overlapping moral consensus to sustain a common content-full political conception of justice in society in general and health care in particular.[1] Terms such as sect, cult, and fundamentalist possess strategic rhetorical force. They serve to marginalize and discount groups that constitute a threat to a broad-based moral unity. They are political terms for condemning and controlling deviance. They identify groups who challenge the hegemony of the liberal cosmopolitan ethos. To be sectarian is to be at variance with those religions that sustain the moral images, moral sentiments, moral structures, and bioethics of the dominant secular culture. Mainstream Christian religions, insofar as their transcendent claims are blunted and their energies turned ecumenical, support the liberal cosmopolitan ethos that is supposed to bind reasonable persons, sustain an overlapping bioethical consensus, and justify the health care policy it should endorse.

The mainstream religions in doctrine, and especially in practice, accord with the dominant mores of our age. They are post-traditional in being distant from the church of the first millennium, especially from its understandings of sexuality, the meaning of death, and appropriate family structure. They embrace the liberal cosmopolitan vision from which they draw a passion for ecumenism.[2] They find themselves sympathetic with the secular culture's moral rationality and its prevailing bioethical fashions. To the discomfiture of a post-metaphysical, liberal culture, sectarians or fundamentalists have a cult of full commitment to a transcendent truth.

The images of reasonable inclusiveness that direct the larger society contrast with the focused and narrow commitments of sects and cults. Sects and cults affirm moral views and take courses out of phase with contemporary conceits. The Latin *cultus*, which identifies occupation, training, dress, and worship, suggests that cults mark out their members with particularities at variance with the moral, bioethical, and religious consensus of the surrounding society. Traditional Christian bioethics is cultic in embedding its moral concerns in a particular life of worship. Traditional Christians pursue ways of life at variance with mainline moral and religious understandings, not to mention secular health care policy. They are cultic in nurturing special ways of living and dying. They may affirm ascetic practices that favor a death of sorrowful repentance concerning past sins to a death of satisfaction with one's life's accomplishments. They are likely to value spiritual health over mental and physical health. Sects in following unpopular viewpoints go against the stream into which the mainstream wishes to channel history. They cut themselves off from its rationality. Traditional Christian bioethics is sectarian in this sense. It leads in directions that go against the prevailing bioethics of public policy which, for instance, supports prenatal screening, abortion, and artificial insemination from donors. Moreover, traditional Christianity is fundamentalist in being opposed to revisionist forms of Christianity, which deny the traditional fundamentals of orthodox belief.[3]

Fundamentalists are the worst of sectarians.[4] They draw their beliefs from and/or ground them in foundational commitments or experiences not open to negotiation, compromise, or discursive rational adjudication. They also hold deeply rooted metaphysical, moral, and bioethical convictions in discord with a hoped-for common morality. Fundamentalists employ language that is moralistic, condemnatory, and divisive on fundamental matters. In a world where law and public policy recognize the availability of abortion as protecting free choice, religious fundamentalists are apt to recognize such "choices" as facilitating murder, indeed, mass murder.[5] Their bioethics not only offends a spirit of toleration that would eschew moralism and require the affirmative acceptance of private choices, it also offends against an aspiration to a consensus, or at least to an overlapping consensus, that can support a common human morality, or at least common bioethical understandings. The strident language of "murder" and "murderer" directed against abortion and abortionists, and "perversion" directed against forms of third-party assisted reproduction which violate the bounds of traditional marriage, highlights differences separating mainstream versus traditional Christian bioethics. Fundamentalists are the heretics of our contemporary post-Christian, cosmopolitan culture: they call into question its unity in matters of foundational concern. In challenging its assumptions they threaten its stability.[6] Fundamentalists are sectarians with foundational, divisive, and non-negotiable commitments who practice an unpopular cult.

Traditional Christian bioethics as sectarian, cultic, and fundamentalist stands over against the now dominant, post-metaphysical, secular public morality that emerged after the Western religious wars and during the Enlightenment.[7] Unlike particular secular, as well as rationalistic, religious moralities, which attempt to camouflage their parochial or particular character under the guise of conceptual analysis and discursive argument, all the while presupposing crucial content-rich premises, rules of moral evidence, and rules of moral inference, traditional Christian morality and bioethics are blatantly particular at their surface and at their roots. Their content is secured in an experience of, indeed communion with, the personal and transcendent God Who works wonders.[8] They are grounded in a noetic, not discursive rationality. Traditional Christians are in this sense fundamentalists.

This chapter addresses the foundations of a Christian bioethics that is fundamentalist in being firmly committed to the unchanging fundamentals of traditional Christian faith, by invoking a view of rationality not accessible in the public forum,[9] and by being committed to a moral view at odds with the surrounding liberal cosmopolitan culture. Traditional Christianity is the counter-pole to those moralities that find their foundations in human choice, immanent reality, and the liberal cosmopolitan ethos. Traditional Christian morality, rather than adapting to the character of the contemporary world, invites the contemporary world to be transformed by a message millennia old. Traditional Christianity's bioethics threatens to invade the secular public forum and its discourse that aspire to be unmarked by transcendent religious claims.[10] Although secular reason cannot justify a content-full, canonical moral vision,[11] and since Christian morality is grounded in an experience of grace, Christians may still enter into the space of a procedural morality grounded in permission. They may make contracts and agreements involving the sparse morality binding moral strangers. However, within that space they should peaceably condemn that which they know to be wrong, even if that wrongness is not justifiable in general secular terms. Traditional Christian bioethics may not forgo what will be perceived by others as an intrusively sectarian presence by camouflaging its true character.

As this chapter turns to the fundamentals of a traditional Christian bioethics, a cardinal ambiguity looms large. In the face of so many Christianities, which should provide the framework for a Christian bioethics? As the first chapter acknowledges, this volume is grounded in the Christianity that once united the Mediterranean littoral in belief and worship. Here a further ambiguity rises as a possible roadblock. From what perspective should one understand this Christianity? Should one regard this Christianity as historically foundational in the sense of being at the historical roots of the contemporary Christianities that developed and took possession of new theological understandings? After all, it does provide the point of departure for these Christianities, no matter how extensively they may have transformed their roots. Or should one instead regard the Christianity of the first millennium as not at all past, antiquated, or obsolete, but as vividly present and alive? It is the second view that this volume embraces, although this option also allows a perspective on these historical roots. This Christianity at the foundations of the contemporary Christianities is found within the experience of Orthodox Christianity, a perspective established before the Renaissance, Reformation, and Enlightenment, as well as over against the immanentized Christianity of the previous chapter. It offers a bioethics from a vantage point that lives in the texts of the first millennium with an immediacy not found in the other Christianities, while also disclosing the ultimate roots of Western Christian culture. It can contribute an understanding of bioethics drawn from a worldview articulated before the dizzying array of diverse Christianities born of the Reformation. It can explore issues from a perspective antecedent to the conflict between Protestantism and Roman Catholicism, which in their dialectic of disputes defined a Christianity for which only the Enlightenment seemed an adequate solution.

"Traditional Christianity" identifies a Christianity that uses first millennium theological texts as contemporary guides for understanding Christian morality and, therefore, bioethics. Traditional Christianity lives not only in the texts, thoughts, and practices out of which all Christianity developed as the testimony of living holiness, but also lives with the authors of those texts. Such a Christianity experiences itself within a life-world thickly nested within the metaphysics and axiology of a substantive morality that guides bioethical choices. This life-world is experienced not just in continuity with the past. It experiences the past and its saints as present in an enduring now. For example, speaking of the Fathers of the Councils, the Church sings

> Those God-mantled Fathers have proclaimed today in concert that the uncreated Trinity is one God and one Lord, explaining to all the agreement of the simplicity of the one Nature through participation of the will, and the simplicity of the deed, and defining all as without beginning and without end. Wherefore, we glorify them, as being like to the Apostles and teaching their Gospel to all.[12]

The Fathers are present in the contemporary life of the Church.

It is here that one finds a decisive contrast. Not just the Orthodox, but also Roman Catholic theologians and Protestant reformers such as John Calvin knew the texts of the Eastern Fathers. Traditional Christianity does not simply know and use such texts. It is immersed in the lifeworld that sustains them. Traditional Christianity experiences itself as not merely reacting to or engaging the texts of the first millennium of Christianity. It lives fully in the mind in which those authors wrote and in the embrace of their theological world-view. In this sense of "traditional" Christianity, the authors of such texts are present as fully relevant contributors to contemporary debates. For this to be the case, there must be a continuity of epistemological, metaphysical, and axiological commitments as well as theological experiences so that questions are framed and answered as the Fathers would pose such questions and answer them. There must be a thick communality and, most importantly, a continuity of the Spirit.

On the one hand, this sense of traditional Christianity embraces all who from any Christian religion affirm and attempt to live in this continuity with the Christianity of the first millennium. Traditional Christianity represents an always and everywhere present possibility of redemption of the Spirit. On the other hand, this sense of traditional Christianity identifies as its exemplar, Orthodox Christianity. Orthodox Christianity interweaves theological experience and reflection through liturgical texts and ascetical practices that have firm roots in the work and sentiments of the Fathers, thus making the Fathers of the Church and their lives present to the contemporary community of believers.[13] By sustaining religious life in the spirit of the first millennium, a framework for moral theology is engaged so that the contemporary believer can engage the moral reflections of early Christians with little conceptual opacity or distance. Contemporary traditional Christian theologians can identify with the work of ancient theologians. As a consequence, later authors can address issues in the same spirit as theologians over a millennium and a half before. Paradigms of analysis and reflection remain intact, supporting (1) a rich resource of literature bearing on the grounding of a Christian moral theology and its bioethics, which (2) provides the roots of Western Christian moral theology, however different that theology may now have become. Within this framework, within this Spirit, a traditional Christian bioethics can be nested in the religious mind of the first millennium.

It might be protested: a reliance on biblical Christianity would more firmly ground a Christian bioethics than one for which the Bible is set within theological texts of the 2nd century and later. However, which construal of biblical Christianity should be used? Even from the outside, a very plausible choice is that of the 4th century, which provided commentaries on the New Testament at the very time the Church was defining the scriptural canon. Indeed, what it is to have canonical Scriptures was understood in the first millennium in terms different from those articulated in the disputes between Roman Catholicism and Protestantism in the 16th century. The question in the first millennium was not simply what books are sacred, can be read for edification, or are divinely inspired, but what books may be read in the church, the place within which Scripture is authenticated. The focus is on the liturgical life within which Scripture has its place and draws its meaning.[14] The liturgical centering of the Scriptures has profound implications for Christian bioethics, as we shall see.

This sense of traditional Christianity is out of phase with elements of what became the Western Christian tradition. After all, Blessed Augustine of Hippo (354-430) plays little role in the tradition framing this book. This may seem odd. From the perspective of the West, Augustine is Christianity's major first-millennium figure. He towers over other Latin Fathers in the scope, depth, and philosophical character of his work. It is impossible to conceive of the subsequent history of Roman Catholicism or of the emergence of Calvinism and Lutheranism in his absence. But for the East, Augustine was a bishop from far northwestern Africa, who wrote in a language inaccessible to many of the major Christian thinkers of his time. On the periphery of Christianity, both geographically and culturally, his theological work was largely unknown and without force for the tradition sustained by the Church of the Councils, the Church of the East.[15] He had little or no role in the tradition so understood. Traditional Christianity, as this volume understands it, compasses a unity of worship and religious sensibility that draws more from the Syrian Christianity of the early 5th century than from the Christianity of northwest Africa.

In the spirit of informed consent, the reader should receive a repeated disclosure of why the author has chosen this perspective for an account of Christianity and Christian bioethics: he knows it is true. Still, it is hoped that even those who do not share the author's conviction, even atheists, will garner a fresh appreciation of contemporary bioethical controversies, when regarded from a perspective nearly a millennium distant from Western Christian thought. After all, it is this perspective that lies at the foundations of Western Christian moral theology and contemporary Christian bioethics. A further warning is also due: as the volume turns to address the foundations of a traditional Christian bioethics, the tone of exposition is often homiletical, if not exhortative. The reason lies in the epistemology of a traditional Christian moral theology. A change of heart, repentance, is integral to an epistemology grounded in a worshipful relationship to, indeed, in a union with, God. If canonical moral knowledge cannot be acquired by analysis and discursive argument, but first and originally through an experiential relationship with God, then the method of this epistemology will be unavoidably tied to living as a traditional Christian. To know well, one must be open to God. One must pray well and worship well in order to know God well. Providing an account of a traditional Christian bioethics requires laying out this invitation to an experiential relationship. An exploration of a traditional Christian bioethics must be conducted in a genre of exposition necessarily having some of the characteristics of a spiritual manual. The knower must be spiritually prepared in order to know truly. Only by spiritual preparation can one successfully enter traditional Christian moral theological and bioethical reflection. After all, the claim is that moral and metaphysical knowledge is to be acquired from the religious life one lives. Since the moral and metaphysical knowledge at the roots of Christian bioethics is acquired not by discursive reasoning but from noetic knowledge made possible by an appropriate relationship with God, much turns on the spiritual state of the knower.

For those who have read the Church Fathers, this approach to moral theology and Christian metaphysics will not seem as exotic as it will to those who are primarily acquainted with contemporary philosophical and bioethical texts. The works of St. John Chrysostom (344-407) and St. Isaac the Syrian (613-c.700) are predominantly in the form of homilies. So, too, the work of the Church Fathers is preponderantly of a devotional or pastoral nature. This may seem out of place to the contemporary reader, unless it is recognized that this account of moral knowledge requires changing the knower so as to be able to be open to God, to be able to come into union with the object of knowledge, rather than devising better arguments so as to argue to or conclude to the object of knowledge. If with the Fathers one recognizes truth as the Persons of the Trinity, rather than as impersonal fact to be known discursively, the genre they have chosen for their writings can be accepted as appropriate to their task, even if one is an unbeliever and does not credit their claims. In this spirit I invite the unbelieving reader to an exploration of a moral epistemological point of view that underlies the project of a traditional Christian bioethics, with the warning that this language is not that usually found in bioethics texts.

From Discursive Reason to Spiritual Change

The project of a post-Christian bioethics freed from transcendent claims is at loggerheads with traditional Christian aspirations to experience and be redeemed by a truth that is both personal and transcendent. An ecumenical faith with its ecumenical bioethics, such as the one described in chapter 3, is not the faith of traditional Christianity, or until recently of most Christianities. It stands over against the radical character of the Jewish acknowledgement of the Father and the Christian recognition of the Incarnation of His Son through the Spirit. The Judeo-Christian focus is on a very particular God. The anaphorae of the Liturgies of St. Basil and St. John Chrysostom take pains to identify and address the right God, the true God, and no one else. This necessity of appropriately directing one's prayer discloses that other attempts at religion fall short of the mark, being significantly distorted by human passions, if not by diabolic presence.

The grounding reality of traditional Christianity is a personal God Who is transcendent, Who became incarnate, and Who rose from the dead: the long-awaited Messiah of Israel. Christianity has traditionally focused on knowing God, recognizing this knowledge to be transforming and very particular, that "grace and truth came through Jesus Christ" (John 1:17). Traditional Christianity has not sought to conform to the prevailing secular consensus, but to be the faith to which God requires agreement. "For if you do not believe that I am *He*, you will die in your sins" (John 8:24). "Now we command you, brethren, in the name of our Lord Jesus Christ, that ye withdraw yourselves from every brother that walketh disorderly, and not after the tradition [*paradosis*] which he received of us" (2 Thes 3:6). Moreover, the experience of God is not determined by the community, nor is it simply an immanent apperception of sanctity and holiness. Instead, the goal is to turn humbly to God with full expectation that one can experience God, Who is transcendent. The experience of God is first and foremost the result of the reality of God.

This experiential character of traditional Christian theology has implications for its bioethics. Traditional Christianity has not sought to devise better arguments to prove God's existence or discursively to discover the character of divine commands. Instead, the cardinal question has been:

> How can I live so as to experience God and know the content of the moral
> life (including that which bears on health care)?

The knowledge that is the focus of this question possesses at best a family resemblance with the knowing involved in the empirical sciences, mathematics, or formal logic. The knowing par excellence at the root of traditional Christian bioethics is not the knowing at the root of immanent knowing. Christianity aspires not to an as-if transcendental reality à la Kant, but to a real union with the actual and only God. Its focus is beyond the immanent. It seeks an intimate knowing between persons, most particularly an illumination of the creature by the Creator. It is only through this illumination that true knowledge becomes possible.

The question of establishing the truth of a moral account and the content of a Christian bioethics is recast. Rather than asking (1) how one can discursively reason successfully to the truth and the nature of morality, or (2) what empirical investigation can disclose regarding religious experience within the sphere of immanent reality, attention turns instead to the experience of God Himself. Where the first engages in rational philosophical argument and analysis to know God and the character of morality, and the second engages in an empirical investigation of the immanent character of religious experience to appreciate better the character of religious behavior, this last focus brings us to a non-discursive, personal knowledge of God. This reorientation takes us from invoking permission, analyzing the character of arguments, and assessing the character of evidence, to a moral and spiritual change in ourselves that can invite illumination by God.

This change in orientation fundamentally redirects how one might consider the project of knowing the character of morality, the existence of God, and the content of bioethics. St. Maximus (580-662) warns, "The way to knowledge is detachment and humility, without which no one will see the Lord."[16] Though one should not involve others without their consent, and though one may begin by attending to arguments and empirical evidence, the project of morally knowing truly is in its core the project of turning away from self-love to love of God and one's neighbor, so as to experience God. Christian bioethics must consequently be more a way of life than a collection of principles, rules, intellectual insights, or conclusions to arguments. Christian bioethics so construed has much more to do with holiness than with social justice. Traditional Christian bioethics will be first and foremost associated with seeking "the kingdom of God and His righteousness" (Matt 6:33), a kingdom not of this world (John 18:36).

Disbelief: A Moral Choice, not a Miscalculation

Traditional Christianity and its Christian bioethics are first and foremost a matter of faith, repentance, and grace. Knowledge of God is not secured by philosophical arguments; in this, Kant is right. We cannot with discursive arguments reach beyond the bonds of possible empirical experience to an infinite God Who is by His nature beyond our sensory, spatio-temporal experience and discursive concepts. "God is Spirit (John 4:24), invisible, immortal, inaccessible, incomprehensible,"[17] as St. Symeon the New Theologian (949-1022) stresses and the anaphorae of Sts. Basil and Chrysostom proclaim.[18] Within the bounds of the immanent, the transcendent is always invisible, as Kierkegaard recognized. The one who says in his heart there is no God (Psalm 13:1, LXX) is not a fool because his philosophical arguments are inadequate and fail to prove God's existence. Nor is he a fool because of philosophical miscalculations. No philosophical argument can disclose God's existence or nature. The non-believer is a fool because, in order not to see God, he must exclude God from the meaning of his life, the purpose of the universe, and the significance of bioethics. The choice is a moral one because it involves how one ought to regard reality. It is a foolish choice with dramatic moral consequences: the fool decides to approach his life, reality, health care policy, and bioethics as if they were without final and enduring personal significance. Reality is regarded as ultimately surd, conveying to a consistent moral life a sense of the absurd: one does what is right even if all that is right and good fails to endure. In the face of a meaningless universe, one acts to pursue meaning, which in the end will be obliterated by the impersonal forces of an uncaring universe. In such circumstances, one implicitly regards oneself as a moral demigod or as one of a community of demigods without a God, and as the only source of moral meaning in a world that is amoral. One can even take the next step and become a rebel against a universe supposedly deaf to morality.[19] In any event, one orients oneself to the universe as if there were no ultimate personal meaning. The fool is a moral fool for affirming less than ultimate personal meaning in a universe that in its foundations is radically personal. The fool chooses to find his ultimate meaning within the horizon of the immanent, the reality he can survey and compass through his senses. He does not direct his life to transcendent personal meaning. By deciding not to turn to reality with an openness to affirming enduring, personal meaning, the fool willfully gives a significance to his life that does not include a positive relationship to God. As the traditional Christian knows, this is a fool's choice, for God awaits us. We need only choose to turn to Him. When the fool approaches his life and the universe as if they had no enduring, personal meaning, this choice against meaning becomes his destiny.

Although there are differences between the atheist and the agnostic, the lives and bioethics of both involve movement from God. The atheist firmly rejects an ultimate personal meaning for his life, the existence of the universe, and bioethics. The agnostic, who is not prayerfully open to the possibility of God's presence, steps back from such an affirmation and determines to make do within the finite significance of the immanent. This, too, is a choice. The agnostic refuses to turn to reality in prayerful search for ultimate personal significance. Life, the articulation of a bioethics, and the universe itself are approached apart from a continuing concern for ultimate and enduring personal purpose. The possibility of the most important truth in the universe, that at the root of everything there is an eternal and loving Person, is not pursued with consuming zeal. God is instead bracketed as a philosophically undeterminable matter. This choice shapes the character of the agnostic's life. Both the agnostic and the atheist affirm themselves, and perhaps others, but not God, or even the search for God. Confronted with a choice for or against the pursuit of God, for or against faith, the fool embraces the finite and the immanent while eschewing the transcendent and the eternal. This choice involves a defining orientation to oneself, bioethics, and the universe. The question is then:

> Will I turn to reality and to my life, worshipfully affirming that there must be ultimate enduring personal meaning, or instead accept a presumptive ultimate meaninglessness?

This crucial question is not how to argue cogently. The question is how to direct one's life so as to experience morality, including bioethics.

The pursuit of God must come from the heart. It requires an affirmative openness to ultimate personal meaning. To that affirmation, Christianity has traditionally held there will be a response: God will move in synergy with one's free act of turning to Him. Through such a faith-filled turn in the heart nature becomes a window to God and an occasion for a dialogue between creature and Creator. In this dialogue nature can become available as creation, as a signpost directing us to God, the Creator. Without this turn of faith, nature cannot even be recognized as creation. Clement of Alexandria (155-220) stressed that the pagan philosophers were not able to see the world as created. "[T]he first cause of the universe was not previously known to the Greeks."[20] The existence of the finite does not logically require the infinite, at least an infinite that is personal.[21] The experience of the world as creation comes from a turn to God.[22] It would be a mistake to consider nature by itself as evidence in an objective proof of the existence of God, for it is impossible to conclude from the finite to the infinite, from human concepts to that which is beyond human concepts. One cannot consider the turn to God or to nature as an engagement in an ontological argument for God's existence or as an argument to a First Cause, as an argument from design, etc. Such so-called proofs for the existence of God do not function as sound rational arguments but instead portray a realization of a reality, not a syllogistic conclusion. They are summaries of an experience of God when one opens one's heart to His existence.

The existence of God is experienced as one turns from oneself, wholeheartedly to Him. Indeed, faith plays the key role in providing knowledge inaccessible through discursive philosophy, as Clement of Alexandria stresses.

> Should one say that Knowledge is founded on demonstration by a process of reasoning, let him hear that first principles are incapable of demonstration; for they are known neither by art nor sagacity. For the latter is conversant about objects that are susceptible of change, while the former is practical solely, and not theoretical. Hence it is thought that the first cause of the universe can be apprehended by faith alone. For all knowledge is capable of being taught; and what is capable of being taught is

founded on what is known before. ... For knowledge is a state of mind that results from demonstration; but faith is a grace which from what is indemonstrable conducts to what is universal and simple, what is neither with matter, nor matter, nor under matter.[23]

Clement does not deny that God can respond to the prayers of pagan Greeks, even of pagan philosophers. However, apart from faith, he recognizes there would be sparse guidance. Our existence in nature is not a step in a proof, but an occasion for us to see God.

The prayerful examination of nature discloses God and in that sense guidance for a Christian bioethics. But this examination does not involve investigating nature as an inert object. It is not a theoretical, scientific, or scholastic examination of nature undertaken in order to conclude to a natural theology. The examination requires turning to reality in the affirmation and expectation of ultimate personal meaning, so that nature can become an occasion for God to reveal Himself. Nature in our encounter with reality will seem ultimately meaningless until it becomes a window to God.

By natural revelation, God leads the man who believes in him towards the goal of union with himself through indirect utterance and through things, making use of the various circumstances, problems, troubles, and pains that man faces and of the thoughts aroused in his conscience so that man can progress towards God through the way in which he faces up to all these things.[24]

When the heart turns toward God, the boundary between natural revelation and supernatural disclosure gives way before the presence of the Creator. To consider natural revelation as simply natural is to assume that God will not respond personally to those who turn to Him. It is to act without taking account of God as personal. When one turns to nature and sees God's presence, one begins to go beyond nature. When God turns back to His creatures through nature, more is said than mere nature can reveal and provide as content for a bioethics.

Considering natural theology, moral philosophy, moral theology, and bioethics as separable from how one lives one's life is a cardinal error.[25] So, too, is imagining that human ingenuity on its own can break through immanent reality to discover the existence of God, ultimate meaning, or even the canonical content-full character of morality. Again, the very notion of discursively discovering transcendent truth, given the finite capacities of human thought, is oxymoronic. As Kant rightly understands, the finite cannot reach to the infinite. The limiting sphere of immanence is broken by worshipfully turning to encounter God. As Paul Evdokimov stresses,

We prove God's existence by worshipping Him and not by advancing so-called proofs. We have here the liturgical and iconographic argument for the existence of God. We arrive at a solid belief in the existence of God through a leap over what seems true, over the Pascalian certitude. According to an ancient monastic saying, "Give your blood and receive the Spirit."[26]

Second, exaggerated expectations regarding natural theology can also lead to exaggerated expectations (indeed, pride) regarding moral philosophy by suggesting that the nature of the moral life and the content of a Christian bioethics can be secured through discursive arguments, rather than from turning to God. Third, the idea of a purely discursive proof for the existence of God is also morally misleading. It dangerously and unjustifiably inflates expectations concerning discursive reasoning, which when disappointed are a temptation to atheism. The notion that the content of a canonical morality (and bioethics) is disclosable by sound rational argument rather than by opening one's heart to grace will like an *ignis fatuus* lead to quicksands of unsustainable expectations from secular philosophy that when disappointed may engender skepticism regarding moral truth, the possibility of a Christian bioethics, and even the existence of God.

The content and substance of theology and morality, including knowledge of the existence of God and of the content of a Christian bioethics, are not acquired by rational argument itself. If Christian bioethics is to have a content beyond that which is historically conditioned and possess an authority more than that derived from the consent of a particular community, Christian bioethics must be given content and authority by God. Traditional Christianity must offer an intimate connection with God Who can set aside the confines of immanence and the historically conditioned character of biblical texts. The foundations of Christian ethics and bioethics cannot merely be scriptural, because Christianity's foundation is in the transcendent beyond any immanent experience or texts. The experience of God grounds the authority of the Scriptures and the Church, which authenticates the Scriptures. St. John Chrysostom even laments that we must at all rely on Scriptures.

> It were indeed meet for us not at all to require the aid of the written Word, but to exhibit a life so pure, that the grace of the Spirit should be instead of books to our souls, and that as these are inscribed with ink, even so should our hearts be with the Spirit. But, since we have utterly put away from us this grace, come, let us at any rate embrace the second best course.
> For that the former was better, God hath made manifest, both by His words, and by His doings. Since unto Noah, and unto Abraham, and unto his offspring, and unto Job, and unto Moses too, He discoursed not by writings, but Himself by Himself, finding their minds pure.[27]

For traditional Christianity, theology par excellence is union with God. All else is analysis and commentary on a gift given from a personal God. Indeed, the good moral life, including keeping the commandments, is not an end in itself but only a means for union with God. Further, as will be clearer shortly, the Scriptures are not a source of moral content outside of the liturgical life of Christians.[28] A traditional Christian bioethics is liturgical, more than scriptural.

In summary, natural theology, Christian morality, and Christian bioethics begin with a turning to God. They begin with a choice about oneself and one's relationship to God. One is affirming or rejecting a connection to a final personal meaning beyond oneself. To regard oneself and to approach reality as if there were no ultimate or final meaning, or not to make the pursuit of that reality important for one's life, is a choice with ultimate significance for oneself and one's relationship to reality. To decide to approach the world as empty of God establishes how one will understand oneself, one's life, and bioethics. Agnosticism is not a miscalculation. Agnosticism is a moral choice about the very tenor, character, and energies of one's life. If one turns to God, one will find oneself in worshipful relation with Him. If one decides to the contrary, one will find oneself separated from Him. Thus, St. John Chrysostom in his account of the perceptibility of natural law distinguishes pagans in general from those who follow the law of God in their hearts, because the latter worship the true God.[29]

> But by Greeks he [St. Paul] here [Rom 1:28] means not them that worshipped idols, but them that adored God, that obeyed the law of nature, that strictly kept all things, save the Jewish observances, which contribute to piety, such as were Melchizedek and his, such as was Job, such as were the Ninevites, such as was Cornelius.[30]

To perceive the natural law, one must turn to God. Melchizedek was, after all, "a priest of the most high God", so that he could bless Abraham (Gen 14:18-19). The thrust of St. John Chrysostom's remarks is that the Greeks of whom St. Paul speaks when he identifies those who recognize and keep "the work of the law written in their hearts" (Rom 2:15) are not just any pagans, but properly pious, monotheistic pagans. To have moral knowledge, one must act with worshipful propriety. Moral action, faith, and knowledge are intimately interwoven so that a Christian bioethics requires for its mastery more than intellectual engagement or even clinical practice. It requires faith.

Christian Bioethics: The Knowledge of the Heart and the Natural Law

The moral epistemology underlying Christian bioethics is unlike that which can be claimed for secular bioethics. Or to put matters another way, the collapse of Christian bioethics into secular bioethics is only avoided when one recalls that the epistemological claims of Christian bioethics are rooted in a real experience of a transcendent God. In the absence of a noetic experience, religious knowledge will always only be immanent.[31] The foundations of a traditional Christian bioethics escape the difficulties besetting secular morality because its foundations are in the end noetic.[32] They are anchored in an experience of God, so that a canonical content-full morality can be (1) received, (2) apperceived as true, and (3) sustained in a community maintained in this experience over the centuries.[33] The church must out of an engagement with God unbroken through the centuries secure and preserve the moral content that it proclaims.

The use of such Greek terms as nous, noesis, and noetic may be off-putting at best and even a stumbling block for biblically oriented Christian bioethicists. They may suggest that more of Proclus[34] and less of Christ is being introduced in such an account of moral theology. This is a misunderstanding, though there is surely a borrowing of terms from Greek philosophy. The term nous should be taken as nothing other than a synonym for the heart of which Christ and St. Paul speak, as well as certain uses of understanding or mind, as when St. Paul enjoins us to be transformed by the renewing of our minds (nous) (Rom 12:2). [35] The traditional Christian account of knowledge is that the nous is the perceptive ability of which the Gospel proclaims, "Blessed are the pure in heart [*kardia*], for they shall see God" (Matt 5:8). This invocation of heart identifies the central faculty of understanding, which when opened and oriented to God transforms us so that we are restored by grace. At stake is a new way of seeing held to be exactly that to which St. Paul exhorts his readers in Ephesus, "[I pray] in order that the God of our Lord Jesus Christ, the Father of glory, may give to you the Spirit of wisdom and revelation, in the full knowledge of Him having the eyes of your heart [*kardia*] enlightened that ye may know what is the hope of His calling" (Eph 1:17-18).

Noetic experience is the sufficient condition required to establish a Christian bioethics, as well as to identify true theologians. Theologians *sensu stricto* are those who know in a direct, non-discursive fashion the content of Christian morality. Only a direct noetic experience of God's transcendent reality can bring human knowledge beyond the sphere of immanence and provide access not only to ultimate personal meaning, but to the experience of the canonical character of a morality. Christianity brings the indwelling of God, so that spiritual comprehension is achieved. The goal is "that the Christ might dwell in your hearts through faith, having been rooted and founded in love, in order that ye might be able to apprehend with all the saints what is the breadth and length and depth and height, and to know the love of the Christ which surpasseth knowledge, that ye might be filled to all the fullness of God" (Eph 3:17-19). As St. John the Theologian stresses, "And ye have an anointing from the Holy One, and ye know all things" (I John 2:20). With the Spirit of God a new form of knowledge is possible.

In this experience of God one's sins become only too apparent, making manifest the unchanging morality of the Church. In this experience, to approach God is to recognize one's sinfulness. As King David sings in Psalm 5, a psalm recited at the first hour: "He that worketh evil shall not dwell near Thee, nor shall transgressors abide before Thine eyes" (Ps 5:3, LXX). To recognize one's unworthiness is also to discern how one has turned away from Him. This morality, which is the content of Christian bioethics, should not be taken as simply an inventory of external prescriptions and proscriptions, nor as an impersonal codebook of divine law, but more fully as the requirements for orienting one's heart to God in worshipful love. Christian morality is thus as truly love as it is all the prescriptions and proscriptions that have been a part of a Christian life from the time of the Apostles. In this union of love with God, Christian morality becomes as well known to theologians today as it was to those who wrote the books of the New Testament. After all, if true experience of God's transcendent reality grounds its moral knowledge, then Christian bioethics possesses a firm foundation in the source of being itself, the personal life of the Trinity. Unless there is the possibility of experiencing God, all is isolated and indeed lost in the immanence of phenomenal appearance, the uncertainty of the correct ranking of moral values and principles, and the socio-historically conditioned character of texts. If God can be experienced, then one can break through the horizon of the finite. A connection with God Who is the aim of all morality is a necessary and sufficient condition for the possibility of maintaining a Christian bioethics that is not ultimately rooted in secular bioethics.

The issue of a noetic grounding for morality is crucial. Only if truth veridically communicates with us can we break out of the horizon of immanence. If we cannot experience a particular moral vision as canonical, then we are returned to a libertarian moral perspective with permission as the only ground for moral authority, even among moral friends. This default position can only be escaped if we can have noetic knowledge of the truth. If we cannot have such knowledge, then moral claims will beg the question or engage in infinite regress, leaving permission as the only source of moral authority, even among moral friends.[36] The position of traditional Christianity is precisely that there is noetic knowledge, so that those who experience it experience the canonical character of traditional Christian morality. Needless to say, for many outside of this experience, this claim will not at all be persuasive. From the outside, the claim can at best be appreciated as the recognition of a possible sufficient condition for a canonical, content-full morality. For traditional Christians, this will not be an outrageous claim because of their first-hand knowledge that this experience is given as both sufficient and necessary. They will also recognize that, for those outside, an argument cannot be developed; one can only offer an invitation to turn in one's heart to God. This approach will always be unsatisfactory for those on the outside. To understand more, they must accept the invitation to taste and see.

This invitation, when accepted, discloses the grounding of a sense of right and wrong action placed in us by God and which grows through prayer and worship. Because of this gift of God in us, we can without external instruction perceive morality. Morality is disclosed without any contribution from the scholarly undertakings of philosophy. Even in our sinful state, this knowledge of the heart is usually sufficient to guide, even in the absence of special illumination by God achieved by theologians. St. John Chrysostom stresses, "a natural law of good and evil is seated within us."[37] This knowledge of the nature of proper conduct "resides within the conscience of all men, and we require no teacher to instruct us in these things."[38] As a consequence, for example,

> ... we account adultery to be an evil thing, and neither is there here any need of trouble or learning, that the wickedness of this sin may be known; but we are all self-taught in such judgments; and we applaud virtue, though we do not follow it; as, on the other hand, we hate vice, though we practise it. And this hath been an exceeding good work of God; that He hath made our conscience, and our power of choice already, and before the action, claim kindred with virtue, and be at enmity with wickedness.[39]

St. Isaac of Syria emphasizes the same point, terming this knowledge natural in being inherent in humans.

> What is natural knowledge? Knowledge is natural that discerns good from evil, and this is also called natural discernment, by which we know to discern good from evil naturally, without being taught. God has implanted this in rational nature, and with teaching it receives growth and assistance; there is no one who does not have it. This power of natural knowledge is a rational soul's discernment of good and evil, which is constantly active in her.[40]

This natural knowledge is the basis of conscience: it allows us to know in our hearts what we ought to do.

In being rooted in us by God, our understanding of the moral law develops us and transforms us by God's grace as we turn to God. St. Basil explains:

> In the same way and even to a far greater degree is it true that instruction in divine law is not from without, but, simultaneously with the formation of the creature – man, I mean – a kind of rational force was implanted in us like a seed, which, by an inherent tendency, impels us toward love. This germ is then received into account in the school of God's commandments, where it is wont to be carefully cultivated and skillfully nurtured and thus, by the grace of God, brought to its full perfection. Wherefore, we, also, approving your zeal as essential for reaching the goal, shall endeavor with the help of God and the support of your prayers, and as power is given us by the Spirit, to enkindle the spark of divine love latent within you.[41]

Virtue is born of a response to a divine command. It is developed by drawing on a power in us from God.

> By means of this power, rightly and properly used, we pass our entire lives holily and virtuously, but through a perverted use of it we gradually fall prey to vice. ... Having received, therefore, a command to love God, we have possessed the innate power of loving from the first moment of our creation.[42]

The moral law is thus a means for the growth of an intimate connection between the creature and the Creator.

Our free choice is an essential element. We must answer the command to love God. As we respond to that command, we are transformed by God. God acts to change those who turn to Him as they cooperate with God Who transforms them. The moral law within, the ability to love God and turn to God and to others in love, makes possible a personal response to God, and leads to the acquisition of moral, including bioethical, knowledge. Again, the moral law that is at the basis of a traditional Christian bioethics is not a set of rules separate from or over against the persons who should obey them – it is part of them and properly their way of life. The moral law is integral to our turning in full love to God. Morality must be lived so as to cure our souls from passions, to make us whole, and to unite us with God. "In order that all may be one, even as Thou, Father, art in Me, and I in Thee, that they also may be one in Us" (John 17:21). If not corrupted, the heart can give guidance, though such guidance requires prayer and is often unreliable, given human passions, without the aid of someone who is a theologian. If one turns to satisfy oneself and not to pursue God, one follows the evil impulses of broken nature; one's sense of morality becomes further distorted and broken. The natural ability to discern good from evil can then be perverted through desire and sin. Once perverted, as St. Isaac the Syrian knows, one turns further from God and the ability appropriately to distinguish good from evil until one repents.

The prophet reproaches those who have destroyed this insight which discerns good from evil, saying, 'Man, being in honour, did not understand.' The honour belonging to rational nature is the discernment that tells good from evil, and those who have destroyed it are justly compared to 'mindless cattle', which have no rational and discerning faculty. With this discernment it is possible for us to find the pathway of God. This is knowledge that is natural; this is the predecessor of faith; and this is the pathway to God. By it we know to discern good from evil and to accept faith. The power of nature attests that it behooves man to believe in Him Who brings forth all things in His creation, to believe the words of His commandments, and to do them. From this belief is born the fear of God. When a man joins righteous works to the fear of God and makes a little progress in this activity, the fear of God gives birth to spiritual knowledge, which we have said is born of faith.[43]

To see clearly, one must in repentance turn from passions to God's grace.[44] Knowledge of the moral law is acquired primarily through a life of repentance and virtue, not one of discursive reflection.

This is not to deny the existence of morally complicated situations where it would be very wrong to follow the first impulse that recommends itself as the voice of conscience. For most persons, it will be important to reflect very carefully on situations so as to determine their character. This often requires well-developed analytic skills. Usually, it will be important to seek instruction from those who combine intelligence with moral experience in addressing complex bioethical issues. This will demand careful examination of issues, the drawing of distinctions, and the framing of discursive arguments about the character of these distinctions. But the content to which the analysis is directed and for which the distinctions are framed is not secured by discursive argument. The discernment necessary to see clearly what is appropriate and what is inappropriate will be drawn from a heart that has turned from itself to God. As we will see, discernment must be developed both ascetically and liturgically. Claims of bioethical knowledge should be tested by the moral experts who have acquired such discernment and who need not be educated.[45] Hence the role, *pace* Kant, of a spiritual father.[46] Finally, discernment in the full guidance of grace will even be free of the need for prior discursive analysis. Such discernment will simply penetrate to the heart of the matter.[47]

Nature, Natural Law, and the Fall

A superficial reading of Clement of Alexandria, St. Basil the Great, and St. John Chrysostom might still indicate a sense of natural law as understood by the Stoics or later by the Scholasticism of the West: an impersonal legislation, discursively available.[48] Gaius in his *Institutes* speaks of "the law that natural reason establishes among all mankind [and which] is followed by all people alike, and is called *ius gentium* [law of nations or law of the world] as being the law observed by all mankind."[49] So, too, Justinian's Code states that "The law of nature is that law which nature teaches to all animals ... this law does not belong exclusively to the human race, but belongs to all animals."[50] In such terms, natural law might not be recognized explicitly as a gift of God to our hearts coeval with our creation. Instead, it could be seen as merely grounded in human inclinations or biological functions. Or natural law can be regarded as expressing rational moral constraints binding both the creature and the Creator. In the first case, natural law will be brought into question by the pleomorphism of human inclinations and possible biological functions. In the second case, as a rational constraint, natural law will be brought into question by the multiplicity of moral rationalities. The first has its expression in biologically oriented natural law manuals of medical ethics,[51] the second has its expression in rationalistically oriented explorations of bioethical issues.[52] In either case, there is a failure intimately to connect natural law with God, from Whom its character comes and to Whom its observance directs us, and the content of which is as available to the ill-educated as to the schooled. Such approaches to natural law construe it as an independent moral reality that can assume the character of a would-be legalistic constraint on God.

William Blackstone (1723-1780) speaks of natural law as if it were a constraint on the Creator and creature extrinsic to the character of the relation of the Creator and the creation itself. He conceives of natural law as a third thing binding creatures and their Creator. In this case, one answers the question as to whether the good and the right are such because God commands them, or whether God commands them because they are good and right, by making the good and the right what creature and Creator both should acknowledge. It is simply that such moral conformity is for God effortless. Blackstone thus speaks of the laws of nature as

> the eternal, immutable laws of good and evil, to which the creator himself in all his dispensations conforms; and which he has enabled human reason to discover, so far as they are necessary for the conduct of human actions. Such among others are these principles: that we should live honestly, should hurt nobody, and should render to every one his due; to which three general precepts Justinian has reduced the whole doctrine of law.[53]

Yet a merciful transcendent God does not give us our due.[54] In addition, He is a radically transcendent Person Whose relationship to us is personal in contrast with natural law construed as an independent and impersonal moral framework. Natural law in Blackstone's interpretation is no longer the spark of God's love within us. It is an independent moral framework, which can be recruited as a foundation for bioethics. Natural law becomes an objective structure constraining God, angels, and humans. There is no realization that one pursues the good and does what is right, and that this conduct is best for oneself and for others, because through it one becomes the kind of person who can come into union with God.

The difficulty in understanding "natural law" lies partly in the ambiguity of "nature". Nature is everything created by God. Nature is also that which is proper to humans as human. In this sense nature compasses both humans and the world within which they were created. In addition, it is natural for man not only to have spatio-temporal, finite knowledge, but also to have noetic knowledge. Man is naturally a being who worships and turns noetically to know God, although the experience of God is beyond his nature. As St. Isaac the Syrian observes, it is as if man had two sets of eyes.

> What the bodily eyes are to sensory objects, the same is faith to the eyes of the intellect that gaze at hidden treasures. Even as we have two bodily eyes, we possess two eyes of the soul, as the Fathers say; yet both have not the same operation with respect to divine vision. With one we see the hidden glory of God which is concealed in the natures of things; that is to say, we behold His might, His wisdom, and His eternal providence for us which we understand by the magnitude of His governance on our behalf. With this same eye we also behold the heavenly orders of our fellow servants. With the other we behold the glory of His holy nature. When God is pleased to admit us to spiritual mysteries, He opens wide the sea of faith in our minds ...
> The intellect is spiritual perception that is conditioned to receive the faculty of divine vision, even as the pupils of the bodily eyes in which sensible light is poured. Noetic vision is natural knowledge that is used [by power] to the natural state and it is called natural light.[55]

It is not simply that after the Fall man is subject to the passions and weakness of will, and is therefore unable to carry through by himself the resolution to do the good. It is also the case that his intellect, his noetic capacities no longer without struggle allow him discernment of good and evil undistorted by desire. He also no longer possesses spiritual knowledge. The impact of the Fall is not so much on man's will as often supposed in the West, but upon his intellect, his noetic capacity for non-discursive knowledge.

Nature as creation is also now broken. In many ways, what is now "natural" is that which is improper for, and turned against, humans. The nature of man himself as well as the physical and biological nature that surrounds him is deaf to human purposes, if not hostile to them.[56] The curse that comes to Adam with the Fall includes the world's malignancy. "Cursed is the ground in thy labors" (Gen 3:18). Nature is natural in defining our taken-for-granted expectations, though it is not the way nature ought to be. Nature's way of being natural has become unnatural with reference to the original intent of the Creator. Everything is marked by the results of man's sin. Man no longer has easy noetic access to the meaning of things, nor can he any longer with facility know as did Adam the appropriate names to give to animals (Gen 2:19-20). Nature has become a limit defined in terms of the sensible, finite, and immanent. Nature is noetically opaque. As St. Symeon Metaphrastis (fl. end of 10th century), paraphrasing St. Makarios of Egypt (c.300-c.390), explains, "When God in His love condemned Adam to death after his transgression, he first experienced this death in his soul: his spiritual and deathless organs of perception, deprived of their celestial and spiritual enjoyment, were quenched and became as though dead."[57] Worse yet, banished from Eden, man no longer has the taken-for-granted possibility of knowing God spiritually, as did Adam.

As man turns to the struggle for survival in painful toil to preserve his physical existence, trusting in his own powers, not in the providence of God, the world closes in around him, highlighting his very tangible concerns. This sphere of lust, greed, and aggression becomes for him the self-evident sphere of the natural. God observes regarding the sinful condition of mankind after the Fall, "And the Lord God [saw] that the wicked actions of men were multiplied upon the earth, and that every one in his heart was intently brooding over evil continually" (Gen 6:6[5]). The world seen through wicked eyes confirms the naturalness of natural evil and of evil inclinations. This view of reality is further strengthened as nature is resituated within the expectations of modern physics and biology. Everything is defined in terms of possibilities for discursive analysis, examination, study, and reasoning, but not for prayer. Construed within the truncated terms of post-Newtonian physics and post-Darwinian biology, nature becomes an all-inclusive sphere of immanence closing man off from God. As a consequence, neither physical nor biological nature is recognized as gesturing beyond itself to the Creator. Approached within these assumptions, within a gaze turned to the sensible world and away from a transcendent Other, nature can only be regarded through discursive rationality. So regarded, it does not lead to God.

It is not just that sensation, sensible experience, analysis, examination, and discursive reasoning are the only modes of access to reality within the bounds of a possible knowledge now restricted to the finite, spatio-temporal, and sensible. In addition, the possibility of any other approach is discounted either in terms congenial to Kant, which reinforce the impenetrability of the boundaries of the sensible, spatio-temporal, and finite, or in terms congenial to Hegel, which render any hint of the transcendent fully immanent, an element of human culture. The world is demythologized and detheologized so that miracles are impossible, communion with God foreclosed, and transcendence immanentized. It is a world without a hint of divine providence or ultimate meaning. Instead of God's providence, human power provides the only hope. Broken nature is then further misperceived in being approached, experienced, and used with reference to human desire and understood relentlessly in the terms of finite, discursive rationality.

In a world defined by sin, the broken character of nature is rendered normative. First, nature is no longer unequivocally good. It is now beset by forces deaf to human purposes. From earthquakes to tornadoes and hurricanes, the physical world is the source of natural evil as well as good. The world of living things is defined by a cycle of conflict, violence, and death. Nature is not just the sphere of the corporeal, finite, and immanent. Nature is experienced as hostile to humans. Second, after the Fall, after being inserted into this cycle of desire, lust, reproduction, conflict, violence, killing, and death, which now frames the natural history of all beings, man apart from God accepts this state of affairs as the moral point of reference. Nature then has its meaning constituted normatively through this web of desires, including inclinations to evil. This context of lust, violence, killing, and death becomes man's "natural" home. The natural world of fallen man is not simply corporeal but interpreted within the passions that embed him in the "natural" cycle of desire, violence, and death, which constitutes the "natural" environment of all beings in the fallen world. Third, this broken world is approached through a discursive rationality formed by post-Enlightenment expectations that discount the possibility of grace and the personal presence of God. Seen in these terms, nature and the natural lead away from God, not to Him, as they should. Nature has become a sphere transformed by sin. It is also a world manipulated by the satisfaction of human passions and explained within a discursive, rational, explanatory framework that excludes the possibility of the spiritual. As we find it, the world is not the world as we should expect it to be.

Natural law properly understood compasses the precepts taught us by God through our being and through the world around us, rendering nature a window to God. [58] To see that law, one must take on the faith that turns us from agnosticism to an encounter with God. God then allows us through His energies to grow in knowledge of His commandments. Conscience is the knowing with (i.e., *conscire*) that discloses God's law, not by learning, study, or deep analysis, but spontaneously within us, from our nature through faith, ascesis, and prayer. It is natural in giving us a knowledge we would have had clearly, had there not been the Fall.[59] It is natural in disclosing obligations that pertain to us, given the kind of embodied beings we are. It is also natural in being put in us by God. But it is not the knowing of a mere set of external moral constraints. It is a knowing along with God about how to approach God. Like the old English term "inwit" for conscience, it involves an internal knowledge that is not solitary. This knowing grows as we free ourselves from passion and turn to God through keeping His commandments. Christians have traditionally approached the task of learning God's commandments through prayer. In the ancient prayer, the kataxioson, said at vespers and at matins, one prays, "Blessed are Thou, O Lord, teach me Thy statutes."[60] In all of this, the commandments, the law taught us by nature, are not external and empirical, but integral to bringing us to union with God.

Moral and Theological Knowledge as a Spiritual Journey

Patristic epistemology presupposes a distinction among body, soul, and spirit, each having its own activity, object, and goal of knowledge. Knowledge through the body is sensible knowledge requiring experience and study, having as its object corporeal reality. The development of this knowledge is often, if not usually, motivated by some form of corporeal desire. This knowledge compasses not just most of ordinary experience, but what would be included under the broad scope of *Wissenschaft*. "It is not difficult to see that in this first and lowest degree of knowledge of which St. Isaac speaks is included virtually the whole of European philosophy, from naïve realism to idealism – and all science from the atomism of Democritus to Einstein's relativity."[61] In contrast, through noesis there is the soul's knowledge of the inner essence of the principles of created things, as Adam knew how to name the animals. It is also by noesis that man perceives the providence of God and sees that "God is always present in an unutterable way."[62] This knowledge is spiritual, natural to man, and acquired not by study, but by a life turned to God in prayer, fasting, almsgiving. This involves a movement in faith from oneself to God, and through God to love of one's fellowman. The good life which this knowledge requires is not that of secular humanitarianism or even a secularly available natural-law-based bioethics. A secular humanitarian approach to health care will from this perspective at best be dangerously one-sided. It will be morally broken and isolated from all spiritual concerns; it will be perverted. A secular humanitarian attempt to provide health care to those in need, if not marked by a love that leads to God, will lead away from God, as St. Isaac the Syrian understands.

The object of the soul's knowledge is incorporeal and the goal supernatural: illumination by God.[63] This third form of knowledge is beyond human nature and involves union with God. It comes through the Holy Spirit, Who leads us to being "partakers of the divine nature, having escaped the corruption which is in the world by desire" (2 Pet 1:4).[64] This knowledge is spiritual in the strong sense of supranatural.

St. Isaac of Syria summarizes these levels or kinds of knowledge under the rubrics natural, spiritual, and supranatural.

> Knowledge that is occupied with visible things and receives instruction concerning them through the senses, is called natural. But knowledge that is occupied with the noetic power that is within things and with incorporeal natures is called spiritual, since perception in this case is received by the spirit and not by the senses. In both of these kinds of knowledge matter comes to the soul from without to give her comprehension. But that knowledge which is occupied with Divinity is called supranatural, or rather, unknowing and knowledge-transcending. The soul does not gain divine vision into this knowledge through material external to herself, as in the former instances, but immaterially it manifests itself within her by the grace of God, suddenly and unexpectedly, and it is revealed from within. "The Kingdom of the Heavens is within you", and you should not hope to find it in a place, nor does it come in observation, according to the word of Christ. But without external cause and without meditation upon it, it is revealed within the hidden image of the intellect, for the intellect cannot find in it any matter.
> The first knowledge comes from constant study and diligence in learning; the second comes from a good manner of life and the intellect's faith; and the third is now allotted to faith alone. For by faith knowledge is abolished, works come to an end, and the employment of the senses becomes superfluous.[65]

All of knowledge should thus ascend towards God. It should move from that which is discursive, particular, and isolated, to that which is finally unified in an experience of the Creator of all.

The epistemology of traditional Christianity is thus not static. It recognizes, as St. Isaac stresses, that as man repents he is illumined by God and then united to God.

> Natural knowledge, which is the discernment of good and evil implanted in our nature by God, persuades us that we must believe in God, the Author of all. Faith produces fear in us, and fear compels us to repent and to set ourselves to work. And thus man is given spiritual knowledge, which is the perception of mysteries, and this perception engenders the faith of true divine vision. Spiritual knowledge is not, however, thus simply begotten of mere faith alone; but faith begets the fear of God, and when we begin to act from the fear of God, then, out of the steady action of the fear of God, spiritual knowledge is born, just as Saint John Chrysostom has said, 'For when a man acquires a will that conforms to the fear

of God and to right thinking, he quickly receives the revelation of hidden things.' And by 'revelation of hidden things' he means spiritual knowledge.[66]

This epistemology involves a pilgrimage from being estranged from God to receiving the vision of God. St. Isaac of Syria summarizes this journey of faith through knowledge to God:

> The first degree of knowledge renders the soul cold to works that go in pursuit of God. The second makes her fervent in the swift course on the level of faith. But the third is rest from labour, which is the type of the age to come, for the soul takes delight solely in the mind's meditation upon the mysteries of the good things to come.[67]

If knowledge is not directed to God, it is then hostage to the desires of the body and leads downward rather than to divine illumination. One either rises to God, or one falls.

The dynamic character of Christian moral epistemology has profound implications for the moral significance of secular bioethics. The secular bioethics of the libertarian cosmopolitan is at best a broken common ground peaceably shared by believer and unbeliever, saint and sinner alike. Knowledge in this context is a privative mode of knowing where "nature" identifies the sphere of immanence separated from the spiritual. If this secular morality is not defined in terms of any content but is purely procedural, then it of itself does not lead away from God. It is like St. Paul's Corinth; Paul allows his Christians into the city, its streets, its markets, and its parks, though prayerfully and watchfully on guard. Though they were forbidden to have close associations with those who were committed sinners, St. Paul recognized that in their general commerce the Christians could not avoid contact.[68] This context is simply the social space shared by believer and non-believer, by Christian and non-Christian, traditional and post-traditional Christians. Since it is a peaceable social space, it affords not only liberty for a market as well as for gravely evil actions, but also a place for proselytizing, a place where traditional Christians can peaceably witness to the possibility of ascending beyond the knowledge of the body and the senses towards God. In and of itself this social space is a decision tree at the fork between heaven and hell. The knowledge that binds common actions in this social space "is called shallow knowledge, for it is naked of all concern for God."[69]

This domain of collaboration and de facto immanence into which believer and non-believer, saint and sinner, can enter of itself requires neither the acceptance nor the rejection of God. Only when human liberty and satisfaction are given lexical priority is there a clear step away from God. This sphere of concerns and its effects on knowledge are then not simply one-sided and incomplete: they are vicious. They cannot serve as an adequate foundation for a traditional Christian bioethics because knowledge of natural goods and evils has been disengaged from their moral and religious significance. It is the world of the body prescinded from the soul and from God. This is the sphere of the natural as it is available to Kant, Hegel, and the secular world generally: immanent reality considered not just apart from God, but in a way that discounts the transcendence of

God. It is a form of knowledge driven by human desires that reconforms the experience of the world so as to place human liberty and thought at its center. As St. Isaac observes, "we find this knowledge blameworthy and declare it to be opposed not only to faith, but to every working of virtue."[70] Natural knowledge so limited does not simply fail to invite us beyond or through nature towards God. It turns us away from God. "But the natural man receiveth not the things of the Spirit of God; for they are foolishness unto him" (I Cor 2:14). Here is where St. Isaac would have placed liberal cosmopolitan secular bioethics and many genre of Christian bioethics. A secular bioethics that does not invite us to a Christian bioethics is at the very least morally deficient, merely natural.

Because the journey through moral knowledge to holiness is a moral movement from ourselves to God, it depends on our moral choices, on our virtuous development. We can obscure our natural sense of moral direction, pervert our conscience, and thus cloud our knowledge of God and make the appreciation of the proper content of a Christian bioethics impossible. Moral knowledge, including bioethical knowledge, is practical knowledge, not in the sense of the application of principles to action, but in the sense of knowledge developed through engaging in moral actions, which actions separate us from our passions and unite us to God. The result of such moral knowledge is that one learns how to act by acting: spiritual knowledge is gained by engagement that changes ourselves. The pursuit of holiness brings persons to a knowledge that transcends the horizon of the immanent, fundamentally recasting the significance of morality and bioethics. Virtue strengthens the appreciation of the law, but it also ties us to the transcendent reality that created us. Natural revelation invites us to a Divine disclosure, resituating bioethics in terms of an ultimate concern for and pursuit of the Holy.

This approach to knowledge allows a further resituating of our understanding of natural law, relocating the relationship between traditional Christian bioethics and natural law. (1) This account of natural law is not bound directly to the biological character of humans, to moral constraints embedded in discursive reasoning, or to the character of moral rationality. (2) Natural law is primarily an expression of a moral sense given by the Creator as an aid in turning to Him and experiencing Him. Natural law is that perception naturally within ourselves, albeit obscured after the Fall. (3) Natural law is not first discovered or primarily disclosed discursively. It is found within our conscience, within our moral self-experience. Though this experience of the moral law can be strengthened by instruction, it grows principally through prayer, virtuous action, and love of God. It is in particular nurtured by a worshipful relationship with God through Whom one discovers that the law within is the spark of divine love, which is in us from our creation. (4) Natural law in this sense is not a set of moral obligations that can be appreciated in purely secular terms as the basis for a bioethics open to all. Natural law or the moral law, as well as the Christian bioethics, are therapeutic. They bring us away from ourselves to God our Creator.

Christian Bioethics and Theological Knowledge

Because the goal par excellence of human life is holiness, union with God, then the moral life, the keeping of the commandments, the acquisition of virtue, along with the articulation of a Christian bioethics, are not ends in themselves. They are means to

carry us to the other side of natural knowledge. They serve to change the person
sufficiently to allow the acquisition of knowledge that goes beyond the person to God.
Without this uniting presence of the Spirit, as St. Symeon the New Theologian stresses,
one cannot see the source of the Scriptures or the goal of morality. "[E]ven he who, as
we have said, has learned all the divine Scriptures by heart will never be able to know
and perceive the mystical and divine glory and power hidden in them without going
through all God's commandments and taking the Paraclete with him."[71] Religious
knowledge is drawn from the choice to follow one's true conscience, to keep the
commandments, and to worship God. Theological knowledge, as a consequence, does
not necessarily presuppose mastery of discursive and analytic skills. This is not to deny
a kind of moral theological knowledge by means of discursive examination and analysis. Nor does this mean that a Christian bioethics should eschew clear expression,
analytic explication, or systematic reflection in favor of contradictory statements and
deliberately ambiguous claims. Careful examination of claims and conceptual analysis
can and should make a contribution, even when inadequately expressing in a discursive
fashion an experience of non-discursive reality.

The difference between theological knowledge as experiential knowledge and that
which can be garnered by discursive examination and analysis can be illustrated by
comparing those who would theorize about wine without ever having tasted it, and
those who have tasted wine and attempt then to report carefully their experiences.
Theological knowledge, which is not rooted in experience, has the character of oenology without experiencing wine. Oenology in such circumstances is at best second hand.
It is radically dependent on those who have actually tasted wines and developed their
discriminative abilities through experience. They know and appreciate the qualities of
wine. Still, those who have never tasted wine but who have developed an analytic
nomenclature may provide something of benefit for the appreciation of wine. Those
who have tasted wine may find such discursive and analytic nomenclature an aid in
better communicating their experiences to others. Or they may find the nomenclature a
misdirected fantasy. Those who would have actually tasted wine will be the final judges
regarding the usefulness of the distinctions developed. Needless to say, any who claim
to engage in oenology without ever having tasted wine or known anyone who has
tasted wine are at the very least parodying themselves.

Those theologians who have truly experienced God will find the encounter incon-
trovertible. After all, the experience of God is unlike the tasting of wine. The experience of God is the finite creature's encounter with the infinite and transcendent Creator. It is for this reason, as St. Isaac observes, that those who experience God

> can soar on wings in the realms of the bodiless and touch the depths of the
> unfathomable sea, musing upon the wondrous and divine workings of
> God's governance of noetic and corporeal creatures. It searches out spirit-
> ual mysteries that are perceived by the simple and subtle intellect. Then
> the inner senses awaken for spiritual doing, according to the order that
> will be in the immortal and incorruptible life. For even from now it has
> received, as it were in a mystery, the noetic resurrection as a true witness
> of the universal renewal of all things.[72]

Moral theological knowledge must always be rooted in the encounter of the finite with the Infinite. At stake is a claim to theological knowledge that transcends both sensory experience and discursive reasoning: a noetic encounter with the reality of God. Out of this experience, Christian theologians can provide a ground for Christian bioethics that is not confined to the bounds of immanent experience or to socio-historically-conditioned documents. The knower will break through the bonds of finite experience and be united with its Creator.

In summary, the problem of immanence and the grounding of content for bioethics generally, and for a Christian bioethics in particular, can only be solved radically. Otherwise, morality along with a Christian bioethics is confined to phenomenal reality and socio-historically conditioned texts. In such circumstances, as we have seen, a canonical, content-full morality or bioethics cannot be justified. A canonical content-full morality cannot be discovered in immanent reality. One would be left to rely on permission not just to frame a sparse secular morality to bind moral strangers. Unless God can be experienced, one would even need to justify moral theologies and their bioethics in permission. This is the defining predicament for contemporary moral philosophy, moral theology, and Christian bioethics. As the Fathers understood, this problem is as old as the Fall, after which humans could no longer walk in the Garden and converse with God (Genesis 3). It characterizes the human condition and its horizon of immanence.

The proposal of traditional Christianity is to turn to God with full faith and ascetic struggle, to invite God to break through our passions to us. Traditional moral theology is experientially based and so is its bioethics, because it relies on God turning to us so that we can know Him and His commandments. Given our confinement in immanence, and our epistemological limits, such an experience of God is a necessary condition for the possibility of a traditional Christian bioethics. It is also a sufficient condition. A traditional Christian bioethics is possible if and only if we come to experience a personal God by grace. When one recaptures the notion of Christian theology as grounded in an experience of God, one not only finds a possibility for securing a Christian bioethics. One is also brought into critical tension with prevailing understandings of philosophy.

Philosophy as primarily a discursive examination of the nature of reality and of the conceptual conditions for valid and true claims about reality, moral philosophy as a discursive examination of the nature of morality, and bioethics as a discursive examination of the moral and ontological issues raised by health care and the biomedical sciences are all brought into question as radically one-sided and incomplete. It is not that the possibility of these enterprises is directly challenged in their own terms. They are regarded as deficient and misleading if not supplemented by grace. They cannot succeed in the terms under which they are usually undertaken. If knowledge of being, of the character of morality, and of the content of bioethics depend on the spiritual character of the knower, then the ability of the knower is dependent on moral deportment and the proper worship of God.

The Fathers of the early Church were generally well-educated in the learning that sustained the culture of the Mediterranean civilization of the first millennium after Christ. In many respects, they took this culture for granted. They even celebrated its beauty. However, they were critical of the philosophy of the Greeks, the secular philosophy of the ancient world: the philosophy of the pagans made claims to knowledge and wisdom it could not fulfill and its practitioners lived lives unbefitting the claims they advanced. Greek or secular philosophers spoke about wisdom but generally showed a lack of true wisdom. They failed to live a moral life or recognize the therapeutic character of morality. Christianity from the beginning insisted that the philosophy of the pagans must therefore be seen in a new light. First, philosophy requires a virtuous life. As St. Neilos the Ascetic (†430) observes, "philosophy is a state of moral integrity combined with a doctrine of true knowledge concerning reality."[73] The Fathers recognized that philosophy as natural knowledge could disclose the content of the moral life only if philosophy involved more than a discursive or analytic undertaking. In particular, philosophy needed to take its name seriously as the love of wisdom and direct itself to a life of true wisdom in order to acquire the truth. If pagan Greek philosophers had truly pursued wisdom, then they would have lived holy lives. "Where now is Plato? ... yea, he betrayed his disciples, and ended his life miserably. ... Thus, for instance, Aristippus was used to purchase costly harlots...."[74] This criticism is not simply an *ad hominem*. Given the epistemological understanding that moral knowledge, not to mention knowledge of God, is acquired through keeping the commandments, growing in faith, and achieving union with God, a criticism of the lives of philosophers as well as bioethicists is analogous to a criticism of the laboratory equipment of scientists. If those working in bacteriology keep dirty laboratories, it will not be possible for them to grow pure cultures. So, too, the argument is that, if philosophers, theologians, and bioethicists are not able to purify their hearts from passions, they will not know truly. What they teach will be distorted.

Second, it is necessary not only that philosophers live morally good lives, they must also aim at pursuing God noetically, not speculatively. By wrongly aiming at truth, they only make their circumstances worse. As St. Neilos observes,

> Many Greeks and not a few Jews attempted to philosophize; but only the disciples of Christ have pursued true wisdom, because they alone have Wisdom as their teacher, showing them by His example the way of life they should follow. For the Greeks, like actors on a stage, put on false masks; they were philosophers in name alone, but lacked true philosophy. ...Some of the Greeks imagined themselves to be engaged in metaphysics, but they neglected the practice of the virtues altogether. ... At times they even tried to theologize, although here the truth lies beyond man's unaided grasp, and speculation is dangerous; yet in their way of life they were more degraded than swine wallowing in the mud.[75]

This account of philosophical and moral knowledge emphasizes the character of the knower because the moral character of the knower and the knower's spiritual intentions determine the possibilities for personal knowledge of God. To recognize the good, the mind must be morally and spiritually healthy.

It is not just that Greek philosophy generally failed to provide a praxis for freeing its practitioners from passions so that they could pursue true wisdom. It is also the case that discursive reasoning, unconnected to faith and an experience of God, fails to bring reasoners to the ultimate truth. Had Greek philosophy been otherwise, it could have produced saints of God such as Job and Melchisedek. A secular bioethics that sought foundations in a secular pretension to a canonical, content-full natural law or human rights-based ethics will always fall short of the mark. At stake is a synergy of the Creator with the creature, through which God reaches out to those who reach to Him, drawing them to Him as they turn to Him, as St. Maximus the Confessor (580-662) underscores.

> The soul would never be able to reach out toward the knowledge of God if God did not allow himself to be touched by it through condescension and by raising it up to him. Indeed, the human mind as such would not have the strength to raise itself to apprehend any divine illumination did not God himself draw it up, as far as it is possible for the human mind to be drawn, and illumine it with divine rightness.[76]

Fundamentally, what is at issue is not a set of discursive principles, but the experience of a personal God.

Moral health and true philosophical success is secured by repentance, moral behavior, and turning to God. As St. Gregory Palamas (1296-1359) observes, "...the fulfillment of the commandments of God gives true knowledge, since it is through this that the soul gains health. How could a rational soul be healthy, if it is sick in its cognitive faculty?"[77] St. Gregory Palamas is here concerned with noetic intelligence, the human ability inspired by God to see God's truth. This moral epistemology focuses on the relationship between created persons and their personal Creator. The epistemology of a traditional Christian bioethics must take into account whether the knowers have turned to their Creator or turned away from Him towards themselves. Moral knowledge requires humility and is extinguished by pride. Moral deportment and right worship are needed to cure the intellect of passions so that it can have acquaintance with the Truth, Who is God.

This circumstance thrice over disables any attempt to give a discursive grounding to Christian bioethics. First, God as transcendent will not be apprehensible in discursive terms. Second, God can be experienced only if one is morally changed through repentance and worship. Third, God as personal cannot be objectified. The knowledge to which Christians are called is a personal knowledge of an infinite Being. The truth is Personal, indeed a Trinity of transcendent Persons, Who were manifested even before Christ's birth.[78] As Sophrony of Essex (1896-1993) warns, the Trinity cannot be the conclusion to a discursive argument.

> Truth as 'WHO' is never arrived at through reason. God as 'WHO' can be known only through communion in being – that is, only by the Holy Spirit. Staretz Silouan [St. Silouan the Athonite (1866-1938)] constantly emphasised this.
> The Lord Himself spoke of it thus:
> 'If a man love me, he will keep my words: and my Father will love him, and we will come unto him, and make our abode with him ... The Comforter, which is the Holy Ghost, whom the Father will send in my name, he shall teach you all things' (John 14:23,26).[79]

The context for a Christian bioethics is thus a personal disclosure. Philosophy as the pursuit of wisdom is best construed as the pursuit of the Persons of God, and theology the fruit of a personal worshipful relationship with this personal God. In short, accounts of philosophy, theology, or bioethics as essentially argumentative, or analytic enterprises are, from this standpoint, radically incomplete.

Philosophy (including bioethics) decoupled from pursuit of true wisdom becomes a caricature of itself; as St. John Chrysostom laments, "all with them is a fable, a stage-play, a piece of acting."[80] This is not to deny the existence of pious pagan philosophers or that such as Plato attained to some portion of the truth, thus serving as a preparation for the coming of Christianity.[81] The philosophy of the Greeks, i.e., secular philosophy, by itself devolves into an intricate maze of analyses and a labyrinth of discursive puzzles, which if they do not lead to immoral conclusions lead nowhere. "They are like some labyrinth or puzzles which have no end to them anywhere, and do not let the reason stand upon the rock, and have their very origin in vanity."[82] The philosophy of the Greeks, rather than providing a reliable road to wisdom, produced a mechanism carried along by its own workings. Philosophy becomes "mere words, and childish toys."[83] There is much reflection and analysis, but little production of reliable moral guidance, as St. John Chrysostom finds.

> [F]or example, they make their women common to all, and stripping virgins naked in the Palaestra, bring them into the gaze of men; and when they establish secret marriages, mingling all things together and confounding them, and overturning the limits of nature, what else is there to say? ...wherefore besides their uncleanness, their obscurity is great, and the labor they require greater. For what could be more ridiculous than that "republic," in which, besides what I have mentioned, the philosopher, when he hath spent lines without number, that he may be able to shew what justice is, hath over and above this prolixity filled his discourse with much indistinctness?[84]

St. Chrysostom recognizes that, in many cases, philosophy has become a parody of itself, leading to confusion rather than wisdom. He would surely lodge a similar criticism against much of contemporary secular bioethics. It cannot secure the canonical content-full moral content. At worst, it leads to the *Republic's* presentation of free love (i.e., reproduction between unmarried couples) and abortion, if not infanticide, as integral to the ideal politeia.

In addition, in its own terms, secular philosophy requires carrying through intricacies of argument that presuppose not only an intelligence denied to most, but, as St. John Chrysostom observes, a leisure available only to a few.

> For if the husbandman and the smith, the builder and the pilot, and every one who subsists by the labor of his hands, is to leave his trade, and his honest toils, and is to spend such and such a number of years in order to learn what justice is; before he has learnt he will often times be absolutely destroyed by hunger, and perish because of this justice, not having learnt anything else useful to be known, and having ended his life by a cruel death.[85]

The philosophy of the Greeks, unlike the Christian pursuit of wisdom, is in this sense elitist: it requires a leisure and intelligence not possessed by many. In contrast, the Christian pursuit of wisdom allows success to those who, while remaining in the midst of life with perhaps only very modest intelligence but with great love, turn in love to God and those around them.

Here, St. John Chrysostom owes the reader a qualification: he not only recognizes but praises ascetic withdrawal from the world as the life of true philosophy.[86] With the early Church, philosophy takes on a new meaning: the ascetic life, usually identified with the life of monks. Yet, not all seem able to assume this life. Although great intelligence is not a prerequisite, goodness and generosity of heart are necessities. Here we also owe Chrysostom a concession: he does not hold that one must be a monk in order to saved, that is, to come to Christian wisdom. He recognizes that the tradition is clear in not enjoining all to be monks and in recognizing that many who are not monks are holier than monks.[87] Those who live in the world can free their hearts from it, for all are called to salvation through asceticism.

St. John Chrysostom notes as well that discursive reasoning and philosophical reflections of a discursive and analytic sort without the guidance of faith lead away from the veridical experience of the Spirit to heresy.

> Let heretics hearken to the voice of the Spirit, for such is the nature of reasonings. ...For being ashamed to allow of faith, and to seem ignorant of heavenly things, they involve themselves in the dust-cloud of countless reasonings.[88]

This is one of the severest of Chrysostom's criticisms of Greek philosophy, and by implication of secular bioethics. "Therefore they who inquire by reasonings, it is they who perish."[89] This criticism, it should be noted, has a deeply Pauline ring. It is St. Paul as the Apostle to the Gentiles who criticizes the wisdom of the Greeks and recognizes the failure of philosophical disputation to reach true wisdom.

> Where is the wise? Where is the scribe? Where is the disputer of this age? Did not God make foolish the wisdom of this world? For since, in the wisdom of God, the world knew not God through its wisdom, it pleased God through the foolishness of the preaching to save those who believe. For indeed, Jews ask for a sign, and Greeks seek wisdom, but we proclaim Christ Who hath been crucified; to the Jews, on the one hand, a stumbling block, and to Greeks, on the other hand, foolishness (1 Cor 1:20-23).

Christianity for St. John Chrysostom, as for St. Paul, is the anti-wisdom of the wisdom of the Greeks. Each is the foolishness of the other. Each is the anti-philosophy of the other. Or to put the dialectic more properly, the philosophy of the Greeks (and for us, by implication, secular bioethics) uninformed by faith is anti-wisdom. It draws one away from God and salvation.

Here, Chrysostom affirms St. Paul's recognition that the message of Christianity "to those who are perishing is foolishness" (1 Cor 1:18) and that salvation is found when people become "fools for Christ's sake" (1 Cor 4:10). "[B]ut now, unless a man become a fool, that is, unless he dismiss all reasoning and all wisdom, and deliver up himself unto the faith, it is impossible to be saved."[90] Again, this is not to deny that pagans, including pagan philosophers and bioethicists, can turn in worshipful pursuit of God so as to find God's law in their heart and through that moral law find God. The point is rather that natural knowledge goes awry if it does not transcend itself in turning to God. St. John Chrysostom's revaluation of philosophy places the philosophy of the Greeks, and by implication bioethics when uninformed by faith, in opposition to the wisdom of the Christians.

In all of this, the very sense of philosophy and bioethics has been recast. There is a powerful judgment offered against a secular philosophy, and by implication a bioethics, uninformed by faith: (1) its practitioners tend to be burdened by their passions so that they cannot know truly, (2) as a consequence, their accounts of ideal deportment are often immoral when (3) they are not also lost in unprofitable musings leading nowhere while at the same time (4) requiring a leisure available to only a few, so that their wisdom is inaccessible to most. Moreover, (5) attempts at discursive reflection uninformed by faith and the experience of God tend to lead to perdition rather than to wisdom. Therefore, (6) true wisdom must be pursued in ways that would be foolish in the light of secular, discursive philosophy. For its part, true philosophy and therefore true bioethics take their point of departure from a natural knowledge which reaches beyond itself through faith to spiritual knowledge. Only by transcending itself can natural knowledge (e.g., secular bioethics) lead beyond itself to divine illumination by the Trinity (the goal of Christian bioethics in the fullest sense). This is not to deny the role that secular philosophical skills can properly play in clarifying claims and even articulating arguments about what one in faith knows and experiences. True philosophy, and by implication true bioethics, by orienting to God leads to virtue, while virtue leads beyond itself to theology as the experience of God. Philosophy, theology, and bioethics apart from that experience are like an oenology whose practitioners have never tasted wine. For St. John Chrysostom, all true philosophy and theology are dependent on those who have truly tasted the presence of God. For us, this will mean that an authentic Christian bioethics must as well draw on this experience of God.

Moral Theology, Christian Bioethics, and the Community of Knowers

The term "theology" is ambiguous. It has a primary and a secondary meaning. The first is rooted in the eucharistic-mystical theology of the Church of the first millennium. The theological knowledge at the core of traditional Christian bioethics is acquired by repentance, love, ascesis, and worship. It is disclosed by the Holy Spirit in the Church to those theologians who experience God. There is also a place for theologians in a secondary sense, those who either (a) explicate what true theologians (i.e., those who experience God) teach, or (b) clarify terms, compare understandings, and discursively and even systematically examine such explications. Traditional Christian theology and bioethics remain rooted in the experience of God. They thus also remain a whole, united in the liturgical life of the Church. True theology is experiential, requires holiness, and declares itself in the worship of the Christian community. As a consequence, it is impossible for a non-believer or a unrepentant sinner to be a theologian, save in a very incomplete, one-sided, and distorted sense. To do well as a theologian, one must always be appropriately aimed at the true source of theological knowledge: God.

Christian bioethics in the second sense (i.e., as a scholarly but still prayerful analysis and study of theological experience) when isolated from the first sense of theology (i.e., as the experience of God) understands itself as a special area of investigation set off within academically defined borders guided by the usual scholarly norms. Christian bioethics in this sense is a special area of religious studies in which anyone of energy, intelligence, and appropriate knowledge can excel and even be distinguished as a Christian bioethicist. It is theological in the sense of accepting particular dogmatic and moral premises as points of departure. Academically departmentalized, it is no longer integral to the challenge to respond to God's presence through repentance, prayer, and love. For example, in the case of Roman Catholic bioethics, there is theoretically an acceptance of bishops and in particular the pope of Rome as being in authority to settle disputes. These disputes are usually regarded by the academic participants as scholarly in nature, making the intrusion of ecclesiastical authority appear incongruous. After the Galileo Galilei affair, would the pope interfere in debates in physics or mathematics? What authority do ecclesiastical hierarchs have in matters of scientific or scholarly investigation? This becomes a significant puzzle, once theology is no longer the experience of God but an independent genre of scholarly investigation. The hierarchy then function as moderators and directors of scholastic or at least scholarly investigation and reflection. As soon as no special holiness is in principle required for doing theology, the hierarchy are then usually experienced as poorly educated seminar leaders. The hand of the Holy Spirit may be considered present in directing the outcomes of discursive arguments and scholarly reflections. But the focus is no longer first and foremost on the pursuit through holiness of noetic knowledge. As a consequence, there is a conflict between academic integrity and ecclesiastical authority.

This contrast does not arise as long as theology is spiritually therapeutic and liturgical in the sense of finding its epistemic vantagepoint in the union of the Christian assembly in the Eucharistic liturgy. It is not liturgical in the sense of a study of liturgics.[91] In particular, it is not liturgical as an isolated dimension or feature of the Christian life. Christian life is at its core worship. This wholeness may be difficult to appreciate. In the West, theology became separated from the Liturgy, leading to the emergence of an academic theology on the one hand, and a science of liturgics on the other hand, both of which were divorced from theological experience. The epistemic significance of the Liturgy was then discounted. The result has been a Western misunderstanding of theology, liturgics, and Liturgy due to an artificial separation of theology into various academic fields. This led to a view that theology is more the product of scholastic rigor than of prayer, worship, and grace. Theology was no longer nested centrally within a liturgical life of worship.

Eucharistic liturgical prayer is the unity of the community with God. It is the reference point of community for the prayers of even the most isolated hermits. On the one hand, the Liturgy of St. Basil explicitly joins believers with those isolated because of their ascetical struggles: "Have in remembrance, O Lord, those who are in the deserts, and mountains, and caverns, and in the subterranean pits of the earth."[92] On the other hand, hermits in their flight from temptation to repentance pray to participate in the fruit of the Liturgy, a prayer that is often miraculously answered.[93] Christian bioethics finds its foundations first and foremost in the task of freeing the heart from passions, of properly directing energies toward holiness, so that one may worthily enter into the Liturgy within which Christians are united with Christ and with each other. This focus on the Liturgy is central not simply because the Christian moral life is lived with others or because Christians are a people who pray not just alone but together. More significantly, if moral knowledge demands a change in the knower because the knower must for salvation's sake come into union with God, and such a change requires not just a moral life but a moral life embedded in right worship, then a culmination in the transformation of the knower will be found in the Liturgy. The "Eucharist ... is a prophetic prefiguration of the Parousia."[94] Yet to enter worthily into the Liturgy, into communion, the soul must first be prepared ascetically. Traditional Christian bioethics is spiritually therapeutic, liturgical, and eucharistic, because true moral knowledge comes from union with God, which can only be achieved after spiritual therapy, after freeing the heart from passions, and because the Christian community achieves, celebrates, and ratifies that union in liturgical worship, all of which conveys theological knowledge.

As a consequence of this epistemology, a traditional Christian bioethics will not only (1) have a pre-Reformation relationship to Scripture, because Scripture will primarily be understood within the Liturgy (as we will presently see in greater detail), but also (2) have a pre-scholastic appreciation of natural law that lodges its paradigmatic presentation within a life of worship. Just as the Scriptures are a closed book to those outside of the Liturgy, so, too, natural law is a closed book to those who live outside of true worship. Persons who have failed to turn to God will not correctly appreciate His commandments because they will have blinded themselves to the law of nature, the conscience within them. If theological knowledge is rooted in noetic experience, then in the absence of rightly directed asceticism and worship theological knowledge will be distorted. A traditional Christian bioethics will be rooted in a turn both to Scriptures and to natural law, but in terms unanticipated by those who regard these sources of moral content in post-Reformation and post-scholastic lights. Scripture and natural law reveal their true and full content only in the ascetic, liturgical life. There is no natural law accessible outside of faith simply by dint of hard reasoning. A secular construal of natural law does not offer bioethics a content-full moral lingua franca that can provide a canonical secular moral substitute for a Christian moral theology and its bioethics. Natural law reasoning without the grace of faith achieved through asceticism and worship produces the philosophical diversity and perversity decried by the Fathers. There is no reliable religiously disengaged road to moral truth. Outside of faith, natural moral knowledge always goes wide of the mark.

We are brought to a fundamental contrast between secular and traditional Christian moral reflection. As with all real contrasts, they are not sharp. Yet, at the center of the differences, there is a divide regarding the roots of moral knowledge that establishes a substantial separation between secular moral thought and traditional Christian moral understanding. The first involves a discursive rationality, which is forever bound within the sphere of immanence. The second is noetic and claims an experiential encounter with the Truth, Who is personal. The first in being secular engages no transcendent faith. The second claims a form of knowledge that breaks through the horizon of immanence. Again, this is not to discount the place and importance of discursive rationality. Discursive rationality brings analytic clarity. It establishes lines of valid argument. It elaborates, explicates, and organizes. Yet, by itself it cannot disclose the substance of truth. In particular, it cannot establish a content-full, moral vision.

Here is where we began the puzzles in the first chapter regarding the possibility of a canonical, secular morality. Because traditional Christian moral theology, and therefore traditional Christian bioethics, is grounded in experience of a transcendent God, the acquisition and nurturing of moral knowledge is never simply discursive. Moral content develops in dialogue with God. It develops in prayer and worship. The natural law disclosed in the human heart is thus not a disengaged, objectively available fact. It is a personally disclosed truth. Conscience is not just a human faculty, but a point of union between Creator and creature. The knowledge of the heart, of which St. Paul speaks in Romans 2:15, is this beginning of noetic perception. For St. Paul, it is the heart that is to be circumcised (Rom 2:29), purified by righteousness, so as to be illumined, so "Christ shall shine on thee" (Eph 5:14). Those who have cleared their hearts from passions and achieved union with God will have knowledge the nature of things. Moreover, the prayers of the Church concerning issues bioethical (e.g., concerning children in their mothers' wombs, miscarriages, illnesses, and death) will express and convey bioethically relevant knowledge. Finally, the moral life, including Christian bioethics, cannot be fully understood except in terms of preparation for and participation in the eucharistic Liturgy, which is at the center of Christianity's claims regarding its epistemic and metaphysical unity with God. The Liturgy frames the sociology of knowledge for a Christian bioethics.

This centering of traditional Christian morality, and therefore of bioethics, on entering with a pure heart into the prime act of Christian worship leads to further points of contrast between traditional Christian bioethics, on the one hand, and secular bioethics, post-traditional bioethics, on the other. Seven of these points will be examined in the passages that follow. First, as already noted, Christian bioethical claims must be construed in terms of a relationship with God achieved through purification of the heart so that, second, one can enter worthily into the liturgical and eucharistic assembly of Christians. Third, this liturgical center of Christian life gives the Scriptures their place, not the reverse: a Christian bioethics is liturgical before it is scriptural. Fourth, the liturgical assembly is in a community that is hierarchical: there are overseers or bishops in authority to maintain the integrity of the faith, including who may enter into or serve in the liturgical assembly, which has implications for resolving bioethical controversies. Bishops are in authority, but not as seminar leaders. They are in authority in presiding over the liturgical assembly that is the center of Christian life. Fifth, the unity of the Church is the unity of the bishops and the faithful, which unity is synodal, conciliar, or sobornost: there is a commitment to assembling together under the Holy Spirit to articulate the truth of which all are the custodians and which they experience, so as to express what seems good "to the Holy Spirit, and to us" (Acts 15:28). Bioethical issues have been addressed at a conciliar level. Sixth, though bishops and synods are in teaching authority, there is the Spirit-established office of prophet, elder, or theologian: those who intimately know God and must proclaim His word, even against emperors, patriarchs, bishops, and would-be ecumenical councils. A kind of balance has thus been created between those in authority and those who are authorities as they together test the spirits (I John 4:1-3, I Thess 5:21).[95] Theologians are authorities regarding the faith. This distance or distinction emerges only insofar as emperors, bishops, and patriarchs are not also holy, living saints. Seventh, as we have already seen, a sense of theology and theologian is maintained in stark contrast with that which developed in the West. Theology is not primarily an academic field. Theology is the expression of an intimate relationship with God.

Knowing Truly: Bishops, Councils, Popes, and Prophets

The skeptic will ask with regard to the grounding of theology and thus ultimately of Christian bioethics in noetic experience: how can one tell if there is in fact anything like such noetic experiences? And if there are such, how can one determine if one has true noetic experience? After all, there are devils who deceive. There is much that must be said, all of which involves locating all authentic knowledge of the transcendent in the life of right worship and belief. Outside of such experiences, the response will always be incomplete and will appear parochial: enter in and experience so that you will see. Some criteria can be appreciated from the outside: a traditional Christian will look for those encounters with God that show His unchanging and humble love in an experience at one with the revelation of the Church from the beginning. Given the traditional Christian recognition as a noetic, founding experience that the faith has been given once and for all to the saints (Jude 1:3), any claim to a new faith, new teachings, or new dogmas must be rejected. A veridical noetic experience will not disclose novel truth. This is the famous criterion of St. Vincent of Lerins (†ca.450), that Christian belief is unchanging, that the truth is that which has been believed every place, always, and by all who have been fully in the Church. Truth in the Church has the marks of universality, antiquity, and consent.[96]

From inside the Christian community, the recognition of authenticity will be the fruit of spiritual struggle, usually undertaken with the aid of an experienced guide. Because traditional Christian theology is experiential, its critical epistemology is primarily an epistemology of testing the spirit: of determining whether an experience of the spirit is of God or the devil. On this subject, there is an immense literature, primarily monastic. St. Silouan the Athonite has offered the following as an internal criterion: "'The Lord is meek and humble, and loves His creature. Where the Spirit of the Lord is, there is humble love for enemies and prayer for the whole world. ... Let no one make so bold as to belittle this 'psychological' canon, for the state it relates to is the direct result of divine action."[97] In this encounter with humble love there is the unique recognition of the Creator by His creature.

For many secularists, indeed for many rationalist Christians, this grounding of the moral content of bioethics in noetic experience will be troubling, even offensive. It will underscore the absence of a common, content-full morality discursively disclosable or apprehensible apart from a life lived in the pursuit of the kingdom of heaven. It will mean that traditional Christians will not be able to clothe their moral claims in a secularly neutral language. Traditional Christian moral claims will explicitly always lead to the Father through Christ. The determination, the experience of truth will be set within what is a very special social context.

These points bear further exploration, beginning with the liturgical foundations of Christian morality and bioethics. From the very beginning, the life of the Christian has been lived with a sense of liturgical engagement, community, spiritual transformation, and hierarchical authority, alongside prophetic asceticism. The ascetic and liturgical centering of the Christian life presupposes the ascetic cure of the soul in order to approach the Eucharist, the center of the Liturgy, so as to bring us towards union with God, the goal of all asceticism. This has broad implications for a Christian bioethics. First, traditional Christian bioethics is not fully understandable outside of a traditional Christian life. Access to its content and its meaning grows within the life of faith, love, alms, asceticism, worship, and participation in the Mysteries of the Church. Since that life is communal, in fact eucharistic, Christian bioethics will only be fully comprehensible when appreciated liturgically. Yet, the Liturgy can only be understood through repentance, asceticism, and the purification of the heart. Christian bioethics finds its context and content in and from worthily entering into worship. It is not simply that Christian bioethics will be appropriately informed and instructed by the liturgical texts that have been sung over the ages: the liturgical texts themselves supply bioethical guidance. More significantly, the liturgical assembly in the Eucharist has from the beginning been recognized as the cardinal encounter with Christ's reality in the world.

This appreciation of the Christian life is found in Acts: from the beginning after Pentecost, the Apostles devoted themselves "in the breaking of the bread, and in the prayers" (Acts 2:42). In the letters of the late first century and early second century bishop of Antioch, Saint Ignatius (A.D. 30-107), this unity in worship is emphasized.

> Take ye heed, then, to have but one Eucharist. For there is one flesh of our Lord Jesus Christ, and one cup to [show forth] the unity of His blood; one altar; as there is one bishop, along with the presbytery and deacons, my fellow-servants: that so, whatsoever ye do, ye may do it according to [the will of] God.[98]

As already noted, this unity of the life of worship and faith is within an ecclesial, hierarchical structure that provides overseers, bishops who are in authority.

> See that ye all follow the bishop, even as Jesus Christ does the Father, and the presbytery as ye would the apostles; and reverence the deacons, as being the institution of God. Let no man do anything connected with the Church without the bishop. Let that be deemed a proper Eucharist, which is [administered] either by the bishop, or by one to whom he has entrusted it. Wherever the bishop shall appear, there let the multitude [of the people] also be; even as, wherever Jesus Christ is, there is the Catholic Church. It is not lawful without the bishop either to baptize or to celebrate a love-feast; but whatsoever he shall approve of, that is also pleasing to God, so that everything that is done may be secure and valid.[99]

It is in this context of worship, hierarchical approbation, and eucharistic transformation that there is fullness. It is through the Liturgy that the Christian moral life, including Christian bioethics, gains its orientation. It is here that the Church is *katho-*

like, that the Church has its wholeness or completeness.[100] The sociology of Christian knowledge, morality, and bioethics is communal, liturgical, eucharistic, and hierarchical.

The importance of the liturgical assembly for acquiring the content of Christian belief and therefore of a Christian bioethics is easily underestimated. The Liturgy is not usually appreciated as the focal point of moral theology, much less of Christian bioethics. One must recognize the Liturgy as a source of the authority of the Scriptures in order to gauge the significance of the Liturgy. The early Church focused on the Scriptures first and foremost in terms of what works could be read in the Church. Though there was a concern to avoid heretical scriptures or false presentations of the life of Christ, for the Christians of the first centuries, the issue was primarily to determine which writings should be read in the Christian assembly. The Council of Laodicea (A.D. 364), for example, requires that "private psalms must not be recited in church, nor uncanonical books, but only the canonical books of the New and of the Old Testament" and the Council of Carthage (A.D. 418/419) prohibits "the reading of anything besides the canonical Scriptures in church under color of divine Scriptures."[101] It is not just that the Scriptures are given their definition and sense within the liturgical assembly of the Christians. It is also the case that the Scriptures can only be appropriately understood within that authentic assembly. Consequently, the Fathers generally discouraged debates with heretics concerning the Scriptures. It is not as if one could sit down with heretics or non-believers to examine the Scriptures in order to find common ground, much less the truth. Such can only be found through repentance and conversion. "The Gospel cannot be understood outside the Church nor dogma outside worship," for "outside the Church the Gospel is a sealed and incomprehensible book."[102]

This position with regard to the centrality of Christian worship for Christian moral theology and bioethics is stronger yet. Because of the acknowledgement of the union with God in prayer, especially in and through the Eucharist at Liturgy, the very character of the Liturgy takes on an inspired standing. As a result, one includes

> among the credal and dogmatic monuments of the Orthodox Catholic Church ... the liturgies of St John Chrysostom and St Basil the Great, complete with their *typikon* or liturgical rubrics and the actual manner of their celebration. For it is not only prayers with dogmatic content but the whole liturgical action and life of the Church that constitutes a unique theological witness and grace.[103]

It is not just that the Liturgy contributes content to theology and a Christian bioethics, it defines the significance of theology and a Christian bioethics. Theology is, after all, the fruit of worship. "Outside the framework of the Divine Liturgy, where God manifests His glory by the offering and self-emptying of His Son, and the faithful confess the Trinitarian truth by their love for another, it is impossible to understand Orthodox faith and theology."[104] For this reason, in developing a Christian bioethics, one can refer for guidance to the prayers of the Church, especially those of the Liturgy. For instance, it is appropriate to indicate as a basis for forbidding abortions the prayer in the Liturgy of St. Basil: "O God, who knowest the age and the name of each, and knowest every man even from his mother's womb."[105] This prayer is sufficient to indicate that abortion at any time is unacceptable to traditional Christian bioethics, for persons must be acknowledged as such from their mothers' wombs. The Liturgy provides the central place for the tradition that sustains Christian moral theology and therefore a traditional Christian bioethics.

It is important to note that tradition in this sense is not merely an oral history, particular artifacts, or Scriptures that support a set of practices and beliefs. Rather, Tradition is the continuing of union with the Holy Spirit, Who is invoked at each Liturgy.[106] It is this tradition that includes and justifies the Scriptures, not the Scriptures that justify the tradition. The Christian tradition is antecedent both in time to the Christian Scriptures, as well as in ontological priority. As St. Silouan stresses:

> The life of the Church mean[s] life in the Holy Spirit, and Sacred Tradition the unceasing action of the Holy Spirit in her. Sacred Tradition, as the eternal and immutable dwelling of the Holy Spirit in the Church, lies at the very root of her being, and so encompasses her life that even the very Scriptures come to be but one of its forms. Thus, were the Church to be deprived of Tradition she would cease to be what she is, for the ministry of the New Testament is the ministry of the Spirit "written not with ink, but with the Spirit of the living God; not in tables of stones, but in the fleshy tables of the heart" (II Cor 3:3).[107]

This claim for tradition recognizes that the Scriptures are not even a necessary condition for the life of the Church. They are not necessary to supply the content of a Christian bioethics.

Contrary to certain Protestant assumptions (e.g., *sola scriptura*), because the Church makes the Scriptures, not the Scriptures the Church, the Scriptures gain their meaning and place from the living Tradition which is the Church. It is for this reason that the actual authorship of particular works of Scripture (whether St. Paul wrote the Epistle to the Hebrews, for example) is not important for their authenticity. What is important is that they have been accepted by the Church as recording the Revelation that was given to the Apostles and the Disciples. The authority and the significance of the Scriptures are derived from the presence of the Spirit in the Church. It is this presence that is crucial.

> Suppose that for some reason the Church were to be bereft of all her books, of the Old and New Testaments, the works of the holy Fathers, of all service books - what would happen? Sacred Tradition would restore the Scriptures, not word for word, perhaps - the verbal form might be different - but in essence the new Scriptures would be the expression of that same "faith which was once delivered unto the saints" (Jude 3). They would be the expression of the one and only Holy Spirit continuously active in the Church, her foundation and her very substance.
> The Scriptures are not more profound, not more important than Holy Tradition but, as said above, they are one of its forms – the most precious form, both because they are preserved and convenient to make use of.[108]

As a consequence, a traditional Christian bioethics, though it may not go against Scripture, will not be dependent only on Scripture. It will need to draw guidance from the fullness of Tradition. In fact, its very traditional character is marked by its reliance on more than the Scriptures.[109]

Who, then, are the custodians of this tradition? Who preserves it and who maintains its purity over time? As the letters of St. Ignatius of Antioch indicate, this task falls explicitly to the bishops, the overseers. We find in Acts that when a major question confronts the Church, overseers assemble to be guided by the Holy Spirit (Acts 15:28). Even before Nicea, the first Ecumenical Council (A.D. 325), there were councils, local in nature, which then came to be accepted by the whole Church. There were, for example, councils held in Carthage, the third of which was presided over by St. Cyprian, whose canon is collected with the others of the Orthodox Church.[110] There was as well the regional council in Ankara (A.D. 314/315), which was later definitively confirmed by canon 2 of the Quinisext Council in A.D. 692, and which included a canon concerning abortion. From the very early Church, one with the history given in Acts, bishops have traditionally assembled together, as Apostolic Canon 34 specifies.

> It behoves the Bishops of every nation to know the one among them who is the premier or chief, and to recognise him as their head, and to refrain from doing anything superfluous without his advice and approval: but, instead, each of them should do only whatever is necessitated by his own parish and by the territories under him. But let not even such a one do anything without the advice and consent and approval of all. For thus will there be concord, and God will be glorified through the Lord in Holy Spirit, the Father, and the Son, and the Holy Spirit.[111]

As with the Council of Ankara (which spoke to the issue of abortion), the judgments reached by one regional council can gradually be discussed by the whole Church and then affirmed.[112] Or, if what was decided by one council is found to be unacceptable, bishops in other regions can then move to correct the error. The model is one of prayerful dialogue among bishops, as well as with laity. The unity of the bishops must be achieved within a communion of the faithful, united by the Spirit in the true catholicity of an assembly bound in love, truth, and grace. The unity must be sobornost: conciliar. It must be in unity with the Church from the beginning. A formal mark of this is apostolic succession. Just as the faithful require bishops, bishops have no apostolic succession in the absence of right-believing, right-worshipping faithful. That is, apostolic succession resides not in bishops considered in isolation, but in bishops within right-believing, right-worshipping communities who together can trace their authority from the Apostles, whose faith they have maintained. There is no apostolic succession after schism combined with heresy.

The canons themselves provide no formal mechanism for an international or worldwide Church administration. Nowhere in the canons of the Church are there explicit rules for calling or conducting an ecumenical council.[113] Each time one has been held, it was convened with the authority of an emperor (e.g., the Empress St. Pulcheria with her husband convened the Council of Chalcedon in 451). Only once did a pope of Rome attend, and in that instance it was Virgilius, who was accused of perjury. The only structure for worldwide administration appears as a recognition of a confederacy of bishops united in right worship and right belief, with special provision being made for regional organization. One finds this model in Canon 6 of Nicea (A.D. 325),[114] Canon 3 of Constantinople I (A.D. 381),[115] and finally in Canon 28 of the Council of Chalcedon (A.D. 451).

> Everywhere following the decrees of the Holy Fathers, and aware of the recently recognized Canon of the one hundred and fifty most God-beloved Bishops who convened during the reign of Theodosius the Great of pious memory, who became emperor in the imperial city of Constantinople otherwise known as New Rome; we too decree and vote the same things in regard to the privileges and priorities of the most holy Church of that same Constantinople and New Rome. And this is in keeping with the fact that the Fathers naturally enough granted the priorities to the throne of Old Rome on account of her being the imperial capital. And motivated by the same object and aim the one hundred and fifty most God-beloved Bishops have accorded the like priorities to the most holy throne of New Rome, with good reason deeming that the city which is the seat of an empire, and of a senate, and is equal to old imperial Rome in respect of other privileges and priorities, should be magnified also as she is in respect of ecclesiastical affairs, as coming next after her, or as being second to her.[116]

The Council does not recognize the priority of old Rome as grounded in any special right of inheritance from St. Peter (i.e., as if St. Peter had the right to bequeath his primacy to a city, and had moreover done so). Rather, the Church recognizes that old Rome had a priority of honor and service because it had been the chief city or capital of the Empire, able to lead with an effective love for all. There is no unique papal teaching office that can with universal and immediate authority speak to bioethical issues, as occurs with the Roman papacy. There is no universal jurisdiction,[117] not to mention no papal infallibility. Each right-believing and -worshipping bishop with his diocese realizes the wholeness, the catholicity of the Church.

The Councils recognize and establish patriarchal administrative structures. The emperor is surely also regarded as providing a quasi-sacral, non-ecclesial unity. As King David was to Israel, the emperor has been to Christendom. Yet there were Christian churches beyond the boundaries of the Empire and the jurisdiction of the emperor (e.g., the Church of Georgia). There were emperors who were heretical and therefore beyond the unity of the Church. The unity for which the Church prays is not pursued through a centralized ecclesiastical administrative structure. Nor should the Councils be regarded as a kind of special ruling assembly, which could by itself definitively answer all bioethical questions. The structure of this and the continuity one finds in Orthodoxy in the second millennium comprise not just a Church of the Councils sans a pope with universal jurisdiction and infallibility. History shows a much more complex structure. To begin with, there are no reliably external criteria by which to determine whether a purported Ecumenical Council is a true or a heretical assembly, save by the absence of novel beliefs. Often only in retrospect can one know if a council is ecumenical and orthodox, as for example in the case of the Robber Council of Ephesus (A.D. 449). Councils are orthodox because they teach orthodox dogma. Ecumenical Councils are large-scale expressions of the faith that the Holy Spirit sustains the Church in true belief through her conciliar or synodal collaboration within an ecclesial structure that encompasses and is dependent on more than Ecumenical Councils. Councils require acceptance by the right-believing and right-worshipping people of God. The Ecumenical Councils function as an act of synodal mutuality among the bishops of the Church and the people in the absence of a central international, ecclesiastical, central administrative structure.

There is also a source of ecclesial, moral, and spiritual authority of a dimension other than that of the hierarchy and the councils. It is those whom Paul describes as prophets (1 Cor 12:28): the holy fathers and mothers who in union with God declare His word. Such a person today is often referred to as an "elder", "geronda", or "staretz". Such a person need not be a priest, an academic, or a member of the hierarchy. The person may even be a holy fool-for-Christ in rags in the gutter outside the church. Theological authority is possessed not because of what the person has studied or published. There is no presumption of academic title or authority conveyed by the hierarchy. Theologians are authorities, though not in authority, at least if this is understood in hierarchical terms. Theologians in the strict sense possess authority because of their relationship to God and because of what they as a consequence know, which can include not only matters of doctrine but also simple matters of fact.[118]

In these two senses of authority, one finds the intertwining, indeed synergy, of the visible hierarchy of the Church and the Spirit's prophetic presence in the Church, the intertwining of the eschatological proclamation of the Liturgy as the Kingdom of God, St. Paul's proclamation of Christ until He comes (I Cor 11:26),[119] and the ascetical taking of the Kingdom by violence (Matt 11:12). In the Liturgy presided over by the bishop and with the holy Fathers able to enter into that liturgical communion, one encounters Christ and His Kingdom. With St. John the Theologian's and St. Paul's prayer for the full and final transformation of the world by Christ at His second coming (i.e., "Maranatha" ["Come, O Lord"], I Cor 16:22; "Amen; yes, come, Lord Jesus" Rev 22:20), the Church in the Liturgy already sees His second coming[120] and recognizes that, in the Liturgy and in the illumination of a pure heart (Matt 5:8), one can already drink of the water of life (Rev 22:17). On the one hand, the Kingdom of heaven is yet to come (Matt 26:29), and on the other hand, it is already within us (Luke 17:21). On the one hand, Christ is still to appear in His glory (Matt 24:30; Mark 13:26; Luke 21:22); on the other hand, He has already shown Himself in His glory (Matt 17:1-13; Mark 9:2-13; Luke 9:28-36) and shows Himself still to all who achieve a pure heart and are illumined by the Spirit.

The theologian who by ascesis seeks a pure heart so as to be restored to paradisiacal communion with God does not simply look back to Eden in which Adam fell, but to Eden as the Paradise[121] into which the thief enters with Christ[122] (Luke 23:43). It is this Paradise into which Paul was caught up (2 Cor 12:14), for he who overcomes not only eats of the tree of life at the end of the age, but like Paul already tastes of it in this life. Indeed, Paul's ministry is that both of Apostle or overseer, as well as of prophet. As Paul emphasizes, after Christ's special revelation to him, Paul "conferred not with flesh and blood" (Gal 1:16) but went into the deserts of Arabia (Gal 1:17). Only after three years did St. Paul go to the then-leading city of the Church, Jerusalem, and meet with Sts. Peter and James. Like the ascetic theologians over the ages, St. Paul first sought to be alone with Christ, although united with all through Christ, since Christ in His body unites all who are baptized.

Theologians in the full sense overcome the need for Scriptures and set aside the lament of St. John Chrysostom that we should be blamed for standing "in need of written words, and not to have brought down on ourselves the grace of the Spirit".[123] Theologians enter into the same Spirit, as did the authors of the Gospels. Their entrance is not contingent on their learning, but on an act of the Spirit. As the Vespers for Pentecost declare,

> The Holy Spirit provideth all; overfloweth with prophecy; fulfilleth the Priesthood; and hath taught wisdom to the illiterate. He hath revealed the fishermen as theologians. He bringeth together all the laws of the Church. Wherefore, O Comforter, equal to the Father in Substance and the throne, glory to thee.[124]

Because the Spirit is one and Christ the same yesterday, today, and forever (Heb 13:8), one can then understand more deeply the meaning of the formula given by St. Vincent of Lerins that the test of Orthodox belief is that it must be that which has been believed everywhere, always, and by all.[125] Because true theologians are united in one Spirit, traditional Christianity authenticates as well the enduring relevance of past moral teachings for current bioethical controversies. If the source of true moral knowledge is the experience of the truth, that experience will remain the same even if it must now be applied in different circumstances and to different challenges. If there are new problems to confront bioethics, the way to approach them will in a deep sense never be novel. Again, because true theology is orientation to a transcendent personal God, it is the unity of belief over time and space that is the formal criterion of true Orthodox belief. The unity of belief is the unity of belief of true theologians over time and space.

A theologian in this strict sense is a person who successfully turns in prayerful worship to God and experiences Him. The exemplar theologian is therefore not an academic but a saint (though one would hope that the two are not mutually exclusive). As Evagrios the Solitary (345-399) stresses, "If you are a theologian, you will pray truly. And if you pray truly, you are a theologian."[126] Recent examples of such individuals include St. John of San Francisco (1894-1966),[127] Elder Joseph the Hesychast, the Cave-Dweller of the Holy Mountain (1895-1959),[128] Elder Paisios of Romania (†1993), Elder Paisios of Mt. Athos (1924-1994),[129] Elder Porphyrios (1906-1991),[130] St. Silouan the Athonite (1866-1938),[131] and Archimandrite Sophrony (1896-1993).[132] Some such as Elder Sophrony were very well educated; others such as St. Silouan, Elder Joseph, and Elder Porphyrios had only an elementary-school education. The life and teachings of these elders show that equating theology with an academic discipline is a prideful and erroneous presumption. It involves a cardinal misunderstanding regarding the nature of moral theology and the foundations of a Christian bioethics, namely, the erroneous view (1) that the exemplar theologians are the great thinkers and scholars, not the great lovers of God, as well as (2) that theology is preeminently a disengaged discursive scholarly enterprise rather than first and foremost the fruit of repentance, worship, and grace.

> In the teaching of the holy Fathers of the Church, the theologian is identi-
> fied with the God-seer. Only he who has seen God and has been united
> with Him through theosis, has acquired the true knowledge of God. Ac-
> cording to St. Gregory the Theologian, theologians are those who have
> reached "theoria", having been previously cleansed of their passions, or
> being at least in the process of purification.[133]

It is important to notice the extent to which this places theology and theologians alongside the hierarchy and as a corrective for the hierarchy. True theologians are the prophets, and true prophets are the theologians *sensu stricto*.

A classical summary of this position is found in the work of St. Symeon the New Theologian. The force of his writings is conveyed by the circumstance that, in the history of the Orthodox Church, only three individuals have formally been given the epithet "Theologian": St. John the Theologian, the fourth Evangelist, St. Gregory the Theologian of Nazianzus, and St. Symeon the New Theologian. Here two points suf-fice. First, St. Symeon provides a vantage point from which one can explicitly criticize the hierarchy: the experience of the theologian in union with God, like the prophets of Israel, may correct a wayward establishment. Such a theologian can, like St. Symeon, put into the mouth of Christ words such as these.

> They [the bishops] unworthily handle My Body
> and seek avidly to dominate the masses...
> They are seen to appear as brilliant and pure,
> but their souls are worse than mud and dirt,
> worse even than any kind of deadly poison,
> these evil and perverse men![134]

Second, St. Symeon stresses that not only priests but also holy, albeit unordained, monks can at times loose and bind, forgive sins. In so doing, he sustains the recognition that the Holy Spirit is not confined to a hierarchical structure. Theologians in this strict sense of those who live in the Holy Spirit function to correct the magisterium of the bishops, when the bishops themselves fail to be theologians, fail to be prophets who live in the Holy Spirit.

This office of theologian is quite different from what one would expect within West-ern Christian assumptions. Unlike the place of academic theology in the Roman Catho-lic church, especially unlike its role in the magisterium or teaching authority of the church, here the core and cardinal element of the office of the theologian is not academ-ic. It is the Church's anchor in the Holy Spirit, the continuity of Christian religious expe-rience. In the Roman Catholic church, in comparison, it is as if the core of theology had atrophied and the periphery hypertrophied. In Orthodoxy the primary appeal to theol-ogy does not involve the engagement of academic reflection, but of those who live in the Holy Spirit. Indeed, even the sense of philosophy is transformed to identify the experi-ence of wisdom in the Holy Spirit. "When thou didst send thy Spirit, O Lord, the Apos-tles ... philosophized, driving the Gentiles to the Faith, as they preached of things divine."[135] There can be analysis of concepts, terms, and injunctions. There can be careful conceptual, discursively argumentative explorations of theological bioethical commitments.

In the secondary sense, this book is a volume in Orthodox theology. Indeed, it is a study in moral theology and bioethics, if one be willing both to use theology in this extended sense and then to divide the wholeness of theology into various academically determined categories. However, theological truth, the acquisition and understanding of the moral theological foundations and content of bioethics, is achieved by ascesis, through becoming free of self-love by loving God and others. Theology in the strict sense is a work of grace: an epistemological source with metaphysical force. St. Symeon and the tradition recognize that the grace that transforms us is not something created by God or owned by the hierarchy, but is a free gift of God of Himself. Grace is the uncreated energies of God Himself. As St. Symeon the New Theologian emphasizes:

> The Holy Ghost is spoken of as a key because through Him and in Him we are first enlightened in mind. We are purified and illuminated with the light of knowledge; we are baptized from on high and born anew (cf. Jn 3:3, 5) and made into children of God.[136]

Therefore, true theologians supply not only the content for a Christian bioethics; they serve as a protection against academic theologians who are tempted to develop or create novel beliefs.

Given this strong faith in the Holy Spirit, despite a firm commitment to a hierarchical church governed by bishops, and with an appreciation of the importance of careful reasoning, the last word on theological, including bioethical, issues is always given by the Spirit, beyond the academy and embracing the hierarchy. It is for this reason that not even Ecumenical Councils are infallible by themselves. Again, the history of Christianity shows that councils can be assembled with marks of being ecumenical and then fail to be ecumenical because their teaching is heretical and therefore not confirmed by the tradition. One of the best examples of such an occurrence, already alluded to, is the second Council of Ephesus in 449, which was later repudiated as a robber council, a *Latrocinium*. Even an "ecumenical council" that would enjoy the concurrence of all patriarchs is by itself neither infallible nor a necessary guide for faith. The conciliar, synodal, or sobornost character of the Church requires not simply the concurrence of a council or its acceptance by all bishops, but its affirmation by the faithful who are in full and proper eucharistic communion, especially by the theologians.[137] The role of the ordinary laity is emphasized in the famous encyclical letter of the patriarchs and synods of Constantinople, Antioch, and Jerusalem in 1848 in reply to Pius IX.

> Moreover, neither Patriarchs nor Councils could then have introduced novelties amongst us, because the protector of religion is the very body of the Church, even the people themselves, who desire their religious worship to be ever unchanged and of the same kind as that of their fathers.[138]

This view of the relationship of patriarch and people is in many ways quite different from that of the Roman Catholic account of papal authority. What is involved is a synergy of moral authority that defies any simple, discursive, hierarchical description: bishops, priests, monastics, holy elders, and laity united in the Holy Spirit, in one spiritual struggle and in one communion. This union in one communion and in one Spirit is the unity of the liturgical and the mystical, the eucharistic and the spiritually therapeutic dimensions of theology.

It would be misleading to think of ecumenical councils as creating or developing new dogma: they develop articulations of dogma. Particular conciliar formations or articulations of belief are generally fashioned out of a confrontation with heresy. Such dogmatic formulations direct the Church away from novel understandings back to the Tradition. If the body of the Church receives these articulations, they have an enduring, infallible, and special therapeutic standing. It is agreed that those who reject these formulations must be treated with excommunication. Before the acceptance of a Council's formulations, this response of excommunication is not universally accepted as a norm, in part out of a concern whether sufficient admonition or direction has been given. A council's dogmatic formulations and its canons are an inspired act of synodal economia.

If one held that it was in dogmatic formulations that one finally determines theological truth rather than that in councils one finally generally agrees to a therapeutic response to theological falsehood (i.e., as a rule one should respond to the use of other formulations by excommunication) by establishing precise diagnostic and therefore therapeutic criteria, then one would have fallen into an endless discursive trap. If one held that it was only in dogmatic formulation that one finally determined theological truth, then as soon as any conciliar formulation had been established, those of bad will or faith could at once dispute the meaning of each and every term in the formulation. This would engender an endless regress of asking when one knows that one knows that one knows what the formulation means. There is no escape until one steps outside of this error and into the light of noetic experience. Only then can conciliar formulations be appreciated as they should be, as established therapeutic rules for responding to error and not as the development of theological truth. The fact of a conciliar formulation and its reception does not diminish the dogmatic standing of belief that remains formally undogmatized. Such generally accepted understandings of faith and morals are not mere theologumena. Traditional faith and morals in all their particularity are just as enduring, unchangeable, and binding as that which is formally dogmatized by councils. It is simply that there is no commitment to a particular formulation or expression, nor to the norm of responding with excommunication to those who reject the formulation. Still, in the absence of conciliar formulations, the truth is present and is experienced as such. All that the Church universally believes, expresses in worship, and follows in its moral convictions is enduring, unchangeable, and infallible, even outside any council's affirmation.

It would also be wrong to distinguish dogma or faith from morals under the supposition that the first has been dogmatized by the Councils, but the second has not. First, such would be an artificial separation of what should be understood as a whole fabric of life. Second, what has been universally recognized as sinful is as true and enduringly a part of what the Church affirms as unchanging as any of what has been formally dogmatized by councils. One will not some day discover that what has always been recognized as directing away from God will later be found to be part of turning to God.

Abortion, adultery, homosexual acts, and suicide, for instance, have always been recognized as sinful. There is no possibility that this could be otherwise. It would be equally obligatory not to be in communion with those who teach that adultery or homosexual acts are not sinful, as it would be to wall oneself off from those who reject or alter the Nicean-Constantinopolitan Creed. It is just that the therapeutic response of excommunication might not be as immediate. There are, after all, differences between what is obvious and widely discussed, and what should be obvious but has not been as widely discussed and made clear to all. Conciliar formulations are aimed at dispelling confusion.

The canons of the Ecumenical Councils, as well as the canons from the Fathers and universally received regional councils, give special orientation to salvation. The canons indicate the way to salvation, though not in a legalistic sense. The canons are spiritual medicine; they must be applied strictly or at times more severely or leniently, so as to bring health. In a sense, once accepted by the whole Church, they apply even when historically conditioned and seemingly irrelevant. They are an articulation of the moral and ecclesiological voice of the Church. Their validity lies in their indicating a truth about how to turn rightly to God. The canons have therapeutic significance: they are to direct us to a fully transcendent God Who can never adequately be captured in any discursive formulation. But the moral commitments of the Church are not exhausted by the canons. Christianity's unchangeable moral commitments are found in the traditional life of right-believing and right-worshiping Christians.

The truth thus experienced and achieved is not simply a cluster of academic distinctions, but the very fabric of life, of right worship and belief. Formulations of dogma regarding God should not be understood as achieving mere correspondence claims of truth. For example, recognizing that God is first and foremost the Father Almighty is not to claim that God is an all-powerful male. It is to recognize precisely and enduringly that, in order successfully to approach God in love, worship, and prayer, one must turn to God as Father. The enduring place of this infallible knowledge is the oneness of love, worship, and action, which unites Christians over the centuries in a substantive content of belief and moral commitment. The Church's eidetic knowledge is expressed in this unity of love, worship, and action, which is incarnate in the dogmas that live in its Liturgy and is experienced by all, but most fully by those who have become theologians. This knowledge aims beyond itself to an encounter with God Who transcends all concepts and categories.

In examining what Tradition gives us, distinctions between Tradition and tradition[139] are precarious. The Spirit is Tradition.[140] The Tradition is the continuation of the Spirit in the Church maintaining its unity of belief and worship over time, sometimes despite the sins and wishes of laity, priests, bishops, and patriarchs. Tradition in this sense is neither simply oral tradition nor ancient customs. However, ancient customs should never be despised; their antiquity has hallowed them with centuries of prayer. The continuity of the Church, its survival despite the efforts of many laity, bishops, patriarchs, and false synods to destroy the Church, is the manifest miracle of the Spirit. Consequently, it is not possible to identify an unambiguous, this-worldly magisterial authority able to resolve bioethical controversies from the top down. In Orthodoxy the solutions are from the bottom up, not just from the top down, as the people and the bishop turn from themselves to God. The infallible whole of the Church is the Spirit in the whole of the Church, which as right-worshipping remains right-believing in the Tradition that is the continuity of the Spirit. The whole as a sociological matter is the assembly in worthy liturgical communion of those who are united by the energies of God in right belief and right worship. The commitment underscored by St. Vincent of Lerins to being one in belief and worship over space and time connects current questions regarding new biomedical challenges to old accepted responses, as will be illustrated in the four chapters that follow.

In summary, theological authority is in every case embodied in the life of the Church. The theologians as the God-seers derive their authority from their union with God in the Church. So, too, the ability of the Church as a whole to resolve controversies by preserving the Tradition is grounded in an experience of God that unites the Church in true worship and belief. This union culminates in worthy eucharistic unity. Eucharistic communion is the final fruit, not the beginning of right belief, worship, and action. Both bioethical immorality and the broken character of our human condition as it is experienced in health care can place persons outside of the possibility of worthy eucharistic communion and in need of special spiritual therapy. As we will see, because the focus of theological union is eucharistic, moral alienation and spiritual estrangement must at times be remedied by excommunication and a special spiritual convalescence so as to lead back to spiritual health and eucharistic unity. All of this locates theological as well as Christian bioethical expertise along with magisterial, theological, and bioethical authority in the experience and presence of the Spirit and in eucharistic union with Christ.

Two Senses of Theology, Two Senses of Christian Bioethics

The West came to a quite different understanding of theology, and therefore to a quite different understanding of bioethics, especially Christian bioethics. It sought foremost to understand more through discursive reflection and less by noetic knowledge. This difference became accented as an innovative theology took a central place in the emerging self-consciousness and identity of the West. There are many historical roots of this difference. One of them is the influence of Blessed Augustine of Hippo (354-430), whose understandings of doctrine and whose aspirations to intellectual knowledge were not the same as those of the Church that produced the Councils. A few initial divergences in accent and then in discipline grew within deviant approaches to the fast and to clerical celibacy.[141] These, combined with a number of significant theological errors (e.g., claims of universal papal jurisdiction, of the filioque, of the Fall as bequeathing an original sin as a matter of personal guilt, of a precedence given to discursive over noetic theology out of failing to recognize that the Fall clouded the nous, of the Fall as making the human will unable to turn initially on its own to God, of all grace as created, of purgatory, of indulgences, of the Immaculate Conception, and of papal infallibility), grew in force as the new empire of the West founded by Charlemagne needed to distinguish itself theologically from the Empire against which it began to define and justify itself. Its theology had to become developmental in order to justify its new religious claims. The West needed to produce a theological content that would set its religious consciousness over against the Empire seated in Constantinople and its religion. To defend its legitimacy, the new empire had to distinguish itself against the old empire and the old religion. This new perspective was sought in part from the scholarship of the early renaissance in Frankfurt and around Charlemagne's court.[142] It was from here that the influential forgery of the Donations of Constantine was likely produced. The West sought to justify a new scope for ecclesiastical governance. It was out of this intellectual and political milieu that the filioque was endorsed and the road taken to the papacy of the High Western Middle Ages.[143] The Roman papacy then sought to put its emperors in their place, and finally, in response to the collapse of papal temporal power, the power of infallibility was asserted. From a few initial steps a new religion took shape, which in time produced quite different understandings of the character as well as the grounds for claims regarding who is *an* authority as well as who is *in* authority about matters bioethical.[144] The West became theologically underdeveloped. Rather than encouraging theological union with God, it focused instead on developing the intellectual framework that became scholasticism. The West lost the central mystical focus core to traditional Christianity.

Changes in the meaning of theology in the West were tied to other developments. In the West, theological education moved in steps away from monasteries to the cathedral schools and then, in the 13th century, to the universities.[145] The sense of theology, theological education, and theological expertise changed. Among other things, theology took on an academic character. The case of the University of Paris, founded in 1208, is illustrative. It was there that Albertus Magnus (1206-1280) taught Thomas Aquinas (1225-1274). It counted among its students Bonaventure (1221-1274), Duns Scotus (1270-1308), and Roger Bacon (1214-1294). In the brilliance of this burst of scholarship, intellectual ability, and recaptured ancient learning, the exemplar theologian came to be an academic scholar. In the process, this produced Scholastic reflections on bioethical issues.[146] In this century of intellectual energy, theology came no longer to be regarded primarily as the fruit of holiness. Theology came instead to be understood more centrally as the fruit of scholarship.

The turn in the West to academic theology, achieved in the 13th century, proved fateful for subsequent moral theology, and indeed for bioethics. Moral theology and bioethics became presumptively academic endeavors that could be understood outside of a life of prayer. The emphasis shifted, such that prayer now at best supplements "scientific" theological or Christian bioethical research, rather than discursive reflection being invoked to clarify the fruits of prayer. This alteration in the character of theology constitutes a fundamental paradigm shift. It involves a revolution in theological thinking, a change in the very notion of what it is to do theology, be a Christian, or engage in Christian bioethics. As Kierkegaard aptly puts it, in this paradigm "the professor is the true Christian."[147] Epistemological assumptions were revised such that true theological knowledge was gained not primarily through prayer and union with God, but through scholarly analysis and reflection. The metaphysical assumptions changed as well: God was no longer recognized as truly transcendent. Instead, an analogy was invoked between created and Uncreated Being, so as to attempt exploration of the nature of God Himself.

These changes were embedded in a revolution in the sociology of theological knowing and valuing, tied to the movement of theology from the hermitage and monastery to the academy. This shift in the sense of what it is to do theology was as important, if not more important, than the actual theological positions taken by such figures as Thomas Aquinas (1225-1274) and Duns Scotus. This new sense of scientific theology was bound to metaphors of scientific progress, so that theology, as other sciences, could come to be doctrinally progressive, rather than united with the unchanging revelation of Christ. New doctrines could emerge (e.g., papal infallibility), not just new expressions of enduring truths (e.g., the introduction of terms such as "Trinity" and "Theotokos"). The result was a weakening of true theology: the praxis of worship and asceticism, which brings union with God. As the gulf between created and uncreated Being was ignored, the place of the good, the right, and the virtuous could approximate that of the holy. Theological development was no longer the development of union with God, but the elaboration of new doctrines. Finally, the exemplar theologians became most plausibly the great scholars. Vatican II (1961-1965) in its instruction regarding the education of priests, underscored the centrality of discursive, speculative rationality. "[S]tudents should learn to penetrate them more deeply with the help of speculative reason exercised under the tutelage of St. Thomas."[148] The West became ever more theologically underdeveloped, ever less engaged in the pursuit of the noetic experience of God.

A recent Roman Catholic instruction to theologians on their role in the church presents well the results of these changes: theology is regarded as primarily a discursive discipline. It presupposes that theology is primarily an academic field, no longer the fruit of prayer but the product of scholarship. As an academic field, it can hope for further progress. It must also meet scholarly standards.

> Through the course of centuries, theology has progressively developed into a true and proper science. The theologian must therefore be attentive to the epistemological requirements of his discipline, to the demands of rigorous critical standards and thus to a rational verification of each stage of his research.[149]

The document is directed against theological dissidence. It seems blind to the circumstance that much of this dissidence is born of the academic incentives that reward novelty. Once theology is academic, it has the aspirations of other academic disciplines to see things anew and to fit in with the secular fashions of the age.

A similar background change frames the grounds for Pope John Paul II's laments regarding the contemporary state of philosophy. His diagnosis of the spiritual problems of our age do not lead him to call for a return to the ancient ascetic practices. He recognizes that "Dechristianization, which weighs heavily upon entire peoples and communities once rich in faith and Christian life, involves not only the loss of faith or in any event its becoming irrelevant for everyday life, but also, and of necessity, *a decline or obscuring of the moral sense*."[150] Yet John Paul II does not attempt to re-institute the spiritual life and asceticism of the Tradition. Instead, he urges philosophers once again to pursue the disclosure of ultimate truth, "to trust in the power of human reason and not to set themselves goals that are too modest in their philosophizing. ... I appeal now to philosophers to explore more comprehensively the dimensions of the true, the good and the beautiful to which the word of God gives access. ... I appeal also to philosophers, and to all teachers of philosophy, asking them to have the courage to recover, in the flow of an enduringly valid philosophical tradition, the range of authentic wisdom and truth – metaphysical truth included – which is proper to philosophical enquiry."[151] Rather than recognizing that Western culture has become neo-pagan because it no longer rightly pursues the holy, the Western pontiff complains that philosophers are no longer engaged in doing what St. John Chrysostom and traditional Christianity in general recognized to be impossible: discursively reasoning one's way to a proper knowledge of being and of God.

John Paul II fails to recognize that well directed philosophical speculation is impossible outside of a Christian ascetical context. If one does not live a spiritual life that leads from oneself to God, then philosophical speculation will always be misguiding. John Paul II's lament that the West has been returned to the skeptical, eclectic, and polymorphous engagement in philosophy that characterized its pagan past is ironic at best. Lamenting the state of philosophy is like whipping the Hellespont, if one does not recapture the true roots of theology in prayer, worship, and asceticism. The pope of Rome does not recognize that it was philosophy as speculative reflection and theology as academic science that have undone the West and his church. Philosophy, even in the context of a religious university, invites non-Christian moral understandings because it has at best only a non-noetic, academic theology to guide it.

This observation concerning academic theology and the place of discursive philosophy is not meant to deny that some of the greatest heresies of the Church developed before there were theological academies or professors of theology as we know them now. The temptations are always the same: novelty is attractive. It is just that certain institutional structures intensify those temptations. If theology and Christian bioethics are regarded as are other academic pursuits, where professors are rewarded for creativity and innovation, advancement will often go to those who create new understandings, develop new doctrines, and fashion new accounts of Christianity. In particular, Christian bioethics under such circumstances will be expected to produce morally innovative solutions to new challenges, rather than to draw from the enduring source of solutions: prayer and the pursuit of holiness. If theology were merely academic, patristic texts would be viewed as the focus of historical scholarly work, rather than as reporting the ever vivid encounter with the Spirit Who constitutes the Tradition.

These changes in the meaning of theology that have rendered it primarily an academic discipline essentially distort how one can appreciate Divine Revelation. Rather than appreciating revelation as (1) abiding, as the Tradition in the sense of the ongoing presence of the Spirit, Who reminds the Church of everything Christ has said (John 14:26), revelation becomes (2) a past event found in documents and oral history or (3) an ongoing disclosure including the presentation of new truths. Initially, the West as it stepped out of the noetic life of the Holy Spirit came to see revelation as a past event recorded in Scriptures and, for the Roman Catholics, also as remembered in oral tradition. As a subject matter to be addressed by scholars, not only were new expositions of that past revelation possible, but new insights could be developed. Revelation as a past event when joined to an academic theology able to disclose new insights into this revelation, produces theology as a discipline capable of new disclosures. In contrast, if revelation is abiding and theology is life in the Holy Spirit, though new expressions may be coined to disclose this enduring experience, there is no new revelation, no new discovery, for the Spirit has come in full to His Church, bringing to mind all of Christ's teaching (John 14:26), and is the same across the ages.

These changes in the meaning of theology inevitably distort Christology, pneumatol-
ogy, and ecclesiology. As the churches of the West separated themselves from noetic theology, the Church as the body of Christ was no longer experienced in the Holy Spirit,
guided by true theologians. There is then a temptation to think of the Church as the
body of Christ embedded in and hostage to the exigencies of history. There is no longer
a recognition that it is the Holy Spirit that compels unity in the revelation of God as the
Council of Jerusalem was compelled to accept the Gentiles because the Spirit of God
accepted them from the beginning (Acts 15:12). The failure to recognize theological
knowledge in the Spirit, which places the human in the eternal, is presented in the radical separation in the West of baptism from chrismation. The Western attempt to become
one with Christ through baptism (Rom 6:1-14; Gal 3:27; Eph 5:30) is severed from the
attempt to be united with His Holy Spirit through chrismation. As Acts makes plain,
baptism without the conferral of the Holy Spirit is radically incomplete (Acts 8:14-19).
This rupture between body and Spirit is presented as well in the Western neglect of the
epiclesis as the transformation of the Eucharist. As St. Paul emphasizes in Ephesians,
there is not only one body but one Spirit (Eph 4:4), so that the body of Christ, the
Church, remains in the unity of the experience of the Spirit. Absent this unity, ecclesiology either (1) construes having a church in a radically incarnate fashion, so that it becomes dominated by history, or (2) subjects the church to whatever spirits speak so that
church structure becomes hostage to a legion of disparate inspirations. On the one hand,
there is an attempt centrally to impose a unity; on the other hand, there is a fracturing
into a legion of new religions, each with its own bioethics.

Traditional Christian theology and its bioethics are rooted in the unity of the
experience of the transcendent that provides the abiding unity of the Church. This
unity and its focus are mystical.

> It is most faulty to think that philosophical terms and expressions could
> confine theological meanings which are purely divine. ... There are many
> mysteries in our religion which we accept with deep acquiescence just
> because they are revealed by God. We believe in them contrary to the
> evidence of our senses and to our reason if we may use the word, just
> because they are proved to be from God. As we believe in God and in His
> omnipotence, so we believe in the mysteries of our religion without any
> need to ask why and how. A philosophical mind cannot agree to this
> mystical faith. But a philosophical mind is not in fact a true religious
> mind. It rather believes in its own capacities and measures. Religion to a
> philosophical mind is a science that could be treated on the same level as
> any other branch of human knowledge. A philosophical mind applies to
> religion the scientific method. Here analysis, classification, philology and
> so on enter into religion, in order to make it more reasonable and accept-
> able to a philosophical mind. Alas, in this kind of dealing with our reli-
> gion we cannot understand the spirit of our religion. Where reason inter-
> feres, mystical experience disappears. We have to use our minds up to a
> certain point, but beyond that we should leave our minds to the guidance
> of a mystical experience.[152]

When scholarly analyses claim a priority over the pursuit of holiness, one loses the central connection to holiness as the source of canonical moral and religious content. Content is drawn from the history and resources of an academic discipline rather than from a tradition of ascesis and worship that secures its content from grace and an encounter with God.

A traditional Christian bioethics will not accept the primary contribution of theology to bioethics as that of academic refinement, analysis, and argument instead of theological experience. As Patriarch Bartholomeus stresses:

> The Orthodox Christian does not live in a place of theoretical and conceptual conversations, but rather in a place of an essential and empirical lifestyle and reality as confirmed by grace in the heart (Heb 13:9). This grace cannot be put in doubt either by logic or science or other type of argument.[153]

Theology and Christian bioethics as a "true and proper science" will resist academic models of science that objectify and depersonalize theology, rendering theology and Christian bioethics into human research programs instead of recognizing true theology as the fruit of love, worship, and deification.

> Therefore we do not engage in idle talk and discuss intellectual concepts which do not influence our lives. We discuss the essence of the Being Who truly is, to Whom we seek to become assimilated by the grace of God, and because of the inadequacy of human terms, we call this the image of the glory of the Lord. Based on this image, and in the likeness of this image, we become "partakers of the divine nature" (2 Pet 1:4). We are truly changed, although "neither earth, nor voice, nor custom distinguish us from the rest of mankind" (To Diognetos 2, PG 2, 1173).[154]

Theology or Christian bioethics that is not tied to a holy life is an anti-theology or anti-bioethics. The theology properly at the foundations of Christian bioethics is one grounded in the experience of God.

This latter sense of theology and its bioethics is quite different from that grounded in the academy and scholarly research. The first is noetic, the second discursive. The first has as its exemplar theologians saints in union with God. The second has as its exemplar theologians the learned scholars of the academy. The first as noetic seeks to disclose or reveal the truth present in the Church from the beginning. The second seeks to develop a theology and bioethics justified and undertaken primarily in terms of discursive reasoning. The two are at odds with each other. The first recognizes that the spirit of the second, if made core to theology, moves away from God and towards human powers. The second will deny dogma and moral constraints if they cannot be justified in general, rational, discursive terms. Discursive theology unrooted in noetic theology and an ascetic life will therefore evacuate the content it may have inherited from noetic theologians of the past, which it once shared with the Church of the first millennium. Similarly, a discursive Christian bioethics will step by step bring into question all that the Tradition has affirmed as its content. After all, noetic disclosures, because they are beyond reason, cannot be justified by reason. If considered as claims subject to scholarly critique, they will need to be abandoned if they cannot be discursively justified.

Bioethics in Time and with Persons

Christianity is not a set of anonymous philosophical principles, an impersonal way of life, or a truth that comes to us without a history. Christian bioethics has to do with Christ. Christian bioethics must be understood in terms of a unique narrative of salvation in which real people play important roles and in which God plays the crucial role through the redemptive act of His Son incarnate as the Messiah of Israel. Christian history is the history of persons caught up in a drama of cosmic significance concerning sin and redemption: Adam and Eve, Abraham and Moses, David and the Prophets, Mary and the Apostles, the martyrs, saintly physicians, holy elders, and many others, are all united to God through Christ in a web of free choices and their consequences. This history involves non-human persons as well: devils and angels. Although the existence of devils, the intervention of angels, and the transformation of nature by holiness[155] may seem strange and un-modern to many, this is fundamental to traditional Christianity. Traditional Christianity is in this sense disturbingly unenlightened. Christian bioethics is located in a very thick narrative: the history of redemption, which as history includes the damnation of Lucifer as much as it includes the redemption of many. It is not a narrative that is simply told. It is rather a narrative into which all reality is actually placed.

The language of a traditional Christian bioethics will thus be quite different from that of a secular bioethics: even in the midst of contemporary biomedical science and technology, Christian bioethics has a central place for miracles, saints, angels, and devils. The miracles of God, as well as the appearances of His saints and angels, are lodged deeply in an apophatic theology that can neither predict God's interventions nor allow them to be construed as merely filling gaps in scientific explanation. Miracles, saints, and angels break in upon us, interrupting the immanent by their presence. Often, they are a kind of *hapax legomenon*: startling, individual, and beyond the evaluation of the scientist. At other times, they are present with a combination of flagrant and humble circumstances, so that those who believe can acknowledge them as miracles, and those who do not believe will not care to investigate. Miracles always bestow a gift, strengthen faith, and give a further occasion for glorifying God. They cannot substitute for faith. They fit into no theory. They are personal. So, too, the presence of the devil is personal. The Adversary knows that he usually does best if he never suggests his existence to any who do not already acknowledge him, allowing himself instead inobtrusively to play the role of tempter, stumbling block, and enemy. Yet his influences are real. As a consequence, a traditional Christian regards illness, medicine, and disease within a thoroughgoing double-bookkeeping of the proportions of a Kantian living in the cleft between the phenomenal and noumenal worlds. On the one hand, the world is approached in fully modern ways. On the other, the world is experienced in traditional terms, as shaped by forces malevolent and holy. While never denying scientifically accessible reality, there will at the same time be a recognition of the ubiquity of holy as well as malign powers.

Persons are central. Moral principles are at best chapter headings and rules of thumb. Too much attention to general principles can even divert attention from the personal character of the communion with God to which all theology and all bioethics should lead. This is not to deny a place in Christian bioethics for moral rules, commandments, or precepts: properly understood, they indicate real boundaries beyond which one will go very wrong rather than enter into union with God. But they cannot be systematized in terms of conceptual foundations. So, too, one should resist the temptation to ground prohibitions against murder or abortion in supposed general moral principles such as the principle of the sanctity of life, rather than in the pursuit of God. Murder and abortion are wrong first and foremost because they lead us away from union with God. Nor can there be a legalistic rule for dealing with particular cases, even cases of murder, though murder will surely always be wrong. As to the murderer, one must at the core of the matter remember the command of Jesus, "Cease judging, that ye be not judged" (Matt 7:1). Still, murder will require repentance. It will profit from a spiritual therapeutic response, although an appropriate response by the Church will not always necessarily require applying the canons strictly. The appropriate response will not be found in a casuistic literature, or at least in a formalized casuistic approach. In each particular case, the appropriate response must be drawn from prayer and grace. A formal casuistry that provided recipes for responses to particular cases would confront the Spirit with our dead letters.

Secular bioethics is quite different from all of this. It is concerned with the right, the good, the just, and the virtuous. In secular bioethics acknowledgement is also made of the conflict between rights-based ethics and goals-based ethics. There is even the hope that this tension can be overcome through a virtue-based ethics able to integrate the moral life. Chapter 2 examined the difficulties involved in the secular project of uniting the right and the good, the deontological and teleological dimensions of morality. As chapter 2 shows, the difficulties at the core of secular morality lead to a conflict between the right and the good. As a consequence, against the temptation of pursuing important goods to the jeopardy of particular individuals and communities, rights have been sought as protections. They have been invoked as checks against the unqualified pursuit of the good. So that good ends cannot justify any means, moral theorists have looked for constraints on the pursuit of the good: forbearance rights. As chapters 1 and 2 indicate, when moral strangers meet, given the multitude of visions of the good, the right as grounded in permission possesses a singular precedence in secular bioethics.

In the face of an encounter with incommensurable moral commitments, it is not possible to justify in general moral terms practices that unambiguously nurture character and dedication to virtue as this once seemed both morally necessary and possible: the development of virtue requires a coherent, content-full understanding of the moral life integrated in a canonical pursuit of human flourishing and moral excellence. This is precisely what is not available in a post-traditional, post-modern society: a canonical moral understanding that can sustain a coherent, unambiguous, and encompassing vision of community, virtue, and character. There is at best virtue and character by half measures. There is also a deep hunger for more moral substance, for an opportunity to dedicate oneself fully and completely to a cause. If this moral fulfillment is sought in secular terms, it can again lead to the slaughter that has marked the twentieth century.

As already noted, from the horrors of Lenin and Stalin's Soviet Union to Hitler's National Socialist Germany to Mao's China to Pol Pot's Cambodia, tens of millions have been slaughtered in the pursuit of various secular visions of heaven on earth. The hunger to realize content-rich views of social justice and mutual respect through the coercive force of the secular state has led to carnage and atrocities of a scope unparalleled in human history.

If the moral life is both aimed towards and guided by a personal God Who is the Source of being, the distance between the right and the good disappears: so, too, does the distance between justification and motivation. After all, to act against a morality grounded in God is to make a damnable mistake. The genesis of morality is also rooted in the very source of Being. The particular individual's good is in the end harmonized by Divine Providence with the good of all: there is a deep grounding of the motivation to be moral. There is then a content-full understanding of the character of the appropriate communal life within which to articulate an understanding of virtue and moral character. Given the focus on holiness, on union with the transcendent, the very meaning of virtue and character is recast. As one pursues through virtue the unity of the right and the good, the life of virtue is in itself shown to be incomplete and insufficient. Virtue cannot be an end in itself. Doing the good, respecting rights, achieving justice, and becoming virtuous are not enough for salvation if the goal is union with God.[156] "If the Lord buildeth not the house of virtues, then vainly do we labour."[157] All must aim to union with God. Virtue is no longer an end in itself.

Christian moral theology aims beyond rights, goods, virtues, and justice to holiness. Because the aim is holiness, union with God Who is One, the very notion of moral theology and Christian bioethics as separate fields can be misleading. Holiness is not discursive and separable into special compartments. It is lived. Simply to talk of Christian moral theology or Christian bioethics might wrongly suggest that what is distinguishable for pedagogical purposes constitute separate domains of theology. It is not just that bioethics cannot be understood apart from the moral life. The moral law cannot be understood apart from its being a vehicle for union with God. Theology is a whole. It is the fruit of worship and grace. Moral theology, dogmatic theology, liturgics, and Christian bioethics must be united in a life directed in worship towards God. Although areas of theology may be distinguished, they do not identify separate areas of reality. Nor can there be an adequate discursive systematic account of theology. "A systematic exposure of this dogmatic teaching could be understood only spiritually...."[158] Christian morality is united in a whole which is theology as a life of worshipful uniting with God. This unity has significant implications for Christian bioethics: Christian bioethics must be understood within a traditional Christian life.

A Christian bioethics grounded in transcendence requires an epistemology grounded in a non-discursive experience of God. This epistemology for its part requires a metaphysics that has at its center a personal, transcendent God, a God Who can at best be indicated in an apophatic theology, although He Himself gives Himself to be experienced. This epistemology and metaphysics are fundamental to the traditional Christianity of the first millennium. This Christianity locates its knowing and valuing preeminently in the Liturgy, although many of the best knowers are hermits. This epistemology is ascetic in its practice. It is mystical and focused on the eucharistic gathering, so that even the most isolated hermit stands in that assembly.[159] Christian bioethics binds morality as well to a unique narrative of human salvation, focusing morality beyond the good, the right, the just, and the virtuous, grounding them all in the holy. It ties the paradise Adam lost to the paradise regained by Christ. Its paradigm experts are not specialized academics, but those united to holiness, usually great ascetics. The axiology of a Christian bioethics is deeply otherworldly. The goal of Christian bioethics is beyond morality.

In summary, the Christian theology within which traditional Christian bioethics finds itself is ascetic, liturgical, noetic, empirical, and practical. It is ascetic in that it arises out of the truth that by turning away from our own self-satisfactions and passions we can worship rightly and enter fully into a liturgical relationship with God. This liturgical relationship is the fullness of right worship and right belief within which there is experience of the unchanging revelation of Christ in His Church. This theology is not primarily a set of intellectual or scholastic dogmas. It is a revelation that must be lived, and that leads to a non-discursive, noetic knowledge of God. It is a theology radically different from what the second millennium produced for the Western Christianities, either in their rational, discursive, scholastic, or biblically oriented forms. The epiphany of the difference lies in the paradigmatic understanding of what is required of the theologian to be a theologian in the exemplary sense and a recognition of the fruit that such theology brings. For the Christians of the first millennium, becoming an exemplar theologian requires neither study nor searching of the Scriptures. Neither is a necessary nor sufficient condition, though each can in its way importantly contribute to the life of the theologian. What is essential is to turn ascetically from oneself to love God with all one's heart, soul, and understanding. At stake is a love that is realized liturgically in true worship, leading to an actual, noetic experience of God. The Christians of the first millennium understood that parousia, transformation as on Mount Tabor, is possible before death for those who are true theologians, for those who rightly pray. In this experience, theology is not a priori but empirical; it is lived. Within this experiential understanding of theology, theology remains practical in its substance, an invitation to become holy, rather than an invitation to become engaged in a specialized area of scholarly research. Theology before anything else is prayer; it is loving worship of God.

Notes

1. The meaning and connotation of terms such as sect, cult, and fundamentalist are protean at best. In the text I have introduced a sense of these terms consonant with their etymology in history, but not necessarily in agreement with their usage by certain sociologists of religion. Some would distinguish between sects as ideological collectives who view their group as uniquely legitimate, versus cults which have a pluralistic understanding and therefore would be open to acknowledging other groups as also legitimate. Sects and cults identify ideological collectives held in a society to be deviant, as opposed to churches and denominations, which are accepted as culturally respectable. Steve Bruce, *Religion in the Modern World* (New York: Oxford University Press, 1996), pp. 82-85.
2. "Ecumenism is the common name for the pseudo-Christianity of the pseudo-Churches of Western Europe. Within it is the heart of European humanism, with Papism as its head." Fr. Justin Popovich (1894-1979), "Humanistic Ecumenism," in *Orthodox Faith and Life in*

Christ, trans. Asterios Gerostergios, *et al.* (Belmont, MA: Institute for Byzantine and Modern Greek Studies, 1994), p. 169.

3. The term fundamentalist has its origins as a contrast to modernist, liberal, or revisionist forms of Christianity. As the *Oxford English Dictionary* indicates in giving the roots of the term, it is "A religious movement which became active among various Protestant bodies in the United States after the war of 1914-18, based on strict adherence to traditional orthodox tenets (e.g. the literal inerrancy of Scripture) held to be fundamental to the Christian faith; opposed to *liberalism* and *modernism*." (Oxford: Clarendon Press, 1933), Supplement, p. 399.

4. The term fundamentalist originated in American Protestantism with the American Bible League, which in 1902 produced twelve pamphlets entitled "The Fundamentals". These were directed against higher biblical criticism and stressed the central authority of the Bible for Christian life. This defense of the fundamentals of Christianity was tied to a 19th-century millenarian movement, which emphasized the inerrancy of the Scriptures, the literal interpretation of the Bible, the Virgin Birth, the Atonement, the Resurrection, and the imminent Second Coming of Jesus Christ. The phenomenon of fundamentalism was also a part of a larger effort to stem modernist re-interpretations of Christianity. Christian fundamentalism emerged in response to the post-traditional culture and its project of rendering immanent the transcendent claims of Christianity. The participants were many-sided. For example, one figure associated with the fundamentalist movement was William Jennings Bryan (1860-1925), a congressman, presidential candidate, secretary of state, populist politician, supporter of the income tax, advocate of Prohibition, and proponent of woman suffrage, as well as committed defender of the literal interpretation of the Bible and opponent of evolution. The term fundamentalist has become a place-marker in the culture wars between traditional Christianity and post-traditional or modernist society. By transference, fundamentalism and fundamentalist have been applied beyond Christianity to those religions or their adherents who hold firmly to their transcendent religious commitments, contrary to the prevailing secular and post-traditional conceits of the age. For those of modernist, post-traditional, revisionary Christian commitments, the term fundamentalist is often used as a conversation-stopper. The implication is that no one in his right, or at least enlightened, mind would admit to being a fundamentalist.

5. Some 36 to 53 million unborn children are killed by abortion every year. The magnitude of this assault on human life dwarfs the other brutalities of this century. Yet, it is accepted as a commonplace, in fact, as a medical triumph. See, for example, an account of contemporary abortion practices as an appropriate contribution to the health of women. Wendy R. Ewart and Beverly Winikoff, "Toward Safe and Effective Medical Abortion," *Science* 281 (July 24, 1998), 520-1.

6. "Unreasonable doctrines are a threat to democratic institutions, since it is impossible for them to abide by a constitutional regime except as a *modus vivendi*. Their existence sets a limit to the aim of fully realizing a reasonable democratic society with its ideal of public reason and the idea of legitimate law." Rawls, "The Idea of Public Reason Revisited," *University of Chicago Law Review* 64 (Summer 1997), 806.

7. For example, John Rawls considers the Enlightenment a reaction against the bloodshed engendered by the fracturing of medieval Western Christianity. Medieval Christianity contrasts with the current civil religion in being (1) an authoritarian religion (headed by the pope of Rome), which was centralized and nearly absolute, (2) a religion of salvation promising the way to eternal life through true belief as taught by the church, (3) with priests able to dispense the means of grace, and (4) committed to convert all. As will become clear in what follows, traditional Christianity, as this volume understands it, differs on the first point and has important items of difference on the third point. For Rawls' commitments in these

matters, *vide Political Liberalism* (New York: Columbia University Press, 1993), especially p. xxiii.

8. The evening prokeimenon of the Kneeling Vespers for the Sunday of Orthodoxy takes from Psalm 76.14 to emphasize God's miraculous intervention in human history. "Who is so great a God as our God? Thou art the God Who worketh wonders. Thou hast made Thy power known among the peoples." *The Liturgikon* (Englewood, NJ: Antakya Press, 1989), p. 408.

9. Traditional Christianity, as we will see, depends on an awareness of truth not "accessible to every person who is normally reasonable and conscientious". John Rawls, *Political Liberalism* [New York: Columbia University Press, 1993], p. xxvi. More is required than being conscientious, namely, repentance as well as a turn to the worshipful pursuit of holiness. The moral epistemology of traditional Christianity collides with that of Rawls' political liberalism in disclosing a moral order derived from God.

10. John Rawls steps away from his apparently more morally and politically neutral position in *A Theory of Justice* (Cambridge, MA: Harvard University Press, 1971) and moves to embrace an account according to which religious or philosophical views should be excluded from the public space when they do not support the political theory and morality of social democratic polity and instead accept it as merely a *modus vivendi*. This position becomes more apparent in *Political Liberalism* (New York: Columbia University Press, 1993) and becomes fully explicit when he argues to disallow considerations from comprehensive doctrines such as a religion entering into political discussions regarding the appropriate character of law and public policy, if they are not in accord with social democratic assumptions. See "The Idea of Public Reason Revisited," *Chicago Law Review* 64 (Summer 1997), 765-807, as well as *The Law of Peoples* (Cambridge, MA: Harvard University Press, 1999).

11. Arguments to show why a canonical, content-full, secular morality cannot be established are addressed in chapters 1 and 2 of this volume, and more fully in *The Foundations of Bioethics*, 2nd ed. (New York: Oxford University Press, 1996).

12. Vespers for Sunday of the Holy Fathers Assembled in the First Six Ecumenical Councils, Seraphim Nassar (ed.), *Divine Prayers and Services of the Catholic Orthodox Church of Christ* (Englewood, NJ: Antiochian Orthodox Christian Archdiocese, 1979), p. 558.

13. Consider the Matins for January 30, the Feast of Sts. Basil the Great (330-379), Gregory the Theologian (330-389), and John Chrysostom (334-407), and how it presents these three individuals as alive and present.

> O Fathers, stars of transcendent splendour set by God as judges over the Church of Christ, ye have illuminated the world with your teachings, abolishing the heresies of all those of evil opinion, and quenching the blazing agitation of blasphemers. Where, being High Priests of Christ, intercede for our salvation.
> Ye approach the meadows of books like bees, gathering well the flowers of virtue. Ye set before all believers the honey of your teachings as a banquet. Wherefore, every individual being sweetened thereby shouteth with joy, Watch over us, who praise you, even after death, O blessed ones.
> Let us glorify today those wise teachers of the universe, who glorified God on earth with their deeds and with their words; for they are concerned in our salvation.
> Nassar, *Divine Prayers and Services*, p. 491.

14. For some of the listings of which books of the Bible are canonical, see Sts. Nicodemus and Agapius, *The Rudder of the Orthodox Catholic Church* (Chicago: Orthodox Christian Educational Society, 1957), Council of Laodicea (A.D. 364), canon 59, p. 575 and Council of Carthage (A.D. 418/419), canon 32, p. 623. Apostolic canon 85 identifies which books are venerable and sacred. *Ibid.*, p. 145. See also the poems of St. Gregory the Theologian and St. Amphilochius (reposed after A.D. 394); *ibid.*, pp. 883-886, and letter 39 of St. Athanasius. Significantly, these lists of the books of the Bible are not the same. For example, the 85th Apostolic Canon includes the two epistles of Clement pope of Rome among the books it

recognizes. Small differences remain between the deuterocanonical books included in the Slavonic Orthodox and in the Greek Orthodox Bible: the Slavonic has 3rd and 4th Ezdras in an appendix, while the Greek has 4th Maccabees in an appendix. Both Greek and Slavonic include among the deuterocanonical books 2nd Ezdras, the Prayer of Manasseh, the 151st Psalm, and 3rd Maccabees. Cf. Bruce Metzger and Roland Murphy (eds.), *The New Oxford Annotated Apocrypha* (New York: Oxford University Press, 1991). Given the traditional Christian understanding of the Bible, there is no need to have strict uniformity. The content of belief is not derived from the Bible. The Church, its life, and its traditions authenticate the Bible.

15. Jaroslav Pelikan observes: "Although some works of Augustine were translated into Greek during his lifetime, 'centuries had to pass before there was an awareness in the Orient of the overwhelming significance of Augustine.' The first Greek translations of so prominent a monument of Western theology as Augustine's *On the Trinity* did not come until the end of the thirteenth century, with the work of Maximus Planudes." *The Spirit of Eastern Christendom (600-1700)* (Chicago: University of Chicago Press, 1974), p. 181.

16. Maximus Confessor, "The Four Hundred Chapters on Love," *Selected Writings*, trans. George C. Berthold (New York: Paulist Press, 1985), IV:58, p. 81.

17. Symeon the New Theologian, *The Discourses*, trans. C. J. deCatanzaro (New York: Paulist Press, 1980), XXIV:4, p. 264.

18. In the Liturgy of St. Basil, the priest prays, "Who art from everlasting, invisible, inscrutable, ineffable, immutable, the Father of our Lord Jesus Christ, our great God and the Savior...." In that of St. John Chrysostom he prays, "For Thou art God ineffable, incomprehensible, invisible, inconceivable...." Isabel Hapgood (trans.), *Service Book of the Holy Orthodox-Catholic Apostolic Church*, 7th ed. (Englewood, NJ: Antiochian Orthodox Christian Archdiocese, 1996), p. 101.

19. The result of failing to recognize God and of then affirming the seeming surdness of reality can lead to the disastrous moral choice of turning from God to love the world in His stead. As Camus appreciates, "the rebel thus rejects divinity in order to share in the struggles and destiny of all men. ...In the light, the earth remains our first and our last love." Albert Camus, *The Rebel* (New York: Alfred A. Knopf, 1961), p. 306.

20. Clement of Alexandria, "The Stromata," Book 2, chapter IV, ANF, vol. 2, p. 350.

21. If one steps outside the framework of discursive, rational epistemology, which grounds knowledge in finite, spatio-temporal experience, and instead turns prayerfully to God, one can in one's heart recognize that the very existence of anything requires Everything: a personal, omnipotent God. Only when one has taken this step does something like Gottfried Wilhelm Leibniz's (1646-1716) principle of sufficient reason point to God. Leibniz records this recognition that the finite calls out to the infinite in asking, "*Why is there something rather than nothing? For nothing is simpler and easier than something.*" Leibniz, *The Principles of Nature and Grace*, in George M. Duncan (ed.), *The Philosophical Works of Leibnitz* (New Haven: Tuttle, Morehouse & Taylor, 1908), p. 303. Martin Heidegger echoes this puzzle as he begins his *Was ist Metaphysik?* (Frankfurt/M.: Vittorio Klostermann, 1949).

22. It is the experience of faith, not philosophical discursive reasoning, that lies at the roots of theology and Christian bioethics. "[T]he greatest things are attained through faith and not through reasonings. ... Whence [does it appear] that God made these things? Reason does not suggest it; no one was present when it was done. Whence is it shown? It is plainly the result of faith. 'Through faith we understand that the worlds were made.' Why 'through faith'? Because 'the things that are seen were not made of things which do appear.' For this is Faith." St. John Chrysostom, Homily XXII on Hebrews XI.3-4, NPNF1, vol. 14, p. 465.

23. Clement of Alexandria, "The Stromata," Book 2, chapter IV, ANF, vol. 2, p. 350.

24. Dumitru Staniloae, *The Experience of God*, trans. Ioan Ionita and Robert Barringer (Brookline, MA: Holy Cross Orthodox Press, 1994), pp. 22-23.

25. Scholastic philosophy gave birth to a literature exploring the existence of God, the nature of God, immortality, and free will by discursive reason in ways that did not directly presuppose opening one's heart to God through ascesis. See, for example, William J. Brosnan, *God and Reason: Some Theses from Natural Theology* (New York: Fordham University Press, 1924).

26. Paul Evdokimov, *The Art of the Icon: A Theology of Beauty* (Redondo Beach, CA: Oakwood Publications, 1972), p. 23.

27. St. John Chrysostom, Homily on the Gospel of St. Matthew, I.1, NPNF1, vol. 10, p. 1.

28. The approach of traditional Christianity to the Scriptures that locates them within the mind of the Church at one with the Fathers and realized in the Liturgy is remarkably different from that in which most contemporary scholars would approach the Bible, even if they are believers. See, for example, Allen Verhey, *The Great Reversal* (Grand Rapids, MI: W.B. Eerdmans, 1984); David Clines, Stephen Fowl, Stanley Porter (eds.), *The Bible in Three Dimensions* (Sheffield, England: JSOT, 1990); and Stephen Fowl, *Engaging Scripture: A Model for Theological Interpretation* (Malden, MA: Blackwell, 1998). The Orthodox Church gives special weight to the homilies of St. John Chrysostom on St. Paul, for it knows that St. Paul's guidance of St. John is verified not only by the Tradition, but by the relic of St. John Chrysostom's skull and incorrupt ear into which St. Paul spoke, preserved to this day in the monastery of Vatopaidi on Mount Athos. See, for example, "Preface," *The Orthodox New Testament* (Buena Vista, CO: Holy Apostles Convent, 1999), pp. xiv-xvi.

29. St. John Chrysostom recognizes that the Holy Spirit can descend on anyone. Even before Christ's coming or the possibility of baptism allowed a fully effective choice to receive the grace of eternal salvation, God's grace was at hand. This point is made, for example, by Clement of Alexandria quoting Proverbs 2:3-5. "For if thou call on wisdom and knowledge with a loud voice, and seek it as treasures of silver, and eagerly track it out, thou shalt understand godliness and find divine knowledge" (*The Stromata*, Book 1, chap. IV). A more recent example of this possibility of the Spirit's choice to illumine even those nominally fully outside the Church is provided by the account given by St. Innocent of Alaska (1797-1879) concerning his encounter with an Aleut who had been instructed in the faith by angels. "Blessed John Smirennikov," *The Orthodox Word* 33 (July 1997), 185-195. See also Ioann Barsukov, *Innokentii, Mitropolit Moskovsii i Kolomenskii po ego sochineniam pis'mam i razskazam sovremennikov* (Moscow, 1883). One might also consult an interesting study of the possibility that Lao Tzu had come to experience Christ hundreds of years before His Incarnation. As this volume points out, quoting from St. Seraphim of Sarov,

> Though not with the same power as in the people of God [the Hebrews], nevertheless the presence of the Spirit of God also acted in the pagans who did not know the true God, because even among them God found for Himself chosen people. Such, for instance, were the virgin prophetesses called Sibyls who vowed virginity to an unknown God, but still to God the Creator of the universe, the all-powerful ruler of the world, as He was conceived by the pagans. Though the pagan philosophers also wandered in the darkness of ignorance of God, yet they sought the Truth which is beloved by God; and on account of this God-pleasing seeking, they could partake of the Spirit of God, for it is said that the nations who do not know God practice by nature the demands of the law and do what is pleasing to God [cf. Romans 2:14]...

> Hieromonk Damascene, *Christ the Eternal Tao* (Platina, CA: Valaam Books, 1999), p. 11.

30. St. John Chrysostom, Homily V on Romans I.28, V.8, NPNF1, vol. 11, p. 363.

31. Christianity of the first millennium understood that theological knowledge is not simply or even primarily articulated in discursive argument or analysis. It is *sensu stricto* an experiential encounter with God Himself. Because of this it transcends the immanent. The Greek term

noesis or noetic knowledge came to identify this immediate experience of God. Traditional Christianity recognizes that "The human mind also, and not only the angelic, transcends itself, and by victory over the passions acquires an angelic form." Gregory Palamas, *The Triads*, ed. John Meyendorff, trans. Nicholas Gendle (New York: Paulist Press, 1983), I:iii,4, p. 32. Father Alexander Golitzin in his translation of the works of St. Symeon the New Theologian speaks to the meaning of *nous* and the challenge of finding a word to compass its meaning. In particular, he identifies some of the difficulty in capturing the full significance of *noesis* with the English term "intellect".

One could wish there were a better choice, especially since the English word has little or none of the sense of "Reality" clinging to it that *nous* has in the Greek. Together with all the fathers who, from Clement of Alexandria on, used it, Symeon means by this expression far more than mere mentation, i.e., the faculty of rational thought and the making of concepts. *Nous* is instead for him an equivalent for the biblical term "heart (*kardia*)," which he also uses, and which signifies the "center" of the human being, the highest faculty, the very point where God and humanity are intended to meet. The "intelligibles" (*ta noeta* or *to noeton*), as that which intellect perceives, are thus the spiritual universe, the angels for example, or the thoughts and intentions which God has with regard to creation. Put another way, nous for Symeon is that by virtue of which human beings may "see" the invisible. It is that in us which enables us to respond to God's uncreated grace.
St. Symeon the New Theologian, *On the Mystical Life*, trans. Alexander Golitzin (Crestwood, NY: St. Vladimir's Seminary Press, 1995), vol. 1, p. 14.

Similarly, Palmer *et al.* give the following definition in their glossary to volume 1 of *The Philokalia*.

Intellect (nous): the highest faculty in man, through which - provided it is purified - he knows God or the inner essences or principles of created things by means of direct apprehension or spiritual perception. Unlike the dianoia or reason, from which it must be carefully distinguished, the intellect does not function by formulating abstract concepts and then arguing on this basis to a conclusion reached through deductive reasoning, but it understands divine truth by means of immediate experience, intuition or 'simple cognition' (the term used by St Isaac the Syrian). The intellect dwells in the 'depths of the soul'; it constitutes the innermost aspect of the heart... The intellect is the organ of contemplation, the 'eye of the heart'.
Sts. Nikodimos and Makarios, *The Philokalia*, trans. and ed. G.E.H. Palmer, Philip Sherrard, and Kallistos Ware (Boston: Faber and Faber, 1988), vol. 1, p. 362.

In the course of this chapter and those that follow, the term "heart" is employed to identify the deep realms of the soul that can be either enthralled to passions or open to God, making conscience possible. Like the subconscious, it can be scarred, twisted, or misdirected beyond our immediate and direct control. It can be harmed by events that we cannot avoid and by sins that are at best involuntary. What happens beyond our control can harm our moral, our spiritual life. As a consequence, the heart must be purified by taking on a Christian life of love and asceticism, so that in the deep roots of our being we turn away from ourselves to God and others with a selfless love. The pure heart is one that turns easily and of its own accord to God and others.

Noesis or intellectual apprehension is to be contrasted with discursive reasoning, as this is found in secular philosophy, as well as in Scholasticism.

Reason, mind (dianoia): the discursive, conceptualizing and logical faculty in man, the function of which is to draw conclusions or formulate concepts deriving from data provided either by revelation or spiritual knowledge or by sense-observation. The knowledge of the reason is consequently of a lower order than spiritual knowledge and does not imply any direct apprehension or perception of the inner essences or principles of created beings, still less of divine truth itself. Indeed, such apprehension or perception, which is the function of the intellect, is beyond the scope of the reason.
Sts. Nikodimos and Makarios, *The Philokalia*, vol. 1, p. 364.

In this contrast of discursive reason with nous, one finds the contrast between philosophy and true theology. As the Fathers warned, philosophy unsupplemented and undirected by theology will lead nowhere or, worse, it will lead astray.

Finally, it must be observed that these distinctions are not merely Greek understandings imposed on Christian reflections. In the Semitic tradition of the Church, these distinctions are finer still, as one discovers in St. Isaac and the Syriac language identifying *hauna*, *mad'a*, *re'yana*, and *tar'itha*. The term nous in the Greek actually covers two distinct ideas in Syriac. First, the intellect as *hauna* is an active faculty that beholds spiritual things, engages in pure prayer, and is placed in rapture by divine vision. Second, "the intellect [*mad'a*] is spiritual perception that is conditioned to receive the faculty of divine vision, even as the pupils of the bodily eyes into which sensible light is poured." (St. Isaac the Syrian, *The Ascetical Homilies of Saint Isaac the Syrian*, trans. Holy Transfiguration Monastery [Boston, Mass.: Holy Transfiguration Monastery, 1984], p. 323.) *Hauna* is the spiritual power that employs *mad'a* as spiritual eyes to receive the light of grace. Admittedly, this distinction is somewhat subtle and is generally captured in the single term nous. The distinction crucially at issue is between intellect and discursive reasoning. "The difference between the intellect (*mad'a-hauna/nous*) and the mind (*re'yana/dianoia*) is much clearer. The mind is a man's faculty of conscious thinking and cogitation which he employs continuously in deliberating and reflecting." (*Ibid.*, p. cix.) *Tar'itha* (which is translated into Greek as *phronema*) identifies thinking in the sense of what is going on in one's mind.

Somewhat similar distinctions existed in the Western Middle Ages, though these were developed within an epistemological framework that had already become different.

The Middle Ages drew a distinction between the understanding as *ratio* and the understanding as *intellectus*. *Ratio* is the power of discursive, logical thought, of searching and of examination, of abstraction, of definition and drawing conclusions. *Intellectus*, on the other hand, is the name for the understanding in so far as it is the capacity of *simplex intuitus*, of that simple vision to which truth offers itself like a landscape to the eye.
Josef Pieper, *Leisure: The Basis of Culture*, trans. Alexander Dru (New York: New American Library, 1963), p. 26.

32. The necessity of a noetic foundation for the content of moral theology is similar to the necessity to which secular morality is subject. Both need fundamental axioms. The difficulty is to determine which axioms are truly axiomatic, truly self-evident. Without a veridical experience of reality, the issue will always be: whose axiomaticity, whose self-evidence?

33. Because all theologians of true worship and belief are illumined by the same Spirit, there is the confidence that no one can "imagine that they will be putting forward something new." Elder Joseph, *Elder Joseph the Hesychast*, trans. Elizabeth Theokritoff (Mount Athos: Vatopaidi, 1999), p. 86.

34. The traditional Christian need not hesitate in recognizing a parallelism between Christian concerns with purification, illumination, and union with God, and similar concerns found in such late pagan theologians as Proclus (410-485). It is not simply a question of who influenced whom. Pagans, as they turn their hearts toward God, also learn about God. In the New Testament, there is a clear understanding that it is those who purify their hearts who will be illumined. "Blessed are the pure in heart, for they shall see God" (Matt 5:8). Not only is illumination by God promised, but union with Him. Christ before His crucifixion prays not just that His apostles be sanctified (John 17:17), but "may they also be in us" (John 17:21). In the course of this volume, the term "heart" will not only be employed in identifying the openness of the soul to God, but also call attention to the ways in which that openness can be marred, the ways in which our involvement in the broken nature of this world can defile us in ways that make it hard for us to open ourselves, our hearts, to God.

35. For an overview of the theological interconnection of these terms (i.e., understanding and heart, as well as nous, soul, reason, attention, and intelligence) in the Tradition, see Archimandrite Hierotheos Vlachos, *Orthodox Psychotherapy*, trans. Esther Williams (Levadia, Greece: Birth of the Theotokos Monastery, 1994), pp. 97-214.

36. Moral friends who commit themselves to a particular way of life as a given cultural understanding, though they share a moral vision, will find their authority for collaboration coming from their common consent. Such a cultural goal or way of life, as a construct of persons, will never have the moral authority to trump the claim of individuals to choose for themselves in the absence of their prior agreement.

37. St. John Chrysostom, "The Homilies on the Statutes," Homily XIII.7, NPNF1, vol. 9, p. 428.

38. *Ibid.*, Homily XIII.9, p. 429.

39. *Ibid.*, Homily XIII.8, p. 429.

40. St. Isaac the Syrian, *The Ascetical Homilies*, Homily 47, p. 226.

41. Saint Basil, "The Long Rules," in *Ascetical Works*, trans. Monica Wagner (Washington, DC: Catholic University of America Press, 1962), response 2, p. 233.

42. *Ibid.*, response 2, p. 234.

43. St. Isaac the Syrian, *The Ascetical Homilies*, Homily 47, pp. 226-27.

44. "In the teachings of the holy Fathers passions are not outside forces which enter us and must thus be uprooted. Rather they are energies of the soul which have been distorted and need to be transformed." Hierotheos Vlachos, *Orthodox Spirituality*, trans. Effie Mavromichali (Levadia, Greece: Birth of the Theotokos Monastery, 1994), p. 84.

45. "For often this capacity to see things according to their true nature comes more readily to simple people, to those whose intellects are free from the hustle and wiliness of this world, once they have submitted themselves to an experienced spiritual father." St. Peter of Damaskos, "Discrimination," in *The Philokalia*, vol. 3, p. 245.

46. Because Kant focuses only on discursive knowledge, having little sense of noetic knowledge, indeed rejecting it, he also has no appreciation of the role of the guidance given by spiritual fathers. *Religion innerhalb der bloßen Vernunft*, AK VI, 175. Kant does speak of intellectual intuition in the *Critique of Pure Reason*; see, for example, B72.

47. Some elders not only see what is at stake spiritually but know detailed empirical states of affairs, although the latter is expressed without scientific theorizing. An account of such knowing is provided in Klitos Ioannidis, *Elder Porphyrios* (Athens: Convent of the Transfiguration of the Savior, 1997).

48. Although the West recognized Scriptural reflections concerning the availability of natural law in the human heart, it located its understanding of natural law within discursive rationality. As a consequence, access to natural law became paradigmatically discursive, rational reflection and therefore most accessible to academicians. "By the moral law of nature (*lex moralis naturalis*) is understood the sum total of those ethical precepts which God has implanted in the rational nature of man. It is that law which St. Paul says is 'written in the hearts' of men, in order to enable them to attain their natural destiny as free beings, capable of doing right or wrong. The moral law of nature is promulgated by reason." Antony Koch and Arthur Preuss, *A Handbook of Moral Theology* (St. Louis, MO: B. Herder, 1925), 3rd ed., vol. 1, p. 122.

49. *Institutes of Gaius*, trans. Francis De Zulueta, 2 vols. (London: Oxford University Press, 1976), vol. 1, p. 3.

50. Flavius Petrus Sabbatius Justinianus, *The Institutes of Justinian*, trans. Thomas C. Sandars (1922; repr. Westport, Conn.: Greenwood Press, 1970), 1.2, p. 7.

51. An example of a biological or physicalist guide to issues in medical ethics is the once very popular volume by Charles McFadden, *Medical Ethics*, 5th ed. (Philadelphia: F.A. Davis, 1961).

52. Through a supposed appeal to the character of moral rationality, Kant is able to deliver very specific moral constraints regarding such matters as masturbation, the sale of body parts, and smallpox inoculation. See his *Metaphysical Principles of Virtue*, AK VI 422-26.

53. William Blackstone, *Commentaries on the Laws of England*, ed. St. George Tucker (New York: Augustus and Kelly, 1969), vol. 1, p. 40.

54. "Do not call God just, for His justice is not manifest in the things concerning you. And if David calls Him just and upright, His Son revealed to us that He is good and kind." St. Isaac the Syrian, *The Ascetical Homilies*, Homily 51, pp. 250-51.

55. St. Isaac the Syrian, *The Ascetical Homilies*, Homily 46, p. 223, and Homily 66, p. 323.

56. "All creatures, when they saw that Adam had been banished from Paradise, no longer wished to submit to him, the criminal: the sun did not wish to shine for him, nor did the moon and the other stars wish to show themselves to him; the springs did not wish to gush forth water, and the rivers to continue their course; the air thought no longer to blow so as not to allow Adam, the sinner, to breathe; the beasts and all the other animals of the earth, when they saw that he had been stripped of his first glory, began to despise him, and all immediately were ready to fall upon him." St. Symeon the New Theologian, *The First-Created Man*, trans. Fr. Seraphim Rose (Platina, CA: St. Herman Press, 1994), p. 92.

57. St. Symeon Metaphrastis, "The Freedom of the Intellect," in *The Philokalia*, vol. 3, p. 349.

58. Over the centuries, numerous accounts of natural law have been developed, many of which are quite distant from that of traditional Christianity. Some have attempted to relocate contemporary understandings within a set of more traditional expectations. Russell Hittinger, for example, tries to resituate the Roman Catholic appreciation of natural law as a point in the human dialogue with God. Natural law is, as he recognizes, knowledge of the moral law found in nature. Calling on insights from the later writing of Thomas Aquinas, Hittinger emphasizes the inaccessibility of natural law without grace:

> In his last recorded remarks on the subject of natural law, made during a series of Lenten conferences in 1273, Thomas's judgment is even more stern: "Now although God in creating man gave him this law of nature, the devil oversowed another law in man, namely, the law of concupiscence ... Since then the law of nature was destroyed by concupiscence, man needed to be brought back to works of virtue, and to be drawn away from vice: for which purpose he needed the written law." As the critical Leonine edition of 1985 confirms, the words are destructa erat– "was destroyed."
>
> How can he say that natural law is destroyed in us? First, he certainly does not mean that it is destroyed in the mind of the lawgiver. As a law, natural law is not "in" nature or the human mind, but is rather in the mind of God. The immutability of natural law, he insists, is due to the "immutability and perfection of the divine reason that institutes it." Insofar as natural law can be said to be "in" things or nature, it is an order of inclinations of reason and will by which men are moved to a common good. While the created order continues to move men, the effect of that law (in the creature) is bent by sin – not so bent that God fails to move the finite mind, for the fallen man is still a spiritual creature, possessed of the God-given light of moral understanding, but bent enough that this movement requires the remediation of divine positive law and a new law of grace.
> Russell Hittinger, "Natural Law and Catholic Moral Theology," in *A Preserving Grace* (Grand Rapids: Eerdmans, 1997), pp. 7-8.

This interpretation of natural law is still distant from that of the Fathers. First, there is an inadequate appreciation of the bond between natural law and conscience: conscience is our perception of the law placed in us at our very fashioning by God. Second, there is a failure sufficiently to recognize the role of asceticism repairing the harm done by the passions. Third, there is a failure to recognize sufficiently that this perception grows through worship: the content of moral law is best disclosed in the liturgical life of prayer. Finally, there is a failure to recognize that natural law is not simply a set of prescriptions and proscriptions instituted by God, but a therapeutic regimen that can unite us with God. This last failure is likely embedded in the West's claim of an analogy between our created being and the uncreated transcendent being of God. This view encourages a cognitive view of natural law rather than a mere therapeutic view.

For an overview of some of the ways in which the language of natural law has taken possession of the jurisprudence and moral theory of the West, see Heinrich A. Rommen, *The Natural Law*, trans. Thomas Henley (Indianapolis: Liberty Fund, 1998). For a view that places Thomas Aquinas closer to the Orthodox and further from the Scholastics who followed him, see Denis J. M. Bradley, *Aquinas on the Twofold Human Good* (Washington, DC: Catholic University of America Press, 1997).

59. "'Original' sin consists in the darkening of the nous and the loss of communion with God." Hierotheos Vlachos, *Orthodox Spirituality*, trans. Effie Mavromichali (Levadia: Birth of the Theotokos Monastery, 1994), p. 41.

60. Father John Breck describes the kataxioson ("Vouchsafe, O Lord...") as an early Christian liturgical prayer, which maintains the same chiastic structure as many of the books of the Bible.

> Vouchsafe, O Lord, to keep us this night without sin.
> 2: Blessed art Thou, O Lord, the *God* of our fathers, and *praised* and *glorified* is Thy
>   Name forever. Amen.
> 1: Let *Thy mercy, O Lord*, be upon *us*, as we have hoped in Thee.
> 0: Blessed art Thou, O Lord: teach me Thy statutes;
>   Blessed art Thou, O Master, let me understand Thy statutes;
>   Blessed art Thou, O Holy One, enlighten me with Thy statutes.
> 1': *O Lord, Thy mercy* is for ever; do not turn away from the *works of Thy hands*.
> 2':To Thee belongs *praise*, to Thee belongs worship, to Thee belongs *glory*, to the
>   *Father* and to the *Son* and to the *Holy Spirit*, now and ever and unto ages of ages.
>   Amen.
> Breck, *The Shape of Biblical Language* (Crestwood, NY: St. Vladimir's Seminary, 1994), p. 291.

61. Justin Popovich, *Orthodox Faith and Life in Christ*, trans. Asterios Gerostergios (Belmont, MA: Institute for Byzantine and Modern Greek Studies, 1994), p. 145.

62. St. Maximos the Confessor, "Various Texts on Theology, the Divine Economy, and Virtue and Vice" II.73, in *The Philokalia*, vol. 2, pp. 202-3.

63. "When the intellect [nous] is pure, sometimes God Himself approaches and teaches it; and sometimes the angelic powers, or the nature of the created things that it contemplates, suggest holy things to it." St. Makarios of Egypt, "Four Hundred Texts on Love," III.94, in *The Philokalia*, vol. 2, p. 98.

64. The third form of knowledge is the completion of Christ's promise regarding the Spirit. "However, when He, the Spirit of truth, has come, He will guide you into all truth" (John 16:13).

65. St. Isaac the Syrian, *The Ascetical Homilies*, Homily 53, p. 264.

66. *Ibid.*, Homily 47, p. 227.

67. *Ibid.*, Homily 52, pp. 261-62. For an introduction to the thought of Saint Isaac, see Justin Popovich, "The Theory of Knowledge of Saint Isaac the Syrian" in *Orthodox Faith and Life in Christ*, trans. Asterios Gerostergios *et al.* (Belmont, MA: Institute for Byzantine and Modern Greek Studies, 1994), pp. 117-168.

68. "I wrote to you in the epistle not to be associating with fornicators; and yet not altogether with the fornicators of this world, or with the covetous, or rapacious, or idolaters, for otherwise then ye are obliged to go out of the world." I Cor 5:9-10.

69. St. Isaac the Syrian, *The Ascetical Homilies*, Homily 52, p. 258.

70. *Ibid.*, Homily 52, p. 260.

71. Symeon the New Theologian, *The Discourses*, trans. C.J. deCatanzaro (New York: Paulist Press, 1980), pp. 264-65.

72. St. Isaac the Syrian, *The Ascetical Homilies*, Homily 52, p. 261.
73. St. Neilos the Ascetic, "Ascetic Discourse," in *The Philokalia*, vol. 1, p. 201.
74. St. John Chrysostom, Homily XXXIII.5 on the Gospel of St. Matthew 10:16 , NPNF1, vol. 10, p. 222.
75. St. Neilos the Ascetic, "Ascetic Discourse," in *The Philokalia*, vol. 1, p. 200.
76. Maximus Confessor, "Chapters on Knowledge," *Selected Writings*, trans. George C. Berthold (New York: Paulist Press, 1985), II, 31, p. 134.
77. Gregory Palamas, *The Triads, Deification in Christ*, ed. John Meyendorff, trans. Nicholas Gendle (New York: Paulist Press, 1983), II, 17, p. 62.
78. The Tradition recognizes that the Trinity was revealed to Abraham. "The Lord appeared to Abraham near the great trees of Mamre while he was sitting at the entrance to his tent in the heat of the day. Abraham looked up and saw three men standing nearby" (Gen 18:1-2). This epiphany of the Trinity is presented in a famous icon by St. Andrey Rublyov (1360/1370-1430).
79. Archimandrite Sophrony, *Saint Silouan the Athonite*, trans. Rosemary Edmonds (Essex: Monastery of St. John the Baptist, 1991), p. 112.
80. St. John Chrysostom, "The Homilies on the Statutes," Homily XVII.7, NPNF1, vol. 9, p. 455.
81. Clement of Alexandria, *The Stromata*, Book 1, chapter XIX. Clement of Alexandria is taken by some as holding that Greek philosophy was equal to the Old Testament in preparing for the coming of Christ. Rather, his position is that God used Greek philosophy in order to prepare for the spread of Christianity. "The Hellenic philosophy then, according to some, apprehended the truth accidentally, dimly, partially; as others will have it, was set a-going by the devil. Several suppose that certain powers, descending from heaven, inspired the whole of philosophy. But if the Hellenic philosophy comprehends not the whole extent of the truth, and besides is destitute of strength to perform the commandments of the Lord, yet it prepares the way for the truly royal teaching; training in some way or other, and moulding the character, and fitting him who believes in Providence for the reception of the truth." ANF, vol. 2, Book I, 16, p. 318.
82. St. John Chrysostom, Homily II on Romans I.8, II.17, NPNF1, vol. 11, p. 350.
83. St. John Chrysostom, Homily III on Philippians I.18-19, NPNF1, vol. 13, p. 194.
84. St. John Chrysostom, Homily on the Gospel of St. Matthew I.10,11, NPNF1, vol. 10, p. 5. John Paul II, who for the most part seeks from philosophy what traditional Christianity knew to be impossible, still admits, "The practice of philosophy and attendance at philosophical schools seemed to the first Christians more of a disturbance than an opportunity." *Fides et Ratio* (Vatican City: Libreria Editrice Vaticana, 1998), p. 56.
85. St. John Chrysostom, Homily I on the Gospel of St. Matthew, NPNF1, vol. 10, p. 5.
86. Chrysostomus Baur, *John Chrysostom and his Time*, trans. Sr. M. Gonzaga (Vaduz: Büchervertriebsanstalt, 1988), pp. 106-115.
87. St. Antony had prayed the Lord to show him to what measure he had attained. And the answer was, that he had not reached the standard of a certain shoemaker in Alexandria. St. Antony made his way to the man and asked him how he lived. The latter replied that he gave a third of his earnings to the church, a third to the poor, and kept the rest for his own needs. Antony, who had himself given up all he possessed and lived in the desert in greater poverty than the shoemaker, found nothing extraordinary in this. It was not here that he excelled. Antony said to him, 'The Lord sent me to you to see how you live.' Then the humble working-man, who looked up to St. Antony and was dismayed by his words, answered, 'I don't do anything special. Only, when I am working I look at passers-by and think, "They'll all be saved, only I shall perish".'
Archimandrite Sophrony, *Saint Silouan the Athonite*, trans. Rosemary Edmonds (Essex: Monastery of St. John the Baptist, 1991), pp. 210-11.
88. St. John Chrysostom, Homily II on Romans I.8, II.17, NPNF1, vol. 11, pp. 349-350.
89. St. John Chrysostom, Homily IV on I Corinthians I.18-20, IV.2, NPNF1, vol. 12, p. 16.

90. St. John Chrysostom, Homily V on I Corinthians I.26-27, V.3, NPNF1, vol. 12, p. 24.
91. See, for example, Alexander Schmemann, *Introduction to Liturgical Theology* (Crestwood, NY: St. Vladimir's Seminary Press, 1986); and Petros Vassiliadis, "Eucharistic and Therapeutic Spirituality," *Greek Orthodox Theological Review* 42 (1997), 1-23.
92. Hapgood, *Service Book*, p. 108.
93. An example of the miraculous provision of communion to hermits is given by Elder Joseph the Hesychast (1895-1959), who one day when he could not attend Liturgy was struck with an intense longing for the Eucharist. He reports that "I...saw in front of me an Angel full of light, just as the Church describes them, and light filled the place, light from the other world. In his hand he held an elegant and radiant vessel, which fitted into his palm. He opened it with care, came as close as he needed and with great reverence and care placed in my mouth a particle of the Lord's Body. Then he looked at me with a modest smile, [and] closed the vessel...." Elder Joseph, *Elder Joseph the Hesychast*, p. 103.
94. Parintele Galeriu, *Jertfa si Rascumparare* (Bucharest: Crescent, 1991), p. 288.
95. The distinction between being in authority and being an authority is somewhat like the distinction between being a judge and being a legal scholar. The first has the authority to make rulings, the second knows the character of the law and may author a brief that will reverse the judge's holding on appeal. Bishops are in authority to govern and teach. The holy fathers and mothers know what the bishops should teach. In their experience of God, they are the authorities regarding theology. However, the bishops must be recognized as presiding over the claims of theologians as the Church tests the spirits (I John 4:1). Moreover, bishops themselves should become holy elders.
96. St. Vincent of Lerins stresses that

> I have often then inquired earnestly and attentively of very many men eminent for sanctity and learning, how and by what sure and so to speak universal rule I may be able to distinguish the truth of Catholic faith from the falsehood of heretical pravity; and I have always, and in almost every instance, received an answer to this effect: That whether I or any one else should wish to detect the frauds and avoid the snares of heretics as they rise, and to continue sound and complete in the Catholic faith, we must, the Lord helping, fortify our own belief in two ways; first, by the authority of the Divine Law, and then, by the Tradition of the Catholic Church.
> Moreover, in the Catholic Church itself, all possible care must be taken, that we hold that faith which has been believed everywhere, always, by all. For that is truly and in the strictest sense "Catholic," which, as the name itself and the reason of the thing declare, comprehends all universally. This rule we shall observe if we follow universality, antiquity, consent. We shall follow universality if we confess that one faith to be true which the whole Church throughout the world confesses; antiquity, if we in no wise depart from those interpretations which it is manifest were notoriously held by our holy ancestors and fathers; consent, in like manner, if in antiquity itself we adhere to the consentient definitions and determinations of all, or at the least of almost all priests and doctors.
> *A Commonitory*, II,4,6, NPNF2, vol. 11, p. 132.

The force of his observation is that heresy lies in rejecting any belief held in the Tradition or in adopting novel dogmas unknown in the past. St. Vincent makes this plain in summarizing the statement of the Fathers at the Council of Ephesus (A.D. 431). "They also set an example to those who should come after them, how they also should adhere to the determinations of sacred antiquity, and condemn the devices of profane novelty." Chap. XXXI,82, p. 155. He fortifies this view with a quote from Pope Sixtus III of Rome. "Let no license be allowed to novelty, because it is not fit that any addition should be made to antiquity. Let not the clear faith and belief of our forefathers be fouled by any muddy admixture." Chap. XXXII,84, p. 156.
97. Archimandrite Sophrony, *Saint Silouan the Athonite*, trans. Rosemary Edmonds (Essex: Monastery of St. John the Baptist, 1991), pp. 162-3.
98. St. Ignatius, "Epistle to the Philadelphians," chap. IV, ANF, vol. 1, p. 81.

99. St. Ignatius, "Epistle to the Smyrnaeans," chap. VIII, ANF, vol. 1, pp. 89-90.

100. The term catholic appears for the first time in Christian writings in this letter of Ignatius. The term καθολικη in the phrase καθολικη εκκλησια has a broad span of meaning, including "general", "universal", and "whole". Here the focus seems to be on wholeness or completeness.

101. Sts. Nicodemus and Agapius, *The Rudder*, p. 575 and p. 623.

102. Archimandrite Vasileios, *Hymn of Entry*, trans. Elizabeth Briere (Crestwood, NY: St. Vladimir's Seminary Press, 1984), p. 18.

103. *Ibid.*, p. 19

104. *Ibid.*, p. 30.

105. Hapgood, *Service Book*, p. 109.

106. Characteristically, Orthodox Liturgies contain an invocation of the Holy Spirit upon the Gifts to transform them into the Eucharist.

107. Archimandrite Sophrony, *Saint Silouan the Athonite*, trans. Rosemary Edmonds (Essex: Monastery of St. John the Baptist, 1991), p. 87.

108. *Ibid.*, pp. 87-88.

109. In the mid-1st century, while the epistles were being written and St. John's Gospel was still to be composed, the early Church conducted its Liturgy in the absence of anything like a completed New Testament. But the fullness of the Gospel was already available in the absence of written Scriptures. The Scriptures are not a necessary condition for the Church or for Christian bioethics, in that the Scriptures can be used outside of traditional Christianity, as well as in opposition to traditional Christianity. They cannot be a sufficient condition for Christianity. The life of the Church has always been directed by understandings that have been drawn from sources other than the Scriptures, as St. Basil the Great underscores.

> Of the beliefs and practices whether generally accepted or publicly enjoyed which are preserved in the Church some we possess derived from written teaching; others we have received delivered to us "in a mystery" by the tradition of the apostles; and both of these in relation to true religion have the same force. And these no one will gainsay; – no one, at all events, who is even moderately versed in the institutions of the Church. For were we to attempt to reject such customs as have no written authority, on the ground that the importance they possess is small, we shall unintentionally injure the Gospel in its very vitals; or, rather, should make our public definition a mere phrase and nothing more. For instance, to take the first and most general example, who is there who has taught us in writing to sign with the sign of the cross those who have trusted in the name of our Lord Jesus Christ? What writing has taught us to turn to the East at the prayer? Which of the saints has left us in writing the words of the invocation at the displaying of the bread of the Eucharist and the cup of blessing? For we are not, as is well known, content with what the apostle or the Gospel has recorded, but both in preface and conclusion we add other words as being of great importance to the validity of the ministry, and these we derive from unwritten teaching. Moreover we bless the water of baptism and the oil of the chrism, and besides this the catechumen who is being baptized. On what written authority do we do this? Is not our authority silent and mystical tradition? Nay, by what written word is the anointing of oil itself taught? And whence comes the custom of baptizing thrice? And as to the other customs of baptism from what Scripture do we derive the renunciation of Satan and his angels? Does not this come from that unpublished and secret teaching which our fathers guarded in a silence out of the reach of curious meddling and inquisitive investigation? Well had they learnt the lesson that the awful dignity of the mysteries is best preserved by silence.
> St. Basil, "On the Spirit," NPNF2, vol. 8, pp. 40-42.

The Christian Mysteries themselves carry with them their own power to teach. They provide their own authenticating experience. As Patriarch Bartholomew emphasizes,

> Holy Tradition for the Orthodox Christian is not just some collection of teachings, texts outside the Holy Scriptures and based on their oral tradition within the Church. It is this, but not only this. First

and foremost, it is a living and essential imparting of life and grace, namely, it is an essential and tangible reality, propagated from generation to generation within the Orthodox Church. This transmittal of the faith, like the circulation of the sap of life from the tree to the branch, from the body to the member, from the Church to the believer, presumes that one is grafted to the fruitful olive tree (Rom 11:23-25), the embodiment in the body (Rom 12:5, 1 Cor 10:16-17, 12:12-17).
Patriarch Bartholomew, "Joyful Light," Address at Georgetown University, Washington, D.C., October 21, 1997.

The Scriptures must be placed within this experience of Tradition: the experience of grace and the Spirit.

110. Sts. Nicodemus and Agapius, *The Rudder*, pp. 483-488.

111. *Ibid.*, p. 50.

112. The Orthodox Church is governed by canons derived not simply from the Seven Ecumenical Councils, but from numerous regional canons as well as from various Holy Fathers. Even with regard to ecumenical councils, qualifications are needed. For example, the canons for the 5th and 6th councils were written at the Quinisext Council, which was held in A.D. 692. There was a council held in Constantinople in 879-80, the council of the Temple of Holy Wisdom, the Hagia Sophia, which also issued important canons. The canons of the regional synods include those of the First and Second Council in the temple of the holy Apostles (A.D. 861), as well as those of Carthage (in the time of St. Cyprian), Ancyra (314/315), Neocaesarea (315), Gangra (340), Antioch (341), Laodicaea (364), Sardica (347), Constantinople (394), and Carthage (418/419). There are in addition the 85 Apostolic Canons. Also included as generally binding on the entire Church are various canons from the Holy Fathers: St. Dionysius the Alexandrian, St. Gregory of Neocaesarea, St. Peter the Martyr, St. Athanasius the Great, St. Basil the Great, St. Gregory of Nyssa, St. Gregory the Theologian, St. Amphilochius, St. Timothy Pope of Alexandria, St. Theophilus of Alexandria, St. Cyril of Alexandria, St. Gennadius, St. John the Faster, St. Tarasius, and St. Nicephorus. See Sts. Nicodemus and Agapius, *The Rudder*. The result is a collage of canons without systematic order, making their legalistic application nigh unto impossible. The canons are not a set of laws to be applied, for example, to bioethical issues. The canons have not given rise to a systematic casuistry, but to an invitation to approach each case guided by the relevant canons and the Holy Spirit. This is surely one of the great strengths of the canons. The canons must be understood not as a law that must be applied following its letter, but as a set of very important spiritual signposts directing Christians toward salvation. In this way, one can understand the difference between the use of economia in the Orthodox Church and the notion of dispensation in the West. A dispensation lifts the law for a particular person or class of persons. An economia recognizes that the purpose of the law, namely, to bring salvation, is best achieved by something other than the strict application of the law. An economia thus should not violate the spirit of the law; rather, it should focus better on the goal of the law by setting aside its letter. It is important to note that the notion of economia includes not only applying a canon less rigorously, but also applying it more rigorously, thus achieving the true purpose of the canon. At times, the spirit of the law is best served by acrivia, the strict application of the law.

113. The roots of traditional Christianity are often identified with the Church of the Councils, the Church that was unified in agreement with the seven Ecumenical Councils: the Council of Nicea I (A.D. 325), the Council of Constantinople I (A.D. 381), the Council of Ephesus (A.D. 431), the Council of Chalcedon (A.D. 451), the Council of Constantinople II (A.D. 553), the Council of Constantinople III (A.D. 680-681), and the Council of Nicea II (A.D. 787). However, matters are not that simple. For instance, the Seventh Ecumenical Council was not accepted by Charlemagne's kingdom and two councils of the West. Constantine Tsirpanlis, *Introduction to Eastern Patristic Thought and Orthodox Theology* (Colle-

geville, MN: Liturgical Press, 1991), p. 23. Moreover, the Orthodox Church accepted the Quinisext Council or the Council in Trullo of A.D. 692, although this was not fully accepted in the West. This Council among other things condemned the West's prohibition of a married clergy. Further, there is no reason to stop listing ecumenical councils with Nicea II. The Orthodox Church, for example, acknowledges the Council of Constantinople IV (A.D. 879-880), also known as the Council of the Temple of Holy Wisdom, which affirmed the position of St. Photios the Great against Pope Nicholas I of Rome. Finally, the approval in Constantinople in 1341, 1347, and 1351 of the position of St. Gregory Palamas against his Scholastic critics has all the marks of an ecumenical council.

114. "Let the ancient customs prevail which were in vogue in Egypt and Libya and Pentapolis, to allow the bishop of Alexandria to have authority over all these, since this is also the treatment usually accorded to the bishop of Rome. Likewise with reference to Antioch, and in other provinces, let the seniority be preserved to the Churches." Sts. Nicodemus and Agapius, *The Rudder*, p. 170.

115. "Let the Bishop of Constantinople, however, have the priorities of honor after the Bishop of Rome, because of its being New Rome." *Ibid.*, p. 210.

116. *Ibid.*, p. 271.

117. The West for the first time in Council clearly announced its claim to universal jurisdiction in a way that at the same time shows that this novel doctrine implies that there is in reality only one episcopacy for its church. "The Roman church, which through the Lord's disposition has a primacy of ordinary power over all other churches..." has this privilege "inasmuch as it is the mother and mistress of all Christ's faithful." This canon of the Fourth Lateran Council was promulgated subsequent to the Fourth Crusade, the pillage of Constantinople, and its occupation by the Latins. To indicate the Roman papacy as the source of episcopal authority, all patriarchs were to receive "from the Roman pontiff the pallium, which is the sign of the fullness of the pontifical office." In short, the bishop of Rome has ordinary episcopal jurisdiction over the entire world and all other bishops have their proper episcopal authority from him. "Fourth Lateran Council – 1215" in *Decrees of the Ecumenical Councils*, ed. Norman Tanner (Washington, DC: Georgetown University Press, 1990), p. 236. Against this background one can see the full force of Paul VI's signature to the documents of Vatican II, "I, Paul, Bishop of the Catholic Church". The Western pope claims to be the bishop of the world.

118. See, for example, Elder Joseph, *Elder Joseph the Hesychast*, trans. Elizabeth Theokritoff (Mount Athos: Vatopaidi, 1999), pp. 132-33.

119. As the Liturgy of St. Basil the Great reads, "This do, in remembrance of me: for as often as ye shall eat this Bread and drink of this Cup ye shall proclaim my death and confess my Resurrection." Hapgood, *Service Book*, p. 104.

120. The Liturgy of St. John Chrysostom reminds the participants in the celebration that, united to Christ, they stand already at His second coming. "Bearing in remembrance, therefore, this commandment of salvation, and all those things which came to pass for us; the Cross, the Grave, the Resurrection on the third day, the Ascension into Heaven, the Sitting on the right hand, the Second and glorious Coming-again." *Ibid.*, p. 104.

121. The Fall does not touch paradise. It remains unchanged. "And God did not curse Paradise, since it was the image of the future unending life of the eternal Kingdom of Heaven." St. Symeon the New Theologian, *The First-Created Man*, trans. Fr. Seraphim Rose (Platina, CA: St. Herman Press, 1994), Homily 45.2, "Adam and the First-Created World," p. 91.

122. "Verily, Adam, because of a tree, became estranged from paradise. But the thief because of the tree of the Cross came to reside in paradise." Nassar, *Divine Prayers and Services*, p. 167.

123. St. John Chrysostom, Homily on the Gospel of St. Matthew I.2, NPNF1, vol. 10, p. 1.

124. Nassar, *Divine Prayers and Services*, p. 995.

125. *A Commonitory* II,4,6, NPNF1, vol. 11, p. 132. See also footnote 96 above.

126. Evagrios the Solitary, "On Prayer," in *The Philokalia*, vol. 1, p. 62.

127. Peter Perekrestov (ed.), *Man of God: St. John of Shanghai and San Francisco* (Redding, CA: Nikodemos Orthodox Publication Society, 1991); Fr. Seraphim Rose and Abbot Herman, *Blessed John the Wonderworker* (Platina, CA: St. Herman of Alaska Brotherhood, 1987).

128. Elder Joseph the Hesychast, *Monastic Wisdom* (Florence, AZ: St. Anthony's Monastery, 1998).

129. Geronda Paisios, *Hagioreitai Pateres kai Hagioreitika* (Thessaloniki: Holy Monastery Monazouson, 1993); Priestmonk Christodoulos, *Elder Paisios of the Holy Mountain* (Holy Mountain, 1998). See also for another example of a great saint and theologian of the 20th century Paisios of Mount Athos, *Saint Arsenios the Cappadocian* (Vasilika, Greece: Convent of the Evangelist John, 1996).

130. Klitos Ioannidis, *Elder Porphyrios* (Athens: Convent of the Transfiguration of the Savior, 1997).

131. Archimandrite Sophrony, *Saint Silouan the Athonite*, trans. Rosemary Edmonds (Essex: Monastery of St. John the Baptist, 1991).

132. Archimandrite Sophrony, *We Shall See Him as He is*, trans. Rosemary Edmonds (Essex: Monastery of St. John the Baptist, 1988).

133. Hierotheos Vlachos, *Orthodox Spirituality*, trans. Effie Mavromichali (Levadia, Greece: Birth of the Theotokos Monastery, 1994), p. 77.

134. St. Symeon, *Hymns of Divine Love*, trans. George A. Maloney (Denville, NJ: Dimension Books, 1975) # 58, p. 288.

135. Vespers of Pentecost, in Nassar, *Divine Prayers and Services*, pp. 998-99.

136. St. Symeon, *Symeon the New Theologian: The Discourses*, trans. C.J. deCatanzaro (New York: Paulist Press, 1980), pp. 343-4.

137. From the outside, the Orthodox Church may seem an unorganized religion with no central administrative structure, though the patriarch of New Rome has all of the authority once enjoyed by the pope of Old Rome. From the inside, the unity is that of the Spirit, a unity not of this world.

138. "Encyclical Epistle of the One Holy Catholic and Apostolic Church to the Faithful Everywhere" being "A Reply to the Epistle of Pius IX to the Easterns," dated January 6, 1848, §17.

139. Some may attempt to draw a line between the tradition as enduring truth and tradition as accumulated ecclesiastical customs.

140. Here Tradition identifies the ongoing presence of the Spirit in the Church, not mere customs or practices (i.e., mere tradition). "Tradition is the constant abiding of the Spirit and not only the memory of words. Tradition is a *charismatic*, not a historical, principle." Georges Florovsky, *Bible, Church, Tradition: An Eastern Orthodox View* (Vaduz: Büchervertriebsanstalt, 1987), p. 47. Yet, one must be cautious when drawing a distinction between Tradition as an expression of the Holy Spirit and tradition as merely human conventions. What has been sanctified by prayer over time may never be dismissed out of hand as a mere human custom. After all, the customs of the Church reflect its therapeutic experience guided by the Holy Spirit, that which has been successful in treating the soul and curing it of passions.

141. The West changed the weekly fast of Wednesday and Friday to Friday and Saturday and ceased to observe abstinence from dairy products.

The first error of the Westerners was to compel the faithful to fast on Saturdays. (I mention this seemingly small point because the least departure from Tradition can lead to a scorning of every

dogma of our Faith.) Next, they convinced the faithful to despise the marriage of priests, thereby sowing in their souls the seeds of the Manichean heresy. Likewise, they persuaded them that all who had been chrismated by priests had to be anointed again by bishops. In this way they hoped to show that Chrismation by priests had no value, thereby ridiculing this divine and supernatural Christian Mystery. Where does this law forbidding priests to anoint with Holy Chrism come from? From what lawgiver, Apostle, Father, or Council? For if a priest cannot chrismate the newly-baptized, then, to be sure, neither can he baptize. Or how can a priest consecrate the Body and Blood of Christ our Lord in the Divine Liturgy, if at the same time he cannot chrismate with Holy Chrism? If this grace, then, is taken from the priests, the episcopal rank is diminished, for the bishop stands at the head of the choir of priests. But the impious Westerners did not stop their lawlessness even here.
St. Photios, *On the Mystagogy of the Holy Spirit*, trans. Holy Transfiguration Monastery (New York: Studion, 1983), p. 50.

142. John S. Romanides, *Franks, Romans, Feudalism, and Doctrine* (Brookline, Mass.: Holy Cross Orthodox Press, 1981). See also Marcia L. Colish, *Medieval Foundations of the Western Intellectual Tradition 400-1400* (New Haven: Yale University Press, 1997), pp. 66-78 and 160-174.

143. The Donations of Constantine are one of the most influential forgeries of all times. They attested to a supposed grant by Emperor Constantine the Great to Pope Sylvester I (314-335) of Rome conveying authority over all other patriarchates in matters of faith and worship. This document was likely written in the latter half of the 8th century either in Rome or in the Frankish kingdom. There is much evidence to support the latter origin. The Donations were first invoked by Pope Leo IX in 1054 when he separated from the other patriarchates.

144. Western Christianity developed under numerous, important influences. On the one hand, it was somewhat natural for the bishop of Rome, the bishop of the capital city of the Empire, to play a centralizing role in the West analogous to that played by the pope of Alexandria. The role of the Roman papacy was strengthened by the circumstance that Rome was the only city in the West associating the origins of its episcopacy with an apostolic visit. This status was further buttressed by the role the patriarch of Rome played in maintaining order during the chaos engendered by Germanic and other invasions. These tendencies to centralization were further fortified in the second millennium by the impact of the monastery of Cluny, which revised Benedictine life to achieve a new systematized structure foreign to the spirituality of monasteries as this had previously existed in the West and still exists in the East. Such a centralizing and external unity collides with the recognition that the Church is not an external, legal entity and above all that monasteries in their struggle to restore paradise should avoid an external, legalistic unity, for

The Church is our body. As a result of the existence of its Head, our Lord and Savior Jesus Christ, before all time, and before creation, the Church coexists with him before all time. The Church is not an imaginary entity, not a legal entity, a mere gathering of the faithful, or a worldly establishment or creation. The Church is Christ and those that He chooses, in one body with Him for all ages. Patriarch Bartholomew, "Joyful Light".

The changes in monastic organization were initially advanced by Benedict of Aniane at a meeting in 817 in Aachen, one of the primary Frankish capitals. This led to the building in France of what was until the 16th century the largest church structure in the West: the abbey-church of Cluny. This monastery and the eventually some 825 dependent monasteries produced numerous popes of Rome with deeply centralist inclinations. These included Gregory VII (Hildebrand; 1020-1085), who was one of the first popes (1073-1085) after the Schism of 1054. Gregory VII was remarkable in having excommunicated a Western emperor, Henry IV, bringing him to plead for forgiveness, thus establishing the priority of the Roman papacy over the Roman emperor. Although it is unclear whether he actually lived at Cluny, Hildebrand was influenced by its centralizing "reforms". His "reforms" included attempts to suppress simony (surely a very good thing to suppress). But he also attempted to forbid married men from becoming priests. This "reform" had significant consequences for the character of the Western church. On the one hand, a celibate clergy was established; on the other hand, many priests came to have mistresses. This reform occasioned an element of the corruption against which Luther and subsequent Reformers would protest.

A novel ecclesiology or church structure gradually emerged in which one bishop, the pope, claimed to be the universal bishop, and in which "reforms" were achieved through one monastery. This monastery of Cluny in France became in many respects, for a time at least, a universal monastery of reform. This centralized ecclesiology was then combined with a new systematic theology that shaped the Western church: the theology of the schools and the schoolmen. It developed out of the immense influence exerted by the Dominican Thomas Aquinas (1225-1274). Though his influence did not at once displace Augustine, Thomas's Aristotelian approach to theology became ever more a part of the Roman Catholic self-understanding. This was especially the case after the Council of Trent (1545-1563). Many forces were involved in framing Western Christianity following the events unleashed by Luther's nailing his 95 theses to the church door in Wittenberg (1517). Yet, there was a continuity in the developments that framed the West. Variations on Augustinian ideas were taken as support for Lutheran and Calvinist practices. The Roman church for its part was more influenced by a Scholasticism with roots in Thomas Aquinas. As Roman Catholicism entered the end of the 19th century, this became more pronounced. The Roman church affirmed the centrality of Thomistic theology, especially with Pope Leo XIII's encyclical *Aeterni Patris*, 4 August 1879. Also after Trent, the Jesuits and their spirituality, which involved an engagement in conquering the world for Christ, came ever more to frame the spirituality of Roman Catholicism in general. The Carmelites, who had a significant role in missionary activity as well as university work, further tied Western monastic spirituality to an engagement in the world rather than in the old monastic model of sanctifying the world through the power of holiness achieved in prayer.

At the end of the 19th century, one found a Roman Catholicism committed to a Dominican theology, guided by a spirituality grounded in the life of orders such as the Carmelites and Jesuits, all the while still possessing a liturgy with roots in the age of the Fathers. It is interesting to note that it is at the end of the 19th century that Roman Catholicism took further steps away from the traditional character of the fasts. Though the West broke with much of the character of the traditional Lenten fast in the 14th century, until the end of the 19th and the beginning of the 20th century, many of the fasts in the West were still similar to those in the Orthodox Church.

Vatican II represented a further rupture with the past that had framed Roman Catholicism. The liturgy was recast, further severing the bond with the Fathers. The remnants of the fasts were nearly totally extinguished. Also, the theology of Thomas Aquinas and the spirituality of the Carmelites and Jesuits were brought into question. The lingering resonances with the spirituality of the first millennium were substantially obscured, if not totally eradicated. The one thing that did remain was a strong focus on central control. The Vatican now found itself attempting to stem through centralized constraint the centripetal forces that the Roman church had itself set into play.

The Protestant churches, for their part, found themselves in various ways bound in dialectical opposition to the church against which they protested. Out of their criticism of the centralized character of Roman ecclesiology and the rationalism of Roman theology, there emerged an ecclesiology and theology that could not maintain a unity of belief and worship. In part, the character of Protestantism was determined by its having been born of protest. In part, the character of Protestantism was shaped by its revolutionary character. Rather than reforming the established church of the West, it instigated a revolution that claimed to start Christianity anew, renewed, and reformed, a millennium and a half after its beginning. Because Protestantism developed as a revolt against an institution and a tradition it rightly recognized as corrupt, Protestantism had a natural critical regard of institutional religion and tradition. It was not able to take up the Tradition of the first millennium. Because of its critical stance towards Tradition, it found itself committed in the end to its own secularization, a point well made by the scholar of comparative religions, René Guénon (1886-1951).

Actually, religion being essentially a form of tradition, the anti-traditional spirit cannot help being anti-religious; it begins by denaturing religion and ends by suppressing it altogether, wherever it is able to do so. Protestantism is illogical from the fact that, while doing its utmost to "humanize" religion, it nevertheless permits the survival, at least theoretically, of a supra-human element, namely revelation; it hesitates to drive negation to its logical conclusion, but, by exposing revelation to all the discussions which follow in the wake of purely human interpretations, it does in fact reduce it practically to nothing ... It is natural that Protestantism, animated as it is by a spirit of negation, should have given birth to that dissolving "criticism" which, in the hands of so-called "historians of religion," has become a weapon of offense against all religion; in this way, while affecting not to recognize any authority except that of the Scriptures, it has itself contributed in large measure to the destruction of that very same authority, of the minimum of tradition, that is to say, which it still affected to retain; once launched, the revolt against the traditional outlook could not be arrested in mid-course.
René Guénon, *Crisis of the Modern World* (London: Luzac and Co., 1975), pp. 58-9.

Though Protestantism may fervently attempt to maintain its bonds to the original Christianity, it remains deeply ambivalent regarding the history of Christianity after the Apostolic Age. It does not find the Church as the Bride of Christ united to Him through and in history, so that as members of the Church we become members of His Body (Eph 5:30). As a consequence, fundamentalist Protestants are estranged from the Tradition that could sustain their fundamentals.

A different dialectic repels Roman Catholicism from the Tradition. Its commitment to reason has become a kind of poison pill that brings into question the commitments of faith and the Tradition. The difficulty lies in Roman Catholicism's understanding of theology as bound to discursive reasoning, rather than to noetic understanding. Any moral content affirmed in Roman Catholicism's tradition, which cannot be justified by discursive reasoning, is brought into question because of the commitment to a scientific, discursive theology. Since the content of traditional Christianity is grounded in a noetic understanding, not a discursive justification, the very core of the Tradition must always ineluctably be brought into question, criticized, and evacuated. On the one hand, Protestantism attempted to recapture the core of the Christian commitment by an appeal to the individual's capacity in the Spirit to read the Scriptures, yet it did not provide the ascesis, the praxis to develop noetic perception, so that the person could enter appropriately into the liturgical context within which the Scriptures could be opened for understanding. The individual outside of this context was drawn in different directions by different spirits leading to the diversity of contemporary Protestantism. On the other hand, Roman Catholicism attempted to secure a unity through discursive reasoning and papal authority. Discursive reasoning turned out not to be the support but the enemy of Tradition. Once disconnected from the ascetic life of true theology and noetic understanding, it brought into question all particular content that declared itself as canonical. As a consequence, Roman Catholic moral theology, as well as Roman Catholic bioethics, both brought traditional content into question and broke into a diversity of moral understandings as discursive reason showed itself unable to establish one particular canonical moral understanding. Moral theology and bioethics became either

vacuous or diverse. Papal authority, disconnected from the conciliar character of the episcopal teaching role and severed from noetic guidance, became a mere external constraint
over against this diversity.

As Ecumenical Patriarch Bartholomew has observed, these factors have led to a separation
of Orthodox and Western theological understandings, which is not rooted in mere cultural
or geographical circumstances.

> Assuredly our problem is neither geographical nor one of personal alienation. Neither is it a problem
> of organizational structures, nor jurisdictional arrangements. Neither is it a problem of external
> submission, nor absorption of individuals and groups. It is something deeper and more substantive.
> The manner in which we exist has become ontologically different.
> Patriarch Bartholomew, "Joyful Light".

The separation lies in fundamentally different models of theology, union with God, and
ecclesial structure.

> No one ignores the fact that the model for all of us is the person of the Theanthropos (God-Man) Jesus
> Christ. But which model? No one ignores the fact that the incorporation in Him is achieved within His
> body, the Church. But whose church? (Ibid.)

As Patriarch Bartholomew stresses, theology must be understood not as a merely academic
undertaking. It is a transformation achieved through grace.

> Consequently the "glory" of the Lord, which we see, as in a mirror, is that which transforms us. This
> glory is that to which we are likened. The reflection of the divine glory recreates or otherwise
> regenerates us into something other or different in essence than our previous nature. Therefore,
> transformation into the image of the Lord and the image of His body becomes the fundamental pursuit
> of our life, accomplished in essence by the intervention of the Holy Spirit. (Ibid.)

One is then left with radically different appreciations of the human condition, our relationship to God, the meaning of the Church, the significance of theology for our salvation, and
the proper character of a Christian bioethics

145. For a brief overview of the development of the understandings of the university, see Francis
Oakley, *Community of Learning* (New York: Oxford University Press, 1992), pp. 11-59.

146. Thomas Aquinas, for example, reflects at length on the status of the fetus, including the
issue of abortion. See, for example, *Summa Theologica* I, 118, art. 2; *Aristoteles Stagiritae:
Politicorum seu de Rebus Civilibus*, Book VII, Lectio XII; *Summa Theologica* II, II, 64, art.
8; and *Commentum in Quartum Librum Sententiarum Magistri Petri Lombardi*, Distinctio XXXI, Expositio Textus.

147. Kierkegaard, *Judge for Yourself*, eds. and trans. Howard Hong and Edna Hong (Princeton,
NJ: Princeton University Press, 1990), p. 195, XII 462. Kierkegaard appreciates the shift
from a Christianity grounded in asceticism to a Christianity grounded in scholarship. "If
the Christianity of the Middle Ages is called monastic-ascetic Christianity, then the Christianity of today could be called professorial-scholarly Christianity." *Ibid.*, pp. 194-195,
XII 462. He also recognizes that a Christianity grounded in scholarship has nothing to do
with traditional Christianity.

> The professor! This man is not mentioned in the New Testament, from which one sees in the first place
> that Christianity came into the world without professors. Anyone with any eye for Christianity will
> certainly see that one is as qualified to smuggle Christianity out of the world as "the professor" is,
> because the professor shifts the whole viewpoint of Christianity. *Ibid.*, p. 195, XII 463.

In this, Kierkegaard's diagnosis of the problems of the age is considerably more perceptive
than that of Pope John Paul II, who sees a remedy for the deChristianization of Europe in
the development of better philosophers, better Christian scholars.

148. Walter Abbott (ed.), "Priestly Formation" in *The Documents of Vatican II* (New York: Herder and Herder, 1966), p. 452.

149. "Instruction on the Ecclesial Vocation of the Theologian," *Origins* 20 (July 5, 1990), 120.

150. Pope John Paul II, *Veritatis Splendor* (Vatican City: Libreria Editrice Vaticana, 1993), p. 158.

151. Pope John Paul II, *Fides et Ratio* (Vatican City: Libreria Editrice Vaticana, 1998), pp. 86, 148, 151.

152. His Grace Abba Gregorios, quoted in Iris Habib el Masri, *The Story of the Copts: The True Story of Christianity in Egypt* (Nairobi, Kenya: Coptic Bishopric for African Affairs, 1987), Book II, pp. 404, 405.

153. Patriarch Bartholomew, "Joyful Light".

154. *Ibid.*

155. "Grace can also be obtained by the presence of the Saints who have influenced and sanctified, and to a degree transformed, natural objects and places." *Ibid.*

156. St. Seraphim of Sarov gives the following account of the insufficiency of virtue for salvation.

> In the parable of the wise and foolish virgins, when the foolish ones lacked oil, it was said: 'Go and buy in the market.' But when they had bought, the door of the bride-chamber was already shut and they could not get in. Some say that the lack of oil in the lamps of the foolish virgins means a lack of good deeds in their lifetime. Such an interpretation is not quite correct. Why should they be lacking in good deeds if they are called virgins, even though foolish ones? Virginity is the supreme virtue, an angelic state, and it could take the place of all other good works.
> I think that what they were lacking was the grace of the All-Holy Spirit of God. These virgins practiced the virtues, but in their spiritual ignorance they supposed that the Christian life consisted merely in doing good works. By doing a good deed they thought they were doing the work of God, but they little cared whether they acquired thereby the grace of God's Spirit. Such ways of life based merely on doing good without carefully testing whether they bring the grace of the Spirit of God, are mentioned in the Patristic books: 'There is another way which is deemed good at the beginning, but it ends at the bottom of hell.'
> Antony the Great in his letters to Monks says of such virgins: 'Many Monks and virgins have no idea of the different kinds of will which act in man, and they do not know that we are influenced by three wills: the first is God's all-perfect and all-saving will, the second is our own human will which, if not destructive, yet neither is it saving; and the third is the devil's will – wholly destructive.' And this third will of the enemy teaches man either not to do any good deeds, or to do them out of vanity, or to do them merely for virtue's sake and not for Christ's sake. The second, our own will, teaches us to do everything to flatter our passions, or else it teaches us like the enemy to do good for the sake of good and not care for the grace which is acquired by it. But the first, God's all-saving will, consists in doing good solely to acquire the Holy Spirit, as an eternal, inexhaustible treasure which cannot be rightly valued. The acquisition of the Holy Spirit is, so to say, the oil which the foolish virgins lacked. They were called foolish just because they had forgotten the necessary fruit of virtue, the grace of the Holy Spirit, without which no one is or can be saved, for: 'Every soul is quickened by the Holy Spirit and exalted by purity and mystically illumined by the Trinal Unity.'
> Lazarus Moore, *St. Seraphim of Sarov* (Blanco, Tex.: New Sarov Press, 1994), pp. 172-73.

157. Nassar, "Hypakoe, Second Antiphony in the Third Tone," in *Divine Prayers and Services*, p. 156.

158. Patriarch Bartholomew, "Joyful Light".

159. Elder Joseph the Hesychast gives accounts of experiences of great ascetics receiving antidoron and communion by miraculous means. See note 93 above. The hermits are never without the community of saints; they never suffer the ecclesial anomie of Kierkegaard. The seeming isolation of great ascetics is set aside in Liturgy, however infrequent, thus ensuring their union with all Christians in the Liturgy. See Elder Joseph, *Monastic Wisdom*, Letter XXVI, p. 139f.

5 Procreation: Reproduction, Cloning, Abortion, and Birth

Out of Step: The Traditional Christian Bioethics of Sexuality versus the Emerging Secular Liberal Cosmopolitan Consensus

Traditional Christianity is not just heterosexist; it appears fundamentally sexist and patriarchal. As the first clause of its Creed proclaims, "I believe in God the Father almighty." The traditional Christian bioethics of human sexuality is outrageous. It offends contemporary secular mores. It is at direct loggerheads with the developing secular moral consensus regarding sexuality and reproduction. Traditional Christian sexual mores conflict with what has come to be accepted as integral to moral sensitivity, the recognition of the lifestyles of others, and the respect accorded to personal choices. Traditional Christian morality is at odds with the cosmopolitan secular ethos.

The secular moral consensus can somewhat procrusteanly be summarized under seven points. (1) Privacy of sexual acts: sexual and reproductive choices with consenting, mutually respecting adult others regardless of gender are regarded as private, not simply in the sense of being exempt from public interference, but also as being free from third-party moral judgment, given the special intimacy of sexual experience. It is not merely that one should not judge the persons involved (surely a Christian maxim), but according to the liberal cosmopolitan ethos one should not even judge the lifestyle (i.e., Christians are not to judge that a particular murderer such as Stalin will go to hell, only that such a lifestyle of murdering is morally forbidden and evil). (2) Moral permissibility of sexual acts: sexuality is regarded as a human experience that enriches human life and whose engagement at least between adults is morally permissible, given the competent consent of the participants, irrespective of their gender. (3) The avoidance of moralisms: moralistic terms such as "fornication" should be avoided.[1] At the very least, moralistic terms must be recast to reflect a concern about (a) acting without adequate consent or with a betrayal of trust (e.g., having sexual relations outside the bonds of marriage without one's spouse's concurrence), or (b) failing to attend to the special goods of sexual intimacy and mutual regard. Otherwise, (c) they involve endorsing the remnants of a sexual morality grounded in concerns no longer justifiable in an age of safe sex, effective contraception, and safe early abortion. (4) The contraceptive ethos is affirmed as supporting signal human goods. Effective contraception provides a liberation from the constraints of nature, thus sustaining contemporary lifestyles in which sex can be enjoyed without consequences (i.e., seemingly without risk of disease or pregnancy) allowing women, while being fully sexually active, to engage in full-time careers, so as to achieve satisfying levels of high affluence. (5) The avoidance of the language of unnatural and perverse: the language of natural versus unnatural acts, normal versus perverted sexual acts, appropriate versus deviant sexual behavior, is regarded as a morally harmful remnant of a teleological biology out of place in a post-Darwinian world in which the moral norms for such judgments are held to be absent. The harm in the language of unnatural, abnormal, perverse, deviant, and immoral, when applied to sexual activities among consenting adults, is that it fails to recognize the values and needs of others; it obscures the diversity of sexual lifestyles and denies the legitimate range of individual self-realization.[2] It is for this reason that the term gender takes preference over sex (e.g., as in the male sex) to indicate the social construction of sexual roles, male and female, homosexual and heterosexual, on analogy with the social construction of the gender of nouns. (6) The avoidance of sexual exploitation: because the core sexual moral issue is consent, and because the liberal cosmopolitan ethos is most fully realized through individual, autonomous, mutually affirming self-realization, sexual ethics addresses matters that impair competent consent because of the exploitation associated with unfair imbalances of power among partners. (7) Embryo and fetus wastage is non-optimal, but not evil: although laboratory zygote wastage as well as embryo and fetal destruction are morally undesirable, these entities are not recognized as possessing sufficient moral weight to defeat the *prima facie* secular rights of women to determine whether they will be mothers, and of couples to determine whether they wish to reproduce. Most importantly, since there is always the risk of contraceptive failure, the availability of abortion is demanded to sustain the ethos of sex without consequences.

Secular sexual morality affirms self-realization, mutual satisfaction, and mutual self-empowerment. Beyond concerns regarding free and informed consent, and non-exploitative and mutually affirming relationships, sexual issues are not directly matters of morality. Liberal cosmopolitan morality translates that which is specifically sexual in sexual ethics into sexual aesthetics, leaving primarily a procedural moral remnant nested within a liberal cosmopolitan concern with self-determination and mutual self-realization. Within these constraints, sexual choices concern the beautiful, the thrilling, the pleasing, the satisfying, the enriching, and the completing. They are elements that in different circumstances within different lifestyles can be variously fitted into the richly diverse mosaics of human fulfillment and flourishing. Within these constraints, sexual lifestyle choices deserve respect, not moralistic condemnation.

In stark contrast, traditional Christian sexual and reproductive bioethics, although it does not judge persons (i.e., judge who is going to hell or heaven), does judge actions, behaviors, and lifestyles. It recognizes and respects persons, but not necessarily their choices, behaviors, and actions. It places particular lifestyles beyond the bounds of the morally acceptable. In particular, unlike the secular moral consensus, (1) traditional Christianity recognizes that third-party judgments are appropriate regarding sexual lifestyles: consensual, mutually affirming, sexual and reproductive choices are not private in the sense of exempt from further third-party moral judgments. Respecting others and recognizing them as able to pursue union with God require honestly but lovingly condemning evil urges, acts, and evil lifestyles, without condemning or even judging the persons beset by these evils. (2) Sexuality is understood primarily in terms of a relation to God: while acknowledging that carnal sexuality can strengthen the bond between husband and wife, traditional Christianity recognizes that more than consent, mutual respect, and mutual empowerment is necessary for sexual acts to be morally acceptable. Sexual acts must be of the sort that are compatible with approaching holiness. The content of sexual morality is therefore recognized as dependent on what leads to union with God; immoral sexual acts are those that deflect away from union with God. (3) The fundamental purpose of the institution of marriage is the companionship of man and woman in the mutual pursuit of salvation (i.e., "it is not good that the man should be alone" [Gen 2:18]), the purpose of the carnal character of sexual relations is the begetting of children (it is after the Fall that Adam calls his wife not simply woman [Gen 2:23], but Eve, the mother of mankind [Gen 3:20]). Though the begetting of children is the purpose of the carnal character of human sexuality, carnal relations within marriage may be undertaken with other than reproductive intent (e.g., to preserve chastity, including the deepening and strengthening of the bond of husband and wife), as long as the possibility of reproduction is always accepted (e.g., one may not use abortion to avoid having a child).[3] The contraceptive ethos with its affirmation of sex without consequences in the pursuit of a life of affluence (e.g., a couple with means decides to have but one child, given their lifestyle commitments) is radically incompatible with the ascetic pursuit of salvation. (4) Sexual acts can be evil, independently of consent and mutual affirmation: in particular, fornication, adultery, and homosexual acts have an evil that consent and mutual respect cannot cure. (5) Natural law is recast: because the focus is from a world broken by sin to union with a perfect God, natural law is not simply a reflection of our biological proclivities or an impersonal structure in nature; it is the law found within our consciences and within nature when nature is recognized as a window to the experience of God. (6) Sexual sins are sins even if involuntary: in our broken condition some immoral sexual behaviors may be genetically determined; nevertheless, they are to be condemned, both by third parties and by those who engage in them because such acts remain evil even if one cannot control one's behavior (i.e., as a second-order volition one must confess: "I could not stop myself, but my action was evil"). As a self-conscious being, one always has power over one's second-order intentions.[4] Finally, (7) all killing of humans must be avoided: because of a fundamental commitment never to be involved in taking human life, all violence against human zygotes, embryos, and fetuses must be recognized as freighted with grave spiritual peril, even if the mother can protect her life only by taking the life of the unborn child.[5]

In all of this, concerns with sexual morality must be judged in terms of the struggle to God, the pursuit of the kingdom of God. The beautiful, the thrilling, the pleasing, the satisfying, and the completing elements of sexual experience must be relocated within the mutual love of husband and wife in their companionship in loving God. Human sexual fulfillment and satisfaction can only be judged through and in terms of a turn through asceticism toward holiness and away from self-love.

Bioethics as a Lived Ethics

Christian bioethics is not a set of rules. It is integral to a liturgical life leading to union with a fully transcendent God. Because the difference between created and uncreated being is ultimate,[6] traditional Christian bioethics contrasts fundamentally with both secular and post-traditional Christian bioethics.[7] A traditional Christian bioethics of reproduction must be approached within its own epistemological, metaphysical, socio-logical, axiological, narrative, and authority-oriented presuppositions. Questions re-garding human sexuality, contraception, third-party-assisted reproduction, cloning, and abortion can only be fully and appropriately answered when considered within framing concerns for redemption, repentance, and union with God. First, Christian epistemology does not ground its moral and theological claims in either sense experi-ence or discursive rational arguments. The claims are in the end grounded in a noetic experience of God. This epistemology is noetically empirical; it is neither mundanely empirical nor rationalistic. It rests on an experience achieved through an ascetic turn away from oneself to God so as to be open to His grace. It is one with the experience of the Church from the first centuries. Second, although God is fully transcendent, He is experienced as personal. Christian bioethics has a personal character. It is about the relations of persons to each other in the pursuit of a relationship with God. Third, the disclosure of the holy and the experience of God are pursued in worship and love, which are rightly oriented only from the vantagepoint of the eucharistic Liturgy. The exemplar epistemic locus is liturgical: the communion of saints disclosed in the wor-ship of God, including the marriage service. Fourth, moral concerns with rights, val-ues, and virtues are transformed and relocated in terms of the pursuit of holiness, union with God. Acting rightly and justly is not enough for salvation and can only be coherently pursued when oriented to holiness. The focus is not primarily on who has a right to do what, but on what aids in the pursuit of the Kingdom of God. Fifth, the pursuit of holiness is lodged within history: the individual pursuit of holiness is placed within the narrative of salvation, the history of redemption within which all reality is placed. Finally, while bishops are in authority to guide, the authorities regarding this way of life, the theologians par excellence, are those who experience God, the holy fathers and mothers across the ages. All of this, as the previous chapter shows, sustains a bioethics that contrasts robustly with secular and other religious bioethics. Questions regarding Christian bioethics are addressed first by calling on the scriptural and liturgi-cal presentations of human reproduction, birth, suffering, and death, as these have been understood by the Fathers and in the prayers of the Church over the centuries.

Christian bioethics is not legalistic. The Christian ethics of reproduction is not merely a set of rules or principles. Its answers to questions about right and wrong conduct should not be understood on the model of juridical determinations of guilt or innocence, but rather in terms of aiming people closer to union with God. The crucial point of focus is not on particular rules but on changing oneself so as to turn from oneself to God.[8] Still, although Christians "are not under the law, but under grace" (Rom 6:14), there are real moral boundaries set to actions. The matter is multi-valent. On the one hand, the focus is on perfection, on holiness, on the pursuit of the Kingdom of God. On the other hand, there is the recognition that all always fall short of the mark and need to rely on repentance and the redeeming grace of

God.[9] Christian bioethics is absolutist in being integral to a response to Christ's invitation to "Ye shall be perfect, even as your Father Who is in the heavens is perfect" (Matt 5:48). Christian bioethics will also appear lax: with sincere repentance forgiveness is always available. Everything is required; anything can be forgiven.[10] The focus on repentance and perfection relocates the concerns of bioethics within the commitment to living a traditional Christian life of love, ascetical striving, repentance, forgiveness, and salvation.

This focus on union with God has cardinal implications. It determines the character of the Christian bioethics of reproduction: the Christian bioethics of reproduction cannot be fully understood outside of a traditional Christian life. It is not just that the bioethics of reproduction will be one-sidedly and incompletely appreciated outside of a Christian life. More fundamentally, Christian morality and bioethics are grounded in the experience of a transcendent God so that for the outsider Christian bioethics can but appear as a perspective profoundly otherworldly and misguided. Entry into this world of traditional Christian experience cannot be accomplished by argument or by the analysis of framing principles, but only through ascesis, love, repentance, prayer, and worship. In this way, human sexuality and reproduction enter through marriage into the human journey to holiness. They are transformed by grace and oriented towards the Kingdom of God. So transformed, they can no longer be considered in merely biological terms or with reference to merely human concerns. All must be relocated with reference to the struggle to holiness.

Although a life directed to union with God cannot be reduced to a set of discursive moral principles, since that life is a whole directed beyond morality to holiness, some general religious moral observations can be offered. These observations should not be confused with principles as sources or foundations for moral claims. The language of principles risks misleading about what is a seamless whole. With this warning, some general moral observations concerning a traditional Christian bioethics of sexuality can be given as guideposts:

1. Humans are in their essence, before and after the Fall and even after the Resurrection, ontologically male and female. For example, Mary the Mother of God is the Theotokos forever. Her very being for eternity is bound up with her motherhood. Christ's resurrected body gives all indications of being recognizable as male. Our existence as male and female endures. "But from the beginning of creation, God 'made them male and female'" (Mark 10:6). There is in this relationship an order, a hierarchy among equals, for as Chrysostom says, "And from the beginning He made one sovereignty only, setting the man over the woman."[11] It is because of this ordering of male and female, of Adam and Eve, that the priest and bishop as icons of the second Adam are always male.[12] In presiding over the assembly of Christians they reflect this authority of Adam.[13] The equality of men and women set in a hierarchy of authority[14] is expressed most perfectly in marriage, in the Church under bishops, and in the admissibility of only men to any priestly order.[15] All genotypic and phenotypic expressions of sexual differences disclose, however inadequately, this deeper ontological reality of the difference between man and woman. As phenotypic and genotypic sexual difference is more profound than social constructions of gender, men and women are from the beginning ontologically different in their realization of humanity.[16]

2. Marriage is an institution established by God for man and woman in mutual love and companionship to achieve salvation. In particular, its carnal character has as its purpose the procreation and the raising of God-loving children. Men and women may also enter into marriage because their need for companionship would otherwise offend against chastity. In the monogamous marriage of man and woman, this companionship touched by carnal sexuality finds its only appropriate expression.

3. Carnal sexuality may be engaged for pursuing goals other than reproductive (the preservation of chastity through the development of the bond between husband and wife). One may enter into marriage without a view to procreation (e.g., after the usual reproductive age or after a disease has made reproduction impossible), as a means for the mutual pursuit of salvation, as is attested by the Church's blessing first marriages of persons beyond reproductive age.

4. Marriage in the Church is a Mystery that leads to holiness.[17] It is ideally a unique union never to be repeated by either spouse, even after the death of one spouse.

5. All human carnal sexuality and reproduction are to be undertaken within the marriage of one man and one woman, therefore excluding as sinful not just pornography and extramarital sexually evoking circumstances and images, but also masturbation, fornication, adultery, homosexuality, and acts of bestiality.

6. It is appropriate to employ counseling as well as psychological and psychiatric treatment to aid those suffering from urges contrary to the union of man and wife, such as urges to engage in homosexual acts or acts of bestiality; such treatment can be used so as to direct sexual desires to heterosexual unions that can be blessed by the Church. Were some inappropriate sexual lifestyles genetically determined and involuntary, they would remain sinful as involuntary sins, requiring repentance through ascetic struggle.

7. Third parties should not be involved in the sexual or reproductive acts of husbands and wives.

8. Human sexuality even in marriage must be placed within the ascetic struggle to union with God; nothing, including marital sexuality, should distract from wholehearted love of God. The contraceptive ethos, instead of focusing on God, focuses on luxury and indulgence and leads away from God. Marriage in its joyful companionship may lead even in this life beyond carnality to that life of the angels that is the destiny of all marriages (Matt 23:30, Mark 12:25, Luke 20:36).[18]

9. The taking of human life, even the life of unborn children in order to preserve the life of the mother, always falls short of the pursuit of holiness: abortion is always wrong. Persons are not just those who can now act as moral agents, but all who are called to worship God eternally.

10. Given the broken character of the world and the circumstance that "the imagination of man's heart is evil from his youth" (Gen 8:21), the preservation of the marriage bond and the protection of human life can involve actions that fall somewhat short but not wide of the mark in not fully preserving the unique intimacy of union between husband and wife directed ascetically toward God, that is, directed away from self-love and self-satisfaction to a pure love of spouse and of God. This circumstance should be seriously mourned through repentance, ascesis, and prayer.[19] Moral reflections on bioethical issues often take on the character of

providing guidance for those who have entered spiritually dangerous territories and are not willing to retreat to the safety of putting all in the hands of God, and yet who still wish to avoid some of the worst of the dangers. Such moral reflections produce a cartography of our broken, sinful world and of some of the less than ideal ways of responding to it.

This cluster of understandings, which without exception places all carnal sexuality within marriage and categorically excludes abortion, is in Christianity from the very beginning. It is found in the first or second century text, the *Didache*: "Thou shalt do no murder; thou shalt not commit adultery; thou shalt not commit sodomy; ... thou shalt not use philtres[20]; thou shalt not procure abortion, nor commit infanticide."[21] It is found as well in the first or second century work, the Epistle of Barnabas: "Thou shalt not commit fornication, thou shalt not commit adultery, thou shalt not commit sodomy... Thou shalt not procure abortion, thou shalt not commit infanticide."[22] Christianity approaches sexuality, reproduction, birth, and abortion within a thick understanding of appropriate and inappropriate conduct, of what leads to God and what leads away from union with God.

The Mystery of Marriage

Sexuality, reproduction, and marriage are lodged within the history of salvation and the journey to God. They have their appropriate meaning in a narrative flowing from the free choices of persons over time whose character is revealed in the tradition of Christian experience embracing the Scriptures. The significance of sexuality is conditioned by the history of sin and salvation. This history cannot be understood without taking into account Eden, the Incarnation, and the Final Judgment. Here is a challenge, a conflict of visions. What are modern men and women to make of Eden, the Incarnation, and the Final Judgment? Especially, how is Eden to be understood by contemporary men and women whose scientific worldview takes for granted not just evolution, but a cosmology reaching back billions of years? For traditional Christians, Eden is central to the history of salvation: it leads from Adam and Eve's sin to the birth of the second Adam, Christ, from the second Eve, Mary.[23]

Eden and the Final Judgment are moral and spiritual vantagepoints from which to assess this world, not events in a paleontological or cosmological account. First, there is the perspective on the world as unbroken by sin: Eden, where Adam and Eve are together without sin. Eden is the original place of relationship to God. There man is in communion with God, unfettered by passions, in a context unbroken by sin. Second, there is the perspective on the world broken by sin. In this broken and unredeemed world, the relationship of woman to man is radically encumbered by Eve's sin, the first to sin and the one who tempted Adam, so that the authority of Adam over Eve was expanded to a dominion that included polygamy, a practice engaged in even by holy patriarchs. The unique union of Adam and Eve became lost in polygamy and the need to reproduce, a need embedded in a cycle of pleasure, pain, striving, and death born of the Fall: the world of the Old Testament. Then there is the world still broken by sin, but redeemed and on its way to restoration. The natural union of marriage can now be completed in the unique union, the monogamy of Adam and Eve as restored in the Mystery of the Church. Only after the Final Judgment is the world fully restored.[24] Eden is then regained, indeed fulfilled in the new Jerusalem. Banished from the original paradise, man is then to be restored to paradise, but unlike Adam and Eve, man will finally again be in full communion with God.

Eden is not a part of the world within which we live. The paradise created for Adam and Eve was separated out of this world, was entered by Christ with the thief on the cross after their deaths, and continues in existence today.[25] Also, the world as we find it, broken by pain, travail, suffering, death, and the often adverse contingencies of evolution, is not that world which God had envisaged for human existence, but rather that into which Adam and Eve were sent because of their Fall. From Paradise Adam and Eve were inserted into this now broken world, which is in a sense a world parallel to that which was to have been.[26] As the anaphora of the Liturgy of St. Basil the Great stresses, "Thou didst banish him, in thy righteous judgment, O God, from Paradise into this present world..."[27] Because of the sin of Adam and Eve, the world in which we find ourselves is distorted by the dialectic of pain and pleasure, birth and death. Because of the sin of Adam and Eve, by the power of their free choice all is somewhat awry, all falls short of the mark which was intended from the beginning.

Adam and Eve were placed in Paradise, the exemplar reference point for the relationship of man and woman. Created for Paradise, God made them male and female. "Male and female he made them. And God blessed them, saying, Increase and multiply, and fill the earth and subdue it" (Gen 1:27-28). Christ Himself emphasizes this deep truth: "the One Who made them from the beginning 'made them male and female'" (Matt 19:4). In this garden of delight, there is still need, relationship, hierarchy, and fulfillment. They are joined in mutual support for the pursuit of salvation. In Eden God announces, "it is not good that the man should be alone; let us make for him a help suitable to him" (Gen 2:18). The only suitable helper for man was created of his very flesh, Eve, whom the man Adam recognizes as "bone of my bones, and flesh of my flesh", whom Adam called woman, "because she was taken out of her husband" (Gen 2:23). With the creation of Eve out of Adam as his helpmate, Genesis gives the defining Christian text for sexuality and marriage: "Therefore shall a man leave his father and his mother and shall cleave to his wife, and they two shall be one flesh" (Gen 2:24). Already in Eden, God anticipates the mystery of marriage. As St. John Chrysostom emphasizes, "indeed, from the beginning, God appears to have made special provision for this union."[28] God created Adam and Eve and placed them in the Garden of Eden, with both the tree of life and the tree of the knowledge of good and evil, free to eat from any but the latter. It was in this garden that Adam and Even embarked on the project of becoming gods on their own (Gen 3:5), rather than seeking union with God through humility, by the energies of God.

After placing humans in dominion over all life (Gen 1:26), the first announced purpose of marriage after the injunction to be fruitful and multiply (Gen 1:28) is marital companionship: "it is not good that the man should be alone" (Gen 2:18). It is to this point that Christ Himself turns regarding marriage: "And He answered and said to them, 'Ye read, did ye not, that the One Who made them from the beginning "made them male and female," and said, "On account of this a man shall leave father and mother, and shall cleave to his wife, and the two shall be one flesh"? Therefore they are no longer two, but one flesh'" (Matt 19:4-6). Christ proclaims a union that cannot be set aside "except it be for fornication [*porneia*]" (Matt 19:9).[29] As the disciples recognize, the seriousness of this obligation is more than a natural man can bear. "If the case of the man is so with the wife, it is not expedient to marry" (Matt 19:10). The sexual companionship of man and woman is set within marriage as an institution whose purpose is reproduction and the nurturing of holy offspring. It is this institution that is the focus of Christ's first public miracle at the very behest of his mother (John 2:1-11). Within this institution and out of this companionship, man and woman join in the work of God in the procreation of offspring. Marriage is therefore not merely a matter of human convenience.

With Christ, marriage becomes an anointed door to heaven, a Mystery of encounter with God, a joining in Christ's redemption of this broken world. Despite the Fall, during the flood, and after the redemption by Christ, God has affirmed the mystery of marriage. The relation of husband and wife is framed in terms of Christ's relationship to the Church, a union of love and submission transformed through death of the old man and life in Christ.

> Wives, be subordinating yourselves to your own husbands, as to the Lord. For the husband is head of the wife, as also Christ is head of the Church; and is Himself Savior of the body. But even as the Church subordinateth herself to the Christ, so also the wives to their own husbands in everything. Husbands, be loving your own wives, even as the Christ also loved the Church, and gave Himself up for her, in order that He might sanctify her, having cleansed her in the laver of the water with the word, that He might present her to Himself the glorious Church, not having spot, or wrinkle, or any such things; but that she may be holy and unblemished. So ought the husbands to love their own wives as their own bodies. He who loveth his own wife loveth himself. For no one ever hated his own flesh, but nourisheth and cherisheth it, even as also the Lord the Church. For we are members of His body, of His flesh, and of His bones; because of this "shall a man leave his father and mother, and shall cleave to his wife, and the two shall be into one flesh." This mystery [*mysterion*] is great; but I speak in regard to Christ and in regard to the Church. However do ye severally be loving in this manner each one his own wife as himself, and the wife in this manner that she be fearing the husband (Eph 5:22-33).

The biblical texts, as well as the life of the early Church, place all carnal sexuality within this relationship of husband and wife as well as in relation to God. Sexuality is lodged in the marital bed within the Mystery of grace.

From the beginning of the Church, only that union of man and woman acceptable to the bishop has been the rightly constituted union of husband and wife.[30] Through the Church, their union in one flesh is restored to its proper focus on the tree of life, the spiritual journey of the husband and wife toward holiness. The Mystery of marriage, as St. John Chrysostom stresses, involves a restoration in part of Eden.

> This then is marriage when it takes place according to Christ, spiritual marriage, and spiritual birth, not of blood, nor of travail, nor of the will

of the flesh. ... Yea, a marriage it is, not of passion, nor of the flesh, but wholly spiritual, the soul being united to God by a union unspeakable, and which He alone knoweth. Therefore he saith, "He that is joined unto the Lord is one spirit."[31]

This union is understood to be not only unique, monogamous, and holy, but also the remedy for desire that would otherwise be a misdirecting passion. "Marriage is not an evil thing. It is adultery that is evil, it is fornication that is evil. Marriage is a remedy to eliminate fornication."[32] Marriage is where fleshly love goes rightly.

The sexual passions Adam and Eve would not have suffered save for the Fall[33] have in marriage a place allowed by God's blessing of marriage. As St. John Chrysostom clearly emphasizes in his commentary on Ephesians, sexual pleasure in marriage involves energies well-directed.

And how become they one flesh? As if thou shouldest take away the purest part of gold, and mingle it with other gold; so in truth here also the woman as it were receiving the richest part fused by pleasure, nourisheth it and cherisheth it, and withal contributing her own share, restoreth it back a Man. And the child is a sort of bridge, so that the three become one flesh, the child connecting, on either side, each to other.[34]

Marriage is the only proper place for carnal desires. St. John of Damascus cites Chrysostom with approval, "matrimony is indulgence of pleasure".[35] Here carnal desires can be aimed rightly so that the married couple can approach God. This union in reproduction and companionship is enough to justify the holy mystery of marriage. In this, St. John Chrysostom is in accord with St. Maximus the Confessor (*Second Century on Love* 17) and the other Fathers, who recognize that having intercourse only for self-gratification falls short of the mark of a holy Christian life. Marital sexuality must be other-regarding: marital sexuality should express not only the mutual love of husband and wife, but also be located within the pursuit of salvation.

As St. John Chrysostom also emphasizes, the carnal union of marriage properly achieves not just reproduction or pleasure, but the union of husband and wife: their becoming one flesh, one union. Marriage exists because it is not good for man to be alone. Marriage has God's blessing even when children are not possible.

What then? when there is no child, will they not be two? Nay, for their coming together hath this effect it diffuses and commingles the bodies of both. And as one who hath cast ointment into oil, hath made the whole one; so in truth is it also here. ... Why art thou ashamed of the honorable, why blushest thou at the undefiled?[36]

As already noted, the Church blesses marriages of couples even at an age when reproduction would be nothing less than miraculous. Indeed, St. John Chrysostom acknowledges that the command in Genesis to be fruitful and multiply (Gen 1:28) has in general been adequately obeyed.

Marriage does not always lead to child-bearing, although there is the word of God which says, "Be fruitful and multiply, and fill the earth." We have as witnesses all those who are married but childless. So the purpose of chastity takes precedence, especially now, when the world is filled with our kind. At the beginning, the procreation of children was desirable, so that person might leave a memorial of his life. ... But now that resurrection is at our gates, and we do not speak of death, but advance toward another life better than the present, the desire for posterity is superfluous.[37]

Marriage provides the appropriate expression of sexual desire in the union of husband and wife, even when reproduction is not achieved.

The Church brings together these diverse insights regarding marriage, which provide not just for reproduction or the avoidance of fornication, but most centrally companionship. The Church recognizes that, although marriage was instituted for reproduction, men and women have legitimate sexual interests within marriage other than reproduction, which interests are rendered appropriate by being made integral to the companionship of husband and wife in their struggle to salvation. Though marriage was instituted so that children could be procreated, this purpose is set within a union of man and woman, which is encompassing in its direction to holiness. The goal of each marriage and of each sexual act in marriage need not be reproduction (e.g., couples who because of age can no longer reproduce) but should always be nested in a context that leads beyond the carnal to God. Marriage can always realize the purpose of the relation of Adam and Eve before the Fall, that man should not be alone: marriage provides mutual love and support in the Christian life, rendering the family a small church. Still, after the Fall, this companionship will usually involve carnal union marked by strong desire.[38] The energies of sexuality even within marriage will challenge salvation if they are not directed through the mystery of marriage toward God.

The Church recognizes the importance of rightly satisfying the mutual desire of husband and wife. Given the demanding character of sexual need, both husband and wife have a unique reciprocal and equal authority over each other in sexual matters. "Let the husband render due goodwill to the wife, and likewise also the wife to the husband. The wife hath not authority over her own body, but the husband; and likewise also the husband hath not authority over his own body, but the wife" (I Cor 7:3-4).[39] It is for this reason that the third canon of St. Dionysius the Alexandrian (†265) declares: "Persons who are self-sufficient and married ought to be judges of themselves. For we are told in writing by St. Paul that it is fitting that they should abstain from each other by agreement for a time, in order that they may indulge in prayer, and again come together (I Cor 7:5)."[40] Traditional Christianity provides what is for many paradoxical: sexual asceticism. Asceticism in marriage, as with respect to food and drink, has always been understood as integral to the struggle to holiness: enjoyment without being distracted by a self-indulgence that turns one's heart from God. Christians have always kept fasts, even with mutual consent fasts from sexual engagement (I Cor 2:5). Indeed, Chrysostom presumes this is the usual practice. "[T]he many abstain even from their wives when it be a season of fast or prayer...."[41] The goal is to delight in God's creation without being mastered by this delight, to find in this enjoyment rightly taken an opportunity through which to pass beyond this enjoyment to His Kingdom, to paradise where there will be neither marriage nor giving in marriage and surely no carnal union.

In all of this, carnal marriage is blessed, as is the goodness of food and drink, as the following illustrates.

> If any Bishop, or Presbyter, or Deacon, or anyone at all on the sacerdotal life, abstains from marriage, or meat, or wine, not as a matter of mortification, but out of an abhorrence thereof, forgetting that all things are exceedingly good, and that God made man male and female, and blasphemously misrepresenting God's work of creation, either let him mend his ways or let him be deposed from office and expelled from the Church. Let a layman be treated similarly.[42]

From the first centuries, the Church has had both to condemn through its fasts[43] a construal of marriage that placed sexuality outside of the ascetic journey to God, while on the other hand condemning those who would consider marital sexuality as itself defiling. The early canons reflect this balancing that required the Church to emphasize the blessedness of marriage, and in particular the undefiled character of the marriage bed (Heb 13:4). The Council of Gangra in A.D. 340, for instance, declares in its first canon that "If anyone disparages marriage, or abominates or disparages a woman sleeping with her husband, notwithstanding that she is faithful and reverent, as though she could not enter the Kingdom, let him be anathema."[44] In 692 the universal Church had even to condemn the Church of Rome's proscription of married priests continuing to sleep with their wives.

> Since we have learned that in the church of the Romans it is regarded as tantamount to a canon that ordinands to the deaconry or presbytery must solemnly promise to have no further intercourse with their wives. Continuing, however, in conformity with the ancient canon of apostolic rigorism and orderliness, we desire that henceforward the lawful marriage ties of sacred men become stronger, and we are nowise dissolving their intercourse with their wives, nor depriving them of their mutual relationship and companionship when properly maintained in due season, so that if anyone is found to be worthy to be ordained a Subdeacon, or a Deacon, or a Presbyter, let him nowise be prevented from being elevated to such a rank while cohabiting with a lawful wife. Nor must he be required at the time of ordination to refrain from lawful intercourse with his own wife, lest we be forced to be downright scornful of marriage, which was instituted by God and blessed by His presence, as attested by the unequivocal declaration of the Gospel utterance: "What therefore God hath joined together, let no man put asunder" (Matt 19:6); and the Apostle's teaching: "Marriage is honorable, and the bed is undefiled" (Heb 13:4), and: "Art thou bound unto a wife? seek not to be free" (I Cor 7:27). ... If, therefore, anyone acting contrary to the Apostolic Canons require any person who is in sacred orders – any Presbyter, we mean, or Deacon, or Subdeacon – to

abstain from intercourse and association with his lawful wife, let him be
deposed from office. Likewise, if any Presbyter or Deacon expel his own
wife on the pretext of reverence, let him be excommunicated; and if he
persist, let him be deposed from office.[45]

As this canon stresses, sexuality as mutual relationship and companionship is affirmed.
Its role is affirmed in the mutual support of husband and wife in their ascetic struggle
so that they can in the end overcome the passions and achieve sanctification.

The Fathers knew that after the Fall, because human energies can no longer be
easily controlled, reproduction is usually a matter as much touched by passion as by
free choice. Man is embedded in the cycle of pleasure and pain.[46] Yet sexual desire
within marriage, in contrast to misdirected desire, is not condemned.

> Thus ... desire is not sin: but when it has run into extravagance, being not
> minded to keep within the laws of marriage, but springing even upon
> other men's wives; then the thing henceforward becomes adultery, yet not
> by reason of the desire, but by reason of its exorbitancy.[47]

Though virginity is esteemed more highly than marriage, still, as St. Gregory the
Theologian stresses, marriage is fully honored.

> Art thou not yet wedded to flesh? Fear not this consecration; thou art pure
> even after marriage. I will take the risk of that. I will join you in wedlock.
> I will dress the bride. We do not dishonour marriage because we give a
> higher honour to virginity. I will imitate Christ, the pure Groomsman and
> Bridegroom, as He both wrought a miracle at a wedding, and honours
> wedlock with His Presence. Only let marriage be pure and unmingled with
> filthy lusts.[48]

Following St. John Chrysostom in his thirteenth homily on Romans, the lusts condemned do not include the proper mutual desire of husband and wife, but adulterous
desire. Instead, in marriage all is to be directed as in a kind of micro-church where
Adam and Eve in mutual love turn in mutual prayer to God.

Sexuality: Rightly and Wrongly Directed

The Church of the first millennium gives major accent to the bond between sexuality
and reproduction without placing marital sexuality within a natural law understanding
grounded in a philosophical account of natural inclinations or of biological teleologies.
To understand human sexual obligations in such terms would be to ground human
moral conduct in fallen nature.[49] If one attempted to read human sexual morality from
the findings of an Aristotelian, Scholastic, or even post-Darwinian sociobiological
account of human sexuality, one would ironically be attempting an account of how to
approach God in terms of nature after the Fall, in terms of the consequences of the sin
of Adam, the array of inclinations salient in a broken human nature, rather than in

terms of the telos of all teleologies: the Kingdom of God. The Christian bioethics of sexuality places carnal union within the mystery of marriage, which is a way to holiness. The focus is on a relationship established in paradise and which will be restored to paradise. A merely biological account would obscure the central telos: God.

The traditional Christian account of marriage takes human embodiment seriously, without reducing appropriate marital sexual behavior to merely biological terms. St. Paul, for example, warns: "Or know ye not that he that is joined to the harlot is one body? For, 'The two,' saith He, 'shall be into one flesh'" (I Cor 6:16). An illicit sexual union is not evil just because promiscuity dissipates intimacy and ignores responsibility. There is also an appreciation of the significance of becoming one flesh and an acknowledgement that the proper carnal union is marital. The embodied union of husband and wife is affirmed, without developing a biological account of natural and unnatural acts. There is an acknowledgement of the embodied importance of carnal union because to accomplish this union falsely in varying degrees alters those involved. Carnal unions have ontological significance. "Keep on fleeing fornication. Every sin whatsoever a man might do is outside the body; but he who commiteth fornication sinneth against his own body" (I Cor 6:18). Wrongly directed carnal unions (*porneia*) are morally and metaphysically disabling by deflecting from the pursuit of holiness and union with God. Because we in our embodied wholeness approach God, how we act with our bodies affects us spiritually.

Natural law is, after all, the spark of God's love in our nature,[50] not the biological state of affairs we find in broken nature. Natural law is not an objective external constraint, but the will of the living God experienced in our conscience. It is this natural law, the law of God in our nature, which calls for carnal sexuality to be accomplished only within marriage. Anything else is unnatural in violating the law God established in Eden and renewed through Christ. Fornication, adultery, masturbation, bestiality, and homosexual acts are condemned in these terms as unnatural to the union of husband and wife, all without such behaviors being placed within a discursive philosophical justification for holding certain acts to be natural and unnatural. Such a discursive account could not penetrate to the spiritual realities that are central to the issue. Unnatural sexual acts are those that in various degrees go against the normative union of Adam and Eve. It is by reference to the affirmation of marriage experienced and celebrated in the Tradition that Christianity possesses a canonical basis for terming certain sexual desires, urges, acts, and unions unnatural, deviant, and perverse. These are not judgments about the unnaturalness, perversity, or deviance of acts in a secularly biological or medical sense of those behaviors constituting unsuccessful adaptations by reference to either inclusive fitness or personal fulfillment. The Christian moral-theological reference point for the appropriateness of sexual behavior is the creation of humans as male and female and the restoration of the union of Adam and Eve in the Mystery of matrimony.

This recognition that by the nature of our creation sexual relations should only occur between husband and wife is not to obscure, much less deny, the special recognition, following St. Paul, that certain sexual activities such as homosexual relations are profoundly unnatural.

> For this reason God gave them up to passions of dishonor. For both their
> females exchanged the natural use into that contrary to nature, and in like

manner also the males left the natural use of the female, and were burned
up in their lust one toward another, males with males working out that
which is unseemly, and receiving in themselves the recompense which was
fitting of their error (Rom 1:26-27).

Nor is this to deny that sexual union with an animal is similarly doubly unnatural
through fully disengaging sexuality from the union of man and woman, not just from
the marriage bed.[51] The law of God found in our nature and announced in Genesis and
the Gospels is to be found in the union of husband and wife. In these terms, fornication
and adultery are unnatural. Sexual acts are condemned by reference to the creation of
humans as male and female, by reference to a revelation that discloses the Mystery of
marriage which blesses the carnal union of husband and wife.

The world in which we find ourselves due to the Fall is broken at its roots so that
the history of the evolution of human sexuality is itself radically unnatural, deviant,
and perverse (e.g., human history has a character determined by sin), so that fornication, adultery, and homosexual acts may in certain circumstances maximize inclusive
fitness.[52] There may be no basis whatsoever in secular medical terms to hold homosexuality to be a form of illness, disease, or disability, or to count homosexuality as
biologically deviant or perverse. Homosexuality, adultery, and fornication may in the
context of this world be biologically normal and wholesome in the sense of being
adaptive. That is, they may appear as expected and even proper behaviors, given an
immanent horizon of concerns and a secular understanding of human evolutionary
history.[53] This Christian focus is not on health and disease in a secular biological or
medical sense of what in terms of secular assumptions can be recognized as requiring
treatment (though this does not foreclose the endorsement of psychological and medical treatment to help overcome deviant urges).[54] Secular concepts of health and disease
are set within liberal cosmopolitan moral and value commitments to the goals of
human adaptation, which go contrary to those of traditional Christianity. It is these
goals of successful adaptation in fully immanent terms that define secular understandings of health and disease. Health and disease are defined by reference to a particular
environment and the goals of adaptation.[55] Traditional Christians recognize the reference environment for humans to be Eden, and the goal of all adaptation to be the
pursuit of holiness. In particular, the focus for appropriate sexuality is provided in
Christ's affirmation of the creation of humans as male and female (Matt 19:4-6) and in
the Church's recognition of their union as holy (Eph 5:22-32). It is for this reason, as
already noted, that carnal desires other than between husband and wife are unnatural
in being disordered, as aiming away from salvation. Homosexual desires, unions, and
acts are signally deviant in radically directing sexuality away from its only appropriate
expression: the union of husband and wife. For traditional Christianity, terms such as
deviant and perverse have deep meaning, given the recognition of the goal of human
life: the recognition that certain actions lead away from holiness. Desires, unions, and
acts are perverse when they misdirect sexual affection, energies, and interest in ways
that in the knowledge of the Church lead away from union with God.

Masturbation has also been recognized as sexuality misdirected, and therefore unnatural, but as at least not involving a misdirected carnal union. The fleshly union of
carnal intercourse has metaphysical weight: "the two shall be into one flesh" (Mark

10:8). Though a wrongful act that misdirects sexuality, masturbation does not achieve a wrongful union. Therefore, it is understandable that with regard to masturbation the canon of St. John the Faster requires only an excommunication for 40 days: "Anyone having committed masturbation is penanced forty days, during which he must keep himself alive by xerophagy and must do one hundred metanies every day."[56] Indeed, even mutual masturbation, because it does not involve an illicit union, receives only a penance of 80 days: "As for sexual intercourse of men with one another, such as practicing double masturbation, it received the stated penance of up to eighty days."[57] The canon recognizes that, although masturbation is sexuality misdirected, it does not involve an even worse act, a misdirected joining in one flesh. This point is also implicit in the canon that specifies: "But as for women, too, if any of them has allowed herself to be kissed and felt by man, without, however, being ravished by him, let her receive the penance provided for masturbation."[58] Sexuality outside of marriage without a physical union, although unnaturally engaging in sexuality outside of the marital bed and although seriously wrong, still avoids a false union.

In summary, fornication involves going against nature by taking a companion not one's own, while adultery adds the injustice of taking the companion of another and the evil of breaking the purity of a union blessed by God. A union with a member of the same sex or with an animal involves fully misdirecting carnal union not just away from the joining of husband and wife, but from that of male and female. The canons of the Church reflect an appreciation of the embodied character of humans, without invoking an account of natural law that roots natural law in the character of our fallen biology. Instead, there is a focus on a biblically affirmed truth: sexuality is directed to the union of husband and wife in one flesh for the purpose of bearing children and companionship in a mutual relationship that will in the end lead beyond passion. This complex appreciation of sexuality is articulated without invoking biological teleologies. Its final ground is in marriage being the presentation of the unique union of Christ with the Church so that fornication, adultery, and sodomy have the character of idolatry.

Anal intercourse may appear to be a counter-example in favor of a biologically oriented account of unnatural acts. Canon XIX of St. John the Faster specifies that "A boy who has been ruined in front of any man cannot come into holy orders. For although on account of his immature age he did not sin himself, yet his vessel was rent and became useless in connection with sacred services. If, however, he received the ejaculation between his thighs, after being suitably penanced he shall not be barred from preferment to holy orders."[59] Rather than inviting a philosophical account of biologically unnatural behavior (both actions must be construed as unnatural), the canon invites an appreciation of defilement, of an injury that can have an impact on one's heart. It involves as well an appreciation of how those who will come closest to that which is holy (i.e., priests) can in that measure be set at risk by the unholy.[60] There is a recognition of harms that may not be fully cured in this world. At stake is an appreciation of the moral significance of penetration for carnal union. Also at stake is the recognition of the contrast between vaginal penetration and reception versus anal penetration and reception, the first fulfilling the carnal union of husband and wife even when reproduction is not possible, and the second achieving a merdous and unclean anti-icon of marital union, clearly condemned in the Tradition. Some canons appended by Sts. Agapius (†1812) and Nicodemus (1749-1809) to those of St. John the Faster

(St. John IV Nesteutes, Patriarch of Constantinople, +595) provide a further appreciation of wrongly directed sexual embodiment through the contrast in the penancing of the illicit sexual relations that can perhaps be performed without a penis or at least an erectable penis (i.e., depending on the age at which the person was castrated and on whether the castration was radical, involving removal of both testes and penis) and the condemnation of anal intercourse even in marriage.[61] "If any woman shall lie with a eunuch, she shall be penanced for three years, faring the while with xerophagy after the ninth hour and doing three hundred genuflections daily. If any man perform arsenocoetia upon his wife, he shall be penanced for eight years, faring the while with xerophagy after the ninth hour and doing two hundred metanies daily."[62] A woman's illicit relationship with a eunuch appears to be treated as a species of simple fornication, despite the likely peculiarity of many such carnal unions.[63]

Misdirected sexual activity does spiritual harm, even if in some sense involuntary, because passion has a compelling force. It is for this reason, as we will see in chapter 6, that Christians have traditionally been allowed to leap to their deaths rather than be sexually violated. Traditional Christianity recognizes sins that are "involuntary" and "of ignorance".[64] Even if there were illicit sexual behaviors that are "genetically determined" so that those who engage in them "do not choose their lifestyle" (e.g., lifestyles shaped from a compulsion to commit adultery or engage in homosexual acts), still those behaviors and lifestyles remain sinful: they disorient from the pursuit of holiness. They would be sins, albeit involuntary. Such behaviors require repentance even when they cannot be controlled. At least at the second order of volition, one must wholeheartedly repent of such behavior: "I know I cannot control myself, but I mourn and repent of my weakness, asking God's forgiveness and aid to flee what I lack the strength to avoid."[65] If one lacks self-control, one must seek circumstances where such lack of control will cause as little harm as possible. One may even be obliged to flee to the wilderness or to a monastery to limit the opportunities to act on such lusts. The often despair-ridden and desperate pursuit of satisfaction, consolation, and love that characterizes much search for intimacy must be relocated in terms of the pursuit of the kingdom of God. Traditional Christian sexual morality shows that the direction back to healing and salvation for those who will engage in carnal sexuality lies only in the marriage of a man and a woman, the union of Adam and Eve, and in wholehearted repentance for and repudiation of all sexual urges and expressions that deviate from this norm. The dignity of those who find themselves in lifestyles that deviate from this norm is expressed in their ability to repent wholeheartedly.

Because the focus should be on orienting one's energies to God, one's attitude to sinners must be one of love, though one must condemn their sin. That is, the Christian must never judge the sinner in the sense of having a view as to whether any particular sinner will find salvation or damnation. The commandment to love others as oneself (Matt 19:19) requires one to love others who are sinners, for one is oneself a sinner who needs mercy. One must respond to sinners only out of full and compassionate love. To respond in any other way would be to compound the sin of another with one's own sins of arrogance, pride, and judgment. Still, out of love for the other, one owes him the truth: that sin is real and that it can only be overcome through repentance, ascetic struggle, and the grace of God. Because the focus is on the act rather than the actor, on the sin rather than the sinner, there is much to be said in many circumstances in favor of avoiding reifying terms such as fornicator, adulterer, or homosexual. As to the last term, one must recognize that, for many, homosexual acts are often only some among many sexual sins in the maelstrom of passions that direct away from the proper expression of human sexuality. In the disordered experience of human sexuality after the Fall, sinful heterosexual and homosexual acts are frequently intertwined in the passion-broken struggle to love God and others properly. Reifications (e.g., referring to sinners as adulterers, fornicators, etc., that is, in terms of a sinful lifestyle that characterizes their identity) may spring from an uncharitable judgment of the sinner (e.g., unloving characterizations of repentant sinners in terms of their sins). Yet such reifications when used with humble love can at times help call attention to how such sins radically distort our lives. Finally, reifications may also be grounded in some sinners seeking to affirm their way of sin as integral to their very identity. On the one hand, as a form of repentance and a petition for the prayers of others it may be appropriate and courageous for those who had engaged in fornication, adultery, bestiality or homosexual acts to identify themselves as captivated by a sin of a particular sort. On the other hand, it would be morally perverse to ask for affirmation of one's immoral acts and dispositions. Affirming others in their lifestyles as adulterers, fornicators, homosexuals, etc., would be to affirm a sinful lifestyle, and this would be wrong.[66] Rather, one must with love affirm all in their struggle from sin to salvation.

In summary, traditional Christianity recognizes that the appropriate focus of all sexuality is on the carnal union of husband and wife – anything else falls short of the mark by being both unnatural and sinful, by involving a turning from the pursuit of holiness. Such acts are condemned because they are outside of or go against marriage as a Mystery of the Church that brings union with God. As one turns to examine issues of bioethics bearing on human sexuality, one finds human sexuality set fully within: (1) the marriage of (2) a man and a woman, which (3) is realized truly only within the Mystery of the Church, which (4) affirms marital sexuality by (5) placing it within a joyful accompaniment in the ascetic struggle to salvation, such that (6) all sexuality flourishes only within a monogamous union of a man and a woman (7) that has its full physical expression in reproduction, but still can (8) realize its meaning in mutual relationship and companionship in the struggle to salvation even in the absence of the procreation of children.

The Fruitful Union of Adam and Eve: Seeking Help to Reproduce

Marriage is meant to be a fruitful union. In the marriage ceremony the prayer asks for the blessing of many children. Although couples find within wedlock many good and legitimate joys besides children, reproduction and companionship constitute the purpose for the institution.

> Blessed art thou, O Lord our God, the Priest of mystical and pure marriage, and the Ordainer of the law of the marriage of the body, the Preserver of immortality, and the Provider of good things; do thou, the same Master, who in the beginning didst make man and set him to be, as it were, a King over thy creation, and didst say: It is not good for man to be

alone on the earth; let us make a helpmeet for him; and taking one of his ribs didst fashion Woman, which when Adam beheld, he said: This is now bone of my bone, and flesh of my flesh; she shall be called Woman, for she was taken out of man; for this cause shall a man leave father and mother, and shall cleave unto his wife, and the twain shall be one flesh ... Grant them of the fruit of their bodies, fair children, concord of soul and of body: Exalt them like the cedars of Lebanon, like a luxuriant vine. Give them seed in number like unto the full ears of grain...[67]

Because marriage was instituted for companionship and reproduction, many who are childless feel a profound loss. Many are not able to pray and accept their circumstances.

Questions then arise: what ways of assistance in reproduction are morally unproblematic? which are forbidden? and which are burdened by spiritual risks? For a traditional Christian, these questions are posed within a religion that orients everything to seeking the kingdom of heaven, a religion that has for the most part interfered little with marital sexuality,[68] and that has eschewed a biologically oriented account of human sexual morality. It is this traditional appreciation of marriage as companionship that leads to holiness and revelation in the experience of God Who is the source for answers to questions posed by new reproductive technologies. Since this revelation is one and the same over the centuries, a guiding criterion for the truth will be the possibility of embedding current answers to questions within the general mind of the Church expressed in its tradition and recorded within the common teaching of the Fathers. Offering reflections on the spiritual harms involved when in ambiguous contexts physicians and patients step away from the clear assurances of the Tradition is not to endorse those steps. This volume seeks instead to give an analysis of where greater or lesser dangers lurk.

Because the marriage bed is to be undefiled, to be the unique union of husband and wife, the tradition has held that sexuality outside that union is misdirected. Human sexuality is realized in the union of husband and wife, of which vaginal intercourse is the usual completion leading to reproduction. However, vaginal intercourse is not a necessary condition for a marriage. Some saints have lived in companionship with their spouses but with full sexual continence; they are considered married.[69] The failure to consummate a marriage sexually does not annul a marriage.[70] The sacramental source of the marital union is in the blessing of the Church.[71] It is from this focus on the unique union of husband and wife and the understanding of marital sexuality found in the Scriptures, the Fathers, and the unbroken experience of revelation that traditional Christianity addresses new reproductive technologies and the various possibilities for third-party intervention. Traditional Christianity understands the union of husband and wife as the uniquely appropriate locus for (1) the realization of sexual companionship, (2) reproduction, as well as for (3) the satisfaction of sexual desire. Because of this uniqueness, it can be concluded that it is forbidden to make other persons partners in reproduction. One may not allow third parties to enter reproductively into the union of husband and wife. So, for example, the use of artificial insemination by a donor or the use of donor ova is adulterous in this very important sense: a third party would be brought into the unique and sacred reproductive intimacy of husband and wife, which no one should separate. The person providing the gametes to a married couple would have become the biological father or mother of a child of that marriage. Because marriage, when complete, is a union in one flesh, such biological issues have real significance.

On the other hand, there are no grounds to condemn interventions that do not make a third party (1) a parent or (2) a participant in the sexual act. Intrafallopian tube transfer of a wife's ova around a blocked salpynx so as to allow fertilization in intercourse does not interfere in the couple's becoming one flesh through their sexual union, or in their reproduction. It is a pre-reproductive, pre-copulative intervention. Nor does artificial insemination by the husband's sperm involve adultery: no third party is engaged as a parent or a sexual partner. That is, no third party becomes a biological or genetic father or mother by donating gametes or gestating a child. Nor does a third party enter into the sexual act. Still, artificial insemination by the husband does involve various risks of disengaging reproduction from the carnal union of husband and wife.

There is a continuum of spiritual difficulties associated with artificial insemination from a husband. These range from cases where there is little moral difficulty, such as when the semen is collected when the husband ejaculates outside the vagina due to the birth defect hypospadias.[72] The husband in this case may place that otherwise lost sperm into his wife's vagina (even when this procedure is enhanced with the use of an instrument such as a turkey baster): the uniqueness of the carnal union of husband and wife has not been broken and the intimacy of the marital act has not been violated. It should also be allowable to concentrate the husband's sperm by laboratory means prior to its being placed in the wife's vagina by the husband. The least problematic approach in this circumstance would involve collection of sperm from the husband during intercourse using a special condom (one not likely to be toxic to sperm) with the husband then inseminating his wife. Again, in this case a third person does not become a reproductive or sexual party to the couple's union. The most problematic would involve the husband engaging in self-stimulation to produce sperm so as to have a physician then mechanically inseminate the wife. A cardinal element of marriage is union in one flesh. It is from this union in one flesh that children are to come. The canons of the Church in distinguishing the sin of masturbation from fornication also indicate the special character of fleshly marital wedlock: the real union of human flesh. Anything else falls significantly short of the mark in the begetting of children. The more one brings the act of reproduction within the intimacy of the marriage bed, the less one falls short of the mark by preserving the union in one flesh of husband and wife. To have concerns of this sort is to recognize that one has entered into a morally broken arena where all choices save to rely on prayer and God's good grace will often involve one in spiritual harm. To proceed to reflect about this geography of spiritual harms, as this volume now does, is not to endorse these choices but instead to provide warnings of where special dangers lie.

The spiritual difficulties with artificial insemination by the husband are not resolved by mechanically removing sperm from the seminal vesicles for artificial insemination. Reproduction is the fruit of the intimacy of husband and wife. Indeed, this would involve a radical distortion of the carnal intimacy of reproduction. The evocation of sperm, though not of ova, is integral to the pleasurable intimacy of marriage, which St. John Chrysostom praises.[73] The carnal union described by St. John Chrysostom involves the personal intimacy of husband and wife in which the man is aroused by desire for his wife, in which she receives his semen with pleasure and then nurtures their child in her body, all of which is undertaken with love for God as its cardinal point of orientation. It is important that one recognize the synergy of body and soul in all human actions, but here with sexuality and reproduction in particular. Traditional Christianity regards the separation of soul and body as unnatural. It appreciates that attempts to deny the intimate unity of body and soul distort human life. The very fabric of worship marries sight, smell, taste, touch, kinesthetic sensations, and hearing in a symphony of body, soul, and spirit in the worship of God. Its elements should not be severed, separated, or their union denied or distorted.

The full union of flesh, the sexual act of marriage, involves a mutual response of bodies: the arousal of the husband, the pleasurable reception by the wife, and her nurturing of their child. This intimacy of love for each other and for their child, directed to God, defines the appropriate orientation of the marital union. Sexuality and reproduction involve this embodied mutuality which should be maintained as far as possible even in borderline cases, when couples desperately seek to have a child of their own. So as not to fall too short from the mark, too far from the path that leads us securely to the kingdom of God, one should at least avoid whatever separates the usual undertakings of the marital bed. Borderline cases in our broken world often include tragic circumstances, in which couples will nevertheless seek to reproduce, as when the husband is a paraplegic and the wife employs technologically supported means to stimulate her husband to produce semen, by which he then inseminates her. Such undertakings are not ideal and must as far as possible maintain the carnal intimacy of marriage. Nor is the broken character of this world as it should be. The successful pursuit of reproduction in our fallen world often requires counter-balancing a strong desire to reproduce, which sustains and fills a marriage, over against means that fall short but not wide of the mark.

The intimacy of the evocation of the husband by the wife and of the wife by the husband, the wife's reception of her husband's semen, and the wife's nurturing of their child within her own womb characterize the union in one flesh of husband and wife: beyond this union one falls far wide of the mark. No one other than the wife may stimulate the husband without involving a form of adultery. No one other than the husband may penetrate the wife to introduce semen into the wife, especially semen of someone other than the husband, without committing a form of adultery. Nor may someone other than the wife nurture a child in her womb for the husband without adulterating the intimacy of the marital union, without improperly introducing a third party into the intimacy of their union which involves not just the sexuality of carnal conversation but that of reproductive sexuality which nurtures the fruit of that conversation. In all these ways, the significance of embodiment in the intimacy of wedlock should be acknowledged. This consideration gives grounds for at least the wife always being the one to stimulate the husband, and the husband always being the one who pushes the plunger to inseminate the wife. Surely, the ideal is to trust in God and with prayer, fasting, and humility to seek God's miraculous help and not to engage in any activity that may sunder the intimacy and sacredness of the marriage bed.[74]

Since a cardinal reason for the institution of marriage is reproduction,[75] some activities on behalf of procreating a child that fall just shy of the mark can fairly easily be reoriented to God through repentance, or at least through sincerely mourning that one has acted in a spiritually flawed fashion. At the very least, one must avoid endorsing a regrettable exception to the norm, that is, one must recognize that one is acting in a way that involves implication in evil, even when one still acts in that fashion. One must at least acknowledge that one's act falls short of the mark. This recognition must be combined with mourning so as to redirect one's heart toward God. Finally, in all cases, actions should fall with certain very important limits which preserve the unity of husband and wife in one flesh. In particular, third-party-assisted reproduction should not involve (1) gametes from outside the marriage, (2) stimulation to produce sperm other than by intercourse or at least by the wife, (3) a party other than the husband placing the husband's sperm in the wife, or (4) some other person besides the wife nurturing the gestating child. In such circumstances, one has at least avoided introducing a third party directly into the reproductive act while still maintaining the experience of sexuality within the mutuality of husband and wife. Under such conditions, traditional Christian health care professionals need not decline to be involved, though they should strongly recommend that the couple seek spiritual guidance so that their struggle to have a child does not distract from their pursuit of the Kingdom of God, does not cause them great spiritual harm.[76] Health professionals should themselves also seek guidance. The concern is not simply to follow particular rules or to avoid improper actions. The driving concern must be to place any attempt to reproduce fully within a prayerful pursuit of the kingdom of heaven. The attempt to overcome sterility can become all-consuming. It can be a passion that not only distracts from the mutuality and companionship of husband and wife. It can also become a stumbling block in the struggle to salvation. It is important that technological and third-party assistance not deflect the orientation of the marriage from God.

To summarize in somewhat different terms, third-party-assisted reproduction must (1) maintain a focus on holiness, (2) not involve third parties as parents, (3) not significantly displace reproduction from the intimacy of the husband and the wife, (4) not displace the nurturing of their child from the body of the wife, and (5) not put the children produced at significant risk of death, a point to which we will turn presently. *In vitro* fertilization and embryo transfer in their various forms, as well as other third-party-assisted forms of reproduction, must be judged primarily in these terms. In this context, concerns regarding the formation of a zygote outside of a woman's womb take on a special character. There must be an attention to (1) the extent to which the engagement of laboratories and third parties overbears the couple by technologically transforming their reproductive act in a way that turns their hearts away from God and instead towards themselves and human power, (2) whether this engagement transforms the mutuality and companionship of husband and wife by an all-consuming passion to have a child, (3) whether sperm and/or ova other than from the married couple are used, (4) whether the husband's sperm used is acquired from other than a sexual act involving the marital partners, and (5) whether all zygotes formed are placed in the wife and only in the wife.

Since conception occurs outside of the wife with *in vitro* fertilization, there is a significant spiritual brokenness: the marital bed has been disrupted, but perhaps not very seriously. Reproductive and unitive sexual functions have been separated. Such a separation is very pronounced in interventions such as partial zona pellucida dissection, in which sperm from the husband are placed into ova from the wife in order to form a zygote. The wrong in such technologically and third-party mediated reproduction is not fully that of adultery, because the child to be born is flesh and blood of the married couple. In addition, the husband's semen can be secured through the intimacy of their love. Also, to introduce semen the wife is not penetrated by someone other than the husband. Reproduction in these important senses has been maintained within the bonds of marriage. The experience of marital sexuality associated with reproduction can still occur within the intimacy of the marriage bed (e.g., the semen can be collected by the use of a special condom during intercourse). What is awry is that conception occurs outside of the body of the wife. Still, *in vitro* fertilization allows the birth of a child, the fruit of the bodies of husband and wife. That the dissociation of unitive and reproductive sexuality is not ideal, that such reproduction falls short of the mark, should be recognized and sincerely lamented, as one should lament if one lies directly and intentionally to save another's life.[77] Yet, *in vitro* fertilization is not something for which one may have grounds strongly and without exception to forbid the involvement of Christian couples or health care professionals. The intervention does not seriously violate the integrity of marriage as a unique reproductive and carnal union.

The most obvious moral issue at stake in *in vitro* fertilization is associated with the production of "excess" zygotes and early embryos that are at risk of being frozen and/or discarded. To understand the seriousness of this technological distortion of reproduction, one must first determine how to regard the moral status of these zygotes and early embryos. One must recognize that a great number of zygotes in the ordinary course of natural reproduction never implant. This number may be as high as 50%, if not more, as has been shown for a number of years.[78] The Liturgy of St. Basil speaks not of conception but of each man from his mother's womb. "O God, who knowest the age and the name of each, and knowest every man even from his mother's womb."[79] To be a person is to be a being whose proper destiny in theosis. What of the zygote or early embryo before it is or would have been in the womb? What of the circumstance that, because of the high loss of zygotes and early embryos, human biological life at this stage may not be of the sort that inevitably leads to the life of a person? As St. Basil the Great holds, a person is

> a murderer who kills an imperfect and unformed embryo, because this though not yet then a complete being was nevertheless destined to be perfected in the future, according to indispensable sequence of the laws of nature.[80]

On the one hand, one must be careful to follow the injunction of St. Basil not to split hairs as to when there is a soul, a person.[81] Yet, on the other hand, while regarding the non-implantation of "excess" zygotes and early embryos as a serious moral matter, it may be appropriate to consider the wrong as not fully equivalent to abortion, especially when no direct violence is done against these zygotes and early embryos. One has entered into a broken area of human biology whose problematic character is brought into sharp highlight by technology.

The use of a surrogate mother would involve such a serious violation. In the case where a surrogate mother is inseminated with the sperm of the husband, there is reproductive adultery. The husband has reproduced outside the union of husband and wife. He has used a woman other than his wife to bear him a child. Where the surrogate mother is a gestational surrogate, where the husband and wife produce a zygote from their sperm and ovum and then have it implanted in another woman, one has separated motherhood from marriage. Because humans are male and female by God's creation, one may not through technological interventions change the fundamental character of their embodied differences or the significance of those differences for reproduction, for their being as fathers and mothers, and for their unity in one flesh through marriage. In particular, one may not alter the centrality to child-bearing of *in vivo* motherhood by bringing motherhood outside of marriage by using another woman as the gestational mother for a couple, or in the future by completely replacing motherhood through *in vitro* gestation, should such become possible. The man and the woman joined in one flesh in marriage would have had their reproductive significance as a pair altered. All interventions to allow reproduction must maintain not just the reproductive integrity (i.e., no donor gametes) and carnal integrity of marriage (i.e., the husband's semen must be procured from a sexual act of the couple), but also gestational integrity. For example, St. John Chrysostom regards the wife's gestation of the child as integral to the intimacy of marriage. "So in truth here also the woman as it were receiving the richest part fused by pleasure, nourisheth it and cherisheth it, and withal contributing her own share, restoreth it back a Man."[82] A special incarnate moral unity is recognized. The wife of the father of the child should be the mother of their child in the full sense. She should nurture their child in her womb. Motherhood may not be exported from the marriage. A woman may not be involved in motherhood who is not the wife of the man whose child she is carrying.

The goal of maintaining the reproductive, sexual, and gestational union of husband and wife need not totally foreclose (1) forming a zygote outside the wife's womb in order that the married couple may have a child (i.e., *in vitro* fertilization), (2) forming or briefly taking the zygote or early embryo outside of the womb for genetic therapy, or (3) transferring the fetus to an artificial womb if there is premature delivery, if such technology becomes available in the future. As already noted, *in vitro* fertilization and embryo transfer do involve a dissociation of elements of sexuality so that it falls short of the mark by impairing and disrupting the intimate integrity of marital reproductive sexuality: fertilization occurs outside the wife. But this does not entail non-involvement of the wife in gestating the children procreated by the couple. Some married couples may be able to use such means to have a child without great spiritual harm, especially if they sincerely mourn the means they use. In the second case in particular, that of *in vitro* fertilization for genetic therapy, a similar answer can be given. This would involve a distortion of reproduction, but one undertaken on behalf of the health of the child, all without violating some very important bounds of marital and gestational integrity. Surely, the couple could at least in theory have raised a less healthy child; yet the parents may be passionately committed to assisting their child as much as possible, while mournfully and without excessive pride in human power using reproductive technology to secure the child's health. The third case, transferring a prematurely delivered fetus to an artificial womb, limits the gestational involvement of the mother to save the life of her child, but without totally eliminating her involvement. However, it must be stressed that, in order to avoid (1) even more serious sundering of the intimacy of human reproduction and (2) actions against early human life, couples should not produce more zygotes than can be at once implanted in the woman's uterus. Moreover, to avoid further harms (e.g., the discarding of excess embryos or the implantation of an embryo in a wife after the death of her husband), should excess embryos be produced, the couple should then be obliged to have them implanted over time in the wife as soon as this is medically prudent. A couple who has produced excess embryos, so as not to be guilty of abortion, likely has a *prima facie* obligation to have children every year or so until all the embryos are given an opportunity to be born.

At stake in the gestational integrity of marriage are not impersonal natural law constraints, but a moral and spiritual orientation to a personal God Who requires locating childbearing within the intimacy of the marital union. Any partial departures from this intimacy in order better to maintain the marital union or to achieve childbearing may only be undertaken with prayer, regret, repentance, and spiritual guidance. The goal must always be to unite marital sexuality, reproduction, and embodiment in the mutual love of the marital couple, their love for their child, and their love of God. Human embodiment provides and defines a sphere of intimacy, union, and tenderness. The achievement of this intimacy through human embodiment has implications even for the issue of nursing. One should not avoid breast-feeding through bottle feeding or wet nurses simply out of concerns for convenience or attractiveness, thus depriving a child without good cause of the special intimacy of this relationship with its mother. Concerns for mere convenience or attractiveness go against the traditional spirit of Christian asceticism: the renunciation of distractions from the selfless love of God and others. Bottle-feeding and wet-nursing may by necessity of health or of other circumstances be unavoidable or nearly unavoidable (although wet-nursing runs the risk of exposing the child to infectious diseases). As far as possible, one should not undermine the special maternal intimacies of nourishing a child within the family. These considerations also bear very strongly against an unmarried woman's being hormonally induced to be a wet-nurse.

One must as well be especially cautious in responding to charitable offers by women to rescue embryos. One might imagine a science fictional circumstance under which an embryo or fetus could no longer be sustained by its mother (e.g., because of the death of the mother) but could be saved by another woman, if taken into her womb. Were this done to save the life of the child, this might be regarded as an extreme example of wet-nursing to save an infant's life. Still, to enter into pregnancy outside of marriage is to set aside the bond of husband and wife, the union of Adam and Eve, which is the sole appropriate locus for human reproduction.[83] By becoming a gestational mother, even for the best of motives, one willfully reproduces outside of the union of husband and wife. Surrogate motherhood, even if undertaken in order to rescue an unborn child, would still involve a significant dissociation of reproduction from the unity of marriage. Though the acceptance of zygotes for surrogate gestation could be interpreted as the saving of early human life, one must avoid immoral actions, even if these will save the life of others. The matter is further encumbered by the ambiguous character of life before it is or could have been in the mother's womb. Because, as we will see, the canons forbid killing, expelling, or poisoning early human life, killing a zygote will count as an abortion. The direct character of such killing will involve spiritual harm. Since many, if not most, zygotes are lost in the natural course of reproduction, actions "to save" such life cannot be on a par with the action to save a child in the mother's womb. This asymmetry between acting and refraining, which will be examined further in chapter 6, gives a further strong consideration against attempts to "rescue" zygotes and early embryos, since such "rescue" involves the spiritual harm of sundering reproduction from the unity of marriage.

The considerations are most strong against rescuing zygotes from *in vitro* fertilization clinics when they would otherwise be discarded. At stake would not usually be the rescue of zygotes conceived *in vitro* for a husband and wife for immediate implantation, but which for some unforeseen reason cannot be implanted in the wife (e.g., because of her death). Such a case does not approximate the transfer of a fetus to the womb of another woman from a woman unable to carry the pregnancy further, if the embryo is not at a stage when it would have been in its mother's womb. In addition, the attempt to rescue zygotes from *in vitro* fertilization clinics adds the harm of implication in the practice by many couples of producing more zygotes than can at once be implanted, leading to an accumulation of unimplanted zygotes. Such a practice directly places at risk early human life. Though acting to rescue unimplanted embryos surely appears benevolent, such a rescue requires an intimate involvement as a gestational mother in a circumstance that should not have occurred in the first place: the production of zygotes beyond the number that can be implanted at once. Traditional Christianity has condemned all direct acts injurious to unborn children, as this chapter's section on abortion will show. In addition, such gestational "rescue" surrogacy is a further step in routinizing forms of reproduction that fall short of the mark. As already noted, all cases of *in vitro* fertilization involve a falling short of the mark. Even when zygotes are not produced beyond the number that can at once be implanted, there is still a dissociation of the unitive and reproductive dimensions of sexuality. Because of the intimate relation of husband and wife as the context for procreation, all forms of technologically assisted reproduction that endanger or sunder this intimacy fall short of the mark of how sexuality and reproduction should be undertaken. The intimate union of husband and wife blessed by the mystery of marriage provides grounds against *in vitro* fertilization, as already noted. It also provides very strong grounds for not producing zygotes beyond those to be implanted at once: the storage of zygotes should never be a part of aiding reproduction. It is not just that such procedures place at risk early human life, should implantation not be possible. The storage of zygotes for future implantation also radically separates in time the act of reproduction and the act of sexual intimacy. No such separation, or at the most very little such separation, should ever be tolerated. When separation does occur, it should be minimal and, as has been emphasized, sincerely mourned. Benevolently serving as a gestational mother for another's zygote or embryo only makes this worse.

Similar considerations regarding the integrity of marital sexual intimacy and reproduction also weigh very strongly, indeed absolutely, against the use of gametes from a married partner who has died. There will be circumstances when, because of interventions such as cancer chemotherapy, reproduction should be delayed until after treatment in order to protect any child that would be conceived from possible direct harm *in utero* from the treatment or from the impact of the treatment on the gametes. A couple in such circumstances may wish to store sperm from the husband or ova from the wife unaffected by chemotherapy or radiation (i.e., prior to treatment), in order in the future to have children. Reproduction using stored gametes falls short of the mark of the appropriate unity of human sexuality and reproduction by significantly separating sexual intimacy from reproduction. But it does not involve the very serious wrong of reproducing after the death of a spouse or with someone other than the spouse. One may not have sex with one's spouse after the spouse's death, for death ends carnal union. After death, there is no joining in one flesh (Matt 22:29-32). The use of gametes after the death of the spouse involves a reproductive act after the fleshly unity of husband and wife has been completed by death. It involves the completion of a sexual act with a dead spouse. Traditional Christianity acknowledges the enduring significance of marriage, even after death, by treating the marriage of widows and widowers as falling short of the mark.[84] However, by permitting such marriages[85] the Church acknowledges that with the death of a spouse the carnal unity of the previous marriage is over. Because of the close bond between unitive and reproductive sexuality, with the death of a spouse reproduction with that spouse should cease. Storing zygotes, which should always be avoided, may lead to a circumstance in which the father dies, leaving the mother to begin a pregnancy months or years after the death of her husband; this radically dissociates reproduction from the intimacy of the marital act. Still, it may be permissible for the mother to rescue the zygote, despite the moral harms involved. In this circumstance, one is in a morally broken context which should have been avoided and where all decisions to act or to refrain are burdened by moral evil.

Finally, attempts to produce embryos from the fusion of human and non-human gametes are under all circumstances profoundly evil. So, too, is any attempt by genetic engineering to fashion a human-animal hybrid. These are special forms of technologically mediated bestiality. This is the case even when the goal is simply to study early reproductive processes or to acquire from hybrid embryos stem-cell lines for therapeutic and experimental use. However, the introduction of specific human genes into non-human life (e.g., in order to produce human insulin through genetic engineering), not in order to change the essential character of the organism but only in order organically to produce a particular hormone or other product (e.g., an organ that can be transplanted with less likelihood of rejection), would not in intention or substance constitute the attempt reproductively to form an organism that is a human animal hybrid. The focus is not on the wholeness of the new organism, but on a trait or set of traits tangential to the organism's life for itself. That a variety of E. coli produces human insulin does not change the character of the bacterium as a particular organism. The same would be the case if one could bring chimpanzees or pigs to produce organs less likely to be rejected by humans if transplanted. However, if the genetic alterations are not just to remove particular bothersome antigens, but are instead global, in particular if they affect the central nervous system of the animal, and most particularly if they involve human gametes one would have acted in a radically evil fashion by creating an organism from the union of human and non-human life.

It is important to recognize that at stake is not merely the issue of taking genetic material from humans and placing this in animals. The future will raise the broader issue of manufacturing genes that are like human genes and placing them in animals. The point is that one may not produce an animal that is human-like save through human reproduction. One may add a new capacity to an animal using human genes, as long as this does not make a new animal that is partially human in the crucial sense of attempting to increase self-consciousness, to produce human-like rationality, or even to make a human-like bodily form. The immense human power to bring self-conscious rational, embodied beings into existence, to produce a living body such as Christ took on, may only legitimately be used within the Mystery of marriage. It is here alone that procreation may be attempted. In all other cases, the attempt to reproduce, procreate, or fashion human life is illegitimate and marked by evil. Thus, in particular, one may not create a human-animal organism, where the human elements mark the organism as a whole. In many areas, the lines will be obscure and it will likely be best to find the guidance of holy elders, those capable of noetic discernment of the essence of matters and regarding animals in particular.

Cloning, Making Embryos, and Using Embryos

Human cloning, by allowing reproduction from one person alone, would violate at least three major norms following from reproduction being established within the union of husband and wife.[86] First, human cloning would involve reproduction outside of the carnal union of husband and wife. Reproduction would be severed from the union of husband and wife, which is normatively sensual. To quote once more from St. John Chrysostom, "the woman as it were receiving the richest part fused by pleasure, nourisheth it and cherisheth it and withal contributing her own share."[87] The reproduction of the human race as blessed by God in the Scriptures (Gen 1:27-28, Gen 2:24, Matt 19:5, Mark 10:2-8) is that of a carnal union in one flesh of husband and wife. Second, cloning would be asexual reproduction; it would not involve the combination of genetic material from husband and wife in procreation. This deviance cannot be remedied by having the nucleus for the clone supplied by one spouse and the rest of the cell by another. One would not have sexual reproduction, even if the spouse supplying the cell would be providing mitochondrial DNA. Third, spouses should not be able to reproduce alone, a point made by St. John Chrysostom in his commentary on Ephesians. "Nor did He enable woman to bear children without man; if this were the case she would be self-sufficient."[88] To seek to reproduce asexually, independently of the sexual union of husband and wife, is to pursue a reproductive self-sufficiency not willed by the Creator. In sexuality and reproduction, more than in any other area, man and wife are to confront each other as indispensable helpmates. Because men and women may not seek to reproduce independently of each other, there is a special wrong involved in the artificial insemination of an unmarried woman, the development of full *in vitro* gestation, or the use of human cloning.

In the developing technologies, one must distinguish (1) reproduction that goes beyond the union of one man and one woman (e.g., as in the introduction of a donor's ovum nucleus into the ennucleated ovum of the wife), from (2) interventions that may only amount to the transplantation of cytoplasm from a donor ovum into the ovum of the wife. There is a difficult line at best between those interventions that can be compared to transplantation or extensive surgery and those interventions that would amount to the manufacture of a child. This issue will become important as artificial chromosomes can be produced. One might be able to replace a chromosome of a parent with a constructed chromosome tailored to be largely equivalent to that of the parent, save for the absence of a defect or the introduction of some needed or desired enhancement. One can imagine an ovum taken from the wife which, after being operated on (e.g., introducing such a constructed chromosome or mitochondrium), would be placed in her uterus for fertilization through normal intercourse. Such interventions by themselves would not be improper, as long as the gametes remain those of the married couple with only some therapeutic or minor enhancing changes. Still, the technological transformation of the character of reproduction itself involves a moral harm. Here there is need for spiritual discernment in determining what constitutes an essential departure from the reproduction of husband and wife. Boundaries must be discerned with prayer, humility, spiritual guidance, and submission to the will of God.

In vitro fertilization for the purpose of forming zygotes, early embryos, or fetuses for research involves a double wrong. First, such fertilization removes the procreation of human life from the intimacy of marriage. The attempt to develop human life other than as a part of the reproduction of husband and wife breaks the bond that ties human procreation to the marital bed. Second, embryo research involves direct actions against an instance of human life. Although it may not be clear how to regard early embryonic life before it is or could have been in the womb, such life cannot be understood as merely disposable. Because St. Basil the Great, as well as the canons of the Church, rejects a distinction between early and late fetuses in favor of treating all that is in the human womb as a child, this position argues against ever directly killing or acting against any early human life that should at its stage of development have been in the womb. Even if such action against human life before it is or could have been in the womb may not clearly be equivalent to abortion and therefore murder, one should not act destructively against such zygotes, embryos, and fetuses. To take a different position is to step outside of the spirit of the Fathers. In the use of zygotes and embryos for non-therapeutic research, there is an intimate involvement in non-benevolent actions against early human life. As already noted, the fusing of human gametes with animal gametes would at best be a special form of bestiality; the attempt to stimulate parthenogenic reproduction would involve the evils associated with cloning.

Employing materials from dead embryos and fetuses such as embryonic stem cells is a different, difficult, and involved matter. The use of fetal cells (as long as they are not totipotential cells) or tissue from dead fetuses should be governed by the same moral considerations that control the use of tissues from adult humans. Under circumstances that allow the use of tissues and organs from persons who die accidentally, it is appropriate to use tissues and organs from fetuses who die accidentally. Under circumstances that allow the use of tissues and organs from persons who were murdered, it is similarly allowable to use tissues and organs from fetuses who have been aborted (for more concerning transplantation, see chapter 6), from "excess" embryos stored in *in vitro* fertilization clinics, or from embryos that have been formed to produce tissues and organs. The same can be said of knowledge derived from embryo and fetal research. There is no bar in principle against using for a good end something that has been acquired by heinous means, as long as one has not been involved in (1) employing these evil means, (2) encouraging their use, (3) avoiding their condemnation, or (4) giving scandal through their use. One can drink water from a well that was dug by unjustly forced labor. However, one must be very careful neither to endorse nor to encourage any illicit circumstances or means. Great spiritual discernment will be needed, and any use of such materials must at the very least be approached penitentially as a concession to human weakness. After all, the postponement of death and the pursuit of health should never become all-consuming obsessions.

Contraception and a World Well Populated

Voluntary contraception and sterilization are not moral issues for secular bioethics. The free choice of competent adults to use contraception or sterilization raises no immediate moral problems in secular bioethics, whether or not the persons are married. Or to put the matter more strongly: contraception is regarded as a means necessary for controlling one's sexual and reproductive destiny. The contemporary sexual ethic has effective contraception and abortion as its linchpins. Since it is taken for granted that consensual sexual activity is morally neutral, if not usually to be valued as personally enhancing, and because pregnancy can alter many lifeplans, it is then accepted that contraception is integral to self-determination and therefore to be valued. This could not be otherwise: general secular morality has no canonical moral perspective or experience from which to judge the moral rightness or wrongness of consensual, mutually respectful sexual activity, especially if the activity is non-reproductive. When sexual enjoyment is separated from reproduction and from any special moral orientation, it becomes a human resource for friendly encounters, personal enjoyment, fulfillment, and amusement. It can be thrilling. It can be a way of passing time and avoiding boredom. Beyond issues of consent, the criteria invoked are usually aesthetic or hedonistic: do what makes you comfortable, do what makes you happy, as long as you respect all those involved. Unplanned reproduction from a secular perspective appears as a surd imposition of nature on the plans and enjoyments of persons. In this light, contraceptive choices are integral to charting one's own destiny, realizing one's own goals, and composing one's own intimate experiences. Indeed, the choice to use contraception and to determine when, if ever, to have children is considered so fundamental that contraceptive choices are regarded as morally open for independent choice as soon as a child can decide to be involved in sexual relations.[89]

The content of sexual choices has been demoralized. Within the constraints of consent, non-exploitation, and mutual respect, the content of sexuality in the sense of how sexual pleasure is experienced and as to who, and of what gender, has sex with whom has become not a matter of moral absolutes but of special aesthetic values associated with sexual intimacy. This demoralization of consensual sexual activities, contraceptive choices, and indeed most choices regarding sterilization is now integral to the secular cosmopolitan re-construal of matters sexual in aesthetic rather than ethical terms. The liberal cosmopolitan ethos is one in which not only consent is central, but other moral considerations are usually out of place. Reproduction, birth, suffering, and death are lodged within alternative possible styles of living, suffering, etc. These passages of life acquire an affirmatively non-moral valence: moral judgment regarding such choices is appreciated as improper moralizing. Post-traditional Christian religious thought has difficulty appreciating why a Christian bioethics should engage matters of contraception at all, other than with regard to issues such as compulsory contraception and sterilization. Why should anyone have moral concerns regarding contraceptive choices by consenting adults? What could possibly be morally at stake? There is no clue available within general secular morality or the morality of many contemporary non-traditional Christian churches to suggest why any hesitations should arise.[90]

In the secular West, questions regarding contraception, if they are at all recognized as involving moral matters (i.e., other than as consequential considerations such as regarding over-population, danger from pregnancy, etc.), tend for historical reasons to appear against the background of Roman Catholic approaches to natural law, which attempted from an often highly biologically rooted account of right reason to show that artificial contraception is unnatural. These approaches are as unpersuasive to most non-Roman Catholics as they are to most contemporary Roman Catholics, and for the same reason. Most have stepped outside of the very particular Aristotelian teleological construal of biology and its language of natural teleologies into a post-Darwinian biological vision. For the contemporary biologist, after all, human inclinations, drives, and passions result from the forces of evolution, which itself is hostage to the vicissitudes of changing terrestrial environments, genetic drift, and various accidental happenings. Human biology within such a perspective becomes a matter to be mastered according to the plans and designs of humans. By raising the issue of the bioethics of contraception and sterilization, one engages the specter of an outworn natural philosophical or biological approach to human sexuality and reproduction: the Scholastic philosophical accounts of biology and natural law that lie at the root of the development of Roman Catholic doctrine in this area.

Traditional Christianity approaches contraception from a radically different perspective. It neither regards human biology as a mere happenstance, nor does it place moral issues within the context of a particular philosophical or empirical scientific account of the human body or of biological teleologies. Traditional Christianity is not embedded in a discursive philosophical system or a particular scientific account of reality. Instead, it begins with knowledge given through the heart which leads to a noetic experience of teleology, of human life as directed to holiness. This experience occurs within a narrative given and confirmed in an experience that is both Scriptural and ongoing in the Tradition. All concerns regarding sexuality and reproduction find their orientation within traditional Christianity's appreciation of the creation of humans as male and female, of their union as husband and wife, of their companionship in the pursuit of union with God.

In the contrast between this traditional Christian ethos of reproduction, which is aimed at offering children to God in love and self-sacrifice, and the contraceptive ethos, which aims at limiting children in order to maintain a luxurious style of life, one encounters two fundamentally different understandings of life's purpose and the meaning of marriage. One confronts two contrasting understandings of our relationship to ultimate meaning, neither of which has a consanguinity with Scholastic philosophical and biological concerns. The contraceptive ethos, whether pursued through "natural family planning" or artificial means, is antagonistic to and unnatural in terms of the ethos of traditional Christian reproduction because it approaches limiting and spacing children as a means (1) for achieving or maintaining a luxurious or affluent life-style, as well as (2) celebrating human self-control and choice in reproduction as highly valued, in (3) allowing marriage to be a companionship in the successful pursuit of the good life, understood as the self-indulgent, self-fulfilling life.[91] In other words, the contraceptive ethos misses the mark ever more widely the more it focuses away from God and instead to self-satisfaction. The Christian reproductive ethos is in contrast other-regarding, and in particular God-regarding.

To begin with, the traditional Christian approach to the issue of limiting the number of children is addressed indirectly through the fasts customarily part of Christian asceticism, even within marriage. Before the question of contraception or sterilization even arises, the ascetical-liturgical life of the Church has a bearing on the likely conception of children. There is first the possibility of keeping those fasts and thus reducing the number of children who would be born. After all, were a couple abstaining from sexual intercourse on Wednesdays and Fridays, during four fast seasons of the year, and on Saturdays, Sundays, and feastdays, as well as prior to communion on other days, there would already be a fair probability that the number of children produced in a marriage would be reduced.[92] Yet, in all of this the focus must be on the nurturing of mutual love of husband and wife in their love of God. A spiritual father, in advising a couple regarding a marital fast, will need to take into account the abilities of each partner, the temptations to which they are subject, the maturity of their mutual love, and the circumstances of their lives.[93] By simply raising the issue of the traditional fast, marital sexuality has already begun to be directed towards God, even when that fast cannot be kept fully. Finally, whatever marital fast is undertaken must be done with the full consent of husband and wife, as St. Paul warns. "Cease defrauding one another, unless by agreement for a time, that ye may devote time for fasting and for prayer; and come together again for the same that Satan may not be tempting you through your incontinence" (I Cor 7:5). It is for this reason that St. John Chrysostom underscores the full equality in sexual matters of husband and wife.

> Elsewhere I grant He gives to the husband abundant precedence, both in the New Testament, and the Old saying, "Thy turning shall be towards thy husband, and he shall rule over thee." Paul doth so too by making a distinction thus, and writing, (Ephes. V.25, 33.) "Husbands, love your wives; and let the wife see that she reverence her husband." But in this place we hear no more of greater and less, but it is one and the same right. Now why is this? Because his speech was about chastity. "In all other things," says he, "let the husband have the prerogative; but not so where the question is about chastity." "The husband hath no power over his own body, neither the wife." There is great equality of honor, and no prerogative.[94]

Both of these saints recognize the power of carnal passions and the great dangers when they are not appropriately directed.

Limiting the number of children, even through a marital fast, if undertaken in a spirit of self-indulgence or without trust in God, always falls short of the ideal. Here again, this volume enters into charting the geography of decisions that fall short of the mark, where one comes to examine broken or indeed very broken choices, and yet where one seeks to aim those involved back to the mark. For example, if one in any way limits the number of children in order to live lavishly, one acts against the spirit of the Gospels.[95] Such an ethos of reproduction does not aim at humbly, selflessly, and ascetically pursuing holiness. The contraceptive ethos directs marriage away from the cardinal goal of all human life: pursuit of union with God. It directs one's life to oneself, not to God. Out of all these considerations and more, Christian marriage is not to be undertaken for self-satisfaction.[96] To the contrary, marriage involves a form of pleasant ascetic struggle of mutual love and sacrifice: a joyful companionship of spouse and children in the pursuit of holiness. Husband and wife are called to turn away from self-love through love of each other and of God. They are called to be chaste with respect to eschewing sexual acts with others and to turn with love to each other and their children. In all of this, they are like martyrs; they are to die to their passions.[97] In this context, the decision to limit children because of health or due to limited familial or societal resources need not suffer from a misdirection of energies; it can be made out of love of others and with humility before God.[98]

Despite detailed considerations of sexual offenses by ecumenical councils, and by generally accepted local councils, and despite a recognition that marriage is oriented toward reproduction, there is no condemnation of limiting births, apart from the condemnation of abortion. In one passage St. John Chrysostom speaks against preventing the birth of children from intercourse with prostitutes, as well as the use of sorceries to avoid reproduction in marriage. This passage might be construed as directed against limiting the number of children. But the concern is with pursuing a life of moral abandon.

> "Not in chambering and wantonness;" for here also he does not prohibit the intercourse of the sexes, but committing fornication. ... Why sow where the ground makes it its care to destroy the fruit? where there are many efforts at abortion? where there is murder before the birth? for even the harlot thou dost not let continue a mere harlot, but makest her a murderess also. You see how drunkenness leads to whoredom, whoredom to adultery, adultery to murder; or rather to a something even worse than murder. For I have no name to give it, since it does not take off the thing born, but prevent its being born. Why then dost thou abuse the gift of God, and fight with His laws, and follow after what is a curse as if a blessing, and make the chamber of procreation a chamber for murder, and arm the woman that was given for childbearing unto slaughter? For with a view to drawing more money by being agreeable and an object of longing to her lovers, even this she is not backward to do, so heaping upon thy head a great pile of fire. ... For sorceries are applied not to the womb that is prostituted, but to the injured wife, and there are plottings without number, and invocations of devils, and necromancies, and daily wars, and truceless fightings, and home-cherished jealousies.[99]

Since masturbation was not considered killing, and since in the ancient world contraceptives were generally confused with abortifacients, such passages are best understood as the condemnation of abortion, not contraception.[100] Still, the condemnation of the contraceptive ethos can be recognized in St. John Chrysostom's placement of the entire enterprise of the Christian life in the ascetical journey from self to God.

Chrysostom, along with the other Fathers, locates human sexuality, as all human undertakings, including limiting the number of children, within the Christian ascetical commitment of love of God and neighbor as well as against our own pride, avarice, and self-seeking. These commitments are fully opposed to the contraceptive ethos.

On the surface, this account of human sexuality and contraception may appear similar to that given by Roman Catholicism. It seemed sufficiently close so that Patriarch Athanagoras (1948-1972) thought it so.[101] Superficial similarities to the contrary notwithstanding, the differences are substantial.[102] Perhaps here as elsewhere the patriarch's goals may have been excessively ecumenical. Traditional Christian concerns with reproduction are embedded in the pursuit of holiness, not constraints set by natural law in a structure of impersonal norms, especially as this came to be understood in the West from the 13th century.[103] The moral dangers of contraceptive ethos have a priority over the concerns regarding national demographics voiced by the patriarch. The focus must remain on the ascetical struggle to salvation. Here is the point of reconciliation between those who would sternly condemn the use of contraception and those who would accept limiting the number of children for some, if not many couples.[104] Marriage should not be transformed from companionship in the pursuit of holiness to companionship in the pursuit of luxury. Limiting births should be tied to the physical health of the wife, the moral health of the marital union (i.e., that it can be lived in peace, concord, and without adultery), the economic circumstances of the couple, and the spiritual health of the marriage (i.e., that the couple turns with a love towards each other that is directed to God).[105]

In very limited circumstances, perhaps the choice may even be made to marry, and still to avoid all reproduction because of very serious health risks to the mother or because of a very significant risk of conceiving a child with a very serious illness (e.g., the risk with advanced age of having a child with Down's syndrome), which might lead the couple to be tempted to abort.[106] Such choices require careful spiritual guidance. In cases of avoiding all reproduction, so as never to produce a child (i.e., in the case of a couple without children already), the seriousness of the risk and the likelihood of its occurring must be very carefully and prayerfully weighed. In particular, one must address the risk of the couple seeking an abortion, should a pregnancy occur. All of this must be recognized as far from ideal, indeed, as broken. It must be approached within the medicinal response of a spiritual father to the challenge of bringing a couple to recognize that they must turn away from pleasing themselves and strive to become saints: the traditional goal of a Christian marriage.

Most couples will limit the number of children not from considerations of health, but because of a perception of limited personal resources or perhaps even out of concerns for over-population. Regarding the last consideration (i.e., filling the earth with humans [Gen 1:28]), it would appear that humans have in general amply discharged their obligation to fill the earth. As St. John Chrysostom observes, "the world is filled with our kind."[107] Still, even in the face of significant population growth and constrained resources, there will always be too few pious parents raising traditional Christian children. The more that couples turn from themselves towards God, the more they should raise pious children as offerings to God despite the risks of poverty or disease. Such couples will have the spiritual resources to nurture devout children who will be the world's most crucial scarce resource. For this reason, the litany during the marriage service asks that God grant the couple virtuous children.[108]

All couples should step away from a contraceptive ethos of self-indulgence to an other-regarding self-sacrificing love of God and neighbor as they approach child-bearing. Only those couples who approach marriage and having children out of a love for God will understand truly why people should enter into marriage, have children, and sustain families. The very meaning of marriage is opaque to those outside of a traditional religious understanding. Outside of this context, the choice of a spouse and the decision to have children is made in terms of concerns for personal happiness, satisfaction, and fulfillment, reducing both spouse and children to sources of pleasure rather than recognizing them as companions in the struggle to salvation. The very meaning of marriage is opaque outside of a traditional religious understanding. Outside of this context, the choice of a spouse and the decision to have children are often made in terms of concerns for personal happiness, satisfaction, and fulfillment, reducing both spouse and children to sources of pleasure, rather then recognizing them as companions in the struggle to salvation. Outside of a traditional Christian love of God and its canonical narrative, marriage, the raising of children, and the sustaining of families will never quite make sense. Nor will there be an appreciation of the usual Christian sexual asceticism of fasting from sexuality prior to communion,[109] as well as during periods of fast.[110] Even when the latter, given the guidance of a spiritual father, are not fully kept, they orient everything, including human sexuality, to God. Such fasts, with the blessing of the spiritual, can also be used to limit the number of children as long as the goal is to purse God's will and not luxury or the avoidance of parental obligations.

Each couple must begin in the actual context where they find themselves. Consider, for example, Elder Porphyrios' complex but fully traditional approach. On the one hand, he supported the Pan-Hellenic Society of Friends of Large Families by stating emphatically, "Tell them not to avoid having children. It's a great sin to avoid having children. It's a good thing that you're involved in that work. You continue, and tell them that avoiding childbearing is not allowed. It's a great sin."[111] On the other hand, he is reported to have addressed matters with particular couples in different ways:

> Elder Porphyrios said different things to different people who may have appeared at first sight to have had the same problem. There were different presuppositions in each case, and each person needed different medicine to overcome his problem. It was for this reason that he often said to us "Don't tell other people what I am now telling you. This is suitable medicine for you, for your situation. Another person, even if his external symptoms are the same, won't get the same beneficial results." I was often amazed, despite his heavenly wisdom, at the answers of unmarried Elder Porphyrios on matters of marriage, marital relations and childbearing etc. His answers weren't 'cliche,' inflexible, harsh, rigid and 'objective.' They were answers full of truth, love, affection and discernment, corresponding to the situation, the need and the receptiveness of each person, at that particular time. Looking to people's salvation, he didn't try to put them into a single mold to create identical individuals. As a man full of the Holy

Spirit he guided each person according to the will of Christ, giving to "each according to his measure" (Eph 4:7) for the welfare of the soul.[112]

At stake is not a pastoral softening of a general rule for a particular couple, but the economical, that is, appropriate application of the rule, the directing of a general rule in a particular way in order to achieve that rule's goal, the salvation of a particular couple in the conduct of their marriage. The rule is followed so as to realize its central meaning: the pursuit of the Kingdom of God in marriage. All of human life, including human sexuality, must be brought to focus on God. This will allow, in fact require, different points of departure for different persons in the pursuit of salvation, as long as they do not go beyond the traditional bounds of the marital union of husband and wife, the focus for all rules for sexual companionship in the pursuit of God.[113]

In summary, the use of family planning, whether through natural or artificial means, is never the norm, is indeed against the norm, and the contraceptive ethos is always to be condemned.[114] The norm is an ascetic trust in the providence of God, while the contraceptive ethos lies at the heart of the liberal cosmopolitan confidence in human power and its pursuit of luxury and self-satisfaction. While ascetic trust in the providence of God takes aim at the transcendent, the contraceptive ethos affirms the immanent with its possibilities for self-fulfillment. Finally and most especially, no form of contraception may be used which is also abortifacient. The difficulty is that often it is unclear whether with particular hormonal and other interventions there is a remote chance of an abortifacient action. Surely, the intention may never be that this action obtains. These are problematic areas in which guidance can only be found through good spiritual direction.

Sterilization, Sex-change Operations, Alterations in Sexual Identity, and Genetic Engineering

There is a traditional Christian abhorrence of surgical interventions that change sexual dispositions or the anatomical expressions of sexuality. The canons bearing on this matter developed around the issue of castration, often radical castration (i.e., removal of testes and penis) for the production of eunuchs. For example, Canon XXII of the Apostolic Canons specifies: "Let no one who has mutilated himself become a clergyman; for he is a murderer of himself, and an enemy of God's creation."[115] This canon was written against persons such as Origen of Alexandria (185-254), the student of Clement of Alexandria (155-220) who read the passage, "And if thine eye should cause thee to stumble, pluck it out" (Mark 9:47), as justifying "plucking out" one's sexual organs if those were the source of one's sins. The canon requires one to engage in spiritual struggle to constrain one's passions and focus one's energies, rather than take surgical shortcuts.

At the same time, the Church recognized the propriety of such operations if undertaken for medical reasons. These matters are addressed in the first canon of the Council of Nicea I (A.D. 325).

> If anyone has been operated upon by surgeons for a disease, or has been excised by barbarians, let him remain in the clergy. But if anyone has

excised himself when well, he must be dismissed even if he is examined after being in the clergy. And henceforth no such person must be promoted to holy orders. But as is self-evident, though such is the case as regards those who affect the matter and dare to excise themselves, if any persons have been eunuchized by barbarians or their lords, but are otherwise found to be worthy, the Canon admits such persons to the clergy. [116]

The canon underscores the importance of not acting against one's physical integrity as a man and, by implication, one's physical integrity as a woman. Castration when undertaken to obliterate a central element of male identity insults creation, a point that can be made for similar operations for similar purposes on women. However, the canon in recognizing medical necessity recognizes as well by implication that with a sufficient reason one may subject oneself to a surgical procedure that sterilizes. It is just that certain reasons for surgical intervention are not only insufficient but improper, such as the goal of altering the embodied basis of one's sexual desires or identity. The moral focus is on the purpose of the intervention, especially on whether it is a rejection of the character of one's embodied identity. Because the focus is on the purpose of the intervention, therapeutic interventions are accepted.

The acceptance of castration for medical purposes but the rejection of surgical interventions to alter one's sexual character are affirmed in the First-and-Second Council, the council held in Constantinople in 861. Canon VIII states:

> The divine and sacred Canon of the Apostles judges those who castrate themselves to be self-murderers; accordingly, if they are priests, it deposes them from office, and if they are not, it excludes them from advancement to holy orders. Hence it makes it plain that if one who castrates himself is a self-murderer, he who castrates another man is certainly a murderer. One might even deem such a person quite guilty of insulting creation itself. Wherefore the holy Council has been led to decree that if any bishop, or presbyter, or deacon, be proved guilty for castrating anyone, either with his own hand or by giving orders to anyone else to do so, he shall be subjected to the penalty of deposition from office; but if the offender is a layman, he shall be excommunicated; unless it should so happen that owing to the incidence of some affliction he should be forced to operate upon the sufferer by removing his testicles. For precisely as the first Canon of the Council held in Nicaea does not punish those who have been operated upon for a disease, for having the disease, so neither do we condemn priests who order diseased men to be castrated, nor do we blame laymen either, when they perform the operation with their own hands. For we consider this to be a treatment of the disease, but not a malicious design against the creature or an insult to creation.[117]

This canon forbids all operations that mutilate the human body out of a rejection of the character of human embodiment.

As with issues bearing on the contraceptive ethos, so here is one returned to the charting of decisions that in various degrees fall short of the mark. In this context, one can discern that, given this concern of the canons with maintaining one's embodied sexual identity and integrity, one has especially strong grounds for avoiding means of sterilization that alter sexual dispositions as opposed to those that leave the person's anatomy generally unchanged (e.g., vasectomies and tubal ligation). Since neither vasectomy nor tubal ligation changes sexual dispositions, since they do not involve a rejection of the anatomy of human male or female embodiment, and since they are often reversible, they are sterilizing operations that do mutilate on analogy with castration. Moreover, if these are employed for reasons of health (i.e., further pregnancies would significantly put the health of the woman at risk) and after having had children, there is no rejection of the reproductive character of being male and female, even if there are other grounds for hesitation. In contrast, there are grounds not to use hysterectomies as means of sterilization, even though simple hysterectomies leave the ovaries in place. Such interventions involve removing an organ integral to sexual identity. Still, the cardinal issue is the purpose for the removal of the organ: is one removing an organ because of how it defines one's functioning and identity (e.g., removing the uterus to be free of menstruation, or because one wishes never to reproduce, or because of legitimate concerns with disease)? But the removal of the uterus or the uterus and ovaries in middle age because of concerns about cancer does not involve rejecting one's sexual identity. Rather, the intervention is undertaken for medical reasons. Clearly legitimate medical reasons are required to justify significantly changing human anatomy, as occurs with a hysterectomy or an oopherectomy (i.e., removal of the ovaries).[118]

The canons regarding the production of eunuchs, as well as these reflections on sterilization, give strong grounds for forbidding operations to change sexual characteristics. Sex-change interventions are relevantly similar to those involved in limiting sexual passions through castration: there is a radical rejection of one's sexual anatomical identity. It is just that with a sex-change operation there is an interest in differently directing one's passions, rather than eliminating them. There is an interest in surgically altering one's body to achieve an identity in terms of a sexual experience of oneself contrary to one's original anatomy. For example, some persons claim to experience themselves as a man in a woman's body, or a woman in a man's body and then want surgically and hormonally to achieve that identity precluded by their current anatomical character. Such surgical and hormonal interventions change sexual bodily form and the expression of desires by cutting off or out body parts taken to be incompatible with a desired identity (e.g., cutting off breast tissue from a woman wishing to have a male bodily identity or testicles from a man wishing to have a female bodily identity) or reshaping tissue (e.g., so as to "create" a "vagina" or a "penis").[119] Surgically- and hormonally-effected alterations are made in sexual anatomy because the original anatomy is not accepted. These interventions also recast people surgically in ways that preclude their entering marriage as reproductively able, not even considering the circumstance that such an attempt at marriage would involve people who had both begun life and entered puberty with the same sexual genotype, primary sexual characteristics, and secondary sexual characteristics, obscuring the marital union as the unambiguous joining of man and woman.

Surgical and hormonal interventions to change sexual phenotype involve surgically restructuring sexual embodiment in a fashion that mutilates original anatomical sexual identity because this anatomical identity is rejected. Such interventions collide with the spirit of the early Church and her canons, which require accepting the sexual character of one's embodiment. One may correct malformations and restore lost functions so as to allow the realization of the embodied identity of being male or female. Although sexual identity may be unclear in many cases, the Christian insight is that gender is not a social creation. The statement in Genesis that God created humans as man and woman, along with its affirmation in the Gospels by Christ provide a normatively canonical account of humans as sexually dimorphic. Genesis declares "male and female he made them" (Gen 1:27), and the Gospel then announces "Ye read, did ye not, that the One Who made them from the beginning 'made them male and female'" (Matt 19:4). The deep reality of humans is as either male or female, no matter how difficult this reality is to discern. All surgical and other interventions should therefore be directed, as far as possible, to maintaining or determining and then restoring a person's sexual identity.

Usually but not always, this identity can be gleaned from the genotypic sexual identity. Here as elsewhere, in a world radically broken by sin, much that should be clear will at times be painfully obscure. Under such circumstances, one must attempt as best one can with medical and spiritual discernment to aim at reconstituting that which ought to have been.[120] This consideration does not bear against attempts to create useful genitalia for children born with deformed genitalia. When there is a discordance between genotypic sexuality and phenotypic sexuality in a new-born with ambiguous genitalia, one should favor the genotypic sexuality. Genotype is a foundational element of embodiment: it is this ground of sexuality that usually defines the sources for sexual identity and functioning. Still, in a broken world in which our bodies are often disabled, maimed, and fail to realize the usual projects of humans, even the appeal to genotypical identity will at times be insufficient. In some cases, it will be unclear as to how one should view particular genotypes without reference to the phenotypes expressed (e.g., Klinefelter's with XXY). One must try the best one can under less than ideal circumstances to achieve normal human sexual identity while both engaging in as little surgical alteration as possible and also pursuing the goal of restoring to a child born with ambiguous genitalia a sexual identity, so that it can authentically participate in the full sacramental life of the Church. Because humans were created male and female, because being man or woman has deep ontological significance, a child should be helped as far as possible to claim its true sexual identity. In some cases, this will require the guidance of someone with profound spiritual discernment.[121] In many cases with regard to marriage this may at best require an appeal to God's mercy and what seems most plausible.[122]

In a world distorted by passion and the consequences of sin where much that should be clear is obscure, there will likely be individuals who surgically and hormonally will have brought themselves to appear phenotypically to be a member of a sex other than that in which they began their childhood and lived their puberty. Some men, especially, who have been surgically altered to appear female, may frequently as easily pass as female as those persons who are genotypically male but who from a feminizing tumor have come to marry and be accepted as women. In continuity with the mind of the first centuries, how should the Church consider such persons who after sex-change procedures wish to enter into a sacramental marriage? Given the strong condemnation of mutilation and because violating events can bar one from entering into a Mystery of the Church (e.g., bar from the priesthood),[123] anyone who underwent surgical interventions to change sexual phenotype should be barred from sacramental marriage, not to mention the priesthood. Medicine should be engaged in preserving and restoring the normatively human, as male or female.

The canons, and in particular Canon VIII of the First-and-Second Council (A.D. 861), while creating no bar to therapeutic castration identify the evil in castration as that of an insult to the Creator, as the rejection of a cardinal aspect of human identity as a male (and by implication as a female; female castration was not possible at the time).[124] Consequently, there should also be no bar to surgical interventions reasonably undertaken on medical grounds to preserve life or achieve appropriate function as this is traditionally understood within Christianity. As long as surgical or medical interventions do not aim to set aside an element of the normatively human and are curative, restorative, or protective of health, where well-being is understood within a traditional Christian context, there should be no moral barriers. Thus, male circumcision undertaken to convey medical benefit to men or their spouses should be allowable.[125] In contrast, female circumcision that is not therapeutic is not allowable because it radically changes the character and nature of female anatomy. In part, female circumcision is undertaken for reasons analogous to castration, namely, to check female sexual desire through the removal of the clitoris. In addition, female circumcision is meant to be significantly mutilative: it rejects the integrity and goodness of female genital anatomy.[126] However, a therapeutic, and therefore allowable, excision would be one undertaken because of cancer of the vulva. Plastic surgery undertaken to restore human form should be acceptable.

The boundaries for proper plastic surgery are set by the Christian ascetic concern not to pursue luxury or to be overly concerned about one's physical attractiveness. Breast augmentation to enhance a career as a nude dancer, for example, would violate a number of traditional Christian norms. Because the governing goal for humans is to turn the heart to God, there will be many gray areas in plastic surgery that will require spiritual guidance. For instance, cosmetic surgery in the attempt to maintain an ever-youthful appearance should give grounds for pause. In other areas of surgery, there may be less grounds for hesitation. Unlike some concerns in Roman Catholic moral theology based on its "principle of totality"[127] regarding the propriety of incidental appendectomies (i.e., the removal of a normal appendix while performing some other operation, recognizing that the appendix has no important function, while also acknowledging the risks of appendicitis), the crucial issue within a traditional Christian bioethical framework is the therapeutic intent and the surgery's lack of any impact on one's normative identity as a human, as a man or a woman.

These reflections offer points of guidance for the use of human genetic engineering.[128] With any genetic engineering, one must at least preserve the character of humans as rational moral agents who, as male and female, procreate humanity. Because sexuality and sexual difference, as well as the ability generally to engage in fertile mating, ontologically define humanity, these may not be set aside without perverting the character of human existence. The general character of being human as male and female, expressed not just in heterosexual marriage but also in procreation, means that neither sexual difference ("male and female He made them" Gen 1:27) nor the possibility of the reproductive unity of humans ("increase and multiply" Gen 1:28) may be set aside. Humans may not be divided into different species incapable of interbreeding.[129] Within these limits, and presuming the guidance of holy elders, much human genetic germline engineering will not just be morally acceptable but laudatory if it cures diseases, not only in the persons affected, but in all of the person's descendants. In addition, the availability of human germline genetic engineering may set aside the temptation to use abortion to avoid the birth of a child with genetic disease. Currently, prenatal screening, save when it aids a family in planning for the birth of a child who will need special care, is primarily a source of a temptation to commit abortion.

This position will undoubtedly be puzzling to many secular bioethicists with a robust commitment to forbidding human germline genetic engineering on principle. There will be no basis for a global condemnation of genetic engineering, even human germline genetic engineering, as there is a basis for condemning abortion on principle. While in some cultures there may be a nigh-unto-pagan exultation of the natural leading to a condemnation of genetic engineering in general and germline genetic engineering in particular, along with an affirmation of abortion as a liberation from biological constraints on women, the opposite is the case for Orthodox Christianity. The cure of disease through genetic engineering will not of itself be evil because of the means, while abortion must always be recognized as unambiguously a very serious moral matter.[130] Because genetic engineering can offer the prospect of less illness, greater health, and diminished interest in abortion (i.e., because children can by genetic engineering be prevented from having the diseases and disabilities that usually provoke abortion), the priority of appropriate moral concerns as understood in secular morality must be reversed. Although the taking of the life of an unborn child is always wrong, the development of genetic germline engineering is generally a matter of prudence and discernment, except in the circumstances noted above (e.g., changing the very character of human embodiment). A similar reversal of appropriate moral priorities is involved in the case of sex selection. Secular bioethical reflection does not generally challenge the evil of abortion employed in sex selection, but focuses only on the supposed evil of assuring a child of a particular sex.[131] Yet, it is far from clear why it would be wrong to engage in sex selection, if the selection procedure does not involve improper means (e.g., abortion). After all, one may surely pray for a son or a daughter. Indeed, what would be wrong in principle if it were found that eating certain foods (e.g., jalapeños) increased the chance of producing a great preponderance of y-chromosome-bearing sperm, thereby assuring the birth of a son? What then if such natural foods were packaged and used toward the end of sex selection? Would it make any difference if this material were produced artificially? There is nothing in the tradition suggesting that any of this would be wrong in principle. And if there were then more males produced than females, then perhaps there would be less of a hindrance for men to become monks. There is nothing clearly wrong in any of this.

Premarital Sex, Contraception for the Unmarried, and AIDS

Not only priests but also physicians see humanity as it is. Priests in confession hear the endless repetition of the same sins laying bare hypocrisy and self-righteousness. They know how people really live. The sinful, broken character of human life is unveiled.

Physicians confront the same reality literally laid bare, although from a different perspective. They are engaged to treat the consequences of sinful choices, infidelity, and imprudence. They see how sin is not limited in its consequences. Diseases such as AIDS that from the perspective of public health would have remained obscure and insignificant problems in the absence of sexual relations outside of marriage (and the illicit use of intravenous drugs) have become worldwide threats to the health of innocent children born of infected parents and to the recipients of blood products. In a world where passion overbears prudence and virtue, physicians are often asked to provide contraceptives for the unmarried and prophylactics for those who intend to engage in illicit sexual acts.

Health care professionals may provide prophylactics to the unmarried and instruct in their use in order to protect persons from serious sexually transmitted disease and diminish the likelihood of abortion, as long as they do not directly encourage or condone the immoral actions against which the prophylactics act as a protection from diseases. Physicians and other health professionals are like people who might provide helmets to individuals who want to attack each other with bats but nevertheless can be persuaded at least to protect their own heads. The failure to encourage the use of condoms among the sexually immoral may increase the risk of adulterous husbands contracting serious sexually transmitted diseases and then infecting their wives and future children. With the advent of HIV, the tragedy for innocent wives and children has become very serious and global. A disease that would have spread only very slowly, if at all, in the absence of illicit sexual acts, both homosexual and heterosexual, and in the absence of the illicit use of intravenous drugs, has within a few decades taken on epidemic proportions. This epidemic of disease and death, the result of millions of individual sinful acts, has injured innocent children and adults, not just those involved in the sinful acts. AIDS has come to define the focus of contemporary concerns regarding sexually transmitted diseases. Without condoning these sinful acts, one can still provide protection against further disease and death. Because traditional Christianity approaches these matters outside of a Scholastic, biological understanding of natural and unnatural acts, and since a child conceived outside of marriage is at great risk of being aborted, prophylactics can be provided to the unmarried with regret, admonition, but without impropriety.

The obligation not to condone illicit sexual acts will often bring traditional Christian health care professionals beyond the "professional value neutrality" expected in a society reluctant to hear that much of what it praises, or at least accepts, is sinful. Health care professionals who break such bounds of neutrality will be viewed as acting unprofessionally, as imposing their values on others. Professional value neutrality properly understood requires physicians and other health care professionals not to impose punishments for immoral actions or to use coercion to impose their own values. For example, physicians should not deny medical treatment because patients are notorious sinners, or because their diseases result from their sins. However, the traditional Christian provision of health care has as its exemplars holy unmercenary saint-physicians committed to a spiritual holism. They were far from value-neutral: they did not provide physical treatment in isolation from the larger context of health and disease, which is not simply moral but spiritual. "They sought no reward for their work, only urging the sick to faith in Christ the Lord."[132] Christian physicians, following the example of the holy unmercenaries, should still encourage right worship and right belief.

The provision of prophylactics to those who plan to engage in illicit sexual acts is ideally undertaken in a way that clearly conveys a sense of the immorality of premarital and extramarital sexual behavior. One is obliged never to condone sin, not to incite to further sin, or to encourage a further hardening of immoral or anti-religious attitudes (Matt 7:6). For example, one may not provide medical treatment to restore sexual function for people in sexual partnerships that are sinful (i.e., outside of the marriage of a man and a woman). This task is not without great difficulty for physicians and other health care professionals. To provide health care with a moral or religious integrity is likely to be received by many as very offensive: many will take any suggestion that they are acting improperly as an invasion of their privacy, as improperly moralistic, or as involving an illicit intrusion of religious convictions. It has become a canon of the liberal cosmopolitan ethos that it is politically incorrect, indeed secularly immoral, to recognize the immorality of fornication and homosexual acts. Particular vehemence is directed against physicians and other health care practitioners who would attempt to counsel and treat morally inappropriate sexual urges. Being a forthright traditional Christian health care professional under such circumstances is likely to evoke considerable hostility from those committed to the liberal cosmopolitan ethos. The holy unmercenary physicians were martyred because of the salience of their Christianity in their medical practice.

Abortion, Miscarriage, and Birth

From the early Church, intentionally killing embryos has been acknowledged as a radical failure of love, as one of the worst of actions, whether or not the embryo is yet a person.[133] The humble submission asked of Christians is incompatible with the endorsement of deadly force against humans.[134] It is for this reason that even involuntary homicide and homicide in the course of a just war have required excommunication.[135] Homicide is involved even in defense of the life of the mother, even if the abortion is to preserve her health or prevent her death. The Church from the beginning rejected speculations regarding the point at which the soul might enter the body.[136] The canons make no distinction between early and late abortions, as this distinction developed in the West.[137] The focus is on not harming human life within the womb. There was also no use of the distinction between so-called direct and indirect abortions, between foreseen and intended versus foreseen albeit unintended abortions, a distinction that allowed the Western church in the second millennium fully to excuse certain abortions.

Christians are called to engage in reproduction with love, with humility, and without taking unborn human life.

> A woman that aborts deliberately is liable to trial as a murderess. This is not a precise assertion of some figurative and inexpressible conception that passes current among us. For here there is involved the question of providing justice for the infant to be born, but also for the woman who

has plotted against her own self. For in most cases the women die in the course of such operations. But besides this there is to be noted the fact that the destruction of the embryo constitutes another murder, at least in the opinion of those who dare to do these things. It behooves us, however, not to extend their confession to the extreme limit of death, but to admit them at the end of the moderate period of ten years, without specifying a definite time, but adjusting the cure to the manner of penitence.[138]

The canons address not just those who perform abortions, but also those who supply abortifacients. "As for women who furnish drugs for the purpose of procuring abortion, and those who take foetus-killing poisons, they are made subject to the penalty prescribed for murderers."[139] And again, "As for women who destroy embryos as professionally, and those who give or take poisons with the object of aborting babies and dropping them prematurely, we prescribe the rule that they be treated economically up to five or even three years at most."[140] Special attention is directed to prostitutes.

Regarding women who become prostitutes and kill their babies, and who make it their business to concoct abortives, the former rule barred them for life from communion, and they are left without recourse. But, having found a more philanthropic alternative, we have fixed the penalty at ten years, in accordance with the fixed degrees.[141]

These canons record a clear and persistent proscription of abortion and tie this proscription of intentional abortion to murder.

The proscription of abortion has dramatic implications for contemporary health care practice. Among other things, it leads to a firm condemnation of prenatal screening and abortion, a practice that has become core to the secular profession of medicine and the secular societal appreciation of responsible parenting. These have come to require the assessment of unborn children and their abortion, should they prove to be defective. One is considered to have a responsibility not just to society in order to avoid the costs of a child with a serious defect, but a responsibility to the child to insure that it will not suffer such burdens.[142] At law physicians have become responsible for not providing parents the information necessary so that they can decide if they wish to kill their unborn children. In some jurisdictions, this has included the possibility of a child suing for the costs of a defect that could have been avoided if the parent had aborted the child.[143] Responsible parenting comes to focus on avoiding congenital defects and deformities even when this can be achieved only by killing the unborn child. This secular sense of responsible parenting, surely a perversion of the traditional meaning, encourages parents not to face the challenge of loving and caring for a child with serious defects and disabilities. With prenatal screening and abortion, parents remain in control of their lives. They can assure themselves that they will have children as perfect as their houses and cars. The circumstance that a child will be born with a serious defect is not grounds for killing that child, even in utero. Nor does the tradition have any sympathy for arguments that one will injure such a child by having it live with a serious defect. Since the prospects are eternal life, not merely temporal suffering, the child is always being offered an immense benefit with temporal life, given the possibility of experiencing the Mysteries of the Church, despite the harms associated with defect, disability, or disease.

This traditional approach to abortion, because it seeks to avoid even involuntary homicide, does not draw a crisp line between abortion and miscarriage. There has been an appreciation that even an involuntary involvement in homicide can harm the human heart. As a consequence, the absolution for miscarriage recognizes (1) the importance of repentance for the ways in which we are implicated in the broken and sinful character of the world, which can even involve involuntary complicity in the death of an innocent person, (2) the need to forgive any involvement on the part of the woman in the loss of her unborn child's life, and (3) the inclusion in prayerful consideration of those around the woman who may have in some way precipitated the miscarriage.

> O Master, Lord our God, Who was born of the Holy Theotokos and Ever-virgin Mary, and Who, as an infant, lay in the manger: According to Your great mercy, be merciful to Your servant, N., who is in sin, having been involved in the loss of a life, whether voluntary or involuntary, for she has miscarried that which was conceived in her. Forgive her transgressions, both voluntary and involuntary, and protect her from every snare of the Devil. Cleanse her stain and heal her infirmities. And grant to her, O Lover of Mankind, health and strength of soul and body. Guard her with a shining Angel from all assaults of the unseen demons; Yea, O Lord, from sickness and infirmity. Purify her from bodily uncleanness and the various troubles within her womb. By Your many mercies lead her up in her humbled body from the bed on which she lies. For we all have been born in sins and transgressions, and all of us are defiled in Your sight, O Lord. Therefore, with fear we cry out and say: Look down from heaven and behold the feebleness of us who are condemned. Forgive this, Your servant, N., who is in sin, having been involved in the loss of a life, whether voluntary or involuntary, for she has miscarried that which was conceived in her. And, according to Your great mercy as the Good God Who loves mankind, be merciful and forgive all those who are here present and who have touched her. For You alone have the power to remit sins and transgressions, through the prayers of Your Most-pure Mother and of all the Saints.[144]

This absolution acknowledges both feelings of guilt as well as actual guilt. It implicitly appreciates how the loss of an unborn child often leads to self-accusation as one recognizes how one might perhaps have acted differently and avoided the miscarriage. The absolution sets this all aside through repentance in the mercy of forgiveness.

Because of the recognition of the sin of involuntary homicide, even if the abortion is part of an action undertaken to save the life of the mother (e.g., the removal of a ruptured ectopic pregnancy), one is not rendered free of the need for repentance. The Church of the first millennium, at least in the case of homicide, did not employ the doctrine of double effect that developed in the West, which held that one is not culpable for foreseen but unintended deaths achieved through means not evil in themselves that are both fatal to one and beneficial to another person.[145] This doctrine was invoked in medicine beginning at least in the 19th century in the Western church to justify without further spiritual concern interventions such as the removal of a cancerous uterus to save a woman's life, even if the woman were pregnant.[146] The non-juridical character of traditional Christianity grounded instead a therapeutic focus that sustains a concern about involuntary sins and sins committed in ignorance.[147] One can become involved in an evil such as the death of a person, which even against one's will can have an effect on one's heart. In particular, homicide, even when involuntary, provides prima facie grounds to undertake a special ascesis. Such "penance" should not be regarded as a punishment, but as treatment. Excommunication for proximal involvement in homicide reflects the insight that implication in killing must literally give one pause before approaching the chalice. One must step back from the chalice and redouble one's spiritual labors until one can commune without harm.[148]

This approach to involuntary homicide recognizes a presumptive difference between acting and refraining. Though intention can turn an otherwise sinless proximity to death into a serious harm (e.g., deciding not to volunteer for extra hours of work at the hospital in the hope that there will be excess deaths), mere omission need not engender such harm (e.g., merely not volunteering for extra hospital service). Still, proximate implication in death against one's intention can produce a circumstance in need of spiritual address (e.g., after borrowing a car that appeared in excellent condition in order to take a sick friend to the hospital, one is negligently involved in the death of a pedestrian after the brakes fail). Intending to kill and proximate involvement in death are both spiritually harmful. Intention and causal proximity are independent considerations in determining the spiritual harm of actions in general, and the involvement of death in particular. That is, both malevolence (i.e., willing to harm another) and maleficence (i.e., having done harm to another, even if involuntarily) are spiritually harmful. In particular, causal proximity in the death of another must be regarded as an involuntary evil for which spiritual therapy should be sought. Proximate versus distant involvement can often be distinguished by reference to the purpose of the practice associated with the death, as well as whether there was the will of another person intermediate between one's action and the death of the person. For example, in a non-negligent fashion to help a woman exercise for the health of her unborn child, although this may in very rare occasions precipitate a premature delivery and death of the child, is not an act of homicide. The intention is to benefit the health of the mother. The purpose of the practice of exercise is also to benefit the child. Moreover, the practice is not one marked by a more than ordinary risk of life to another. The engaging in exercise is thus a harmless practice and the death of the child through miscarriage can be attributed to unknown factors. In addition, the person merely helping has a certain causal distance, which is maintained by the free choice of the woman to exercise. The distance of the exercise coach from the death of the child may be sufficient not to require special therapy through penance, while the woman's intimate involvement likely will. The line between involuntary homicide and various remote and indirect implications in death should not be legalistically but instead therapeutically drawn by a spiritual father between an involvement in death that should lead to special penance and that which need not.[149]

What then can one say of abortion to save the life of the mother? Since no distinction between direct and indirect abortion was admitted by the Church of the first millennium during which period, as the canons attest, abortions were undertaken, one must approach the matter within a moral concern not to exonerate from guilt, while at the same time seeking to have any guilt transformed through repentance into forgiveness. This is not to deny that there may be less of a volition to kill when the death of a fetus occurs *en passant*, as when a cancerous uterus is removed to save the mother's life, than when an abortion is undertaken to save the life of a mother in congestive heart failure. In the first case, one need not directly will the killing of the embryo. One simply foresees it as a highly regrettable side-effect. In the second case, one must will to kill. The abortion is the direct goal of the intervention. Such differences in willing make a difference to the human heart. Still, even if in the first case the act can be described as a removal of a cancerous organ, it is also a homicide, even if abortion is not the intention one has in mind. The second case where there is a direct intention will likely in general be much more spiritually harmful.

At stake is not (1) a juridical determination, but (2) the spiritual treatment of the heart. The absence of a doctrine of double effect reflects the experience of the Church emphasizing that when there is an abortion the woman and the health care professionals who perform the act are involved in homicide, no matter how involuntary. They need to turn to God in repentance. They must mourn the broken character of our fallen world and our often involuntary complicity in its sinful character. One must turn one's heart away from oneself, from violence, to humble submission to God. Spiritual treatment may require convalescence through excommunication with mourning over involvement in death through prayer, fasting, and almsgiving.

This position regarding abortion can only be adequately understood outside of a language of rights, even one of a right to life. The language of the tradition regarding abortion, as well as other bioethical matters, is preeminently that of commands, proscriptions, injunctions, and invitations to holiness, which direct to a life aimed at the pursuit of the kingdom of heaven. Even to talk of a right to life may obscure the integral character of the Christian life by suggesting that there are ultimate reference points for the moral law outside of the pursuit of the kingdom through Jesus Christ. Fully discursive understandings of natural law can dangerously mislead in suggesting that morality can be adequately understood outside of a life appropriately directed to God. Therefore, while inviting others to join in condemning the great moral evil of abortion, one should at the same time seek to avoid moral confusion. While collaborating with others in condemning a moral evil (e.g., abortion), one must not lose sight of the real significance of this evil. The appreciation of evil, as well as of the good, must always be situated in terms of the pursuit of holiness.

This approach to the issue of abortion may seem bizarre to those in search of a legalistic account of the morality of abortion that will find those accused of sin either clearly innocent or guilty. The approach of traditional Christianity in being spiritually therapeutic is instead non-juridical. It treats the issue of guilt in terms of the pursuit of salvation through repentance. Unlike the Pharisee who seeks a finding of complete innocence, we are called to be like the publican who first and foremost recognizes his sinfulness and turns to God (Luke 18:10-14). For example, if, when faced with a choice between the life of the mother versus the life of the child *in utero*, one chooses to abort the child, then one must sincerely mourn this circumstance and truly repent.[150] One must still seek spiritual guidance and attempt to involve no one who would be excommunicated through participation (i.e., no Orthodox). One must fully recognize how far a choice to kill in order to save life falls short of the mark and that this is the case whether the abortion is undertaken "indirectly" (i.e., the abortion as a side effect of another intervention), as when one removes a cancerous uterus containing a child, or when one performs a "direct" abortion (i.e., acts to abort) for a woman with severe congestive failure. Even in cases where the abortion is "indirect", where in the absence of intervention both mother and child would have died and where the mother may have a duty to her other children as well as to her husband at least to save her own life, there must still be an acknowledgement of sin and the brokenness of our condition. In such difficult cases, one should seek expert theological guidance (e.g., that of one's spiritual father or a holy elder or a holy mother and mourn one's sins if one nevertheless kills an unborn child).

One may not kill an unborn child in order to reduce the number of children in a multiple pregnancy. Nor would pregnancy due to incest or rape justify abortion. In the latter two cases, one encounters the moral horrors of this world with such an intimacy that mercy and forgiveness must be first and foremost. In the case of pregnancy due to rape, the impact on the woman and, if she is married, on her husband and family may be considerable and may even lead to significant spousal abuse. A spiritual father must attempt to guide in a context marked by great evil.

A number of puzzles remain. For example, how should one consider the induction of a premature delivery of a child who will die even if brought to full term (e.g., an anencephalic child), especially since Canon XXI of St. John the Faster forbids abortion through premature delivery?[151] Should such an intervention be treated as an abortion, and therefore as a homicide? The answer can only be given by a discerning spiritual guide. Surely the most significant is whether an earlier delivery will decrease the likelihood of a stillbirth and therefore increase the chance of being able to baptize the child. If the child will die in any event and one is acting to provide baptism, then one will not have an intimate causal involvement in bringing about death, if one delivers the fetus at a gestational stage when a child could otherwise (without the defects) have survived with special care, had that been appropriate. The canon of St. John the Faster appears to focus only on acts that will kill an unborn child who would otherwise live. The canon does not appear to require us to consider premature delivery by itself to be abortion when the child will in any event die immediately after birth. Surely the child so delivered should be given a Christian burial.

Although any act to kill a zygote or early embryo should count as murder in the sense of an abortion,[152] there is the issue of medicines that do not expel, kill, or abort a fetus, but might incidentally prevent a zygote from implanting. Since there is evidence of considerable early zygote loss even prior to implantation[153] and since in the Liturgy of St. Basil the Great one prays, "O God, who knowest every man even from his mother's womb,"[154] such events, which occur before implantation in the mother's womb, are not clearly acts of abortion, though they are surely morally broken.[155] If one considered such events abortions, would one not need also to consider the routine loss of early zygotes as miscarriages and treat them accordingly? Very likely, one can prayerfully, although with serious misgivings and mourning, step back from considering as abortion interventions regarding which there is no clear evidence that they cause abortion hinder implantation and where there is no direct act of violence against an embryo. Where there is no intention to expel a zygote from the womb, and there is only a remote risk that the medication may prevent implantation, and where there is good reason to use the medicine, one can probably proceed without being guilty of deliberate abortion or of using a drug to procure an abortion,[156] though surely not without fault. As the likelihood of a medicine's causing non-implantation increases, so, too, should one's concern about the use of such medication. There will also be very good grounds to condemn the use of intrauterine devices (IUDs), since these may even expel zygotes. Also, the directness of their action in the uterus would engage an intimacy of proximal causal involvement in embryonic death.

Since the focus of the Church has not been on establishing the moment of ensoulment, and since the evil of abortion was not dependent on having taken the life of a person, one must condemn as an abortion (1) any action taken to expel an embryo from the womb, as equivalent to murder, as well as any action to kill an embryo at any stage, while (2) not necessarily considering actions that might incidentally prevent the implantation of the early embryo as abortion. Yet, it is an action burdened by considerable evil because of its closeness to abortion. The central insight is that all actions to kill unborn human life or to use it for the good of others (e.g., as in embryo research) are gravely wrong. Distinctions between embryos and pre-embryos are irrelevant to this point. As we have already seen, St. Basil warns that one is

> a murderer who kills an imperfect and unformed embryo, because this though not yet then a complete being was nevertheless destined to be perfected in the future, according to indispensable sequence of the laws of nature.[157]

In his warning, St. Basil is clear both that abortion should be treated as murder even before ensoulment (i.e., before being formed) and that the embryo is such that it will in the natural course of things become a child. It is therefore safe to say that any action against a zygote or embryo at any stage must be forbidden. Also, at the very beginning (i.e., with the zygote and embryo), though one is dealing with an instance of human life that is not clearly destined, according to the usual course of nature, given the high proportion of embryo loss and some chance of twinning, to become a child, one is dealing with an entity that will often become a child. It is appropriate to build a moral and spiritual fence around early life (i.e., zygotes or early embryos) so that harms *en passant* to such life are regarded as wrongly directed, even when they may not be regarded as abortion. Pre-implantation genetic diagnosis and embryo selection will need to count as a homicide (i.e., abortion), especially given the project of using *in vitro* fertilization to produce surplus embryos so as to assess which are "normal" and then only implanting these. [158] Such interventions would carry a much greater moral burden than the use after rape of morning-after pills which prevent ovulation but also secondarily impede implantation, yet do not expel a zygote (i.e., an intervention that would primarily act to expel the embryo must categorically be forbidden as an abortion). Their use in the case of rape may be faulted without necessarily considering the intervention an abortion. If the procedure does not expel a human life established in the mother's womb, the intervention may be regarded as one that requires repentance and mourning because of possible involvement in the loss of at least human biological life, but not the full penance due for abortion.[159]

Since such occurrences may be very similar to the frequent but unnoticed loss of zygotes with the menstrual cycle, the appropriate spiritual response under such very broken circumstances may at the least be to delay communion subsequent to confession until after the next menstruation and after the completion of a time of prayer. One finds here with regard to married, sexually active women an additional way to understand the Church's admonition that women refrain from communion and couples from intercourse during menstruation.[160] To approach the Chalice worthily, one should step away from all defilement and corruption, recognizing that in our broken state after the Fall the human condition is overshadowed by sin and darkness, a condition ever in need of being reclaimed by the light of the Mysteries of the Church worthily received.

A traditional Christian bioethics must always recognize frankly spiritual needs as it addresses reproduction. It must recognize the need to reclaim our biology spiritually. Most especially, the Church must reclaim the broken character of our biology where our biology joins with the Creator in procreating new human life: birth-giving. Here women engage intimately with God's creative act. Still, this act has a broken character: this joining with God after the Fall is entwined with pain, travail, and often death. "I will greatly multiply thy pains and thy groanings; in pain thou shalt bring forth children" (Gen 3:17). All of anesthesia and obstetrics cannot fully set this aside, at least in the absence of complete *in vitro* gestation, a possibility that is morally unacceptable, as we have seen earlier in this chapter. Even under the best of circumstances, birth-giving is traumatic: birth-giving changes a woman's anatomy.[161] Into this broken circumstance for procreation, the Church reaches to restore by bringing grace. By her absolution and blessing she restores by resituating the world in the promise of its final redemption. It is not just for psycho-therapeutic reasons that the Church through her blessings takes account of the upheaval, distress, pain, and bodily trauma that mark birth-giving.[162] The Church spiritually acknowledges how these traumas, especially during delivery, can turn the heart and occasion harsh even if involuntary remonstrations, and how this all must be set aside in the purifying mystery of the Church. She recognizes as well the unique act of love involved in birth-giving, an act of deep love of God, husband, and child that can be a special window to God, to salvation, not open to men, but only to women, for a woman can "be saved through the childbearing" (I Tim 2:15).

The Church reaches in to nourish spiritually, recognizing the privilege of this experience. In the blessing for the first day after delivery, the Church prays:

O Master, Lord our God, Who was born from our Most-holy Sovereign Lady, the Theotokos and Ever-virgin Mary; Who lay in a manger as an infant and was carried as a little child: Have mercy on this, Your servant, who has given birth today to this child. Forgive all her transgressions, both voluntary and involuntary, and protect her from all torments of the Devil. Preserve the infant who has been born of her from all woes, cruelty and storms of adversity, and from evil spirits, whether of the day or of the night. Preserve this woman under Your mighty hand and grant her a speedy recovery. Cleanse her of every stain and heal her sufferings. Grant health and strength of soul and body, and surround her with bright and radiant angels. Preserve her from every assault of the invisible spirits; Yea, Lord, from sickness and infirmity, from jealousy and envy, and from the evil eye. Have mercy on her and on the infant, out of Your great mercy, and cleanse her from bodily uncleanness and the various afflictions of her womb. By Your quick mercy lead her to recover in her humbled body. Grant that the infant who has been born of her may worship in the earthly temple which You have prepared for the glorification of Your holy Name. For to You is due all glory, honor and worship: to the Father, and to the Son, and to the Holy Spirit, now and ever and unto ages of ages. Amen.[163]

Most significantly, the Church reaches out to bring each new mother and her child out of the broken world and into the assembly of grace, the Church, the Kingdom of God: the focus of the ritual of churching.

O Lord our God, Who didst come for the redemption of the human race, come Thou also upon Thy servant, N., and grant unto her, through the prayers of Thine honorable Priest, entrance into the temple of Thy glory. Wash away her bodily uncleanness, and the stains of her soul, in the fulfilling of the forty days. Make her worthy of the communion of Thy holy Body and of Thy Blood.[164]

As through all of her blessings, the Church claims back from the prince of this world (John 12:31) what is God's and restores Christ's dominion over that which is rightfully His.

Pain, suffering, the loss of human life, and birth-giving are all relocated in the human struggle to turn away from self-love and the brokenness of passion to the love of others and the wholeness that comes from loving God. Because traditional Christian bioethics as a theological morality has its full attention oriented to seeking the Kingdom of Heaven, one does not find the usual bioethical accent on natural virtues, rights, and the realization of the good. Everything is resituated in terms of the pursuit of salvation. A Christian bioethics must underscore the place of sacramental attention to the biological and medical in the unchanging mind of the Church. Such a bioethics is out of phase with usual bioethical expectations.

Summary: Why a Christian Bioethics of Reproduction is so Strange

Having completed this exploration of the Christian bioethics of sexuality, one can now in summary see more fully why the traditional Christian bioethical approach to sexuality and reproduction is radically out of step with what contemporary secular and post-traditional Christian moral theology would lead one to expect from a bioethics. Yet, how could a traditional Christian bioethics be anything but out of step? The ethos of this bioethics is rooted in the mind-set of the Church Fathers of the first millennium, instructed by an experience of God unreconstructed by Scholasticism or the Enlightenment. This bioethics is focused on freeing our hearts from passion, turning our attention from ourselves, and redirecting our energies to union with God. The categories of Christian bioethics include an appreciation of involuntary sin and sins committed in ignorance. It acknowledges that our involvement in the broken character of the world, if not spiritually remedied, can mar the heart: our openness to God. A traditional Christian bioethics is focused critically on anything that can deflect or distract from the pursuit of the Kingdom of God. A traditional Christian bioethics is not confined to considerations of the good, the right, and the virtuous. The language of the Gospels is not the language of rights, goods, or virtues. Traditional Christian bioethics is first and foremost concerned with how, despite our involvement not just in illness, disease, and health care, but in sin and moral brokenness, we can pursue holiness, the Kingdom of Heaven.

Traditional Christian bioethics is in this sense primarily therapeutic.[165] It is only secondarily focused on imposing a set of rules, regulations, or canons. Christian bioethics is not legalistic. It points beyond the law to the purpose of the law: union with God. The Church is uncompromising in her demand that we open our hearts to God, that we become perfect, that we become saints. She is therapeutic in her approach to making us perfect. She recognizes that she must begin by treating us where she finds us in our sins. This general point is key to understanding the ascetical character of a traditional Christian bioethics: it seeks to liberate through repentance, fasting, almsgiving, and vigils from the involvement in sin that has broken our world. On the one hand, Christianity calls all to a perfection impossible even for the saints, to be perfect as the Father is perfect (Matt 5:48). On the other hand, traditional Christianity recognizes that it must reconcile us to the pursuit of holiness in the midst of our sinfulness. Such a Christian bioethics is not in its core an intellectual discursive enterprise. It is part of a way of life that must engage us in the journey to God.

For all of these reasons, a traditional Christian bioethics contrasts starkly with a secular bioethics. A general secular bioethics provides a common moral framework for individuals who do not share the same moral vision or live within the same moral community. It is a bioethics for people who share neither a common, content-full, moral life nor a sense of moral rationality. These are individuals who by the very moral logic of their circumstances do not possess a common understanding of how to resolve content-full moral controversies by sound rational argument or by an appeal to a commonly acknowledged authority. These are people who disagree about what is good to do, about the content of right- and wrong-making conditions, about the nature of virtue and the significance of moral character. It is because of this conflicted character of the moral geography that secular bioethics has its procedural, even its adversarial character. Because of the controversies defining the contemporary moral environment, the emphasis is on claims and counter-claims, visions of the good and contrary visions of the good, rights and the impeachment of rights. Because secular bioethics does not have a canonical content, the default position for resolving moral controversies is common agreement.

Within such a procedural morality, the accent falls on determining who has consented to what and under what circumstances. The focus is on the adequacy of consent and determinations of when humans have a standing such that they can invoke forbearance rights or have others speak on their behalf. The secular bioethics of sexual relations, reproduction, and abortion is primarily a matter of the adequacy and the nature of consent among moral agents. The moral issues at stake in the web of possible collaborators and partners in third-party-assisted reproduction tend similarly to be clarified. One is brought to address consent, the sufficiency of consent, the presence of coercion, and other matters that might limit the free agreement of moral agents in the use of their gametes, zygotes, embryos, and fetuses. In this circumstance, there is often a sense that certain undertakings are wrong, but no sense of why. Cloning, for example, is a moral puzzle that cannot be adequately understood in general secular terms: there is a haunting sense that something is profoundly morally askew. This moral discomfort cannot be articulated in secular terms. After all, to understand the wrongness would require turning to God. Regarding *in vitro* fertilization with embryo transfer, fetal experimentation, and abortion, the general secular moral focus falls on when human biological life becomes human personal life, as well as on who has the right to dispose of what instances of human biological life. The bare focus on consent tends to be augmented through a secular search for further meaning in an emerging cosmopolitan ethos of liberation from traditional constraints. The result is a celebration of the new and a search to break the bonds of traditional restraints within a liberal cosmopolitan sexual ethos announcing its repudiation of the remnants of Christian ascesis. The bioethics formed by this ethos endorses as integral to human dignity the right to have others affirm one's sexual acts and choices as integral to mutual respect, even when they are sinful and perverse.

Some may share or think they share sufficient moral premises to allow the rational resolution of content-full moral controversies. However, insofar as these moral premises are not successfully secured in a self-authenticating ultimate truth, the light of rational analysis and the force of persistent inquiry will disclose the secular arbitrariness of any particular moral vision, leading to its collapse or fragmentation into a diversity of moral visions: the cacophony of post-modernity. As the first chapter rehearsed, secular morality, along with its secular bioethics, is destined to become either procedural or many bioethics.

In all of these matters and more, this chapter has shown a traditional Christian bioethics to be of quite a different character. The primary focus is not on moral controversies. The focus is not on resolving through discursive rationality disputes among conflicting stake-holders. Attention is not on how to mediate among competing understandings of the good, the right, and the virtuous. One is invited through prayer, asceticism, and worship towards unity with God. Because traditional Christian bioethics is focused on the experience and pursuit of holiness, its challenge is not from moral diversity but from temptation. Its attention falls on what separates from holiness, what seduces from holiness, and what restores to its pursuit and experience. This spiritual therapeutic character of traditional Christian bioethics must be understood not just in terms of aiding in better hitting the mark or in restoring wholeness to the broken character of human life, but also in how Christian bioethics aids us in turning away from evil, which evil in the end is always ultimately personal. The language of such a bioethics is therefore strikingly different from that of a secular procedural bioethics, or of a bioethics of any sort that would attempt to lay out an immanently directed morality in terms of purely discursive considerations. A traditional Christian bioethics deals with the relation of human persons with the Persons of the Trinity. In such a context, morality is a truth that out of an experience of the transcendent securely binds across history. Here one encounters the most fundamental difference defining a traditional Christian bioethics. Its morality is radically personal. There is no moral truth outside of persons and their relations. As a result, traditional Christian bioethics appropriately has the character of a cosmic narrative, a story into which persons are placed on their way to or away from God.

Notes

1. T. M. Scanlon expresses this secular attitude well regarding the moralisms of traditional sexual morality in *What We Owe to Each Other* (Cambridge, MA: Harvard University Press, 1998), p. 174: "Sexual morality gets a bad name from being identified with a list of prohibitions, such as those concerning masturbation, sodomy, and other 'deviant' sexual practices."

2. There is a failure in secular morality to recognize how sexual activity that directs away from God harms not just oneself, but others. "[S]pecific moral prohibitions against certain forms of sexual conduct – against masturbation, for example, or against sexual relations between two men or between two women – has no plausibility whatever when the term 'moral' is understood to refer to 'what we owe to each other.'" Scanlon, *What We Owe to Each Other*, p. 172.

3. Very much as ears may legitimately be used to support the earpieces of glasses, though the design and purpose of ears have nothing to do with glasses, within marriage carnal relations may legitimately be used for the preservation of chastity, including the strengthening of the marriage bond, though the purpose of the institution of carnal relations remains that of begetting children.

4. For a discussion of the distinctions between first- and second-order intentions, see Harry Frankfurt, "Freedom of the Will and the Concept of a Person," *Journal of Philosophy* 68 (1971), 5-20; "Coercion and Moral Responsibility," in *Essays on Freedom of Action*, ed. T. Honderich (London: Routledge, 1972), pp. 72-85; and Harry Frankfurt and D. Locke, "Three Concepts of Free Action," *Proceedings of the Aristotelian Society*, suppl. Vol. 49 (1975), 95-125. These are then applied to bioethical issues in Irving Thalberg, "Motivational Disturbances and Free Will," pp. 201-220, and Caroline Whitbeck, "Towards an Understanding of Motivational Disturbance and Freedom of Action," pp. 221-231, in *Mental Health: Philosophical Perspectives*, eds. H. T. Engelhardt, Jr., and S. F. Spicker (Dordrecht: Reidel, 1978).

5. In the course of this chapter and those that follow, in addressing moral perils or difficulties, terms such as "spiritual peril", "spiritual difficulty", "spiritual risk", etc., will be used. "Spiritual" is employed to indicate that the focus is on holiness. A traditional Christian bioethics is not simply concerned with a science of immanent morality, nor with an immanently directed ethic, mores, or cluster of consuetudinary matters. Christian bioethics is meant to lead us beyond the good, the right, the just, and the virtuous to the holy, to the Kingdom of God.

6. Traditional Christianity recognizes that there is no *analogia entis*, no analogy between created and uncreated being. One cannot apply by analogy to God predicates appropriate to created being. For example, St. Maximos the Confessor states: "Created beings are termed intelligible because each of them has an origin that can be known rationally. But God cannot be termed intelligible, while from our apprehension of intelligible beings we can do no more than believe that He exists. On this account no intelligible being is in any way to be compared with Him." "Two Hundred Texts on Theology and the Incarnate Dispensation of the Son of God," in *The Philokalia*, eds. Sts. Nikodimos and Makarios, trans. G.E.H. Palmer, Philip Sherrard, and Kallistos Ware (Boston: Faber and Faber, 1984), vol. 2, p. 115. Terms applied from revelation to God aid us to approach Him, although the meaning of their attribution to God remains obscure.

7. Because they assume one can reason to the character of morality, both secular and post-traditional Christian bioethics attempt to provide a fully immanent account of sexual bioethics. Human sexual morality is thus to be made reasonable in human terms. As chapters 1, 2, and 3 show, this project has important consequences. (1) As Christian bioethics is reduced to secular bioethics, so, too, Christian sexual bioethics is reduced to secular sexual bioethics. (2) Christian bioethics and therefore Christian sexual bioethics are then construed in fully immanent terms, more specifically in terms of the liberal cosmopolitan ethos.

8. The traditional Christian focus is not juridical but therapeutic, a point well made by Metropolitan Hierotheos, who draws on an instance recorded in *The Sayings of the Desert Fathers*. "A brother questioned Abba Poemen saying: 'I have committed a great sin and I want to do penance for three years.' The old man said to him, 'That is a lot.' He added, 'I myself say that if a man repents with his whole heart and does not intend to commit the sin any more, God will accept him after only three days.' The example shows that to be deprived of Holy Communion, the so-called penance, is a therapeutic medicine; it should be included in the therapeutic training of the Church." *The Mind of the Orthodox Church*, trans. Esther Williams (Levadia, Greece: Birth of the Theotokos Monastery, 1998), p. 183. See also "Poemen (called the Shepherd)" #12 in *The Sayings of the Desert Fathers*, trans. Benedicta Ward (Kalamazoo: Cistercian Publications, 1975), p. 169.

9. Human life is marked by sin: "For all have sinned, and come short of the glory of God" (Rom 3:23). The word for sin used by Paul and generally in the Greek biblical text is *hamartia*. This term is etymologically tied to missing the mark, as with a spear throw. The term in the Greek compasses the idea of failing in one's purpose, being deprived of something important, having been wrong or mistaken, being involved in a failure, fault, or error. See H.G. Liddell and R. Scott, *Greek-English Lexicon* (Oxford: Clarendon Press, 1996), p. 77. It is associated with the concept in Aristotle's *Poetics* of *hamartia*, the failure, fault, or guilt, including mistakes made in ignorance leading to the fall of a tragic hero. This concept of fault is not bound simply to a voluntary choice, a choice made in full and unconstrained knowledge. The image of missing the mark also brings to mind in the Christian context that the aim of a Christian life is perfection, of which all fall short. To convey the recognition that while aiming at holiness all fall short of the mark, phrases are used such as the one to which this footnote is tied. Included in this sense of sin is all that leads us away from God, whether or not done knowingly or voluntarily: all will always fall short of the mark.

10. We are called to recognize sin along with the radical possibility of complete forgiveness. "If you forgive anyone his sins they are forgiven; if you do not forgive them, they are not forgiven." John 20:23.

11. Chrysostom, Homily XXXIV.7 on First Corinthians xiii.8, NPNF1, vol. 12, p. 205. In this homily, St. John explains "Further, in order that the one might be subject, and the other rule; (for equality is wont oftentimes to bring in strife;) he suffered it not to be a democracy, but a monarchy; and as in an army, this order one may see in every family. In the rank of monarch, for instance, there is the husband; but in the rank of lieutenant and general, the wife; and the children too are allotted a third station in command." *Ibid.*, p. 204.

12. Traditional Christianity recognizes man and woman as equal within an order or *taxis*, where men and women have different reproductive as well as liturgical roles. The role of the presbyter as the icon of the second Adam makes priestesses impossible, for Christ, the second Adam, was clearly understood in this male role. "Christ revealed Himself as of the male sex when He opened the Virgin's womb." *The Pentecostarion* (Boston, MA: Holy Transfiguration Monastery, 1990), p. 29. See also Kenneth Wesche, "Man and Woman in Orthodox Tradition: The Mystery of Gender," *St. Vladimir's Theological Quarterly* 37 (1993), 213-251; Brian Mitchell, "Scandal of Subjection," *St. Sophia Quarterly* 30 (Autumn 1996), 8-9; and Patrick Mitchell, *The Scandal of Gender* (Salisbury, MA: Regina Orthodox Press, 1998).

It is important to note that the passage in Galatians read by some nowadays in favor of the ordination of Christian priestesses was never so understood by the Church of the first millennium. Instead, it was read as showing that baptism allowed all salvation, whether male or female. "For as many as were baptized into Christ, yet put on Christ. There is neither Jew nor Greek, there is neither slave nor free, there is neither male and female; for ye are all one in Christ Jesus. And if ye are Christ's, then are ye Abraham's seed, and heirs according to promise" (Gal 3:27-29). As St. John Chrysostom stresses in commentary, "that is, ye have all one form and one mould, even Christ's. What can be more awful than these words! He that was a Greek, or Jew, or bondman yesterday, carries about with him the form, not of an Angel or Archangel, but of the Lord of all, yea displays in his own person the Christ." Chrysostom, Commentary on Galatians iii.28, NPNF1, vol. 13, p. 30. Tarazi supposes that St. Paul is here stressing that being baptized in Christ is in no way related to the natural sexual order of things. "Finally, my interpretation leads to a more plausible explanation for the quotation from Gen 1:27. That text stresses sexuality even more than is at first apparent; it continues, "And God blessed them, and God said to them: Be fruitful and multiply..." (v.28). Therefore, by quoting Gen 1:27 but negating it ("there is no male and female"), Paul was emphasizing that baptism in Christ was in no way related to the "natural-sexual" order of things...". Paul Nadim Tarazi, *Galatians: A Commentary* (Crestwood, NY: St. Vladimir's Seminary Press, 1994), p. 176. See also Patrick Mitchell, *The Scandal of Gender* (Salisbury, MA: Regina Orthodox Press, 1998), p. 21f.

13. St. Paul makes this point on a number of occasions with regard to ecclesiastical order or hierarchy. "And I do not permit a woman to teach, nor to have authority over a man, but to be in silence" (I Tim 2:12). "For a man indeed is not obliged for his head to be covered, since he is the image and glory of God; but the woman is the glory of man. For man is not of woman, but woman of man. For also man was not created on account of the woman, but woman on account of the man. For this cause ought the woman to have authority on the head on account of the angels" (I Cor 11:7-10). As Fr. John Breck points out, St. Paul is making reference to the angels, who are responsible for the *taxis* or order of the house of worship. Wearing a headcovering not only shows this order and curbs "a lustful wandering of male eyes", but also avoids any confusion between the sexes. *The Sacred Gift of Life* (Crestwood, NY: St. Vladimir's Seminary Press, 1998), p. 86.

14. "If we have insisted so adamantly on this point, it is because of its implications for the realm of sexual behavior. Most basically, if gender and its sexual expression have neither ontological nor spiritual significance, then sexual behavior is limited to earthly life, with no eternal consequences. In such a case, sexual morality would be a psychological or sociological issue, not a theological one. On the other hand, if the sexes are ontologically equal and complementary, sharing a common nature yet reflecting in ways appropriate to their specific gender the beauty and perfection of the divine nature, then sexual conduct impacts directly on the person's growth toward the likeness of God. Orthodox Tradition unquestionably holds the latter to be the case." *Ibid.*, p. 87.

15. "I grant that in other matters Paul gives the husband superior authority, when he says, 'Let each one of you love his wife as himself, and let the wife see that she respects her husband' (Eph 5:33). He also says, 'The husband is the head of the wife,' and, 'The wife ought to be subject to her husband' (Eph 5:23, 24)." St. John Chrysostom, *On Marriage and Family Life*, trans. Catherine Roth and David Anderson (Crestwood, NY: St. Vladimir's Seminary Press, 1986), p. 87.

16. Though the term gender has taken on new life in the past decades, its first meaning, now obsolete, identifies "kind, sort, class; also, genus as opposed to species" and its second meaning is "Each of the three (or in some languages two) grammatical 'kinds', corresponding more or less to distinctions of sex." *Oxford English Dictionary* (1970), vol. 4, p. 100.

Sex, in the sense of male and female sex, has as its first meaning "either of the two divisions of organic beings distinguished as male and female respectively" and as its second meaning "quality in respect of being male or female". Even the third meaning indicates a reality of difference prior to those focused on reproduction: "the distinction between male and female in general" (*OED*, vol. 9, pp. 577-8).

17. In the Church that employed the New Testament in the Greek, the term "mystery" was used to identify what in the West have come to be called sacraments. Although the Eastern Church acknowledges at least seven sacraments, she has not drawn a rigid line between sacraments and sacramentals, recognizing that in all these ways the Church is bringing the world into contact with the energies that flow from the unknowable, transcendent God. In addition, the term "mystery" is particularly appropriate for marriage, for it is that which St. Paul himself uses in Ephesians when he says, "This mysterion is great" (Eph 5:32). The term sacrament gained currency in the West through Tertullian, drawing on a Latin term that identified both a sum of money deposited by parties in a suit to be forfeited by the losing party and used to support religious purposes (e.g., the *sacra publica*), as well as a military oath, a *sacramentum*. The Greek *mysterion* is tied to notions of sacred and secret rites, divine worship, and secrets revealed by God. See Henry George Liddell and Robert Scott, *A Greek-English Lexicon* (Oxford: Clarendon Press, 1978), pp. 1609-1610, and Charlton T. Lewis, *A Latin Dictionary* (Oxford: Clarendon Press, 1980), pp. 1611-1612.

18. Consider, for example, the couple Sts. Adronicus and Athanasia, who lived during the time of Theodosius the Great (379-395) and who after the deaths of their children separated to pursue the ascetic struggle as monastics (feastday October 9). See St. Demetrius of Rostov, *The Great Collection of the Lives of the Saints*, trans. Fr. Thomas Marretta (House Springs, MO: Chrysostom Press, 1995), vol. 2, pp. 150-159.

19. Here an important observation is introduced regarding the spiritual life: the importance of mourning our broken, sinful state and our involvement in it. This emphasis identifies the distance between traditional Christianity and later legalistic or pietistic developments. The moral choices of traditional Christians should not be regarded in a legalistic fashion as simply a choice between being either guilty or innocent with respect to some law, canon, or moral principle. Moral choices when placed in terms of their full spiritual significance involve the pursuit of God, which within the broken character of the world and the sinfulness of one's life will often, if not always, require special repentance in the recognition of how far one falls short of perfection. This attitude towards the moral life sets traditional Christianity over against legalistic understandings that developed in Roman Catholicism. In its accent on repentance, prayer, almsgiving, and mourning through fasting and vigils, traditional Christianity turns us through repentance away from ourselves to God and our neighbor.
An example of this approach to the moral life is provided in the counsels of St. Dorotheos of Gaza (500-580). "There are times when urgent necessity arises and unless a man conceals the bitter fact, the affair gives rise to greater trouble and affliction. When, therefore, such circumstances arise a man should know that in such cases of need he may adapt his speech so as to avoid the greater disaster or danger. As Abba Alonios said to Abba Agathon: 'Suppose two men committed a murder in your presence and one of them fled to your cell. Then the police, coming in search of him, asks you, "Is the murderer with you?" Unless you dissimulate, you hand him over to death.' But if a man did such a thing, in extreme necessity, let him not be without anxiety but let him repent and sorrow before God and consider it, as I said, a time of trial and not let it become a habit but done once and for all." Dorotheos of Gaza, *Discourses and Sayings*, trans. Eric Wheeler (Kalamazoo, MI: Cistercian Publications, 1977), pp. 160-1.

20. The term philtres identifies love potions and in general spells and charms. The term translated as magic is *pharmakoi* and has a similar scope including not just medicines, but also potions and magic spells.

21. "Didache," in *Apostolic Fathers*, trans. Kirsopp Lake (Cambridge, MA: Harvard University Press, 1965), II 2, vol. 1, p. 311f.

22. "Epistle of Barnabas," in *Apostolic Fathers*, trans. Kirsopp Lake (Cambridge, MA: Harvard University Press, 1965), XIX 4-5, vol. 1, p. 403.

23. St. Irenaeus of Lyons (A.D. 130-202), for example, speaks at length concerning Jesus and Mary as the second Adam and Eve.

... so did He who is the Word, recapitulating Adam in Himself, rightly receive a birth, enabling Him to gather up Adam [into Himself], from Mary, who was as yet a virgin. If, then, the first Adam had a man for his father, and was born of human seed, it were reasonable to say that the second Adam was begotten of Joseph. But if the former was taken from the dust, and God was his Maker, it was incumbent that the latter also, making a recapitulation in Himself, should be formed as man by God, to have an analogy with the former as respects His origin. Why, then, did not God again take dust, but wrought so that the formation should be Mary? It was that there might not be another formation called into being, nor any other which should [require to] be saved, but that the very same formation should be summed up [in Christ as had existed in Adam], the analogy having been preserved. ... In accordance with this design, Mary the Virgin is found obedient, saying, 'Behold the handmaid of the Lord; be it unto me according to thy word.' But Eve was disobedient; for she did not obey when as yet she was a virgin. And even as she, having indeed a husband, Adam, but being nevertheless as yet a virgin (for in Paradise 'they were both naked, and were not ashamed,' inasmuch as they, having been created a short time previously, had no understanding of the procreation of children: for it was necessary that they should first come to adult age, and then multiply from that time onward), having become disobedient, was made the cause of death, both to herself and to the entire human race; so also did Mary, having a man betrothed [to her], and being nevertheless a virgin, by yielding obedience, become the cause of salvation, both to herself and the whole human race. ... because what is joined together could not otherwise be put asunder than by inversion of the process by which these bonds of union had arisen; so that the former ties be cancelled by the latter, that the latter may set the former again at liberty. ... He having been made Himself the beginning of those that live, as Adam became the beginning of those who die. ... And thus also it was that the knot of Eve's disobedience was loosed by the obedience of Mary. For what the virgin Eve had bound fast through unbelief, this did the virgin Mary set free through faith. Irenaeus, "Irenaeus Against Heresies," in ANF, vol. 1, pp. 454-5.

24. Revelations foretells the final restoration. "Then I saw a new heaven and a new earth, for the first heaven and the first earth had passed away, and there was no longer any sea. I saw the Holy City, the new Jerusalem, coming down out of heaven from God, prepared as a bride beautifully dressed for her husband." Rev 21:1-2.

25. "For this God banished them from Paradise, as from a royal palace, to live in this world as exiles. At that time also He decreed that a flaming sword should be turned and should guard the entrance into Paradise. And God did not curse Paradise, since it was the image of the future unending life of the eternal Kingdom of Heaven." St. Symeon the New Theologian, *The First-Created Man*, trans. Fr. Seraphim Rose (Platina, CA: St. Herman of Alaska Brotherhood, 1994), p. 91.

26. Philip Sherrard, in his criticism of *Humanae Vitae*, accents the importance of drawing a distinction between the nature of the world in which we find ourselves, and the nature of the world in which we ought to have been. That is, he reminds us to take the Fall seriously.

And this breach, this dislocation, in man's natural state, this fall into a materialised space-time universe, has, it will then be understood, not only resulted in a loss of spiritual vision and in the contracting of the human mind to the perspectives of a fundamentally unreal world; it has also introduced a corresponding alteration in the laws of nature itself, so that these two are now tainted by something of the abnormality and corruption which vitiates human life itself. They are not the laws as they are ordained by God. They are these laws deformed and denaturalised by the fall of Adam – a fall which itself is profoundly unnatural and *contrary to the will of God*. To accept the laws of nature and natural processes as they appear to the human mind in this fallen world as expressing the will of God and therefore as intuiting the norm for the moral law, is to shift the responsibility for a human act that is contrary to the will of God from man to God, and to make God the ultimate author not only of man's crime but also of the

abnormal and corrupt conditions of the world which issues from it. God becomes responsible for that state of servitude to which man reduces himself and the whole natural order as a result of his assertion of a false liberty in the face of his Creator.
Philip Sherrard, *Sobornost* (London: Fellowship of St. Alban and St. Sergius, 1969), p. 578.

27. Isabel Hapgood (trans.), *Service Book of the Holy Orthodox-Catholic Apostolic Church* (Englewood, NJ: Antiochian Orthodox Christian Archdiocese, 1983), p. 103.
28. Chrysostom, Homily XX on Ephesians v.22-24, NPNF1, vol. 13, p. 143.
29. In the interpretation of Deuteronomy's account of the grounds for divorce, Rabbi Shammai proclaims a position regarding marriage largely in accord with that of Christ, but not with that of Rabbi Hillel who gave a broad interpretation to the passage: "If a man married a woman who becomes displeasing to him because he finds something indecent about her" (Deut 24:1).
30. "But it becomes both men and women who marry, to form their union with the approval of the bishop, that their marriage may be according to God, and not after their own lust. Let all things be done to the honour of God." St. Ignatius, "Epistle of Ignatius to Polycarp," chapter 5, in ANF, vol. 1, p. 95.
31. Chrysostom, Homily XX on Ephesians v.22-24, NPNF1, vol. 13, p. 147.
32. St. John Chrysostom, "Sermon on Marriage," in *On Marriage and Family Life*, p. 81.
33. "God, in the beginning when He created man, created him holy, passionless, and sinless, in His own image and likeness." St. Symeon the New Theologian, *The First-Created Man*, trans. Fr. Seraphim Rose (Platina, CA: St. Herman of Alaska Brotherhood, 1994), p. 51.
34. Chrysostom, Homily XII on Colossians iv.12,13, NPNF1, vol. 13, p. 319.
35. "Matrimonium libidinis indulgentia est." *Sacra Parallela*, Littera Π, Tit. X, "De virginitate, et pudicitia, et honestis nuptiis." *Patrologiae Graecae*, ed. J. Migne (Paris, 1891), vol. 96, col. 247B.
36. Chrysostom, Homily XII on Colossians iv.12,13, NPNF1, vol. 13, p. 319.
37. St. John Chrysostom, "Sermon on Marriage," in *On Marriage and Family Life*, p. 85.
38. St. John Chrysostom emphasizes that the urge for the union between husband and wife is rooted in God's drawing Eve from Adam. Separated as the two sexes, there is a drive felt by each for joining, an urge for love that Chrysostom indicates is among the strongest human drives. "For there is no relationship between man and man so close as that between husband and wife, if they be joined together as they should be. ... For indeed, in very deed, this love is more despotic than any despotism: for others indeed may be strong, but this passion is not only strong, but unfading. For there is a certain love deeply seated in our nature, which imperceptibly to ourselves knits together these bodies of ours. Thus even from the very beginning woman sprang from man, and afterwards from man and woman sprang both man and woman. Perceivest thou the close bond and connection? And how that God suffered not a different kind of nature to enter in from without? And mark, how many providential arrangements He made. He permitted the man to marry his own sister; or rather not his sister, but his daughter; nay, nor yet his daughter, but something more than his daughter, even his own flesh. ... For there is nothing which so welds our life together as the love of man and wife." Chrysostom, Homily XX on Ephesians v.22, NPNF1, vol. 13, p. 143.
39. St. John Chrysostom's commentary on this passage in St. Paul's first letter to the Corinthians emphasizes a unique equality of husbands and wives in matters sexual. "Why does Paul introduce so much equality? Although in other matters there needs to be a superior authority, here where chastity and holiness are at stake, the husband has no greater privilege than the wife." "Sermon on Marriage," in *On Marriage and Family Life*, pp. 87-88.
40. Sts. Nicodemus and Agapius (eds.), "The Four Canons of our Father Among the Saints Dionysius," in *The Rudder*, trans. D. Cummings (New York: Luna Printing, 1983), Canon III, p. 720.

41. Chrysostom, Homily LXIII on John xi.30,31, NPNF1, vol. 14, p. 235.

42. "The 85 Canons of the Holy and Renowned Apostles," *The Rudder*, Canon LI, p. 91. See also Constantine Cavarnos, *St. Nicodemos the Hagiorite*, vol. 3 of *Modern Orthodox Saints* (Belmont, MA: Institute for Byzantine and Modern Greek Studies, 1994).

43. The fasts in their fullness invoke not just abstaining from certain foods, at times going without food, praying more zealously, and giving more alms, but also avoiding marital conversation. Generally, there has also been a fast, among others, from at least the night before Communion, as attested in Question V and its answer from St. Timothy, Pope of Alexandria (fl. 370-2nd Ecumenical Council). "If a woman has coition with her husband during the night, or, as likely as not, a man with his wife, and a church meeting ensues, ought they to partake of communion, or not? Answer: They ought not to do so, because the Apostle says emphatically: 'Deprive yourselves not of each other, unless it be for a time by agreement, that ye may give yourselves leisure to pray; and then come ye again together, to avoid having Satan tempt you on account of your failure to mingle' (I Cor 7:5)." *The Rudder*, p. 892. To the question, "What days of the week ought to be assigned to those who are conjoined in marriage for them to abstain from communion with each other? And on what days ought they to have it?" St. Timothy responded, "Though I have already answered this question, I will answer now once more. The Apostle says, 'Deprive ye not yourselves of each other, unless it be for a time by agreement, in order that ye may have leisure to pray' (I Cor 7:5). And again 'Come ye together again, that Satan tempt you not on account of your failure to mingle' (*ibid.*). But one must necessarily abstain on Saturday and Sunday, on account of the fact that on these days the spiritual sacrifice is being offered to the Lord." "The 18 Canons of Timothy," in *The Rudder*, Question XIII, p. 897. As the commentary also indicates, they are to refrain from sexual intercourse because "they had to prepare themselves and get ready to partake of the divine Mysteries" (*ibid.*).

44. "The Twenty-One Canons of the Regional Council held in Gangra," *The Rudder*, Canon I, p. 523.

45. "The One Hundred and Two Canons of the Holy and Ecumenical Quinisext (or Quinisextine) Council," *The Rudder*, Canon XIII, pp. 305-6. This endorsement of a married clergy by the Fathers at the Quinisext Council (i.e., the Council in Trullo) represents a restatement of the position affirmed by the Fathers for the universal Church at Nicea I (A.D. 325) in response to an attempt from the West to forbid a married, sexually active clergy. Regarding the first Council of Nicea, Socrates Scholasticus records the following: "It seemed fit to the bishops to introduce a new law into the Church, that those who were in holy orders, I speak of bishops, presbyters, and deacons, should have no conjugal intercourse with the wives whom they had married while still laymen. Now when discussion on this matter was impending, Paphnutius having arisen in the midst of the assembly of bishops, earnestly entreated them not to impose so heavy a yoke on the ministers of religion: asserting that 'marriage itself is honorable, and the bed undefiled'; urging before God that they ought not to injure the Church by too stringent restrictions. 'For all men,' said he, 'cannot bear the practice of rigid continence; neither perhaps would the chastity of the wife of each be preserved': and he termed the intercourse of a man with his lawful wife chastity." Socrates Scholasticus, *The Ecclesiastical History*, trans. A. C. Zenos, NPNF1, vol. 2, p. 18. Sozomen confirms the account of Socrates: "but Paphnutius, the confessor, stood up and testified against this proposition; he said that marriage was honorable and chaste, and that cohabitation with their own wives was chastity." Sozomenus, *The Ecclesiastical History*, trans. Chester Hartranft, NPNF1, vol. 2, p. 256. See also Nicon Patrinacos, *The Orthodox Church on Birth Control* (Garwood, NJ: Graphic Arts Press, 1975), p. 21.

46. "The most basic consequence [of the Fall] is the fact that the physical mode of man's life is changed and marked by pleasure and pain. Man was destined to live eternally, but through

his choice of temporal, sensible pleasure he called upon himself – according to God's good counsel – a pain, which introduced into his life a law of death, which – seen from the aspect of the divine purpose – is there to put an end to his destructive escape from his natural goal. Death is thus the culmination of pain. On the other hand, man is still created to live, and mankind gains its life, after the fall, by means of that very lust, sexual intercourse, which is an excellent example of sense pleasure, and which also leads to a birth through pain. The law of death, putting an end to individual life, has its counterpart in a law of pleasure, regulating new physical life. These laws constitute the collective imprisonment of fallen man, from which he cannot escape, except through Christ." Lars Thunberg, *Microcosm and Mediator. The Theological Anthropology of Maximus the Confessor* (Copenhagen: C.W.K. Gleerup, Lund and Einar Munksgaard, 1965), p. 169.

47. Chrysostom, Homily XIII on Romans vii.14A, NPNF1, vol. 11, pp. 427-8.

48. St. Gregory Nazianzen, "Oration on Holy Baptism," NPNF1, vol. 7, p. 365.

49. Sherrard provides a heuristic overview of the significant errors involved in attempting to read natural law from the characteristics of nature without taking the Fall into account. "It is the laws and processes of this fallen and corrupted nature that are said to express the will of God, to express God's pleasure and purpose, and this even where man himself is concerned. They reflect the divine scheme of things. We are here within a sphere of theology according to which the fall of man and the deformations it introduces into creation are regarded as natural events, events, that is to say, which conform to the will of God. Man's fallen life, and the natural processes to which he is subject in the fallen world, constitute the norm on which the moral law of the Church is to be based. Man's natural life is regarded as that which he lives within the world as it is, as it is perceived by the senses, that in which he has fallen away from his original glory. There is no longer any recognition that this life is profoundly abnormal and unnatural where man is concerned. There is no acknowledgment that it is not that which God created or intended for man, but is what man has brought on himself as a result of his own defection and lapse. And there is consequently no recognition that the norm for what is natural for man, and hence for what constitutes the moral law, may lie in a completely different order of reality, and that to derive it from this world as it is, and man's life as it is in this world, is to mistake human error and its consequences for divine ordinances." Philip Sherrard, *Sobornost* (London: Fellowship of St. Alban and St. Sergius, 1969), p. 572.

50. Saint Basil, "The Long Rules," in *Ascetical Works*, trans. Monica Wagner (Washington, DC: Catholic University of America Press, 1962), response 2, p. 233.

51. This appreciation of the unnaturalness of fornication and adultery does not undercut the special unnaturalness St. Paul and the Fathers, indeed the Church, recognize in homosexual acts and bestiality as going against not just the marital union of husband and wife, but the proper union of male and female. All these moral assessments of improper sexual acts are made without invoking a particular philosophical account of natural and unnatural acts. Instead, natural sexuality is defined in terms of the undefiled character of the marriage bed (Heb 13:4) and the intention of the Creator. As a result, for instance, the canonical condemnation of masturbation is advanced without a particular biological or philosophical account of natural law.

   Improper carnal unions, along with the self-mutilation of castration, are often compared to murder in order to recognize their profoundly wrong-directed character in rejecting the normative character of humans. Canon VII of St. Basil the Great states, for example: "Sodomists and bestialists and murderers and sorcerers and adulterers and idolaters deserve the same condemnation, so that whatever rule you have as regarding the others observe it also in regard to these persons." *The Rudder*, p. 793. Canon IV of St. Gregory of Nyssa presents a detailed picture of the attitude of the Church regarding these sins. "As for sins done for the satisfaction of desire and for pleasure, they are divided as follows: It has pleased some of the more accurate authorities, indeed, to deem the offense of fornication to be tantamount to adultery; for there is but one lawful state of matrimony and conjugal relationship, namely, that of wife to husband and of husband to wife. Everything, then, that is not lawful is unlawful at any rate, including even the case in which has no wife of his own, but has that of another man. For only one helper was given to man by God (Gen 2:20), and only one head was set over woman. 'That every one of you should know how to possess his vessel in sanctification and honor,' as divine Paul says (I Thes 4:4-5), the law of nature permits the right use of it. But if anyone turns from his own, he will infringe upon another's in any case; but another's is whatever is not one's own, even though its owner is not acknowledged. Hence it is evident that fornication is not far removed from the offense of adultery, as has been shown by those who give the question more accurate consideration, seeing that even the divine Scripture says: 'But not too intimate with another man's wife' (Prov 5:20). Nevertheless, inasmuch as a certain concession was made by the Fathers in the case to weaker men, the offense has been distinguished on the basis of the following general division to the effect that whenever a man fulfills his desire without doing any injustice to another man, the offense is to be called fornication; but when it is committed by plotting against and injuring another man, it is to be called adultery. Copulation with the lower animals, too, and paederasty are considered to belong to this class of offenses, because they too are a sort of adultery, or in the nature of adultery. For the wrongfulness consists in infringing upon what belongs to another or acting contrary to nature. This division, then, having been made also in connection with this kind of sin, the general remedy for it consists in the man's becoming purified and being made pure as a result of regret for the passionate madness for such pleasures. But inasmuch as no injustice has been made admixed with the sin of those polluting themselves by fornication, therefore and on this score the length of time fixed for the return of those tainted by adultery has been double that fixed for the other forbidden evils. For, the penalty for copulation with lower animals and for the madness practiced upon males has been doubled, as I have said, because such cases involve one sin consisting in the enjoyment of a forbidden pleasure, and another sin consisting committing an injustice with what belongs to another man, after the manner of abusing another man's wife." *The Rudder*, pp. 871-2.

52. Robert Trivers, "Parent-Offspring Conflict," *American Zoologist* 14 (1974), 259-64.

53. I have discussed these issues at greater length in *The Foundations of Bioethics,* 2nd ed. (New York: Oxford University Press, 1996), chapter 5. See, also, Ronald Bayer, "Politics, Science, and the Problem of Psychiatric Nomenclature: A Case Study of the American Psychiatric Association Referendum on Homosexuality," in *Scientific Controversies*, eds. H. T. Engelhardt, Jr., and A. L. Caplan (New York: Cambridge University Press, 1987), pp. 381-400; Robert L. Spitzer, "The Diagnostic Status of Homosexuality in DMS-III: A Reformulation of the Issues," pp. 401-415; and Irving Bieber, "On Arriving at the American Psychiatric Association Decision on Homosexuality," pp. 417-436.

54. Regarding ways in which psychology and medicine might be recruited in helping individuals overcome deviant sexual urges (the deviance of which will not be perceivable within a fully secular moral perspective, including a secular medical or secular psychological perspective), see the following volume, which includes, among other things, an examination of the proposed therapeutic taxon, Same Sex Attraction Disorder (SSAD). Christopher Wolfe (ed.), *Homosexuality and the American Public Life* (Dallas: Spence, 1999). See also J. Nicolosi, *Reparative Therapy of Male Homosexuality: A New Clinical Approach* (Northvale, NJ: Jason Aronson, 1991) and C.W. Socarides, *Homosexuality: Psychoanalytic Therapy*, 2nd ed. (Northvale, NJ: Jason Aronson, 1989).

55. H. T. Engelhardt, Jr., *The Foundations of Bioethics*, 2nd ed. (New York: Oxford University Press, 1996).

56. "The Thirty-five Canons of John the Faster" (+619), in *The Rudder*, Canon VIII, p. 936. Xerophagy refers to eating only uncooked foods. A metanie can be a bow from the waist, touching the right hand to the ground, or a prostration, falling on one's knees and touching the forehead to the ground. The canons of St. John the Faster, though widely affirmed, have never been ratified by a Council.

57. *Ibid.*, Canon IX, p. 936.

58. *Ibid.*, Canon XI, p. 939.

59. *Ibid.*, Canon XIX, p. 943.

60. It is essential to recognize that what is at stake is not simply a matter of ritual uncleanliness or simply moral judgment. Instead, the focus is on the challenge of adequately preparing for approaching the holy. This will be further explored in chapter 6.

61. Obviously, it is precarious to reconstruct what exactly was taking place in such illicit liaisons with eunuchs. As to the issue of anal intercourse, the canon appears to be referring to an act performed by men on men and men on women, with no mention of an act performed by women on men. Since fellatio was well known in the ancient world, the assumption must be that this particular canon is directed to anal intercourse. Interestingly, in his summary of Roman Catholic reflections, the term sodomy is restricted among heterosexuals to rectal intercourse. § 230, p. 151. This is not to suggest that Jone and the Roman church considered ejaculation in the mouth anything but a serious sin. Heribert Jone, *Moral Theology*, trans. Urban Adelman (Westminster, MD: Newman Press, 1952). As Payer remarks, "The weight of evidence suggests that reference to heterosexual oral practices is not to be found in these early penitentials, nor is it found in the later manuals except for a canon in the *Tripartite of St Gall*, which makes the only unambiguous reference to a heterosexual oral relation in the Latin penitentials: 'He who emits semen into the mouth of a woman shall do penance for three years; if they are in the habit they shall do penance for seven years.'" Pierre J. Payer, *Sex and the Penitentials* (Toronto: University of Toronto Press, 1984), pp. 29-30. The matter of allowable marital sexual foreplay prior to intercourse has apparently been left to the direction of spiritual fathers.

62. "The Thirty-five Canons of John the Faster," in *The Rudder*, commentary on Canon XXXV, p. 952.

63. There would appear from Juvenal that women had sexual relations with eunuchs in order to avoid becoming pregnant. It is unclear what kind of sexual activity was involved. Juvenal, *Satires*, vi 365-378. See also Norman Himes, *Medical History of Contraception* (New York: Gamut Press, 1963), p. 93.

64. "Wherefore, I beseech Thee, have mercy upon me, and forgive my transgressions, whether voluntary or involuntary; whether of word or of deed; whether committed with knowledge or in ignorance." Hapgood, *Service Book*, pp. 116-117.

65. At the first order volitions, one may find oneself overwhelmed by a compulsion to pursue some activity. If this activity is sinful, one must at least at a second level judge that compulsion to be an evil and to take steps to eradicate the compulsion, if possible, and to contain the opportunities for it to be acted upon. For some reflections on first and second order volitions and related issues, see Harry Frankfurt, "Freedom of the Will and the Concept of a Person," *Journal of Philosophy* 68 (1971), 5-20; "Coercion and Moral Responsibility" in T. Honderich (ed.), *Essays on Freedom of Action* (London: Routledge, 1972), pp. 72-85; H. Frankfurt and D. Locke, "Three Concepts of Free Action," *Proceedings of the Aristotelian Society*, Supp. Vol. 49, pp. 95-125. For a review of Frankfurt's views, see Irving Thalberg, "Motivational Disturbances and Free Will" in H. T. Engelhardt, Jr., and S. F. Spicker (eds.), *Mental Health: Philosophical Perspectives* (Dordrecht: D. Reidel, 1977), pp. 201-220.

66. A traditional Christian could but recognize as deeply morally perverse a dignity march for compulsive adulterers, child molesters, or others who find themselves habitually beset by a

weakness of will that brings them repeatedly to commit immoral acts of a particular sort, if this suggested approval of such behavior. Equally perverse would be a notion of "outing" individuals (i.e., making public a hidden sinful lifestyle of others) and expecting them, once "outed", to affirm this sinful way of life rather than in repentance to declare their sorrow and ask for the prayers of others.

67. Hapgood, *Service Book*, pp. 295-6. Matters would be quite different if it were a procession of penitents asking for God's mercy and the prayers of their fellow-sinners.

68. Likely under influence from the West, which did produce a thick web of sexual regulations bearing on marital sexuality (see, e.g., Pierre J. Payer, *Sex and the Penitentials: The Development of a Sexual Code 550-1150* [Toronto: University of Toronto Press, 1984]), particular Orthodox churches at times had local regulations limiting and constraining marital sexuality. These were never affirmed by the whole Church, which instead maintained a therapeutic approach free of the detailed casuistry of the West. See, for example, Eve Levin, *Sex and Society in the World of Orthodox Slavs, 900-1700* (Ithaca, NY: Cornell University Press, 1989).

69. One of the recent saints living in full continence is St. John of Kronstadt (1829-1907). Bishop Alexander, *The Life of Father John of Kronstadt* (Crestwood, NY: St. Vladimir's Seminary Press, 1979). Though the marriages of continent saints did not involve sexual intercourse, there was no question of their having used their union for the selfish purpose of mere self-satisfaction while avoiding children or of the validity of their marriages. They offered their lives to God. They would therefore not have collided with the conclusion that Zaphiris draws: "From the material we have surveyed above, it should be obvious that there can be no question of entering into marriage without the intention of procreating children as part of the marriage and still remain faithful to the Orthodox moral tradition." Chrysostomos Zaphiris, "The Morality of Contraception: An Eastern Orthodox Opinion," *Journal of Ecumenical Studies* 11 (1974), 682. The offering of themselves and their marriage would have taken priority.

70. Although non-consummation is not grounds for annulment, for holding that a marriage never occurred, "impotence existing prior to marriage and continuing two years after" is a ground for granting divorce and permitting remarriage. Athenagoras Kokkinakis, *Parents and Priests as Servants of Redemption* (New York: Morehouse-Gorham, 1958), p. 54.

71. For a brief treatment of marriage as being rooted in the grace of the Church, not in a contract between the partners, see Athenagoras Kokkinakis, *Parents and Priests as Servants of Redemption* (New York: Morehouse-Gorham, 1958), pp. 38-39. See also John Meyendorff, *Marriage: An Orthodox Perspective* (Crestwood, NY: St. Vladimir's Seminary Press, 1984).

72. Hypospadias is an embryological developmental failure of the male urethra to extend to the end of the penis so as to allow ejaculation of semen in the vagina. It can often be remedied with reconstructive surgery.

73. St. John Chrysostom, Homily XII on Colossians iv.12, 13.

74. Traditionally, there has been a reliance on prayer for the cure of infertility, especially asking the Theotokos to intercede that fertility be granted. The Holy and Great Monastery of Vatopedi on Mount Athos provides to pilgrims a small belt touched to a relic of the Theotokos, her belt, with instructions for special fasting and prayer for those seeking to have children.

75. The first mention of the creation of man and woman is followed by "be fruitful and increase in number; fill the earth" (Gen 1:28).

76. When artificial insemination from the husband involves self-stimulation, it might be appropriate to impose the traditional 40-day excommunication for masturbation so as to recognize the broken character of such an undertaking.

77. As observed in note 19 above, Dorotheos of Gaza's admonitions regarding direct intentional lies to save the life of a person include seriously mourning one's involvement in actions that fall short of the mark. This will usually require the guidance of a spiritual father.

78. Arthur Hertig in 1967 showed that at least 28%, if not 50%, of all conceptions seem to terminate in early unnoticed miscarriages. "Human Trophoblast: Normal and Abnormal," *American Journal of Clinical Pathology* 47 (March 967), 249-68. These findings were reviewed by John D. Biggers, "Generation of the Human Life Cycle," in W. B. Bondeson *et al.* (eds.), *Abortion and the Status of the Fetus* (Dordrecht: Reidel, 1983), pp. 31-53.

79. Hapgood, *Service Book*, p. 109.

80. *The Rudder*, p. 789, note.

81. St. Basil the Great, Letter 188.

82. Chrysostom, Homily XII on Colossians iv.12,13, NPNF1, vol. 13, p. 319.

83. The case of the Theotokos' childbearing is unique. She responded to the will of the Father even more wholeheartedly than Abraham. What then occurred is beyond human comprehension. Yet even here, the icon of Adam and Eve's relationship is maintained by Joseph the Betrothed, who within wedlock without relations nurtures the Christchild Who is God.

84. John Meyendorff, *Marriage: An Orthodox Perspective* (Crestwood, NY: St. Vladimir's Seminary Press, 1984), pp. 18-24.

85. For a exploration of some issues at stake in remarriage as well as the status of second marriages, see Athenagoras Kokkinakis, *Parents and Priests as Servants of Redemption* (New York: Morehouse-Gorham, 1958), esp. chap. 10, "Moral and Physical Death Break the Marriage Bond".

  The marital union of husband and wife is ideally fully monogamous. Therefore, remarriage even after the death of a spouse falls short of the mark. See, for example, Canon VII of the Council of Neocaesarea, which in A.D. 315 held that "the plight of a digamist is one demanding repentance." *The Rudder*, p. 312. See also Canon II of St. Nicephorus, *The Rudder*, p. 963. As St. John Chrysostom emphasizes, a second marriage is not in itself forbidden. "For it is not the union that is objectionable, but the multitude of cares that attend it." Chrysostom, Homily VII on Timothy iii.1-7, NPNF1, vol. 13, p. 503. In that a man remarried should not be a priest or a bishop, St. John Chrysostom recognizes that a second marriage betrays the memory of and union with the first spouse. "For he who retains no kind regard for her who is departed, how shall he be a good president?" "Homilies on Titus," NPNF 1, vol. 13, Homily II, p. 524. There is a real sense in which the first marriage continues, hence those who remarry are termed digamists and trigamists. Indeed, after divorce, if a person separates from a second or third spouse, it is possible to return to a previous spouse. One is not remarried. Instead, a previous marriage is reinstated. In the "Office at the Re-establishment of the Marriage of Divorced Persons" the priest prays, "For the servants of God, N. and N., who are now being rejoined in marriage; that there may be granted unto them an undisgraced life and a blameless state and conduct uncondemned, let us pray to the Lord." David F. Abramtsov, *An Abridged Evchologion* (Philadelphia: Orthodox Catholic Literature Association, 1954), p. 106.

86. For a contrasting secular view of cloning, see Martha Nussbaum and Cass Sunstein (eds.), *Clones and Clones* (New York: W.W. Norton, 1998).

87. Chrysostom, Homily XII on Colossians iv.12,13, NPNF1, vol. 13, p. 319.

88. St. John Chrysostom, "Homily 20 on Ephesians 5:22-33," in *On Marriage and Family Life*, p. 44. "For man did not come from woman, but woman from man ... In the Lord, however, woman is not independent of man, nor is man independent of woman. For as woman came from man, so also man is born of woman. But everything comes from God" (I Cor 11:8,11-12).

89. By 1977, the Supreme Court struck down a New York statute forbidding the distribution of non-prescription contraceptives to children under the age of 16. To understand that one wanted contraceptives was sufficient to consent to their use. *Carey v. Population Services Int'l*, 431 U.S. 678, 97 S.Ct. 2010, 52 L.Ed.2d 675 (1977).

90. For an example of post-traditional Christian justifications of sexual liaisons Christians have for centuries understood to be sinful, see John Shelby Spong, *Living in Sin?* (San Francisco: Harper & Row, 1988). See also Raymond J. Lawrence, Jr., *The Poisoning of Eros* (New York: Augustine Moore Press, 1989).

91. S. F. Spicker, I. Alon, A. de Vries, and H. Tristram Engelhardt, Jr. (eds.), *The Use of Human Beings in Research* (Dordrecht: Kluwer, 1988).

92. See also a general account of the fast from marital conversation and its extent, *The Rudder*, pp. 125-126 footnote.

93. When I speak here as elsewhere in this volume concerning how to give counsel, I do so merely from the experience of a physician, a perspective that possesses no special grace, yet still some knowledge of how carnal passions if not appropriately directed can produce great evil. Wrongly directed carnal passions can lead in addition to divorces and adulteries to sexually transmitted diseases, which in the case of AIDS can cause not only the death of an innocent spouse, but even infection of a child in utero. In this last case, the child very likely faces not only death from the disease if born, but the risk of being aborted. Adultery in such circumstances can be a form of murder. God forgive me when my concerns in these matters move me to suggest actions with more force than I should or in ways in which I should not.

94. Chrysostom, Homily XIX on I Cor vii.1,2, NPNF1, vol. 12, p. 105.

95. In all that we do, including marriage and the begetting of children, we are called insofar as we have strength to trust fully in Christ. This should be done with spiritual guidance, prayer, and vigilance, trusting that the Lord will provide. The injunction of the Gospels is "Therefore I tell you, do not worry about your life, what you will eat; or about your body, what you will wear. ... And do not set your heart on what you will eat or drink; do not worry about it. For the pagan world runs after all such things, and your Father knows that you need them. But seek his kingdom, and these things will be given to you as well" (Luke 12:22,29-31). This injunction is not to avoid storing food for the winter, but instead to avoid being consumed by such projects.

96. Recent Orthodox reactions to the contraceptive ethos include the encyclical of the Greek bishops signed by Archbishop Chrysostom of Athens with 55 other bishops. "Encyclical of the Hierarchy of Greece," October 14, 1937. The encyclical speaks to the moral sea-change in the view of marriage and sexuality introduced with the secularization of the West and the introduction of effective contraception. Although the medical facts advanced by the encyclical may be incomplete, the bishops were morally on target in focusing on the dangers of a contraceptive ethos, which would regard (1) the limitation of the number of children as morally indifferent, (2) even if this is undertaken to maximize wealth and luxury, (3) while eschewing faith in God's Providence, and (4) construing marriage as merely a means for the couple's self-satisfaction. A similar position was taken by the Romanian church. Demetrios Constantelos, *Marriage, Sexuality, & Celibacy: A Greek Orthodox Perspective* (Minneapolis: Light & Life, 1975), pp. 63-67.

97. In the Orthodox marriage service, the husband and wife circle the analogion while the choir sings, "O holy martyrs, who fought the good fight and have received your crowns: Entreat ye the Lord that he will have mercy on our souls. Glory to thee, O Christ-God, the Apostles' boast, the Martyrs' joy, whose preaching was the consubstantial Trinity." Hapgood, *Service Book*, p. 300.

98. The Coptic monk Matthew the Poor taught that "The Church cannot possibly tell a woman suffering from diabetes or severe albuminuria to stick to the commandment of absolute faith and embark on a career of pregnancy trusting to God and disregarding the doctor's advice, for this would be an instigation to suicide. Nor is it fitting for the Church to commend a destitute woman or man to stick to the commandment of absolute faith and

reproduce any number of children trusting to God alone, without the Church's contribution to the expenses of pregnancy, birth, nursing and bringing up the children. But the Church can speak out to those who are uninhibited by impediments of economy or health to beget children without resorting to contraceptives. This we have always advocated with all our heart." Fr. Matta El-Meskeen, "A Viewpoint on Birth Control" (Cairo: Monastery of St Macarius, 1994), p. 12. There is here a recognition of the importance of rejecting the contraceptive ethos.

99. Chrysostom, Homily XXIV on Rom xiii.11, NPNF1, vol. 11, pp. 518, 520.

100. For an account of the confusion of contraception with abortifacients, see Keith Hopkins, "Contraception in the Ancient World," *Comparatives Studies in Society and History* 8 (October, 1965), 124-151. There is a passage from Blessed Jerome (340-420) apparently directed both to contraception and to abortion. It is clear from the passage that Jerome's concern focuses on dangerous contraceptive potions, which may involve not only abortion, but death to the woman. "Others, however, drink before [coitus] a potion in order to remain sterile, and go on even to practice abortion. Many, when they become aware of the results of their immorality, meditate on how they may deliver themselves by means of poisonous expedients, and, often dying themselves for that reason, go to hell as threefold murderesses: as suicides, as adulteresses to their heavenly bridegroom Christ, and as murderesses of their still unborn child." *De custodia virginitatis*, in P. Leipelts, *Bibl. der Kirchenväter*, liv, 211 f. St. Methodius (+311?) mentions with approbation a method for lowering both libido and fertility. *Symposium* 4.3 (GCS 48-49).

101. Patriarch Athanagoras of Constantinople expressed the view that the position of the Orthodox Church regarding contraception is the same as that of the Roman Catholic religion. In one sense, this is true: both religions appreciate the wrongness of the contraceptive ethos that considers as morally neutral the choice to limit the number of children in the pursuit of wealth, luxury, and self-satisfaction. The focus of Patriarch Athanagoras is correctly on preserving a godly understanding of the family. He appears to interpret *Humanae Vitae* in this light. "I am completely in agreement with the Pope. Paul VI could not have expressed himself in any other way. The interests and the survival of the family and of entire nations are at stake. ... The Pope's encyclical is coherent with the doctrine of the Bible. All the religious books, including the Bible and the Koran, favor the safeguarding of the family, and in his encyclical the Pope has followed the line laid down in the Bible. It was not possible to expect that a different position might be taken." Fernando Victorino Joannes (ed.), *The Bitter Pill*, trans. IDO-C (Philadelphia: Pilgrim Press, 1970), p. 147. Yet having said this, Patriarch Athanagoras resituates the issue of contraception in a non-Latin context. "Our Church has granted full authority to the spiritual father. It is for him, conscious of his responsibility and his mission, to give the advice and the direction that are appropriate." *Eastern Churches Review* 2 (Spring 1968), 69-70. This reaction to *Humanae Vitae* appears to have been to reinterpret it and resituate it within the Orthodox ascetic understanding of life as a turning away from self and towards God, thus placing matters in terms of the guidance of the spiritual father. A statement in 1968 with regard to *Humanae Vitae*, for example, reads that "the Orthodox adopt this position on account of the evangelical principle of Christian ascesis so dear to them, while recognizing at the same time the legitimacy of the *oikonomia*, which permits a certain amount of attenuation of the general law." *Ibid.*, p. 146. Some local churches appear to have taken a stance that turned Malthus on his head: they judged that the impact of a contraceptive ethos would be that some Christian nations might come close to dying out. In their encyclical of July 29, 1968, Greek bishops held that a condemnation of the contraceptive ethos was also "in the national interest. A greater number of children is necessary." *Ibid.*, p. 146. See also regarding the Bulgarian church, Demetrios Constantelos, *Marriage, Sexuality, & Celibacy: A Greek Orthodox Perspective* (Minneapolis: Light & Life, 1975), pp. 63-67.

102. The differences between the Orthodox and the Roman Catholic views regarding contraception lie in the first being primarily articulated in terms of an asceticism directed to approaching holiness and the second being directed to conforming to impersonal norms, including those rooted in a highly biological interpretation of natural law. The Orthodox focus with respect to contraception is primarily on maintaining the asceticism of marriage on behalf of an orientation to holiness, as well as maintaining the "marriage-bond in peace and concord" ["Divine Liturgy of St. Basil the Great," in Hapgood, *Service Book*, p. 109]. It is for this reason that even Orthodox bishops who strongly oppose contraception still generally allow avoiding conception for medical reasons with the guidance of one's spiritual father. The spiritual father is recognized as playing a central role. Athenagoras Kokkinakis, *Parents and Priests as Servants of Redemption* (New York: Morehouse-Gorham, 1958), p. 57. By recognizing natural law as the spark of Divine love within nature, the Orthodox position avoids a legalistic approach to contraception, as well as what is usually termed a natural law approach. The traditional Christian application of law is spiritually therapeutic: it focuses on pursuing the integrity and holiness of the marriage bed. For an overview of issues involved in the Orthodox approach to contraception, see William Basil Zion, *Eros and Transformation* (New York: University Press of America, 1992), chapter 7, "Orthodoxy and Contraception," pp. 239-261. See also Stanley Harakas, *Health and Medicine in the Eastern Orthodox Tradition* (New York: Crossroad, 1990), pp. 140-141. None of these qualifications should discount the very serious moral dangers of the contraceptive ethos, which *inter alia* threatens to trivialize the significance of marriage.

103. The Roman Catholic understanding of reproduction and human sexuality is rooted in a synthesis of moral attitudes, which developed in the West and were combined in views articulated in the 13th century, especially by Thomas Aquinas (1225-1274). As noted in this chapter, there had already emerged early in the West a suspicion regarding marital sexuality, leading to a movement to proscribe a married clergy and to forbid priests who were married from having intercourse with their wives. This understanding finds an early expression in canons regulating married priests, which were adopted in northern Africa under the influence of the Church of Rome. Thus, among the 141 canons of the Council of Carthage, held A.D. 418/419, Canon IV decrees: "It is decided that Bishops, Presbyters, and Deacons, and all men who handle sacred articles, being guardians of sobriety, must abstain from women." *The Rudder*, p. 607. Canon XXXIII also requires: "It is decreed that Subdeacons who attend to the Mysteries, and Deacons and Presbyters, and even Bishops, on the same terms, must abstain from their wives, so as to be as though they had none; which if they fail to do they shall be removed from office. As for the rest of the Clerics, they shall not be compelled to do this, unless they be of an advanced age; but the rule ought to be kept in accordance with the custom of each particular church." *The Rudder*, p. 624. This attitude towards sexuality spread to Northern Africa from Rome and was subsequently condemned by the Council in Trullo (692). "Interpretation [of Canon IV]. ... This custom, being prevalent in Rome, according to c. XIII of the 6th, was carried from Rome into Africa by the legates of the bishop of Rome. For the man who offered this Canon to this Council was none other than Faustinus, the bishop of Picenum in the Potentine province of Italy and also legate of the bishop of Rome, as may be seen in the minutes of this Council." *The Rudder*, p. 607. This adverse view of marital sexuality is associated with views articulated by Augustine of Hippo (354-430) bearing on the inheritance of guilt from original sin. This foundational distrust of marital sexuality was then combined with Thomas Aquinas's affirmation of Aristotelian philosophy and natural science. Aristotle was of the view that everything following its essence has a nisus to a particular end. Every object is held to have a discursively intelligible structure, a form, with an intrinsic end to which it is directed. Every organ has its proper function, goal, or teleology. For example, noses have

their function, goal, or teleology in breathing and smelling; holding up glasses is not the function, for example, for which they were designed. In terms of such an understanding of intelligible structures and proper functions, Roman Catholicism attempted to give a legalistic, moral account of what is sexually allowable and forbidden. Its attitudes toward marital sexuality led to the imposition of celibacy on all priests, thereby engendering abuses (e.g., priests taking mistresses). The novelty of mandatory priestly celibacy in part gave rise to the moral difficulties that provoked the Protestant Reformation.

104. The Orthodox condemnation of the contraceptive ethos is rooted in the rejection of any marital sexuality that regards marriage as a matter of mere self-gratification, that does not recognize marital sexuality as rightly ordered only in the ascetic turn from oneself to the love of God, spouse, children, and others, and that rejects trust in God's providence.

105. A core Orthodox pastoral care concern regarding marriage is to maintain the marriage bond in peace and concord. The Church recognizes how each married couple within its own circumstances must journey toward God. Consequently, the Church has in great measure stepped back from interfering with the intimacy of the marital bed. "The Church Councils clearly respected the honour and intimacy of the marital bed, and did not legislate or permit a third party to regulate the relationship of two who became one." George S. Gabriel, *You Call my Words Immodest* (Dewdney, Canada: Synaxis Press, 1995), p. 19. This can be seen to be the force of the third canon of St. Dionysius the Alexandrian, already quoted in the text, where he stresses "Persons who are self-sufficient and married ought to be judges of themselves." "The Four Canons of our Father Among the Saints Dionysius," *The Rudder*, Canon III, p. 720.

106. The decision to avoid all reproduction should only be made in very extraordinary circumstances, with appropriate spiritual guidance, and in the face of very significant concerns (e.g., the husband has become infected with AIDS due to a blood transfusion). One view taken is that "It is generally acknowledged that couples who have given birth to more than two children may use their discretion and obey the dictates of their conscience." Demetrios Constantelos, *Marriage, Sexuality, & Celibacy: A Greek Orthodox Perspective* (Minneapolis: Light & Life, 1975), p. 67. It is important to note that even after two children one is not simply free to limit the number of children and embrace the contraceptive ethos.

107. St. John Chrysostom, "Sermon on Marriage," in *On Marriage and Family Life*, p. 85.

108. "That he will grant unto them the procreation of virtuous offspring...." Hapgood, *Service Book*, p. 294.

109. See, for example, the 18 Canons of St. Timothy of Alexandria (+388), Questions V and XIII, as well as Canon III of St. Dionysius the Alexandrian (+265).

110. See *The Rudder*, pp. 125f.

111. Klitos Ioannidis, *Elder Porphyrios* (Athens: Convent of the Transfiguration of the Savior, 1997), p. 135.

112. Ioannidis, p. 91.

113. Bishop Athanagoras Kokkinakis, in developing a contrast between the Roman Catholic religion and that of the Orthodox with respect to contraception stresses that "The Orthodox Church takes a different approach. These questions are subjects that the individual may reveal in confession. Studying carefully every individual case from every angle the confessor priest may advise properly the persons involved." Athenagoras Kokkinakis, *Parents and Priests as Servants of Redemption* (New York: Morehouse-Gorham, 1958), p. 57. For a further exploration of the difference between the two religions, see Paul D. O'Callaghan, "Pseudosex in Pseudotheology," *Christian Bioethics* 4 (1998), 83-99. Also see N. Aerakis, *The Will of God on the Issue of Childbearing* (Greece: Agion Oros, 1988). In all cases, the ascetical focus of the pursuit of salvation must be maintained.

114. For a recent article in condemnation of the contraceptive ethos, see Bishop Artemy, "The Mystery of Marriage in a Dogmatic Light," *Divine Ascent* 1 (March 1999), 48-60.

115. Canon XXII of the Apostolic Canons in *The Rudder*, p. 34. See also, for example, "A Eunuch, whether he became such by influence of men, or was deprived of his virile parts under persecution, or was born thus [i.e., undescended testicles], may, if he is worthy, become a Bishop." Canon XXI of the Apostolic Canons in *The Rudder*, p. 33. "If anyone who is a clergyman should mutilate himself, let him be deposed from office. For he is a self-murderer." Canon XXIII of the Apostolic Canons in *The Rudder*, p. 35. There is both violence against oneself and a rejection of one's God-given gender.

116. Canon 1 of the First Ecumenical Council in *The Rudder*, p. 163.

117. "The Seventeen Canons of the So-called First-and-Second Council," in *The Rudder*, Canon VIII, p. 465.

118. The incidental removal of ovaries with a medically indicated hysterectomy in order to avoid a general 1% chance of ovarian cancer can be justified more easily, especially given a family history of cancer or once a woman has entered menopause.

119. The matter is quite different in the case of a man or a woman whose phenotypic sexual characteristics were altered through surgery for cancer and who seeks to have the anatomy restored as far as possible.

120. In facing difficult decisions, Christians have traditionally sought a spiritual father's guidance to help them judge how to free themselves from their own passions, to test the spirits (I John 4:1), and thus discern the will and judgment of God. "He who pursues his own will, however slightly, will never be able to observe the precept of Christ the Savior...Do not be alone by yourself, lest you be seen carried off by the wolf who destroys souls, or succumb to one disease after the other and so die spiritually, or, as you succumb, you attain to that woe. He who gives himself in the hand of a good teacher will have no such worries, but will live without anxiety and be saved in Christ Jesus our Lord, to whom be glory forever." St. Symeon the New Theologian, *Symeon the New Theologian, the Discourses*, trans. C. J. de Catanzaro (New York: Paulist Press, 1980), pp. 232, 237. In many circumstances, only a very holy father or mother (e.g., a staretz or geronde) with true spiritual discernment may be able to give appropriate guidance about the proper sexual identity of a child.

121. To stress a point made earlier, traditional Christianity recognizes that the relation of man and woman is defined in terms of their creation in Eden. "For man did not come from woman, but woman from man; neither was man created for woman, but woman for man" (I Cor 11:8-9). It recognizes as well that this relationship is shaped by not just the consequences of the Fall, but by the ontology of the sexes rooted in the original intention of God. As already noted, "A woman should learn in quietness and full submission. I do not permit a woman to teach or to have authority over a man; she must be silent. For Adam was formed first, then Eve. And Adam was not the one deceived; it was the woman who was deceived and became a sinner. But women will be saved through childbearing—if they continue in faith, love and holiness with propriety" (I Tim 2:11-15).

122. In our broken world, it may at times be very difficult for some children unambiguously to take possession of their proper sexual identity. In some cases, for example, genotypic males may display, because of a benign feminizing tumor, female secondary sexual characteristics. As a consequence, they may marry as a woman and only later come to medical attention when unable to bear a child. Under such circumstances and with spiritual guidance, health care professionals may be able to acquiesce in accepting this manifest female sexual identity as the sexual identity of the person. There would be strong grounds for not doing so if the woman were the wife of a priest, for their union should be an unambiguous icon of the unique joining of Adam and Eve.

123. "The Thirty-five Canons of John the Faster," in *The Rudder*, Canon XIX, p. 943.

124. "The Seventeen Canons of the So-called First-and-Second Council," in *The Rudder*, Canon VIII, p. 465.

125. A medical justification for circumcision appears tenuous at best. See Edward Wallerstein, *Circumcision: An American Health Fallacy* (New York: Spring, 1980). The absence of a medical justification for male circumcision notwithstanding, male circumcision for religious reasons should always be allowable, for the intention is clearly not to affront the Creator, even if we as Christians know it no longer to be required. In addition, circumcision does not significantly mutilate human male anatomy, nor does it involve a rejection of male identity. From a religious perspective, since male circumcision is mandated in Genesis, it is clear that its practice is not immoral.

126. See Loretta Kopelman, "Female Circumcision/Genital Mutilation and Ethical Relativism," *Second Opinion* (Oct. 1994), 55-71; "Medicine's Challenge to Relativism: The Case of Female Genital Mutilation," in R.A. Carson and C.R. Burns (eds.), *Philosophy of Medicine and Bioethics* (Dordrecht: Kluwer, 1997), pp. 221-237.

127. The Roman Catholic "principle of totality" can be summarized as justifying mutilating operations only if they are conducive to the bodily health of the person as a whole: "A mutilating operation or procedure is lawful if it is necessary for the good of the whole body or for the preservation of life." John P. Kenny, *Principles of Medical Ethics*, 2nd ed. (Westminster, MD.: Newman Press, 1962), p. 154. The articulation of this principle can be traced back at least to the time of Thomas Aquinas, *Summa Theologica* II.2 Q 65 A 1. In reflecting on incidental appendectomies to avoid the future risk of an appendicitis, the following moral principle was generally accepted: "The removal of a healthy appendix while the abdomen is open for some other reason is lawful." John P. Kenny, *Principles of Medical Ethics*, 2nd ed. (Westminster, MD: Newman Press, 1962), p. 178. Others held that it would be morally acceptable to have an appendectomy to avoid the risk of an appendicitis on a missionary expedition where there would be no physicians. Similar reasoning was applied to elective tonsillectomies. See Charles J. McFadden, *Medical Ethics* (Philadelphia: Davis, 1961), especially pp. 268-70.

128. For a brief but very helpful review of secular moral issues involved in germ-line genetic engineering, see Nelson Wivel and LeRoy Walters, "Germ-Line Gene Modification and Disease Prevention: Some Medical and Ethical Perspectives," *Science* 262 (October 22, 1993), 533-538. See, also, LeRoy Walters and Julie Gage Palmer, *The Ethics of Human Gene Therapy* (New York: Oxford, 1996).

129. Humans may not become so significantly altered that they are no longer clearly of the same species as the humans at the time of Christ. Christ's assumption of humanity rendered our humanity normative. Through baptism a new race is created, the Christian race, by being united to Christ, the incarnate Son of God. In this new race the separation of humans into diverse races and the various evils this has engendered, including racism, are to be set aside and overcome through all being united to Christ in true belief and true worship. Thus, the priest prays during the Kairon, the entrance prayers of the priest prior to the Liturgy: "Open unto us the door of thy compassion, O blessed Theotokos. As we set our hope in thee, may we not be confounded; through thee may we be delivered from all adversities, for thou art the salvation of the race of Christians." *The Liturgikon* (Englewood, NJ: Antiochian Orthodox Christian Archdiocese, 1989), p. 231. As members of one race, Christians should not through genetic engineering be rendered so different that they may no longer fruitfully enter into the Mystery of marriage.

130. Elder Paisios reported a terrible vision that he experienced at midnight in Tuesday of Bright Week in 1984, in which he heard the roar of thousands of heartbreaking cries from the souls of infants killed by abortions. Priestmonk Christodoulos, *Elder Paisios of the Holy Mountain* (Holy Mountain, 1998), p. 174.

131. Remarkably, Wertz and Fletcher give the following reflection concerning the proscription of abortion for the purpose of sex selection. In the course of the account, the analogy

between murdering adults and murdering fetuses never occurs to the authors. "In the United States it would be possible, within the framework of *Roe v. Wade* and recent Supreme Court decisions, to prohibit abortions done for a specific reason, such as sex selection, using the analogy of laws that prohibit the sale of guns to those who say they will use them to murder people. This is not a particularly helpful analogy, for few would-be murderers tell gun-shop owners that they intend to shoot people, and few prospective parents tell doctors that their real reason for having prenatal diagnosis is to discover fetal sex. Even unenforceable laws against sex selection in Western societies, however, pose real dangers to civil liberties and abortion rights." Dorothy C. Wertz and John C. Fletcher, "Sex Selection Through Prenatal Diagnosis: A Feminist Critique," in *Feminist Perspectives in Medical Ethics*, eds. Helen Holmes and Laura Purdy (Bloomington: Indiana University Press, 1992), p. 248.

132. Nicholas Velimirovich, *The Prologue from Ochrid* (Birmingham, England: Lazarica Press, 1986), vol. 3, p. 5

133. "Father Philotheos Zervakos (+1980) was a disciple of St. Nectarios. He had the gift of clairvoyance and his tomb is now fragrant. He said that there is no worse crime than abortion. It surpasses all heresies and evils. If they had let their children be born, baptized them, and then with a knife killed them, their children would die as Christians and their responsibility would be smaller. He says that whenever parents commit abortion it exceeds the evil of the inhabitants of Sodom and Gomorrah." Tom and Georgia Mitrakos, *The 1998 Daily Lives and Wisdom of the Saints* (Allison Park, PA: Orthodox Calendar Company, 1997), August 28.

134. "But I say to you do not resist the evil one; but whosoever shall strike thee on the right cheek, turn to him the other also" (Matt 5:39). "Then Jesus saith to him [Peter], 'Turn back thy sword to its place; for all those who take the sword shall perish by the sword'" (Matt 26:52).

135. See Canon 66 of the Apostolic Canons in *The Rudder*, pp. 113-17, and Canon 13 of the Canons of St. Basil the Great (+378) in *The Rudder*, pp. 801-2. These matters will be explored further in chapter 6.

136. As already noted in the text, the Liturgy of St. Basil recognizes the personal existence of the child from the mother's womb, indicating that a child in utero must be treated as a person. "O God, who knowest the age and the name of each, and knowest every man even from his mother's womb." Hapgood, *Service Book*, p. 109. Here it is worth stressing again that St. Basil rejects speculations that would erode this attitude via a contrast between formed and unformed fetuses, drawn from the Septuagint version of Exodus (Ex 21:22). Such distinctions were used in the West to justify discriminating between early and late abortions. The distinction in the Septuagint can be understood as a mere juridical distinction. After all, the Jewish understanding of abortion is that it is a capital crime if committed by a Gentile. See Baruch A. Brody, "The Use of Halakhic Material in Discussions of Medical Ethics," *Journal of Medicine and Philosophy* 8 (August 1983), 317-328. Thomas Aquinas drew on a supposed distinction between the fetus before and after it received a rational soul. See Aristotle, *De Generatione Animalium* 2.3.736a-b and *Historia Animalium* 7.3.583b. This distinction justified Aquinas's favorable view of Aristotle's condemnation of late abortions, but tolerance of early abortions. See Aquinas, *Aristoteles Stagiritae: Politicorum seu de Rebus Civilibus*, Book 7, Lectio 12, in *Opera Omnia* (Paris: Vives, 1875), vol. 26, p. 484. See also *Summa Theologica* 1, 118, art. 2, and 2-2, 64, art. 8; and *Commentum in Quartum Librum Sententiarium Magistri Petri Lombardi*, Distinctio 31, Expositio Textus, in *Opera Omnia*, vol. 11, p. 127. For an account of these debates within Roman Catholic moral theology regarding mediate versus immediate animation, see J. Donceel, "Abortion: Mediate v. Immediate Animation," *Continuum* 5 (Spring 1967), 167-71, and "Immediate

Animation and Delayed Hominization," *Theological Studies* 13 (March 1970), 76-105; and Canon Henry de Dorlodot, "A Vindication of the Mediate Animation Theory," in E.C. Messenger (ed.), *Theology and Evolution* (London: Sands, 1952), pp. 259-83. In contrast, as a footnote in *The Rudder* indicates, the position of St. Basil and traditional Christianity is:

> For in ch. 21 of Exodus, v. 22, it is written that if anyone should happen to strike a pregnant woman and cause her to miscarry, or to expel the embryo, in case the latter comes out unformed and imperfect, he is to pay as much money as the husband of the woman shall demand, seeing that it is not yet a perfect human being, and does not possess a rational soul, according to Theodoret and Theodore; but if it be formed and perfect, the one who killed it is to be put to death as a murderer of a perfect human being possessing both a perfect body and a rational soul. But St. Basil the Great states that this observation is not in effect with us. (*The Rudder*, p. 789.)

As already noted, St. Basil's Canon II states, "a woman that aborts deliberately is liable to trial as a murderess." One is

> a murderer who kills an imperfect and unformed embryo, because this though not yet then a complete being was nevertheless destined to be perfected in the future, according to indispensable sequence of the laws of nature. (*The Rudder*, p. 789, note)

In rejecting all early abortions, no claim is advanced by traditional Christianity regarding when the soul enters the body. Instead, the requirement is that one must give recognition to new human life, even if the soul may not have entered. Killing that life will involve being implicated in a person's not having life. St. Basil explicitly eschews any "hair-splitting" as to when the soul enters. St. Basil the Great, Letter 188. In short, the position regarding abortion is independent of concerns regarding personhood, ensoulment, or distinctions in utero between human personal and human biological life.

137. A Western canon law case from the 12th century led to a Roman Catholic canon in the 13th century recognizing a difference between abortion as the crime of murder versus abortion as the act of killing an unformed, that is, supposedly unensouled, fetus. *Corpus Juris Canonici Emendatum et Notis Illustratum cum Glossae: decretalium d. Gregorii Papae Noni Compilatio* (Rome, 1585), *Glossa ordinaria* at book 5, title 12, chap. 20, p. 1713. From 1234 until 1869, the Roman Catholic canons did not hold early abortion to be equivalent to murder. John T. Noonan, Jr., "An Almost Absolute Value in History," in John T. Noonan, Jr. (ed.), *The Morality of Abortion* (Cambridge, MA: Harvard University Press, 1971), pp. 1-59. From 1588-1591 under the reign of Pope Sixtus V there was a three-year rejection of the milder treatment of early abortions. Cf. Pope Sixtus V, *Contra procurantes, Consulentes, et Consentientes, quorunque modo Abortum Constitutio* (Florence: Georgius Marescottus, 1588).

138. "The Ninety-two Canons of our Father among Saints Basil the Great," in *The Rudder*, Canon II, p. 789.

139. "The One Hundred and Two Canons of the Holy and Ecumenical Sixth Council" [A.D. 691], in *The Rudder*, Canon XCI, p. 395.

140. "The Thirty-five Canons of John the Faster," in *The Rudder*, Canon XXI, p. 944.

141. "The Twenty-five Canons of the Holy Regional Council held in Ancyra" [A.D. 315], in *The Rudder*, Canon XXI, p. 501.

142. For example, courts in some jurisdictions have held not only that parents can recover the costs associated with raising a child with birth defects, which costs they could have avoided had they been given sufficient information to allow them in a timely fashion to kill the child in utero, but also that the child can recover for the costs it must sustain, given its defects. One court even ruled that the child could sue the parents for not having been

aborted, though this holding was reversed on appeal. See *Curlender v. Bio-Science Laboratories and Automated Laboratory Sciences*, 165 Cal. Rptr. 477 (Ct. App. 2d Dist. Div. 1, 1980); and *Turpin v. Sortini*, 31 Cal. 3d 220, 643, P.2d 954, 182 Cal. Rptr. 337 (1982). See also *Harbeson v. Parke-Davis, Inc.*, 98 Wash. 2d 460, 656 P.2d 483 (1983).

143. For an account of the development of the notion of tort for wrongful life, see Angela R. Holder, "Is Existence Ever an Injury? The Wrongful Life Cases," in S.F. Spicker *et al.* (eds.), *The Law-Medicine Relation: A Philosophical Exploration* (Dordrecht: Reidel, 1981), pp. 225-39; G.M. Lehr and H.L. Hirsch, "Wrongful Conception, Birth and Life," *Medicine and Law* 2 (1983), 199-208; E. Haavi Morreim, "Conception and the Concept of Harm," *Journal of Medicine and Philosophy* 8 (1983), 137-57; Jeffrey Botkin, "The Legal Concept of Wrongful Life," *Journal of American Medical Association* 259 (March 11, 1988), 1541-1545; and Deborah Mathieu, *Preventing Prenatal Harm* (Dordrecht: Kluwer, 1991).

144. Monk of St. Tikhon's Monastery, *Book of Needs* (South Canaan, PA: St. Tikhon's Seminary Press, 1987), pp. 6-7.

145. The doctrine of double effect can be summarized as follows. "*Undertaking an act* that has an *evil effect* is lawful only if the following four conditions are simultaneously verified. (a) The action itself must be *good* or at least morally *indifferent*. (b) A good effect must follow from the action at least *as immediately as* the evil effect. (c) The *intention* must be directed to the good effect exclusively. (d) There must be a *sufficient reason* to permit the evil effect." Heribert Jone, *Moral Theology*, trans. Urban Adelman (Westminster, MD: Newman Press, 1952), §14, p. 5.

146. See, for example, Heribert Jone, *Moral Theology*, trans. Urban Adelman (Westminster, MD: Newman Press, 1952), pp. 136-140.

147. Engelhardt, "Sins, Voluntary and Involuntary," *Christian Bioethics* 3 (1997), 173-180.

148. One must recall St. Paul's stern warning regarding the dangers of participating in the Eucharist unworthily. "Therefore, whoever eats the bread or drinks the cup of the Lord in an unworthy manner will be guilty of sinning against the body and blood of the Lord. A man ought to examine himself before he eats of the bread and drinks of the cup. For anyone who eats and drinks without recognizing the body of the Lord eats and drinks judgment on himself. That is why many among you are weak and sick, and a number of you have fallen asleep." I Cor 11:27-30.

149. A spiritual father in attending with care to the spiritual needs of a spiritual child must determine when a specific penance or excommunication will effectively aid in healing the penitent. The goal is not legalistic but therapeutic, to cleanse the heart of the penitent, so that he can turn humbly toward God.

150. For those of a juridical mind, it will appear highly disingenuous to hold that one can both (1) plan to engage in a less than optimal behavior and (2) then engage in penance for that act. This disingenuity is dispelled, once penance is understood as spiritual therapy, not as punishment, and once the broken character of the world is fully recognized. Often no matter what we do, we will be involved in sin.

151. "The Thirty-five Canons of John the Faster," in *The Rudder*, Canon XXI, p. 944.

152. At stake is the spiritual harm due to active involvement in killing human life that will become a child.

153. Arthur Hertig in 1967 showed that at least 28%, if not 50%, of all conceptions seem to terminate in early, unnoticed miscarriages. See footnote 78.

154. Hapgood, *Service Book*, p. 109.

155. God has foreknowledge of all persons, even before they are conceived. In addition, the Scriptures give special acknowledgement of persons coming into existence in their mothers' womb. On the one hand, "Before I formed thee in the belly, I knew thee; and before thou

camest forth from the womb I sanctified thee" (Jer 1:5). On the other hand, in Isaiah the Scripture reads: "the Lord that formed me from the womb to be his own servant" (Is 49:5).

156. At the very least, the advice of one's spiritual father should be sought. The spiritual father may wish to seek the direction of some holy person experienced in giving guidance in such matters.

157. *The Rudder*, p. 789, note.

158. For a secular bioethical exploration of some of these issues, see Christian Munthe, *Pure Selection* (Göteborg: Acta Universitatis Gothoburgensis, 1999).

159. Although the Church sings of the conception of the Theotokos, St. John the Baptist, and St. Ann, when the Church speaks in detail and exactly, she focuses on life in the womb. "Behold! The promises of the Prophets are realized for the Holy Mountain is planted in the womb, the Divine Ladder is set up, the great Throne of the King is ready, the place for the passage of the Lord is prepared..." (Vespers for the Feast of the Conception of the Theotokos, December 9).

160. The Church provides numerous indications that, when morally appropriate, women should refrain from taking Communion during their menstrual periods. St. Dionysius the Alexandrian in his canon 2 includes the response that "Concerning menstruous women, whether they ought to enter the temple of God while in such a state, I think it superfluous even to put the question. For, I opine, not even they themselves, being faithful and pious, would dare when in this state either to approach the Holy Table or to touch the body and blood of Christ." *The Rudder*, p. 718. Similarly, St. Timothy, Pope of Alexandria, provides the following response: "Question VI: If a woman who is a catechumen has given her name in order to be enlightened, and on the day appointed for the baptism she incurs the plight which regularly afflicts women, ought she to be enlightened on that day, or defer, and how long ought she to defer? Answer: She ought to defer, until she has been purified." *The Rudder*, p. 893. St. John the Faster, in his canon XVII, reflecting on that of St. Timothy, enjoins: "As for women occupying a separate seat, let them not touch holy things for as many as seven days, the second Canon of St. Dionysius, but in particular the seventh Canon of Timothy bids. ... But as for a woman who has been so scornful of the same uncleanness during this period and has touched the divine Mysteries, they bid her to remain communionless for forty days." This canon also suggests that intercourse during menstruation is forbidden. *The Rudder*, p. 941. These considerations regarding menstruation are part of a larger concern to convey to Christians a sense of the clean and undefiled versus the unclean and the defiled as a focus on the approach to the holy, which persists even after the completion of the law of Moses in Christ: one must with watchful care move away from the defilement of the world so as to focus wholeheartedly on the pursuit of perfection. One must with great care approach the chalice. This connection between the "clean" and the holy will be further explored in chapter 6. The point is that as one approaches the holy, one must take special care to avoid defilement. Thus, one finds as well a concern by St. Dionysius the Alexandrian with respect to nocturnal emissions. See his Canon IV, *The Rudder*, p. 721. St. John the Faster also holds that "Anyone who has been polluted in sleep by reason of an emission of semen, shall be denied communion for one day; but after chanting the fiftieth Psalm and making forty-nine metanies, it is believed that he will thus be purified." *The Rudder*, Canon VI, p. 935. The goal is a spiritually therapeutic one. It directs our energies more fully to the pursuit of the kingdom of heaven. After the Fall, our nature is broken so that we lose mastery of ourselves. As a consequence of this loss of control we must be especially vigilant. These canons convey a concern with uncleanness or defilement that should not be confused with the guilt associated with voluntary sin. As Canon II of St. John the Faster emphasizes, "An assault of sensual pleasure against the heart through mentation is to be regarded as a sin not yet committed and not subject to the

least penance." *The Rudder*, p. 932. Still, even matters fully beyond voluntary control or the involvement of our will may invite the equivalent of a penance, because penance is therapeutic. On the one hand, we should not confuse the voluntary choice of evil with temptation. On the other hand, we must recognize the precariousness of our control over our own bodies and passions.

161. Although after the Fall birth-giving brings trauma to the anatomy of the mother, this was not the case for the Mother of God. Traditional Christianity has affirmed the account given in the Proto-Evangelium of James that Mary remained virginal not only before and after the birth of Christ, but also during the birth as well. In that she gave birth to the God-man his passage was free of the curse of the Fall. Protevangelium Jacobi XX.1.

162. The Orthodox Church, for example, provides special blessings for women in hard labor and women on the first day after childbirth.

163. *Book of Needs*, pp. 2-3.

164. Hapgood, *Service Book*, pp. 268-9. The Church in her wisdom makes reference to stains of her soul, likely recognizing that many women during the pains of childbirth may be moved with thoughts and even express ideas regarding their husbands and their marital union that may not be fully pious. The Jewish account why a woman who had given birth was to be presented in the Temple for purification was not focused on some "mere" consideration of ritual uncleanliness, but was addressed to this situation, as is attested in the Babylonian Talmud Niddah 31b. "When she kneels in bearing, she swears impetuously that she will have no intercourse with her husband. The Torah...ordained that she should bring a sacrifice." Jacob Neusner, *The Religious Study of Judaism* (Lanham, MA: University Press, 1988), p. 97. The Orthodox Christian understanding of the purification necessary should be seen neither in legalistic terms nor in terms of ritual purity, but in terms of spiritual therapy. The focus should be on addressing harms to the heart due to the travail of childbirth.

165. The traditional Christian understanding of authentic theological knowledge contrasts robustly with that which developed later in the West: it offers spiritual therapy rather than primarily discursive metaphysical insights. Traditional Christian theology is only secondarily and indirectly about discursive metaphysical truth. Traditional Christianity recognizes theologians not as successful academicians or scholars but as those who have purged their hearts from passion, been illuminated by the energies of God, and been united to Him. As such, the role of theology is spiritually curative.

Western theology however has differentiated itself from Eastern Orthodox theology. Instead of being therapeutic, it is more intellectual and emotional in character. In the West, Scholastic theology evolved, which is antithetical to the Orthodox tradition. Western theology is based on rational thought whereas Orthodox is hesychastic. Scholastic theology tried to understand logically the Revelation of God and conform to philosophical methodology. Characteristic of such an approach is the saying of Anselm of Canterbury: 'I believe so as to understand'. The Scholastics acknowledged God at the outset and then endeavoured to prove His existence by logical arguments and rational categories. In the Orthodox Church, as expressed by the Holy Fathers, faith is God revealing Himself to man. We accept faith by hearing it not so that we can understand it rationally, but so that we can cleanse our hearts, attain to faith by 'theoria' and experience the Revelation of God.
Hierotheos Vlachos, *Orthodox Spirituality*, trans. Effie Mavromichali (Levadia, Greece: Birth of the Theotokos Monastery, 1994), pp. 25-26.

6 Suffering, Disease, Dying, and Death: The Search for Meaning

What Does it All Mean? Facing Finitude

Suffering is not just an encounter with human limits, with human finitude, but most significantly with sin and its consequences. Because health care is a theater for the drama of human disability, suffering, and death, it occasions not just questions about the treatment of disease, the control of suffering, and the postponement and management of death, but reflection concerning the meaning of life, suffering, and death. Nowhere are questions about meaning more intrusive than in health care. Hospitals are the arena where disease, disability, and death play themselves out on humans. There is often devastating tragedy. There is the torment of the innocent whose disability, pain, and premature death demand an explanation and challenge the infinite: if there is real, ultimate meaning, why is suffering permitted? Suffering reaches into our hearts. It pulls us back from our hubris, from denying our finitude, from not facing death. Suffering is a foretaste of death. It tells us: we are limited and will all die. It confronts us with the precariousness of existence: everything in this world, solar system, and galaxy will in the end come to naught. In the long run, everything particular will be blotted out. Will anything survive?

Suffering brings us to metaphysical questions with an individual focus: Why is this happening to me? Is there any meaning to my suffering? Is there any ultimate meaning to human life, our striving, even the universe, beyond what we ourselves provide? Why is there suffering, disease, disability, and death? Does our suffering and death have any significance beyond our brief life in this transitory world? And if there is meaning, can that meaning redeem the enormity of human suffering and loss? Is there life after death? In the face of suffering, the child's global "why" is returned to the adult. The painful finitude of life raises questions regarding the possibility of infinite meaning, the existence of God, and final redeeming love. A positive answer to questions about truly enduring meaning, if adequate, must be powerful. A meaning by which to redeem human suffering and death must not be transient. A more limited answer would again provoke the search for truly enduring meaning. The answer may not be marked by the limits of this universe. It cannot simply be a principle, law, or enduring singularity. To be fully satisfying, it must speak to us in personal terms, person to person. An impersonal reality or meaning is always less than we, who are self-conscious and at least recognize ourselves as adrift in this world. For us who are self-conscious beings, a commensurate answer to our sufferings must be a living, self-conscious, enduring meaning that can speak to self-conscious sufferers as a reality of greater, not lesser, standing or reality. To find deep and enduring purpose for our suffering, to find deep and persistent significance for our lives requires recognizing the human condition within a meaning that is infinite, personal, enduring, and transcendent. Anything else is less than the full meaning for which one might hope.

How can one search for, much less characterize, such enduring meaning? Can one successfully undertake such a metaphysical quest for a deep account of suffering? How can one proceed, especially this side of Immanuel Kant (1724-1804) and skepticism regarding reason's ability to reach beyond this world? Kant sets the context for contemporary questions regarding the ultimate significance of our lives, our suffering, and our deaths by reminding us that discursive reason is restricted to the horizon of empirical experience. In these terms, quests for deep meaning are mistaken. According to Kant, such a search for meaning cannot engage true transcendence. For Kant such questions require rephrasing in terms of the conditions of possible experience and the character of morality, the undertakings of practical reason. At that point they cease to be questions about transcendent reality. They are domesticated within the confines of immanence. Until the transcendent breaks through to us, we are hopelessly encircled by the limited and the immanent. In secular terms, deep questions regarding ultimate meaning are unanswerable. They are the fuel of myths. In secular terms, the world's meaning is as one finds it within the horizon of immanence. There is no deep drama or cosmic narrative of salvation. Secular bioethics by its nature eschews all meaning beyond the immanent. It cannot reach to deep meanings beyond the domain of the finite.[1]

Even if the sciences that frame our culture give no final meaning, medicine intimates that pain is controllable, suffering escapable, and death ever more postponeable. Medicine fails: these promises cannot be kept. Suffering cannot in the end be avoided. Death finally claims the day. Within an ethos of control and progress these failures spur the search for meaning in the face of suffering, disability, and death. The temptation arises, if meaning cannot be found, at least to cheat suffering by one's own hand, thus securing at least the meaning of having chosen for oneself. Although nature inevitably brings death, one can select the time and the circumstance. If the universe were without purpose and the human condition circumscribed by inevitable suffering and death, one could still realize that meaning that comes from self-determination. Contemporary support for euthanasia within the liberal cosmopolitan ethos resonates with Seneca's (4 B.C.-A.D. 65) pagan stoicism expressed in his letter concerning suicide: self-inflicted death conveys nobility even to the condemned criminal. "It is a great man who not only orders his own death but contrives it."[2] Seneca's understanding of the appropriateness of directly acting to terminate one's life approximates that of the emerging liberal cosmopolitan ethos. Seneca affirms, for example, "Living is not the good, but living well. The wise man therefore lives as long as he should, not as long as he can... He will always think of life in terms of quality, not quantity."[3] In a way that applies to decisions to accept physician-assisted suicide or euthanasia, Seneca reasons that when "one death involves torture and the other is simple and easy, why not reach for the easier way? ... Must I want for the pangs of disease...when I can strike through the midst of torment and shake my adversaries off?"[4] Seneca's death provided for the ancient pagan world an image of self-possession and autonomy. Rather than be subjected to possible torture by Nero, he and his wife together committed suicide. "Then by one and the same stroke they sundered with the dagger the arteries of their arms. ... Even at the last moment his eloquence failed him not; he summoned his secretaries and dictated much to them which, as it has been published for all readers in his own words, I forbear to paraphrase."[5] Similarly, interest in euthanasia is tied to autonomy and the quest for meaning through self-determination. [6] Physician-assisted suicide and voluntary active euthanasia in the confrontation with suffering or indignity offer self-determination and control, however meager. They are integral to the ethos of personal dignity as self-rule, which lies at the root of the liberal cosmopolitan ethos.[7]

Within the liberal cosmopolitan ethos, access to physician-assisted suicide and euthanasia appears only too plausible.[8] Who would not want physician-assisted suicide available, at least under certain circumstances? After all, although significant pain can often be avoided, there will always be exceptions. Are not physician-assisted suicide and voluntary active euthanasia important for just such exceptions? Even if pain can be medically controlled, much suffering cannot. From the loss of physical control with multiple sclerosis and amyelotropic lateral sclerosis, to the deterioration of mental function with Alzheimer's, many experience illness as marked by not just intolerable discomforts, but unacceptable indignities and the loss of self-control. The blind course of physical or mental deterioration can take away the opportunity to mark the end of one's life with one's own will. Why should nature be allowed to despoil the final chance to bequeath an example of a life self-possessed, a death completed with dignity, and a dying that does not burden others? Why should one not be free to die on one's own terms, rather than at the whim of natural forces? If rationality, freedom, dignity, and self-determination distinguish the good life, should they not characterize the good death? These moral concerns resonate in popular phrases such as "Whose life is it anyway?" "Who has a right to decide for others?" "My death is my own!"

The issues are political and moral. Their entrance into legislative agendas betokens a sea-change in cultural assumptions. Because the American Supreme Court in 1997 acknowledged a substantial legal history forbidding physician-assisted suicide and voluntary active euthanasia reaching back in England at least to A.D. 673, the American Court did not recognize a constitutional right to physician-assisted suicide and voluntary active euthanasia, at least from the cases presented.[9] For the interim, any legal right to physician-assisted suicide must be created legislatively. Steps towards such legislation have already been taken in the United States.[10] The long and well-developed history of the proscription of physician-assisted suicide in Anglo-American law makes such legalization a dramatic cultural and moral rupture: a departure from the religious assumptions that have traditionally shaped Anglo-American law. Yet, for all the reasons already noted, a secular society cannot avoid taking this step away from its religious past and to a new morality of suffering, dying, and death. The Kingdom of the Netherlands illustrates this acceptance of physician-assisted suicide and euthanasia as a development fully in concert with the liberal cosmopolitan ethos.[11]

If one values (1) self-determination as well as (2) affirmative mutual respect, then one must go beyond merely tolerating decisions in favor of physician-assisted suicide and euthanasia. One must endorse these practices, at least in principle. Toleration requires only living peaceably with a state of affairs held to be improper. It does not require approval or forbid disrespectful condemnation. It requires only the eschewal of force to suppress behavior. Toleration is compatible with the public judgment, "You are at liberty to engage in physician-assisted suicide although it is very wrong." Such concepts of toleration took their modern form out of the political toleration of religions which particular societies held to be false. Toleration in this originary sense requires suffering the presence of the viewpoints of those one takes to be misguided. In contrast, "acceptance" requires forgoing the judgment of wrongness: "You are at liberty to engage in physician-assisted suicide; for many it is an appropriate choice, though it is not the right one for me." In this circumstance, characterizing those involved in physician-assisted suicide and voluntary active euthanasia as self-murderers or murderers becomes morally offensive, insensitive, politically incorrect, and therefore unacceptable within the liberal cosmopolitan ethos. If personal freedom and human dignity are central to secular morality, the conclusion is drawn: it is appropriate for secular health care and educational institutions to support the acceptance of individual, intimate decisions about death, including physician-assisted suicide and euthanasia.[12] If a society values individual choice and self-determination regarding ways of life, it should presumptively value individual choice and self-determination regarding death. In a liberal cosmopolitan culture that celebrates autonomy, life or death outside of personal control will be experienced as personally demeaning, alienating, and undignified.

The liberal cosmopolitan ethos in endorsing self-determination, liberation from the constraints of the past, and self-fulfillment has a moral content beyond what a general secular morality can justify to moral strangers. It involves a particular ethos calling for a break with the traditional Christian past. It involves a more accepting approach to suicide and euthanasia. This new secular cosmopolitan culture invites religion to reorient its commitments. In the terms of this culture, religion should aid caregivers and family members in accepting the choices of patients who use physician-assisted suicide and voluntary active euthanasia. Christians who love their neighbors should in terms of this liberal cosmopolitan reorientation encourage choices concerning death that support the values, freedom, and dignity of their neighbors. Indeed, because the very character of death in highly technological societies has rendered death a matter of free choice, a contemporary moral theology in accord with the liberal cosmopolitan ethos should now recognize that physician-assisted suicide and voluntary active euthanasia can be undertaken from a commitment to dignity and love. A positive moral reevaluation of physician-assisted suicide and voluntary active euthanasia within this autonomy-affirming ethos becomes appropriate not just for contemporary secular society but for post-traditional Christianity as well.[13]

The Presbyterian Church (USA) provides a good example of a shift in the attitude of post-traditional Christianity away from an unambiguous condemnation of not only abortion but also physician-assisted suicide and euthanasia as well. In a volume addressing euthanasia and physician-assisted suicide the PC(USA) reprints a sermon of a minister who encourages not condemnation but a positive evaluation of ending one's life by suicide. The cases to which he responds include one woman who committed suicide[14] and another with a seemingly suicidal intent seeking to have all treatment stopped so that she might die, though otherwise she could live fifteen to twenty years.[15] "But should we not also respond compassionately to a Diane or an Elizabeth, not condemning, but valuing a different kind of courage and faithfulness?"[16] The Presbyterian Church itself adopted the following in 1981:

> "Active euthanasia" is extremely difficult to defend morally. There are, however, extreme circumstances in which we may have to at least raise the question of a fundamental conflict of obligations. There is an analogy between such cases of "active euthanasia" and abortions, questions that are based on the circumstances of the fetus. There is an accompanying prejudice against the taking of life in both cases, since the conflict between doing no harm and protecting from harm has reference to one and the same individual. The ambiguity of this situation serves to reinforce what has already been said about cautious and consultative decision making.[17]

In all of this one sees a perceptible turn to an affirmation of decisions to take life directly in order to avoid pain and suffering.[18]

Placing suffering in the context of immanent meaning involves an invitation to turn to the immediate and tangible. In the face of the seeming senselessness of suffering, and until one decides to exit by one's own hand, one can seek succor in the pleasures, beauty, and the engagements of this world. One can hope that sensual, aesthetic, and intellectual pleasures will distract until the end, the final night of death. One can seek to quench the thirst for the transcendent in pursuing the satisfactions of this world and the flesh. Camus (1913-1960) portrays this strategy in his "Summer in Algiers", suggesting that the allure of the otherworldly can be lost through engagement in physical beauty "on which no deceptive divinity has traced the signs of hope or of redemption." Camus hoped to find a secure home for immanence. "Between this sky and these faces turned toward it, nothing on which to hang a mythology, a literature, an ethic, or a religion, but stones, flesh, stars, and those truths the hand can touch."[19] Though initially the flesh comforts and satisfies, it always finally fails. The flesh weakens, becomes diseased, grows old, and dies. Inevitably, one confronts suffering, dying, and death. The question then returns: is there any enduring and ultimate significance to it all? The immanent cannot still the hunger for the transcendent.

Death, Temptation, and Sin: The Cosmic Narrative

The deep meaning of suffering that Christianity discloses is personal and radically at odds with the liberal cosmopolitan ethos. This personal character speaks to the heart and declares, "even the hairs of your head are all numbered. Therefore do not become afraid" (Matt 10:30). For many, this meaning is also disturbing, for it literally breaks through the horizon of immanence. If truth is a person, truth will lack (or more precisely, be beyond) the discursive universality sought in the impersonal logic of secular reason. Truth will not be a principle, an axiom, or an ultimate rational ground, but a living free will: "I am Who am."[20] In its particularity, the traditional Christian account of transcendent meaning is jarringly contrary to ecumenical aspirations. Christianity's deep account of life, suffering, and death is a particular story involving particular people and their relationship with a transcendent but personal God. The Christian account of suffering is a narrative about persons: suffering is tied to a drama of sin and salvation involving not only humans, but angels, devils, and God in which free choice is central and cosmic in its power.[21] For traditional Christianity, disease, suffering, and death are recognized within a cosmic narrative of sin, forgiveness, and salvation.

As in the last chapter, a central focus is on man in paradise: Adam and Eve. The Genesis account discloses the power of freedom and the destructiveness of sin. Once paradise is lost, the very ground is cursed because of Adam (Gen 4:17). Mankind must toil and travail with a nature now inclement, full of thorns and thistles. In response to the question of why there is suffering, the answer is to be found within this cosmic narrative. It is human willfulness that took Adam and Eve out of paradise and placed them within this world's history of suffering and its proclivity to harm even the innocent. On behalf of Eve, Adam was to have offered all creation back to God, thus uniting all to God. Instead, Adam with Eve joined Satan in prideful separation, binding all humans in the consequences of their sin, including suffering and death. As Saint Symeon the New Theologian (949-1022) summarizes: "The first-created Adam lost this garment of sanctity, not from any other sin but from pride alone, and became corruptible and mortal, all people also who come from the seed of Adam are participants of the ancestral sin from their very conception and birth. He who has been born in this way, even though he has not yet performed any sin, is already sinful through this ancestral sin."[22] One is born full of evil inclinations, "because the imagination of man is intently bent upon evil things from his youth " (Gen 8:21). Suffering is the fault of mankind, of all who have sinned.

It is not that Adam's sin is passed on as a hereditary guilt. It is rather a defining catastrophe for the universe. The consequences of Adam's sin touch us all. "As sin came into the world through one man, and through sin death, so death spread to all men, because all men have sinned" (Rom 5:12). As the head of humanity, Adam involved all in the consequences of his sin as no other man could. Like a father who in sin contracts a disease he passes to his children without his children inheriting the guilt, all inherit the consequences of Adam's sin, though not his guilt. Nevertheless, our lives are distorted by that sin. Adam and Eve infected our nature with sinful inclinations, suffering, and death. Each of us then further compounds the problem by adding the consequences of our own voluntary pride and rebellion. We are involved with one another in all our own sins. They mark the character of our world.[23]

The resulting suffering is not simply a punishment. It can be a chastising medicine we receive from our own prideful acts, from our own sins. The consequences can bring us to our senses and help cure our pride as we experience what our sin does to ourselves and others, especially innocent bystanders. Suffering can offer an opportunity to conquer pride, control the passions, seek forgiveness, and look beyond the immanent. It can help us turn beyond ourselves to God. But suffering itself may generally be evaded. It is for this reason the Church prays for a "Christian ending to our life, [which is] painless, blameless, [and] peaceful," as St. John Chrysostom's Liturgy puts it. Still, if suffering cannot be avoided, one must face it with humility so as to have "a good defense before the fearful judgment seat of Christ".[24] Indeed, with spiritual insight, pain and suffering offer a road from pride to humility. As "an old monk said, 'For one to be ill is a divine visitation. Illness is the greatest gift from God. The only thing that man can give to God is pain.'"[25] As St. Paul teaches, "but we boast in afflictions also, knowing that the affliction worketh out patience; and patience, a tested character; and a tested character, hope. And the hope doth not put to shame, for the love of God hath been poured out in our hearts through the Holy Spirit Who was given to us" (Rom 5:3-5). By humbly accepting the suffering we cannot avoid and by mourning the impact of suffering on the innocent, all of which is in some way due to sin, we can give substance to our repentance, abandon pride, and purge the heart from the passions that control us. That is, we can redirect our energies. If we humbly and patiently bear suffering, the consequence of sin, we will cure our passions and repent. Our suffering patiently borne does not make up for a legalistic debt of temporal punishment due to sin.[26] However, it can help us learn humility and cure the effects of sin. The role of suffering should therefore be understood therapeutically, not legalistically.

The undoing of the results of our sins has been accomplished in the personal drama of the second Eve and the second Adam. The focus is again on free choice and humility. The second Eve, a teenage girl like others save in her humility and her voluntary submission, made possible the second Adam's birth. "Although Mary is a chosen vessel, still she was a woman by nature, not to be distinguished at all from others," as St. John of San Francisco (1896-1966) reminds us.[27] Unlike the first Eve, Mary the Mother of God shared in our corrupted nature, its sinful inclinations, and its proclivities to turn from God. Like us, she required correction by our and her Savior.[28] Although as frail as we and not untouched by sin as was Eve, she did not succumb to pride.[29] Barely a girl of sixteen, she freely chose to do God's will. Because she resisted temptation and obeyed, giving birth to the second Adam, the only sinless one, her free choice led to our being severed from Satan and death, the ultimate consequence of sin. At stake is the recognition of the truly cosmic force of free choice. As the Liturgy of St. Basil proclaims, "He gave himself a ransom to Death, whereby we were held, sold into bondage under sin. And having descended into Hell through the Cross, that He might fill all things with Himself, He loosed the pains of death, and rose again from the dead on the third day, making a way for all flesh through the Resurrection from the dead – for it was not possible that the Author of Life should be holden of corruption."[30] Christ also chooses freely, thus breaking the bond with Satan, sin, and death, so that we can transcend our suffering and death through His suffering and Resurrection. Christ as the second Adam through the submission of the second Eve has taken on our nature so that we can be freed from Satan and united with God.

Suffering remains, but its meaning is transformed. Even seemingly senseless death is placed within the drama of redemption. For example, the birth of Christ, Who is the solution to human sin and suffering, redeems the surd suffering of the innocent. St. Matthew records Herod's slaughter of the innocents in Bethlehem as an attempt to kill the Christchild (Matt 2:16-18). The pain of their parents is emphasized by St. Matthew, quoting the prophet Jeremiah, "A voice was heard in Rama, of lamentation, and of weeping, and wailing; Rachel would not cease weeping for her children, because they are not" (Jer 38[31]:15). St. Nicholas of Zica (1880-1956) stresses the brutality: "[Herod's] soldiers cut off some of the children's heads with their swords, dashed others on the stones, trampled some of them underfoot and drowned others with their own hands."[31] How could such suffering, especially that of children, ever be made whole, or the parents' loss redeemed? St. Matthew does not mention the verse that follows in Jeremiah, although it is present for all who know the Bible well: "Thus saith the Lord; Let thy voice cease from weeping, and thine eyes from thy tears: for there is a reward for thy works" (Jer 38[31]:16). The meaning of their suffering and its redemption lies in the God of Israel, in His Messiah Jesus, and in His holy Church which recognizes their sainthood (Dec. 29). These children in dying because of Christ were saved as martyrs for Christ. Their suffering and death have been transformed through His suffering, death, and Resurrection. But so can the death of all innocent children now be redeemed through baptism.[32]

The cure of the Fall and its consequences, and the source of our triumph over death and suffering, are to be found in the history of redemption. This is the triumph of salvation that is proclaimed yearly in the Paschal homily of St. John Chrysostom, which announces the new context for suffering, death, and resurrection.

> He that was taken by death has annihilated it! He descended into hades and took hades captive! He embittered it when it tasted his flesh! and anticipating this Isaiah exclaimed, "Hades was embittered when it encountered thee in the lower regions." It was embittered, for it was abolished! It was embittered, for it was mocked! It was embittered, for it was purged! It was embittered, for it was despoiled! It was embittered, for it was bound in chains!
>
> It took a body and, face to face, met God! It took earth and encountered heaven! It took what it saw but crumbled before what it had not seen! "O death, where is thy sting? O hades, where is thy victory?" Christ is risen, and you are overthrown! Christ is risen, and the demons are fallen! Christ is risen, and the angels rejoice! Christ is risen, and life reigns! Christ is risen, and not one dead remains in a tomb! For Christ, being raised from the dead, has become the First-fruits of them that slept. To Him be glory and might unto ages of ages. Amen.[33]

The cross is transformed by being oriented to the victory of the Resurrection. It confirms Christ's prayer on the cross: "O God, my God, attend to me; why hast Thou forsaken me?" (Psalm 21:1, LXX), which reaches from this first line through the whole psalm, declaring "and when I cried unto Him, He hearkened unto me" (Psalm 21:24, LXX), ending with a prophecy of His revelation to those who will be born of water and the spirit. "The generation that cometh shall be told of the Lord, and they shall proclaim His righteousness to a people that shall be born, which the Lord hath made" (Psalm 21:31, LXX).[34]

Against Medicine as an Idol: Withholding and Withdrawing Treatment

Medicine outside of a Christian understanding generally aims somewhat short of the mark. It usually fails to direct its energies as all human activities ought to be directed: in a worshipful orientation toward God. Without this orientation, which must aim at God through the crucifixion and resurrection, medicine's place in culture threatens to be dangerously distorted. If one does not know that each of our deaths leads to resurrection and final judgment, then the postponement of death can take on a dominating and distorting importance. If one does not recognize that suffering and disability can break our pride and help us to turn to God, then a science that can ameliorate suffering and disability will be regarded as a commanding good. Because medicine has the power effectively to relieve much suffering and often postpone death, medicine has been able to claim immense social, political, and economic attention and resources. It is for this reason among others that medical centers have taken on the cultural roles that cathedrals once claimed in the West. Medicine has become a cardinal focus of cultural investment and energy. Health care in many countries now exacts more than a tithe of the Gross Domestic Product. Few individuals will sell all that they have to pursue eternal salvation, while many will sell all they have to secure a few more years of life. Medicine possesses a commanding place in contemporary culture. Medical centers are now the place where many, if not most, seek to resolve the problems of their sexuality, suffering, dying, and death. Even spirituality and religion become reinterpreted in terms of medicine's understanding of health and well-being. A healthy spirituality becomes a spirituality that passes the muster of a secular understanding of health and well-being. When life, sexuality, reproduction, dying, death, and spirituality are articulated only in immanent terms, the role, place, and meaning of medicine is fundamentally deformed.

Against this dominating vision of medicine, Christianity offers a radical reorientation. This life is not all there is. Full meaning is to be found beyond death, and therefore medicine is not the art most needed for a healthy life. Instead, all human challenges must be approached with an eye to health that leads beyond this world. The focus should first and foremost be on spiritual health, on nurturing through Christian asceticism, the discipline of becoming watchful so as not to be mastered by passions, temptations, or even particular goals and projects, in order to turn fully to God. Christian asceticism, the mastery of influences that would misdirect energies, is compatible with a discerning use of medicine. As St. Basil the Great (329-379) emphasizes,

> Each of the arts is God's gift to us, remedying the deficiencies of nature ... And, when we were commanded to return to the earth whence we had been taken and were united with the pain-ridden flesh doomed to destruction because of sin and, for the same reason, also subject to disease, the medical art was given to us to relieve the sick, in some degree at least.[35]

Christians have traditionally understood that they may engage medical interventions, as long as these do not impede the spiritual life. There is also the recognition that medicine should not be used if it significantly distracts from our life of prayer or brings us to being obsessed with preserving this life. As St. Basil the Great warns, we should avoid "Whatever requires an undue amount of thought or trouble or involves a large expenditure of effort and causes our whole life to revolve, as it were, around solicitude for the flesh...."[36] Such uses of medicine are inappropriate, disproportionate, extraordinary, and morally misguiding. It is not just that such treatments *may* be withdrawn or withheld. They *should* be withdrawn or withheld. The postponement of death, the avoidance of suffering, and the correction of disabilities should not become all-consuming projects.

Medicine and its cure of disease, amelioration of disability, and postponement of death must be placed within the pursuit of the kingdom of heaven. As with all human talents, abilities, sciences, and technologies, those of medicine are appropriately used only as long as they do not take central stage and become all-consuming. When the pursuit of health and life in this world becomes an all-absorbing project, medicine distracts from the cardinal human goal that lies beyond this world, the kingdom of God, and medicine becomes an idol. Medical interventions should be withheld or withdrawn whenever they distract from the pursuit of the Kingdom. The test is not merely one of burdens, costs, or the likelihood of success, but a matter of spiritual misdirection. The issue is not one of futility but spiritual threat, though one is surely never required to use treatment that is absolutely useless. Instead, futility language usually masks judgments about the extent to which one is obliged to provide treatment when the quality of life is restricted, the length of life achieved likely to be short, and/or the possibility of success guarded. The important questions must be addressed by the traditional Christian, though in a different context. Here the focus is on costs, in particular, spiritual costs. This point is appreciated even if only darkly by Plato in his account of how Herodicus postponed death by involving his whole life in his treatment (Rep III 406a-b). Plato recognized a moral distortion that a Christian should also see more clearly as involving a spiritual deformation when one's energies are primarily devoted simply to maintaining physical life. To avoid such a spiritual threat, treatment may properly be withheld or withdrawn, even when it could secure years of life.

The appropriate focus is on a way of life, rather than just on saving or preserving life. It is in terms of this way of life that health care decisions, in particular end-of-life decisions should be made. Health care decision-making should be focused on the ascetic turn from all that distracts so as to pursue the Kingdom of Heaven. Decisions to withhold or withdraw treatment made in the light of this commitment have some similarities with decisions following the Roman Catholic distinction between ordinary or proportionate versus extraordinary or disproportionate treatment: a line is drawn between obligatory and non-obligatory treatment based on the burden to the patient, the family, and/or society, as well as the likelihood of restoring health.[37] The traditional Christian focus makes plain that at stake is not merely a set of considerations that defeat a prima facie obligation to seek treatment in order to preserve life. Instead, the focus is on hitting the mark, on seeking the Kingdom of Heaven. The concern is to remain on target and not be deflected by either distractions from or confusions about the proper target: holiness. Health care can absorb our energies, distract us, and confuse us, leaving us less focused on the proper goal: union with God.

St. Basil the Great's concern about avoiding anything that makes our whole life revolve around solicitude for the flesh compasses both the reception of health care and the provision of health care.[38] At times, health care will attempt to involve patients and their families in an all-consuming engagement in medicine and its technologies. At times, the distortion will be indirect by leaving patients in a state such that they can only be sustained by all-embracing technological interventions (i.e., such as life in an intensive-care unit), which may distort the lives not only of patients and their families, but also of their caregivers. All-encompassing medical interventions that will not leave one able to engage in one's spiritual life (e.g., a resection of a brain tumor that might save one's life but leave one obtunded) or only marginally postpone death with significant burdens (e.g., a chemotherapeutic protocol that will cause significant side effects and only increase one's likely life expectancy a few months) should be approached with great caution. The improper use of medicine may lead patients, family members, and caregivers into situations where, if they do not make physician-assisted suicide and euthanasia temptations, they may burden hearts or lead to cynicism born of misusing human energies and resources. Paradoxically, the technological imperative to use all available resources to save life can lead to the temptation to take life. Neither patients nor families and caregivers should be given more than they can bear. Health care practices focused on saving life at all costs will in moral and spiritual terms cost far too much: the spiritual lives of both caregivers and care-receivers will be imperiled. Health care interventions that can become inappropriate by involving our whole life in the solicitude of the flesh are not only those that are highly technological, such as critical care. They can at times even include artificial hydration and nutrition or antibiotics. At the end of life, even normal eating may become too burdensome for a particular patient. The issue turns on discerning when attempts to postpone death or bring health distract from preparation for eternal life with God.

What is important is often not what one does or does not do medically, but why and how one does it, as long as one's actions and omissions are not what proximately lead to death, as long as the underlying disease process existing before the action or omission, and continuing independently of the action or omission brings death. In withholding and withdrawing treatment, it is essential that one make such omissions in order to avoid acting in a way that would be harmful to the patient. The omission must be a stepping back from spiritual injury. Treatment should be withheld or withdrawn because its burdens would cause the patient or others to fall short of the mark. All health care interventions must be given in parallel with care for the soul of the patient, to paraphrase a passage in St. Basil's Long Rule 55. Indeed, to quote St. Basil, "To place the hope of one's health in the hands of the doctor is the act of an irrational animal."[39] Instead, our final reliance must be on God. We are not obliged to postpone our deaths indefinitely in a highly technologically mediated environment that would be strange to the Fathers and contrary to St. Basil's warning against allowing medical care to encompass our lives. In such circumstances, one should allow broken nature, as God wills, to take its course.

At stake is avoiding not just acting without an intention to effect an earlier death, but also avoiding intimate and proximate involvement in the taking of a human life. This issue cannot easily be captured in an ordinary examination of causal factors and events. In a sense, withholding or withdrawing of treatment can be as much a sufficient cause of the death of a patient as any of the elements of the disease process.[40] The same can be said of any intervention to provide pain relief, which may somewhat increase the likelihood of dying earlier. Such actions can as much cause the patient's death as any of the pathological processes. To see matters rightly, one must not simply attend to causal factors, but to an account of causation, to use a distinction developed by Hart and Honoré in their classical account of causation in the law.[41] They offer the example of a garden in which the flowers die because of the failure of the gardener to water them. The gardener is held to have caused the flowers' death, although the failure of others to water, as well as the lack of sufficient rain, are as much causes as the gardener's malfeasance. The gardener is identified as the cause of the death of the flowers because of the gardener's obligation. The dying of the flowers is appreciated within a practice in which gardeners discharge particular duties of caring for flowers in gardens. Most other causal factors are ignored as background conditions in terms of this practice. Analogously, Christians approach disease, disability, and death with the recognition that these are the result of sin and "often [also] a punishment for sin imposed for our conversion; 'For whom the Lord loveth,' says the Scripture, 'he chastiseth' [Prov 3:12]."[42] As a consequence, in the right circumstances and with the proper disposition, as well as intention, Christians may stop treatment and "let nature take its course" in humble acceptance of God's will. As such, they do not cause death.

This interpretation of causation highlights particular duties and discloses particular spiritual dangers. It recognizes a distinction between withholdings or withdrawings that are passive homicide or passive euthanasia, versus withholdings and withdrawings that amount to letting God's will be done. Even outside of traditional Christianity, one can distinguish between omissions not undertaken in order to bring an early death and those that are intentionally focused on achieving an earlier demise. The second are properly instances of passive euthanasia. Similarly, within a secular bioethical context, one can distinguish between actions directed to an important good that may bring an earlier death and those undertaken in order to achieve an earlier demise. The latter are properly instances of active euthanasia, which can be further distinguished as voluntary (i.e., if done at the behest of the patient to be killed), involuntary (i.e., if done against the wishes of the patient to be killed), and non-voluntary (i.e., if done without the concurrence of the patient, albeit presumptively in the patient's best interests and likely in accord with the patient's wishes). The traditional Christian approach does not fully fit within this classification: it focuses primarily (albeit not exclusively) on intention and the avoidance of proximate causal involvement in the death of a human.

The last qualification is important. Even in purely secular interpretations, there is generally an appreciation that one may not merely engage in an action that will kill in order to achieve one's purposes, while claiming that one is not in fact intending to kill. To recall, the Roman Catholic doctrine of double effect purportedly allows one without guilt to engage in an action that has two effects, one good and the other involving natural evil. One is held to be acting without sin if (1) the action in which one engages is not itself morally evil, e.g., giving analgesics, (2) the good effect is not a result of the evil effect (e.g., one is not attempting to kill the patient in order to relieve the patient's pain), (3) the evil effect is sincerely not intended (e.g., the possible shortening of life due to the use of analgesics), and (4) there is a proportionate good to be achieved (e.g., more good must be realized than harm).[43] Distinctions in the matter of double effect have been notoriously unsatisfactory because the designation of a particular effect as primary and others as secondary appears arbitrary if not question-begging. As we have seen, calling on Hart and Honoré, one can resolve this problem by distinguishing between direct and indirect or secondary effects within an established understanding of human obligations to God and to other humans. Within such a framework, ambiguities can be dispelled in terms of traditional roles, obligations, and expectations.

Still, in the traditional Christian understanding, the intention and disposition of the persons withholding or withdrawing treatment play a central role. They must not intend to kill by omission but instead to withdraw a spiritually harmful medical intervention out of love and concern for the salvation of the patient. Such an intention is central to the spiritual health of the one withholding or withdrawing treatment. Yet having the right intention (to protect against spiritual harm) and a proper disposition of love (prayerfully to do God's will) is not sufficient. At stake as well is a recognition of the spiritual danger of being proximately involved in taking the life of another, even if this be fully involuntary. This concern is recognized in the canons bearing on involuntary homicide. The canons require repentance not only for someone who kills another inadvertently in an altercation,[44] but also for those who take life during a just war.[45] In a footnote commenting on the Apostolic Canon addressed to involuntary homicide (Canon LXVI), there is a reflection not only on why executioners acting at the behest of a Christian emperor, as well as those who kill a robber in defense of property, must still do penance, but also on those who ride out in a posse to kill a thief.

> But whosoever after being many times begged to do so goes forth and searches and finds a thief and puts him to death for the sake of the common interest of the public at large, he is to be deemed to deserve rewards. Nevertheless, for safety's sake, it has been found to be reasonable that he too should be penalized for three years.[46]

A canon of St. Gregory of Nyssa [?-394] also penances those involved in manslaughter "through failure to pay attention to the situation".[47]

As a result of this canon of St. Gregory of Nyssa, a Christian layman would be excommunicated or a priest deposed in most circumstances in which an automobile accident leads to the loss of life. The commentary on this canon indicates that it applies even when fully against a person's will he is involved in manslaughter. Why, then, would withdrawing or withholding treatment not count as a form of manslaughter? The answer appears twofold. First, the action in which one is engaged is best understood not as manslaughter but as an action integral to a practice of avoiding spiritually harmful intrusions, here in particular, harmful medical over-treatment. One acts not to kill, but to secure life, in this case spiritual life. The omission is undertaken as a form of defense against a spiritual threat. Second, one does not kill; the disease kills. In the practice of medicine as St. Basil describes it, the physician must not be construed as the master of life and death. God is the Master Who permits the disease to kill. Consequently, the physician or patient who withdraws or withholds treatment out of love and trust in God and from a love of the neighbor which aims at salvation, and not out of self-love, leaves the final outcome humbly in the hands of God. In the face of human finitude and given the prize of immortality and the wholehearted love of God, the practice of avoiding excessive medical treatment is not manslaughter when death is not postponed.

It is another matter if through medical negligence or lack of appropriate commitment and attention, not just due to the limits of human abilities and skills, a physician mortally injures a patient. Such an active fatal harm will likely count as manslaughter. It will be no different from manslaughter committed in an automobile accident. Still, negligently failing to provide appropriate treatment leading to a patient's death, though this surely can be sinful, should not be treated as manslaughter in the absence of an intent to do harm. The practice of considering an action a form of homicide with the canonical penalties it involves (i.e., from excommunication to deposition, as well as preclusion from being ordained to the priesthood) appears focused on fatal forms of violence and intentional killings by omission, including intentional breaches of duty.[48] An omission, however culpable, if not intending to kill, is not an instance of such active violence against another and has not been usually considered as having the same harmful spiritual consequences. There is an appreciation that violence can distance us from the holy. A priest may not strike another.[49] Also, out of appreciation for the holiness of the altar, priests should generally avoid involvement in surgery as a profession,[50] not just because of its bloody character, but because of the risk of being proximately causally involved in the death of a patient. It is not appropriate for the one who presides over the bloodless sacrifice of the Eucharist to have bloody hands.

Treating pain, even when this risks an earlier death, if done to comfort the patient and avoid despair, is neither a violent act nor manslaughter, if it is the sort of intervention that would not have caused death in the absence of the disease. The treatment may not be independently lethal and surely may not aim at preventing pain by taking life. However, one can provide analgesia to comfort the patient and avoid despair, recognizing that, as a result, death may occur earlier. Within such constraints, the treatment of pain should be acknowledged as acceptable, as St. Basil the Great understood: "...with mandrake doctors give us sleep; with opium they lull violent pain."[51] Analgesics may even help the ill to pray. Suffering is not in itself good, even though pain can be our offering to God.[52] It is appropriate to use medicine to avoid suffering. One may not only pray to avoid the temptations that for some may be associated with suffering, but one may also act to avoid the temptations suffering may bring, rather than to confront them ascetically.

Finally, high-technology, highly invasive treatment may be morally necessary for those who have not faced and undertaken the tasks of repentance and the pursuit of the Kingdom of Heaven. Patients who find themselves still focused simply on pursuing whatever treatment will increase the quality of the life left to them or their dignity in dying, instead of focusing on entering into a pious and prayerful relationship with God, should if morally and medically possible be treated until they face their finitude and turn to the Kingdom of Heaven. If at the end of life a patient is still engaged in this world rather than turning to God, further treatment should be encouraged in the hope that the patient will in repentance turn to God. High-technology care can provide additional time to achieve a good death, one of prayer and repentance.[53] In this regard, if at all possible, analgesics should not be used to the point that they make the patient's repentance and preparation for death difficult by clouding the patient's sensorium. It is for all these reasons that traditional Christians should use advance directives not only to avoid medical interventions likely to be useless or spiritually burdensome, but also positively to ensure appropriate spiritual guidance as death approaches. They should name not only a appropriate proxy decision-maker, but also indicate the patient's spiritual father, so that choices to pursue further treatment or to "let nature take its course" can be made with a proper spiritual focus. These spiritual concerns should be clearly conveyed to the patient's proxy, family, and physicians. This means that the person appointed as a proxy decision-maker may need to be someone other than the usually expected family member, someone else more likely to make decisions in accord with the goals of a traditional Christian. One must seek surrogate or proxy decision-makers who will not be stumbling blocks to salvation. They should instead be those most likely to aid in one's pursuit of the kingdom of heaven.

Because appeals to death with dignity often engage a misguiding ideal, appropriately spiritually directed decisions at the end of life should not invoke this moral exemplar. The slogan "death with dignity", which has been invoked against the medico-technological postponement of death, in particular against the prolongation of dying, has been set in a context of meaning focused on a genre of terminal self-fulfillment. It has served not simply as a rallying cry in opposition to the technological envelopment of death, including its usual occurrence in a hospital setting. It has also been understood in robust secular terms at one with the liberal cosmopolitan ethos with an accent on a self-regarding concern for control and the determination of the circumstances of one's own death: a death over which one has as much control and from which one garners as much satisfaction as possible. The ethos of dying one's own way, of choosing autonomously, or of fulfilling one's own wishes may lead to a very bad death, if one's way, choices, and wishes are not focused on humble repentance in search of forgiveness. We conquer death, the outcome of Adam's sin, only by uniting ourselves to the Resurrection through Christ's Cross.

There is much to be said about the virtues of dying in a hospice rather than in a hospital. Indeed, home hospice care can blunt the temptations of high-technology attempts to postpone death at all costs. One can avoid false technological promises that can convey the misperception that one can postpone facing death, even though death is at one's doorstep. One can avoid the invasive routines of hospital life and have the support of one's family in prayerfully approaching death. In a familiar environment, surrounded by the icons in front of which for a lifetime one has prayed, one can prepare for death. All of this is good. Matters go wrong when one conceives of hospice care as primarily directed to enabling a more pleasant or dignified death rather than as a resource in one's final turn from oneself to God, from pride to holiness. The task is to make sure that everything is focused on the love of God and neighbor, rather than on self-indulgence. In contrast, the forces of a secular society, especially those of the emerging dominant secular global culture, move everything toward the immediate, the immanent, and away from that which is otherworldly, especially that which is transcendently Christian. This culture attempts to domesticate, transform, and assimilate that which is traditionally Christian, while at the same time offering a generic, neo-pagan spirituality. As with everything in Christian bioethics, the focus must be on reaching God through Christ. Suffering, disease, dying, and death must be located within the journey to His kingdom. Only then will their true meaning be disclosed.

Why This is all so Different

The traditional Christian account of bioethical decision-making is firmly nested in a spiritual quest: the pursuit of the kingdom of heaven. At the surface, many of the responses may seem similar to those provided by other Christian bioethics, as well as by secular morality. On closer inspection, each of the choices differs from those of a secular bioethics in being explicitly directed by spiritual concerns. The enterprise of ethics and bioethics for the traditional Christian always leads beyond this world to the next. As a consequence, decisions will differ because of the concern to treat the soul and achieve salvation. In comparison with the ethics and bioethics of other Christian religions, traditional Christian ethics and bioethics will also diverge because of different understandings of the nature of moral knowledge and of moral authority. Where among other Christian religions there will be a central reliance on discursive moral rationality or biblical exegesis, instead noetic experience, the role of the spiritual father, and concerns with spiritual, ascetic therapy will be central for traditional Christians.

The reconstruction that has been offered of a traditional Christian approach to withholding and withdrawing treatment, as well as to sins of involuntary homicide, is illustrative of this difference. The traditional Christian approach is set within a web of understandings that attribute to God ultimate responsibility for the death of each patient. Responsibility is not assigned to the one who withholds or withdraws treatment or provides appropriate analgesic care so as to protect against a spiritual threat. Acting with appropriate motivation (i.e., to do God's will) and with right intention (i.e., protection against a spiritual threat), cannot count as an involuntary homicide when the disease can be regarded as the cause of death. Having united one's will with God's will, one can step back and say "let God's will be done." However, because of the concern with the spiritual impact of being proximately causally involved in the death of another, one must seek remedies when one is involved even in a fully involuntary homicide (e.g., because of an unforeseeable mislabeling on a vial, an injection given non-negligently to cure a disease kills the patient). That the death of a patient is neither willed due to negligence nor foreseeable will not do away with the need to seek spiritual remedy because of the proximate causal involvement. As already noted, traditional Christianity takes involuntary sins quite seriously. She recognizes that only the pure of heart can see God (Matt 5:8) and that being intimately involved in the death of another can harm the heart.

It is important to note once again that traditional Christianity does not engage a principle analogous to the Roman Catholic doctrine of double effect. It is clear that this doctrine is rejected as is shown in cases of involuntary homicide, as well as in the discussion in chapter 5 regarding abortion. The moral theological doctrine of double effect is nested in a religious context that, even in its best circumstances, remains juridical. Within this context, the question is whether or not one is guilty of or accountable for a homicide, not whether one may need spiritual therapy. If one can show that (1) one did not act from a bad intent (a *mens rea*) but (2) according to one's obligations in the circumstance and (3) without negligence, then one cannot be held guilty or accountable. Matters look quite different if the issue is nested in spiritual therapy designed to free our hearts from passion so that we can be united with the holiness of God.

In the traditional Christian context, the focus is instead on (1) the intention of the agent (e.g., avoiding a spiritual threat), (2) the disposition or motivation of the agent (e.g., acting humbly to submit to the will of God), and (3) the nature of the causal involvement in human death (i.e., one is to seek spiritual therapy if one is involved in violent or aggressive actions that bring about the death of a human being). As a consequence, one can gain some insight into three special clusters of cases. (4) One may withdraw from spiritual threats (e.g., withhold or withdraw medical interventions that would cause a spiritual burden); (5) in the case of threats to chastity, as we will see, one may even act so that only God would be able to preserve one's life. (6) Under the appropriate circumstances and with spiritual discernment, it is allowable to expose oneself to martyrdom (i.e., in conformity with God's will, one may witness to Him with one's death).

Traditional Christianity completes the fundamental Jewish concern that in our relationship to God we are called not simply to be good but to be holy, and that these are distinct though inseparable categories. Christ's criticism of the Pharisees was for separating the pursuit of the holy from the pursuit of the good (see, for example, Matthew 23:25-26, Mark 7:19, and Luke 11:39). Christ performs a ministry that involves setting aside the unclean. As Jacob Neusner argues, when Christ cleanses lepers, He conjoins curing with cleansing (Matt 8:14, Mark 1:40-44, Luke 7:22). [54] As Neusner also shows, the focus on cleanliness was primarily a focus on holiness, which he correctly understands to be an ontological, not simply a moral category. [55] The concerns with cleanliness are understood appropriately only when they are seen to be concerns with holiness. "The opposite of unclean is holy, precisely as, throughout the priestly code, e.g., the book of Leviticus, the antonym of unclean is holy, far more than it is merely clean (tamé, qaddosh, appears far more regularly than tamé/tahor)." [56] It is just that the holy cannot be approached without a concern for virtue, for acting morally. On the other hand, one cannot effectively pursue the good, act morally, unless one also aims at holiness. This connection between holiness and morality is emphasized in the passage from the Mishna tractate Sotah (9:15), which Neusner quotes.

> Heedfulness leads to physical cleanliness, cleanliness to levitical purity, purity to separateness, separateness to holiness, holiness to humility, humility to the shunning of sin, shunning of sin to saintliness, saintliness to the Holy Spirit, the Holy Spirit to the resurrection of the dead. [57]

The concern with cleanliness of the heart so that one can approach the holiness of God is core to the traditional Christian spiritual therapeutic concern with the effect of involvement in the death of humans. As Neusner also notes, that which can more easily be rendered unclean is that which is closer to the holy. [58] It is for this reason that an ordinary layman may be a surgeon, but a priest may not. The special character of the holiness of the priestly office must be protected against possible proximate causal involvement in death, not to mention usual involvement in blood.

When placed in a traditional Christian context, the concern is neither juridical nor one of ritual cleanliness. There is instead a recognition that evil events, involuntary sins, can harm our hearts by intimately involving us in the broken character of our fallen world. We find ourselves enmired in sin, which we ourselves have willed to avoid, and therefore in special need of opening our hearts more fully to God. Being closely causally involved in killing another human should touch us deeply and should require a profound spiritual response, including praying for the person one has killed. Once a juridical framework is rejected and the focus restored to one of spiritual therapy, invocations of double effect as ways to exonerate guilt and dismiss the need for compensatory ascetical struggles can be seen to be deeply malicious. Such juridical understandings fail adequately to recognize that theology is primarily a way to union with God achieved through freeing our hearts from passions, which requires recognizing the ways in which evil can touch our being, even against our will. It is for this reason that the Church engages us in prayers and asceticism, especially when we contact evil, so as to remove impurities, distractions of our hearts, to free us from the results of involuntary sins. Such spiritual therapy focuses on restoring us so that we can approach the Mysteries recognizing the danger of approaching them with inadequate preparation. Beyond the sphere of morality as the domain of responsible action, there is holiness which we will not be able to endure unless our hearts are purged from defilement.

This complex of spiritual concerns with medical decision-making can be summarized around six points along with case illustrations.

1. One may not directly will to kill the innocent. To intend directly to kill the innocent who are not even unwilling aggressors is voluntary and unmitigated homicide in the full sense. The evil is not cured by the consent or even pleadings of the victim for euthanasia or any other form of death.

2. Even killing the guilty in the defense of others can harm our souls, thus requiring spiritual therapy. So, too, killing in self-defense, killing in a just war, and killing as an executioner require spiritual treatment.

3. It is generally appropriate, indeed obligatory, to use medicine to cure disease, ameliorate disability, and postpone death. St. Basil's concerns regarding the ways in which medicine can become all-absorbing indicate that we must approach all medical care with circumspection.

4. The level of therapeutic intervention chosen should not be
   a. so encompassing or burdensome as to harm the spiritual life of the patient.
      Heart transplants, complicated surgical procedures that must be repeated, and long-term artificial hydration and ventilation fall under this category, whether provided for oneself or for one's children. A hermit's traveling to a dialysis center to treat renal failure could be an example of treatment that should be avoided.
   b. or, so little as
      i. to fail to care adequately for our own health and life through appropriately using the blessings of medicine God has allowed to develop.
         Generally, for example, one is obliged to use insulin for the treatment of diabetes and antibiotics to cure otherwise fatal, sub-acute bacterial endocarditis; to fail to use such treatment would usually be sinful.
      ii. or to fail to accept the cross of suffering and pain medicine cannot set aside by instead accepting a premature death.
   Generally, one is obliged if one has diseases such as multiple sclerosis and amyelotropic lateral sclerosis not to reject treatment at the earlier stages, so as to avoid struggling with these difficult diseases as a labor of purification from one's passions. As the disease progresses and complications develop and the needed treatments become more onerous and intrusive, matters change.

5. Pain control should be used not only to comfort the patient but to aid the patient in preparing for death. If in the terminal stages of disease or when treatment has become too burdensome and it has been decided to remove artificial ventilation, it would not be inappropriate to provide sufficient analgesia to diminish the anguish

of hunger for air so as to prevent despair at the moment of death, as long as the analgesia provided is not of a dose sufficient in itself to be lethal, i.e., the disease process must be what brings the death of the patient.

6. Medicine should be used to sustain life for a patient who has not yet begun to repent and prepare for death. Here one might consider the case of a patient with cancer of the large bowel with metastases to the liver who will likely die within a few weeks without aggressive support, but who with intensive care could live for a number of months. If that person has not yet begun to repent and prepare for death, such a use of resources would be appropriate.

Suicide and Euthanasia

The ethos of approaching suffering and death is changing both in secular society and within much of Christianity itself. There are developments heralding conflicts within Roman Catholicism and other Christian religions as euthanasia comes to be accepted. David Thomasma puts it this way: "I further suggest that requesting assisted suicide and/or euthanasia from the motive of love of one's family or care givers might possibly qualify as one instance of justifiable euthanasia, although I acknowledge that the Church will not be making changes in its stance any time soon."[59] Thomasma indicates that for Roman Catholicism a concept of justified euthanasia on the model of justified homicide may develop. He advances this possibility against the backdrop of a suggestion taken from another author that Christ's death on the cross should be interpreted as a kind of suicide.[60]

Contemporary misunderstandings of the Christian view of suicide stem from a failure to appreciate how the early Church distinguished suicide from actions regarding oneself that to the modern mind can only appear suicidal. Some have even held that certain saints in their martyrdom in fact committed suicide.[61] Others have argued that it was not until centuries after Christ's death that Christianity appreciated suicide's sinfulness.[62] Such contemporary Western misunderstandings of the martyrdom and the death of certain saints surface in Compassion in Dying v. Washington.[63] Such claims are shown to be false by the early canons of the Church.[64] The early Church understood suicide to be forbidden but possessed an understanding of the appropriate involvement in one's own death somewhat different from most contemporary views, as we have begun to see. To begin with, to confess the Faith expecting and hoping to be martyred is not to commit suicide. Acting with appropriate intent to die as a martyr is not self-murder: it is submission to a death like Christ's. Martyrdom can only be understood within the fullness of the Faith that takes on the death of Christ. Martyrdom is not suicide, because martyrdom involves uniting selflessly with the Author of life, although putting oneself at a similar risk of death with an intent to die, but not for the Faith, purity, or holiness, could be a form of suicide. The Church of the first millennium recognized that, as long as one does not lay direct and violent hands on oneself against the will of God, even intentionally aiding others in the completion of one's own martyrdom cannot be counted as suicide. With proper spiritual preparation, discernment, and guidance, it has always been considered appropriate to go to certain martyrdom. However, seeking martyrdom requires moral discernment, as indicated by Canon IX of Pope Peter of Alexandria.[65]

Consider the following account by St. Nicholas Velimirovich (1880-1956) of an embrace of martyrdom by an early 18th century saint.

> Our Holy Father, the Martyr Nicodemus. Born in Elbasan, he was married and had children. Duped by the Turks, he embraced Islam and forced his children to do likewise, with the exception of one son who fled to the Holy Mountain and became a monk. Nicodemus went to Athos to take his son back, but the place made such an impression on him that he repented, returned to the Christian faith and became a monk himself. He bewailed his apostasy for three years, then decided to return to Albania, to expiate his sin there where he had committed it. He therefore returned, informed the Turks that he was a Christian and was beheaded on July 11th, 1722. His wonderworking relics are preserved today whole and uncorrupt.[66]

The lives and deaths of martyred saints carry with them a vivid appreciation of the importance of locating life and death within the pursuit of the Kingdom of God. As a result of this orientation towards holiness, what counts as suicide, as self-murder, for the Church of the first centuries is not fully equivalent to what most moderns mean by suicide. There are acts in which one can intend one's death that are not suicide because they appropriately aim at eternal life by avoiding a particular form of spiritual threat.

Christianity experiences martyrdom as a special opportunity to heal one's soul and to unite oneself with God. It also recognizes how certain experiences can profoundly harm the heart. Sexual violation, especially sexual seduction by one's torturers, is appreciated as a fundamental threat to spiritual health and integrity against which one is permitted to take radical measures. Intentionally putting oneself in death's way to preserve chastity was and still is not considered suicide. In this light, the stories of saints, puzzling to many moderns, take on a different light. Consider St. Nicholas Velimirovich's account of the life of St. Martinian (†422).

> When a woman came to tempt him and he saw that he would fall into sin with her, he leapt barefoot into the fire and stood in it until the pain brought forth tears from his eyes and he had killed all lust within himself. When other temptations arose, he fled to a lonely rock in the sea and lived there. When, though, in a shipwreck, a woman swam to the rock, he leapt into the sea intending to drown himself. But a dolphin took him upon its back and brought him, by God's providence, to the shore.[67]

The sympathy with which St. Nicholas Velimirovich presents St. Martinian's actions places the reader in the spirit of the early Church, within which such behavior is not suicidal but an exemplary affirmation of life: the pursuit of eternal life.

An account similar to that regarding Martinian is given of the twentieth-century ascetic, Augustinus the Russian (†1965), by the Elder Paisios. An account of Father

Augustinus' subsequent transfiguration in the light of God's uncreated energies is provided by Alexander Golitzin.[68]

> [Augustinus was called Antonius until he was clothed.] As he told me, he was at a monastery that was almost entirely composed of old men and they despatched him to serve as an aide for an employee of the monastery in the fishery, for the monastery was supported by the fishery. One day, the daughter of the employee came and told her father that there was an urgent task at home, so she sat in his place to help [the novice]. Temptation overcame the poor woman and without thinking she threw herself on the novice with sinful intentions. At that moment, Antonius lost control because the event happened so suddenly. He made the sign of the Cross and said, "My Christ, it is better to drown than to sin" and flung himself from the shore into the deep river! But the good God, viewing the great heroism of the holy youth, who acted like a new St. Martinianos in order to preserve his virtue, held his head up above the water without even getting wet. As he told me, "Although I flung myself headfirst, I did not understand how I found myself standing above the water without even getting my clothes wet!"
>
> At that moment, he also felt an internal peace and an inexpressible sweetness, which made every sinful thought and every carnal urge disappear, which had been provoked beforehand by the impious gestures of the girl. When the girl saw Antonius standing upright, she began to weep in repentance because of her sin and also because she was moved by the great miracle itself.[69]

It is clear from the Church's reception of his life that his leap to apparently certain death was never considered to be an act of suicide. Such actions, though they would appear to invite certain death, are not self-murder. Even Western churchmen such as St. Ambrose[70] (339-397) and Blessed Jerome (345-419) could recognize that going to certain death to preserve chastity is not sinful. Jerome argues that one should not die by one's own hands "except when chastity is threatened."[71]

Saints and holy monastics, those who are infused with theology, have never actively hastened their own death even when their dying imposed burdens on themselves or others. They have accepted with humility the indignities and sufferings of dying, recognizing as well that to kill oneself or another to escape the burdens of caring and of dying would be spiritually harmful. The exemplars of good living and dying, the saints, live and die in a way that has had no place for physician-assisted suicide or euthanasia. They have never acted to avoid suffering by suicide or euthanasia. One learns from them, from their lives and deaths, how to draw the lines between murder, suicide, and humble self-sacrifice. What is offered is an experiential knowledge of how to aim at union with God. This experiential, noetic knowledge of progress from oneself to God opens the door to understanding why one should voluntarily accept suffering.

The general contemporary secular understanding of suicide is thus radically different from that of the traditional Christian, as the foregoing shows. Early Christianity did not regard intentionally facilitating one's death as a sufficient condition for holding a death to be suicide. There are numerous instances of Christians acting in ways they hope will lead to martyrdom, as the death of St. Nicodemus the New Martyr illustrates. There are also instances of saints avoiding the loss of chastity in ways that, in the absence of a direct divine intervention, will lead to death, as the life of St. Martinian illustrates. These classes of actions have not been considered acts of suicide because they are directed to spiritual health. They are acts of love to God in the fullness of the Tradition. Suicide as self-murder includes only those actions intentionally leading to one's death that are not directed towards holiness, towards love of God. Such misdirected actions collide with the Tradition which reflects the guidance of the Spirit. Within the Tradition's experience of life, death, and the pursuit of holiness, Christ's voluntary acceptance of His death, *pace* Thomasma,[72] could never appropriately be interpreted as an act of suicide.[73] Within this experience of life, truth, and the pursuit of holiness, facilitating one's own death so as not to be a burden to others has always been recognized as a rejection of Christian asceticism. Patiently bearing burdens is integral to the Christian life. There has been no provision to regard such homicide to avoid burdens as other than self-murder. One would have missed the force of the crucial moral issue: if the purpose of life is worship of God so that a martyrdom freely accepted or a death suffered to avoid the loss of chastity is an appropriate selfless offering to God, the distinction with regard to death will be between those acts through which one turns to oneself or others versus those through which one turns oneself first and foremost ascetically to God. The boundaries of appropriate action are grounded in the ascetical experience of the Church. The boundaries of what is allowable will at times be unclear and will require spiritual discernment. Yet, the crucial point is clear: suicide is a form of turning away from God which the death of a saint cannot be.

Puzzles regarding suicide and the death of certain martyrs derive from confusions between two profoundly divergent understandings of the moral life. First, there is the spiritually therapeutic and liturgical vision of early Christianity. It is framed and directed by the experiences of the saints and is not a deductive moral system. Second, there are various moral juridical accounts, which emerged in later Western Christianity. These have been lodged within systematic, deductive accounts. In the first case, divine laws are not legal proscriptions regarding which one can have oneself found innocent or guilty by appealing to special justifying or excusing circumstances. Rather, the laws of God are crucial points of orientation in the ascetic struggle to turn to the Kingdom of Heaven. They indicate how appropriately to enter into the intimacy of eucharistic worship. The laws of God turn us away from loving ourselves and toward loving God and others. In the second case, God's laws are interpreted as one would a mundane code of law, where justifying and excusing grounds are crucial. In contrast, within the therapeutic model one is interested in what mars the heart, what turns a person away from God. Excuses are as out of place as would be an appeal to be excused from insulin for one's diabetes. At stake is one's state of spiritual health, which must be achieved by ascetic struggle rather than through juridical pleadings.

In all of this, it must again be emphasized, suffering is not a good in itself. Although one should always accept suffering that cannot be avoided, one may ask God to take the life quickly of someone whose dying is prolonged and painful. In the office of the parting of the soul from the body, the priest prays, "Wherefore, O Master, command that the soul of thy servant, N., may depart in peace, and may rest in thine everlasting mansions with all Thy Saints."[74] If the person has suffered long and is on the point of death, the priest entreats that "this destructible bond, which as the God of our fathers Thou hadst sanctified by Thy divine will, should be dissolved, and that his body should be dissolved from the elements of which it was fashioned, but that his soul should be translated to that place where it shall take up its abode until the final Resurrection."[75] As with Christ's prayer to His Father in Gethsemane (John 17:1-26), one may pray for deliverance, but one must accept the Divine will, not one's own. The deaths of Christ and the saints teach the good death. Christ's voluntary acceptance of the Cross is the best icon of how to accept suffering; His death leads to the Resurrection. The death to be feared is the one that comes suddenly, unanticipated, giving no opportunity for repentance. The death that sets eternal life at jeopardy is the one that affords little chance to forgive all one's enemies, to ask the forgiveness of all whom one has harmed, to make amends for the evil one has done, to confess one's sins, and to beg the forgiveness of God, turning one's life around in order to aim at God. As the West once prayed, *a subitanea et improvisa morte, libera nos, Domine* [from a sudden and unprovided-for death, deliver us, O Lord].[76]

The issue of physician-assisted suicide discloses foundational differences in the understanding of moral theology. One genre of theology attempts to reason discursively to the character of the good death. It attempts by sound argument to produce a systematic morality to address physician-assisted suicide and euthanasia, and then logically to persuade believer and unbeliever alike. In contrast, a second genre of theology, the theology of the first centuries, is a way to experience God. Christ and the saints disclose in their lives and deaths a morality of living and dying inaccessible by rational argument alone. As a morality of dying and death grounded in Christ's humble acceptance of crucifixion, this life has no place for the self-assertion of physician-assisted suicide or euthanasia. In contrast, the first genre of theology will be rent by divisions as different basic premises are recruited to secure different conclusions regarding the morality of physician-assisted suicide and euthanasia. Doctrines will develop in novel ways as a consequence of accepting new axioms at the foundation of this discursive theology in the service of adapting to new moral contexts, towards the goal of accommodating to moral concerns such as death with dignity and the value of self-determination. In this fashion, many of the Christian religions will likely accept physician-assisted suicide and euthanasia, at least in certain circumstances. Physician-assisted suicide offers us a moral and theological Rorschach test to disclose foundational commitments regarding morality and theology. Further doctrinal development is likely to occur in many of the Western Christian religions, so that they can seemingly in good conscience embrace a new morality that will allow them to accept physician-assisted suicide and euthanasia.[77]

Where, then, does this leave Christians when confronting suffering, dying, and death? Traditional Christianity is fundamentally opposed to physician-assisted suicide and euthanasia. The traditional Christian life has always experienced such a death as a separation from the humility and holiness of the life and death of Christ.[78] This opposition to suicide, assisted suicide, and euthanasia is rooted in the experience of the Christian life as a life directed to humility. To be a Christian is to take on Christ, not only His life, but also His submissive death on the Cross (Romans 6). To avoid confusing traditional Christian and contemporary, post-traditional Christian and secular moral understandings of murder, killing, and suicide, one must recognize the humble submission involved in acquiring moral and spiritual health. Terminology can help guide and draw out important distinctions. For example, Abraham does not embark on the project of murdering but on that of sacrificing his son Isaac.[79] Because Abraham submits to the will of God, not his own will, even using the word "kill" instead of "sacrifice" is morally confusing. One must draw similar distinctions among self-murder, self-killing, and self-sacrifice, especially when the last is an instance of an appropriate offering of oneself, a proper sacrifice of one's life. Describing Christ's death, the martyrdom of the saints, or the choice to die rather than lose one's chastity as suicide goes awry: (1) involvement in one's own death is conflated with suicide as self-murder (i.e., the traditional Western usage), while in addition, (2) even the term "self-killing" obscures the submission of Christ, the martyrs, and the saints in general to the Father's will, because (3) such terms (e.g., suicide and assisted suicide) are profoundly out of place in cases of appropriate "self-sacrifice". When one truly acts to follow the will of God, one's actions are inappropriately described by terms that usually identify sins.[80]

The life and death of Christ with which Christians unite themselves conflict radically with secular culture. Because the times have changed with the emergence of a vigorous, post-Christian, post-traditional, indeed neo-pagan culture, the Cross is ever more a stumbling block. It is the epiphany of an undignified death, a humiliating death, a death of submission. Traditional Christianity provides bioethics a language out of step with a culture of self-determination and pride. It sees matters of suffering, dying, and death without a central focus on considerations of rights, dignity, and self-satisfaction. Instead, the focus is on how life in the body of Christ teaches us to live and die. At stake is a goal beyond freedom, dignity, and virtue: union with the transcendent God[81] through taking on Christ's divinity, as He took on our humanity.[82] The culture of traditional Christian belief focuses on life regained through the humiliation of death on the Cross.

Death and Transplantation

The nature of death is both a metaphysical and an empirical issue. Although Christians recognize that human beings are not just their bodies, but a whole of body, soul, and spirit, so that the resurrection of the body gives completeness to human life, they also recognize through the appearances of the saints that there is life after death before resurrection. Also, Christians, as others, understand the difference between actions against a living body, such as murder, and actions against a dead body, such as the desecration of a corpse. Although bodies can remain hallowed by the person whose body they were, corpses are no longer the embodied presence of a person. For example, the canons of the Church make it clear that the Eucharist may be given only to living humans, not to corpses.[83] The question then arises of how to determine the moment of death. In part, this is a metaphysical question: when does the soul depart the body? In part, this is a question regarding the ontology of embodiment: what part of the body is necessary for the presence of the soul?

To some extent, this last question must be approached in empirical terms. To quote St. Gregory Palamas,

> If we ask how the mind is attached to the body, where is the seat of imagination and opinion, where is memory fixed, what part of the body is most vulnerable and so to say directs the others...in all such matters each man may speak his opinion.... [I]t is the same with all question of this sort about which the Spirit has given us no plain revelation; for the Spirit only teaches us to know the Truth which penetrates everything.[84]

It has become increasingly clear as neurophysiological information and experience with transplantation have developed that the substitution of a person's organs other than the brain by transplanted or prosthetic ones does not change the identity of a person. Though the soul is in the hand (as the soul is in all of the body), destroying the hand will not kill a person. Though the soul is in the heart, people can have their hearts removed and remain alive, even without an organic heart. The last 200 years have shown the necessity of the brain, if not particular portions of the brain for the presence of a person.[85] To transplant a heart, lung, or liver is not to transplant a person. A quadriplegic is alive and so, too, would be a quadriplegic whose whole body was removed and destroyed but whose head was maintained. The earthly presence of a person is manifestly dependent on the brain; every other organ can be transplanted without transplanting the person. Indeed, to transplant a brain would be to transplant a body. As Roland Puccetti once put it, where the brain goes, there goes the person.[86]

This leads to an empirically guided ontological appreciation of the embodiment of persons: once persons have a brain, their presence in this world is tied to that brain, though it would be a mistake to say that they or their souls are only in their brains, unless the rest of the body is destroyed. Nor are persons reducible to their brains or to cognitive function. After the early periods of gestation, when a person's brain is destroyed, that person is dead, although certain human biological life may continue in cell cultures, tissues, and organs. The remains of the body can be transplanted without transplanting the person. The kind of human life sustained in cells, tissues, organs, and even in decapitated bodies is not that of a person. Because (1) these parts of the body are not sufficient for the life of a person, i.e., sensing the world and responding to the world, (2) these parts are not integral to the embodied life of a person (i.e., persons can continue reasoning and willing even when parts of the body other than the brain have been destroyed or transplanted), and (3) other organs can be transplanted without transplanting the person. Aside from the brain, all body parts appear fungible so that a body could at least in principle be transplanted to the head of another person. One would not be uniting two persons, but what had been the body of one person to the head of a living person.[87]

These reflections regarding the death of adult humans cannot be transferred to speculations regarding when the soul enters the body of an embryo, so as to determine whether zygotes are persons or what parts of early embryos constitute the embodiment of a person. As the last chapter shows, the Church has recognized the obligation to protect the life from the mother's womb, eschewing metaphysical speculations about the actual moment of ensoulment. After all, until a brain is formed, one cannot talk about the brain death of an embryo. In addition, there has been a special focus on protecting early life: for this last reason, as the previous chapter indicated, one may not engage in any non-therapeutic experimentation with human zygotes, embryos, or fetuses. These restrictions against drawing a line between animated versus unanimated embryos and fetuses do not bar exploring the appropriateness of at least some higher-brain-oriented definitions of death of children and adults. One may seek to determine when persons are no longer present in this world.

One can only determine that a portion of the body is not necessary for life when one knows it can be destroyed without killing the person. If it becomes clear that certain brain structures are not necessary for sentience or consciousness, but rather perform only reflex-like functions, then their continued existence after the death of the rest of the brain would not be an index of the life of a person. Such determinations will likely occur only through experience in determining which parts of the brain can be replaced by transplanted or prosthetic parts without affecting the presence of a person. One can only determine that a part of the body is not necessary for human embodiment when there is moral certainty it can be transplanted without in principle transplanting or killing the person. For example, it would seem that one can transplant every organ save the whole brain without transplanting the person or without in principle killing the person. Even then, there will likely be so many gray areas that one will not usually be able to distinguish between the absence of personal life and compromised human personal life (e.g., a human person in coma). One can only declare death when the embodiment of a person has been destroyed. Also, since persons are a unity of body, soul, and spirit, persons must be recognized as present even when they are asleep, under deep anesthesia, or comatose, as long as their embodiments are intact. In addition, there is no question that both newborn infants and the profoundly mentally retarded are persons: they have traditionally been given the Mysteries of the Church.

Finally, it may turn out that the brain can incrementally be replaced while still leaving the person in this world. That is, the person may incarnate the new material as his own. If such is the case, one will have learned even more concerning our ability to enliven and ensoul matter and make it our personal embodiment. At stake is an empirical truth about the scope of human dominion. Even now in the case of transplantation, an organ or tissues from another person or even from an animal can be incorporated within a person, and thus rendered a part of the embodiment of a person. The children of Adam still retain dominion over nature and have a power, albeit limited, to transform the world and render it an offering to God.

In establishing a definition of death, it is crucial to avoid definitions that in the absence of brain death, or at least of higher-brain death, identify as death only the cessation of spontaneous respiration and cardiac function. Such purely cardiorespiratory definitions of death may be devices that allow the transplantation of organs, without first appropriately determining the death of the signal embodiment of persons in this world: the death of the brain. That is, holding that a person is dead when there is only cardiopulmonary arrest, but in the absence of true brain death, so as to remove vital organs, may involve killing that person.[88] Such "pragmatic" approaches to the definition of death (i.e., non-heartbeating but not necessarily brain-dead donors) may depend on the assumption that the person called dead by such practices would at best only be able to be resuscitated with severe brain damage and therefore might as well be treated as if dead. Such definitions of death do not take seriously determining when a person is no longer present in this world. We now know that brain death must directly or indirectly always be the focus of any declarations of death. Interest in transplantation cannot be allowed to obscure this crucial focus.

When there is an appropriate determination of death, even an appropriate determination of whole-brain death, there should be no bar to Orthodox Christians' donating their organs or to their families consenting to such donations after determination of brain death, if they undertake this with love for others. When there is a reliable determination of death, transplantation involves neither the killing nor the mutilation of a living person. Indeed, even the living donation of an organ or tissue not necessary for life has none of the marks of a sinful mutilation, which the Canons have characterized in their condemnation of non-therapeutic castration. One is not ungrateful for the body God has given. One does not attempt to set aside the differences between man and woman. One does not fail to accept the goodness of human embodiment. Instead, one turns in love to aid another. As long as this does not involve a risk of certain death (e.g., donating one's heart), such acts of love, depending on the circumstances, are not only tolerable, but laudable.

As long as such provision is out of love for others, there is no moral bar in principle to accepting, even seeking payment. The poor may out of their need, or the need of their families, ask for funds in exchange for an organ or tissue that may be licitly provided before or after death. A kind of exploitation is involved in forbidding the poor from selling their organs. If the poor are allowed to donate their organs, but not to ask for payment in return, thus holding the poor to a very high moral ideal, one may be guilty of imposing a burden too heavy for many. In particular, since greater wealth and social status is correlated with better health and greater longevity, the policy of forbidding organ sales may condemn some of the poor to remain poor and be short-lived.[89] Health care policy should encourage assistance for the poor while overseeing organ sales where these are legal, so as to prevent the poor from being defrauded of the payments for their organs.[90] In any case, transplantation should not be viewed as evil in itself. As long as what is done does not change the sexual identity of men and women, make persons parents through the use of another's gonads (e.g., through the transplantation of testicles, thus engaging in a genre of adultery), or alter their ability to be moral agents in an embodiment recognizably similar to that of Christ's, there should be no bars in principle.

In all of such circumstances, the human bodies, organs, and tissues should be accorded respect.[91] Faithful Christians have taken on Christ in baptism and united themselves to Christ (Gal 3:27) and in the Eucharist they have brought Him into themselves. Their bodies have become temples of the Holy Spirit.[92] This may give grounds for never directly killing a brain-dead but otherwise alive human body (e.g., never injecting a lethal drug in order to bring bioethical death). The bodies of all (for the Holy Spirit goes where He wills), but especially those of faithful Christians, should be respected as one would the body, the relics, of a holy saint. The bodies of faithful Christians have been one with Christ and therefore, except in the case of great necessity (e.g., a dangerous, contagious disease), should be given a traditional Christian burial and never be cremated. This consideration also bears against the donation of bodies for dissection, although not so strongly, as long as in the end a proper burial is performed. Yet the grounds for hesitation are considerable. With the donation of a body, the family and the church community are denied both the sobering and spiritually therapeutic encounter with death and the immediate evocation of their prayers on behalf of the dead person. At the very least, if a body is donated, these prayers should not be postponed, much less omitted. Special care should always be taken to treat the human body, especially that of a faithful traditional Christian, with special regard not only because it has been with God through the Mysteries of the Church, but because it is always potentially to be discovered to be the relic of a holy saint. The bodies of saints are holy, for they (1) testify through their preservation from corruption and the miracles they work to the paradisiacal restoration of nature through union with God and (2) manifest the very energies of God.

Miracles, Sins, Devils, and Forgiveness

Christianity abounds with miracles. It began with miracles. Miracles remain with it. Alongside, indeed within highly secular scientific cultures, traditional Christianity nourishes a parallel insight: God is omnipotent, personal, and merciful. Not only is death conquered through the Resurrection, but the Resurrected One before the General Resurrection reaches out to some miraculously to bring them health. Before death, in the midst of our suffering, God partially restores nature to its paradisiacal state, miraculously setting aside particular disabilities and sufferings. The seemingly arbitrary character of God's miraculous mercy may bring troubling doubts to some, especially those who suffer, pray for relief, but whose prayer is not answered with healing. Why are some cured and others not? In response to such puzzles one meets the silence of God's transcendence, even if it is of His transcendent mercy. There is no accounting for how and when the transcendent God will choose to restore the broken character of our lives and this world. Confronted with God Who is transcendent, personal, and free, philosophical reflection fails.

St. John Chrysostom stresses this point in his Second Homily on the incomprehensibility of God.

> Why does this man escape vengeance, while the other is overwhelmed with sufferings? Why did this man find pardon and another fail to find it? Such are the things they were seeking to learn. How do we know this? From the words Paul spoke just before the text I quoted. I mean when Paul said: "Therefore, he has mercy on whom he wills, and whom he wills he hardens. You will then say to me: 'Why, then, does he find fault? For who has opposed his will?'" [Rom 9:18-19] It was then Paul went on to say: "My friend, who are you to answer God back?"[93]

Chrysostom restates Job: man cannot impeach God's justice (Job 40:8) or His mercy. However difficult for prideful and suffering humans, the appropriate response when tempted to judge God is Job's declaration, "Therefore I despise myself and repent in dust and ashes" (Job 42:6). Despite his suffering, Job repents for suggesting that God might have been wrong. As with the Fiftieth Psalm, in which David as everyman acknowledges that because of his sins he has no grounds for complaint against God's chastisements (Psalm 50:4, LXX), so, too, we are left without grounds for complaint for our or others' suffering, disability, and death – or for the miraculous deliverance of only some.

Christ's miracles not only often focus on the forgiveness of sin, but on demonic powers as well: cure is often associated with driving out a devil.[94] For the modern mind, this is surely a stumbling block. There is little appreciation of the world's requiring exorcism and reclamation by the Church. Yet every baptism involves preliminary exorcisms and every blessing is an entry into the world of the kingdom of God: the Church sanctifies. So, too, all miraculous cures involve restoring a part of the world to its paradisiacal character: it is taken back from Satan and the consequences of the Fall. Because this reclamation has occurred ultimately for all practicing, truly believing Christians rightly baptized, it is infrequently appropriate to recognize a direct demonic presence in a baptized person's illness. However, when present, as with many of the disorders Christ miraculously cured, it can camouflage itself within the usual symptoms of disease, like a Kantian noumenal reality lurking in the shadows of phenomenal appearance.[95] It can also declare its presence unambiguously, breaking the ordinary character of reality.[96]

Because all empirical science approaches appearance in terms of regularities in the physical world, unless a spiritual presence wishes to declare itself, it will usually not be noticed. The unbeliever will easily dismiss most intrusions of bodiless powers as "noise" or as an element of physical phenomenal experience. However, for the believer even the ordinary temptations of life will not only have obvious empirical explanations, they will also be regarded as the result of personal evil. First, the world and human nature incline to evil as the result of the Fall, which involves an intimate engagement with Satan. Second, intrusions of temptations will be considered the result of malign spiritual interventions. As in science fiction where one might imagine clever extraterrestrials tipping the balance of causal influences so as to cascade events to the production of a particular outcome, so, too, forces both benevolent and malevolent may be envisaged as inobtrusively intervening in the flow of circumstances. Thus, within the Tradition temptations can easily be regarded as the product of evil spirits.[97]

Evil is ultimately personal in being either the consequence of personal choices or the direct expression of personal choice. Because this recognition of the personal character of evil was never taken to discount the independent role of science, science and the recognition of the demonic have coexisted in traditional Christianity. *Pace* Kant, who as a good son of the Enlightenment had no place for spirits, this coexistence can be understood on a model somewhat analogous to Kant's bifurcate account of reality: a two-world theory of phenomenal and noumenal, apparent and hidden reality.[98] Behind a seemingly unbroken web of phenomenal causal associations, there are other realities. However, given a secular commitment to non-psychical explanations in sorting information from noise, findings will usually be constituted without attention to any marks of spiritual presence. In addition, usually a demonic force will have good reason not to call attention to its presence. In any case, there must be a recognition with St. Paul that "our struggle is not against flesh and blood, but ... against the spiritual forces of evil in the heavenly realms" (Eph 6:12). If one fails to acknowledge the demonic, one fails fully to appreciate the seriousness of the spiritual struggle.

At times there must be a strikingly un-Enlightenment (and in this sense unkantian) acknowledgement of both miraculous interventions and demonic manifestations. At times disease and healing can only be understood as encounters with personal good and evil. There will be no other way reasonably to construe some occurrences.[99] Not only are miracles recognized, but special measures are provided for spiritual combat. There are not just exorcisms and the anointing of the sick but also prayers against the evil eye as a protection against spells and curses.[100] Traditional Christianity does not incline to medicalizing or depersonalizing evil. Rather than medically reifying as diseases inclinations to particular sins (e.g., alcoholism and homosexuality), the Tradition has regarded all such inclinations as due to the Fall and demonic influence, while providing no grounds for excluding a concurrent, fully naturalistic account or enlisting the aid of medicine.

Traditional Christian bioethics is thus embedded in a philosophy of medicine that resolutely takes spiritual powers seriously. Healing should surely always be pursued medically within the taken-for-granted everyday of the empirical. Healing must always also be pursued spiritually as an occasion to recognize sinfulness, repent, seek forgiveness and be ready, God willing, to accept a miraculous cure. Christian bioethics is thus involved with more than disclosing the goods, harms, rights, duties, wrong-making conditions, and virtues associated with engagements in health care and the biomedical sciences. Most importantly, it discloses how health care and the biomedical sciences are involved in the cosmic drama of salvation involving God, saints, angels, and demons. The metaphysics of a Christian bioethics and philosophy of medicine relocates disease, disability, suffering, and death in transcendently personal terms. Because these personal relations have a specially liturgical development through which persons move from Satan, sickness, and evil to God, holiness, and ultimate health, the Christian bioethics of suffering has a liturgical character. Where a secular bioethics would need to attend to goods, rights, duties, and virtues, a Christian bioethics must attend to spiritually therapeutic and liturgical obligations associated with suffering and death. It must recognize how encounters with health care needs should not be estranged from liturgical needs, in fact can only be fully understood within a liturgical context. The Christian liturgical response to disability and disease both locates suffering in the drama of salvation and points to spiritual cure, directing one's energies to the wholehearted love and worship of God.

As Therese Lysaught recognizes, the Christian anointing of the sick inscribes the sufferings of Christians into the sufferings of Christ.[101] Since the sufferings of Christ are directed to the Resurrection, it does more. The Christian response to suffering is to inscribe our suffering, disability, and death into the liberation from sin and death which comes only with Christ's Resurrection. As a consequence, traditional Christianity focuses on liberating the sick not just from suffering, but from sin, because sin is the cause of suffering. Illness, suffering, and the imminence of death should recall the bond between suffering and sin. Because sin is the root of suffering, the most important response of the Church to the sick is to forgive sins and reconcile with Christ. This is always the greatest and most significant miracle: forgiveness. The Synoptic Gospels recall Christ's association of the forgiveness of sin with healing (Matt 9:1-8; Mark 2:1-12; Luke 5:17-26). Even though St. John the Theologian records Christ's denial that the man born blind suffered because of either his sins or those of his parents (John 9:1-3), he records the warning of Jesus to the man healed at Bethesda, "Behold, thou hast become well; no longer go on sinning, lest a worse thing should befall thee" (John 5:14). It is for this reason that the anointing of the sick is a core Christian response to sickness and ill-ness,[102] making Holy Unction integral to Christian bioethics. Holy Unction discloses the reality within which Christians must approach disease, suffering, and death.

By focusing on sin and its forgiveness, the rubrics join Holy Unction to repentance and confession, as well as to the assembly of the Church and the Liturgy. Spiritually therapeutic concerns are integral to the liturgical.

> The sick person who receives this Sacrament must be of the Orthodox faith, and must prepare himself by repentance and confession; and before or after this Sacrament he receives the Sacrament of the Holy Communion. Holy Unction ... is performed in church, in the presence of an assembly, if the sick person be able to leave his bed; or at home, before an assembly of people.[103]

Although sickness may be solitary, and repentance alone before the face of God, salvation is within a community. If at all possible, one must enter into the right-worshiping, right-believing community in continuity with the Apostles. The several absolutions of Holy Unction are, for example, broad, encompassing, and focused within the community of the faithful, as this excerpt from the prayer of the Sixth Priest[104] illustrates.

> We beseech thee, and entreat thee, in thy goodness loose, remit, forgive, O God, the errors of thy servant, N., and his (her) iniquities, whether voluntary or involuntary, whether of knowledge or of ignorance, whether of excess or of disobedience, whether of the night or of the day; whether he (she) be under the ban of a priest, or the curse of father or mother; whether through the sight of his (her) eyes, or his (her) sense of smell; whether through the union of adultery or the taste of fornication, or through whatsoever impulse of the flesh and of the spirit he (she) hath departed from Thy will, and from Thy holiness. If we, also, have sinned in like manner, forgive; forasmuch as Thou art a good God who rememberest not evil, and lovest mankind: and let not him (her) or us fall into evilness of life, neither run in hurtful ways.[105]

The connection between sin and illness is recognized not only in the case of the sick person, but regarding all, since all are sinners.

The seventh prayer acknowledges both the self-destructive character of sin and the role of the devil. Again, our struggle is with the supernatural. "For we wrestle not against flesh and blood, but against principalities, against powers, against the rulers of the darkness of this world, against spiritual wickedness in high places" (Eph 6:12).

> Give ear unto our supplication, and receive it as incense offered unto thee; and visit thy servant, N.; and if he (she) hath done aught amiss, either by word, or deed, or thought, either by night or by day; if he (she) hath fallen under the ban of a priest, or under his (her) own anathema; or hath been embittered by an oath, and hath cursed himself (herself): We beseech thee,

and supplicate thee: loose, pardon, forgive him (her), O God, overlooking his (her) sins and wickednesses, both those which he (she) hath done knowingly, and those which he (she) hath committed in ignorance. And if he (she) hath transgressed thy commandments, or hath sinned because he (she) bearest flesh, and dwelleth in the world, or through the wiles of the Devil, do thou, forasmuch as thou art a good God and lovest mankind, forgive; for there is no man who liveth and sinneth not.[106]

The focus on making the suffering person whole by forgiving sin is also central in the final absolution at the end of the office of Holy Unction.

O holy King, compassionate and all-merciful Lord Jesus Christ, Son and Word of the living God, Who desirest not the death of a sinner, but rather that he (she) should turn from his wickedness and live: I lay not my sinful hand upon the head of him (her) who is come unto Thee in iniquities, and asked of Thee, through us, the pardon of his (her) sins, but Thy strong and mighty hand, which is in this, Thy Holy Gospels, that is now held by my fellow-ministers, upon the head of Thy servant, N. And with them I also beseech and entreat Thy merciful compassion and love of mankind, which cherisheth no remembrance of evil, O God our Savior, who by the hand of Thy prophet Nathan didst give remission of his sins unto penitent David, and didst accept Manasses' prayer of contrition: Do Thou, the same Lord, receive also with Thy wonted tender love towards mankind this Thy servant, N., who repenteth him (her) of his (her) sore transgressions, regarding not all his (her) trespasses. For Thou art our God, Who hast commanded that we forgive, even unto seventy times seven, those who fall into sin. For as is Thy majesty, so also is Thy mercy: and unto Thee are due all glory, honor and worship, now, and ever, and unto ages of ages. Amen.[107]

The health offered is of soul and body. Because suffering and sin touch us all, in many Orthodox churches all Orthodox are invited to be anointed on Wednesday in Holy Week.[108]

Christianity is about cure: it is radical therapy. As Bishop Hierotheos provocatively notes: had Christ lived in the twentieth century, Christianity would have been more associated with medicine than with religion, at least in the non-Orthodox sense of religion.[109] Christianity is the method for curing suffering, disability, and death by the uncreated energies of God. Suffering is not only an occasion for patience,[110] but for uniting us with God. Christian physicians and health care institutions must be ready to aid suffering patients in more than just secular terms. They must control pain while helping their patients approach the Mysteries of the Church in repentance and through spiritual therapy (e.g., confession, communion, and Holy Unction). The role of the chaplain is thus properly particular and non-ecumenical: the traditional Christian approach to suffering and sin is not generic. It is rich with very particular concerns. Christian bioethics must attend not just to the bounds of appropriate medical care, but also to how medical care must be placed within the context of spiritual care.

Notes

1. Immanuel Kant in the last of his famous three questions raises the issue of the existence of God and immortality. "All the interests of my reason, speculative as well as practical, combine in the three following questions: 1. What can I know? 2. What ought I to do? 3. What may I hope?" Immanuel Kant, *Immanuel Kant's Critique of Pure Reason*, trans. Norman Kemp Smith (New York: St. Martin's Press, 1964), p. 635, A804f=B332f. For Kant, the last question turns out not to secure a truly metaphysical answer. He does not encounter true transcendence. Kant will only allow practical, "as if" knowledge about God and immortality. The transcendent thus becomes an idea that has its meaning in giving direction to our actions, our moral lives. The meaning given is integral to the sphere of moral action and the organization of knowledge. See *Critique of Practical Reason*, Dialectic of Pure Practical Reason, and *Critique of Pure Reason*, Appendix to the Transcendental Dialectic. The meaning found does not transcend the horizon of our finite undertakings. When this volume refers to the deep meaning of life, suffering, and death, reference is made to metaphysical concerns regarding immortality and God, concerns that Kant would denominate both transcendent and noumenal.
2. Seneca, *The Stoic Philosophy of Seneca*, trans. Moses Hadas (New York: Norton, 1958), Letter 70, p. 207.
3. *Ibid.*, p. 202.
4. *Ibid.*, pp. 204-5.
5. Moses Hadas (ed.), *The Complete Works of Tacitus* (New York: Random House, 1942), pp. 391-92.
6. For an exploration of historical and cultural relationships between concerns with self-control and euthanasia, see Ezekiel Emanuel, "Euthanasia: Historical, Ethical, and Empiric Perspectives," *Archives of Internal Medicine* 154 (September 12, 1994), 1890-1901.
7. For an analysis of traditional professional (Hippocratic) ethics towards the goal of showing its compatibility with physician-assisted suicide, see Richard Momeyer, "Does Physician-Assisted Suicide Violate the Integrity of Medicine?" *Journal of Medicine and Philosophy* 20 (February 1995), 13-24.
8. Ronald Dworkin, *Life's Dominion: An Argument About Abortion, Euthanasia, and Freedom* (New York: Alfred A. Knopf, 1993).
9. *Compassion in Dying v. Washington*, 79 F.3d 790 (9th Cir. 1996), rev'd sub nom. *Washington v. Glucksberg*, 117 S. Ct. 2258 (1997); *Quill v. Vacco*, 80 F.3d 716 (2d Cir. 1996), *rev'd*, 117 S. Ct. 2293 (1997).
10. Until 1972, the Republic of Texas and the state of Texas were exceptions to the Anglo-American legal history concerning suicide in proscribing neither suicide, attempted suicide, nor aiding and abetting suicide. H.T. Engelhardt, Jr., and Michele Malloy, "Suicide and Assisting Suicide: A Critique of Legal Sanctions," *Southwestern Law Review* 36 (November 1982), 1003-37. The history of Texas suggests how difficult it is for Texans to be committed Christians and why as of yet there are no recognized Texan saints. For a study of the cultural roots of the Texian *Weltanschauung*, see the author's pre-conversion essay, "Texas: Messages, Morals, and Myths," *Journal of the American Studies Association of Texas* 21 (October 1990), 33-49. God's grace has now found a special acceptance in Texas marked by the founding of Orthodox monasteries. Perhaps some day Texas will have her own Saint Bubba of Texas, Fool for Christ. The Oregon referendum, by legalizing physician-assisted suicide through its Death With Dignity Act, took the first step in refashioning state legislation in the matter of physician-assisted suicide. See Oregon Death with Dignity Act, Or. Rev. Stat. § 13 (1996), *implementation stayed*; *Lee v. Oregon*, 891 F. Suppl. 1439 (D. Or. 1995), *rev'd*, 107 F.3d 1382 (CA9 1997), *cert. denied sub nom.*; *Lee v. Harcleroad*, 118 S. Ct. 328 (1997).

11. For a review of euthanasia in the Netherlands, see P.J.M. van der Maas, J.J.M. van Delden, and L. Pijnenborg, *Euthanasia and Other Medical Decisions Concerning the End of Life* (Holland: Elsevier, 1992). See, also, P.J.M. van der Maas, G. van der Wal, I. Haverkate, *et al.*, "Euthanasia, Physician-assisted Suicide, and Other Medical Practices Involving the End of Life in the Netherlands, 1990-1995," *New England Journal of Medicine* 335 (1996), 1699-1711.

12. Sylvia Law provides an argument regarding the secular moral obligation of physicians not to make statements that would dissuade a patient from seeking an abortion. These arguments are general enough to have an application to issues such as physician-assisted suicide and euthanasia. Sylvia A. Law, "Silent No More: Physicians' Legal and Ethical Obligations to Patients Seeking Abortions," *New York University Review of Law and Social Change* 21 (1994-95), 315-321.

13. One can envisage market opportunities for physician-assisted suicide and euthanasia services for the affluent seeking a luxurious final exit: "Club Dead: Depart this life with the luxury in which you lived it!", "Final Departure: Experience the death you have always wanted! Leave with dignity, pleasure, and style!", or "Executive Death: For those who have always been in control!"

14. It would appear that the minister is identifying a case made famous in Timothy E. Quill, "Death and Dignity – A Case of Individualized Decision Making," *The New England Journal of Medicine* 324 (March 7, 1991), 691-694.

15. Very likely, the minister is making reference to the case of Elizabeth Bouvia. Though it is not clear, Bouvia may have not simply wished treatment stopped because of the moral burden, that is, because the treatment was distracting her from her spiritual task, but also with a direct intent to die. *Bouvia v. Riverside General Hospital*, No. 159780 (Cal. Super. Ct. Dec. 16, 1983). The Appellate Court in addressing this case made it clear that a suicidal intent was not a bar to stopping treatment. One of the three judges of the court, Justice Compton, held that it fell within Bouvia's rights to seek assistance from her physicians, should she wish to have a quicker, more painless death. In this minority opinion, Justice Compton affirmed an at least limited right to suicide and assisted suicide. *Bouvia v. Super. Ct. of Cal.*, L.A. County, No. C583828 (Cal. Sup. Ct., Apr. 16, 1986).

16. Eugene C. Bay, "The Christian Faith and Euthanasia," in *In Life and in Death We Belong to God*, Christian Faith and Life Area, Congregational Ministries Division, PC(USA) (Louisville, KY: Presbyterian Distribution Services, 1995), p. 35.

17. 121st General Assembly of the Presbyterian Church in the United States, "The Nature and Value of Human Life," in *In Life and in Death We Belong to God*, p. 41.

18. This crucial shift in Western Christian theological sentiments regarding decisions to terminate life actively is perceptively sketched by Hans Küng.

So as a Christian and a theologian I feel encouraged, after a long 'consideration of the benefits', now to argue publicly for a middle way which is responsible in both theological and Christian terms: between an anti-religious libertinism without responsibility ('unlimited right to voluntary death') and a reactionary rigorism without compassion ('even the intolerable is to be borne in submission to God as given by God'). And I do this because as a Christian and a theologian I am convinced that the all-merciful God, who has given men and women freedom and responsibility for their lives, has also left to dying people the responsibility for making a conscientious decision about the manner and time of their deaths. This is a responsibility which neither the state nor the church, neither a theologian nor a doctor, can take away. This self-determination is not an act of arrogant defiance of God....
Hans Küng and Walter Jens, *Dying with Dignity*, trans. John Bowden (New York: Continuum, 1995), p. 38.

19. Albert Camus, *The Myth of Sisyphus and Other Essays*, trans. Justin O'Brien (New York: Alfred A. Knopf, 1961), p. 151.

20. The Jewish Publication Society of America offers the following translations of God's answer to Moses' question regarding His name, "Ehyeh-Asher-Ehyeh," as "I am that I am," "I am Who I am," and "I will be What I will be" (Ex 4:14). *The Torah: The Five Books of Moses* (Philadelphia: Jewish Publication Society of America, 1962), p. 102.

21. Orthodox theology appreciates that the Fall did not abolish human freedom. The Fall made us subject to passions and immoral inclinations in addition to darkening the mind so that we lost communion with God. This communion with God can only be reestablished through repentance, purifying the heart of passions, and by being illumined by God's grace so that one can know through union with God. Knowledge of the meaning of suffering does not require the successful completion of a rationalist investigation. It is acquired through purifying one's heart from the passions so as through God's grace to see the meaning of things, including suffering. See, for example, Hierotheos Vlachos, *Orthodox Psychotherapy*, trans. Esther Williams (Levadia, Greece: Birth of the Theotokos Monastery, 1994) and *Orthodox Spirituality*, trans. Effie Mavromichali (Levadia, Greece: Birth of the Theotokos Monastery, 1994).

22. St. Symeon the New Theologian, *The First-Created Man*, trans. Fr. Seraphim Rose (Platina, CA: St. Herman of Alaska Brotherhood, 1994), p. 70.

23. The results of Adam's sin show that human freedom is powerful and potentially dramatically destructive. In sin man's freedom links us with Satan, the prince of this world (John 12:31, 14:30, 16:11). The translation of Romans 5:12 in this paragraph is from John Meyendorff *Byzantine Theology* (New York: Fordham University Press, 1979), p. 144.

24. "The Divine Liturgy" in *The Liturgikon* (New York: Antakya Press, 1989), p. 281.

25. Archimandrite Ioannikios, *An Athonite Gerontikon*, trans. Maria Mayson and Sister Theodora (Kouphalia: Monastery of St. Gregory Palamas, 1997), p. 430.

26. The Latin doctrine of purgatory attempts to impose a quasi-economic meaning on the reality of suffering: the discharge of temporal punishment due to sin. The view is that, even after repentance, contrition, absolution, and forgiveness of sins, the reformed sinner still owes punishment. Suffering is then given a new meaning: out of considerations of justice, it supposedly allows one to avoid suffering later in the fires of purgatory. Suffering wipes away temporal punishment that would otherwise be experienced in purgatory, at least in the absence of securing an indulgence. As the Roman church decreed in Canon 30 of the Council of Trent, "If anyone says that after the reception of the grace of justification the guilt is so remitted and the debt of eternal punishment so blotted out to every repentant sinner, that no debt of temporal punishment remains to be discharged either in this world or in purgatory before the gates of heaven can be opened, let him be anathema." H. J. Schroeder (trans.), *Canons and Decrees of the Council of Trent* (Rockford, IL: Tan Books, 1978), p. 46.

The early Church taught neither that such temporal punishment is required, nor that purgatory exists. There was a clear understanding of the importance of freeing ourselves from the effects of our prior sins and thus truly repenting. There was and is a recognition that suffering humbly borne can aid us in our repentance. Whenever one truly repents and is forgiven, one is fully forgiven. There is no punishment after death but the love of God, which because of persistent rebellion is experienced as fire. Because we as humans are united in one nature, before the Final Judgment even the dead, depending on the character of their repentance when alive, can be aided to turn towards God. One of the best commentaries on these points is provided by St. Mark of Ephesus (1392-1444). "Of the fact that those reposed in faith are without doubt helped by the Liturgies and prayers and almsgiving performed for them, and that this custom has been in force from antiquity, there is the testimony of many and various utterances of the Teachers, both Latin and Greek, spoken and written at various times and in various places. But that souls are delivered thanks to a certain purgatorial suffering and temporal fire which possesses such [a purgatorial] power and has the character of a help – this we do not find either in the Scriptures or in the prayers and hymns for the dead, or in the words of Teachers. But we have received that even the souls which are held in hell and are already given over to eternal torments, whether in actual fact and experience or in hopeless expectation of such, can be aided and given a certain small help, although not in the sense of completely loosing them from torment or giving hope for a final deliverance." First Homily, "Refutation of the Latin Chapters Concerning Purgatorial Fire" in Fr. Seraphim Rose, *The Soul After Death* (Platina, CA: Saint Herman of Alaska Brotherhood, 1980), p. 199. The difference can in part be summarized in terms of fundamental differences in moral orientation between the West and the Orthodox, the first being jurisprudential in its understanding of sin and the second therapeutic.

27. St. John Maximovitch, *The Orthodox Veneration of Mary the Birthgiver of God* (Platina, CA: St. Herman of Alaska Brotherhood, 1994), p. 54.

28. St. John Chrysostom understands Christ's response to His mother's attempt to interrupt Him (Matt 12:48-50) as a spiritual correction. What she was about to do was "of superfluous vanity; in that she wanted to show the people that she hath power and authority over her Son, imagining not as yet anything great concerning Him; whence also her unseasonable approach. ... [thus] correcting her weakness ... He both healed the disease of vainglory, and rendered the due honor to His mother, even though her request was unseasonable." St. John Chrysostom, Homily 44 on Matthew 12.46-49, NPNF1, vol. 10, pp. 279-280. Blessed Theophylact of Bulgaria (1050-1108) affirms that Jesus acted not "to offend His mother, but to correct this vainglorious and human thought of hers." Blessed Theophylact, *The Explanation by Blessed Theophylact of the Holy Gospel According to St. Matthew* (House Springs, MO: Chrysostom Press, 1993), p. 109.

29. St. John [Maximovitch] of San Francisco recognizes that Mary, who inherited all the results of Adam and Eve's sin, nevertheless submitted wholeheartedly to the will of God. Her glory is thus even greater. "There is no intellect or words to express the greatness of her who was born in the sinful human race but became 'more honorable than the Cherubim and beyond compare more glorious than the Seraphim'." St. John Maximovitch, *The Orthodox Veneration of Mary the Birthgiver of God* (Platina, CA: St. Herman of Alaska Brotherhood, 1994), p. 68.

30. Isabel Hapgood (trans.), "Divine Liturgy," in *Service Book of the Holy Orthodox-Catholic Apostolic Church* (Englewood, NJ: Antiochian Orthodox Christian Archdiocese, 1996), p. 103.

31. St. Nicholas Velimirovich, *The Prologue from Ochrid: Lives of the Saints*, trans. Mother Maria (Birmingham, England: Lazarica Press, 1986), vol. 4, p. 384.

32. The Orthodox Church has not concerned itself extensively with the status of infants who die without baptism. However, in his exploration of death, Vassiliadis quotes from St. John Chrysostom, "A 'sheep' that does not bear the seal of the Holy Baptism becomes the portion of the wolf-Satan. The seal of Christ (Holy Baptism) protects the one who has it from Satan." PG 61, 786. Nikolaos Vassiliadis, *The Mystery of Death* (Athens, Greece: Orthodox Brotherhood of Theologians "The Savior", 1993), p. 322.

33. St. John Chrysostom, "Paschal Homily" in *The Liturgikon* (New York: Antakya Press, 1989), p. 392.

34. In exegesis on this last verse of Psalm 21 (LXX), Blessed Augustine of Hippo comments: "To a people that shall be born of the Lord through faith." *Expositions on the Book of Psalms*, NPNF1, vol. 8, p. 60. In his gloss, Cassiodorus explains, "A generation to come means that which is to be begotten through the Lord's generosity of water and the holy Spirit." *Explanation of the Psalms*, trans. P. G. Walsh (New York: Paulist Press, 1990), vol. 1, p. 233.

35. St. Basil, *The Long Rules*, trans. Sister Monica Wagner (Washington, DC: Catholic University of America Press, 1962), Question 55, pp. 330-31.

36. *Ibid.*, p. 331.
37. For a comprehensive historical study of the development in Roman Catholicism of the line between obligatory and non-obligatory, that is, between ordinary and extraordinary treatment, see Daniel A. Cronin, "The Moral Law in Regard to the Ordinary and Extraordinary Means of Conserving Life," Dissertation for Pontifical Gregorian University, Rome, 1958. This dissertation has been reprinted in *Conserving Human Life* (Braintree MA: Pope John XXIII Medical-Moral Research and Educational Center, 1989). See also H. T. Engelhardt, Jr., and Thomas J. Bole, "Entwicklungen der medizinischen Ethik in den USA: Die Verführung durch die Technik und der Irrtum einer Lebenserhaltung um jeden Preis," *Arzt und Christ* 36 (1990), 113-21. Recent Roman Catholic statements of importance include Pope Pius XII, Allocution "Le Dr. Bruno Haid," Nov. 24, 1957, *Acta Apostolicae Sedis* 49 (1957), p. 1031, English translation as Pius XII, "Address to an International Congress of Anesthesiologists," November 24, 1957, *The Pope Speaks* 4 (Spring 1958), 395-96; Sacred Congregation for the Doctrine of the Faith, "Declaration on Euthanasia" of May 5, 1980, in *Origins* 10 (August 14, 1980), 154-57, Latin text in *Enchiridion Vaticanum* VII, pp. 332-351 (nn.346-373).
38. St. Basil, "The Long Rules," Q 55, p. 333.
39. *Ibid.*
40. For an account of the causal equivalence of acting and refraining in the sense that both can be seen as causally efficacious, see Jonathan Bennett, who contends that the only essential difference is that in the case of acting most things that one could do will not lead to the outcome in question. Only a few do. In the case of omissions, most things one could do would prevent the results of the omission. Bennett, "Whatever the Consequences," *Analysis* 26 (January 1966), 83-102. For a reflection on Bennett and his arguments, see Daniel Dinello, "On Killing and Letting Die," *Analysis* 31 (April 1971), 83-86. See also P.J. Fitzgerald, "Acting and Refraining," *Analysis* 27 (Mar. 1967), 133-39; and James Rachels, "Active and Passive Euthanasia," *New England Journal of Medicine* 292 (Jan. 9, 1975), 78-80.
41. "The 'failure' on the part of persons other than the gardener to water the flowers would, accordingly, be a normal though negative condition and, just because such negative conditions are normal, no mention of them would usually be made. The gardener's failure to water the flowers, however, stands on a different footing. It is not merely a breach of duty on his part, but also a deviation from a system or routine." H. L. A. Hart and A. M. Honoré, *Causation in the Law* (Oxford: Clarendon Press, 1959), p. 36.
42. St. Basil, "The Long Rules," Q 55, p. 334.
43. A good summary of the principle of double effect is provided by Fr. Kelly.

> The principle of the double effect, as the name itself implies, supposes that an action produces two effects. One of these effects is something good which may be legitimately intended; the other is an evil that may not be intended... The main point in this presupposition is that some good effect is produced, because, if an action produces *only* an evil effect, that effect is necessarily intended.
> Granted the presupposition of good and evil effects, an action is permitted, according to the principle, if these conditions are fulfilled:
> 1) The action, considered by itself and independently of its effects, must not be morally evil....
> 2) The evil effect must not be the means of producing the good effect....
> 3) The evil effect is sincerely not intended, but merely tolerated....
> 4) There must be a proportionate reason for performing the action, in spite of its evil consequences.
> Gerald Kelly, *Medico-Moral Problems* (St. Louis, MO: Catholic Hospital Association, 1958), pp. 12-14.

For two recent studies of double effect, see Joseph Boyle (ed.), "Intentions, Christian Morality, and Bioethics: Puzzles of Double Effect," *Christian Bioethics* 3 (August 1997), 87-180; and Thomas J. Bole, III (ed.), "Double Effect: Theoretical Function and Bioethical Implications," *Journal of Medicine and Philosophy* 16 (October 1991), 467-585.

44. See Canon 66 of the Apostolic Canons in Sts. Nicodemus and Agapius, *The Rudder of the Orthodox Catholic Church*, trans. D. Cummings (New York: Luna Printing, 1983), pp. 113-117.

45. See "The Canons of St. Basil the Great" in *The Rudder*, Canon 13, pp. 801-802.

46. *Ibid.*, p. 116.

47. "The Canons of St. Gregory of Nyssa" in *The Rudder*, Canon 5, p. 874.

48. "Women who expose their babies at the entrance to churches, are chastised as murderesses, even though some persons picking them up take care of them." "The 35 Canons of John the Faster" in *The Rudder*, Canon 26, p. 947.

49. "As for a Bishop, or Presbyter, or Deacon that strikes believers for sinning, or unbelievers for wrong-doing, with the idea of making them afraid, we command that he be deposed from office. For the Lord has nowhere taught that: on the contrary, He Himself when struck did not strike back; when reviled, He did not revile His revilers; when suffering, He did not threaten." "The 85 Canons of the Holy and Renowned Apostles" in *The Rudder*, Canon 27, p. 38.

50. This traditional Christian appreciation of the necessity of Christian priests to keep distant from blood and the shedding of blood was still understood in the West in the High Middle Ages. For example, Canon 18 of the Fourth Lateran Council (1215) requires that "no cleric may be put in command of mercenaries or crossbowmen or suchlike men of blood; nor may a subdeacon, deacon or priest practise the art of surgery, which involves cauterizing and making incisions..." Norman Tanner (ed.), *Decrees of the Ecumenical Councils* (Washington, DC: Georgetown University Press, 1990), vol. 1, p. 244. It is for such reasons that Thomas Aquinas quotes Nicholas I, pope of Rome (the Nicholas condemned by St. Photios), in his reflections regarding homicide in self-defense. "Concerning the clerics about whom you have consulted Us, those, namely, who have killed a pagan in self-defense, as to whether, after making amends by repenting, they may return to their former state, or rise to a higher degree; know that in no case is it lawful for them to kill any man under any circumstances whatsoever." Thomas Aquinas, *Summa Theologica* II-II Q 64 art 7, (Westminster, MD: Christian Classics, 1981), vol. 3, p. 1465. In reply to this objection, Aquinas takes a position that shows no appreciation of the spiritually therapeutic significance of the irregularity incurred by a cleric who is involved in the taking of life. "I answer that, Nothing hinders one act from having two effects, only one of which is intended, while the other is beside the intention. Now moral acts take their species according to what is intended, and not according to what is beside the intention, since this is accidental as explained above (AQ. 43, A. 3; I-II, Q. 72, A. 1). Accordingly the act of self-defense may have two effects, one is the saving of one's life, the other is the slaying of the aggressor. ... Reply Obj. 3. Irregularity results from the act though sinless of taking a man's life, as appears in the case of a judge who justly condemns a man to death." Aquinas, *Summa Theologica* II-II, Q 64, art 7, vol. 3, p. 1465.

51. "The Hexaemeron," Homily 5, §4, NPNF2, vol. 8, p. 78.

52. A decision to forgo analgesics and ascetically to face severe pain should be made only with the guidance of one's spiritual father.

53. For the foregoing reflections, I am especially indebted to my spiritual father, the Rev. Fr. Thomas Joseph. See his "Secular vs. Orthodox Chaplaincy: Taking the Kingdom of Heaven Seriously," *Christian Bioethics* 3 (1998), 276-8.

54. Jacob Neusner, *Ideas of History, Ethics, Ontology, and Religion in Formative Judaism* (New York: University Press of America, 1988), pp. 98-106.

55. "Virtue and holiness constitute distinct classifications, the one having to do with morality, the other with ontology." *Ibid.*, p. 83.

56. *Ibid.*, p. 83.

57. *Ibid.*, p. 87.

58. "To be able to become unclean formed a measure of the capacity to become holy, so that, the more susceptible to uncleanness, and the more differentiated the uncleanness to which susceptibility pertained, the more capable of becoming holy, and the more differentiated the layers and levels of holiness that entered consideration." Neusner, p. 83.

59. David Thomasma, "Assisted Death and Martyrdom," *Christian Bioethics* 4 (1998), 122.

60. L. Boros, *The Mystery of Death* (New York: Herder and Herder, 1965).

61. For a discussion of martyrdom as suicide, see Darrel Amundsen, "Suicide and Early Christian Values," in *Suicide and Euthanasia*, ed. Baruch Brody (Dordrecht: Kluwer, 1989), pp. 77-153.

62. See, for example, A. Alvarez, "The Historical Background," in *Suicide: The Philosophical Issues*, eds. M.P. Battin and D.J. May (New York: St. Martin's Press, 1980), pp. 7-32.

63. *Compassion in Dying v. Washington*, CA9, 1995 (49 F.3d 586, 63 LW 2569).

64. "Question XIV. If anyone having no control of himself lays violent hands on himself or hurls himself to destruction, whether an offering ought to be made for him, or not? Answer: The Clergyman ought to discern in his behalf whether he was actually and truly out of his mind when he did it. For oftentimes those who are interested in the victim and want to have him accorded an offering and a prayer in his behalf will deliberately lie and assert that he had no control of himself. Sometimes, however, he did it as a result of influence exercised by other men, or somehow otherwise as a result of paying too little attention to circumstances, and no offering ought to be made in his behalf. It is incumbent, therefore, upon the Clergyman in any case to investigate the matter accurately, in order to avoid incurring judgment." "The 18 Canons of Timothy, the Most Holy Archbishop [Pope, fl. 372] of Alexandria" in *The Rudder*, p. 898.

65. Pope Peter of Alexandria warns against impetuously seeking to have oneself martyred. This lengthy canon gives spiritual direction to the would-be martyr. "The 15 Canons of our Father among Saints Peter, Archbishop [Pope, fl. 304] of Alexandria and a Martyr" in *The Rudder*, Canon IX, p. 746.

66. St. Nicholas Velimirovich, *The Prologue from Ochrid,* trans. Mother Maria (Birmingham, England: Lazarica Press, 1985), vol. 3, p. 49.

67. *Ibid.*, vol. 1, pp. 168-69.

68. "At night, he [Fr. Augustine the Russian, †1965] had no need of a kerosene lamp. 'God gives me another light,' he used to say, 'and I can see more clearly than during the day.' In his simplicity, he believed that everyone could see, just like he could, the uncreated light of God." Alexander Golitzin (trans.), *The Living Witness of the Holy Mountain* (South Canaan, PA: St. Tikhon's Seminary Press, 1996), p. 140.

69. Geronda Paisius, *Hagioreitai Pateres kai Hagioreitika* (Thessaloniki: Holy Monastery Monazouson, 1993), pp. 74-75. For this translation I am indebted to the monastics of Holy Archangels Monastery, Kendalia, Texas.

70. St. Ambrose supports the view that it is licit to jump to certain death to preserve chastity in *De virginibus*. In particular, he argues that, with regard to "virgins placed in the necessity of preserving their purity", this is appropriate because this is a mode of death that has been used by saints, "that there exists an instance of martyrdom." He then proceeds to examine the martyrdom of St. Pelagia and her mother and sisters. The latter, in order to preserve themselves from defilement, had jumped from a bridge into a torrential stream to certain death. Although St. Ambrose is not as precise as one would wish, it is clear that his view is that one may put oneself in the way of death "as a remedy against evil [i.e., loss of chastity]" and that "God is not offended" (VII.32-33, p. 386). It is important to underscore that his argument is directed not only to virgins, but to anyone preserving chastity. St. Ambrose, "Concerning Virgins" VII.35, NPNF2, vol. 10, p. 387.

71. *Commentarius in Ionam Prophetam* 1.6.

72. David Thomasma, "Assisted Death and Martyrdom," *Christian Bioethics* 4 (1998), 122-142.

73. The anaphora of the Liturgy of St. John Chrysostom underscores Christ's voluntary acceptance of His death on the Cross. "... who, when he had come and had performed all the dispensation for us, in the night in which he was given up, in the which, rather, he did give himself for the life of the world..." Hapgood, "The Divine Liturgy," *Service Book*, p. 102. St. Basil's anaphora reads similarly: "For when he was about to go forth to his voluntary, and ever-memorable, and life-creating death, in the night in which he gave himself for the life of the world..." *Ibid.*, p. 104. In the Liturgy of St. James, the priest also prays: "in the night in which He was betrayed, nay, rather delivered Himself up for the life and salvation of the world...." ANF, vol. 7, p. 544.

74. Hapgood, "Office at the Parting of the Soul from the Body," *Service Book*, p. 366.

75. *Ibid.*

76. "Litany of the Saints," in *The Roman Ritual*, trans. Philip T. Weller (Milwaukee: Bruce Publishing, 1952), vol. 2, p. 454.

77. The author and his wife have received accounts of the provision in the Netherlands of the Roman Catholic sacraments as a part of the administration of voluntary active euthanasia and physician-assisted suicide. These events have been reported to him as occurring in Roman Catholic-sponsored institutions with the knowledge and support of the administration, indicating the beginning of a further development in Roman Catholic moral theology.

78. Consider, for example, the prayer of the priest over someone who has attempted suicide. "O Almighty God, the Creator and Redeemer of mankind; Who gives us our life in this world so that we may prepare for the life to come; Who has delivered Your servant, N., from blood-guiltiness: Have pity, we implore You, upon him who rashly would have thrown away Your gift; and as You, in mercy, have defeated his intention, grant him time and grace for repentance. Graciously look upon him, and in Your compassion forgive him the wrong he has done on account of the malice of the Enemy. Restore him by Your Grace; strengthen him by Your might; and bring forth from his heart tears of sorrow that he may weep for his sins committed against You, and by Your mercy obtain pardon for them. For You are the God of those who repent, and to You we ascribe glory: to the Father, and to the Son, and to the Holy Spirit, now and ever and unto ages of ages. Amen." A Monk of St. Tikhon's Monastery, *Book of Needs* (South Canaan, PA: St. Tikhon's Seminary Press, 1987), pp. 28-29.

79. Once outside of the framework of traditional Christianity, Abraham's willingness to sacrifice his son appears problematic at best. As John Caputo puts the matter, "The story of Abraham poses a scandal for ethics. It belongs to the 'sacred scriptures' but it seems to tell quite an unholy tale about how it is permissible to commit murder, provided the right conditions are met." *Against Ethics* (Bloomington: Indiana University Press, 1993), p. 9.

80. St. John Chrysostom makes clear that acting in accord with God's will defines the character of an action. "I should not call Phinehas a murderer, though he took two lives with one blow [Num 25:7-8], nor Elijah, in spite of the hundred soldiers and their captains [2 Kings 1:10,12] and the great river of blood he made flow from the slaughter of those who sacrificed to devils [1 Kings 18:40]. If we were to allow that description, a man could strip all action of the intention of the agents, examine it out of context, and, if he liked, condemn Abraham for murdering his son [Gen 22:10], and accuse his grandson and his descendant of evil-doing and fraud, since it was by this means that the one gained the privileges of the first-born [Gen 27], and the other transferred the wealth of the Egyptians to the host of the Israelites [Ex 11:2]. But this will not do, it will not do! Perish the presumption! We not only acquit them of blame, we revere them for these very things, since God praised them on their account." Chrysostom, *On the Priesthood*, trans. Graham Neville (Crestwood, NY: St. Vladimir's Seminary Press, 1984), p. 51.

81. In the mid-14th century, Mount Athos affirmed St. Gregory Palamas (1296-1359), thereby underscoring that developments in Scholastic philosophy had separated Western Christianity from rightly understanding theological knowledge, grace, and virtue. Scholastic philosophy in claiming an *analogia entis*, an analogy of being between created and uncreated being, lost sight of the fundamental distinction between the merely good life and the holy life, theosis. "The grace of deification is therefore beyond nature, beyond virtue and knowledge." "Tomos of Mount Athos in Defense of the Hesychasts," Alexander Golitzin (trans.), *The Living Witness of the Holy Mountain* (South Canaan, PA: St. Tikhon's Seminary Press, 1996), p. 114. In addition, a life of virtue cannot be secured unless it is grounded in God. "If the Lord buildeth not the house of virtues, then vainly do we labour; but if He defend and protect our lives, none shall prevail against our city." Second Antiphon, Third Tone, Matins, in S. Nassar, *Divine Prayers and Services of the Catholic Orthodox Church of Christ* (Englewood, NJ: Antiochian Orthodox Christian Archdiocese, 1979), p. 156.

82. The doctrine of theosis recognizes that "For He was made man that we might be made God." St. Athanasius, "De incarnatione verbi dei" § 54.3, NPNF2, vol. 4, p. 65, interpretation, *The Rudder*, pp. 387-390.

83. See Canon 83, Quinisext Council (A.D. 691-2).

84. *Defence of the Holy Hesychasts* II.2.30, cited in John Meyendorff, *A Study of St. Gregory of Palamas* (Bedfordshire, England: Faith Press, 1964, p. 148. As Meyendorff comments regarding this passage, "while maintaining the general Biblical conception of the ontological unity of man's composition, Palamas had no desire to dogmatize about any physiological system, and so left full freedom to scientific research. Revelation was only concerned with eternal verities necessary to salvation, and not with physiology." *Ibid.*

85. H. T. Engelhardt, Jr., "John Hughlings Jackson and the Mind-Body Relation," *Bulletin of the History of Medicine* 49 (Summer 1975), 137-51; Robert Young, *Mind, Brain, and Adaptation in the Nineteenth Century* (Oxford: Clarendon Press, 1970); Engelhardt, *Mind-Body: A Categorial Relation* (The Hague: Martinus Nijhoff, 1973). The centrality of the brain for life is not defeated by the observation that in many if not most cases isolated brain cells may remain alive after death of the brain as an organ. See for example, Amir Halevy and Baruch Brody, "Brain Death: Reconciling Definitions, Criteria, and Tests," *Annals of Internal Medicine* 119 (Sept. 15, 1993, 519-525.

86. Roland Puccetti, "Brain Transplantation and Personal Identity," *Analysis* 29 (1969), 65.

87. There would be important moral constraints in these matters. For example, one would not be at liberty to transplant a body to the brain of a person of the opposite sex.

88. For a review of the pressures to relax definitions of death in order to acquire more organs for transplantation, see Robert M. Arnold and Stuart J. Youngner, "The Dead Donor Rule: Should we Stretch it, Bend it, or Abandon it?" *Kennedy Institute of Ethics Journal* 3 (1993), 263-78. See also Stuart J. Youngner, Robert M. Arnold, and R. Shapiro (eds.), *The Definition of Death* (Baltimore: John Hopkins University Press, 1999).

89. There is evidence that the affluent live longer, even in societies with a considerable welfare safety net. John Iglehart, "Canada's Heath Care System Faces its Problems," *New England Journal of Medicine* 322 (1990), 562-8; R. Wilkins, O. Adams, and A. Brancker, "Changes in Mortality by Income in Urban Canada from 1971 to 1986," *Finding of a Joint Study Undertaken by the Policy, Communications, and Information Branch, Health and Welfare Canada, and the Canadian Centre for Health Information* (Canada, 1989). Similarly, higher socio-economic status has been correlated with better health for children. National Crime Prevention Council of Canada, "The Determinants of Health and Children" (Ottawa, 1996). Studies have shown that life expectancy is improved, especially among men in non-manual occupational classes with more control over their environment. See, for example, Edwin Locke and M. Susan Taylor, "Stress, Coping and the Meaning of Work," in A. Monat and

R.S. Lazarus (eds.), *Stress and Coping* (New York: Columbia University Press, 1991), pp. 140-58; M.G. Marmot and M.E. McDowall, "Mortality Decline and Widening Social Inequalities," *The Lancet* (August 2, 1986), 274-6; M.G. Marmot *et al.*, "Health Inequalities Among British Civil Servants: The Whitehall II Study," *The Lancet* 337 (1991), 1387-92; M.G. Marmot, "Contribution of Job Control and Other Risk Factors to Social Variations in Coronary Heart Disease Incidence," *The Lancet* 350 (1997), 235-9; and David Goldstein, *Stress, Catecholamines, and Cardiovascular Disease* (New York: Oxford University Press, 1995).

90. For an account of a policy to select and protect individuals who would wish to sell their kidneys, see C.M. Thiagarajan, K.C. Reddy, *et al.*, "The Practice of Unconventional Renal Transplantation at a Single Centre in India," *Transplantation Proceedings* 22 (June 1990), 912-914. See also K.C. Reddy, C.M. Thiagarajan, *et al.*, "Unconventional Renal Transplantation in India," *Transplantation Proceedings* 22 (June 1990), 910-911.

91. Many indeed consider it appropriate for Christians to bury their amputated limbs in order to recognize the holiness of the body.

92. St. Paul, for example, emphasizes that God's temple is sacred and that we are that temple (I Cor 3:16-17). In particular, he underscores that it is our body that is the temple of the Holy Spirit (I Cor 6:19, II Cor 6:16).

93. St. John Chrysostom, *On the Incomprehensible Nature of God*, trans. Paul Harkins (Washington, DC: Catholic University of America Press, 1982), p. 86.

94. See, for example, Matt 4:24; 9:32; 12:22.

95. As with Immanuel Kant's account of the relationship between free choice and the causal web of empirical reality, where the spontaneity of free choice never perceptibly breaks the web of empirical causal connection, so, too, here there need be no assumption that the expected web of etiology and pathogenesis will be perceptibly distorted by the immediate action of personal, diabolic evil.

96. For example, "And after He came into the country of the Gergesenes, there met Him two possessed by demons coming out of the sepulchers, exceedingly fierce, so that no one was able to pass by that way. And behold they cried out, saying, 'What have we to do with Thee, Jesus, Son of God? Art Thou come here to torment us before the time?'" (Matt 8:28-29). Or to take another example, this time from Luke: "And in the synagogue there was a man who had an unclean demon; and he cried out with a loud voice, saying, 'Ha! What is it to us and to Thee, Jesus, O Nazarene? Art Thou come to destroy us? I know Thee Who Thou art—the Holy One of God!' And Jesus rebuked him, saying, 'Be thou muzzled, and come forth out of him.' And after the demon threw him in the midst, he came out from him and by no means hurt him. And amazement came upon all, and they were talking together with one another saying, 'What word is this, for with authority and power He commandeth the unclean spirits, and they come out?'" (Luke 4:33-36).

97. "The demons, murderers as they are, push us into sin. Or if they fail to do this, they get us to pass judgment on those who are sinning, so that they may defile us with the stain which we ourselves are condemning in another." St. John Climacus, *The Ladder of Divine Ascent* (Boston: Holy Transfiguration Monastery, 1991), p. 91.

98. Moltke Gram offers a critical exploration of these Kantian models. See *The Transcendental Turn: The Foundation of Kant's Idealism* (Gainesville: University of Florida Press, 1984).

99. The author of this volume can report, for example, the following occurrence related to him by an Orthodox pharmacist and fellow reader at St. George Antiochian Orthodox Church in Houston. Reader Cleopas Kennedy had received on a cotton ball oil from a weeping icon and stored it in an airtight container. He reported to me returning months later to find it with an inch of oil, to which he remarked, "Now I understand the meaning of something from nothing."

100. "Prayer Against the 'Evil Eye'," in *Sacraments and Services, Book Two*, trans. Leonidas Contos (Northridge, CA: Narthex Press, 1995), pp. 147-48.

101. M. Therese Lysaught, "Suffering, Ethics, and the Body of Christ: Anointing as a Strategic Alternative Practice," *Christian Bioethics* 2 (1996), 172-201.

102. Holy Unction is biblical: "Is any one of you infirm? Let him call for the presbyters of the Church; and let them pray over him, having anointed him with oil in the name of the Lord. And the prayer of faith shall save the one who is sick; and the Lord shall raise him up; and if he be one who hath commited sins, it shall be forgiven him." James 5:14-15.

103. Hapgood, "Office of Holy Unction," *Service Book*, pp. 332, 608

104. Emphasizing the communal nature of this prayer and faithful to St. James' injunction to priests in the plural (James 5:14), the Church provides for the participation of up to seven priests.

105. Hapgood, "Office of Holy Unction," *Service Book*, p. 355.

106. *Ibid.*, p. 357.

107. *Ibid.*, p. 358.

108. In Russia before the Communist Revolution, general anointing of the congregation was held on Holy Thursday after Liturgy in the Cathedral of the Falling-Asleep of the Theotokos in Moscow. Hapgood, *Service Book*, pp. 607-8.

109. "If Judaism and its successor, Christianity, had appeared in the twentieth century for the first time, they would most likely have been characterised not as religions but as medical sciences related to psychiatry." Hierotheos Vlachos, *Orthodoxy Psychotherapy*, p. 29. At stake here is not a secular notion of medical or psychiatric therapy, but a therapy of the soul itself. That therapy is found in faith itself, which "faith frees the intellect from the categories of the senses and sobers it by means of fasting, by pondering on God and by vigils." Justin Popovich, "The Theory of Knowledge of Saint Isaac the Syrian," in *Orthodox Faith and Life in Christ*, trans. Asterios Gerostergios, *et al.* (Belmont, MA: Institute for Byzantine and Modern Greek Studies, 1994), p. 125. This therapeutic approach to religion is to recognize that spiritual growth and knowledge involve not just moral, but ontological change in the character of the human personality. "The problem of the nature of knowledge becomes an ontological and ethical problem which, in the last resort, is seen to be the problem of human personality. The nature and character of knowledge depend ontologically, morally, and gnoseologically on the constitution of the human person, and especially on the constitution and state of its organs of knowledge. In the person of the ascetic of faith, knowledge, of its very nature, turns into contemplation." *Ibid.*, p. 152.

110. Stanley Hauerwas and Charles Pinches, "Practicing Patience: How Christians Should be Sick," *Christian Bioethics* 2 (1996), 202-221.

7 Providing Health Care: Consent, Conflicts of Interest, the Allocation of Medical Resources, and Religious Integrity

Putting Medicine in its Place: Health and the Pursuit of Salvation

Life is encircled by death. Health holds death at bay, though health is never secure. Salvation conquers death. Nearly five millennia ago, Egypt began to build pyramids in the pursuit of immortality. The medieval West erected cathedrals, grasping for eternal life. At the beginning of the third millennium, our contemporary culture builds medical centers and devotes an ever-increasing percentage of the gross domestic product to health care in order to push back death. Each of these monumental projects discloses what a civilization takes to be important. In each case, one confronts a society's struggle with finitude, suffering, and death. In the first two instances, societies sought an encounter with the divine. They hoped to reach beyond death to enduring life. In the last case, there is an attempt to control suffering and to postpone death as long as possible by human means. Unlike the pagan culture of Egypt or the Christian culture of Western Europe, our contemporary society's focus on health care is, at least on the surface, predominantly this-worldly. Contemporary health care offers the only salvation, the only healing many can imagine: healing through secular knowledge and human power. To secure this healing, societies are increasingly willing to pay more than a tithe of their gross domestic product for health care. Where few individuals will sell all they have to pursue eternal salvation, many will gladly expend all they have for a few more years of temporal life.

Christianity at once knows the obvious. Health care is at best a temporary expedient. Medicine only postpones death. It can only ameliorate, not banish, human suffering. In our hearts, we know that the prize is the cure of death itself. Nietzsche's Zarathustra knows, "All joy wants eternity – wants deep, wants deep eternity."[1] Christ's invitation is to defeat death by accepting the cross and participating in His Resurrection, to cure death by uniting ourselves with God. Traditional Christianity announces that the goal is nothing less than salvation through union with God, theosis or deification.[2] In terms of this transcendent goal, all immanent concerns are reordered. After all, once the prize is not simply immortality but union with God, what else could compare in importance? Still, health care remains important. Avoiding suffering and postponing death are generally good. In addition, health care can be located within the Christian life. Oriented towards the love of God, the health care professions take on an earnestness of dedication to God and others. But it is not worldly cure, care, and health that are most important. They have enduring significance only if they lead to the only true cure of death: salvation. If not aimed at this ultimate goal, they lead to ultimate death. Traditional Christianity re-orients secular, taken-for-granted appreciations of health care's importance.

Commitments to ameliorating pain, postponing death, and providing care must be set within the constraints of traditional Christian morality and its pursuit of the kingdom of heaven. First, outside of these constraints, what might appear an act of love may misdirect from the pursuit of the kingdom of God. To a secular individual, providing abortion services for the poor may seem an act of love. So, too, may offering artificial insemination from a donor for an unmarried woman wanting a child or providing euthanasia for a suffering person asking to be killed. Second, beyond such particular issues, there is health care's all-consuming character. Health care as a surrogate, however inadequate, for the pursuit of eternity can evoke nearly boundless passions for postponing death and avoiding suffering. The Christian must place health care, the amelioration of suffering, and the postponement of death within the pursuit of holiness. The vocation of medicine can only be rightly understood when ordered in terms of the pursuit of the kingdom of heaven.

This relocation of health care within the pursuit of the kingdom of God places moral obligations and bioethics in a new light. Once God is recognized as the source of being and meaning, the derivation of medical authority must be relocated as well. This also requires re-examining how health professionals should relate to their patients. This requires re-exploring the obligations of free and informed consent and truth-telling. If medicine should be directed primarily to the pursuit of the kingdom of God, it becomes a major challenge to maintain the integrity of health professionals as traditional Christians and of health care institutions with a traditional Christian mission. How can one be a Christian health professional in a post-Christian world, which takes for granted the provision of services Christians must condemn? The issue of involvement or cooperation in evil is addressed within the obligation to confess the faith at all costs. After addressing the issue of individual and corporate moral as well as spiritual integrity, this chapter turns to the allocation of resources for health care services in a secular world. The chapter concludes by exploring how Christians can provide health care in a world indifferent, if not hostile, to traditional Christian medical morality.

Consent, Deceit, and Physicians: Free and Informed Consent Reconsidered

Why is permission the cardinal moral principle for secular bioethics? Why is it not central for Christian bioethics? To begin with, gaining permission from persons is cardinal to secular bioethics because there is no other general source of secular moral authority. Deaf to God and in the face of an intractable moral pluralism, authority is derived from persons. After all, if selecting the appropriate moral or value vision requires already having a particular value-informed position to guide choice, as shown in chapter 1, the resolution of foundational moral controversies is not possible by sound rational argument without begging the question or engaging an infinite regress.[3] One must already know what values one should have. To make that determination, one must again already have a value perspective, which itself must be chosen, and so on ad infinitum. Different rankings of values have significantly different moral implications. To recall an earlier example, if individuals give different rankings to liberty, equality, and security, they commit themselves to a different moral vision. In the absence of unity in the experience of God, moral visions diverge and conflict.

The clefts separating moral visions are deepened by conflicting views of the significance of life and death, as for example regarding abortion and physician-assisted suicide. Choices about issues that matter are directed by different understandings of the good and the right. To act together with moral authorization in the face of diverse and indeed antagonistic moral and religious commitments, and in the absence of a common experience of God, one can appeal to neither God nor reason. An appeal in such circumstances to God is divisive, for not all recognize God's existence, and many worship false images of God, if not false gods. The appeal to reason fares no better; either reason is formal and empty or it has the content of one among a number of moral rationalities. There is no way free from this condition of moral epistemological incapacity without re-establishing noetic knowledge, which can only be achieved through asceticism and by grace. Reliable moral knowledge must be anchored in the Holy Spirit.

In the face of a multiplicity of moral understandings, one can still decide what one will or will not do with others. Confronted with intractable moral controversies, in order to act with moral strangers with an authority that is mutually justifiable, one must settle for persons and their consent. It is from one's collaborators that one gains authorization: one can only establish areas of collaboration by agreement. The appeal to permission is the default strategy for establishing areas of agreement, given foundational disagreement. To withhold information deceptively in such circumstances is to abandon the project of resolving controversies through mutual agreement: deception constitutes a kind of force. It constrains agreement through closeting important information under the cloak of misinformation. More needs to be said about the circumstances under which deception occurs, as to when persons have a right to particular information, how such rights to information and against deception are waived, etc. Here it is enough to recognize that secular morality has finite human persons as the source of authority, and that unconsented-to deception is an act against this morality, against the derivation of authority from permission. Therefore, one would expect matters to be as one finds them in secular bioethics and health care policy: practices of consent are central. They focus on (1) identifying who can and may give authorization and (2) determining whether information has been withheld or coercion employed that might invalidate an agreement.

As chapter 3 has shown, this centrality of permission as the source of authority is often conflated with autonomous individualism as a valued moral ideal. In the search for a source of values, the source of permission becomes an object of value: the person as a chooser. The libertarian cosmopolitan ethic is transformed into the liberal cosmopolitan ethos. As a result, giving permission, conveying authority is elided with affirming action that is autonomous in the sense of being free from significant external influences. As a consequence, an idealized view of personal dignity and autonomy emerges which portrays patients as individuals meeting outside of the constraints of any particular community. In this portrayal of consent, it is not just that one ideally chooses free from driving passions: one chooses without substantive inducements or strong limiting obligations (such as, "I must choose this treatment because my husband insists and I should obey him"). Patients are ideally to consent as (1) lucid, (2) autonomous, and (3) independent individuals. In contrast, significantly ill persons tend to come to medical care (1) somewhat confused, (2) conditioned by heteronomous concerns, and (3) embedded in a matrix of family and friends who constrain their choices in particular directions. People usually do not choose outside of history, family, and community. They act within a thick web of concerns, feelings of guilt, and interests in others, as well as issues imposed by others. When they choose, they do not choose autonomously in the sense of acting solely out of their own interests. Instead, they find their choices influenced by the concerns, desires, and demands of others. Some in fact recognize choices as most authentically theirs when they are made in the context of constraints derived from their religion, family, and cultural commitments. Moreover, Christians ideally choose (1) free from passions, (2) illumined by God's grace, and (3) humbly submitting to each other (Eph 5:21).

Traditional Christians draw authority not from the consent of particular individuals, nor from conclusions to discursive moral philosophical arguments, but instead from the experienced revelation of the requirements of God. Nor is ideal Christian decision-making atomistic or individualistic. Rather, choice within the body of Christ, the communion of saints, the Church, should be directed by the Holy Spirit so as to turn humbly, selflessly, and wholeheartedly to God the Father. Although persons are recognized as free and able even without grace to choose between good and evil,[4] still persons are also appreciated as in the grip of passions and therefore unable on their own consistently to keep their lives directed to God. As a consequence, humans must be approached not as lucid free agents engaged with equals, but as enmired in their passions, faced with obeying God in a relationship of radical inequality.

The meaning of lying and deceit is thus radically different within a traditional Christian context. First and foremost, lying does not have an intrinsic, indefeasible wrong-making character, as it does either for the secular libertarian moralist or for Blessed Augustine of Hippo. On the one hand, for the traditional Christian, moral authority is drawn from God, not from permission. Therefore, the appeal to permission does not establish an indefeasible wrong-making character for all unconsented-to deception in the use of others. Nor did the tradition ever develop the view embraced by Augustine, namely, that intentional deception by stating a falsehood constitutes an intrinsic evil, which cannot be counter-balanced by other considerations. Instead, although deception has been recognized consistently as involving a harm to the deceiver, at the same time it has been recognized that in this broken world one may be obliged to use deception in the pursuit of salvation and goods closely associated with salvation.[5] The pursuit of salvation may require struggling with the consequences of having used deceit in the pursuit of holiness. Finally, traditional Christian morality does not affirm an ideal of autonomous individualism that would exclude all use of deceit. It emphasizes freedom of the intellect from its darkening due to the Fall and of the will from the passions that beset it. It emphasizes that freedom from passion through struggle and by grace is essential, if one is effectively to will to be united with God. Traditional Christianity emphasizes the freedom of the intellect in the sense of opening the intellect (i.e., nous), so that one can accept the illumination of God.[6] It does not categorically exclude the use of deception in the pursuit of salvation.

The story of Abraham and Isaac discloses the gulf between secular and traditional Christian portrayals of moral interaction. It also emphasizes the radical authority of God and the obedience to which God calls us.[7] The story of Abraham shows as well that God tailors information to the task at hand, knowing how hard it is for us to obey. When Sarah hears the Lord tell Abraham that within a year she will bear a son, she laughs to herself, "The thing has not as yet happened to me, even until now, and my lord is old" (Gen 18:12). While stressing the need for reliance on God, God does not in this conversation with Abraham refer to Sarah's doubts about the aged Abraham's abilities. "And the Lord said to Abraham, 'Why is it that Sarah has laughed in herself, saying, "Shall I then indeed bear? But I am grown old." Shall anything be impossible with the Lord?'" (Gen 18:13-14). The West could come to terms with this part of the story of Abraham by making a distinction: God does not lie, He simply withholds a particular truth.[8]

Blessed Augustine (354-430) gave the West its view that not only is lying spiritually harmful, but also an intrinsic evil: one may never state a falsehood, hoping to deceive. Augustine held that "a lie is an utterance of a person wishing to utter a false thing that he may deceive."[9] Augustine's exceptionless position became the West's view.[10] As this position evolved, it differentiated lies into three genre: (1) lies told with a pernicious intent to damage or injure another's life, property, or good name; (2) officious or courteous lies, whose purpose is to prevent injury or inconvenience; and (3) lies told simply in jest.[11] This tradition of analysis developed a labyrinth of distinctions to allow withholding particular truths from those with no right to those truths. As a result, this approach allows one to deceive as long as the utterance one makes is not strictly false in explicitly stating something other than what one knows to be true. Although lying itself is considered intrinsically evil, and therefore something never to be directly undertaken, one may licitly engage in equivocations. One is at liberty, at least in certain circumstances, to employ ambiguous expressions with the intention of being misunderstood by others. Because in such circumstances one does not state a falsehood, such deceptions are not considered lies, although one's intention is to deceive. The fault is ascribed to the hearer: the hearer could have known better.

An account of mental reservation also developed in Roman Catholicism toward the end of safeguarding important truths. For a while, it was even held that one could in the mind reserve, that is, not disclose, the context needed to understand a proposition uttered. When asked a question, the speaker, for example, would say "no," but not to answer the question posed. A patient, for example, might ask a physician, "Will I die of this disease?" and the physician, while thinking of the question, "Will I [the physician] die of this disease?" could say "No." The "no" only makes sense in terms of some special or peculiar interpretation on the part of the responder of the question or the answer. On the one hand, the "no" did correspond to the truth in the speaker's mind. On the other hand, the response was strictly deceptive in terms of the discourse outside of the speaker's mind. There was clearly a false statement with the intent to deceive. Such robust forms of mental reservation were condemned by Pope Innocent XI (1611-1689).[12]

The accepted position is that a person making a statement to a question could rely on any generally accepted interpretation of the statement, even though the speaker recognized that in the circumstances at hand the hearer would be deceived. To a patient's question, "Will I die of this disease?" the physician may answer, "Many patients recover without any difficulty," all along recognizing that this patient will not recover. The general principle is one of "let the hearer beware."[13] In terms of the discourse of questioner and responder, at least in terms of the meaning of the words, the answer was not false. The careful crafting of discourse to allow misleading without "lying" is one among the epiphanies of the Roman Catholic legalistic approach to morality. On the one hand, stating what one knows to be false in order to deceive is understood to be wrong in itself. On the other hand, a number of devices are available to mislead one's interlocutor purportedly without guilt.

The Church of the Councils did not adopt Augustine's view concerning deception. Nor did it engage in such analytic gymnastics. The general moral rule is not to deceive but to answer simply and straightforwardly, as Christ had commanded (Matt 5:37). Yet, it was recognized that in special circumstances the prophets and saints of the Old and New Testaments directly and intentionally engaged in deception. It was appreciated that, under certain circumstances, one can be obliged to deceive. Deception was and is accepted when there is:

(1) urgency (under the press of circumstances only deception can achieve an important goal, which otherwise cannot be realized), as well as

(2) necessity (a significant moral good is at stake, involving doing God's will, especially bringing one's self or others to God, saving someone's life, etc.), at the same time

(3) mourning the deception in order to protect one's own heart from the damage of lying, while all along maintaining

(4) a purity of purpose (i.e., one must aim at doing God's will, not one's own, so that one does not become a liar but aims at the truth of God).

Under these conditions, deception is like a very strong medicine used sparingly and carefully to achieve an appropriate important good. The goal of acting autonomously and without deception, though generally good, is not an overriding good. It must be radically situated within the pursuit of the kingdom of heaven.

The Platonic metaphor of lying as a strong and dangerous medicine needed to be employed for desperate cases is widely engaged by the early Fathers. Plato had considered "falsehood...useful to people as a form of drug" (Republic 389b), especially when employed by physicians: "Clearly, we must allow only doctors to use it" (Republic 389b).[14] However, the traditional Christian account of the morality of lying does not accord with that of Plato, who would have permitted it to no citizen of the polis save physicians. For the Fathers, deceit by physicians as a form of treatment serves as an exemplar for its wider use.

Origen (185-232) affirms that "it is sometimes allowable to employ deceit and falsehood by way, as it were, of medicine."[15] Origen's student, Clement of Alexandria, similarly holds that one should tell the truth "unless at any time, medicinally, as a physician for the sake of the sick, he may deceive or tell an untruth."[16] Clement attributes this understanding to the Sophists. By the 5th century, this medicinal image of the necessary lie is well established. As St. John Cassian the Just Roman (360-432) emphasizes,

> And so we ought to regard a lie and to employ it as if its nature were that of hellebore; which is useful if taken when some deadly disease is threat-

ening, but if taken without being required by some great danger is the cause of immediate death.[17]

As will shortly be seen more amply, St. John Cassian requires a serious reason for deception.

As already noted, the traditional Christian approval of therapeutic deceit is not drawn from Plato. It comes from an abiding recognition that important figures in the Old and New Testaments (e.g., St. Paul, I Cor 9:20-22) employed deceit. Therefore, deceit cannot be incompatible with holiness. St. John Cassian states:

> Holy men and those most approved by God employed lying, so as not only to incur no guilt of sin from it, but even to attain the greatest goodness; and if deceit could confer glory on them, what on the other hand would the truth have brought them but condemnation? Just as Rahab, of whom Scripture gives a record not only of no good deed but actually of unchastity, yet simply for the lie, by means of which she preferred to hide the spies instead of betraying them, had it vouchsafed to her to be joined with the people of God in everlasting blessing. But if she had preferred to speak the truth and to regard the safety of the citizens, there is no doubt that she and all her house would not have escaped the coming destruction, nor would it have been vouchsafed to her to be inserted in the progenitors of our Lord's nativity, and reckoned in the list of the patriarchs, and through her descendants that followed, to become the mother of the Saviour of all. ... To which end the patriarch Jacob also had regard when he was not afraid to imitate the hairy appearance of his brother's body by wrapping himself up in skins, and to his credit acquiesced in his mother's instigation of a lie for this object. For he saw that in this way there would be bestowed on him greater gains of blessing and righteousness than by keeping to the path of simplicity: for he did not doubt that the stain of this lie would at once be washed away by the flood of the paternal blessing, and would speedily be dissolved like a little cloud by the breath of the Holy Spirit; and that richer rewards of merit would be bestowed on him by means of this dissimulation which he put on than by means of the truth, which was natural to him.[18]

The position is not just that lying, in the sense of stating what one knows to be false so as to deceive, can under certain circumstances be excusable. The position is far stronger. Lying can be justified in the robust sense of not merely being meritorious, but indeed in some circumstances obligatory.[19]

As noted, deceit is at least permitted when a significant good hangs in the balance and there is no ready alternative. St. John Cassian explains:

> When then any grave danger hangs on confession of the truth, then we must take to lying as a refuge, yet in such a way as to be for our salvation troubled by the guilt of a humbled conscience. But where there is no call of the utmost necessity present, there a lie should be most carefully avoid-

ed as if it were something deadly, just as we said of a cup of hellebore
which is indeed useful if it is only taken in the last resort when a deadly
and inevitable disease is threatening, while if it is taken when the body is
in a state of sound and rude health, its deadly properties at once go to find
out the vital parts. And this was clearly shown of Rahab of Jericho, and
the patriarch Jacob; the former of whom could only escape death by
means of this remedy, while the latter could not secure the blessing of the
first-born without it.[20]

Dorotheos of Gaza similarly stresses that deception may only be used when necessary
for discharging an important obligation.

There are times when urgent necessity arises and unless a man conceals
the bitter fact, the affair gives rise to greater trouble and affliction. When,
therefore, such circumstances arise a man should know that in such cases
of need he may adapt his speech so as to avoid a greater disaster or danger.
As Abba Alonios said to Abba Agathon: "Suppose two men committed a
murder in your presence and one of them fled to your cell. Then the
police, coming in search of him, asks you, 'Is the murderer with you?'
Unless you dissimulate, you hand him over to death."[21]

Dorotheos takes a robust position: to protect life one may deceive, even to legitimate
authority (i.e., the police) responding to a real wrong (e.g., murder).

There is also the appreciation that, although one may be obliged to lie, nevertheless
this must be mournfully followed by repentance: one should take necessary steps so
that one's heart is not harmed. As Abba Dorotheos of Gaza stresses,

But if a man did such a thing, in extreme necessity, let him not be without
anxiety but let him repent and sorrow before God and consider it, as I
said, a time of trial and not let it become a habit but done once and for all.
... Just as an antidote for snake poison or a powerful purge is beneficial
when taken in time and in case of need, it does harm if taken habitually,
without necessity. It may be appropriate to dissimulate once in a while in
a case of dire necessity but not to make a practice of it; and if ever the need
and the occasion arise, and one acts with fear and trembling in the sight of
God, he will be sheltered from transgression, since he is under constraint;
otherwise he would be doing himself harm.[22]

Deceit should generally be undertaken only with regret, so that one remains directed
towards union with God.[23] Both the deceit of another and moral regard for oneself are
placed within a spiritual therapeutic context.

Here repentance takes on a form different from that of the West, which requires a
sincere resolution never to repeat the act for which one repents. Following Abba
Dorotheos, one must sincerely mourn what one has done. One prays that one will
never need to repeat such a deception again. However, one also recognizes that in
similar circumstances one will be obliged once more to deceive. Repentance is focused

on the attitude of one's heart, one's sincere mourning for having deceived, and one's prayer for God's mercy never to have to face such a trial again. The focus is therapeutic rather than juridical. That is, the focus is not directly or immediately on being exonerated from guilt, but on being free from the effects of those actions and volitions that may direct away from the pursuit of the kingdom of heaven. Since freeing oneself from the effects of actions and volitions involving evil (e.g., deceiving in the pursuit of an appropriate important good) will require forgiveness, the concern for guilt is recaptured. The concern to recognize guilt and seek forgiveness is located within a larger concern: how to be the kind of person who can turn to God with wholehearted love and can love his neighbor as himself. Once deception or lying is placed in this non-juridical therapeutic understanding of the pursuit of salvation, the significance of deception or lying becomes radically non-Augustinian. "Great is the power of deceit; only it must not be applied with a treacherous intention. Or rather, it is not right to call such action deceit, but good management and tact and skill enough to find many ways through an impasse, and to correct the faults of the spirit."[24] As a consequence, truth-telling, *pace* Blessed Augustine and Kant, can be vicious.

Because one must maintain purity of heart, one's purpose is crucial. One's goal must be to achieve a good integral to the humble and loving pursuit of union with God.

> For God is not only the Judge and inspector of our words and actions, but He also looks into their purpose and aim. And if He sees that anything has been done or promised by some one for the sake of eternal salvation and shows insight into Divine contemplation, even though it may appear to men to be hard and unfair, yet He looks at the inner goodness of the heart and rewards the desire of the will rather than the actual words spoken, because He must take into account the aim of the work and the disposition of the doer, whereby, as was said above, one man may be justified by means of a lie, while another may be guilty of a sin of everlasting death by telling the truth.[25]

The same point is made by St. John Chrysostom with regard to the importance of intention in determining the significance of an action.

> If we were to allow that description, a man could strip all action of the intention of the agents, examine it out of context, and, if he liked, condemn Abraham for murdering his son, and accuse his grandson and his descendant of evil-doing and fraud, since it was by this means that the one gained the privileges of the first-born, and the other transferred the wealth of the Egyptians to the host of the Israelites. But this will not do, it will not do! Perish the presumption! We not only acquit them of blame, we revere them for these very things, since God praised them on their account.[26]

On the one hand, we have already seen that, although certain actions can as a rule be tolerated only with tears (e.g., homicide in self-defense or in just warfare), this does not usually obviate the need for penance to cure the heart from the harms involved. On the other hand, though usually spiritually harmful, some actions can nevertheless be so connected with the will of God that no harm occurs.

St. John Chrysostom acknowledges a wide range of occasions for justified deceit. "A husband needs it for a wife, a wife for a husband, a father for a son, a friend for a friend, and sometimes even children for a father. Saul's daughter could not have rescued her own husband by any other device from her father's grasp except by tricking him."[27] St. John clearly endorses an obligation to deceive in cases of necessity. Indeed, it would not be too strong to say that under certain circumstances he would hold it sinful not to deceive. "The straightforward man does great harm to those he will not deceive."[28] Even though deceit can be obligatory, it will also always be prima facie appropriate to proceed with mourning and repentance.

Therapeutic deception by physicians is accepted within this context as often appropriate and in general as paradigmatic: (1) the tradition uses medical therapeutic images with (2) deceit by physicians taken as a moral exemplar. Save for cases from the lives of saints, therapeutic deceit is thus best presented in medicine.

> To discover how useful deceit is, not only to the deceivers but to the deceived, go to any doctor and inquire how they cure their patients of diseases. You will hear them say that they do not rely on their skill alone, but sometimes they resort to deceit, and with a tincture of its help they restore the sick man to health. When the plans of doctors are hindered by the whims of their patients and the obstinacy of the complaint itself, then it is necessary to put on the mask of deception, in order to conceal the truth about what is happening – as they do on the stage.[29]

St. John Chrysostom then provides an example of appropriate medical deception.

> I will relate to you one of the many tricks which, I have heard, doctors devise. Once a fever fell suddenly upon a patient very violently, and his temperature kept rising. The sick man refused the medicine which would have allayed the fever, but longed and insisted, with requests to everyone who visited him, that he should be given a long drink of neat wine and be allowed to take his fill of the deadly thing he wanted. It would not only have inflamed the fever but have thrown the poor man into a hemiplegia, if anyone had granted him this favour. ... The doctor took an earthenware vessel fresh from the kiln and steeped it in wine. Then he took it out empty and filled it with water. Next he gave orders for the room where the patient was lying to be darkened with thick curtains, for fear that the daylight might show up the trick. He then gave the vessel to the patient to drink from, pretending it was full of neat wine. The patient was deceived.... He did not stop to examine closely what was offered to him. Convinced by the aroma, ...he immediately shook off the fever and escaped his imminent danger.[30]

Although this example could meet Roman Catholic criteria for allowable equivocation, it is clear from the rest of the text that Chrysostom accepted direct and intentional deception.

Chrysostom's approach to truth-telling by physicians conflicts with the accepted standard American version of bioethics. On the one hand, his account of the medical practice of his time is such that one could as little go to a physician as to a poker game expecting no deceit. The practice of medicine was framed by deceptive ploys. One could very well argue that, in the case of physicians in Chrysostom's era, there had to be a tacit acquiescence by patients in deception by physicians. On the other hand, this approach to health care goes against the grain of empowering patients as autonomous decision-makers. His ideal is not one of a morally neutral physician, committed disinterestedly to empowering patients. Chrysostom considers it quite appropriate for physicians to deceive their patients to secure important health interests. Physicians are expected to act paternalistically to realize their patients' good. Yet it is not an unacknowledged paternalism, one for which there are not at least clear warnings. Still, tacit permission is not presupposed as a necessary condition for allowable deception. To accomplish an important therapeutic goal, deception is not only permitted, it is required. Elder Paisios gives the account of a person suffering from an apparent psychiatric problem rooted in a deeper spiritual disorder who was disinclined to take his medication. Elder Paisios advises that "someone else should put the medicine in his food and show him spiritual love and try to correct his thoughts."[31] There would appear to be no bar against deceptively providing medication not just to one's children, the mentally ill, and the disoriented elderly in one's family, but to anyone to whom one has special moral obligations.

To the contemporary moralist, this approach to deception and consent can at best appear antiquated and morally underdeveloped, if not ethically outrageous. This approach is radically egregious. It is lodged within a moral framework directed to the ultimate cure: salvation. Salvation in this context is not understood legalistically but therapeutically. What is important is being oriented towards God. The result is a complex appreciation of what it means to give consent, so as to turn to God. To begin with, loving God with one's whole heart, mind, and soul can only be an act of unqualified free choice. Otherwise, the love would lack the completeness demanded: such full love cannot be given under coercion. When accomplished wholeheartedly, such love requires a choice made selflessly: a crucified love free of utilitarian concerns and framed by humble directedness towards God. Still, in coming to this free choice, one may begin with many misunderstandings and even be motivated by strong passions.[32] The crucial issue is that in the end one must turn wholeheartedly from one's self towards God. On the one hand, employing force to achieve conversions has from the beginning been forbidden.[33] On the other hand, peaceable deception to bring another to the point of beginning to accept salvation has been regarded as relatively unproblematic, if not praiseworthy. Violence against another is recognized as highly improper, especially on the part of the clergy.[34] However, one may meet misconceptions and passions with therapeutic responses that may appropriately include deceptions aimed at redirecting the one deceived towards God and towards important duties, including duties to accept needed and appropriate medical treatment.

This approach to deception is possible because the source of moral authority is first and foremost not individual permission; it is God. Given that ideal moral deportment is exemplified not in self-directed, autonomous choices, but in humble, other-directed love, appropriate decision-making requires one's assent to the will of God, not to self-directed, individualistic choice. Choice is important not because it is fully autonomous in the sense of expressing the capricious wishes of an agent, but because the choice is the right one. True, one must freely choose. However, there is no requirement that the choice be experienced as having been made without the influence of others, only that it be made in the absence of anyone's having used physical violence or coercion to secure that choice. The last would harm the heart of those who used violence and importantly qualify the freedom of deciding to love God. Violence or coercion is spiritually counter-therapeutic.

What does this mean for medical decision-making? First, there is no special virtue in patients choosing their own medical treatment with lucid autonomy. Lucidity and authenticity in medical decision-making do not make a special contribution to the pursuit of the kingdom of heaven. What is important is that patients make medical decisions conducive to salvation. It is important fully and wholeheartedly to love God and others. If embedding medical decision-making within the structure of the family will lead (1) to decisions better directed to life and health (2) in the sense of aiding the patient's pursuit of salvation, then (3) this will be the preferable approach to patient consent. For example, if (1) there is a medical decision to be made regarding the use of (a) life-saving treatment, (b) abortion, or (c) physician-assisted suicide, and (2) if the family is more likely to guide the patient to the morally obligatory choice, then (3) they and not the patient should be the primary focus for therapeutic decision-making.

To summarize, true autonomy is not capricious choice, but rightly directed choice free of the passions. It is a false autonomy to choose as one wills, moved by powerful urges. Even free of passions, one's autonomy is false if wrongly directed. Such wrongly directed autonomy, if realized in full clarity, is deeply diabolic: it mirrors the free choice of Lucifer to turn from God. Autonomy in its fullest sense is not just choice uninfluenced by the passions, but choice that unites to God, thus completing one's being through union with one's Creator. Free and informed consent, when it bears on matters of salvation, should focus not just on aiding a person to choose as that person would. It should involve helping that person to choose as that person should. Given the condition of humans, this will include aiding the patient in resisting passions and urges that would misdirect choice. Moreover, it involves orienting the patient's choice not just to health, but to holiness. Free and informed consent for the Orthodox thus would not be value-neutral, nor non-directive. Nor would it be individualistic in attempting to treat the patient as an isolated decision-maker. It would instead seek to embed the patient in an Orthodox social context that can support the patient and properly direct the patient's choices. Such decision-making appropriately orients the patient and aids the patient in making the morally right choice. Ideally, choices should be made free of passion and wholeheartedly directed to God. Thus understood, autonomy involves virtue, the energy of holiness, which comes from God. As Archimandrite Vasileios stresses, "The gift of God is what has a motive force of its own: it is what is autonomous and balanced. 'For it befits virtue to be free of all fear and autonomous.'"[35]

This understanding of appropriate medical decision-making is at loggerheads with the liberal cosmopolitan account of bioethics, which focuses on ensuring unmanipulated choice by adults, even by mature minors. Instead, the focus should be on peaceably guiding decisions so that patients acquiesce in appropriate choices. Rather than attempting to liberate patients in their medical choices from the thick guiding matrices of peaceable family constraints, pressures, and manipulations, the focus should be on recruiting all incentives that lead the patient to affirming the morally appropriate choice. Physicians should collaborate with whoever is available in the family, especially within the traditional Christian structure of the family, to ensure that medical decisions lead to salvation, that they lead to a humble love of God and others rather than self-love. Parents, for example, are presumed to be in authority over their unmarried children, especially when, with regard to abortion, the parents decide in favor of preserving life. In this case, there is a confluence of the obligation of children to obey their parents, and of parents to restrain their children from evil: in this last example, murdering an unborn child.

Appropriate proxy decision-making is primarily determined by reference to who has spiritual insight and by a concern not to deform traditional lines of authority and submission (i.e., wives to husbands, children to parents). Physicians should, if possible, not deform the traditional structures of familial authority, but draw on these supports, as well as those of the community of believers. A 17-year-old patient may have more understanding than parents in their 40s. Yet, submission to the parents' guidance in making medical decisions where the choice is not constrained by moral considerations supports obedience and humility. The Christian goal is not to nurture individualistic, self-regarding decisions. Ideally, there should be a synergy of those in authority and the proper goals for human choice, so that decisions direct the patient away from involvement in evil and towards God. In addition, there is a recognition that the moral life is appropriately lived within the moral community. Even, indeed especially, hermits in the desert are embedded in this community of saints living and dead whose vivid presence is fully available only within a humble, obedient, submissive love.

The very focus of consent is recast. The focus is not on an autonomous authenticity in the sense of conformity to one's settled views, congenial passions, and established inclinations. Autonomous authenticity is found instead in the creature's free submission in love and worship to the Creator. To respect the latter autonomy in health care is to aid patients to choose in a way that leads to salvation. This will among other things involve a turning away from the liberal cosmopolitan view of the good life. This approach to medical decision-making subordinates therapeutic choices to non-medical priorities. The interaction among physician, patient, and family is relocated in a matrix of spiritual father and religious community. This requires not just good medical judgment. It requires spiritual direction. Choices need to be embedded within the context of repentance, metanoia, and the pursuit of the Kingdom of Heaven. In social contexts where the usual lines of moral authority have weakened, if not broken, advance directives and medical powers of appointment are needed to insure that a decision-maker is selected who will not be overborne by the seduction of medical priorities that go against the goals of spiritual health. Often, the appropriate surrogate decision-makers will not be those in the family. Proxy decision-makers should be committed to traditional Christian understandings.

Medical concerns must be subordinated to the pursuit of a heart freed from passions, hungering for union with God. To some extent, the Christian ideal of appropriate medical decision-making has similarities with non-Christian, traditional, family-oriented decision-making. Both recognize and take connectedness seriously. Both emphasize the community-embedded character of a full moral life. But there are significant differences. Although Christianity presumptively affirms traditional lines of family authority,[36] it requires that the pursuit of salvation trump all traditional familial commitments.[37] Christianity relocates all moral concerns, including patient consent to treatment, within the all-encompassing and all-demanding pursuit of the kingdom of heaven. The health of the body becomes secondary to the health of the soul.

Providing Health Care in a Post-Christian Age

During the preparation prayers of the Liturgy (i.e., the prayers of the prothesis), the priest remembers "the holy Unmercenaries and wonder-working Cosmas and Damian, Cyrus and John, Panteleimon, Hermolaus; and all the holy unmercenaries".[38] These saints provide Christian exemplars of medical caring: (1) they united the medical and the spiritual and (2) took advantage of their role as physicians to bring their patients to the faith, while (3) often working miraculous cures.[39] They followed the radical Christian call of unqualified love – to "sell as much as thou hast and give to the poor" (Mark 10:21). They gave freely from what they had received (Matt 10:8). Even when physicians, nurses, and other health care professions are not willing to give with the radical love of the holy unmercenaries, they, like the Good Samaritan (Luke 10:30-37), are still called to respond to those in need. In this response the provision of health care is subordinated to the pursuit of holiness. All concerns with health and well-being are to be placed within and constrained by Christian morality, as well as oriented to the kingdom of heaven. The pursuit of the kingdom of heaven has moral and ontological priority. "But be seeking first the kingdom of God and His righteousness, and all these things shall be added to you" (Matt 6:33).

This centrality of the pursuit of the Kingdom of Heaven should still transform the practice of Christian physicians, nurses, and other health care providers. The holy unmercenaries integrated their roles as physicians and caregivers within their lives as Christians. At the very least, health care professionals must not deny their faith in the practice of their profession. This will be ever more difficult. Like the holy unmercenary physicians whose careers ended in martyrdom, contemporary Christian health care professionals in a secular, neo-pagan culture will likely be brought to explain why their health care commitments collide with those of the dominant, secular, liberal cosmopolitan culture. Their conscientious objection to providing what many regard as necessary services, indeed as elements of the standard of appropriate medical care (e.g., prenatal diagnosis and abortion) will itself be an affront. When the traditional Christian health care professional asks not to be required to participate in much that the secular society judges morally appropriate, from third-party-assisted reproduction and abortion to euthanasia, there is an implicit judgment of the immorality of the surrounding society. Conscientious objection as a requirement of conscience is at its core an act of protest directed against the moral commitments of the surrounding culture. By declining to be involved in actions others consider necessary and appropriate, the traditional Christian judges those actions and the morality that supports them as misguided at best and perverted at worst. When a poor woman pregnant out of wedlock begs for an abortion, the Orthodox Christian must respond that to provide an abortion will be to harm that woman severely and to murder her unborn child. To state clearly this blunt truth as gently and lovingly as possible will be an act of kindness. Love requires declaring the truth: sin is an injury.

So, too, when a person is dying in intractable pain, begging for physician-assisted suicide, the Orthodox Christian must out of love attempt to ameliorate the pain while resolutely denying the request. In such circumstances, these denials may appear as immoral affronts, not only to those who ask but to those in the culture generally who will see the denial as unfeeling, if not disrespectful and outrageous. In a culture that demands mutual respect in the sense of avoiding judgment of another's way of life, traditional Christianity will fail to respect the core commitments of the liberal cosmopolitan ethos. When traditional Christian health care professionals refuse to be involved in core elements of the liberal cosmopolitan understandings of decent health care, it will be clear that traditional Christians stand for moral views at odds with the health care values of the surrounding society. By being true to their own moral commitments, traditional Christians in liberal cosmopolitan terms will appear profoundly insensitive to the understandings and commitments of others, if not enemies of civil probity.

One need only consider the reaction if the only physicians in a small town are traditional Christians who will provide neither abortion, physician-assisted reproduction (artificial insemination by a donor), nor physician-assisted suicide. Many in the town may consider themselves burdened by the need to travel some distance to abort their unborn children. If they find none of the state-licensed physicians in their town willing to aid them in avoiding the pain, suffering, and indignities of death, they may view these physicians as acting unprofessionally. Matters will be even worse if the only hospital in town is a religiously-affiliated hospital that will not provide services held to be integral to maintaining control over human destiny with respect to reproduction and death. Yet a further step in the outrage will be engendered by the refusal even to assist through referral to those practitioners and institutions willing to provide the desired services. After all, not only must one not murder, but also one may not even refer others to those who will commit murder. Similarly, for those who recognize abortion and physician-assisted suicide as illicit killings tantamount to murder, it will follow that one must not only not perform abortions or help in assisted self-murder, one may also not refer to those who would perform abortions or aid in physician-assisted suicide.[40] Even where Christians are not the only health care providers or in control of the only health care institution in the area, traditional Christians will be stumbling blocks for secular health care policy. Their non-participation in abortion and physician-assisted suicide will require accommodations of schedule and adjustments in staffing. At the very least, the presence of traditional Christians imposes transaction costs. From the perspective of a liberal cosmopolitan society, the presence of traditional Christians will be a burden and a moral affront.

The question can then be put from the perspective of the Christians as to how much and what sort of involvement in evil activities may be allowed. How distant may an involvement be so that one remains sinless? At what point must one lodge a conscientious objection to any involvement in a forbidden procedure or practice? Is it permissible, for example, to work as a physician in a clinic that provides abortions, as long as one does not personally perform or assist in abortions? May nurses and others arrange medical equipment, which eventually will be used in whole or in part for abortion, illicit third-party-assisted reproduction, or physician-assisted suicide? To what extent may one focus on one's immediate tasks and not worry about how they may be co-opted within various immoral projects? At what point must one wall oneself off from those bent on doing evil? This is a question that existed even in the time of the Apostles. A wine merchant's wares may be used to celebrate the Eucharist, to make glad the heart of man, or to debauch oneself and others. At what point must the wine merchant refuse to sell the wine? At what point and how extensively must the wine merchant inquisit would-be buyers about how the wine will be used?

Unlike the Roman Catholic church, which developed in the Middle Ages, the Christianity of the first millennium did not elaborate crisp distinctions among different degrees of cooperation in the evil activities of others.[41] Nevertheless, the Christianity of the first millennium possessed very clear views that particular involvements in evil practices, however unwilling, could never be condoned. For example, when addressing the case of Christian slaves who had been compelled to sacrifice to pagan gods on behalf of their masters, the Church did not find them innocent simply because their masters had ordered them to do so. Here one must recall that in Graeco-Roman society, unlike the antebellum South,[42] a slave could have been peremptorily tortured and killed by his master.[43]

> As touching the Christian slaves who sacrificed vicariously, the slaves as being in the control of others, and themselves in a way imprisoned by their masters, and having been frightfully threatened by them, and for fear of them having consented and slipped, they shall exhibit works of repentance for a full year, learning henceforth as servants and slaves of Christ to do the will of God, and to fear Him, the more so when they are told that everyone, if he do what is good, shall receive a recompense from the Lord, whether he be bond or free (Eph. 6:8).[44]

Actions such as idolatry, adultery, fornication, and murder are evil in themselves in a way that cannot be excused by any external threat of torture or death.

In drawing lines and ordering one's life in a secular medical culture that accepts much that is evil and indeed praises it (e.g., prenatal diagnosis and abortion as elements of responsible parenting), one must be careful not to find oneself unwittingly enmired in evil undertakings. Even unwitting involvement can have harmful effects. One must note once again that even involuntary homicide or miscarriage requires the therapeutic response of asceticism and prayer. As a consequence, one must withdraw from and purge one's heart from close causal involvement in evil. That one may be involuntarily involved in evil does not necessarily protect against the results of the involvement, as the tradition of ascetic responses to involuntary homicide shows. In determining how closely one may be involved in the evils without taking special ascetic counter-measures to protect oneself, one can say at least the following:

1. One may not be voluntarily involved in evil; that is, one must not want or will evil to occur.
2. One must not be immediately causally involved in the production of evil. That is, one should be separated from causing the evil by at least the agency of another person who is not under one's direct control or authority. For example, if a wine merchant sells wine to a customer knowing that the customer means to engage in

debauchery while not encouraging such use, the merchant is not intimately involved in the evil that comes from the misuse of the wine, though the merchant will still be involved in an evil.

3. One must be clearly opposed to the evils in which one finds oneself enmired, given the broken character of this world. At the very least, the wine merchant must not advertise the wine in a way that would suggest that it should be used in any way except properly. When there is a suspicion of misuse, the merchant should at least oppose that use. If possible, the merchant should advertise the wine in a way that opposes misuse.

4. When one is free to refuse to be involved in supplying resources to someone who one knows will engage in evil, one should refuse to be involved. The merchant should not sell wine to a person who announces that it will be used in debauchery.

5. When one is a servant or employee of another, one may with deep regret and with no approval simply supply materials that others at law can claim and that will be used improperly. A clerk may provide wine purchased by a customer, albeit for evil purposes.

6. With prayerful regret one may be involved in complex relationships in which one is not directly causing, encouraging, or approving of the evils in which others with whom one is involved are engaged. For example, one may pay taxes, knowing that the funds will be used by the state for immoral purposes. After all, Christ Himself countered the concern whether it was legitimate to pay one's taxes to Caesar: "Render therefore the things of Caesar to Caesar, and the things of God to God" (Matt 22:21).

7. One's actions should not give scandal to others. One should not be seen to have compromised oneself in a way that would undermine the resolution of others to stand firmly against evil.

8. In a world within which it will be almost impossible not to be partially coopted and somewhat enmired in the production of evil (e.g., a man may visit a monastery with a woman in the hopes of gaining her confidence in order later to seduce her), one must pray both for oneself and for those others who will involve one in evil.

In summary, Christians should avoid direct causal involvement in such undertakings as abortion, physician-assisted suicide, or euthanasia. Yet, in a society where mores are so broken that such practices are integral to ordinary life, it will be impossible to be totally causally uninvolved in some way in the provision of evil. As usual, each person will need to find the guidance of a spiritual father. Given the intrusiveness of our secular culture, each will need with redoubled strength through prayer and repentance to turn his heart in repentance to God. Also, as far as possible, as the general culture, and health care in particular, become aggressively secularized, Christians must find ways of providing health care that unambiguously make plain their Christian commitments.

Quarantining and Secularizing Christianity: Religion as a Private Matter

The financial, social, and moral burdens imposed by traditional Christians on secular society give the state considerable incentives to quarantine traditional Christianity by first rendering it a private matter and then requiring even matters of private life to conform to the canons of secular morality and justice. To begin with, religion will be construed as private in the sense of precluded from intrusion into the lives of others. In the framework of a secular society, religion is something that should be closeted within special buildings (e.g., churches) or in one's own home. Like the viewing of child pornography, it should take place with the doors closed. This sense of private recaptures its etymological roots in the Latin *privo, privare, privatum*, whose first meaning is to bereave, deprive, rob, or strip of something, and whose second meaning is to be free, released, or delivered of something. It is from this verb that the adjective *privatus* is derived, whose first meaning is: "apart from the State, peculiar to one's self, of or belonging to an individual, private."[45] It is also from this that the meaning of private as a private person not engaged in public or official life is derived. The substantive *privatus* also takes its origin here as "a man in private life" and especially "in the time of the emperors, *private*, i.e., *not imperial, not belonging to the emperor or to the imperial family.*"[46] The private is thus defined in privative terms as the absence of the civic so that it does not have a standing in its own right. It is that which does not or should not enter into the civic sphere. In this sense, religion is to be a private matter that does not have a standing on its own and should not be allowed to intrude into public life. The private is understood in terms of what it is not.

This sense of privacy circumscribes religion and reinterprets its meaning within the requirements of secular public reason. The claim is robust. Religion may offer a historical source of orientation or morality. However, the liberal cosmopolitan ethos cannot tolerate religion as a source of transcendent claims over against secular justice, civil society, secular morality, or public reason. Such a religion would advance non-negotiable claims contrary to its foundational commitments. It is out of such considerations that liberal cosmopolitan societies oppose the role of religion in public life. The position usually is that if religious concerns cannot be articulated in terms of public secular reason, which reason is to be understood fully through the assumptions of a secular, democratic polity, then they should not appear in the public forum. Public secular reason is to provide the canonical point of justification for public justice, morality, and civil society. In the process, the liberal cosmopolitan ethos seeks to secure a civil discourse in conformity with aspirations that give a lexical priority to human liberty from history and from nature. Public conversations should not even introduce considerations adverse to the liberal cosmopolitan ethos. In the process, a content-full secular ethos focused on the value of liberty as defining the basis for mutual respect requires that religion be transformed so that the moral authority of secular morality and justice are primary.

John Rawls' (1921–) *Theory of Justice,*[47] perhaps the most important 20th century work in English regarding the moral foundations of justice and political theory, offers a systematic reconstruction of the liberal cosmopolitan ethos. It is the exemplar of a moral and political account grounded in an immanent ethos committed to liberty and equality, but not to the cardinal authority of individual permission-giving: the liberal cosmopolitan ethos. *Political Liberalism* [48] discloses that his is the morality of social democratic life and that it is committed to transforming the institutions compassed by his just society. Rawls' account in particular and the liberal cosmopolitan ethos in general will not tolerate dissenting social structures and institutions. Such toleration would involve acquiescence in injustice. It is out of such grounds that Rawls takes pains to sever the family from a robust sense of privacy that would allow families a moral independence over against the larger society and its moral demands. The liberal cosmopolitan vision appreciates the family in civic terms: "The adult members of families and other associations are equal citizens first: that is their basic position."[49] It follows as well that members of religion are equal citizens before they are members of a religion. Citizenship has moral and social-ontological priority over religious commitments. Rawls offers an influential exemplar of the liberal cosmopolitan regard for traditional religious commitments.

In these terms, the secular civil society within which traditional Christian physicians, nurses, and patients find themselves is not merely neutral to their commitments. It endeavors to be subtly if not overtly corruptive of authentic Christian belief, always inviting Christianity to restate its commitments in general secular terms. Everything, including belief, is relocated within strong moral and political constraints, which in secular terms are morally primary. For Rawls, "No institution or association [including churches] in which they [persons] are involved can violate their rights as citizens."[50] It is not merely that the rights of citizens may not be violated. A corollary is that there should be no sphere of discourse not preemptively defined in terms of public reason. This brings into question spheres of life and education whose views of human reproduction, relationship, suffering, and death go against the prevailing secular content-rich views of justice. Rawls makes this clear. "If the so-called private sphere is alleged to be a space exempt from justice, then there is no such thing."[51] In terms of this position, one can better understand why Rawls employs the phrase, "citizens of faith", and why this so clearly discloses the commitments of the liberal cosmopolitan ethos. One is first and foremost a citizen, and only secondarily a person of faith. One's commitments as a citizen are to be lexically prior to one's commitments as a person of faith. After all, for Rawls, "citizens of faith" must be "wholehearted members of a democratic society who endorse society's political ideals and values and do not simply acquiesce in the balance of political and social forces."[52] Citizens of faith should not encourage actions that go contrary to the general secular morality and its claims of justice. For example, traditional Christian physicians, according to this account, should not refuse, because of revealed religious reasons, to provide abortions to women who desperately want them. Those who attempt to convert others to this view will appropriately be subject to moral reeducation.

Such individuals are for Rawls fundamentalists because (1) they are committed to a morality unjustifiable in general secular terms, which (2) they nevertheless hold should influence their activities with others and (3) even their activities in the public forum, and (4) which moral understandings they also hold all others should by conversion embrace. Religious fundamentalism is thus defined by reference to those religious views that "assert that the religiously true, or the philosophically true, overrides the politically reasonable."[53] To be a fundamentalist for Rawls is to have a religious conviction that is lexically prior to one's commitment as a citizen. For Rawls, to be a fundamentalist is to put God before the social democratic state. If a religion claims a priority in knowledge or moral authority over the civic so as to criticize the polity in terms not open to secular reason, it is by definition fundamentalist, and as such to be criticized and reformed. On the one hand, "fundamentalist" becomes a pejorative term in secular discourse, while on the other hand the refusal to embrace the fundamentals of secular social justice becomes grounds for being judged guilty of secular heresy. The secularly politically reasonable must trump any requirements of religion that cannot be reduced to its own terms. If the ways of God are not the ways of the state, then the ways of the state must prevail. In these terms, traditional Christianity is robustly fundamentalist.

One might still attempt to interpret the claims of the liberal cosmopolitan ethos and of Rawls as placing only weak demands on religious integrity: as requiring only that one peaceably abide by the laws of a tolerant, democratic society. However, this will be too much of a requirement if the law enjoins on "citizens of faith" violations of obligations to God such as requiring physicians to refer patients for abortion and physician-assisted suicide (if the physicians will not provide the services themselves). Moreover, Rawls demands even more than obedience to law: he requires conformity to the expectations of a social democratic understanding of political correctness. He does this in part by expanding the meaning of toleration: a social democratic polity involves a commitment to public reason which compasses more than just complying with democratic procedures out of religious commitments to acquiescing peaceably in public authority as long as this does not require violations of religious duties. Rawls' proviso requires participation in the societal framework out of the correct general political reasons.

> [R]easonable comprehensive doctrines, religious or nonreligious, may be introduced in public political discussion at any time, provided that in due course proper political reasons – and not reasons given solely by comprehensive doctrines – are presented that are sufficient to support whatever the comprehensive doctrines introduced are said to support. This injunction to present proper political reasons I refer to as *the proviso*, and it specifies public political culture as distinct from the background culture.[54]

By this proviso Rawls requires more than he acknowledges: he does not simply distinguish political culture from the background culture. The political culture he affirms is recognized as the point of view from which one should criticize, revise, and reform the background culture.

The requirements are thoroughgoing. One must not only act in conformity with the requirements of secular justice and morality, but out of those requirements. The ties of "civil friendship" require a foundational affirmation of public reason, which provides the ground of a liberal, democratic polity along with a sense of toleration that requires affirmation and respect of each other's views as citizens, including each other's religious and moral views. It is not enough to respect others as persons while being critical of their religion, if the criticisms cannot be reduced to considerations articulable within public reason. The ideal is to meet as citizens committed to the moral unity of a social democratic policy and the mutual recognition of each other as first and foremost equal stakeholders in a liberal cosmopolitan society. This ideal is incompatible with confronting others with moral declarations that cannot be justified in terms of social democratic morality. In particular, it would not be proper to criticize another's religion for failing to be properly oriented to the transcendent and only true God. For Rawls and for the liberal cosmopolitan generally, the religious dimension of life must be reduced to the requirements of secular morality.

Areas often held to have a privileged political independence in belonging to private life, in the sense of being exempt from public regulation and the intrusion of unwanted values, become appropriately a focus of social concern, control, and reeducation. The liberal cosmopolitan vision must ensure that there are no spheres immune from its values. It is out of such a commitment to securing the general governance of liberal cosmopolitan values that John Rawls, for example, nests the family and other would-be areas of private association within the liberal cosmopolitan ethos. Rawls is willing to recognize spheres of association as being private only in the sense of not as easily, efficiently, or usefully shaped by direct social control. It is only by default that such areas are partially freed from the full governance of civic norms, public reason, and the demands of justice. The sense of privacy in this context is a privative notion. It identifies an area deprived of direct and full governance by civic norms, public reason, and the demands of justice. It is an area of moral privation in that moral rationality is public (1) as the reason of free and equal citizens, (2) as addressing the public good appropriately constituting society, as well as (3) matters of basic justice. In this sense, spheres of privacy are areas not fully subject to the demands of public reason and of liberal cosmopolitan moral requirements, only insofar as one needs room for "a free and flourishing internal life appropriate to the association in question,"[55] that is, insofar as the political principles of justice do not clearly inform us about how to govern such areas, or insofar as the political principles of justice best apply indirectly rather than directly to such associations, so as to allow their successful functions.

Even in such spheres of privacy, the requirements of liberal cosmopolitan justice and morality still apply, setting the background conditions of justice. Rawls takes pains to emphasize that, once one has such an appropriately robust notion of public reason and its governance (i.e., a social democratic, that is, liberal cosmopolitan notion), private associations such as churches and families do not exist in exclaves free from the intrusion of political conceptions of justice and moral probity.

> A domain so-called, or a sphere of life, is not, then, something already given apart from political conceptions of justice. A domain is not a kind of space, or place, but rather is simply the result, or upshot, of how the principles of political justice are applied, directly to the basic structure and indirectly to the associations within it.[56]

This view gives grounds for a state to regard religious groups as fundamentalist, extremist, and illiberal, and therefore to mount educational efforts to counteract their beliefs, if they hold as a matter of revelation that services should not be provided that are generally recognized as integral to a just society (e.g., prenatal diagnosis and abortion), or hold that interpersonal relations should have a character judged to be unjust in secular moral terms (e.g., that wives should submit respectfully to their husbands). Thus, there would be public grounds to respond to physicians who not only refuse to perform abortions or assist in suicide, but also refuse to refer to those performing such services. The same would hold of a religion that taught that wives should submit to their husbands with respect, that women cannot be priests, that homosexual lifestyles (i.e., lifestyles involving homosexual acts) are perverted, and that consensual fornication is deeply immoral.

Spheres of private life and association within a liberal cosmopolitan ethic, as exemplified by Rawls, contrast fundamentally with how these spheres appear if one takes a libertarian cosmopolitan perspective, that is, if one recognizes the authority of the state as derived from the people, rather than from a governing account of justice. A libertarian cosmopolitan morality, as a default morality grounded in the authority of individuals, requires robust areas for private choice and association. It is this sense of privacy as rooted in the rights of persons that lies behind some of the features of English and American law. Such notions of privacy have roots in English law, as Warren and Brandeis observed as early as 1890. "That the individual shall have full protection in person and in property is a principle as old as the common law...."[57] Almost forty years later, this notion of privacy, drawn from tort law, began to have standing in constitutional law. As an American Supreme Court justice, Brandeis transformed these considerations into the beginnings of a constitutional principle with a deep resonance with the libertarian cosmopolitan ethic.

> The makers of our Constitution undertook to secure conditions favorable to the pursuit of happiness. They recognized the significance of man's spiritual nature, of his feelings and of his intellect. They knew that only a part of the pain, pleasure, and satisfactions of life are to be found in material things. They sought to protect Americans in their beliefs, their thoughts, their emotions and their sensations. They conferred, as against the government, the right to be let alone – the most comprehensive of rights and the right most valued by civilized men.[58]

This dissenting opinion was then further developed by Justice Warren Burger before he was a member of the U.S. Supreme Court in yet another dissenting opinion.

> Nothing in this utterance suggests that Justice Brandeis thought an individual possessed these rights only as to *sensible* beliefs, *valid* thoughts, *reasonable* emotions, or *well-founded* sensations. I suggest he intended to include a great many foolish, unreasonable and even absurd ideas which do not conform, such as refusing medical treatment even at great risk.[59]

From such holdings an American constitutional understanding of rights to privacy as disclosing limits on governmental intrusions and as defining spheres for private choice and association gradually took shape.[60]

Under this rubric of constitutional rights to privacy, the contemporary American secular sexual morality with its acceptance of consensual fornication, the contraceptive ethos, open homosexual lifestyles, and abortion received constitutional protection.[61] Such rights to privacy, and the spheres for free association they allowed, established areas for voluntary action, in the pursuit of not only sin, but also salvation. Rights to privacy in this strong sense indicate not just that sinners are at liberty to perform their immoralities with consenting others in the sense that coercive force will not be used against them, but also that consenting persons should be free to pursue the kingdom of

God as they see fit. This idea of protected rights to privacy thus gives secure political space not only for immorality, but also for the pursuit of holiness.

Rights to privacy were derived not just from the 1st and 4th Amendments but especially from the 9th Amendment,[62] which has language clearly indicating rights of individuals over against claims of justice and publicly established morality. "The enumeration in the Constitution of certain rights shall not be construed to deny or disparage others retained by the people."[63] For this reason, Justice Arthur Goldberg in his 1965 opinion in *Griswold v. Connecticut* drew on the 9th Amendment in defending his view of rights to privacy. As Goldberg argued, the 9th Amendment is

> almost entirely the work of James Madison. It was introduced in Congress by him and passed the House and Senate with little or no debate and virtually no change in language. It was proffered to quiet expressed fears that a bill of specifically enumerated rights could not be sufficiently broad to cover all essential rights and that the specific mention of certain rights would be interpreted as a denial that others were protected.[64]

Indeed, it is in the 9th Amendment that the notion of a constitutional right to act on one's own moral and religious commitments has its most forceful expression.

> There is no clause in the Constitution, except the Ninth Amendment, which makes a declaration of the sovereignty and dignity of the individual....
> The Ninth Amendment announces and acknowledges in a single sentence that (1) the individual, and not the State, is the source and basis of our social compact and that sovereignty now resides and has always resided in the individual; (2) that our Government exists through the surrender by the individual of a portion of his naturally endowed and inherent rights; (3) that everyone of the people of the United States owns a residue of individual rights and liberties which have never been, and which are never to be surrendered to the State, but which are still to be recognized, protected and secure; and (4) that individual liberty and rights are inherent, and that such rights are not derived from the Constitution, but belong to the individual by natural endowment.[65]

In recognizing that secular political authority is drawn from individual consent, the 9th Amendment offers a source of moral authority similar to that which grounds the libertarian cosmopolitan morality.

Rights to privacy in this libertarian cosmopolitan sense reflect not simply an important sphere of individual interests in enjoying seclusion from others, the protection of embarrassing facts, or the use of one's name or likeness only with one's own permission. At stake are the limits of public authority to interfere in private choices and consensual associations. However costly the results of rights to privacy in allowing sinners space to sin as they wish with consenting others, they also offer the possibility of a protected space for traditional Christians to pray and associate with consenting others as they pursue union with a transcendent and highly politically incorrect God.

At least in theory, space was established within which religious fundamentalists could pursue their views of proper association and behavior, even if these were at odds with the surrounding secular society. Rights to privacy in this sense contrast with Rawls' account of "private" areas of association and choice, which in accord with the liberal cosmopolitan ethos offer only a privative and limited understanding of privacy. In this, Rawls shows himself to be a true son of the Enlightenment who wishes to order human life in terms of a rationally disclosable account of justice. In contrast, rights to privacy that are rooted in individual permission set immediate limits to the intrusion by society on individual religious commitments or the integrity of religious associations. The contrast between Rawls' position and rights to privacy as spheres for peaceable action into which even the ingression of public reason and demands of justice are severely limited, if not excluded, discloses the extent to which Rawls wishes to introduce a powerfully intrusive secular ethics through which to break down the separation allowed within a libertarian moral vision between the public and the private. For Rawls and the cosmopolitan liberal, religion should become a private matter in the radical sense that any moral content not in accord with social democratic morality should at most be a matter of belief but never expressed in action.

The liberal cosmopolitan ethic has found further influence through a view of the state as less limited and therefore more authoritative, which has sent the American constitutional recognition of rights to privacy into retreat. The current choice in American constitutional law of identifying "liberty interests" in preference to "rights to privacy" is of fundamental significance. The notion of liberty interests fits more congenially within the liberal cosmopolitan ethic, while rights to privacy fit more securely within a libertarian cosmopolitan understanding.[66] Liberty interests can in principle be rendered fully congenial with the liberal cosmopolitan ethos, such that freedom comes to be understood as acting in conformity with its goals. Liberty interests, unlike the moral and political trumps provided by rights to privacy rooted in a ninth amendment-like vision of moral authority independent of the framework of a liberal social democratic polity, do not secure morally deviant exclaves, where among other things traditional Christians can peaceably pursue their salvation. By appealing to liberty interests rather than rights to privacy, one can justify the state's reeducating and remotivating believers who make moral claims inarticulable in the general language of the public forum or that criticize the liberal cosmopolitan ethos. Commitments to a liberal cosmopolitan understanding of liberty bear against claims of religious integrity grounded in a mystical apprehension of a transcendent God, because these claims cannot be expressed within the public discourse required by social democratic moral rationality.

This gives a secular ground for further concern regarding traditionally Christian health care professionals: they may abuse or exploit their power over patients by introducing religious values opaque to the values of the liberal cosmopolitan ethos. In particular, those who are in authority over others, as physicians over the treatment of their patients, if they are religious fundamentalists, may draw on an unfair power differential to wrest their patients from their commitments to the ideals of public reason. They will recognize their authoritarian role as health professionals as giving them an opportunity to direct patients away from sin and toward salvation. From a liberal cosmopolitan moral point of view, traditional Christian health care professionals will have a dangerous proclivity to exploit the existential angst of sick and dying patients to influence their choices and perhaps even bring them to convert. It is in such contexts that proselytization is given an adverse connotation: appeals to the compromised or distressed circumstances of individuals in order to bring them to consider conversion. Religious suasion and conversion are to occur only in circumstances of unhindered autonomy, though it will be held appropriate to draw on any emotions and nearly any circumstances in order to strengthen commitments to toleration and equality. The intrusion of religious values of Christian health care professionals will be regarded in general as immoral in being exploitative, and as unethical in particular in being contrary to an emerging commitment to professional value neutrality. Traditional Christian physicians and other health care professionals in such circumstances will endanger the neutrality of health care decision-makers.

Any attempt by Christian physicians and other health care professionals to bring patients to avoid choices whose moral harms can only be appreciated within a religious perspective (e.g., to choose not to have an abortions or to use physician-assisted suicide) are considered inappropriate violations of professional value neutrality from a liberal cosmopolitan moral perspective. These intrusions of guidance violate the canons of professional value neutrality because the potential patient choices are not considered truly harmful. "Value" in considerations of professional value neutrality is a shorthand to identify value concerns considered not just matters of opinion, but involving an illegitimate intrusion of religious or non-cosmopolitan liberal moral commitments. Values intrude at all levels in the professional guidance given to patients. Any view that it is best to treat a disease and accept certain side effects in order to avoid early death and disability involves an appeal to values. Health professionals will vary in their judgment as to what counts as a prudent balance between different exposures to the chance of suffering and dying, contingent on the choice of one over another diagnostic or therapeutic intervention. Many consider it appropriate for physicians in their discussions with patients to offer their own views. It is generally considered proper for physicians to warn patients about their health care obligations to their dependents and to reinforce conduct in accord with liberal cosmopolitan commitments (e.g., reassuring a patient of the moral propriety of having chosen to abort an unborn child). When the professional guidance does not comport with the general commitments of the liberal cosmopolitan ethos, matters are different (e.g., responding to a patient's question about the propriety of a decision to secure an abortion with the answer that the choice is equivalent to murder of an unborn child). In both cases, values are engaged. It is only that, when choices in accord with the liberal cosmoplitan ethos are at stake, they are neutral in the very special sense of not deviating from the background moral commitments of the dominant culture.

Of course, the difficulty arises in that traditional Christians are not committed to the liberal cosmopolitan ethos, but to the pursuit of holiness. This special religious commitment violates the value-neutral role that professionals are to have in a liberal cosmopolitan society. That is, physicians and patients are to meet in terms of their roles within civil society and the state. They are to meet in their special office as citizens: as citizen health professionals treating citizen patients. They are not within this role to meet in terms of their religious commitments. Physician-patient relationships are to be structured in accord with the liberal cosmopolitan ethos. As a consequence, health professionals are to be neutral to all values save those core to the liberal cosmopolitan ethos. The value-rich perspective of the liberal cosmopolitan ethic is affirmed as the morally neutral perspective from which health care professionals should relate with patients. If their moral concerns cannot be translated into considerations of social democratic morality, these commitments are to remain private in the sense of excluded not only from public expression, but also from guiding even consensual actions in professional roles that are contrary to the requirements of social democratic morality.

The more professional integrity and conduct are brought within the control of a content-rich ideal of secular public reason, the more suspect the open expression of traditional Christian belief and commitments will be. A liberal cosmopolitan ethos will require the peaceable assimilation as far as is possible of all deviant moral perspectives to its own understanding. Thus, it will seem quite appropriate to engage tax policy, public education, public propaganda, and state regulation to bring deviant, that is, fundamentalist religious and moral understandings in line with the liberal cosmopolitan establishment. Even voicing religious views in a public context will go against the demands of justice if they undermine the equality and justice a secular social democracy takes to be essential. For Rawls, secular understandings of equality and justice are to transform the lives of all.

> Recall that public reason sees the office of citizen with its duty of civility as analogous to that of judge with its duty of deciding cases. Just as judges are to decide cases by legal grounds of precedent, recognized canons of statutory interpretation, and other relevant grounds, so citizens are to reason by public reason and to be guided by the criterion of reciprocity, whenever constitutional essentials and matters of basic justice are at stake.[67]

One must also recall that Rawls' feminist and democratic concerns about the family, drawing on John Stuart Mill,[68] lead him to conclude that the principles of justice may enjoin that "a reasonable constitutional democratic society can plainly be invoked to reform the family."[69] Out of such roots, a secular society may find intolerable as violating basic rights the refusal of traditional Christian health practitioners not to provide certain forms of third-party-assisted reproduction, or to treat sexual dysfunction among homosexual couples. This "intolerance" will be seen to be ever more unacceptable, insofar as such religious moral positions are advanced in terms of a mystical experience of God's truth, and not in terms of arguments articulable in general secular terms.

Committed traditional Christian health care professionals will find themselves twice-over going against the grain of a public reason which is largely in the image and likeness of John Rawls. On the one hand, traditional Christians by their conscientious objections to particular medical interventions will impede access to health care services, which many as a matter of justice will claim as a basic secular right. On the other hand, in terms not open to general secular public reason, they will condemn the availability and use of such services. Where in terms of an account of public reason à la Rawls one would be forbidden to advance religious claims unjustifiable in social democratic secular moral terms, traditional Christian health care professionals, following the holy unmercenary physicians of the first centuries, will properly look for opportunities to bring their patients to salvation. At the very least, they will always be required to confess their faith when asked about the roots of their moral commitments. There is, after all, Christ's stern warning:

> Everyone therefore who shall confess in Me before men, I also will confess in him before My Father who is in the heavens. But whosoever shall deny Me before men, him will I also deny before My Father Who is in the heavens. Never think that I came to cast peace on the earth; I came not to cast peace, but a sword. For I came to divide in two a man against his father, and a daughter against her mother, and a daughter-in-law against her mother-in-law; and a man's enemies shall be they of his own household (Matt 10:32-36).

Traditional Christians will be morally disruptive. Contrary to the liberal cosmopolitan ethic, they will indeed seek opportunities for converting others and directing them away from sin, as did the holy unmercenaries of the first centuries. The liberal cosmopolitan is right in discerning a real conflict between the duties of physicians as citizens of a social democracy and physicians as committed traditional Christians. The religious moral integrity of the traditional Christian will be expressed both in stepping back from any involvement in forbidden activities (e.g., abortion, artificial insemination from a donor, physician-assisted suicide) and in providing a witness to the truth of Christianity, which is always an invitation to repentance and conversion.

The Integrity of Christian Health Care Institutions

The preservation of life and the avoidance of suffering are not overriding goals. Christ charges us to visit the sick (Matt 25:36), not to secure the best available physicians and health care for the sick. In the time of Christ's earthly ministry, there were physicians regarded as able to provide superior care. In the first century, patients with means often invested considerably in medical services (Mark 5:26): then as now the pursuit of health and a longer life through medicine could become an all-consuming project, deflecting both the giver and the receiver of care away from the pursuit of the kingdom of God. St. Basil the Great in question 55 of his *Long Rules* makes this clear: we are not to immerse ourselves wholeheartedly in the pursuit of health through medicine.[70] There are strong moral grounds to be cautious about involvement in any social understanding of health care that makes medicine into a cultural obsession in the sense of an overriding human practice or project. There are independent and equally strong grounds against embedding the provision of health care within a single, all-encompassing state system, when its morality is at odds with traditional Christianity. An encompassing health care system combined with a cultural obsession with health care becomes a major spiritual threat, because health care touches all passages of life likely to be integral to a cosmopolitan liberal society's attempt to establish fully its moral vision. It will serve as a vehicle for reforming religious understandings of sexuality, reproduction, and death. Such an all-encompassing health care system will be the powerful embodiment of an anti-Christian ethos.

In the face of a dominant secular society, traditional Christians must often settle for a limited space within which to pursue the kingdom of God with like-minded persons. The preservation of this may involve peaceably resisting the intrusion of all-encompassing secular health care systems, which would disallow such space for health care guided by traditional Christian assumptions. In order to garner as much space as possible for traditional Christian approaches to health care, Christians will have strong grounds for

1. opposing all-encompassing, state-supported health care systems, especially one-payer systems as exist in Canada that do not allow opting out through private insurance and private payments;
2. criticizing appeals to social justice forwarded to support health care reform. Invocations of "social justice" tend to transform spiritual commitments into social democratic moral commitments, thus discounting their transcendent significance in terms of the secular ideology of social democratic states; and
3. counteracting the influence of political or religious groups and movements that centrally enshrine commitments to social justice. They are at least involuntarily hostile to traditional Christianity.

Traditional Christianity is committed to personal responses to those in need in ways that focus wholeheartedly on love of God and others. Anonymous state and social interventions on the part of the needy cannot substitute for responses to those in need by individual Christians and Christian communities. Since the poor will always be with us (Matt 26:11), the goal cannot be the abolition of poverty or its results. God can always provide for those in need. The response to those in need must be an expression of personal love – of love for the poor and of love for God. The focus must be on the character of the charity, the character of the love that motivates the giver. If the giver gives other than out of a love that sets others within an overriding love of God, the giving will not lead to the kingdom of heaven. "And if I dole out all of my goods, and if I deliver up my body that I may be burned, but I have not love, I am being profited nothing" (I Cor 13:3). The provision of health care should be as saliently Christian as that offered by the holy unmercenaries.

To take a recent contrast in moral visions, one might compare pre-Vatican II and contemporary Roman Catholic health care. Until Vatican II and the moral, liturgical, and spiritual chaos it engendered, Roman Catholics were able, through the lifelong dedication of religious brothers and sisters, to provide health care to the indigent. They reached to others with love from the thoroughgoing offering by nuns and brothers of their own lives to God. They provided health care that was flagrantly Christian. For example, in some Roman Catholic hospitals all employees addressed each other and the patients with the salutation, "Praised be the Incarnate Word."[71] In addition, Roman Catholic institutions assiduously avoided any cooperation in evil acts such as abortion and physician-assisted suicide. With Vatican II and the dramatic collapse in vocations and the exit of religious from their vows, Roman Catholic hospitals lost an important resource from which to provide indigent care with a clearly Christian character. It lost as well the strength of will to be distinctively religious. It is not just that employees and patients are no longer addressed with the salutation, "Praised be the Incarnate Word." Nor is it only that Roman Catholic hospitals often find themselves entering into associations with hospitals that provide services they find immoral. Most significantly, there is no longer a commitment to embedding all actions in an all-pervasive and particular Christian self-consciousness.

In an age that is post-Christian if not anti-Christian, traditional Christians will need to seek to provide care while both avoiding forbidden interventions (e.g., abortion) and giving care with a clear and particular religious character. The establishment of hospices may offer an opportunity to care in contexts in which those approaching death can be helped to turn from themselves and to Christ. To provide hospice as would the holy unmercenary physicians will require remaining as free as possible from the morality of the surrounding society. This may necessitate refusing any government payments for services that would disallow an uncompromisingly particularist character for such health care institutions. After all, a Christian hospice should with love and patience attempt to bring all under its roof to repentance and conversion. To provide health care in such circumstances will require robust acts of charity. The requirements of the Gospel leave little justification for feeling at ease if one has not done all one can to help those in need. After all, Christ demands that we give our very coats to those in need. "The one who hath two tunics, let him share with him who hath not" (Luke 3:11). At the same time, one must not confuse the demand of charity with a demand for an egalitarian, all-encompassing health care system. Christ calls us to be good Samaritans, to turn personally to persons in need. Christ did not call us to use the coercive force of the state to ensure that others will be cared for by an anonymous, secular welfare system. Moreover, an egalitarianism of envy, a commitment against some having more, that would require the imposition of an all-encompassing health care system in order to achieve a unified, egalitarian level of health care for all, would be five times evil.

1. Christians should not be concerned that some have more than others, only that some have too little for their needs. Traditional Christianity condemns evil and praises humility. From the circumstance that some have more health care, it does not follow that they must give from the surplus of their health resources, rather than from some other surplus or possession, in order to give to those in need of health care.

2. Christianity should resist and indeed condemn ideologies that make health care a matter of overriding concern. To engage the force of the state in establishing an all-encompassing egalitarian health care system morality distorts behavior by giving a disproportionate focus to the postponement of death and the alleviation of suffering.

3. Christians should resist an all-encompassing secular health care system because it will invite patients and care-givers to enter into a medical morality hostile to traditional Christian commitments.

4. Christians should seek opportunities to give care in ways so that their Christian commitments are open, unambiguous, unconstrained, and uncompromised.

5. Christians should act with ascetical works of charity to reach out to care for the sick, suffering, disabled, and dying in ways that with love fully express the Christian understanding of the Truth that can lead to holiness.

The goal should be to care for others in ways that do not involve compromises with one's commitments as a Christian. Indeed, one should seek circumstances under which giving care to others will nurture and not threaten those commitments.

Within a political structure framed in terms of a libertarian cosmopolitan ethic, the provision of Christian health care to the ill would be limited only by the generosity of Christians. Quite different global health care systems could take shape within a political structure that took seriously: (1) persons as the source of secular moral authority, and (2) the substantive moral diversity that separates moral communities. Two possibilities can be advanced as heuristic examples: (1) a global Roman Catholic health care system (perhaps under the brandname Vaticare), and (2) a global Orthodox Christian health care system (perhaps under the brandname Orthocare). Roman Catholics could fashion a worldwide health care system that would:

1. avoid the provision of morally forbidden health care services (e.g., artificial insemination from donors, abortion, and physician-assisted suicide);
2. offer a preferential option for the poor through an internal taxing system that would redistribute resources
   a. from rich patients to poor patients within a hospital,
   b. from affluent to impoverished of the same country, and
   c. from rich to impecunious countries;
3. provide care in a context that is marked by Christian, indeed, Roman Catholic religious commitments.

Commitments to a particular moral character for health care could be protected through special criminal and civil law applicable only to the facilities of the particular health care system. Thus, those who would attempt to provide abortion or euthanasia on Vaticare premises would be subject to civil recovery and criminal prosecution. There might also be different levels of health care and amenities following the Roman Catholic moral theological principle of providing care *proportionem status*. The result might be levels of health care such as Papalcare, Cardinalcare, Monsignorcare, and MotherTeresaCare ranging in the compass of their services from luxury hospital suites with access to all of the most expensive diagnostic and therapeutic interventions to straw mats in large wards where only the most basic care would be offered. The extent to which such an international Roman Catholic health care system might be of spiritual interest would turn on the extent to which it looked beyond a secular view of justice and aimed at holiness. That is, the crucial issue would be the extent to which the Roman Catholic religion is post-traditional, alienated and distant from the Christianity of the first millennium. This would determine the extent to which such a health care system could place all of its moral concerns, from those of social justice to the avoidance of the violation of particular norms, within the spiritual concern of bringing all to holiness through conversion to Christianity.

An Orthodox health care system would be the result of agreements among different bishops across the world. After all, the diocese is the basic as well as complete Christian community. "Wherever the bishop appears let the congregation be present; just as wherever Jesus Christ is, there is the Catholic Church."[72] Such a health care system should provide a basic level of care nested within a spiritual life for both staff and patients. One might imagine the various shifts in the working day beginning with common prayer. All patients would find themselves in a context that invited conversion away from sin, to right worship and belief. The constraints and goals of the authentic Christianity of the first millennium would be nourished as the raison d'être for the health care institution.

The integrity of the health care system, indeed of such a confederacy of health care systems, could be nurtured by criminal and civil law applicable only to Orthocare premises. Given the resources of the Orthodox Church in various countries, one would expect that diverse arrangements would be made out of charity to transfer resources to those in need. In addition to providing basic adequate medical care, there should be the provision of special opportunities for prayer, access to the Mysteries, anointing with oil from the vigil lamps of wonder-working icons, and blessings with the relics of saints. Holy elders would be invited to visit and give their blessing to the patients. Special prayers for the ill and exorcisms for those in need would be available. In short, the usual taken-for-granted interventions of medical care would be relocated within the pursuit of the kingdom of God. Though medical care would be an important focus, the staff would be directed first and foremost to ensuring that the medical care was compatible with the care of the soul. All would be directed to seeking first the kingdom of heaven: "But be seeking first the kingdom of God and his righteousness, and all these things shall be added to you" (Matt 6:33). The pursuit of physical health and the postponement of death would have their place in terms of the struggle to salvation.

The extent to which a religion locates health care in terms of the pursuit of salvation discloses the extent to which it takes transcendence seriously. The more the energies of a religion are displaced to the pursuit of secular moral goods, the more one must suspect that that religion has lost its way, indeed, abandoned its character as a worshipful pursuit of the transcendent God. Friedrich Hayek has seen this clearly in his criticism of the displacement of transcendent concerns with concerns for social justice. As he observes,

> [Social justice] seems in particular to have been embraced by a large section of the clergy of all Christian denominations, who, while increasingly losing their faith in a supernatural revelation, appear to have sought a refuge and consolation in a new "social" religion which substitutes a temporal for a celestial promise of justice, and who hope that they can thus continue their striving to do good. The Roman Catholic church especially has made the aim of "social justice" part of its official doctrine; but the ministers of most Christian denominations appear to vie with each other with such offers of more mundane aims – which also seem to provide the chief foundation for renewed ecumenical efforts.[73]

A Christianity that takes the biblical call to holiness (Lev 11:44) seriously will place all moral concerns in terms of this pursuit of the kingdom of heaven. After all, "the kingdom of the heavens is like treasure which hath been hidden in the field, which, after a man found he hid, and for the joy of it, he goeth and selleth all things, as much as he hath, and buyeth that field" (Matt 13:44).

Notes

1. Friedrich Nietzsche, *The Portable Nietzsche*, ed. & trans. Walter Kaufmann (New York: Penguin, 1982), *Thus Spoke Zarathustra: Third Part*, pp. 339f. "Doch alle Lust will Ewig-

keit–,–will tiefe, tiefe Ewigkeit!" Friedrich Nietzsche, *Werke in Drei Bänden* (München: Carl Hanser, 1969), vol. 2, p. 473.

2. As already noted, St. Athanasius (295-373) emphasizes regarding Christ and salvation, "For He was made man that we might be made God." Athanasius, "De incarnatione verbi dei" §54, NPNF2, vol. 4, p. 65. For a commentary on deification or theosis, see Georgios Mantzaridis, *The Deification of Man*, trans. Liadain Sherrard (Crestwood, NY: St. Vladimir's Seminary Press, 1984) and Panayiotis Nellas, *Deification in Christ*, trans. Norman Russell (Crestwood, NY: St. Vladimir's Seminary Press, 1987). In its focus on deification, the Church of the first millennium took seriously the passage in Psalm 81, "Ye are gods, and all of you the sons of the Most High" (Ps 81:6, LXX).

3. The argument that it is impossible by discursive reason to establish a particular content-full moral understanding as canonical is developed at greater length in chapter 1 of this volume, as well as in *The Foundations of Bioethics*, 2nd ed. (New York: Oxford, 1996), chapters 2 and 3.

4. St. John Cassian the Just Roman, *pace* Blessed Augustine of Hippo, recognizes the power of human free choice, even in our sinful state. St. John acknowledges that "Where then is there room for free will, and how is it ascribed to our efforts that we are worthy of praise, if God both begins and ends everything in us which concerns our salvation?" "Conference of Abbot Paphnutius," chap. 11, NPNF2, vol. 11, p. 325. In St. John Cassian's account, he answers this question by recognizing that we can turn to God for salvation, though it is only with His grace that we succeed in coming to salvation. "And truly the saints have never said that it was by their own efforts that they secured the direction of the way in which they walked in their course towards advance and perfection of virtue, but rather they prayed for it from the Lord, saying 'Direct me in Thy truth,' and 'direct my way in Thy sight.'" *Ibid.*, chap. 13, p. 326. However, St. John Cassian also knows that human freedom remains operative despite the Fall; we are still able on our own to make small, albeit over the long run ineffectual, efforts to our own salvation. "And none the less does God's grace continue to be free grace while in return for some small and trivial efforts it bestows with priceless bounty such glory of immortality, and such gifts of eternal bliss." "Third Conference of Abbot Chaeremon", *ibid.*, chap. 13, p. 430. The matter is not one of predestination. "But the person who has opted for the path of evil, and actually commits evil, should blame only himself, for no one can force him to commit it, since God created him with free will. Hence he will merit God's praise when he chooses the path of goodness; for he does so, not from any necessity of his nature, as is the case with animals and inanimate things that participate passively in goodness, but as befits a being that God has honoured with the gift of intelligence." St. Peter of Damaskos, "A Treasury of Divine Knowledge," in Sts. Nikodimos and Makarios (eds.), *The Philokalia*, trans. G.E.H. Palmer, Philip Sherrard, and Kallistos Ware (Boston: Faber and Faber, 1986), vol. 3, p. 80. In all of this, free choice is central, as St. Gregory Palamas makes plain: "He willed that by the free inclination of their will towards Him they should achieve union with Him..." "Topics of Natural and Theological Science and on the Moral and Ascetic Life," in *The Philokalia*, vol. 4, §91, p. 389.

5. For a discussion of the requirements of truth-telling within a general secular morality, see *The Foundations of Bioethics*, pp. 309-319.

6. For an account of the impact of Adam's sin on the intellect, see "The Freedom of the Intellect" from "St. Symeon Metaphrastis [10th century] Paraphrase of the Homilies of St. Makarios of Egypt [300-390]," in *The Philokalia*, vol. 3, pp. 337-353.

7. It is crucially important to discern between the voice of God and hallucinations due to mental illness. When God truly commands, as with Abraham and Isaac, He is beyond the constraints that usually guide human conduct. The Creator may decide when His creatures will die.

8. Western moral traditions concerning lying have their roots in Blessed Augustine of Hippo's *De mendacio* and *Contra mendacium*. For a treatment of these matters, see Boniface Ramsey, "Two Traditions on Lying and Deception in the Ancient Church," *Thomist* 49 (1985), 504-533.

9. "On Lying," NPNF1, vol. 3, p. 459.

10. Thomas Aquinas's position regarding deceit, though similar to Blessed Augustine's, does not require an intent to deceive as a necessary condition for there being a lie. See *Summa Theologica* II/II, Q 110 art 1. For a brief discussion of the difference between these two positions, see Antony Koch, *A Handbook of Moral Theology*, ed. Arthur Preuss (St. Louis, MO: B. Herder, 1933), vol. 5, pp. 60-1. The Roman Catholic moral theological manuals vary in the accent given to the Augustinian or the Thomistic understanding of lying. At times, the definitions offered follow Augustine by including as a criterion the intention to deceive. Génicot states: "Mendacium est locutio contra mentem ad fallendum prolata (S. Aug. contra Mend. c.4)." Eduardus Génicot, *Theologiae Moralis* (Lovanii: Polleunis et Ceuterick, 1902), 4th ed., vol. 1, §413, p. 390. "Mendacium definitur: locutio contra mentem (ad fallendum prolata)." H. Noldin and A. Schmidt, *De Praeceptis Dei et Ecclesiae* (Oeniponte: Feliciani Rauch, 1938), 25th ed., vol. 2, §636, p. 577. Alphonsus Liguori for his part defines lying as: "Mendacium est locutio vel significatio contra mentem cum voluntate fallendi." A. Konings, *Theologia Moralis Sancti Alphonsi* (New York: Benziger Brothers, 1879), §510, p. 229. Often, the reference to or paraphrase of Blessed Augustine omits his difference from Thomas. Sabetti simply quotes from Augustine: "Mendacium est locutio contra mentem, vel, ut ait S. Augustinus, est 'dicere aliquid scienter aliter ac sentimus.'" Aloysio Sabetti and Timotheo Barrett, *Compendium Theologiae Moralis* (Cincinnati: Frederick Pustet, 1931), 33rd ed., §310, p. 300. Others do not begin with a reference to Blessed Augustine. For example, J.B. Ferreres writes: "*Mendacium* est sermo prolatus cum intentione dicendi falsum." *Compendium Theologiae Moralis* (Barcinone: Eugenius Subirana, 1918), 9th ed., vol. 1, §542, p. 364. "Mendacium est falsa significatio contra mentem." Arthurus Vermeersch, *Theologiae Moralis* (Romae: Universita Gregoriana, 1937), 3rd ed., vol. 2, §652, p. 632. "Mendacium est locutio contra mentem." Joseph Aertnys, *Theologia Moralis* (Galopiae: M. Alberts, 1918), vol. 1, §994, p. 388.

11. "Triplex distinguitur mendacii genus: 1.° *damnosum*, quo mediante injustum damnum alicui infertur; 2.° *officiosum*, quod utilitatis propriae vel alienae gratia profertur; 3° *jocosum*, quod fit ex joco et sola nugandi causa." J.B. Ferreres, *Compendium Theologiae Moralis* (Barcinone: Eugenius Subirana, 1918), 9th ed., vol. 1, §542, p. 364.

12. See Pope Innocent XI, Propositiones LXV damnatae in Decr. S. Officii 2. Mart. 1679, especially sections 25-27.

13. For a treatment of equivocation and mental reservation, see Antony Koch, *A Handbook of Moral Theology*, ed. Arthur Preuss (St. Louis: B. Herder, 1933), pp. 73-90.

14. Plato, *Republic*, trans. G.M.A. Grube (Indianapolis: Hackett, 1992), p. 64.

15. Origen, "Origen Against Celsus", Book 4, chap. 19, ANF, vol. 4, p. 504.

16. Clement of Alexandria, "The Stromata," Book 7, chap. 9, ANF, vol. 2, p. 538.

17. Cassian, "Second Conference of Abbot Joseph," NPNF2, vol. 11, p. 465.

18. *Ibid.*

19. The Fathers provide numerous illustrations of morally appropriate deceit. St. Paulinus of Nola (†ca.431) offers the example of St. Felix's (3rd century) deceiving his pursuers to avoid capture. "He himself recognised the stratagem afforded by Christ's help, and smilingly addressed the inquisitors: 'I do not know the Felix you are looking for.'" *The Poems of St. Paulinus of Nola*, trans. P.G. Walsh (New York: Newman Press, 1975), Poem 16, p. 97. In this case, the facts are sufficiently ambiguous, so that St. Felix's reply might be interpreted as one of equivocation rather than outright deceit. However, St. Maximus of Turin's (†464)

account of how St. Eusebius (283-371) extricated St. Dionysius, Bishop of Milan, from the Arians involves blatant deception. St. Eusebius indicated agreement with the Arian heresy in order to retrieve St. Dionysius from the clutches of heretics. "But I do not think that this should be passed over in silence, namely, that when the hateful perfidy of the Arians had thrown all of Italy into tumult, along with the rest of the world, and the priests of this plague had taken captive the simplicity of the martyr Saint Dionysius and had enchained him by his signature, Eusebius cleverly freed him from their hands. For as the holy Apostle says: *I became a Jew to the Jews in order to win the Jews*, so also Saint Eusebius feigned that he was a heretic before the heretics in order to snatch his son from heresy." *The Sermons of St. Maximus of Turin*, trans. Boniface Ramsey (New York: Newman Press, 1989), Sermon 7.3, p. 244.

20. Cassian, "Second Conference of Abbot Joseph," NPNF2, vol. 11, p. 465

21. Dorotheos of Gaza, *Discourses and Sayings*, trans. Eric Wheeler [Kalamazoo, MI: Cistercian Publications, 1977], p. 160-1.

22. Dorotheos of Gaza, *Discourses and Sayings*, trans. Eric Wheeler (Kalamazoo, MI: Cistercian Publications, 1977), p. 161.

23. Elder Paisios warns, "It is a sin for someone to lie. When he lies for a good cause, i.e. to save someone else, then it is half a sin, because the lie is for the benefit of his fellow man and not for himself. However, it is also considered a sin; therefore, we should keep it in mind, and not fall into the habit of telling lies for insignificant things." Priestmonk Christodoulos, *Elder Paisios of the Holy Mountain* (Holy Mountain, 1998), p. 140.

24. St. John Chrysostom, *Six Books on the Priesthood*, trans. Graham Neville (Crestwood, NY: St. Vladimir's Seminary Press, 1984), p. 50-51.

25. Cassian, "Second Conference of Abbot Joseph," NPNF2, vol. 11, pp. 464-5.

26. St. John Chrysostom, *Six Books on the Priesthood*, trans. Graham Neville (Crestwood, NY: St. Vladimir's Seminary Press, 1984), p. 51.

27. *Ibid.*, pp. 48-49.

28. *Ibid.*, p. 51.

29. *Ibid.*, p. 49

30. *Ibid.*, pp. 49-50.

31. Priestmonk Christodoulos, *Elder Paisios of the Holy Mountain* (Holy Mountain, 1998), p. 36.

32. St. Cyril of Jerusalem indicates how God uses carnal allures to help us on our way to salvation. "Perhaps you have come with a different motive: perhaps you are courting, and a girl is your reason – or, conversely, a boy. Many a time, too, a slave has wished to please his master, or a friend his friend. I allow the bait, and I welcome you in the trust that, however unsatisfactory the motive that has brought you, your good hope will soon save you. Maybe you did not know where you were going, or what sort of net it was in which you were to be caught. You are a fish caught in the net of the Church. Let yourself be taken alive: don't try to escape. It is Jesus who is playing you on His line, not to kill you, but, by killing you, to make you alive. For you must die and rise again. Did you not hear the Apostle say, 'dead to sin, but living to justice'? Die, then, to sin, and live to righteousness; from today be alive." Roy Deferrari (ed.), *The Fathers of the Church*, trans. Leo McCauley and Anthony Stephenson (Washington, DC: Catholic University of America Press, 1969), vol. 61, pp. 74-5.

33. Canon 119 of the Council of Carthage (A.D. 418/19) records the proscription of coercive conversion. "There has been given a law whereby each and every person may by free choice undertake the exercise of Christianhood." Sts. Nicodemus and Agapius, *The Rudder of the Orthodox Catholic Church* (New York: Luna Printing, 1983), p. 673. This canon was affirmed by the whole Church through Canon 2 of the Quinisext Council (A.D. 692).

34. "As for a Bishop, or Presbyter, or Deacon that strikes believers for sinning, or unbelievers for wrong-doing, with the idea of making them afraid, we command that he be deposed from office. For the Lord has nowhere taught that: on the contrary, He Himself when struck did not strike back; when reviled, He did not revile His revilers; when suffering, He did not threaten." *The Rudder*, Canon 27 of the Apostles, p. 38. The early Church thus had a view of matters quite different from that of the Western High Middle Ages.

> But most of the Bishops [of the early Church] absolutely condemned the infliction of the death penalty for heresy, even if the heresy was incidentally the cause of social disturbances. Such was the view of St. Augustine, St. Martin, St. Ambrose, many Spanish bishops, and a bishop of Gaul named Theognitus; in a word, of all who disapproved of the condemnation of Priscillian. As a rule, they protested in the name of Christian charity; they voiced the new spirit of the Gospel of Christ. At the other extremity of the Catholic world, St. John Chrysostom re-echoes their teaching. "To put a heretic to death," he says, "is an unpardonable crime."
> E. Vacandard, *The Inquisition*, trans. Bertrand Conway (New York: Longmans, Green, 1908), pp. 28-29.

However, the Christian state is not constrained to support freedom of religion, as St. John Chrysostom acknowledges in his commentary on the Gospel of St. Matthew 13:24-30, the parable of the tares. "He doth not therefore forbid our checking heretics, and stopping their mouths, and taking away their freedom of speech, and breaking up their assemblies and confederacies, but our killing and slaying them." Chrysostom, Homily XLVI.1 on the Gospel of St. Matthew, NPNF1, vol. 10, p. 289.

35. Archimandrite Vasileios, *Hymn of Entry*, trans. Elizabeth Briere (Crestwood, NY: St. Vladimir's Seminary Press, 1984), p. 111. Quotation from St. Gregory of Nyssa, *On the Lord's Prayer, Or.3*; PG 44:1156C.

36. The traditional Christian view of authority in the family is robustly in conflict with the liberal cosmopolitan ethos. "Wives, be subordinating yourselves to your own husbands as is fitting in the Lord. Husbands, be loving your wives and cease being embittered against them. Children, be obeying your parents in all things, for this is well-pleasing to the Lord. Fathers, cease provoking your children, that they may not be disheartened." Col 3:18-21.

37. "The one who loveth father or mother more than Me is not worthy of Me; and the one who loveth son or daughter more than Me is not worthy of Me." Matt 10:37.

38. The office of oblation of the Divine Liturgy, Hapgood, *Service Book*, p. 73. The Holy Unmercenaries include as well Sts. Diomedes, Tryphon, Anicetus, Thalleleus, Samson, and Mocius.

39. Christian physicians were reported to the pagan authorities and prosecuted because they used their position, power, and influence as physicians to proclaim the Gospel and convert their patients. In his remarks concerning the life of St. Panteleimon, St. Nicholas notes "he studied medicine as a young man. The priest Hermolaus befriended him, instructed him in the Christian faith and baptised him. Panteleimon miraculously healed a blind man whom other doctors had treated in vain: he healed him by the name of Christ and baptised him." St. Panteleimon was martyred on July 27, 304. Nikolai Velimirovich, *The Prologue from Ochrid*, trans. Mother Maria (Birmingham, England: Lazarica Press, 1986), vol. 3, p. 115.

40. In Texas it is often remarked that there is nothing wrong with Bubba So-and-so that a good killing would not cure. A well acculturated, secular Texan will understand at once the power of this moral insight. However, once truly baptized in the Faith, the traditional Christian Texan must not only forgo doing harm to Bubba So-and-so, but even forgo wishing him harm. When J. R. Smith comes to visit our newly illumined Texan and asks, "Please, blow Bubba away," it will not be enough for the converted Texan to say, "I got me religion now, so I can't blow Bubba away, but I know someone who can do you a right good job of it." One

may not even give referral for a hit man. The same applies for abortion, physician-assisted suicide, and euthanasia.

41. Alphonsi de Ligorio, *Theologia Moralis* (Paris: Le Clere, 1862), Book 3, Tract 3, Cap. 2. De proec. charit. erga prox. Dub. 5, Art. 3, pp. 347-356. Also, for example:

    1.   Co-operation is formal when A helps B in an external sinful act, and intends the sinfulness of it, as in deliberate adultery.

    2.   Co-operation is material when A helps B to accomplish an external act by an act that is not sinful, and without approving of what B does.

        (a) This material co-operation is immediate, if it is co-operation in the sinful act of the other, as to help a burglar to empty the jewels that he is stealing into the burglar's wallet.

        (b) Material co-operation is mediate, if it is an act that is secondary and subservient to the main act of another, as to supply a burglar with tools for his burglary.

        (i)   Mediate co-operation is proximate, if the help given is very intimately connected with the act of another, as to hold a ladder for the burglar as he climbs up to a window for the purpose of burglary.

        (ii) Mediate co-operation is remote, if the help given is not closely connected with the other's act, as to purchase tools for a burglar.

        Henry Davis, S.J., *Moral and Pastoral Theology* (New York: Sheed and Ward, 1936), vol. 1, p. 341-342.

42. Though in most Southern states slaves were not persons before the law in the sense of able to sue their masters, they had a certain standing within a Christian society and at law. In some states, slaves even had limited legal rights against their masters. See, for example, A. E. K. Nash, "Texas Justice in the Age of Slavery: Appeals Concerning Blacks and the Antebellum State Supreme Court," *Houston Law Review* 8 (1981), 438-456.

43. For an overview of the peremptory rights of masters over their slaves in Graeco-Roman society, see Thomas Wiedeman, *Greek and Roman Slavery* (Baltimore: Johns Hopkins University Press, 1981).

44. Canon VI, "15 Canons of St. Peter of Alexandria," in *The Rudder*, p. 744.

45. Lewis and Short, *A Latin Dictionary* (Oxford: Clarendon Press, 1980), p. 1447

46. *Ibid*.

47. John Rawls, *A Theory of Justice* (Cambridge, MA: Harvard University Press, 1971).

48. John Rawls, *Political Liberalism* (New York: Columbia University Press, 1993).

49. John Rawls, "The Idea of Public Reason Revisited", *University of Chicago Law Review* 64 (Summer 1997), 791. This essay of Rawls is reprinted in Rawls, *The Law of Peoples* (Cambridge, MA: Harvard University Press, 1999), pp. 131-180.

50. Rawls, "The Idea of Public Reason Revisited," p. 791.

51. *Ibid*., p. 791.

52. *Ibid*., p. 781.

53. *Ibid*., p. 806. In *The Law of Peoples*, Rawls defines fundamentalism thus:

Many persons – call them "fundamentalists" of various religious or secular doctrines which have been historically dominant – could not be reconciled to a social world such as I have described. For them the social world envisaged by political liberalism is a nightmare of social fragmentation and false doctrines, if not positively evil. To be reconciled to a social world, one must be able to see it as both reasonable and rational. Reconciliation requires acknowledging the fact of reasonable pluralism both within liberal and decent societies and in their relations with one another. Moreover, one must also recognize this pluralism as consistent with reasonable comprehensive doctrines, both religious and secular. Yet this last idea is precisely what fundamentalism denies and political liberalism asserts (pp. 126-127).

54. Rawls, "The Idea of Public Reason Revisited", pp. 783-784.

55. *Ibid*., p. 790.

56. *Ibid*., p. 791.

57. Samuel Warren and Louis Brandeis, "The Right to Privacy," *Harvard Law Review* 4 (1890), 193. These common-law protections of the person find expression in the Magna Carta (June 15, 1215), especially in section 39, and generally in ancient Germanic codes proscribing the unauthorized touching of persons. See, for example, Katherine F. Drew (trans.), *The Lombard Laws* (Philadelphia: University of Pennsylvania Press, 1973), and Drew (trans.), *The Burgundian Code* (Philadelphia: University of Pennsylvania Press, 1972). In ancient pagan German law, these legal protections were nested within a general notion of a limited government. See, for example, Henry Charles Lea, *Torture* (Philadelphia: University of Pennsylvania Press, 1866; repr. 1973), pp. 24-25.

58. *Olmstead v. United States*, 277 U.S. 438, 478 (1928) (Brandeis, J., dissenting).

59. *In re President & Directors of Georgetown College, Inc.*, 331 F.2d 1000, 1017 (D.C. Cir.) *cert. denied*, 337 U.S. 978 (1964) (Burger, W., dissenting) (emphasis in original).

60. For a study of the development of legal concepts of privacy, see Tom Gerety, "Redefining Privacy," *Harvard Civil Rights-Civil Liberties Law Review* 12 (Spring 1977), 233-296. See also David M. O'Brien, *Privacy, Law, and Public Policy* (New York: Praeger, 1979), esp. pp. 177-199.

61. See, for example, *Griswold v. Connecticut*, 381 U.S. 479, 85 S.Ct. 1678, 14 L.Ed.2d 510 (1965); *Eisenstadt v. Baird*, 405 U.S. 438, 92 S.Ct. 1029, 31 L.Ed.2d 349 (1972); and *Roe v. Wade*, 410 U.S. 113 (1973).

62. John E. Nowak, Ronald D. Rotunda, and J. Nelson Young, *Constitutional Law* (St. Paul, MN: West, 1983), pp. 1412-1414.

63. Amendments of the Constitution of the United States, Article IX.

64. *Griswold v. Connecticut* 381 U.S. 479, 488.

65. Bennett B. Patterson, *The Forgotten Ninth Amendment* (Indianapolis: Bobbs-Merrill, 1955), pp. 1-2.

66. *In re Cruzan* 58 LW 4916 (June 25, 1990).

67. Rawls, "The Idea of Public Reason Revisited," *University of Chicago Law Review* 64 (Summer 1997), 797.

68. John Stuart Mill, *Subjection of Women*, chap. 2.

69. Rawls, "The Idea of Public Reason Revisited," *University of Chicago Law Review* 64 (Summer 1997), 791.

70. "Whatever requires an undue amount of thought or trouble or involves a large expenditure of effort and causes our whole life to revolve, as it were, around solicitude for the flesh must be avoided by Christians. Consequently, we must take great care to employ this medical art, if it should be necessary, not as making it wholly accountable for our state of health or illness, but as redounding to the glory of God and as a parallel to the care given the soul." St. Basil, *Ascetical Works*, trans. Sister M. Monica Wagner (Washington, DC: Catholic University of America Press, 1962), pp. 331-332.

71. Personal communication by Beulah Karbach Engelhardt, God give rest to her soul. In the 1930s while a Protestant, she entered training as a surgical nurse at Santa Rosa, a Roman Catholic hospital in San Antonio, in which this greeting was to be used by all, including Protestant nurses, such as was my mother at that time.

72 St. Ignatius, "Ignatius to the Smyrnaeans," in *Apostolic Fathers*, trans. Kirsopp Lake (Cambridge, MA: Harvard University Press, 1965), VIII.2, vol. 1, p. 261.

73 Friedrich Hayek, *The Mirage of Social Justice* (Chicago: University of Chicago Press, 1976), p. 66.

8 Christian Bioethics in a Post-Christian World

Living after Christendom

Traditional Christians in a post-Christian world are cultural deviants. They approach everything out of joint with the society around them. Everything is set within an all-encompassing project: salvation. They know that the long-awaited Messiah of Israel has come and that He is Jesus Christ, the Son of the living God. Moreover, they know that He took on our humanity to free us from bondage to eternal death: the prize of life is now theosis. Humans are commanded to become gods by grace. In the experience of this grace, they know that God is not an underachiever: He has from the Apostles been able to reveal His truth in the Church. As a consequence, theological development is the growth of each person in grace through worship of God and love of others, especially moral strangers. In this experience, there are no dogmatic or moral truths accessible to us today unavailable to Christians after the revelation to the Apostles was complete (Jude 3). The sum and the parts of all of this are radically counter-cultural.

Though traditional Christians will recognize other Christian groups as struggling to be fully Christian, they will recognize as well that attempts outside of the bounds of right worship and right belief fail to be complete. They are one-sided and distorted. In this important sense, the Church has no branches. It is whole. Indeed, this is an article of faith. Traditional Christianity confesses that the Church is one.[1] The Church may once have had two lungs, but one developed the cancer of novel beliefs and the development of new doctrines. Yet, there is truth in this metaphor of the two lungs. Indeed, the Western rites of Christianity are being returned to the fullness of Orthodoxy, restoring the chorus of worship from the ancient Church.[2] In this chorus, the Church as the community of Christians united in right worship and right belief possesses Tradition whole and unimpaired: the Holy Spirit dwells in Her. In this context, as we have seen, Tradition is not just oral history. Nor is Tradition just the Scriptures, practices, and writings of the Fathers, along with oral history. Tradition is the abiding presence of the Holy Spirit Who sustains the Church's truth and the content of all that is carried from generation to generation. After all, the Church is the body of Christ (Eph 4:12,16) in the Spirit of God so that there is only one Body and one Spirit (Eph 4:4). Surely, the Holy Spirit goes to whom He wishes (John 3:8). But the Spirit is only in one tradition, the body of Orthodox worship and belief. Just as Ultimate Truth is not a what but a Who, the Holy Trinity, Tradition is not a what but a Who, the Holy

Spirit. "The Spirit is the truth" (I John 5:6). In this Spirit, the generations are not isolated one from the other, for "Thou has been our refuge from generation to genera-tion."[3] The Church is united in Liturgy across the ages.

Within this abiding continuity sustained by the Holy Spirit across time, traditional Christians are out of step in their attitudes regarding the major passages of human life from marriage, reproduction, and birth to suffering, disability, and death. In contrast with the pagan Greco-Roman civilization of the Mediterranean littoral, Christians of the first centuries were similarly odd in not having priestesses, in condemning fornica-tion and homosexual acts, in not allowing abortions, in denouncing infanticide, and in accepting unavoidable pain, disability, and disease as opportunities to learn humility and to endure patiently. In contrast to Seneca, they firmly refused physician-assisted suicide and euthanasia. Because of Christ's resurrection, they knew death not to be the end but the beginning of life. They understood, as do traditional Christians now, that the prize is not a long, healthy, and satisfying life but salvation. This insight relativizes health and health care. As a result, traditional Christians are as deviant in our contem-porary society as they were in the world of the pagan Roman empire.

Contemporary Christians may fail fully to recognize the challenges they confront because of the remembrance of Christendom. They may not have noticed that their cultural hegemony has passed. Christianity was until recently the established religion in most countries of Europe. But the Empire is no more; it has fallen. On that terrible Tuesday morning, May 29, 1453, Constantine XI (1405-1453), having betrayed the city spiritually, walked through the breached walls of the Second Rome, Constantino-ple, dying in battle under the swords of the army of Mohammed II (1431-1481). The ersatz empire that Charles the Great (842-914) accepted after the third Mass on Christ-mas, 800, in defiance of the original and continuing Christian empire, fell with the abdication of Franz II (1768-1835) on August 6, 1806, defeated by Napoleon (1769-1821), the herald of a new and secular Europe. Finally, although Holy Russia with the marriage of Sophia Paleologus (1450-1503), niece of Constantine XI, to Ivan III (1440-1505) maintained the lineage of Constantinople, it ended in martyrdom. With the brutal assassination of St. Nicholas II (1868-1918), Czar (the Slavic assimilation of the Latin Caesar) of Russia, on July 4 in 1918 (on the Gregorian calendar, July 17), the throne of the Christian empire was left vacant. Christendom passed away. Though in a sense there are remnants of established Christianity in some European countries, they and their influence have been radically secularized. Christendom remains a disturbing, if not misguiding memory.

The United States itself was far from secular in the 19th century and the first half of the 20th. The First Amendment, which guaranteed freedom of religion and forbade the establishment of a religion,[4] constrained only federal law until after the Late Unpleas-antness (more commonly known as the War Between the States).[5] It was only much later that the Fourteenth Amendment was interpreted as applying the First Amendment to the states, requiring the constitutional secularization of American public life.[6] For a long time America's Christian character was taken for granted. The Supreme Court in the 19th century could affirm without embarrassment that the Americans are "a Chris-tian people".[7] Christianity, and by this was meant Protestant Christianity, was integral to the generally accepted common law of the United States.[8] "Evidence that Protestant Christianity [was] the functional common religion of the society would overwhelm us if we sought it out. What is of more interest here is how observers concerned with American society simply took this phenomenon for granted."[9] The legal watershed in the United States occurred in the 1950s and 1960s as the Supreme Court came to interpret American constitutional law through fully secular eyes.[10]

The difficulty is that secular morality cannot offer what religious morality promised: the unity in reason which religion strives to provide through a unity in faith. There are as many secular moralities as there are religious moralities. It turns out that both must first convert dissidents to agreement about basic premises, rules of evidence, and rules of inference. There is consequently a diversity of secular bioethics, as there is a diversity of religious bioethics. Nor can secular rationality secure the unity of morality that can be justified through the power of a personal, omnipotent, and transcendent God. Secular rationality cannot guarantee a harmony of the right and the good. Nor can it show that it is always rational to follow the morality that is rationally justifiable. Finally, secular morality cannot offer the metaphysical guidance that many seek in the face of suffering, disability, and death. Secular morality cannot offer a personal answer to the meaning of suffering and loss: within the secular moral framework the deep roots of being are impersonal, surd, and uncaring. Secular morality can authorize various personal and communal narratives, but these remain aesthetic-moral creations on the surface of an unaffected cosmos. In contrast, Christian morality discloses the narrative into which God has told the very universe and in which persons and angelic powers play real and enduring roles. Over against what Christian morality promises through its grounding in a personal, transcendent God, secular morality is superficial in its immanence. It is ephemeral in the face of personal death and the otherwise ultimately transient character of everything in the universe.

This volume has explored the character of a Christian morality that takes seriously its grounding in an enduring experience of the transcendent, personal God. It has done this by examining the issues of sexuality, reproduction, birth, suffering, disease, disability, health care, dying, and death that fill the scope of bioethics. It has tried taking seriously the consequences of grounding morality in our ascetical pursuit of union with the transcendent, personal being of God. This has involved exploring a mystical or, better put, noetic epistemology that secures its truth in an immediate and enduring experience of God's revelation. Because this truth is pursued first and foremost through changing ourselves so that we can experience God, this epistemology is at its roots ascetic and liturgical. It involves a turning from oneself to God and one's fellowman within the liturgical worship of the Church. Moral knowing is dependent on loving and praying rightly. As a consequence, the bioethics offered is in its roots therapeutic. It is about how one should act in order properly to cure one's soul so that one can approach God.

Will Austin, Texas, be the Fourth Rome? When will the Orthodox Mounted Posse Ride into Constantinople and Restore the Second Rome? Would St. Autonomous Burn down Abortion Clinics? How Can One Teach Bioethics?

As every young Texian Christian of school age knows,[11] Austin shall surely be the fourth Rome, and if not Austin, then Dallas or perhaps even Abilene. Or, when Texas is restored to its rightful boundaries, then Santa Fe, the city of the Holy Faith. The patriarch of all the Texans will then bear the weight of that priority among the bishops which is the Primacy of St. Peter that will be preserved by that Church, that future diocese of Santa Fe. As the capital of the Empire of Holy Texas, it will preside as first in loving care for all true believing and worshipping churches. The first Rome fell to heresy, the second to the Mohammedans, and the third to the Bolsheviks. Once all is put in order, the Empire can be reestablished and the populace of Texas baptized in the Brazos de Dios. Then the Orthodox Mounted Posse can saddle up and ride out to the Second Rome to restore the Hagia Sophia, Christendom's great temple, carrying the Bonnie Blue Flag next to the Empire's banner of gold with the proud double-headed eagle. The Posse would have to decide whether to depart from Galveston or Indianola. Needless to say, when riding through Europe, they would have to stop to baptize the pope of the first Rome in the waters of the Tiber. All of this is vivid in the millennial hopes of the young and the dreams of old men. All of this will some day surely take place, God willing, of course. In the meantime, Christians are as always required to be patient – the day of the Last Emperor and then the restoration of all things lies, for all we know, in the very distant future.

For the time being, we must live within a society that is both post-Christian and neo-pagan. This will require not just courage. It requires peaceable endurance in the face of the postponement of one's hopes. Christians will need to learn to be Christian in a world growing ever more hostile to their way of life. It is not just that Christianity is disestablished and traditional social structures brought into question. Many of the Christian religions have fallen into internal chaos, and the relevancy of their religious bioethics has been radically brought into question and then transformed in the image and likeness of liberal cosmopolitan moral commitments. This religious faith and its bioethics have been largely immanentized. Traditional Christianity finds itself surrounded by a culture that is pagan, even when in Christian trappings. Unlike the ancient paganism in which Christianity first preached the Gospel, the contemporary neo-paganism is dialectically set over against the Christian past. It is specifically and consciously post-Christian. It seeks to set traditional Christianity aside. As a consequence, traditional Christians find themselves in a society bent on inducting them and their children into an all-embracing, liberal, post-Christian, cosmopolitan ethos. When they resist, they will be found intolerant, fundamentalist, and opponents of the core values shaping the dominant culture.

In this neo-pagan culture, traditional Christians will survive as Orthodox Jews and Orthodox Christians have known to survive over the ages in the face of persecution: they will have to be different from the core and strictly observant. They will have to transform every moment of their lives with their peculiar love of God and of their neighbor. Their love must be peculiar, for they must understand that many of what the liberal cosmopolitan ethos takes to be loving acts are indeed harmful. Traditional Christians will not be value-neutral in the ways in which the surrounding culture demands. Namely, they will not have a neutrality over against the possible range of choices acceptable within the liberal cosmopolitan ethos. Instead, they will recognize this supposed neutrality as fraudulent. They will recognize the domain of acceptable choices as framed by the values of the liberal cosmopolitan ethos. Through sharing this recognition with others, they will be critics of the fundamentals of their surrounding culture. Such critics will be seen as disloyal provocateurs. When they are health care professionals, they will be found to be unprofessional. Such conduct can only make them the enemies of the liberal cosmopolitan culture.

To be the enemy of the dominant culture is to be called to martyrdom. It requires witnessing against that which is generally accepted, against that which frames the very logic of the emerging global civilization. It means to act on behalf of a truth which that culture rejects. This is a life of conflict. It is also a life of temptation, the temptation to abandon one's difference and to be absorbed into the surrounding ethos. If one resists this absorption, the temptation is to respond with hostility, indeed violence, rather than with patience and love. This last temptation is as profound as it is evil. To face this temptation, traditional Christians must remember the Christian calling to change the world through the force of holiness, not through violence. This is not to deny that the Christian emperor may use coercive state force.[12] But in his absence, we are called to endurance, remembering that we may not take the law into our own hands. The only law we can justify with moral strangers is that sparse fabric of a libertarian cosmopolitan ethic. If accepted, this ethic will give space for traditional Christians to live in peace. From the outside, its justification will be in the permission of those who collaborate in a polity. This will secure the moral place within which traditional Christians can peaceably turn in love to God and to their neighbors. It will provide the peaceable domain in which the Gospel can be preached. From the inside, it will be justified within a thick commitment to love. It will be integral to a traditional Christian way of life.

As the example of St. Autonomous teaches, we must use love, not violence. This martyr under Diocletian (ruled 284-305) steadfastly warned the Christians of his age who were being tortured and slaughtered by the empire not to do any damage to the pagan temples.[13] Christians are called instead to respond to all, but especially to their enemies, with love. Like the Christians under Bishop Autonomous, traditional Christians living in our post-Christian, neo-pagan world must resist all temptation to violence, even against those who murder unborn children or aid in the self-murder of patients. St. Autonomous would have neither burnt down nor bombed abortion clinics, nor threatened abortionists. Instead, we must recognize with the Christians of the first centuries that we must care for pregnant women who need support, adopt children who would otherwise be killed, provide care for the dying such that self-murder does not become a temptation, and lovingly pray for those who murder.

Through a Christian life, we will learn Christian bioethics. Christian bioethics is not merely an academic field over against the everyday fabric of life. If it succeeds truly in being a Christian bioethics, it is a Christian way of living, experiencing, and engaging in sexuality, reproduction, suffering, disease, disability, health care, and dying. It is a living response to all the challenges that frame bioethics. It is a communal response uniting right-believing and right-worshiping Christians across the ages with each other as well as with the bodiless powers and the triune Deity. Christian bioethics is correctly taught only within and through an ascetic, liturgical life. Only then will we correctly understand its significance. Access to this bioethics will always be one-sided and incomplete, insofar as it is considered only as a body of doctrine amenable to didactic instruction, as a set of principles to be analyzed, or as a set of controversies to be resolved. It must first and foremost be experienced as integral to the pursuit of holiness. A merely scholarly bioethics is tame and domesticated. Its demands are too easily evaded. It lives in a set of books, articles, and reflections that can be set aside as one turns to relax and enjoy this world. A Christian bioethics is not merely a philosophical bioethics, for philosophy outside of Christianity will misguide. As the Matins of Thursday of the third week in Lent reminds us,

> Simple in speech but wise in knowledge, they have destroyed the webs of words spun by philosophers, the cunning tapestries of the orators.... Peter speaks, and Plato falls silent; Paul teaches, and Pythagoras is heard no more. The company of the apostles, preaching the mysteries of God, has buried the dead voice of the pagan Greeks and called the world to the worship of Christ.[14]

 A Christian bioethics must live in the experience of the unbroken tradition of theology. Christian bioethics properly understood is integral to God's claim on us, which must in the end consume all of us.

Notes

1. "And [we believe] in one, holy, Catholic and Apostolic Church." "The Holy Creed which the 150 Holy Fathers Set Forth," NPNF2, vol. 14, p. 163.
2. There are now various Western Orthodox rites. These include an augmented version of the Book of Common Prayer (the Divine Liturgy of St. Tikhon), as well as a restored Roman rite (the Divine Liturgy of St. Gregory). See *Saint Andrew Service Book* (Englewood, NJ: Antiochian Orthodox Christian Archdiocese, 1996). There are even Orthodox Latin masses.
3. "The Great Doxology" of Matins, in *The Liturgikon* (Englewood, NJ: Antakya Press, 1989), p. 147.
4. The first article added as an amendment to the compact styled "the Constitution of the United States" reads: "Congress shall make no law respecting an establishment of religion, or prohibiting the free exercise thereof; or abridging the freedom of speech, or of the press; or the right of the people peaceably to assemble, and to petition the government for a redress of grievances."
5. After the Late Unpleasantness, the sense and significance of the American Constitution and its Supreme Court changed. See Charles Warren, "Legislative and Judicial Attacks on the Supreme Court of the United States – a History of the Twenty-fifth Section of the Judiciary Act," *American Law Review* 47 (Jan. 1913), 1-34 and (Mar. 1913), 161-189.
6. *Everson v. Board of Education* (1947) 330, U.S. 1.
7. *Church of the Holy Trinity v. United States*, 143 US 457 (1892).
8. See, for example, *United States v. Macintosh*, 283 US 605 (1931).
9. John Wilson, "Common Religion in American Society," in *Civil Religion and Political Theology* (Notre Dame, IN: University of Notre Dame Press, 1986), p. 113.
10. See, for example, *Tessim Zorach v. Andrew G. Clauson et al.*, 343 US 306, 96 L ed 954, 72 S Ct 679 (1951); *Roy R. Torcaso v. Clayton K. Watkins*, 367 US 488, 6 L ed 2d 982, 81 S Ct 1680 (1961); and *School District of Abington Township v. Edward L. Schempp et al.*, *William J. Murray et al. v. John N. Curlett et al.*, 374 US 203, 10 L ed 2d 844, 83 S Ct 1560 (1963).
11. As the Methodist theologian Stanley Hauerwas understands, "In God's love of us we do not cease being Jew or Greek, male or female, or the ultimate ontological categories – Texan and

everyone else – but rather God's love of us only intensifies our particularity as we are made precious in God's life." Hauerwas, *Unleashing the Scripture* (Nashville: Abingdon Press, 1993), p. 96.

12. It is not for nothing that traditional Christianity has counted among its Mysteries not only the Great Blessing of Waters at Epiphany, the tonsure of monks, and the burial of the dead, but also the anointing of the Emperor. When one embarks on anointing an emperor, one has like the ancient Jews embarked on consecrating a king. God willing, one has brought into existence David, not Saul, for whom one must in any event pray. "Have in remembrance, O Lord, our most God-fearing and Christ-loving Ruler, N., to whom thou hast given the right to reign in the earth. Crown him with the armour of truth, with the panoply of contentment. Overshadow his head in the day of battle. Strengthen his arm, exalt his right hand; make mighty his kingdom; subdue under him all barbarous nations which seek wars; grant unto him peace profound and inviolate; inspire his heart with good deeds toward thy Church, and toward all thy people; that through his serenity we may lead a quiet and tranquil life, in all godliness and soberness." Liturgy of St. Basil, in *Service Book of the Holy Orthodox-Catholic Apostolic Church*, trans. Isabel Hapgood (Englewood, NJ: Antiochian Orthodox Christian Archdiocese, 1996), p. 109.

13. The following is an excerpt from the life of St. Autonomous (feastday September 12). "He preached not only the word of Jesus Christ, but also a policy of non-violence... At the same time, this [the conflicts of the pagans and the Christians] kindled emotional hatreds to the point that even the gentlest of Christians would storm the temples and destroy pagan idols in retaliation for the persecution of their friends. It was at the height of these conflicts that he urged non-violence, even though restraint was easier said than done for oppressed Christians." George Poulos, *Orthodox Saints* (Brookline, MA: Holy Cross Orthodox Press, 1991), vol. 3, pp. 189-90.

14. *The Lenten Triodion*, trans. Mother Mary (Bussy-en-Othe, France: Monastery of the Veil of the Mother of God, 1979), Matins of Thursday of the third week in Lent, Second Canon, pp. 147-148.

Index